"For the first time, we have a book that takes a nov ation. Using an intersectional lens, Meredith Worthe stigma and a method for investigating how the inte normativity, gender/sexuality, and racial/ethnic identities relate to differences in the stigmatization of a whole array of different queer identities. The elegance of the argument, breadth of scholarship marshalled, and the author's crisp and engaging writing make this book a pleasurable read for beginners and experts alike."

**Verta Taylor, Professor of Sociology and Feminist Studies,
University of California, Santa Barbara**

"Despite hard-earned progressive social change that has enhanced the status and welfare of LGBTQ people, they are still stigmatized. *Queers, Bis, and Straight Lies* is a must read if you want to understand the cultural sources of that stigma, how LGBTQ stigma manifests in the lives of the stigmatizers and the stigmatized, and the constancy and variation in the stigmatization of lesbian women, gay men, bisexual women, bisexual men, trans women, trans men, non-binary and genderqueer people, queer women, and queer men. This book scores on multiple fronts: it provides an encyclopaedic treatment of what is known about LGBTQ stigma; it advances an innovative theory of LGBTQ stigma, Norm-Centered Stigma Theory; it draws on original survey data to test the theory and, as a result, presents a dizzying array of provocative empirical findings; and it ultimately enables us to understand the intersectional nature of LGBTQ stigma. The result is a significant advancement in stigma research and an empirically grounded unpacking of the complicated ways LGBTQ stigma is anchored by hetero-cis-normativity that interfaces with gender, race and ethnicity, social class, and other axes of social stratification. Seen in this way, this book begins as a sociological study of stigma, but it turns out to be more than that. It is a compelling treatise on power, including the power to define social types, and the production of social differentiation connected to prejudice, discrimination, and violence."

**Valerie Jenness, Professor of Criminology,
Law and Society, University of California, Irvine**

"This book is essential reading for people looking for a powerful theory on stigma that helps explain the lives of LGBTQ people. Based on extensive research, the author fastidiously details LGBTQ groups' and individuals' experiences with discrimination, harassment, and violence. Criminologists, especially those with a special interest in LGBTQ welfare, will want this book for themselves and for their students. Included are scales for measuring stigma and other important, and validated, resources. It's a relief to have a study that is both a practical and scholarly approach to this important issue."

**Pepper Schwartz, Professor of Sociology,
University of Washington**

"This book's deep dive into anti-LGBTQ stigma reveals why the topic remains fundamentally important, despite recent gains in equality. Theoretically informed and with exacting analyses, this book challenges popular discourses about who LGBTQ people are, what they experience, and why."

**Vanessa R. Panfil, Ph.D., Assistant Professor, Department of Sociology and Criminal Justice, Old Dominion University**

"Meredith Worthen has done us an invaluable service—providing the first detailed roadmap for developing a true science that can challenge the kind of social stigmas with which every queer is all too familiar."

**Riki Wilchins, author of *TRANS/gressive and Burn the Binary!***

"Finally, a look at stigma that disaggregates the experiences of nine subgroups within the LGBTQ+ community, including bisexual, pansexual, queer, and non-binary people, and does so through an intersectional lens! This book not only covers stigmatizing attitudes and perspectives, but also LGBTQ+ people's experiences with discrimination, harassment, and violence."

**Robyn Ochs, Speaker and LGBTQ+ Advocate, Editor, *Bi Women Quarterly***

# QUEERS, BIS, AND STRAIGHT LIES

Though there have been great advances for LGBTQ people in recent years, stigma, intolerance, and prejudice remain. *Queers, Bis, and Straight Lies: An Intersectional Examination of LGBTQ Stigma* offers an in-depth exploration of LGBTQ negativity through its ground-breaking use of Norm-Centered Stigma Theory (NCST), the first ever theory about stigma that is both testable and well-positioned in existing stigma scholarship.

Based on research with more than 3,000 respondents, hetero-cis-normativity and intersectionality are highlighted as fundamental in understanding separate but interconnected discussions about LGBTQ individuals' experiences with discrimination, harassment, and violence. With chapters dedicated to lesbian women, gay men, bisexual women, bisexual men, trans women, trans men, non-binary/genderqueer people, queer women, and queer men, *Queers, Bis, and Straight Lies* brings together empirically-driven findings that work toward dismantling "straight lies" in an innovative and impactful manner.

Through its novel and critical approach, *Queers, Bis, and Straight Lies* is the ideal resource for those who want to learn about LGBTQ stigma more broadly and for those who seek a nuanced, theory-driven, and intersectional examination of how LGBTQ prejudices and prejudicial experiences differ by gender identity, sexual identity, race/ethnicity, and class.

**Meredith G. F. Worthen** is a professor of sociology. Her main interests are in the sociological constructions of deviance and stigma, gender, sexuality, and LGBTQ identities, as well as feminist and queer criminology. As a researcher, teacher, and activist, her work dissects multiple dimensions of prejudice in efforts to cultivate understanding, empathy, and social change.

# QUEERS, BIS, AND STRAIGHT LIES

An Intersectional Examination of LGBTQ Stigma

*Meredith G. F. Worthen*

Routledge
Taylor & Francis Group
NEW YORK AND LONDON

First published 2020
by Routledge
52 Vanderbilt Avenue, New York, NY 10017

and by Routledge
2 Park Square, Milton Park, Abingdon, Oxon, OX14 4RN

*Routledge is an imprint of the Taylor & Francis Group, an informa business*

© 2020 Taylor & Francis

The right of Meredith G. F. Worthen to be identified as author of this work has been asserted by her in accordance with sections 77 and 78 of the Copyright, Designs and Patents Act 1988.

All rights reserved. No part of this book may be reprinted or reproduced or utilised in any form or by any electronic, mechanical, or other means, now known or hereafter invented, including photocopying and recording, or in any information storage or retrieval system, without permission in writing from the publishers.

*Trademark notice*: Product or corporate names may be trademarks or registered trademarks, and are used only for identification and explanation without intent to infringe.

*Library of Congress Cataloging-in-Publication Data*
Names: Worthen, Meredith Gwynne Fair, author.
Title: Queers, bis, and, straight lies: an intersectional examination of LGBTQ stigma/Meredith G. F. Worthen.
Description: New York, NY: Routledge, [2020] | Includes bibliographical references and index. Identifiers: LCCN 2019044850 (print) | LCCN 2019044851 (ebook) | ISBN 9781138241442 (hardback) | ISBN 9781138241459 (paperback) | ISBN 9781315280332 (ebk)
Subjects: LCSH: Homophobia. | Transphobia. | Sexual minorities–Social conditions. | Heterosexism. | Stigma (Social psychology)
Classification: LCC HQ76.4 .W67 2020 (print) | LCC HQ76.4 (ebook) | DDC 306.76–dc23
LC record available at https://lccn.loc.gov/2019044850
LC ebook record available at https://lccn.loc.gov/2019044851

ISBN: 978-1-138-24144-2 (hbk)
ISBN: 978-1-138-24145-9 (pbk)
ISBN: 978-1-315-28033-2 (ebk)

Typeset in Bembo
by Swales & Willis, Exeter, Devon, UK

To anyone who has ever had their light stolen, this book is proof that you can get it back.

# CONTENTS

*About the Author*   xi
*Acknowledgments*   xii
*Preface*   xiv

1 Introduction   1

**PART I**
**Foundations in Understanding LGBTQ Stigma**   7

2 Theorizing Stigma and Norm-Centered Stigma Theory   9

3 Identifying Hetero-cis-normativity and Intersectionality in LGBTQ Stigma   24

4 Hetero-cis-normativity and Common Explanations for LGBT(Q) Stigma   60

5 Measuring LGBTQ Stigma and Hetero-cis-normativity in NCST   83

6 The LGBTQ Stigma Scales   101

## PART II
## NCST and Understanding LGBTQ Stigma — 123

  7  Part II Overview — 125

  8  Lesbian Women Stigma — 166

  9  Gay Men Stigma — 196

10  Bisexual Women Stigma — 222

11  Bisexual Men Stigma — 250

12  Trans Women Stigma — 274

13  Trans Men Stigma — 300

14  Non-binary/Genderqueer Stigma — 323

15  Queer Women Stigma — 349

16  Queer Men Stigma — 373

17  LGBTQ Stigma, NCST, and Future Research — 397

*Appendix A: Data and Methods* — *403*
*Appendix B: Supplemental Tables* — *408*
*Index* — *420*

# ABOUT THE AUTHOR

**Meredith Gwynne Fair Worthen**, Ph.D. (the University of Texas at Austin, 2009), is a professor of sociology, elected faculty member of the Department of Women's and Gender Studies, and faculty affiliate of the Center for Social Justice at the University of Oklahoma. Her main interests are in the sociological constructions of deviance and stigma, gender, sexuality, LGBTQ identities, as well as feminist and queer criminology. She is the author of nearly fifty academic articles and book contributions and currently serves as an associate editor of *Deviant Behavior*. Dr. Worthen has received multiple awards for her work including the Irene Rothbaum Outstanding Assistant Professor award, given to a model teacher recognized for dedication, effectiveness and ability to inspire students to high levels of achievement, the Robert D. Lemon Social Justice Award, given to a faculty member who demonstrates courage, compassion, and leadership while working to eliminate discrimination, oppression, and injustice locally and globally, and the Jill Irvine Leadership Award, given to a faculty member who exemplifies collaborative spirit, expansive vision, commitment to advancing women's and LGBTQ issues, service to campus, and dedication to leadership.

In addition to her work in academia, Dr. Worthen is the creator of The Welcoming Project, a non-profit organization that promotes LGBTQ-friendly businesses, organizations, churches/congregations, and health care providers by providing "All Are Welcome" rainbow signs to post in their windows and on their websites. She also developed @MeTooMeredith, an Instagram platform where survivors of sexual violence and harassment can share their stories anonymously. As a researcher, teacher, and activist, Dr. Worthen's work dissects multiple dimensions of prejudice in efforts to cultivate understanding, empathy, and social change.

# ACKNOWLEDGMENTS

I would like to acknowledge the following people for their contributions to the creation and execution of this book. Many at the University of Oklahoma significantly helped shape the last decade of my life in academia. To the members of the Department of Sociology in particular, I am eternally grateful for the support, mentorship, and guidance you all have provided. For this book especially, I am forever indebted to Melissa Jones who was there for me to bounce ideas off of, which included her review of many, many iterations of the chapters in this book (all while completing her dissertation as a graduate student at OU) and numerous lengthy phone calls as I struggled through the theory construction and book writing processes. I am also grateful to Amy Goodin, Trina Hope, Tonya Maynard, and Marc Musick for their help with the survey instrument that was used to collect data for this project, Haley Cook for her help with the review of the literature, and Mitch Peck for his help with statistical methods. I would also like to thank the 3,104 survey respondents who contributed their experiences to this project and the anonymous manuscript reviewers who have helped me build critical insight into LGBTQ stigma over the years. I would be remiss not to thank Mark Stafford who taught me the foundations of deviance and stigma, who has supported and mentored me for nearly twenty years, and who let me know (upon reading my first draft of NCST) that "*It is the most well-conceived treatment of stigma I have ever read.*" I would also like to acknowledge my family. My parents' unwavering commitment to my thirst for knowledge and lifelong teachings of social justice made me who I am today. My husband, Brian, who has been with me every step of this academic journey was there to lift me up, give me motivation, and supply me with unyielding support when I needed it (and even when I didn't). To my daughter, Gwyneth. You teach me more about the importance of kindness, respect, and the joy of diversity every day. It is my true honor to be your mother and to watch you grow. To all these wonderful people in my life and those not explicitly mentioned here, thank you. Without you, I would not be able to write about the experiences of marginalized people like myself with such candor and respect. I am forever appreciative of the insight you have given me.

# PREFACE

In this book, I argue that we must build separate but interconnected discussions about the experiences of lesbian women, gay men, bisexual women, bisexual men, trans women, trans men, non-binary/genderqueer individuals, queer women, and queer men to best understand LGBTQ stigma and negativity. I first outlined portions of this argument in an article published in *Sex Roles* entitled "An Argument for Separate Analyses of Attitudes toward Lesbian, Gay, Bisexual Men, Bisexual Women, MtF and FtM Transgender Individuals" (Worthen 2013). The goal of this piece is to encourage future researchers to investigate prejudices toward LGBT individuals as separate from one another. In particular, I highlight how the intersections of gender and sexual identity contribute to differing attitudes toward L, G, B, and T individuals. The manuscript offers no empirical analyses of its own but rather functions as a "think piece." As a relatively new scholar (I first submitted this piece to *Sex Roles* in 2011, less than two years after obtaining my Ph.D. in 2009), I was unsure how my first non-empirical manuscript would be received—especially since the *Sex Roles* editor-in-chief, Irene Frieze, invited me to submit this theoretical paper *after* rejecting an empirical piece I submitted to *Sex Roles* using a similar framework (that empirical article was later published in 2012 in *Sociological Focus*). Dr. Frieze expressed interest in my arguments and after its initial peer review was favorable, she assigned my theoretical paper to a special issue (68:11/12) on intersections of gender, sexual identity, and racial/ethnic identities, co-edited by Mike Parent, Cirleen DeBlaere, and Bonnie Moradi. Much to my pleasure, it was exceedingly well received. I continue to be astounded by the positive response to this manuscript. Since its publication in 2013, it has been one of the top most-frequently cited and downloaded articles from *Sex Roles* and as of January 2020, it has been cited over 200 times according to Google Scholar Citations. The success of this manuscript stimulated many of my subsequent publications and of course, the writing of this book.

However, since first writing this "think piece" back in 2011, I have been working on refining my arguments and building a deeper understanding of these issues. In particular, in my search to explain LGBTQ negativity, I coined the construct of *hetero-cis-normativity* in 2012 (first published in "Hetero-cis-normativity and the Gendering of Transphobia," Worthen 2016a). I identify hetero-cis-normativity as a system of norms, privilege, and oppression that organizes social power around sexual identity and gender identity whereby heterosexual cisgender people are situated above all others and thus, LGBTQ people are in a place of systemic disadvantage. Hetero-cis-normativity dictates an intersectional perspective that considers how our social positions in society, including gender, race, ethnicity, and class identities (among others) shape experiences with oppression and privilege (e.g., Collins 2000; Crenshaw 1991; Davis 2008). Thus, hetero-cis-normativity serves as the theoretical construct that helps to explain LGBTQ negativity in an intersectional context.

The original framework of this book was initially entirely focused on hetero-cis-normativity and intersectionality. However, after a year into writing this book, in spring of 2018 it became obvious that I needed to think more about LGBTQ stigma in particular. While it is clear that hetero-cis-normativity underlies LGBTQ stigma, the links between hetero-cis-normativity and LGBTQ stigma needed further clarification. In other words, I knew there was something missing; there was something about norms and stigma that needed more attention. At this point, I looked to Erving Goffman (1963), the "father" of the scholarly investigation of stigma. I also refreshed my memory on the widely recognized update to contemporary stigma research, Bruce Link and Jo Phelan's (2001) "Conceptualizing Stigma." I did not know exactly what I was looking for but I believed I could find it there. Although I had read both of these pieces dozens of times and poured over them in great detail during numerous graduate seminars I had led over the past decade, something exciting popped out at me this time; much to my surprise, it was not Link and Phelan's (2001) work (which I knew well) but rather a piece that they cited written by Mark C. Stafford and Richard R. Scott way back in 1986 (when I was just a toddler). In Link and Phelan's (2001:364) discussion of variations in the definition of stigma, they list Stafford and Scott's definition: "stigma is a characteristic of persons that is contrary to a norm of a social unit" (Stafford and Scott 1986:80). When I reread this singular sentence, I was delighted. Not only was this the "missing link" between norms and stigma that I believed I had been looking for, but also, I had known the author of it (Mark C. Stafford) for nearly half of my life! Mark taught me sociology and deviance while I was an undergraduate and graduate student at the University of Texas at Austin from 2001 to 2009, and he served as my thesis committee chair. He is, for all intents and purposes, my academic mentor. He is also my colleague and friend.

So of course I emailed him immediately and asked him to send me his 1986 piece. As I waited for his response, I began to brainstorm more deeply about these ideas and it just came to me while I was driving: Norm-Centered Stigma Theory (NCST). I would build my own stigma theory focusing on the importance of norms.

Only hours later, I received an email back from Mark:

*Hi Meredith,*
*Here is the chapter. Happy reading! While it is an oldie, I believe it is still a goodie.*
*Mark*

Mark was right, it *was* "a goodie." In fact, I was not sure if I was on the right track with my norm-centered theory building until I read this piece. With a skeleton of the theory in place, I searched for additional work that drew connections between stigma and norms while keeping close hold to the importance of intersectionality and social power. Only a week later, I had my first draft of NCST written along with dozens of chicken scratches of theoretical models I had drawn. I continued to craft NCST in the subsequent months of writing this book in an effort to build something helpful to other scholars of stigma. In the end, I believe I have created something valuable and unique. It is my hope that NCST will be a powerful fixture in future scholarly work investigating stigma.

Beyond my enthusiasm about NCST, I am also excited about the data in this book. Thanks to a grant I received from the Norman Campus Research Council's Faculty Investment Program at the University of Oklahoma, I was able to obtain a nationally representative sample of heterosexual-cisgender (n = 1,500) and LGBTQ (n = 1,604) U.S. adults aged 18–64 stratified by U.S. census categories of age, gender, race, ethnicity and census region. In the social sciences, nationally representative data is the "gold standard" for which quantitative survey projects are evaluated because using such data allows for scholars to offer findings that can be generalized to the general population. Despite this, it is extremely rare for social scientists exploring LGBTQ attitudes to use nationally representative data because obtaining such data is so expensive that it can be cost-prohibitive. In fact, I am aware of only two manuscripts in this area of inquiry that have utilized such data in recent years: Norton and Herek (2013) and Hatzenbuehler, Flores, and Gates (2017). No existing research (whether nationally representative or not) explores attitudes toward all nine groups of LGBTQ individuals as done in this book. So I am excited to say that this study is innovative in that it is the first to examine LGBTQ attitudes among a nationally representative sample of heterosexual-cisgender and LGBTQ U.S. adults. Notably, it offers the only generalizable findings about LGBTQ attitudes among heterosexual-cisgender and LGBTQ American adults, making this especially impactful research. By using nationally representative data that appeal to the social sciences' utmost data standards, this book will ideally have a major influence on the existing literature that speaks to the complexities of LGBTQ stigma. As a result, unlike any other previously published scholarly works, I am proud to say that this book has the potential to have broad impacts on society at large, helping to improve the LGBTQ cultural climate.

## Author's Note

Portions of this book have been drawn from my previous published works including Worthen (2011, 2012a, 2012b, 2013, 2014, 2016a, 2016b, 2018; 2019), Worthen, Lingiardi, and Caristo (2017), and Worthen et al. (2019).

## References

Collins, Patricia Hill. 2000. *Black Feminist Thought* (Second Edition). New York, NY: Routledge.
Crenshaw, Kimberlé. 1991. "Mapping the Margins: Intersectionality, Identity, Politics, and Violence against Women of Color." *Stanford Law Review* 43:1241–1299.
Davis, Kathy. 2008. "Intersectionality as Buzzword: A Sociology of Science Perspective on What Makes A Feminist Theory Successful." *Feminist Theory* 9:67–85.
Goffman, Erving. 1963. *Stigma: Notes on the Management of Spoiled Identity*. New York, NY: Penguin Books.
Hatzenbuehler, Mark L., Andrew R. Flores, and Gary J. Gates. 2017. "Social Attitudes regarding Same-Sex Marriage and LGBT Health Disparities: Results from a National Probability Sample." *Journal of Social Issues* 73(3):508–528.
Link, Bruce and Jo Phelan. 2001. "Conceptualizing Stigma." *Annual Review of Sociology* 27:363–385.
Norton, Aaron T. and Gregory M. Herek. 2013. "Heterosexuals' Attitudes toward Transgender People: Findings from a National Probability Sample of US Adults." *Sex Roles* 68:738–753.
Stafford, Mark and Richard Scott. 1986. "Stigma, Deviance, and Social Control." Pp. 77–91 in *The Dilemma of Difference: A Multidisciplinary View of Stigma*, edited by Stephen C. Ainlay, Gaylene Becker, and Lerita M. Coleman. Boston, MA: Springer.
Worthen, Meredith G. F. 2011. "College Student Experiences with an LGBTQ Ally Training Program: A Mixed Methods Study at A University in the Southern United States." *Journal of LGBT Youth* 8(4):332–377.
Worthen, Meredith G. F. 2012a. "Understanding College Student Attitudes toward LGBT Individuals." *Sociological Focus* 45(4):285–305.
Worthen, Meredith G. F. 2012b. "Heterosexual College Student Sexual Experiences, Feminist Identity, and Attitudes toward LGBT Individuals." *Journal of LGBT Youth* 9(2):77–113.
Worthen, Meredith G. F. 2013. "An Argument for Separate Analyses of Attitudes toward Lesbian, Gay, Bisexual Men, Bisexual Women, MtF and FtM Transgender Individuals." *Sex Roles: A Journal of Research* 68(11/12):703–723.
Worthen, Meredith G. F. 2014. "The Interactive Impacts of High School Gay-Straight Alliances (GSAs) on College Student Attitudes toward LGBT Individuals: An Investigation of High School Characteristics." *Journal of Homosexuality* 61(2):217–250.

Worthen, Meredith G. F. 2016a. "Hetero-cis-normativity and the Gendering of Transphobia." *International Journal of Transgenderism* 17(1):31–57.

Worthen, Meredith G. F. 2016b. *Sexual Deviance and Society: A Sociological Examination.* London: Routledge.

Worthen, Meredith G. F. 2018. ""Gay Equals White?" Racial, Ethnic, and Sexual Identities and Attitudes toward LGBT Individuals among College Students." *Journal of Sex Research* 55(8):995–1011.

Worthen, Meredith G. F. 2019. "A Rainbow Wave? LGBTQ Liberal Political Perspectives during Trump's Presidency: An Exploration of Sexual, Gender, and Queer Identity Gaps." *Sexuality Research and Social Policy*, Online First, DOI: 10.1007/s13178-019-00393-1.

Worthen, Meredith G. F., Vittorio Lingiardi, and Chiara Caristo. 2017. "The Roles of Politics, Feminism, and Religion in Attitudes toward LGBT Individuals: A Cross-Cultural Study of College Students in the United States, Italy, and Spain." *Sexuality Research and Social Policy* 14(3):241–258.

Worthen, Meredith G. F., Annalisa Tanzilli, Chiara Caristo, and Vittorio Lingiardi. 2019. "Social Contact, Social Distancing, and Attitudes toward LGT Individuals: A Cross-Cultural Study of Heterosexual College Students in the United States, Italy, and Spain." *Journal of Homosexuality* 66(13):1882–1908.

# 1
# INTRODUCTION

*I Abstained From Sex for a Year to Donate Blood*[1]
*Gay Veteran, 91, Gets Honorable Discharge After 69 Years*[2]
*Supreme Court Ruling Makes Same-Sex Marriage a Right Nationwide*[3]
*Bathroom Law Repeal Leaves Few Pleased in North Carolina*[4]
*Boy Scouts, Reversing Century-Old Stance, Will Allow Transgender Boys*[5]

These headlines pulled from *The New York Times* evoke feelings of victory, triumph, prejudice, and stigma for LGBTQ individuals and their allies. Indeed, the current global socio-political climate is loaded with contention regarding LGBTQ rights (Kollman and Waites 2009; McCarthy 2019; Worthen, Lingiardi, and Caristo 2017). In the United States, there have been obvious improvements for gay men and lesbian women and the vast majority of public opinion research demonstrates a significant attitudinal shift toward support of lesbian women and gay men in recent years (McCarthy 2019; Pew Research Center 2014, 2017). However, amidst these gains, stigma and prejudice remain. Gay men and lesbian women endure legal barriers to adoption and state family leave protections (Goldberg et al. 2014). Bisexual men and women lack recognition and significant cultural presence (Brewster and Moradi 2010; Worthen 2013). Trans people face a variety of unique challenges that situate their daily experiences within a nexus of hostility and misunderstandings (Serano 2007; Stryker 2008). Queer and non-binary/genderqueer people and issues are missing from the vast majority of socio-political legal and cultural discourse (Morandini et al. 2016; Stein and Plummer 1994). Many U.S. states do not have employment and housing non-discrimination laws, leaving non-heterosexual and non-cisgender individuals exceedingly vulnerable (Becker 2014).

While many situate these conversations within the monolithic category of "LGBTQ" rights, much can be learned from a more nuanced investigation. In particular, I argue that we must build separate but interconnected discussions about the experiences of lesbian women, gay men, bisexual women, bisexual men, trans women, trans men, non-binary/genderqueer people, queer women, and queer men to best understand LGBTQ stigma and negativity (see Worthen 2013). In addition, I suggest that a norm-centered intersectional examination of hetero-cis-normativity is integral to understanding LGBTQ stigma. This approach will be further specified in Part I and explored in depth in Part II.

## Outline

This text is divided into two parts. Part I, Foundations in Understanding LGBTQ Stigma, introduces the concepts that are used in this text to build a deeper understanding of LGBTQ stigma and explanations for it. Chapter 2 specifies NCST building from Goffman's (1963) foundational book and works by modern scholars of stigma (e.g., Link and Phelan 2001; Stafford and Scott 1986) as well as intersectional (e.g., Collins 2000; Crenshaw 1991; Davis 2008) and queer (e.g., Butler 1990, 1993; Sedgwick 1991) theorists in order to expand the current landscape of stigma research. An emphasis on the relationships between norms, social power, and stigma is highlighted in the three tenets of NCST identified in Chapter 2. A theoretical model for NCST and accompanying hypotheses are also provided.

In Chapter 3, the key concepts that are explored throughout the text are further specified. First, hetero-cis-normativity is defined as the overarching norm that secures the cultural devaluation of LGBTQ people. Next, the relationships between hetero-cis-normativity, multiple axes of social power, and LGBTQ stigma are discussed in an intersectional context. Building from these arguments, race, ethnicity, and social class are examined as interlocking systems of oppression and privilege that relate to LGBTQ stigma. Specifically, three norms common in the West that inform these relationships are interrogated: "gay equals White," "trans equals White," and "gay equals rich." Finally, I consider the sexualization processes involved in LGBTQ stigma, objectification, and victimization as they relate to stereotypes about LGBTQ sex, relationships, and bodies.

Chapter 4 overviews the explanations and correlates of LGBT(Q) stigma most commonly found in past work (i.e., LGBT contact, religiosity, political perspectives, and beliefs about gender) and considers both hetero-cis-normativity and intersectionality and their overlapping relationships to common explanations of LGBT stigma. The "Q" is largely missing from this chapter because "common" existing explanations fail to encapsulate attitudes toward queer people and queer-related stigma. This chapter concludes with a discussion of hetero-cis-normativity as the social construct that underlies these common explanations for LGBT stigma.

Chapter 5 examines ways to measure LGBTQ stigma, starting with an overview of the socio-historical contexts of previously published tools (and problems therein) and then provides new ways to measure LGBTQ stigma. Seven LGBTQ Measurement Principles are offered to help guide future inquiry. In addition, hetero-cis-normativity measurement tools are detailed. Finally, these measurement principles and tools are situated into NCST.

Chapter 6 provides the LGBTQ Stigma Scales that speak to the Measurement Principles outlined in Chapter 5. Specifically, six key areas of the LGBTQ Stigma Scales are discussed as they relate to LGBTQ people's experiences with stigma: (1) social and familial relationships; (2) positions of importance and social significance; (3) basic human rights; (4) sex-related stigma; (5) LGBTQ identity permanency; and (6) the achievement of femininity or masculinity. This chapter concludes with the integration of the LGBTQ Stigma Scales into NCST.

Part II, NCST and Understanding LGBTQ Stigma, provides one of the first-ever empirical investigations of NCST. Specifically, Part II considers how violations of hetero-cis-normativity (as they relate to multiple axes of social power) are key to understanding stigma directed toward LGBTQ people (stigmatizer lens) and LGBTQ people's experiences with discrimination, harassment, and violence (stigmatized lens). Chapter 7 describes the data, sample, and survey and also provides an overview of the overarching trends and patterns that are found throughout Part II. Each of the following chapters in Part II follows a similar pattern whereby NCST is applied to understand LGBTQ stigma. This includes three interrelated methods: (1) rank-ordering and *t*-test comparisons of the LGBTQ Stigma Scales and individual scale items; (2) Ordinary Least Squares (OLS) regression models of NCST, social power axes, and the LGBTQ Stigma Scales; and (3) logistic regression models of NCST and LGBTQ gender- and sexuality-based discrimination, harassment, and violence. Chapter 8 focuses on lesbian women, followed by gay men in Chapter 9, bisexual women in Chapter 10, bisexual men in Chapter 11, transgender women in Chapter 12, transgender men in Chapter 13, non-binary/genderqueer people in Chapter 14, queer women in Chapter 15, and queer men in Chapter 16.

Chapter 17 offers additional considerations, suggestions for future research, and concluding remarks. It both summarizes the text and its novel approach of breaking LGBTQ prejudices down into separate but related concepts and then builds these ideas together by acknowledging their significant overlap. Finally, future research areas are offered including the importance of understanding how LGBTQ people resist stigma and oppression as well as the roles of other identities including cultural origin, age, and ability in additional investigations.

## Goals

The goals of this text are three-fold: (1) to introduce a theory about stigma that is testable and grounded in previous research (NCST), (2) to highlight the significance of hetero-cis-normativity and intersectionality in understanding LGBTQ stigmatization (stigmatizer lens) and the stigmatizing experiences of LGBTQ people (stigmatized lens), and (3) to continue to stress the importance of separate but interconnected discussions about lesbian women, gay men, bisexual women, bisexual men, trans women, trans men, non-binary/genderqueer people, queer women, and queer men to uncover both similarities and differences across their experiences.

## Notes

1 https://www.nytimes.com/2017/01/12/opinion/i-abstained-from-sex-for-a-year-to-donate-blood.html?rref=collection%2Ftimestopic%2FHomosexuality&action=click&contentCollection=timestopics&region=stream&module=stream_unit&version=latest&contentPlacement=1&pgtype=collection
2 https://www.nytimes.com/2017/01/10/nyregion/gay-veteran-air-force-undesirable-honorable-discharge.html?rref=collection%2Ftimestopic%2FHomosexuality&action=click&contentCollection=timestopics&region=stream&module=stream_unit&version=latest&contentPlacement=2&pgtype=collection
3 https://www.nytimes.com/2015/06/27/us/supreme-court-same-sex-marriage.html
4 https://www.nytimes.com/2017/03/30/us/north-carolina-senate-acts-to-repeal-restrictive-bathroom-law.html?_r=0
5 https://www.nytimes.com/2017/01/30/us/boy-scouts-reversing-century-old-stance-will-allow-transgender-boys.html

## References

Becker, Amy B. 2014. "Employment Discrimination, Local School Boards, and LGBT Civil Rights: Reviewing 25 Years of Public Opinion Data." *International Journal of Public Opinion Research* 26(3):342–354.

Brewster, Melanie E. and Bonnie Moradi. 2010. "Perceived Experiences of Anti-Bisexual Prejudice: Instrument Development and Evaluation." *Journal of Counseling Psychology* 57(4):451.

Butler, Judith. 1990. *Gender Trouble: Feminism and the Subversion of Identity*. New York NY: Routledge.

Butler, Judith. 1993. "Critically Queer." *GLQ: A Journal of Lesbian and Gay Studies* 1:17–32.

Collins, Patricia Hill. 2000. *Black Feminist Thought* (Second Edition). New York, NY: Routledge.

Crenshaw, Kimberlé. 1991. "Mapping the Margins: Intersectionality, Identity, Politics, and Violence against Women of Color." *Stanford Law Review* 43:1241–1299.

Davis, Kathy. 2008. "Intersectionality as Buzzword: A Sociology of Science Perspective on What Makes a Feminist Theory Successful." *Feminist Theory* 9:67–85.

Goffman, Erving. 1963. *Stigma: Notes on the Management of Spoiled Identity*. New York, NY: Penguin Books.

Goldberg, Abbie, Lori Kinkler, April Moyer, and Elizabeth Weber. 2014. "Intimate Relationship Challenges in Early Parenthood among Lesbian, Gay, and Heterosexual Couples Adopting via the Child Welfare System." *Professional Psychology: Research & Practice* 45:221–230.

Kollman, Kelly and Matthew Waites. 2009. "The Global Politics of Lesbian, Gay, Bisexual and Transgender Human Rights: An Introduction." *Contemporary Politics* 15(1):1–17.

Link, Bruce and Jo Phelan. 2001. "Conceptualizing Stigma." *Annual Review of Sociology* 27:363–385.

McCarthy, Justin. 2019. "Gallup First Polled on Gay Issues in '77. What Has Changed?" Gallup. Retrieved August 21, 2019 (https://news.gallup.com/poll/258065/gallup-first-polled-gay-issues-changed.aspx).

Morandini, James S., Alexander Blaszczynski, and Ilan Dar-Nimrod. 2016. "Who Adopts Queer and Pansexual Sexual Identities?." *The Journal of Sex Research* 54(7):911–922.

Pew Research Center. 2014. "Views about Homosexuality." *Pew Research Center*. Retrieved August 21, 2019 (www.pewforum.org/religious-landscape-study/views-about-homosexuality/).

Pew Research Center. 2017, October 4. "Majorities in both Parties Now Say Homosexuality should be Accepted." *Pew Research Center*. Retrieved January 31, 2020 (www.people-press.org/2017/10/05/5-homosexuality-gender-and-religion/5_1-8/).

Sedgwick, Eve Kosofsky. 1991. *Epistemology of the Closet*. Berkeley, CA: University of California Press.

Serano, Julia. 2007. *Whipping Girl: A Transsexual Woman on Sexism and the Scapegoating of Femininity*. Berkeley, CA: Seal Press.

Stafford, Mark and Richard Scott. 1986. "Stigma, Deviance, and Social Control." Pp. 77–91 in *The Dilemma of Difference: A Multidisciplinary View of Stigma*, edited by Stephen C. Ainlay, Gaylene Becker, and Lerita M. Coleman. Boston, MA: Springer.

Stein, Arlene and Ken Plummer. 1994. "'I Can't Even Think Straight' Queer Theory and the Missing Sexual Revolution in Sociology." *Sociological Theory* 12(2):178–187.

Stryker, Susan. 2008. *Transgender History*. Berkeley, CA: Seal Press.

Worthen, Meredith G. F. 2013. "An Argument for Separate Analyses of Attitudes toward Lesbian, Gay, Bisexual Men, Bisexual Women, MtF and FtM Transgender Individuals." *Sex Roles: A Journal of Research* 68(11/12):703–723.

Worthen, Meredith G. F., Vittorio Lingiardi, and Chiara Caristo. 2017. "The Roles of Politics, Feminism, and Religion in Attitudes toward LGBT Individuals: A Cross-Cultural Study of College Students in the United States, Italy, and Spain." *Sexuality Research and Social Policy* 14(3):241–258.

PART I

# Foundations in Understanding LGBTQ Stigma

# 2
# THEORIZING STIGMA AND NORM-CENTERED STIGMA THEORY

Since Erving Goffman's work thrust the concept of stigma forward in the 1960s, scholars across numerous disciplines have recognized the value of stigma in understanding the experiences of vulnerable and marginalized populations who endure negativity. Myriad concepts have been defined throughout the endeavors of stigma-based research—including nearly 50 stigma-related terms identified by Goffman (1963) (e.g., the stigmatized, the normal, the wise, etc.)—as well as concepts defined by notable scholars of stigma such as Gerhard Falk (e.g., existential and achieved stigma, Falk 2001:11) and Bruce Link and Jo Phelan (e.g., stigma as a "persistent predicament," Link and Phelan 2001:379). As Falk (2001) succinctly states, "Stigmatization is a social fact and will always be with us" (339). While the value of stigma is indisputable, theories of stigma are largely missing from extant literature. Instead, scholars often focus on clarifying and/or identifying types of stigma (e.g., Goffman's "abominations of the body" 1963:4), the processes involved in stigma (e.g., labeling: Becker 1963; Lemert 1951; Link and Phelan 2001; Schur 1984; Tannenbaum 1938), the dimensions of stigma (Jones et al. 1984), or stigma as related to specific experiences (e.g., stigma and mental illness, Fink and Tasman 1992; stigma and HIV/AIDS, Liamputtong 2013). Such work is tremendously valuable and has brought much sophistication to the study of stigma. Still, most modern-day scholars have not chosen to focus on developing stigma theory.

There are three likely reasons why this is the case. First, Goffman literally wrote the book on stigma. It is often thought of as the foundation of all social science research on stigma. Goffman's book is cited by nearly all stigma researchers and has been translated (in full) into Danish (Goffman 2009) and German (Goffman 2016). Yet Goffman's *Stigma: Notes on the Management of Spoiled Identity* (1963) does not offer a "theory of stigma." As a result, scholars often integrate Goffman's key terms about stigma into their own work without theorizing about stigma itself. Second, while scholars agree that stigma is a useful concept, there is some level of disagreement about how it should be defined (see Link and Phelan 2001 for a review). Third, and related, there is also disagreement about what the focus of research about stigma should be (e.g., discrimination, status loss, social avoidance, social control, etc.) (Falk 2001; Schur 1984; Stafford and Scott 1986). Thus, amidst copious amounts of scholarly work about stigma, theory about stigma remains relatively scarce.

## Norm-Centered Stigma Theory (NCST)

In this book, I propose an addition to the well-established scholarly work about stigma that focuses on the importance of norms. I call this *Norm-Centered Stigma Theory* (NCST). To introduce this theory, I first identify the concepts that the foundations of NCST are derived from. These are: norms, social power, and stigma. NCST defines these concepts as follows:

- Norms are established standards and expectations about beliefs, behaviors, and identities maintained by a particular group and/or society that are culturally bound and organized by social power. All societies have those who follow norms and those who violate norms.
- Social power is privilege based on access to and embodiment of social, cultural, economic, and political advantages afforded to certain beliefs, behaviors, and identities and not others.
- Stigma is the negativity and other social sanctions (e.g., stereotyping, discrimination, devaluation, and denigration) directed toward norm violations and norm violators which is organized and justified through social power dynamics between the stigmatized and the stigmatizers, and is situated on a spectrum.

Below, I further explain these concepts as they relate to the three tenets of NCST.

### *The Three Tenets of NCST*

#### *NCST Tenet #1: There Is a Culturally Dependent and Reciprocal Relationship between Norms and Stigma*

Using the definitions of both norms and stigma outlined above, it becomes clear that stigma *depends* on norms. Without norms, and in particular, norm violations, there is no stigma. In other words, the central element of identifying and understanding stigma *is* norms. Under NCST, this is defined as *norm centrality*. Because both norms and stigma are dependent on culturally bound established standards and expectations about beliefs, behaviors, and identities, they feed off one another. As norm following and norm violations are defined, so is stigma. Thus, the relationship between norms and stigma is reciprocal.

I am by no means the first scholar to highlight the overlap between norms and stigma. As Goffman (1963) noted:

> One can therefore suspect the role of the normal and the role of the stigmatized are parts of the same complex, cuts from the same standard cloth (130)...In conclusion, may I repeat that stigma involves not so much a set of concrete individuals who can be separated into two piles, the stigmatized and the normal, as a pervasive two-role social process in which every individual participates in both roles, at least in some connections and in some phases of life. The normal and the stigmatized are not persons but rather perspectives.
>
> *(137–138)*

Thus, according to Goffman (1963) and NCST, norms are central to understanding stigma and lead to processes that code certain beliefs, behaviors, and identities into "the normal" (norm following) and "the stigmatized" (norm violating). As will be discussed later in Tenets #2 and #3, NCST further expands Goffman's (1963) conceptualization of two easily discernible groups (norm followers and norm violators) by considering how both social power and the *spectrum of stigma* relate to these processes.

Goffman (1963) also identified the importance of understanding the *relationships* between norms and stigma in his widely cited definition of stigma:

> The term stigma, then, will be used to refer to an attribute that is deeply discrediting, but it should be seen that a language of relationships, not attributes, is really needed ... A stigma, then, is really a special kind of relationship between an attribute and a stereotype.
>
> *(3–4)*

To rephrase Goffman (1963:3–4), "stigma" (the "deeply discrediting attribute") has a "special kind of relationship" with a "stereotype." Or in other words, there is an important connection between stigma and stereotypes. While norms are not the same as stereotypes, both represent ideas about how people should or should not behave, identify, and think in a particular society with the former more focused on known trends and patterns and the latter less based on realities and more concentrated on perceptions and biases. Even so, it is reasonable to suggest that Goffman's (1963) definition of stigma fits within NCST.

NCST also has foundations in Stafford and Scott's (1986) work. In calling attention to their own observation that "conceptualization and use of the term [stigma] have been so vague and uncritical that one may reasonably ask: What is stigma?" (77), Stafford and Scott (1986) offer the following response: "Stigma is a characteristic of persons that is contrary to a norm of a social unit" (80) where a "norm" is inclusive of "shared beliefs as to what individuals ought to be (behaviorally and otherwise)" (81). Thus, Stafford and Scott (1986) emphasize two components in their definition of stigma: behavioral and nonbehavioral norm violations. Much like Stafford and Scott (1986), NCST also calls attention to stigma as the violation of norms about beliefs, behaviors, and identities.

Notably, Link and Phelan's (2001) widely popular and impressively developed conceptualization of stigma does not specifically emphasize norms. In fact, the only mention of "norms" in Link and Phelan's (2001) article is referencing Stafford and Scott's (1986) work (and is somewhat incorrectly done[1]). Even so, Link and Phelan (2001) do call attention to the importance of distinguishing, labeling, and "identifying [human] differences that will matter socially" (367) which "differ dramatically according to time and place" (368). Although Link and Phelan (2001) do not state as such, it is not unreasonable to assume that the "differences" from socially valued characteristics they describe can be perceived of as norm violations (e.g., sighted people differ from blind people: the norm and socially valued characteristic is to be sighted and blind people violate this norm). This is at least somewhat in line with NCST's emphasis on stigma and norm violations yet lacks the nuances that a norm-centered approach to stigma offers.

Link and Phelan (2001) (see also Jones et al. 1984) also describe a process whereby these so-called differences are linked to undesirable characteristics that form stereotypes. As they note, their conceptualization of the stigma process is similar to Goffman's (1963) in that it calls attention to the "relationship between an attribute and a stereotype" (4). As previously described, although stereotypes are not the same as norms, both Goffman's (1963) definition of stigma and Link and Phelan's (2001) process of linking socially valued human differences to stereotypes relate to NCST.

To summarize, the emphasis on the relationship between norm violations and stigma as outlined in Tenet #1 of NCST is not new. In particular, both Goffman (1963) and Stafford and Scott (1986) specifically highlight the role of norms in identifying stigma as well as the relationships between norms and stigma. However, NCST is unique from this past work in that its additional tenets emphasize the role of social power in conjunction with *norm centrality*. In doing so, NCST situates the importance of social power within the nexus of norm violations and stigma. These relationships within NCST are further discussed below.

### NCST Tenet #2: the Relationship between Norms and Stigma Is Organized by Social Power Dynamics between the Stigmatized and the Stigmatizers

NCST defines social power as an organizational element within the links between norms and stigma. In other words, established standards and expectations maintained by a particular group and/or society are embedded within and organized around existing culturally bound infrastructures that privilege some beliefs, behaviors, and identities, and oppress others. Norm followers secure privileges that go along with the embodiment/adoption of certain social, cultural, economic, and political norms while norm violators experience oppressive disadvantages and stigma. This creates a hierarchy of non-stigmatized norm followers and stigmatized norm violators that is organized by social power. In other words, NCST recognizes *social power as organizational* in the relationship between norms and stigma.

Again, I am by no stretch of the imagination the first to draw links between norms, social power, and stigma. Indeed, in his description of social identity norms (Goffman 1963:126–130), Goffman proposes that:

> there is only one complete unblushing male in America: a young married, white, urban, northern, heterosexual Protestant father of college education, fully employed, of good complexion, weight, and height, and a recent record in sports. Every American male tends to look out upon the world from this perspective, this is constituting one sense in which one can speak of a common value system in America. Any male who fails to qualify in any of these ways is likely to view himself—during moments at least—as unworthy, incomplete, and inferior.
>
> *(128)*

This "unblushing male" is an *ideal* social identity, or in other words, an *ideal type*. If "he" existed, "he" would occupy the top of the social hierarchy and would retain both privilege and social power. Persons existing outside of these ideal social identity norms lack social power and are stigmatized according to their non-normative status. It is clear that this "single set" of norms (ideal beliefs, behaviors, and identities) is virtually unattainable yet reinforced within society by most of its members. Goffman (1963) states:

> It can be assumed that a necessary condition for social life is the sharing of a single set of normative expectations by all participants, the norms being sustained in part because of being incorporated ... The common ground of norms can be sustained far beyond the circle of those who fully realize them.
>
> *(127–129)*

Goffman (1963) claims that even those who could by no means achieve this ideal type (e.g., women, atheists, LGBTQ people) share these normative expectations about ideal beliefs, behaviors, and identities. Goffman (1963) goes on to say that such "general identity-values of a society may be fully entrenched nowhere, and yet they cast some kind of shadow on the encounters encountered everywhere in daily living" (128–129). In this way, we all suffer from the inability to adhere to this ideal social identity norm, but the further away from this norm we are, the less social power and the more stigma and suffering we will endure. Goffman (1963), however, does not explicitly mention "power" in his book on stigma and perhaps because of this, he neglects to acknowledge anything beyond norm consensus (i.e., a single ideal type) including the existence of norm dissensus (i.e., multiple—even conflicting—ideal types) (Rossi and Berk 1985).

Further identifying these relationships, Link and Phelan (2001) squarely locate the importance of social power in their updated conceptualization of stigma when they state:

> stigmatization is entirely contingent on access to social, economic, and political power ... Thus, we apply the term stigma when elements of labeling, stereotyping, separation, status loss, and discrimination co-occur in a power situation that allows the components of stigma to unfold.
>
> *(367)*

Here, Link and Phelan (2001) propose that all of the converging elements involved in stigma should be understood as related to power (see also Jones et al. 1984; Schur 1980). Much like such previous scholars have done, NCST situates stigma within power dynamics between the stigmatized and stigmatizers. NCST's emphases on *norm centrality* and *social power as organizational* in understanding stigma add to these complexities.

In addition, according to NCST, social power organizes the lens from which the relationship between norm violations and stigma is examined. In particular, there are two lenses: the *stigmatized lens* and the *stigmatizer lens*. The *stigmatized lens* considers how the target of stigma's (i.e., the stigmatized) own axes of social power impact their own experiences with negativity, prejudice, and stigma. In contrast, the *stigmatizer lens* examines how the stigmatizer's (i.e., the individual who is potentially expressing negativity or passing judgement on another) own axes of social power impact their feelings about the target of stigma. Because the stigmatizer most commonly has more social power than the stigmatized (though not always, consider when the stigmatized becomes the stigmatizer, e.g., Syke's and Matza's technique of "condemnation of the condemners" 1957:668), these two lenses are organized by social power and thus, shape the ways NCST is investigated.

For example, consider the relationships between HIV/AIDS-related stigma and racial identity. Using the stigmatized lens, one might examine how the race (their own axis of social power) of the person with HIV/AIDS impacts their own experiences with enduring the stigma associated with HIV/AIDS. Here, the focus is on the target of stigma and their experiences with social power and stigma as they relate to their own norm violations. Using the stigmatizer lens, one would examine how the stigmatizer's race (their own axis of social power) impacts their feelings about HIV/AIDS. Here, the focus is on the stigmatizer and their experiences with social power as they relate to attitudes toward norm violations and accompanying stigma. In other words, there is an important distinction between two types of questions: (1) how does being a Black person with HIV/AIDS impact experiences with HIV/AIDS-related stigma (stigmatized lens)? or (2) how does being a Black person impact stigmatizing perspectives about HIV/AIDS (stigmatizer lens)? In both examples, the relationship between HIV/AIDS (norm violation) and its associated stigma is examined; however, the lens from which this relationship is viewed shapes how race (social power) is investigated as it relates to HIV/AIDS-related stigma. In the stigmatized lens example, we might explore internalized HIV/AIDS stigma among a sample of those living with HIV/AIDS with special attention to race (e.g., Overstreet et al. 2012). In the stigmatizer example, we might explore HIV/AIDS-related stigmatizing attitudes among those without HIV/AIDS but also with special attention to race (e.g., Earnshaw and Chaudoir 2009). Both projects would examine HIV/AIDS-related stigma and racial identity; however, they would differ in their lens of social power (stigmatized lens or stigmatizer lens) and most likely, in the social power and composition of their populations (sample of stigmatized people or sample of potential stigmatizers). Making the distinction between the stigmatized lens and the stigmatizer lens allows for the exploration of important complexities in these relationships regarding *social power as organizational* and thus, this distinction is an essential component of NCST.

### NCST Tenet #3: Stigma Is Inclusive of Negativity and Social Sanctions Directed toward Norm Violations and Norm Violators Justified through Social Power Dynamics and Situated on a Spectrum

NCST's third tenet provides a norm-centered, social power justification for negative treatment of the stigmatized. Because societies value upholding norms and rewarding norm followers, the stigma, social sanctions, and negativity norm violators endure become culturally validated. In other words, stigma (and its accompanying negativity) is justified by norms that reflect the privileging of those with social power and the simultaneous oppression of those lacking social power. NCST emphasizes *social power as justification* for the enduring negativity that stigmatized people experience.

Here, there is overlap between NCST and Link and Phelan's (2001) work. Specifically, they note that power differentials lead to the placement of individuals into distinct categories and this creates "some degree of separation of 'us' from 'them'" (Link and Phelan 2001:367). This in turn provides the "rationale" for "smoothly accomplished" labeling and stereotyping "because there is little harm in attributing all manner of bad characteristics to 'them'" (370).

Link and Phelan (2001) describe power differentials as a "rationale" for stigma. Thus, differences in power allow for "the full execution" of social sanctions ("disapproval, rejection, exclusion, and discrimination") to occur (Link and Phelan 2001:367). In other words, much like NCST, Link and Phelan's (2001) conceptualization of stigma both situates stigma within power dynamics and suggests that these power differentials permit or even authorize a wide range of negativity and other social sanctions directed toward the stigmatized. NCST expands these ideas by bringing together the role of social power in *norm centrality* while also emphasizing *social power as justification* in understanding the accompanying social sanctions toward the stigmatized norm violators.

Other scholars have also taken care to highlight social power as a rationale or justification for stigma. For example, in his book, *Labeling Women Deviant: Gender, Stigma, and Social Control*, Edwin Schur (1984) links stigma to powerlessness in patriarchal societies. In particular, due to women's inferior social power as compared to men's, they are deemed deviant subordinates and the social sanctions they endure (because they are women) are justified through the fact that they are lacking in social power. Schur (1984) uses gender norms to support these claims. For example, women's appearance norms related to visual objectification and sexuality norms related to heteronormativity mean that men can legitimize the stigmatization of women who do not meet these ideals. The (lesser) complement to Goffman's (1963:128) "unblushing male," this "unblushing female," is also an *ideal* social identity, one that men expect women to achieve but that is unattainable. Thus, women's stigmatization is built from norm violations (specific to women) that are predicated on powerlessness. In these ways, those with more social power, in this case men, have the power to determine who is stigmatized (women) *and* who is "normal" (men). The system of norms that value patriarchy secures this process in place and women's stigmatization becomes "a key mechanism that backs up and 'enforces' many of the restrictions and limitations placed on women" (Schur 1984:11). In line with NCST, Schur's (1984) work specifically considers how the negativity and stigma women endure is "backed up" by patriarchal gender norms that give social power to men (over women).

Also focusing on *social power as justification* for stigma, Gregory Herek (2007) first defined his construct of "sexual stigma" as "the negative regard, inferior status, and relative powerlessness that society collectively accords to any nonheterosexual behavior, identity, relationship or community" (906–907). Herek (2007) then explained two overlapping heterosexist cultural assumptions that "legitimate and perpetuate sexual stigma and the differentials in status and power" that secure the "inferior status" of nonheterosexuals as compared to heterosexuals (907). These are: (1) the "heterosexual assumption" and (2) the assumption that nonheterosexuals will be problematized when made visible (Herek 2007:907–908). As Herek (2007) explains, because nonheterosexuality does not fit the heterosexual assumption,

> Nonheterosexuals, homosexual behavior, and same-sex relationships are presumed to be abnormal and unnatural, and, therefore, are regarded as inferior, as requiring explanation, and as appropriate targets for hostility, differential treatment and discrimination, and even aggression. By contrast, heterosexuals are regarded as prototypical members of the category people, and heterosexual behavior and different-sex relationships are presumed to be normal and natural.
>
> *(907–908)*

In these ways, Herek's (2007) concept of sexual stigma is justified through power differentials that are reflected by heterosexism. Through *norm centrality* as defined in NCST, sexual stigma can perhaps be better understood as a violation of the norm of heteronormativity (a term which is strangely missing from Herek's 2007 piece). As NCST's Tenet #3 states, stigma is built from norm violations justified through social power dynamics. Therefore, we would expect to see violations of heteronormativity relate to sexual stigma in a process that socially sanctions those that violate heteronormativity and socially rewards those who adhere to heteronormativity. This process further secures the social power of heteronormative people over non-heteronormative people. In this way, NCST's focus on *norm centrality* helps expand Herek's (2007) conceptual framework by providing a theoretical lens with which to examine the relationships between heteronormativity, social power, and sexual stigma.

The final element of NCST's Tenet #3 is the norm-centered, social power justification for the *spectrum of stigma*, whereby some beliefs, behaviors, and identities are stigmatized more than others and thus, the associated social sanctions of stigma also vary. As seen in Figure 2.1, in the spectrum of stigma, some are situated on one end as highly stigmatized, illegitimate, invisible, and denigrated while others are situated on the opposite end as legitimate, recognized, and supported. In the middle lies the "zone of transition." Here, enhanced cultural awareness about some beliefs, behaviors, and identities results in contemporary debate about their status as normative or stigmatized. They are being actively challenged thus they are permitted, visible, and tolerated.

Goffman (1963) does not specifically describe a spectrum of stigma but he does state that stigma can vary depending on "degree of obtrusiveness" including "how much it interferes with the flow of interaction" (49). Similarly, Jones et al. (1984:24) define "disruptiveness" as a unique dimension of stigma that impairs communication. Some discrediting attributes are more obtrusive and disruptive than others due to the ways they impact social situations. Goffman (1963:49) provides the example of a person in a wheelchair sitting behind a conference table as compared to a person speaking who has an obvious speech impediment. He notes that social responses and associated social sanctions toward these individuals will certainly vary. Furthermore, Goffman (1963:50) states that the "perceived focus" of the stigma (e.g., medical, social,

**18** Foundations in Understanding LGBTQ Stigma

| Stigmatized Identities, Behaviors, and Beliefs | Actively Debated Identities, Behaviors, and Beliefs | Normative Identities, Behaviors, and Beliefs |
|---|---|---|
| Illegitimate | Permitted | Legitimate |
| Invisible | Visible | Recognized |
| Denigrated | Tolerated | Supported |
| | *Zone of Transition* | |

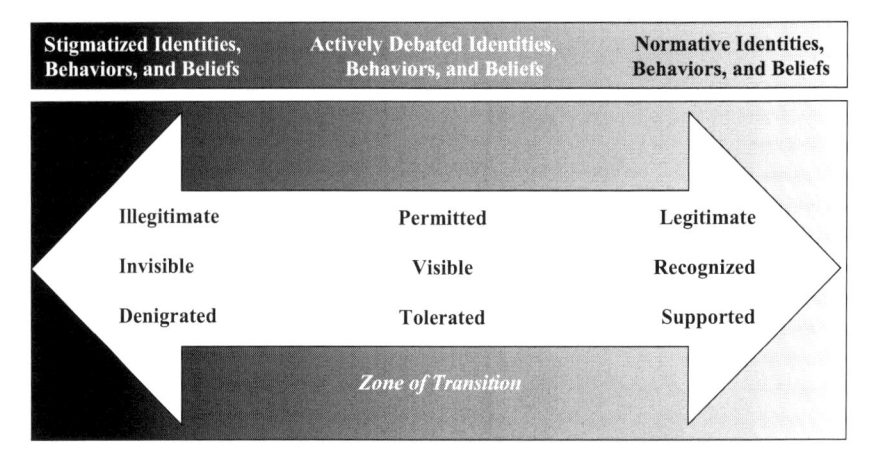

**FIGURE 2.1** Spectrum of Stigma

etc.) will also result in differing social responses and associated social sanctions toward the stigmatized. NCST states that these differences and variations should be understood on a spectrum of stigma, as seen in Figure 2.1.

Adding the necessary link to social power to these ideas, Link and Phelan (2001) discuss stigma as "a matter of degree" that can "vary from group to group" (377) based on "power differences" between those who have "available resources to resist the stigmatizing tendencies of the more powerful group" (378) and those who do not. In other words, those with more access to social power have more resources to prevent stigma and accompanying negativity. Succinctly stated, "The amount of stigma that people experience will be profoundly shaped by the relative power of the stigmatized and the stigmatizer" (Link and Phelan 2001:378). Thus, those who endure high levels of stigma are also severely lacking in social power. There is a relationship between the two (stigma and social power). Link and Phelan (2001:379) also emphasize "stigma as a persistent predicament" due to its far-reaching mechanisms of individual and structural discrimination and multiple outcomes. Such differences across stigma experiences imply the importance of thinking about stigma as situated on a spectrum. Link and Phelan (2001) go on to solidify these dynamics by stating that "In the extreme, the stigmatized person is thought to be so different from 'us' as to be not really human. And again, in the extreme, all manner of horrific treatment of 'them' becomes possible" (370). Somewhat similarly, Jones et al. (1984:66) describe "peril" as a dimension of stigma that is associated with threat such that the more strongly a certain belief, behavior, or identity becomes associated with danger, the more strongly stigmatized the belief, behavior, or identity will be (e.g., violent crime). These ideas are reflected in the left end of NCST's spectrum of stigma (see Figure 2.1) whereby beliefs, behaviors, and identities are highly stigmatized, illegitimate, invisible, and denigrated.

NCST's "zone of transition" in the spectrum of stigma whereby some beliefs, behaviors, and identities are being actively challenged and thus they are permitted, visible, and tolerated, can also be seen, at least partially, in Jones et al.'s (1984) work. Specifically, Jones et al. (1984:302) describe a "destigmatization" process that occurs when a discredited or devalued belief, behavior, or identity becomes more positively evaluated over time. Jones et al. (1984:302) offer several examples of the destigmatization process (e.g., positive shifts in valence toward divorce, ethnic minorities, obesity, "homosexuality") and locate some of these within organized movements (e.g., the Black Power Movement, the Gay Rights Movement). While Jones et al. (1984) identify such shifts away from stigma, they do not situate their arguments in the context of *norm* transitions. Link and Phelan (2001) do allude to the importance of norm transitions when they note that "to really change stigma … the deeply held attitudes and beliefs of powerful groups that lead to labeling, stereotyping, setting apart, devaluing, and discriminating" must also change (381). In a similar fashion, NCST proposes that changing norms is the key to changing stigma and that the "zone of transition" is where some of these changes are taking place in the spectrum of stigma.

Intersectional theorists (e.g., Collins 2000; Crenshaw 1991; Davis 2008) further locate these relationships within a framework that takes into consideration how our social positions in society, including gender, race, ethnicity, and class identities (among others) shape perspectives, life experiences, and trajectories. Intersectionality frameworks acknowledge differences across these identities as well as power imbalances embedded within them. In doing so, intersectional approaches locate negative social sanctions and oppression within a nexus of power imbalances built from systemically problematic "isms" (e.g., sexism, racism, classism, etc.). In addition, queer theorists (e.g., Butler 1990, 1993; Sedgwick 1991) also consider social power imbalances through interrogating, problematizing, critiquing, and deconstructing heterosexism and presumptions about gender and sexual identity (e.g., cisnormativity and heteronormativity) (Stein and Plummer 1994; Valocchi 2005). Queer theorists often focus on gender and sexuality norm violations (e.g., "the anatomies, genders, sexual practices, and identities that do not neatly fit into either category of the binaries or that violate the normative alignment of sex, gender, and sexuality") and "the ways, for example, gender is sexed and sexuality is gendered in nonnormative ways" (Valocchi 2005:753). In doing so, both intersectional and queer theorists consider how multiple, intersecting axes of social power (e.g., sexism, racism, classism, heterosexism, etc.) shape life experiences.

Such power-driven "isms" can be conceived of as norm violations of socially valued behaviors, beliefs, and identities that, according to NCST, are stigmatized. NCST recognizes that these norm violations occur in a constellation of differing ways that exist on a spectrum of stigma. Those who violate multiple norms (e.g., working-class queer women of color) experience stigma in different ways than those who occupy multiple positions of social power (e.g., upper-class White heterosexual men). It is easier for those with social power to be norm followers than it is for those lacking in social power. In addition, among those with social power who do violate norms, social power can help them to resist/deflect stigma. According to NCST, there is a relationship between norm violations and stigma that is significantly impacted by the presence (or absence) of social power. A spectrum of stigma exists because such variations in social power lead to different experiences with norm violations.

In sum, numerous scholars note the importance of norms (especially Goffman 1963; Stafford and Scott 1986) in defining stigma. Others, in particular, Link and Phelan (2001), identify the role of social power in conceptualizing stigma. Still others (e.g., Collins 2000) recognize diverse, interacting axes of social power that shape varying life circumstances that lead to a spectrum of stigma and signal the importance of considering these experiences from both the stigmatized lens and stigmatizer lens. None, however, have created a solidified, norm-centered, power-driven stigma theory. NCST brings these ideas together through its theoretical model and accompanying testable hypotheses.

## *NCST Theoretical Model and Hypotheses*

At the outset, NCST identifies norms as organized by social power. Thus, the norms and norm violations examined using NCST should be recognized as built from and embedded in social power. In addition, there are two important relationships that NCST outlines (see Figure 2.2). First, there is a direct relationship between norm violations and stigma. For example, as norm violations become more numerous and/or more threatening, stigma increases. Second, the relationship between norm violations and stigma is moderated by social power. Social power impacts the relationship between norm violations and stigma.

Together, this leads to the four testable hypotheses of NCST:

- *Hypothesis 1a:* there is a significant relationship between norm violations and norm violation stigma.
- *Hypothesis 1b:* there is a significant relationship between individual axes of social power and norm violation stigma.
- *Hypothesis 2a:* the relationship between norm violations and norm violation stigma is moderated by interactions between axes of social power and norm violations.
- *Hypothesis 2b:* the relationship between norm violations and norm violation stigma is moderated by interactions between axes of social power.

```
                    ┌─────────────────────────┐
                    │  Axes of Social Power   │
                    │     Interactions        │
                    ├─────────────────────────┤
                    │ Norms or Norm Violations*│
                    │   Axes of Social Power  │
                    ├─────────────────────────┤
                    │  Axes of Social Power*  │
                    │  Axes of Social Power   │
                    └─────────────────────────┘
                                │
┌──────────────┐  ┌──────────┐  │
│   Norms      │  │  Norm    │  ▼               ┌──────────────┐
│ Organized by │─▶│Violations│  ───────────────▶│Norm Violation│
│ Social Power │  │          │                  │   Stigma     │
└──────────────┘  └──────────┘                  └──────────────┘
┌───────────────────────────────┐
│     Axes of Social Power      │
└───────────────────────────────┘
```

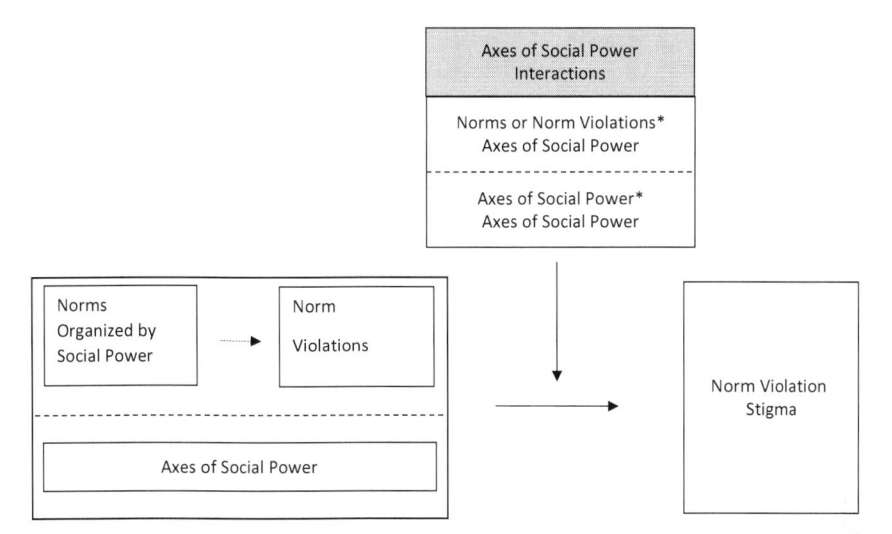

**FIGURE 2.2** Theoretical Model of Norm-Centered Stigma Theory

*Note:* The * indicates an interaction.

## Summarizing Norm-Centered Stigma Theory

In sum, NCST is an addition to the existing scholarly work about stigma that focuses on *norm centrality*. Unlike previous work, NCST offers both a theoretical model and accompanying testable hypotheses. In doing so, scholars interested in exploring the relationships between norms, social power, and stigma can utilize the tenets of NCST in their own investigations. In the next chapter, I outline one of the first empirical investigations of NCST that will take place in the remainder of this book which examines the relationships between hetero-cis-normativity, intersectionality, and LGBTQ stigma.

## Note

1 Link and Phelan (2001:365) somewhat incorrectly state that Stafford and Scott's (1986) definition of stigma relies on the definition of a norm as a "shared belief that a person ought to behave in a certain way at a certain time (Stafford and Scott 1986:81)." This is inaccurately quoted and misrepresents the broader conception of norms (both behavioral and nonbehavioral) that Stafford and Scott (1986) emphasize. The exact quote from Stafford and Scott's (1986:81) more general conception is that norms "are depictions of 'ideal' persons, shared beliefs as to what individuals ought to be (behaviorally and otherwise)."

## References

Becker, Howard. 1963. *Outsiders*. New York, NY: Free Press.
Butler, Judith. 1990. *Gender Trouble: Feminism and the Subversion of Identity*. New York, NY: Routledge.

Butler, Judith. 1993. "Critically Queer." *GLQ: A Journal of Lesbian and Gay Studies* 1:17–32.
Collins, Patricia Hill. 2000. *Black Feminist Thought* (Second Edition). New York, NY: Routledge.
Crenshaw, Kimberlé. 1991. "Mapping the Margins: Intersectionality, Identity, Politics, and Violence against Women of Color." *Stanford Law Review* 43:1241–1299.
Davis, Kathy. 2008. "Intersectionality as Buzzword: A Sociology of Science Perspective on What Makes A Feminist Theory Successful." *Feminist Theory* 9:67–85.
Earnshaw, Valerie A. and Stephenie R. Chaudoir. 2009. "From Conceptualizing to Measuring HIV Stigma: A Review of HIV Stigma Mechanism Measures." *AIDS and Behavior* 13:1160–1177.
Falk, Gerhard. 2001. *Stigma: How We Treat Outsiders*. Amherst, NY: Prometheus Books.
Fink, Paul Jay and Allan Tasman (Eds.). 1992. *Stigma and Mental Illness*. Washington, D.C: American Psychiatric Press, Inc.
Goffman, Erving. 1963. *Stigma: Notes on the Management of Spoiled Identity*. Englewood Cliffs, NJ: Prentice-Hall.
Goffman, Erving. 2009. *Stigma: Om Afvigerens Sociale Identitet*. København: Samfundslitteratur. Retrieved January 31, 2020 (http://samples.pubhub.dk/9788759325629.pdf).
Goffman, Erving. 2016. "Stigma: Über Techniken Der Bewältigung Beschädigter Identität." in *Kriminologische Grundlagentexte*, Wiesbaden: Springer VS. Retrieved January 31, 2020 (http://irwish.de/PDF/Goffman/Goffman-Stigma.pdf).
Herek, Gregory M. 2007. "Confronting Sexual Stigma and Prejudice: Theory and Practice." *Journal of Social Issues* 63(4):905–925.
Jones, Edward, Amerigo Farina, Albert Hastorf, Hazel Markus, Dale Miller, and Robert Scott. 1984. *Social Stigma: The Psychology of Marked Relationships*. New York, NY: W.H. Freeman and Company.
Lemert, Edwin. 1951. *Social Pathology*. New York, NY: McGraw-Hill.
Liamputtong, Pranee (Ed.). 2013. *Stigma, Discrimination, and Living with HIV/AIDS: A Cross Cultural Perspective*. New York, NY: Springer.
Link, Bruce and Jo Phelan. 2001. "Conceptualizing Stigma." *Annual Review of Sociology* 27:363–385.
Overstreet, Nicole M., Valerie A. Earnshaw, Seth C. Kalichman, and Diane M. Quinn. 2012. "Internalized Stigma and HIV Status Disclosure among HIV-positive Black Men Who Have Sex with Men." *AIDS Care* 25(4):466–471.
Rossi, Peter H. and Richard A. Berk. 1985. "Varieties of Normative Consensus." *American Sociological Review* 50(3):333–347.
Schur, Edwin. 1980. *The Politics of Deviance: Stigma Contests and the Uses of Power*. Englewood Cliffs, NJ: Prentice-Hall, Inc.
Schur, Edwin. 1984. *Labeling Women Deviant*. New York, NY: McGraw Hill Publishing.
Sedgwick, Eve Kosofsky. 1991. *Epistemology of the Closet*. Berkeley, CA: University of California Press.
Stafford, Mark and Richard Scott. 1986. "Stigma, Deviance, and Social Control." Pp.77–91 in *The Dilemma of Difference: A Multidisciplinary View of Stigma*, edited by Stephen C. Ainlay, Gaylene Becker, and Lerita M. Coleman. Boston, MA: Springer.
Stein, Arlene and Ken Plummer. 1994. "'I Can't Even Think Straight' Queer Theory and the Missing Sexual Revolution in Sociology." *Sociological Theory* 12(2):178–187.
Sykes, Gresham M. and David Matza. 1957. "Techniques of Neutralization: A Theory of Delinquency." *American Sociological Review* 22(6):664–670.

Tannenbaum, Frank. 1938. *Crime and the Community*. New York, NY: Columbia University Press.

Valocchi, Stephen. 2005. "Not yet Queer Enough: The Lessons of Queer Theory for the Sociology of Gender and Sexuality." *Gender & Society* 19(6):750–770.

# 3
# IDENTIFYING HETERO-CIS-NORMATIVITY AND INTERSECTIONALITY IN LGBTQ STIGMA

To begin to understand LGBTQ stigma and the interlocking complexities involved in the oppression of LGBTQ people, this book offers one of the first ever empirical investigations of NCST. Using NCST, hetero-cis-normativity (defined below) is conceptualized as the centralized overarching concept that helps us to understand LGBTQ stigma and the cultural devaluation of LGBTQ people. Specifically, the relationships between hetero-cis-normativity, social power, and LGBTQ stigma are highlighted in this chapter using an intersectional lens that considers the ways multiple marginalized identities interact to privilege and disadvantage certain individuals (Collins 2000; Crenshaw 1991; Davis 2008). In particular, this intersectional perspective acknowledges the importance of gender- and sexuality-based oppression in line with queer theorists' interrogations of cisnormativity and heteronormativity (e.g., Butler 1990, 1993; Sedgwick 1990), and the importance of investigating the simultaneous and interacting effects of other identities (e.g., race, ethnicity, class, culture) on negative life experiences and prejudicial circumstances. This approach centers "issues of difference and diversity" (Davis 2008:71) as they relate to LGBTQ stigma and investigates how social identities converge and differentially situate LGBTQ individuals' experiences.

In this chapter, I first identify and define hetero-cis-normativity as the overarching theoretical concept that secures the cultural devaluation of LGBTQ people. Next, I outline the relationships between hetero-cis-normativity, power, and the spectrum of stigma. Then, I introduce how axes of social power, including race, ethnicity, and social class, relate to LGBTQ stigma and create a hierarchy of non-stigmatized norm followers and stigmatized norm violators that is organized by social power. Specifically, I interrogate three norms common in the West that inform these relationships: "gay equals White," "trans equals White," and "gay equals rich." Following this,

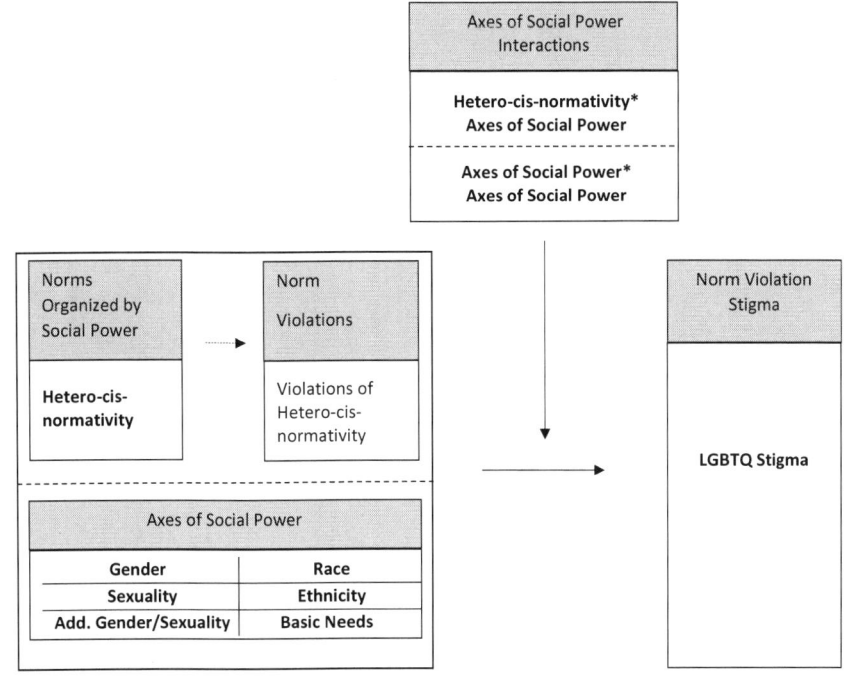

**FIGURE 3.1** Theoretical Model of NCST, Hetero-cis-normativity, and LGBTQ Stigma
*Note:* The * indicates an interaction.

I consider the sexualization processes involved in LGBTQ stigma, objectification, and victimization as they relate to stereotypes about LGBTQ sex, relationships, and bodies. Finally, I revisit the importance of NCST in understanding LGBTQ stigma. Overall, this chapter connects LGBTQ stigma and prejudice with hetero-cis-normativity by locating their social constructions within a discussion of social power informed by an intersectional perspective. Social power is contextualized as built from hetero-cis-normativity and White upper/middle-class privilege. This investigation of NCST and LGBTQ stigma is illustrated in Figure 3.1.

## Identifying Hetero-cis-normativity and LGBTQ Stigma

In most parts of the world, there is a system of norms, privilege, and oppression that situates heterosexual cisgender people above all others and thus, places LGBTQ people in a place of systemic disadvantage. This system of *"hetero-cis-normativity* whereby it is 'normal' to be both heterosexual and cisgender and it is not normal (and therefore acceptable to be prejudiced toward) non-heterosexual and non-cisgender individuals" (Worthen 2016a:31) organizes social power around sexual identity and gender identity. Hetero-cis-normative thinking is built from norms, stereotypes, and presumptions that often begin with sex assigned at birth

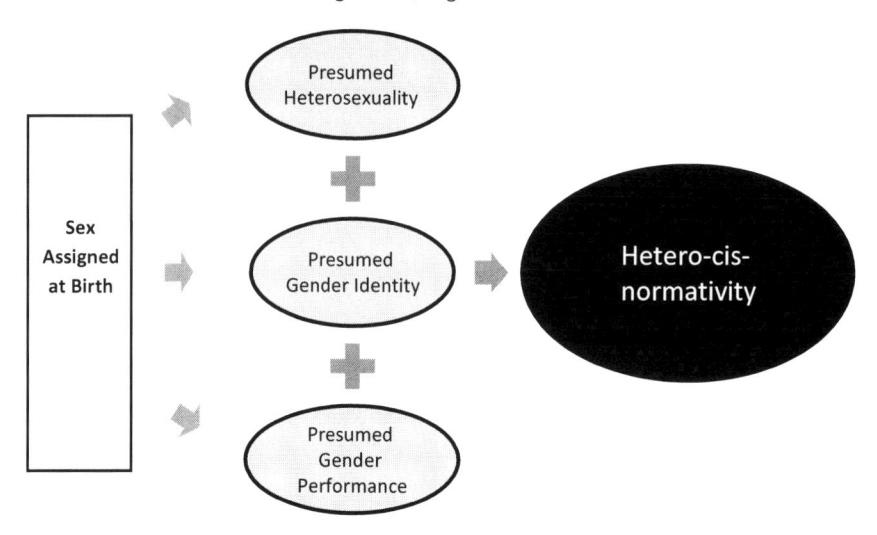

**FIGURE 3.2** The Relationships between Sex Assigned at Birth, Heterosexuality, Gender Identity, Gender Performance, and Hetero-cis-normativity

(which is frequently confined to a male/female dichotomy). From there, presumptions about gender identity, gender performance/expression, and heterosexuality flow as part of the larger system of hetero-cis-normativity, as seen in Figure 3.2 (Ingraham 1994; Rich 1980; Schilt and Westbrook 2009; West and Zimmerman 1987; Worthen and Dirks 2015). For example, a baby is born and the baby's sex assigned at birth is "male," then it is presumed this baby will identify as a boy (and later a man), that he will perform and express gender in a masculine way throughout his life course, and that he will be heterosexual. In this system, a person's privilege and/or stigma is built from sex assigned at birth. If this person follows hetero-cis-normativity (i.e., is a norm follower), privilege will likely follow. If this person goes against hetero-cis-normativity (i.e., is a norm violator), stigma will likely follow.

In most societies, culturally bound and socially enforced standards and expectations about gender and sexuality secure hetero-cis-normative beliefs, behaviors, and identities as advantageous and powerful. Thus, hetero-cis-normativity situates non-hetero and non-cis people in a place of social disadvantage whereby they are at risk for enduring negativity, stigma, and other social sanctions because they are violating the norms of hetero-cis-normativity. In this way, hetero-cis-normativity *is* the set of norms linked to LGBTQ stigma and social power both *organizes* and *justifies* these relationships.

## *Spectrum of Stigma: Gender and Sexual Identities*

The system of hetero-cis-normativity described above differentially impacts the stigma experiences of L, G, B, T, and Q people. This is illustrated on NCST's spectrum of stigma (as previously described in Chapter 2) with examples of gender and sexual identities in Figure 3.3. Looking at gender identities, cis men and cis women occupy a place of power and privilege on the right end of the spectrum as legitimate, recognized, and supported while trans people occupy the left end of the spectrum of stigma as highly stigmatized, illegitimate, invisible, and denigrated. In between are cis people in the "zone of transition" who perform gender in ways that challenge traditional notions of masculinity and femininity and thus, they are permitted, visible, and tolerated. Looking at sexual identities, heterosexuals exist on the powerful end of the spectrum and gay men and lesbian women are currently in the "zone of transition" due to the recent shifts in policy and public opinion that indicate increasing support of lesbian women and gay men (McCarthy 2019; Pew Research Center 2014, 2017). Queer people remain on the margins in stigmatized statuses. According to NCST, the role of social power should be emphasized in conjunction with *norm centrality* as they both relate to stigma. As illustrated in Figure 3.3, social power *organizes* the spectrum of LGBTQ stigma and differentially situates violators of hetero-cis-normativity.

Considering LGBTQ stigma on a spectrum of social power like this allows us to see some variations in the societal prejudices associated with gender, sex, and sexual identities, which will be further discussed throughout this text. However, before this, it is important to recognize that there are additional, intersectional layers of advantage and disadvantage involved in hetero-cis-normativity beyond sex assigned at birth, genders, and sexualities. In particular, hetero-cis-normativity is also closely entwined with Western White upper/middle-class norms. Race, class, and other experiences shape

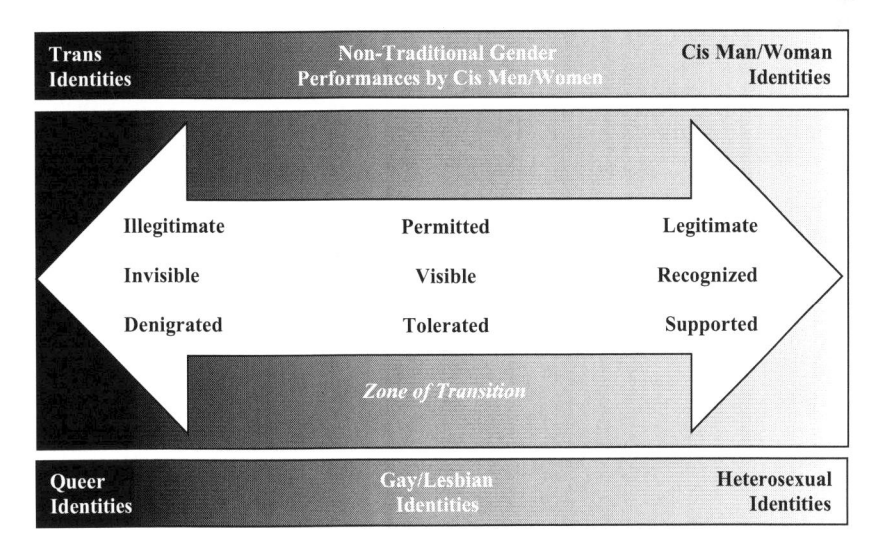

**FIGURE 3.3** Spectrum of Stigma with Examples of Gender and Sexual Identities

access to socially valued performances of gender and sexual identity (see more below). Indeed, "in many instances, constructions of gender are about being white [and] being perceived to be white" (Vidal-Ortiz 2014:264). Furthermore, "whiteness is a structuring and structured form of power that, through its operations, crystallizes inequality while enforcing its own invisibility" (Vidal-Ortiz 2014:264). As a result, there are multiple moving parts built into hetero-cis-normativity that inform places of privilege and oppression as well as power and stigma. Western White upper/middle-class norms often reinforce this system of hetero-cis-normativity and situate non-hetero, non-cis, non-White, and non-upper/middle-class people in vulnerable positions as stigmatized norm violators. Thus, at this juncture, it is important to introduce how race, ethnicity, and class experiences contribute to hetero-cis-normativity, social power, and LGBTQ stigma.

## Introducing Race, Ethnicity, and LGBTQ Stigma

Many discussions about race, ethnicity, and LGBTQ issues center on racial/ethnic differences in various experiences, attitudes, and perspectives (i.e., social contact, religiosity, political conservatism, and beliefs about gender) as they relate to LGBTQ stigma. These arguments will be described in Chapter 4 and explored in Part II. Here, I offer a brief overview of some unique and distinct cultural understandings of LGBTQ identities and stigma to further contextualize the relationships between race, ethnicity, and LGBTQ issues. In particular, I demonstrate how violations of hetero-cis-normativity (i.e., being LGBTQ) and accompanying experiences with LGBTQ stigma are impacted by race and ethnicity. In line with NCST, race and ethnicity are conceptualized as axes of social power that shape hetero-cis-normativity and the links between being LGBTQ and experiencing LGBTQ stigma.

To illustrate these patterns, I discuss two norms common in the West: "gay equals White" and "trans equals White." Both generally reflect a deeply embedded sociocultural historical focus on Whiteness and the erasure of people of color. These stereotypes also identify LGBTQ people of color as norm violators in multiple, interacting ways within a nexus of power imbalances built from systemically problematic "isms" (e.g., heterosexism, cisgenderism, racism, etc.). Interestingly, the solidification of these norms likely emerged at the same time out of the same cluster of events (the Stonewall Uprising). However, because gay and lesbian people are currently in the "zone of transition" (see Figure 3.3), scholarly discussions about gay and lesbian people of color are more prominent as compared to work focusing on trans people and trans people of color. It is also important to note that research on queer-identified people's experiences and non-binary people's lives is also not as abundant as work focusing on gay and lesbian people. Thus, in this chapter I review how the norms of "gay equals White" and "trans equals White" impact African American and

Black, Native American, Asian American, South Asian, Southeast Asian, and Pacific Islander, and Latinx LGBTQ people and the processes behind their stigmatization while also recognizing that not all experiences are monolithic.

## Gay Equals White?

In the West, there is a problematic norm that "gay equals White" and male (Han 2007:53; Whitley, Childs, and Collins 2011; see also Bérubé 2001; Battle, Pastrana, and Harris 2017b). Indeed, research suggests that the vast majority of people associate "homosexuality" with "Whiteness" and the term "homosexual" with a "gay man" (Whitley, Childs, and Collins 2011). This is evident in both heterosexual and LGBTQ communities as well as White communities and communities of color (Han 2007; Hunter 2010; Whitley, Childs, and Collins 2011). This typecasting restricts social understandings and awareness of non-gay (male), non-White issues and people. In doing so, it effects the ways LGBTQ people of color see themselves and the processes involved in their stigmatization. Furthermore, there are distinct cultural patterns that contribute to additional complexities in these relationships.

For example, being Black and being gay have been historically described as antithetical (Cohen 1996). Indeed, over three-quarters (77%) of Black LGBTQ people indicate that "homophobia" is a problem in the Black community (Battle, Pastrana, and Harris 2017b) and the silencing and invisibility of Black lesbian, gay, and bisexual people are evidenced in numerous studies (Bowleg 2013; Choi et al. 2011; Jeffries, Dodge, and Sandfort 2008; Ward 2005). Bowleg (2013) even found that Black gay and bisexual men sometimes "pass" as heterosexual in a process that both reduces experiences with sexual prejudice (in Black community, church, and family life especially) and simultaneously increases the saliency of one's Black identity over gay/bisexual identities (see also Battle et al. 2002; Hunter 2010). Furthermore, because Black lesbian, bisexual, and trans women endure *triple jeopardy* whereby they experience racial, gender, and sexual identity oppression (Greene 1996), they may sometimes obscure their stigmatized identities that are less overtly visible (i.e., their LGBTQ identities) to avoid oppressive experiences. These coping processes further contribute to the sociocultural equation of "gayness" and "Whiteness," the stigmatization of LGBTQ people of color, and the enforcement of hetero-cis-normativity.

There are also sexual identities often found in Black and African American cultural communities that shape these patterns, including same-gender-loving (SGL). Originally coined by activist Cleo Manago in the early 1990s, SGL is an identity predominantly used by Black and African American people with same-gender sexual and romantic attractions (Nagle 2000). Moving away from terms such as "gay" and "lesbian" which are often associated with "White" cultural scripts (Han 2007; Whitley, Childs, and Collins 2011), SGL is a culturally affirming identity that highlights the uniqueness of Black and African American same-gender relationships (Nagle 2000). Research shows that Black SGL men and women experience relatively high levels of family support and comfort in LGBTQ communities (Battle and Harris 2013; Harris and Battle 2013) but the vast majority of SGL people (82%) agree that "homophobia" is a problem in Black communities (Battle, Pastrana, and Daniels 2012). Thus, even among SGL people whose identities evoke the interconnectedness of African American culture and same-gender love, there is evidence of feeling stigmatized within Black communities.

In addition, many Native American cultures are inclusive of diverse expressions of gender and sexuality in family life and spiritual practice, including those of Two-Spirit people. Two-Spirit is an identity often within Native American and Alaskan/Inuit/Eskimo cultures that expresses sexual and gender diversity, moves away from White cultural definitions of "gay" or "transgender," and embraces non-hetero-cis identities. Two-Spirit people may "follow some or all of the parameters of alternate gender roles—which may include specific social roles, spiritual roles, and same-sex relationships—specific to their tribe or pan-ethnicity" (Adams and Phillips 2006:274). In doing so, Two-Spirit connects non-heteronormative and non-cisgender indigenous peoples with Native traditions that have historically valued their uniqueness (Adams and Phillips 2006; Elhakeem 2007; Jacobs, Thomas, and Lang 1997; Walters, Evans-Campbell, Simoni, Ronquillo, and Bhuyan 2006).

Even though Two-Spirit is embedded in Native traditions, most culturally conservative Native American communities (especially those that are Christian) reject LGBTQ and Two-Spirit people on the grounds of "tradition" (Gilley 2010:47). For example, Gilley's (2006, 2010) research with Two-Spirit men revealed that most believed that they had to hide their sexual desires and gender expression to be included in gendered tribal social and ceremonial practices (e.g., Powwow Princess and Head Man Dancer) and to spare their families from hostility, embarrassment, and shame. Additional research shows that Two-Spirit women feel connected to their traditional spiritual values but also struggle with being out and open in their own communities in fear of rejection (Walters et al. 2006). As one Two-Spirit woman noted "[In Indian Country] it's safe to be homophobic" (Walters et al. 2006:144). Furthermore, Native American LGBTQ and Two-Spirit people often feel disconnected and silenced. They experience a great deal of invisibility and many feel ostracized from larger society because they do not fit the "White" standard of gay Western culture and they also feel out of place in their own tribal nation (Adams and Phillips 2006; Han 2007; Walters et al. 2006). Indeed, 68% of Two-Spirit people agree that "homophobia" is a problem in their communities (Battle, Pastrana, and Daniels 2012). Thus, religious ceremonial participation, gendered obligations to family, and community norms drive hostility toward Native American LGBTQ and Two-Spirit people and perpetuate the relative invisibility of non-White LGBTQ people and the stigma they endure.

There are also diverse understandings of gender and sexuality within Asian American/Pacific Islander cultures beyond the LGBTQ acronym. For example, *Tom boys* or *Toms* (cis women who present themselves as masculine) are amongst the most visible in Thailand. Toms typically partner with extremely feminine cis women, frequently referred to as *Dees*. Interestingly, Tom and Dee relationships often reflect the "butch/femme" duality found among Western lesbian relationships but unlike them, Toms and Dees do not identify as "lesbians" and they have carved out their own unique Tom–Dee social scene (e.g., see Sinnott 2004 for a discussion of the Lesla community). Furthermore, despite their cultural presence, Toms and Dees remain relatively stigmatized in Thailand (Jackson and Sullivan 1999; Sinnott 2004). Although the Tom–Dee culture originated in Thailand, its increasing visibility in media reflects both rising cultural awareness and a global bridge for Toms and Dees who are not confined exclusively to the borders of Thailand. Indeed, Asian American/Pacific Islander people are one of the largest growing immigrant groups in the United States and the blending of Asian American/Pacific Islander gender and sexual diversity into American LGBTQ communities is evident (Battle, Pastrana, and Harris 2017a; Radford 2019).

Despite this, Asian American/Pacific Islander LGBTQ people face hostilities. For example, 69% of Asian American/Pacific Islander LGBTQ people believed that "homophobia" was a problem in the Asian American/Pacific Islander community in a large-scale American survey and about one-third of Asian American/Pacific Islander people indicated discomfort in the LGBTQ community due to their race or ethnicity (Battle, Pastrana, and Daniels 2012). Existing outside of the White stereotype associated with LGBTQ cultures can be particularly problematic for Asian American/Pacific Islander LGBTQ people. Indeed, one study found that LGBTQ Asian American/Pacific Islander individuals reported significantly more frequent experiences with racism in the LGBTQ community, racism in dating and close relationships, and heterosexism in racial/ethnic minority communities when compared to LGBTQ African American and Latinx individuals (Basalm et al. 2011). Such overlapping experiences with racism and LGBTQ stigma can lead some Asian American/Pacific Islander LGBTQ people to feel socially isolated and rejected from both heterosexual and LGBTQ spaces.

Within Latinx communities, there is also gender and sexual diversity. Historically, a great deal of research about LGBTQ identities in Latinx cultures focused on an activo/pasivo dymanic in the coupling of men—reflective of a masculine dominant/insertive (activo) partner and an effeminate submissive/receptive (pasivo) partner. However, more recent research examines a much wider range of relationships and numerous identities for members of LGBTQ Latinx communities (Daniel and Esteinou 2014; Jeffries, Dodge, and Sandfort 2008; Rodríguez 2003). For example, some Latinx people identify as Two-Spirit and connect with Native American indigenous communities (Estrada 2017). However, overlapping sociocultural practices including familial closeness (*familismo*), *machismo* and *marionismo*, and religiosity (Cauce and Domenech-Rodriguez 2002) can lead to the closeting of LGBTQ Latinx people (see more in Chapter 4). This may reflect the harsh sentiment evident in some Latinx communities that "being gay is the worst thing a man can do" (Estrada et al. 2011:359; see also Mirandé 1997). Indeed, 71% of Latinx LGBTQ people agreed that "homophobia" was a problem in their community in a large-scale American survey and less than half (48%) felt connected to the "LGBT" community (Battle, Pastrana, and Daniels 2012).

Latinx LGBTQ people also experience racism and stigma within LGBTQ communities. For example, qualitative research shows that Latino MSM (men who have sex with men) sometimes conceal their gay/bisexual identities and avoid spaces that they perceive cater to White gay men (Choi et al. 2011). Additional work indicates that lesbian and bisexual Latinas experience invisibility, alienation, and marginality within the larger LGBTQ community due to their multiple intersecting experiences of oppression based upon their gender (as women), race/ethnicity (as Latinas), and sexuality (as lesbian and bisexual people) (Alimahomed 2010). Together, such experiences shape the stigmatization of LGBTQ Latinx people and further the coupling of "Whiteness" and "gayness."

These examples only begin to scratch the surface of the complex relationships between race, ethnicity, and LGBTQ stigma. There are numerous additional ways these experiences intersect and myriad diverse dynamics beyond those mentioned here. For example, biracial and multiracial individuals experience these cultural influences in different ways, immigrants differ from first, second, and third generation citizens, and some non-Western conceptualizations of gender and sexuality simply do not translate into Western cultures (La Fountain-Stokes 2009; Luibhéid and Cantú 2005). Furthermore, while the "gay equals White" norm is vividly palpable in the West today, it is increasingly challenged by the growing visibility of LGBTQ people of color. Even so, as outlined in NCST, axes of social power strongly shape the relationships between violations of hetero-cis-normativity and accompanying LGBTQ stigma in ways that continue to be heavily informed by race, ethnicity, and culture (recall Figure 3.1).

## *Trans Equals White?*

Corresponding to the "gay equals White" phenomenon, there is also evidence of a "trans equals White" discourse. Indeed, Battle, Pastrana, and Harris (2017b:17) list "All trans* people are White" as one of the top LGBTQ myths in the current social climate. As scholar Susan Stryker notes, the field of transgender studies "has been criticized for the perceived Whiteness and Eurocentrism (or, even more pointedly, the US-centrism) of the term transgender: a term that originated among White, middle-class, American male cross-dressers" (Stryker 2009:89). This association may also serve a larger, and perhaps more insidious function. The equation of "trans" and "White" can be conceived of as a "colonizing move" whereby all understandings of "trans" are embedded in Whiteness (Stryker 2009:89; see also Valentine 2007). Related, most contemporary trans rights movements are predominantly led by White trans people while trans people of color are often "tokenistic[ally]" mentioned (Vidal-Ortiz 2014:265). In these ways, much of the dominant cultural awareness about trans issues is shaped by White-washed dialogue that marginalizes and further stigmatizes trans people of color in multiple, intersecting ways.

In line with other representations of marginalized peoples, trans individuals have served as specters, fools, and spectacles in side/freak show attractions, cabaret shows, and popular media. Rather unfortunately, perspectives about marginalized groups can be fully shaped by such media representations (in part because some people may have no known personal contact with some groups) and this may be especially the case for trans issues because unlike lesbian and gay people who are in the "zone of transition," trans people remain on the illegitimate, invisible, and denigrated side of the spectrum of stigma (recall Figure 3.3). Indeed, much of society currently relies on pop culture to illustrate what it means to be "trans" and in doing so, the complexities of trans peoples' lives and the lives of other relatively invisible and marginal groups are swept into simplistic stereotypes that do not accurately reflect the experiences of anyone. This process upholds the social power of norm followers (cisgender people), justifies the negativity and stigma that violators of cisnormativity (i.e., trans people) endure, and secures the devaluation of trans people and especially, trans people of color who experience interacting layers of oppression.

For example, popular media recently exploded with stories involving Caitlyn Jenner, an Olympic gold medal-winning decathlete who very publicly transitioned from male to female in 2015. Jenner was featured in various media outlets including the reality television series *I am Cait* (2015–2016) and the July 2015 *Vanity Fair* cover story "Call me Caitlyn" complete with glamorous photographs (Bissinger 2015). Her experiences are eerily similar to Christine Jorgensen's. Although transgender history began much earlier than her global media appearances in 1950s, Christine Jorgensen was the first widely known trans person.[1] Born in 1926 and assigned "male" at birth, Jorgensen's transition to female in 1951/1952 "brought an unprecedented level of public awareness to transgender issues, and helped define the terms that would structure identity politics in decades ahead" (Stryker 2008:49). With Danish American parents, her "young, pretty, gracious, and dignified," (Stryker 2008:47) White, upper-class appearance led to an immediate branding of what being "trans" looked like. Indeed, the 1952 New York *Daily News'* front-page headline "Ex-GI Becomes Blonde Bombshell" (White 1952) was the first of many newspapers worldwide that plastered her image across their covers not unlike the numerous 2015 media displays of Jenner's transition. Jorgensen "embodies the White, fashionably self-fashioning, glamorous ethos associated with the post-World War II US material culture" (Stryker 2009:89) as does Jenner in today's hyper-image-focused social media (e.g., in 2020 @CaitlynJenner had over 10 million Instagram followers). Interestingly, when presenting as men, both Jenner and Jorgensen had experiences in masculine, valorized institutions: Jenner, an Olympic athlete and Jorgensen, an Army veteran of WWII. As women, their White "pretty" appearances and social class privileges allowed them to become visible faces of what it means to be "transgender" both then and now.

The links to social power in both of these examples are unquestionable. Although they were/are both norm violators, because both Jorgensen and Jenner had/have access to multiple axes of social power (i.e., race, class, Western beauty), their trans-related stigma was/is shaped into a media-frenzy that upholds the "trans equals White" norm. Undeniably, not all violations of cis-normativity have the same (or even similar) outcomes. Within the trans umbrella, there is a hierarchy of stigmatized norm violations that is organized by social power which results in very different stigma experiences among White trans people and trans people of color.

Unlike Jorgensen and Jenner, trans people of color have endured systemic cultural erasure. For example, resistance and public demonstrations in working-class and poor urban neighborhoods among trans women of color in the 1960s, including the Compton's Cafeteria Riot in 1966[2], arguably helped shape the modern American LGBTQ rights movement. Even the 1969 Stonewall Uprising, which is often credited as the watershed demonstration that began the U.S. gay and lesbian movement, was instigated and supported by trans women of color Sylvia Rivera and Marsha P. ("Pay it no mind") Johnson, and drag king Stormé DeLarverie. Yet these women and others have been historically repeatedly erased from discussions about LGBTQ rights. This is likely because Stonewall and its accompanying activism became dominated by those with access to multiple axes of social power (i.e., upper/middle-class White gay cis men) starting with the Gay Activists Alliance, while people of color, especially trans women of color, were relegated to the margins of LGBTQ liberation. In particular, Rivera and Johnson were excluded from the Gay Activists Alliance and then formed their own organization, the Street Transvestite Revolutionaries, which focused on urban, homeless, impoverished trans youth (Stryker 2008). The race, class, gender, and power dynamics shaped in the aftermath of Stonewall sealed the privileges of upper/middle-class White gay cis men to the top of the LGBTQ rights movement confirming the associations between Whiteness and LGBTQ identities we still see today. At the same time, LGBTQ people of color and especially trans women of color have been further marginalized in the LGBTQ rights movement and in larger society due to their multiple, intersecting oppressed identities. This constellation of norm violations significantly impacts the stigma that trans people of color endure.

Taking a look back to pop culture (as we are often forced to do with marginalized groups still situated on the "denigrated" side of the spectrum of stigma, recall Figure 3.3), Laverne Cox certainly stands out. An African American trans actress and outspoken LGBTQ advocate, Cox brings a voice to trans women of color and is reshaping the "trans equals White" discourse. Like Jenner, she has been featured in various media outlets including the (2013–2019) Netflix series *Orange is the New Black* and the June 2014 *Time* magazine cover story "The Transgender Tipping Point: America's Next Civil Rights Frontier" (Steinmetz 2014). But unlike Jenner, Cox brings a much needed focus on race and class to media discourse surrounding trans issues. Indeed, today there is increasing visibility of trans people and their lives, especially trans women of color, defying the "trans equals White" stereotype.

Beyond these simplistic pop culture examples, scholarly research solidifies the continued need for a focus on trans people generally and trans people of color specifically. Studies consistently show that many trans people live in extreme poverty, endure abusive home lives, encounter numerous experiences with stigma and discrimination in schooling, housing, employment, and healthcare, suffer from mental and physical health issues including HIV, and are at life-threatening risk for victimization (James et al. 2016; Meyer 2008; Schilt and Westbrook 2009). Indeed, a U.S. nationwide study conducted by the National Center for Transgender Equality with nearly 28,000 respondents revealed that transgender and gender non-conforming people face pervasive difficulties in nearly all aspects of their lives (James et al. 2016). For example, as seen in Table 3.1, over half (54%) report intimate partner violence in their own relationships and close to half indicate that they have been sexually assaulted (47%). Forty percent report attempting suicide in their lifetimes (James et al. 2016).

Trans people of color are at a greater risk for experiences with stigma, discrimination, harassment, victimization, and negative health experiences as compared to White trans people, as seen in Table 3.2. For example, nearly three-quarters (73%) of Native American trans people report intimate partner violence in their own relationships as compared to just over half (54%) of White trans people and nearly two-thirds (65%) of Native American trans people indicate they have been sexually assaulted as compared to slightly less than half (45%) of White trans people (James et al. 2016). Over half (57%) of Native American trans people report attempting suicide as compared to about one-third (37%) of White trans people (James et al. 2016). A complex constellation of racism, classism, and trans prejudice shapes the experiences of trans people of color. Even so, there are numerous ways that trans people of color resist stigma and oppression and redefine the "trans equals White" discourse (see more in Chapter 17).

In addition, there are many terms beyond "trans" and "transgender" that people use to self-identify. Indeed, a survey conducted by the National Center for Transgender Equality with nearly 28,000 respondents revealed more than

**TABLE 3.1** Stigma, Discrimination, Harassment, Victimization, and Health Experiences of Transgender and Gender Non-Conforming People in the United States

| | | |
|---|---|---|
| **School (K-12)** | Verbally harassed | 54% |
| | Not allowed to dress in accordance with gender identity or expression | 52% |
| | Physically attacked | 24% |
| | Left school | 17% |
| | Sexually assaulted | 13% |
| | Expelled | 6% |
| **Home Life** | Intimate partner violence in their own relationships | 54% |
| | Family rejection | 50% |
| | Homelessness (lifetime) | 30% |
| | Homelessness (past year) | 12% |
| | Sent to professional to "stop" being transgender while growing up | 14% |
| | Ran away from home | 10% |
| | Kicked out of home | 8% |
| **Public Sphere** | Verbally harassed due to trans status (past year) | 46% |
| | Physically attacked due to trans status (past year) | 9% |
| | Sexually assaulted (past year) | 10% |
| | Sexually assaulted (lifetime) | 47% |
| | Discomfort asking police for help (lifetime) | 57% |
| **Public Restrooms (past year)** | Avoided using public restrooms | 59% |
| | Limited eating/drinking to avoid public restrooms | 32% |
| | Verbally harassed, physically attacked, and/or sexually assaulted | 12% |
| | Denied access due to trans status | 9% |
| | Developed a health problem due to avoiding public restrooms | 8% |
| **Workplace** | Verbally harassed, physically attacked, and/or sexually assaulted | 15% |
| | Quit job in fear of trans-based discrimination | 15% |
| | Job loss due to trans bias | 13% |
| **Identity Documents** | Documents do not have preferred name | 49% |
| | Documents do not have preferred gender | 67% |
| | Harassed due to presumed mismatch with identity documents | 25% |
| | Assaulted due to presumed mismatch with identity documents | 2% |
| **Mental Health** | Serious psychological distress (past year) | 39% |
| | Attempted suicide (past year) | 7% |
| | Attempted suicide (lifetime) | 40% |
| **Health Care** | Negativity from providers | 33% |
| | Avoided services in fear of harassment | 23% |
| | Professional tried to "stop" them from being transgender | 18% |

*Source*: Data come from 27,715 transgender, trans, genderqueer, and non-binary respondents from all fifty states, the District of Columbia, American Samoa, Guam, Puerto Rico, and U.S. military bases overseas (James et al. 2016).

**TABLE 3.2** Stigma, Discrimination, Victimization, and Health Experiences of Transgender and Gender Non-Conforming People in the United States by Racial and Ethnic Identity

|  |  | *Percentage of each race/ethnicity that responded affirmatively* |  |  |  |  |  |  |
|---|---|---|---|---|---|---|---|---|
|  |  | White | Asian | Latinx | Black | Middle Eastern | Native American | Multi-racial |
| **School (K-12)** | Verbally harassed | 55% | 53% | 52% | 51% | 61% | **69%** | 58% |
|  | Physically attacked | 23% | 17% | 24% | 28% | 36% | **49%** | 31% |
|  | Left school | 16% | 11% | 16% | 22% | 36% | **39%** | 21% |
| **Home Life** | Intimate partner violence in their own relationships | 54% | 43% | 54% | 56% | 62% | **73%** | 62% |
|  | Family rejection | 49% | 50% | 52% | 52% | 48% | **66%** | 49% |
|  | Sent to professional to "stop" being transgender while growing up | 14% | 15% | 16% | 14% | **31%** | 24% | 16% |
|  | Ran away from home | 8% | 12% | 12% | 15% | **25%** | 18% | 14% |
|  | Kicked out of home | 6% | 9% | 11% | 12% | **17%** | 14% | 11% |
| **Public Sphere** | Physically attacked due to trans status (past year) | 8% | 11% | 9% | 9% | 14% | **19%** | 12% |
|  | Sexually assaulted (lifetime) | 45% | 41% | 48% | 53% | 58% | **65%** | 59% |
|  | Discomfort asking police for help (lifetime) | 53% | 58% | 59% | 67% | **70%** | 59% | 67% |
| **Public Restrooms (past year)** | Verbally harassed, physically attacked, and/or sexually assaulted | 12% | 12% | 12% | 10% | 13% | **24%** | 16% |
|  | Denied access due to trans status | 8% | 13% | 10% | 9% | 12% | **18%** | 11% |
| **Workplace** | Verbally harassed, physically attacked, and/or sexually assaulted | 15% | 13% | 15% | 15% | 26% | **28%** | 18% |
|  | Quit job in fear of trans-based discrimination | 14% | 11% | 17% | 19% | 17% | **23%** | 17% |

(*Continued*)

**TABLE 3.2** (Cont.)

| | | White | Asian | Latinx | Black | Middle Eastern | Native American | Multi-racial |
|---|---|---|---|---|---|---|---|---|
| **Identity Documents** | Job loss due to trans bias | 12% | 8% | 11% | 17% | 14% | **21%** | 18% |
| | Harassed due to presumed mis-match with identity documents | 24% | 24% | 27% | 26% | **44%** | 39% | 33% |
| | Assaulted due to presumed mis-match with identity documents | 2% | 3% | 2% | 4% | **9%** | 6% | 3% |
| **Mental Health** | Attempted suicide (past year) | 6% | 8% | 9% | 9% | 8% | **10%** | **10%** |
| | Attempted suicide (lifetime) | 37% | 40% | 45% | 47% | 44% | **57%** | 50% |
| **Health Care** | Negativity from providers | 34% | 26% | 32% | 34% | 40% | **50%** | 38% |
| | Avoided services in fear of harassment | 22% | 24% | 26% | 26% | 34% | **37%** | 28% |
| | Professional tried to "stop" them from being transgender | 19% | 14% | 17% | 16% | **32%** | 27% | 21% |

*Source:* Data come from 27,715 transgender, trans, genderqueer, and non-binary respondents. The racial and ethnic categories include: White or European American (62%), Latinx or Hispanic (17%), Black or African American (13%), Asian, Asian American, Native Hawaiian, or Pacific Islander (5%), American Indian or Alaska Native (.7%), Middle Eastern or North African (.4%), and biracial or multiracial (2.5%) (James et al. 2016). The largest percentage in each row is bolded to highlight racial and ethnic differences in these experiences.

500 unique gender identity terms other than "transgender" (65%) or "trans" (56%) written in by respondents to capture their own identities including "non-binary" (31%), "genderqueer" (29%), and "gender fluid" (20%) (James et al. 2016:44). This is especially important because non-binary individuals may have experiences that are distinct from binary individuals. For example, one Australian study (N = 7,479) found that those that identify as non-binary were significantly younger and more likely to live in urban capital cities than individuals who identify within the binary of male and female (Whyte, Brooks, and Torgler 2018). Other research indicates that non-binary individuals are more likely than trans men (but less likely than trans women) to experience underemployment and being denied a job promotion (Davidson 2016). Thus, non-binary individuals' lives may be unique from trans people's experiences in important ways that are informed by intersections with class privilege and oppression (see more in Chapter 14).

Furthermore, it is also important to recognize the experiences of "trans" people are often understood through a Western lens. Indeed, the term "transgender" is both White and Western (Stryker 2009). However, there are numerous culturally specific examples of gender diversity that may not resonate with this type of framing. For example, as noted earlier, Two-Spirit identities in Native American cultures encompass non-cisgender and non-heteronormative indigenous peoples (Adams and Phillips 2006; Elhakeem 2007; Jacobs, Thomas, and Lang 1997; Walters et al. 2006). In India, *hijras*, who are typically born and identified as male based on the appearance of their genitalia but present themselves as women, form a third gender category (Monro 2007). The *kathoey*, sometimes described by Westerners as "lady boys" due to their male genitals and feminine gender presentation, also form a third gender category in Thailand (Jackson and Sullivan 1999). The term "transgender" is rarely used in these cultures to describe these groups of people, although Westerners do impose such labels on them. Two-Spirit people, hijras, and kathoeys experience culturally-specific discrimination and stigma that may not reflect the experiences of Western trans individuals (Gilley 2010; Jacobs, Thomas, and Lang 1997; Monro 2007).

Together, these diverse understandings of gender and sexuality are necessarily entwined with Western norms such as "gay equals White" and "trans equals White." This means that violations of hetero-cis-normativity look different depending on the cultural lens from which they are viewed. Being "hetero" and being "cis" are Western concepts that may not translate with cross-cultural significance, and the "White" terms of "gay," "lesbian," "bisexual," "trans," "non-binary," and "queer" also have various culturally-bound meanings. Even in non-hetero-cis-normative spaces, some of these identities can carry more social power than others. For example, White gay cis men are often situated in places of privilege above others in non-hetero spaces while trans and non-binary people remain on the margins in most cultural contexts (recall Figure 3.3). These patterns will be further explored throughout this text. What is evident here, however, is that

Western social privilege and power coincide with White hetero-cis-normativity and devalue LGBTQ people, especially LGBTQ people of color. Together, as suggested by NCST, violations of hetero-cis-normativity and accompanying LGBTQ stigma are significantly impacted by the presence (or absence) of social power.

## Introducing Social Class and LGBTQ Stigma

While race and ethnicity shape perspectives about LGBTQ issues and people in ways that necessitate nuanced investigations, another layer that adds to this complexity is social class—and the two are not separate. As Bérubé (2001) notes, many conceive of "gay" people as a monolithic category that is both "White" and "well-to-do" (234). This norm is at least partly rooted in early twentieth century America where "the notion of the homosexual" appeared first in middle-class predominantly White communities (Valocchi 1999:211). From there, some of the largest visible collective "homosexual" rights organizations in America (i.e., the Mattachine Society[3] and the Daughters of Bilitis[4]) sometimes "ignored either implicitly or explicitly the class, racial, and erotic diversity that existed in the subcultures of homosexuals" (Valocchi 1999:217). From here, the most visible LGBTQ issues remain White-washed and upper/middle-class focused. This process marginalizes LGBTQ people of color and low-income LGBTQ people, placing them on the outskirts of dominant discourse about LGBTQ issues amidst enduring stigma shaped by multiple, intersecting experiences with oppression.

### *Gay Equals Rich?*

A prominent Western cultural myth is that "All LGBT people are wealthy" (Battle et al. 2017a:18). Indeed, numerous media representations depict gay men in particular "as being overwhelmingly upper-middle class—if not simply rich—and white" (Han 2007:53). Being "rich" implies not only economic wealth, but also high status class privilege that includes access to social power often based on occupation, income, and education but entwined with other privileged positions such as gender, race, and sexuality. The "gay equals rich" norm actively shapes how others understand the LGBTQ community and how LGBTQ individuals see themselves. In particular, social class effects LGBTQ stigma as well as access to resources that influence an individual's abilities and willingness to openly express non-hetero-cis-normative sexual and gender identities. For example, higher levels of both income and education were found to be related to a higher likelihood of identifying as "gay," being active in gay subcultures, and living in a gay neighborhood among a probability sample of men who have sex with men (MSM) living in Chicago, Los Angeles, New York, and San Francisco (N = 2,881) (Barret and Pollack 2005). In addition, Whites were more likely than racial/ethnic minorities to self-label as gay (Barret and Pollack 2005). Together, these patterns contribute to a more visible "White" and "well-to-do" gay American culture which can be seen elsewhere in the West. For example, in a U.K study, middle-class professionals (i.e., those in managerial or professional positions) were 60% more likely to self-identify as gay, lesbian, or bisexual as compared to those in working-class/manual labor/low-skilled positions (Spillett 2014). In addition, non-binary individuals indicated higher education levels than those who identified with the binary identities of female or male in one large scale Australian study (N = 7,479) (Whyte, Brooks, and Torgler 2018).

Within the working-class milieu, there are norms that shape LGBTQ people's experiences with stigma and oppression. In particular, Connell, Davis, and Dowsett's (1993) qualitative study with working-class Australian MSM (N = 21) revealed widespread homophobia. Specifically, they found that many working-class MSM did not adopt a gay identity "because it connotes effeminacy, or class privilege, or both" and they also completely rejected "bisexual" as a recognized identity (Connell, Davis, and Dowsett 1993:125). Instead, working-class MSM adhered to more conventional working-class masculinities linked to physical prowess, aggressive heterosexuality, and dislike of "queens," "flamboyance," and "campness" (Connell, Davis, and Dowsett 1993:128). More recently, Balay's (2014) qualitative study with LGT steelworkers in Indiana revealed that most took measures to keep their "gay" (LGT) selves separate from their "mill" working selves in an environment she describes as the *Steel Closet*. In particular, Balay identified "the cultural impossibility of embodying both gay male and working-class masculinity" among the steelworkers she interviewed (2014:114). Interestingly, sex between men in the *working-class closet* can be relatively common and is not necessarily tied to gay or bisexual identities (Balay 2014; Humphreys 1970). Consider men who participate in "the Down Low"—a lifestyle that is "predominately practiced by young, urban, African American men who have sex with other men and women, yet do not identify as gay or bisexual" (Heath and Goggin 2009:17). Men having sex with other men in this instance and others (e.g., steel mill sex, Balay 2014; tearoom sex, Humphreys 1970) does not bring about gay/bisexual/homosexual labels. Instead, the *working-class closet* often renders same-sex sexual acts as rather meaningless encounters while simultaneously silencing LGBTQ people and reinforcing hetero-cis-normativity and LGBTQ stigma. In these ways, the relationships between being LGBTQ and enduring LGBTQ stigma are shaped by experiences with class, culture, and race, as demonstrated in NCST (recall Figure 3.1).

Furthermore, working-class people that do adopt an LGBTQ identity can experience negativity from the larger LGBTQ community. For example, gay and bisexual working-class men have indicated that they are "more apt to experience discrimination from the middle-class queers than from the straights" (Appleby 2001:60). Indeed, working-class LGBTQ people often see themselves and their experiences as distinct from middle- and upper-class LGBTQ people and their experiences. For example, gay and bisexual working-class men have reported that middle-class LGBTQ people "try too hard to be accepted" while their own "blue collar mentality" focuses on "work" and "self-reliance" (Appleby 2001:60). In particular, working-class LGBTQ people must manage their economic vulnerability along with their marginalized sexual identities. Meyer's (2008) work with LGBTQ hate crime victims shows that working-class and low-income LGBTQ people of color were often preoccupied with other more pressing concerns related to living at or near the poverty line rather than concerns about the role that "homophobia" played in their victimization while middle- and upper-class LGBTQ and White people were significantly more introspective about how their victimization experiences related to their LGBTQ identities. In addition, White LGBTQ people were more likely than racial minorities to view their victimization experiences as hate crimes motivated by their LGBTQ identities and to report them as such (Meyer 2008). Middle- and upper-class privilege affords some LGBTQ people with the time to analyze their anti-LGBTQ experiences, arms them with power and knowledge to identify their anti-LGBTQ experiences as problematic (even criminal), and secures their legitimacy when reporting their anti-LGBTQ experiences to law enforcement officials. Thus, class experiences shape LGBTQ stigma and violence in distinct ways informed by racial/ethnic privilege and oppression.

It is worth noting that the "gay equals rich" norm is often only associated with gay and bisexual cis men. This is most likely because lesbian women, bisexual women, trans, and non-binary people lack the social power that gay and bisexual cis men have within patriarchal societies. Indeed, LGBTQ women experience lower levels of economic security as compared to gay and bisexual cis men as well as heterosexual women. For example, in the U.S., 24% of lesbian and bisexual women live in poverty, compared to 19% of heterosexual women, while the poverty rate among gay and bisexual men is similar to the rate among heterosexual men (13%) (Sears and Badgett 2012). In addition, trans people face life-threatening economic hardships with close to one-third (29%) living at or below the poverty level—a rate that is over twice the poverty rate among the general U.S. adult population. As seen in Table 3.3, trans people of color are highly likely to live in poverty with more than one-third of Latinx (43%), Native American (41%), Multi-racial (40%), Black (38%), and Middle Eastern (34%) trans people living at or near the poverty level. Unemployment is high, as is the receipt of public assistance and the inability to afford health services. Between 1 in 10 (9% White) and 1 in 5 (19% Black) trans people live on an annual income of less than $10,000 USD (see Table 3.3). In addition, trans women are more likely than trans men to live in poverty and to participate in the underground economy for survival (e.g., income-based sex work, illicit drug sales) (James et al. 2016). Beyond this, in

**TABLE 3.3** Economic Hardships of Transgender and Gender Non-Conforming People in the United States by Racial and Ethnic Identity

|  | *Percentage of each race/ethnicity occupying each category* |  |  |  |  |  |  |  |
| --- | --- | --- | --- | --- | --- | --- | --- | --- |
|  | All | White | Asian | Latinx | Black | Middle Eastern | Native American | Multi-racial |
| Poverty[a] | 29% | 24% | 32% | **43%** | 38% | 34% | 41% | 40% |
| Unemployment[b] | 15% | 12% | 10% | 21% | 20% | **35%** | 23% | 22% |
| Currently receive public assistance (WIC, SNAP)[c] | 15% | 13% | 5% | 18% | **23%** | 8% | 19% | 17% |
| Household income < $10,000 USD | 12% | 9% | 15% | 18% | **19%** | 8% | 16% | 10% |
| Could not afford health services | 33% | 31% | 27% | 37% | 40% | 36% | 41% | **42%** |

a Respondents were designated as living in or near poverty if their total family income fell under 124% of the official poverty line as defined by the U.S. Census Bureau.
b The unemployment rate was calculated using data from the March 2015 U.S. Census Bureau's Current Population Survey Annual Social and Economic Supplement in which the overall U.S. unemployment rate was 5.5%.
c Respondents received the following definition for SNAP: "The Supplemental Nutrition Assistance Program (SNAP) is sometimes called the Food Stamp program. It helps people who have low or no income to buy food, usually with an EBT card." Respondents received the following definition for WIC: "'WIC' stands for 'Women, Infants, and Children.' It's the short name for the Special Supplemental Nutrition Program for Women, Infants, and Children. WIC is a federal program to help women who are pregnant or breastfeeding and children less than five years old get health care and healthy food."
*Source*: Data come from 27,715 transgender, trans, genderqueer, and non-binary respondents. The racial and ethnic categories include: White or European American (62%), Latino/a or Hispanic (17%), Black or African American (13%), Asian, Asian American, Native Hawaiian, or Pacific Islander (5%), American Indian or Alaska Native (.7%), Middle Eastern or North African (.4%), and biracial or multiracial (2.5%) (James et al. 2016). The largest percentage in each row is bolded to highlight racial and ethnic differences in these experiences.

contrast to being stereotyped as "rich" as gay and bisexual cis men are, lesbian, bisexual, and trans women are often sexually objectified placing them at risk for sexual stigma and sexually-based violence (see more below). Together, class experiences and stigma entwine with race, gender, sexuality to marginalize LGBTQ people of color and low-income LGBTQ people.

## *Working-Class/Working-Poor LGBTQ Perspectives*

Class experiences not only shape LGBTQ people's lives, but also, how individuals view LGBTQ issues. For example, the social marginalization of low-income and working-class people can relate to the disparagement of LGBTQ people. Indeed,

"Working-class/working-poor people claim the dubious honor of being dubbed more homophobic (and more racist, and more sexist) than rich people. This holds true in mainstream society, queer organizations, and other progressive movements" (Kadi 1997:34–35). For example, Anderson and Fetner's (2008) global study of 35 countries found that, generally, the countries that are most supportive of "homosexuality" tend to be those with high levels of economic development. More specifically, managers and professionals are more supportive of "homosexuality" than working-class (e.g., skilled and unskilled blue-collar manual labor) individuals (Anderson and Fetner 2008).

In particular, working-class and impoverished environments can shape hetero-cis-normative perspectives and LGBTQ stigma. For example, there is evidence of a unique working-class hegemonic masculinity that is more restrictive and less supportive of gender and sexual diversity (Connell 1995). Working-class men often assert their own hegemonic masculinities while simultaneously policing and stigmatizing non-hegemonic (non-hetero-cis-normative) masculinities (Balay 2014; Connell 1995). Indeed, one ethnographic study found that straight White working-class men in one of the largest baked goods companies in the U.S. felt outright disgust toward gays and lesbians and many felt they should be excluded from the workplace (Embrick, Walther, and Wickens 2007). Balay's (2014) research with steelworkers in Indiana also revealed rampant sexual prejudices directed toward LGT people.

Furthermore, hegemonic masculinity can often be one of the only forms of social capital working-class and inner city poor men have access to and they may embody it in ways that reinforce hetero-cis-normativity and the stigmatization of LGBTQ people. For example, C.J. Pascoe's (2007) ethnography of working-class high school students in California revealed ritualized heterosexist and homophobic discourses that shaped the masculinity performances of young men especially. Policing gender and sexuality in ways that disparage and denigrate LGBTQ people (often embodied through the phrase "*Dude, you're a fag*") were common hetero-cis-normative tropes among teenage boys which were reinforced by working-class high school norms. Furthermore, compulsive heterosexuality, popularity with the ladies, and heterosexual prowess among working-class and inner city young men (Anderson 1999) work together to emphasize the importance of hetero-cis-normativity and devalue LGBTQ people from an early age.

Alongside hegemonic masculinity sits a certain type of femininity which has been described as "emphasized femininity focused on compliance to patriarchy" (Connell and Messerschmidt 2005:848) and as "hegemonic femininity" consisting of "the characteristics defined as womanly that establish and legitimate a hierarchical and complementary relationship to hegemonic masculinity and that, by doing so, guarantee the dominant position of men and the subordination of women" (Schippers 2007:94). Like the maintenance of hegemonic masculinity, embodying hegemonic femininity involves reinforcing the value of hetero-cis-normativity and denigrating LGBTQ people (e.g., *dissident femininities*, Bettie 2003:132, or *pariah femininities* that challenge hegemonic masculinity and patriarchy such as lesbian femininities, Schippers 2007:99). Within working-class and working-poor environments, hegemonic femininity is a significant mode of social capital. For example, Elijah Anderson's (1999) research in Philadelphia, Pennsylvania with inner city youth revealed that girls' frequent use of sex as a bargaining tool for attention from young men often resulted in pregnancy and the babies derived from these relationships served as a "prize" that teenage mothers used to play up their social status in inner city neighborhoods (163). This process reinforces both the value of hetero-cis-normative sex and the devaluation of LGBTQ people and relationships. Indeed, the overt focus on a heterosexually desirable personal appearance among working-class and working-poor girls reflects the value of hegemonic femininity and the social capital of using of sexuality as a tool to navigate class constraints (see also, Bettie 2003).

Together, class, race, gender, and sexuality combine to reflect norms such as "gay equals rich" or more generally, "gay" as a reference to an upper-class White man. Furthermore, the importance of hegemonic masculinity and femininity among working-class and working-poor youth and adults influenced by their relative oppression can contribute to the further stigmatization of LGBTQ people's lives. This in turn shapes the *working-class closet* as a space where sex between men can be thought of as nothing more than a simple social encounter and sex between women can be largely invisible or highly sexualized for the male gaze (see more below). Hetero-cis-normativity, then, is situated in a class context whereby the normalcy of being heterosexual and cisgender is shaped by upper-class, middle-class, working-class, and working-poor norms. In these ways, gendered, racialized, and sexualized social privilege and power converge in a process that devalues LGBTQ people, especially working-class and working-poor LGBTQ people of color, and significantly impacts LGBTQ stigma.

## The Sexualization of LGBTQ Stigma

An underlying layer in the relationship between hetero-cis-normativity, power, and LGBTQ stigma that is sometimes missing from public discourse is related to sexual behaviors. Hetero-cis-normativity not only devalues non-hetero and non-cis people but also legitimizes and justifies the sexualizing, fetishizing, and stigmatizing of non-hetero and non-cis people. The pattern of objectifying those lacking in social power is a very real part of sexual cultural dynamics with the objectification of cis-women by cis-men organizing many global patterns of gender inequality, patriarchy, and hegemonic masculinities and femininities. With hetero-cis men on the top of this hierarchy, this places all others below and at risk for oppression and stigma. In particular, LGBTQ people are sexualized (although in different ways informed by gender, class, and race privilege) and this contributes to their inferior stigmatized status, lack of social power, victimization, and (sometimes) criminalization. For example, the stereotypes about the sex that takes place in LGBTQ relationships carry various loaded meanings which can in turn shape LGBTQ stigma. In addition, there are other dynamics, including the objectification of bisexual women and working-class men as well as the vulnerability of trans women, that contribute to differences in social power both in and out of the LGBTQ community. Thus, LGBTQ stigma and oppression are informed by presumptions about LGBTQ sexual behaviors and LGBTQ people's bodies.

## LGBTQ Stigma and LGBTQ Sex

The presumed non-hetero-cis-normative sex acts of LGBTQ people can drive stigmatizing perspectives toward these groups. LGBTQ people have long been associated with deviant, risky, and criminal sex acts. These include (but are not limited to) sex work and anal sex, as well as HIV and other STIs. While all of these experiences have been widely culturally deviantized, many are also criminalized. For example, over one-third of the sovereign states in the world have laws criminalizing "homosexuality" (largely defined as sex acts between two persons of the same sex) and there are least 10 locations where "homosexuality" can be punishable by death: Brunei, Iran, Mauritania, Nigeria, Qatar, Saudi Arabia, Somalia, Sudan, United Arab Emirates, and Yemen (Erasing 76 Crimes 2017; Human Dignity Trust 2016; Human Rights Campaign 2019). In these places, it is most often not the self-proclaimed identity of LGBTQ people that is most culturally and criminally problematic, but rather, it is the presumed norm-violating sexual behaviors of LGBTQ people that secure them into a place of systemic disadvantage and oppression. In other words, it is the opposition to non-hetero-cis-normative sex acts between persons of the same sex that can lead to the stigmatization of LGBTQ people.

In addition, there are subcultures within the LGBTQ community that can be highly sexualized. For example, the leathermen community has eroticized leather, the bear community is often hyper-focused on certain types of bodies (beefy and hairy) and their sexual value (Hennen 2008; Lahti 1998), and the "twink" is yet another group among LGBTQ men that is sexually objectified based on their hairless and youthful body type (Filiault and Drummond 2007). The "butch" and "femme" dynamic is also often accompanied by sexualized stereotypes in the LGBTQ community (Blair and Hoskin 2015). More generally, non-vanilla sex and sexual "kink" are associated with LGBTQ people and their sexual behaviors (Dominguez 1994; Galupo, Mitchell, and Davis 2015; Sprott and Hadcock 2018; Worthen 2016b). Together, these associations reinforce the stereotyping of LGBTQ people with deviant sex.

## "LGBTQ Sex" Equals Anal?

LGBTQ stigma is most certainly entwined with what is perceived to be "LGBTQ sex." Although often based on uninformed stereotypes, many think about LGBTQ sexual behavior as primarily or even solely involving anal sex (although of course opposite sex partners can engage in anal sex and same-sex sexual behavior may not entail anal sex at all, perhaps especially in the case of sex between two women). This is partly because people are generalizing "LGBTQ" to mean "gay men" (Whitley, Childs, and Collins 2011). A further generalization is that sex acts between gay men necessarily or always involve penile–anal sex acts. In one swiping overgeneralization, "LGBTQ sex" becomes equated with a singular sex act: penile-anal sex between men. Some research has found that anal sex, in general, is viewed quite negatively, especially when it is between two men (compared to anal sex between a man and a woman) (Heflick 2010). Because people may have a general aversion toward anal sex and a specific aversion toward anal sex between two men, they may also attach a specific stigma toward LGBTQ sex and more generally, LGBTQ people (Worthen 2016b). Indeed, across the 78 jurisdictions in the world in which same-sex sexual acts are criminalized, only about half (n = 44, 56%) criminalize sex acts between women (although that number has been increasing in recent years). Furthermore, while there are 21 jurisdictions which *only* explicitly criminalize sex between men, there are *no* jurisdictions which only explicitly criminalize sex acts between women (Human Dignity Trust 2016). Clearly sex between men (most often perceived as anal sex or just "gay sex" in general) is commonly stigmatized. In this way, it is not just being LGBTQ that violates hetero-cis-normativity, it is also the presumed sex acts that LGBTQ people participate in. Thus, LGBTQ stigma is shaped by presumed violations of hetero-cis-normative sex acts that are further impacted by the presumed body parts and genders of those involved in the sex act.

Another layer that impacts these sexualized patterns of LGBTQ stigmatization involves the behavioral dynamics of the sex act itself. Penile–vaginal, penile–oral, and penile–anal sex involve two similar behaviors: (1) the insertion of a penis and (2) the reception of a penis. The insertive partner is frequently described as the "dominant" partner while the receptive partner is designated as the "submissive" partner. These labels hold true for opposite-sex and same-sex sexual acts. Furthermore, the receptive partner in a sex act is not only defined as submissive, but also, the receptive partner is often feminized and stigmatized as inferior to and weaker than the insertive partner. Put another way, a man who inserts his penis into another person holds more social power than his receptive partner and as the inserter, he can resist both the stigma and negative labels associated with being penetrated. Indeed, some men who engage in only insertive (never receptive) sex acts with other men do not self-identify as "gay" or "bisexual" despite their participation in sex with men (e.g., Balay 2014; Heath and Goggin 2009; Humphreys 1970) while their insertive partners more frequently self-identify as "gay" or "bisexual" and are more often stigmatized for their participation in sex with other men. Furthermore, there are cultural dynamics that solidify these patterns. For example, researchers examining sexual behaviors between Latinx men regularly identify an *activo* (dominant/insertive/masculine) and *pasivo* (submissive/receptive/effeminate) partner arrangement (Daniel and Esteinou 2013; Jeffries, Dodge, and Sandfort 2008; Rodríguez 2003). Thus, insertive/receptive sexual roles shape a larger system of social power in hetero-cis-normative relationships as well as LGBTQ relationships. Of course, not all sex experiences involve penises or insertive/receptive dynamics and in many relationships, partners switch between insertive and receptive roles. Even so, the larger system of hetero-cis-normativity that defines hetero-cis sexual behaviors as normative also defines insertive partners as dominant, powerful, masculine, and valorized while receptive partners are viewed as submissive, weak, effeminate, and stigmatized. Thus, LGBTQ stigma is reflected in prejudices toward non-hetero-cis-normative people and sexual behaviors as well as the body parts involved (or not involved) in them.

## *Heterosexual Men Fetishizing Bisexual Women*

While anal sex between two men is largely stigmatized within hetero-cis-normative culture (Heflick 2010; Worthen 2016b), sex acts between women are often fetishized by Western heterosexual men. Indeed, women kissing and fondling other women are often objects of the male gaze. The college party scene with bars, clubs, fraternity parties, etc., is a notorious home for heterosexual men fetishizing "girl-on-girl" sexual behavior (Fahs 2009; Rupp and Taylor 2010). Often, however, these fetishizing patterns are limited to White upper/middle-class "pretty" and "femme" (i.e., stereotypically heteronormative and attractive) women who are perceived to be "bisexual" (meaning they may also have sex with the male "gazer") and rarely involve any behaviors beyond "petting in public" (e.g., vaginal–oral sex or vaginal sex with objects/digits between women are not as commonly fetishized because they move beyond the tropes of the male gaze into lesbian-coded behaviors). Indeed, some women engage in public bisexuality because they believe that it may help them "garner sexual-validation within their heterosexual relationships or the heteronormative culture at large" (Fahs 2009:432). While eroticized images of bisexuality among women contribute to more accepting attitudes toward bisexual women among heterosexual men (Worthen 2013), this "acceptance" is tainted by their objectification and sexualization. So while bisexual women have some socially valued significance due to their potential to be the sexual partners of heterosexual men, the fetishizing of bisexual women's sexuality limits their social power and contributes to their stigma as "sex objects." In this way, conceptualizations of bisexual women as "sexy" and the eroticization of their sexual behaviors are a part of hetero-cis-normative culture whereby heterosexual men retain social power and the objects of their gaze (i.e., their potential receptive sex partners that include bisexual women) are inferior and stigmatized (see more in Chapter 10).

## Gay Men Fetishizing Gay Men

While White upper-class hetero-cis men retain social power in the larger system of hetero-cis-normativity, there are also specific dynamics within the Western cultures of gay men that reflect a hierarchical and sexualized organization of social power worth mentioning here. For example, upper/middle-class gay men sometimes fetishize working-class gay men in a process that eroticizes their abilities to do manual labor and their accompanying masculine, muscular bodies (Connell 1995). Indeed, the gay and "beefy" lumberjack, leatherman, military man, construction worker, cop, and bear are all eroticized working-class gay archetypes (Han 2007; Hennen 2008; Lahti 1998). As classed sex objects, their social power is sometimes limited within gay culture, as one working-class gay man noted, "They [upper/middle-class gay men] think we are just a piece of meat for the taking" (Appleby 2001:60). Indeed, the Western appeal of working-class gay men's bodies was perhaps most aptly solidified by Finnish artist Tom of Finland whose semi-naked renditions of muscular mechanics, sailors, and bikers present the "proletarian man as an object of desire" (Lahti 1998:198) (see Image 3.1).

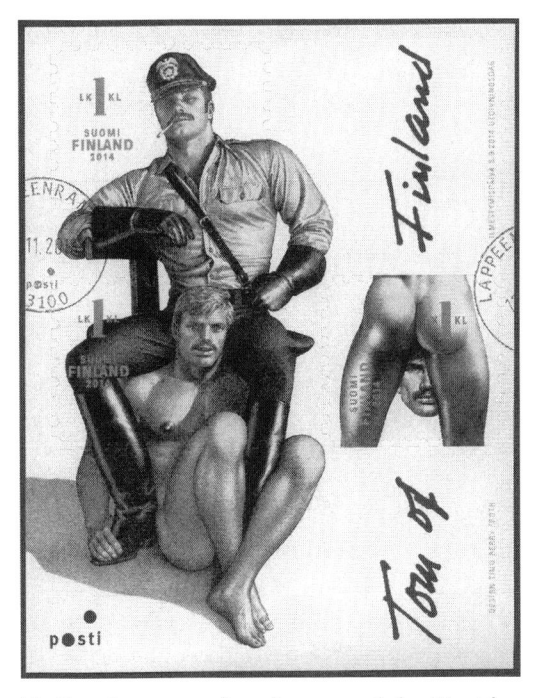

**IMAGE 3.1** Finnish first class stamp featuring artwork by Finnish cartoonist Touko Laaksonen (1920–1991) known as "Tom of Finland" released on September 8, 2014. Tom of Finland produced more than 3,500 drawings throughout the 1950s to 1970s. His work is featured in the New York Museum of Modern Art (MOMA), the Los Angeles Museum of Contemporary Art (MOCA), and the San Francisco Museum of Modern Art (Lahti 2008).

Gay men of color are also objectified within Western gay communities in a process that allows White gay men to retain social power. Indeed, gay men of color, especially Black gay men, are sometimes reduced to stereotypes about their penis size "existing only as props for white male consumption" (Han 2007:57). In addition, fetishized as "Latin meat" (Engardio 1999:7), one study found that a majority (62%) of Latino gay and bisexual men indicated that they were frequently sexually objectified and that other gay and bisexual men paid more attention to their Latino identity than to who they were as people (Diaz et al. 2001). Because White masculinity is valued in the West, gay men of color are often either ignored or eroticized in gay communities "as a consumable product for white male fantasy" (Han 2007:56). Even gay men of color have been found to express an explicit dating and sexual preference for White men (Han 2007; Phua and Kaufman 2003). These experiences are entwined with class as well, with working-class gay men of color both fetishized in Western gay communities and lacking in social power. Although Western gay communities are generally stigmatized and situated outside of larger hetero-cis-normative culture, social power dynamics connected to gender, race, ethnicity, sexuality, and class remain solidly in place in Western gay communities as well. Together, these processes secure a relationship between violations of hetero-cis-normativity and LGBTQ stigma that is significantly impacted by social power.

## *The Sexualization of Trans Stigma and Violence*

Trans individuals, especially trans women as well as "lady boys" in Thailand (Jackson and Sullivan 1999), are stigmatized, fetishized, and objectified. In particular, many trans women are at extreme risk of oppression and sexual violence. For example, a survey conducted by the National Center for Transgender Equality with nearly 28,000 respondents revealed that 12% of trans women overall and 42% of Black trans women participated in income-based sex work at some point in their lives. Furthermore, as compared to trans women who had never participated in income-based sex work, trans women sex workers were significantly more likely to live in poverty (26% vs. 46%) and to have experienced intimate partner violence (51% vs. 77%) and/or sexual assault (44% vs. 72%) (James et al. 2016).

Trans women are especially vulnerable to sexualized violence, especially when their trans status is unknown to their sexual partners but later revealed. In some extreme situations, the exposure of a trans woman's male sex assigned at birth and/or penis can result in fatal violence. Indeed, Westbrook's analysis of 7,183 individual U.S. news stories about 232 homicides with trans women victims that occurred between 1990 and 2005 revealed that the perpetrators of violence (who were cis men) felt "deceived" and "as a result, killed the victim" (Schilt and Westbrook 2009:454). Most were brief sexual encounters between strangers, some of which involved the open exchange of money. Of central concern to these murderers was that these men believed they were "'tricked' into homosexuality by 'gender deceivers'" (Schilt and Westbrook 2009:452). Using this argument, because these men were involved (or almost involved) in a sexual encounter with a person who at some point had male-identified genitals, sex with this person could be perceived as "homosexual." In other words, the fear of participating in "gay sex" underlined these murderers' feelings of outrage and perhaps (in their minds) legitimized the violence they enacted toward their victims as an ultimate display of masculine valor. Indeed, their need to "prove" that they are *not* gay and the importance of defining, defending, and "showing off" their heterosexual orientation are a key part of some heterosexual men's masculine identity (Connell 1995; Pascoe 2007) and central to supporting hetero-cis-normative cultural dynamics. Coupled with their high likelihood of experiencing income-based sex work, poverty, and racial/ethnic discrimination (James et al. 2016), trans women of color remain vulnerable to stigma, oppression, and victimization which are built from a process of sexualization of their bodies within an overarching system that supports and values hetero-cis-normativity and stigmatizes LGBTQ people (see more in Chapter 12).

Together, hetero-cis-normativity secures the success of hetero and cis people (especially hetero-cis men) while simultaneously devaluing non-hetero and non-cis people. Part of this process involves the sexual objectification of LGBTQ people as well as a heightened focus on stereotypes about LGBTQ bodies and the sex that takes place in LGBTQ relationships. Certain sexual behaviors are more often criminalized (e.g., anal sex between men) while others are subject to the hetero-male gaze (e.g., public displays of kissing between women). The context of the sex act can further heighten the vulnerability of LGBTQ people (e.g., trans women in brief sexual encounters with strangers). These dynamics simultaneously reinforce the normalcy of hetero-cis people and the devaluation of LGBTQ people. Thus, LGBTQ stigma and oppression are impacted by hetero-cis-normative sexual scripts and other axes of social power that interact to create a spectrum of LGBTQ stigma.

## Intersectionality and LGBTQ Stigma

Together, the intersectional layers involved in LGBTQ stigma are extremely complex. So much so that it can be difficult to identify the underpinnings of oppression that LGBTQ people experience. Are LGBTQ people stigmatized because they identify as LGBTQ? Because of their gender and gender performances? Because of their sexual behaviors? Because of their genitals? Because of their race? Because of their ethnicity? Because of their class? *YES*. What's more, these experiences differ for a Latino bisexual middle-class cis man, an Asian straight working-class trans man, and a White lesbian upper-class non-binary person. This is because people, identities, and behaviors are situated on a spectrum of stigma with one end as highly stigmatized, illegitimate, invisible, and denigrated (e.g., trans and queer identities) while others are situated on the opposite end as legitimate, recognized and supported (e.g., cis and straight) (recall Figure 3.3). Because much of the dominant cultural awareness about LGBTQ issues is shaped by White-washed and upper/middle-classed dialogue, this spectrum of stigma is further impacted by race/ethnicity and class experiences. Examples include: hijra, kathoey, Two-Spirit, SGL, and Down-Low sex in the *working-class closet*. All are informed by hetero-cis-normativity and access to social power.

There are additional issues including immigration, housing, employment, education, school bullying, welfare, healthcare, hate crimes, public accommodations, and changes on identification documents that effect LGBTQ people's experiences with stigma, not to mention the thousands of anti-LGBTQ laws introduced annually across the globe. So while I briefly cover a few myths here (i.e., "gay equals White," "trans equals White," and "gay equals rich") there are certainly more. For example, "gay equals urban," "gay equals educated," or "gay equals victim" are all stereotypes floating around. Additional layers that shape differences across the LGBTQ spectrum are also important to recognize, such as that lesbian trans lives differ from bisexual non-binary lives, for example. Some of these ideas were touched upon in this chapter and some will be discussed throughout this book—but certainly not all. The purpose here is to begin to dissect the intersectional dynamics that shape both hetero-cis-normativity and LGBTQ stigma. From here, we can learn to understand the cultural dynamics that shape social power and place LGBTQ people in a place of systemic disadvantage.

## Hetero-cis-normativity Equals LGBTQ Stigma

The overarching theme of this chapter utilized hetero-cis-normativity to connect LGBTQ stigma and oppression with a discussion of social power. Hetero-cis-normativity, race, ethnicity, social class, sexual behaviors, and sexual objectification were all introduced as interlocking cultural experiences that inform LGBTQ stigma, objectification, and victimization. Overall, the links between hetero-cis-normativity and LGBTQ stigma are impacted by race, ethnicity, social class, and other axes of social power.

### *NCST and LGBTQ Stigma*

To summarize, here are the three tenets of NCST informed by the arguments outlined in this chapter:

1. NCST Tenet #1: There is a culturally dependent and reciprocal relationship between *hetero-cis-normativity* and *LGBTQ stigma*.
2. NCST Tenet #2: The relationship between *hetero-cis-normativity* and *LGBTQ stigma* is organized by social power dynamics between *LGBTQ people* and those that stigmatize *LGBTQ people*.
3. NCST Tenet #3: *LGBTQ stigma* is inclusive of negativity and social sanctions directed toward violations and violators of *hetero-cis-normativity*, justified through social power dynamics and situated on a spectrum.

As illustrated throughout this chapter, starting with Figure 3.1, hetero-cis-normativity is the centralized overarching concept that helps us to understand LGBTQ stigma. Multiple axes of social power, discussed here as gender, race, ethnicity, class, sexuality, and culture, impact the relationship between violations of hetero-cis-normativity and accompanying LGBTQ stigma. Together, this leads to the following testable hypotheses as outlined by NCST:

- *Hypothesis 1a*: there is a significant relationship between hetero-cis-normativity/violations of hetero-cis-normativity and LGBTQ stigma.
- *Hypothesis 1b*: there is a significant relationship between individual axes of social power and LGBTQ stigma.
- *Hypothesis 2a*: the relationship between hetero-cis-normativity/violations of hetero-cis-normativity and LGBTQ stigma is moderated by interactions between axes of social power and hetero-cis-normativity/violations of hetero-cis-normativity.
- *Hypothesis 2b*: the relationship between hetero-cis-normativity/violations of hetero-cis-normativity and LGBTQ stigma is moderated by interactions between axes of social power.

Overall, using NCST to explore hetero-cis-normativity and LGBTQ stigma allows for a careful examination of the interlocking complexities in these relationships. The centrality of hetero-cis-normativity to understanding LGBTQ stigma is upheld through multiple sources of social power which can be critically investigated using this theoretical perspective and NCST's two lenses (the stigmatized lens and the stigmatizer lens). Here, I defined the foundational concepts central to this exploration (i.e., hetero-cis-normativity, intersectionality, and social power). In the next chapter, I review common explanations for LGBT(Q) stigma and situate them within the theoretical model of NCST and LGBTQ stigma offered here.

## Notes

1 Born as George Jorgensen, Jr. on May 30, 1926 to parents George Jorgensen (a carpenter/contractor) and Florence Davis Hansen Jorgensen in the Bronx, NY, Jorgensen grew up in a middle-class neighborhood but struggled with her gender identity from a young age.

After graduating from high school, Jorgensen was drafted into the U.S. Army but was honorably discharged due to illness. After spending time in photography school, Jorgensen traveled to Denmark in 1950 to meet Dr. Christian Hamburger who performed her gender affirming surgeries in 1951 and 1952. She chose the name "Christine" in his honor. The press coverage of her transition began in 1952 and she remained in the spotlight for decades doing public speaking events and media interviews. She also published an autobiography (Jorgensen 1967). Jorgensen died in 1989 of complications from bladder and lung cancer. In June 2019, Jorgensen was one of fifty inaugural activists inducted into the National LGBTQ Wall of Honor located in the Stonewall Inn on the 50th anniversary of the Stonewall Uprising (National LGBTQ Task Force 2019).

2 The Compton's Cafeteria Riot occurred in San Francisco, California in August 1966. Trans women customers who were regulars at the 24-hour restaurant were frequently harassed by police at this establishment and one night, a riot broke out that resulted in damage to the building and the alleged arrests of several trans women. Compton's then banned trans women from the restaurant and many protested and picketed their decision the next day. This collective uprising is one of the first recorded LGBTQ-related demonstrations in U.S. history. Unlike many who have proclaimed the 1969 Stonewall Uprising as the watershed moment in the U.S. gay and lesbian movement, Trans Studies scholar Susan Stryker (2008) describes the Compton's Cafeteria Riot and accompanying activism as the first turning point in LGBTQ activism in the U.S. In 2017, the Compton's Transgender Cultural District was founded where Compton's Cafeteria once stood and is the first legally recognized transgender district in the world (transgenderdistrictsf.com).

3 The Mattachine Society was established by Harry Hay (1912—2002) in Los Angeles, California in 1950 and is one of the oldest American national gay rights organizations. Chapters across the U.S. (first in San Francisco, then New York, Washington D.C., Chicago, and other locations) emerged throughout the 1960s and although the national chapter disbanded, the Mattachine Society is recognized as one of the first organized collectives of the gay and lesbian movement (Myers 2013) (see also Chapter 9).

4 The Daughters of Bilitis (DOB) was founded in 1955 in San Francisco and is one of the first lesbian-only organizations in the U.S. It was initially a non-political social group but later became more politically focused. DOB chapters existed across America and in Australia but most eventually dissolved in the 1970s due to tensions between lesbian separatists and those that believed they should align with groups like the Mattachine Society which included gay men (Myers 2013) (see also Chapter 8).

## References

Adams, Heather and Layli Phillips. 2006. "Experiences of Two-Spirit Lesbian and Gay Native Americans: An Argument for Standpoint Theory in Identity Research." *Identity* 6(3):273–291.

Alimahomed, Sabrina. 2010. "Thinking outside the Rainbow: Women of Color Redefining Queer Politics and Identity." *Social Identities* 16(2):151–168.

Anderson, Elijah. 1999. *Code of the Street: Decency, Violence, and the Moral Life of the Inner City*. New York, NY: Norton.

Anderson, Robert and Tina Fetner. 2008. "Economic Inequality and Intolerance: Attitudes toward Homosexuality in 35 Democracies." *American Journal of Political Science* 52(4):942–958.

Appleby, George Alan. 2001. "Ethnographic Study of Gay and Bisexual Working-Class Men in the United States." *Journal of Gay & Lesbian Social Services* 12(3/4):51–62.

Balay, Anne. 2014. *Steel Closets: Voices of Gay, Lesbian, and Transgender Steelworkers*. Chapel Hill, NC: The University of North Carolina Press.

Barret, Donald and Lance Pollack. 2005. "Whose Gay Community? Social Class, Sexual Self-Expression, and Gay Community Involvement." *The Sociological Quarterly* 46(3):437–456.

Basalm, Kimberly, Yamile Molina, Blair Beadnell, Jane Simoni, and Karina Walters. 2011. "Measuring Multiple Minority Stress: The LGBT People of Color Microaggressions Scale." *Cultural Diversity and Ethnic Minority Psychology* 17:163–174.

Battle, Juan, Cathy Cohen, Dorian Warren, Gerard Fergerson, and Suzette Audam. 2002. *Say It Loud, I'm Black and Proud: Black Pride Survey, 2000*. New York, NY: National Gay and Lesbian Task Force Policy Institute.

Battle, Juan and Angelique Harris. 2013. "Connectedness and Sociopolitical Involvement of Same-gender-loving Black Men." *Men and Masculinities* 16(2):206–267.

Battle, Juan, Antonio (Jay) Pastrana, and Jessie Daniels. 2012. *Social Justice Sexuality Project 2010 Cumulative Codebook*. City University of New York – Graduate Center. Retrieved January 30, 2020 (http://socialjusticesexuality.com/files/2014/09/Codebook-Reformatted.pdf).

Battle, Juan, Antonio (Jay) Pastrana, and Angelique Harris. 2017a. *An Examination of Asian and Pacific Islander LGBT Populations across the United States*. New York, NY: Palgrave.

Battle, Juan, Antonio (Jay) Pastrana, and Angelique Harris. 2017b. *An Examination of Black LGBT Populations across the United States*. New York, NY: Palgrave.

Bérubé, Allan. 2001. "How Gay Stays White and What Kind of White It Stays." Pp. 234–265 in *The Making and Unmaking of Whiteness*, edited by B. B. Rasmussen, E. Klinenberg, I. J. Nexica, and M. Wray. Durham, NC: Duke University Press.

Bettie, Julie. 2003. *Women without Class: Girls, Race, and Identity*. Los Angeles, CA: University of California Press.

Bissinger, Buzz. 2015. "Caitlyn Jenner: The Full Story." *Vanity Fair*. Retrieved January 30, 2020 (www.vanityfair.com/hollywood/2015/06/caitlyn-jenner-bruce-cover-annie-leibovitz).

Blair, Karen L. and Rhea Ashley Hoskin. 2015. "Experiences of Femme Identity: Coming Out, Invisibility and Femmephobia." *Psychology & Sexuality* 6(3):229–244.

Bowleg, Lisa. 2013. ""Once You've Blended the Cake, You Can't Take the Parts Back to the Main Ingredients": Black Gay and Bisexual Men's Descriptions and Experiences of Intersectionality." *Sex Roles* 68(11):754–767.

Butler, Judith. 1990. *Gender Trouble: Feminism and the Subversion of Identity*. New York, NY: Routledge.

Butler, Judith. 1993. "Critically Queer." *GLQ: A Journal of Lesbian and Gay Studies* 1:17–32.

Cauce, Ana Mari and Melanie Domenech-Rodriguez. 2002. "Latino Families: Myths and Realities." Pp. 3–25 in *Latino Children and Families in the United States*, edited by J. Contreras, K. Kerns, and A. Neal-Barnett. Westport, CT: Greenwood.

Choi, Kyung-Hee, Chong-suk Han, Jay Paul, and George Ayala. 2011. "Strategies for Managing Racism and Homophobia among U.S. Ethnic and Racial Minority Men Who Have Sex with Men." *AIDS Education and Prevention* 23(2):145–158.

Cohen, Cathy. 1996. "Contested Membership: Black Gay Identities and the Politics of AIDS." Pp. 362–394 in *Queer Theory/Sociology*, edited by S. Seidman. Malden, MA: Blackwell Press.

Collins, Patricia Hill. 2000. *Black Feminist Thought* (Second Edition). New York, NY: Routledge.
Connell, Raewyn. 1995. *Masculinities*. Berkeley, CA: University of California Press.
Connell, Raewyn and James Messerschmidt. 2005. "Hegemonic Masculinity: Rethinking the Concept." *Gender and Society* 19(6):829–859.
Connell, R.W., M.D. Davis, and G.W. Dowsett. 1993. "Bastard of a Life: Homosexual Desire and Practice among Men in Working-class Milieux." *Journal of Sociology* 29(1):112–135.
Crenshaw, Kimberlé. 1991. "Mapping the Margins: Intersectionality, Identity, Politics, and Violence against Women of Color." *Stanford Law Review* 43:1241–1299.
Daniel, Nehring and Rosario Esteinou. 2014. *Intimacies and Cultural Change: Perspectives on Contemporary Mexico*. London, UK: Routledge.
Davidson, Skylar. 2016. "Gender Inequality: Nonbinary Transgender People in the Workplace." *Cogent Social Sciences* 2(1):1–12.
Davis, Kathy. 2008. "Intersectionality as Buzzword: A Sociology of Science Perspective on What Makes A Feminist Theory Successful." *Feminist Theory* 9:67–85.
Diaz, Rafael, George Ayala, Edward Bein, Jeff Henne, and Barbara Marin. 2001. "The Impact of Homophobia, Poverty, and Racism on the Mental Health of Gay and Bisexual Latino Men: Findings from 3 US Cities." *American Journal of Public Health* 91(6):927–932.
Dominguez, Ivo. 1994. *Beneath the Skins: The New Spirit and Politics of the Kink Community* (Second Edition). Los Angeles, CA: Daedalus Publishing.
Elhakeem, Norhan. 2007 "A Place to Belong: Two-Spirit Movement Welcomes Discriminated-Against Native Gender-Variants." *Manitoba Student Newspaper* 94(25). March 21. Retrieved January 30, 2020 (web.archive.org/web/20090129230209/www.themanitoban.com/2006-2007/0321/121.A.place.to.belong.php).
Embrick, David, Carol Walther, and Corrine Wickens. 2007. "Working Class Masculinity: Keeping Gay Men and Lesbians Out of the Workplace." *Sex Roles* 56:757–766.
Engardio, Joel. 1999, April 14. "You Can't Be Gay–You're Latino." *SF Weekly*. Retrieved January 30, 2020 (https://archives.sfweekly.com/sanfrancisco/you-cant-be-gay-youre-latino/Content?oid=2136378).
Erasing 76 Crimes. 2017, May 19. "76 Countries Where Homosexuality Is Illegal." *Erasing 76 Crimes*. Retrieved January 30, 2020 (https://76crimes.com/76-countries-where-homosexuality-is-illegal/).
Estrada, Fernando, G. Marybeth Rigali-Oiler, Miguel Arciniega, and Terence J. G. Tracey. 2011. "Machismo and Mexican American Men: An Empirical Understanding Using a Gay Sample." *Journal of Counseling Psychology* 58(3):358–367.
Estrada, Gabriel S. 2017. "Two-Spirit Mexica Youth and Transgender Mixtec/Muxe Media: La Mission (2009), Two Spirit: Injunuity (2013), and Libertad (2015)." *Journal of Religion & Film* 21(1):38.
Fahs, Breanne. 2009. "Compulsory Bisexuality?: The Challenges of Modern Sexual Fluidity." *Journal of Bisexuality* 9(3/4):431–449.
Filiault, Shaun M. and Murray J. N. Drummond. 2007. "The Hegemonic Aesthetic." *Gay and Lesbian Issues and Psychology Review* 3:175–184.
Galupo, M. Paz, Renae C. Mitchell, and Kyle S. Davis. 2015. "Sexual Minority Self-Identification: Multiple Identities and Complexity." *Psychology of Sexual Orientation and Gender Diversity* 2(4):355–364.
Gilley, Brian. 2006. *Becoming Two-Spirit: Gay Identity and Social Acceptance in Indian Country*. Lincoln, NE: University of Nebraska Press.

Gilley, Brian. 2010. "Native Sexual Inequalities: American Indian Cultural Conservative Homophobia and the Problem of Tradition." *Sexualities* 13(1):47–68.

Greene, Beverly. 1996. "Lesbian Women of Color: Triple Jeopardy." *Journal of Lesbian Studies* 1(1):109–147.

Han, Chong-suk. 2007. "They Don't Want to Cruise Your Type: Gay Men of Color and the Racial Politics of Exclusion." *Social Identities* 13(1):51–67.

Harris, Angelique and Juan Battle. 2013. "Unpacking Civic Engagement: The Sociopolitical Involvement of Same Gender Loving Black Women." *Journal of Lesbian Studies* 17(2):195–207.

Heath, Jessie and Kathy Goggin. 2009. "Attitudes Towards Male Homosexuality, Bisexuality, and the Down Low Lifestyle: Demographic Differences and HIV Implications." *Journal of Bisexuality* 9(1):17–31.

Heflick, Nathan. 2010, February 6. "EWWW..Anal Sex Is Icky! Men, Women and Anal Sex." *Psychology Today*. Retrieved January 30, 2020 (www.psychologytoday.com/blog/the-big-questions/201002/ewwwanal-sex-is-icky).

Hennen, Peter. 2008. *Faeries, Bears, and Leathermen: Men in Community Queering the Masculine*. Chicago, IL: University of Chicago Press.

Human Dignity Trust. 2016. "*Breaking the Silence: Criminalisation of Lesbian and Bisexual Women and Its Impacts*." Retrieved January 30, 2020 (http://www.humandignitytrust.org/uploaded/Library/Other_Material/Breaking_the_Silence-Criminalisation_of_LB_Women_and_ its_Impacts-FINAL.pdf).

Human Rights Campaign. 2019. "*Criminalization around the World*" Retrieved January 30, 2020 (http://hrc-assets.s3-website-us-east-1.amazonaws.com//files/assets/resources/Criminalization-Map-042315.pdf).

Humphreys, Laud. 1970. *Tearoom Trade: Impersonal Sex in Public Places*. New York, NY: Aldine de Gruyter.

Hunter, Marcus. 2010. "All the Gays are White and All the Blacks are Straight: Black Gay Men, Identity, and Community." *Sexuality Research & Social Policy* 7:81–92.

Ingraham, Chrys. 1994. "The Heterosexual Imaginary: Feminist Sociology and Theories of Gender." *Sociological Theory* 12(2):203–219.

Jackson, Peter A. and Gerard Sullivan. 1999. "A Panoply of Roles: Sexual and Gender Diversity in Contemporary Thailand." Pp.1–28 in *Lady Boys, Tom Boys, Rent Boys: Male and Female Homosexualities in Contemporary Thailand*, edited by Peter Jackson and Gerard Sullivan. New York, NY: Haworth Press.

Jacobs, Sue-Ellen, Wesley Thomas, and Sabine Lang. 1997. *Two-spirit People: Native American Gender Identity, Sexuality, and Spirituality*. Urbana, IL: University of Illinois Press.

James, Sandy, Jody Herman, Susan Rankin, Mara Keisling, Lisa Mottet, and Ma'ayan Anafi. 2016. *The Report of the 2015 U.S. Transgender Survey*. Washington, DC: National Center for Transgender Equality.

Jeffries, William, Brian Dodge, and Theo Sandfort. 2008. "Religion and Spirituality among Bisexual Black Men in the USA." *Culture, Health & Sexuality* 10(5):463–477.

Jorgensen, Christine. 1967. *Christine Jorgensen: A Personal Autobiography*. New York, New York: Bantam Books.

Kadi, Joanna. 1997. "Homophobic Workers or Elitist Queers?." Pp. 29–42 in *Queerly Classed*, edited by S. Ruffo. Boston, MA: South End Press.

La Fountain-Stokes, Lawrence. 2009. *Queer Ricans: Cultures and Sexualities in the Diaspora*. Minneapolis, MN: University of Minnesota Press.

Lahti, Martti. 1998. "Dressing Up in Power: Tom of Finland and Gay Male Body Politics." *Journal of Homosexuality* 35(3/4):185–205.

Luibhéid, Eithne and Lionel Cantú. 2005. *Queer Migrations: Sexuality, U.S. Citizenship, and Border Crossings*. Minneapolis, MN: University of Minnesota Press.

McCarthy, Justin. 2019. "Gallup First Polled on Gay Issues in '77. What Has Changed?" Gallup.Com. Retrieved August 21, 2019 (https://news.gallup.com/poll/258065/gallup-first-polled-gay-issues-changed.aspx).

Meyer, Doug. 2008. "Interpreting and Experiencing Anti-Queer Violence: Race, Class, and Gender Differences among LGBT Hate Crime Victims." *Race, Gender & Class* 15(3/4):262–282.

Mirandé, Alfredo. 1997. *Hombres Y Machos: Masculinity and Latino Culture*. Boulder, CO: Westview Press.

Monro, Surya. 2007 "Transmuting Gender Binaries: The Theoretical Challenge." *Sociological Research Online* 12(1). Retrieved January 30, 2020 (www.socresonline.org.uk/12/1/monro.html).

Myers, JoAnne. 2013. *Historical Dictionary of the Lesbian and Gay Liberation Movements*. Lanham, MD: Scarecrow Press, Inc.

Nagle, Jill. 2000. "When I Get that Feeling: A Conversation with Cleo Manago about Black Male Lust." Pp. 239–248 in *Male Lust: Pleasure, Power, and Transformation*, edited by John Dececco, Kerwin Brook, Jill Nagle, and Baruch Gould. Binghamton, NY: Harrington Park Press.

Pascoe, C. J. 2007. *Dude, You're a Fag: Masculinity and Sexuality in High School*. Los Angeles, CA: University of California Press.

Pew Research Center. 2014. "Views about Homosexuality." *Pew Research Center*. Retrieved January 30, 2020 (www.pewforum.org/religious-landscape-study/views-about-homosexuality/).

Pew Research Center. 2017, October 4. "Majorities in Both Parties Now Say Homosexuality Should Be Accepted." *Pew Research Center*. Retrieved January 30, 2020 www.people-press.org/2017/10/05/5-homosexuality-gender-and-religion/5_1-8/).

Phua, Voon and Gayle Kaufman. 2003. "The Crossroads of Race and Sexuality: Date Selection among Men in Internet "Personal" Ads." *Journal of Family Issues* 24(8):981–994.

Radford, Jynnah. 2019. "Key Findings about U.S. Immigrants." *Pew Research Center*. Retrieved January 30, 2020 (www.pewresearch.org/fact-tank/2019/06/17/key-findings-about-u-s-immigrants/).

Rich, Adrienne. 1980. "Compulsory Heterosexuality and Lesbian Existence." *Signs* 5(4):631–660.

Rodríguez, Juana Maria. 2003. *Queer Latinidad: Identity Practices, Discursive Spaces*. New York, NY: NYU Press.

Rupp, Leila and Verta Taylor. 2010. "Straight Girls Kissing." *Contexts* 9:28–32.

Schilt, Kristen and Laurel Westbrook. 2009. "Doing Gender, Doing Heteronormativity: 'Gender Normals', Transgender People, and the Social Maintenance of Heterosexuality." *Gender & Society* 23(4):440–464.

Schippers, Mimi. 2007. "Recovering the Feminine Other: Masculinity, Femininity, and Gender Hegemony." *Theory and Society* 6:85–102.

Sears, Brad and Lee Badgett. 2012. "Beyond Stereotypes: Poverty in the LGBT Community." *TIDES | Momentum* 4. Retrieved January 30, 2020 (https://williamsinstitute.law.ucla.edu/headlines/beyond-stereotypes-poverty-in-the-lgbt-community/).

Sedgwick, Eve Kosofsky. 1990. *Epistemology of the Closet*. Berkeley, CA: University of California Press.

Sinnott, Megan. 2004. *Toms and Dees: Transgender Identity and Female Same-Sex Relationships in Thailand*. Honolulu, HA: University of Hawaii Press.

Spillett, Richard. 2014, October 8. "Middle-class Professionals 60 Percent More Likely to Be Openly Gay than Working-class Men and Women." *The Daily Mail*. Retrieved January 30, 2020 (www.dailymail.co.uk/news/article-2784665/Middle-class-profesionals-60-cent-likely-openly-gay-working-class-men-women.html).

Sprott, Richard A. and Bren Benoit Hadcock. 2018. "Bisexuality, Pansexuality, Queer Identity, and Kink Identity." *Sexual and Relationship Therapy* 33(1/2):214–232.

Steinmetz, Katy. 2014. "The Transgender Tipping Point." *Time* 183(22). Retrieved January 30, 2020 (https://time.com/magazine/us/135460/june-9th-2014-vol-183-no-22-u-s/).

Stryker, Susan. 2008. *Transgender History*. Berkeley, CA: Seal Press.

Stryker, Susan. 2009. "We Who are Sexy: Christine Jorgensen's Transsexual Whiteness in the Postcolonial Philippines." *Social Semiotics* 19(1):79–91.

Valentine, David. 2007. *Imagining Transgender: An Ethnography of a Category*. Chapel Hill, NC: Duke University Press.

Valocchi, Steve. 1999. "The Class-Inflected Nature of Gay Identity." *Social Problems* 46:207–224.

Vidal-Ortiz, Salvador. 2014. "Whiteness." *TSQ: Transgender Studies Quarterly* 1(1/2):264–266.

Walters, Karina, Jane M. Teresa Evans-Campbell, Theresa Ronquillo Simoni, and Rupaleem Bhuyan. 2006. ""My Spirit in My Heart": Identity Experiences and Challenges among American Indian Two-Spirit Women." *Journal of Lesbian Studies* 10:125–149.

Ward, Elijah. 2005. "Homophobia, Hypermasculinity and the US Black Church." *Culture, Health & Sexuality* 7:493–504.

West, Candace and Don H. Zimmerman. 1987. "Doing Gender." *Gender & Society* 1(2):125–151.

White, Ben. 1952. "Ex-GI Becomes Blonde Beauty." *The Daily News* 3. December 1.

Whitley, Bernard, Christopher Childs, and Jena Collins. 2011. "Differences in Black and White American College Students' Attitudes toward Lesbians and Gay Men." *Sex Roles* 64:299–310.

Whyte, Stephen, Robert C. Brooks, and Benno Torgler. 2018. "Man, Woman, 'Other': Factors Associated with Nonbinary Gender Identification." *Archives of Sexual Behavior* 47(8):2397–2406.

Worthen, Meredith G. F. 2013. "An Argument for Separate Analyses of Attitudes toward Lesbian, Gay, Bisexual Men, Bisexual Women, MtF and FtM Transgender Individuals." *Sex Roles* 68(11/12):703–723.

Worthen, Meredith G. F. 2016a. "Hetero-cis-normativity and the Gendering of Transphobia." *International Journal of Transgenderism* 17(1):31–57.

Worthen, Meredith G. F. 2016b. *Sexual Deviance and Society*. London, UK: Routledge.

Worthen, Meredith G. F. and Danielle Dirks. 2015. "Gender and Deviance." Pp. 277–297 in *Handbook of Deviance*, edited by Erich Goode. Hoboken, NJ: Wiley-Blackwell Press.

# 4
# HETERO-CIS-NORMATIVITY AND COMMON EXPLANATIONS FOR LGBT(Q) STIGMA

Using NCST to explore the relationships between hetero-cis-normativity and LGBTQ stigma allows for a critical examination of the multiple, interacting complexities embedded within these cultural patterns. Interestingly, however, the majority of existing studies that have investigated "explanations" for LGBT(Q) stigma have been largely atheoretical. Many lack conceptual arguments that distinguish L, G, B, and T stigma and most fail to examine queer (Q) and non-binary-related stigma (these will be explored more closely in subsequent chapters). On the whole, previous work typically investigates heterosexuals' attitudes toward LGBT individuals as they relate to the following common explanations: (1) LGBT contact, (2) religiosity, (3) political perspectives, and (4) beliefs about gender. In other words, most existing research uses the stigmatizer lens to examine correlates of LGBT stigma. Overall, past studies are generally lacking in the theoretical focus that NCST can provide. The purpose of the current chapter is to review the most commonly investigated explanations for LGBT stigma (as a byproduct of the existing literature, nearly all use the stigmatizer lens and examine heterosexuals' attitudes) and situate them within the theoretical model of NCST and LGBTQ stigma described in Chapter 3. In doing so, this chapter identifies the existing landscape of research about LGBT(Q) stigma while also highlighting the importance of using NCST to examine numerous experiences and beliefs that are shaped by social power, maintain hetero-cis-normativity, and contribute to LGBTQ stigma.

## LGBTQ Stigma and LGBTQ Contact

With close to 9 out of 10 (88%) Americans indicating that they personally know someone who is gay or lesbian (Pew Research Center 2015) and 37%

of Americans saying that they personally know someone who is transgender (Brown 2017), contact with those that identify as LGBT is likely more common in the U.S. today than at any other time in modern history. Even so, hetero-cis-normativity continues to be the expectation among the majority and prejudice and stigma from norm followers (stigmatizers) directed toward hetero-cis-normativity violators (i.e., stigmatized LGBTQ people) remain prominent. Some ways to understand such prejudices using the stigmatizer lens include the degree of contact individuals have with LGBTQ people. Past researchers have developed methods to examine such contact experiences that help us to better understand the relationships between social contact with hetero-cis-normativity violators and LGBT stigma. These are reviewed below.

## LGBT Stigma and Allport's Contact Hypothesis

Allport's (1954) contact hypothesis suggests that intergroup contact may help to reduce biases and negative attitudes between ingroups (norm followers, potential stigmatizers) and outgroups (norm violators, potentially stigmatized). The premise of the contact hypothesis is rather simple: "if, on the one hand, interpersonal contact with minority group members is an effective way to reduce prejudices against them, on the other hand, a lack of interpersonal contact may be associated with greater hostility against them" (Lingiardi et al. 2016:96; see also Costa, Pereira, and Leal 2015). Furthermore, the effects of social contact are far reaching: "Not only do attitudes toward the immediate participants usually become more favorable, but so do attitudes toward the entire outgroup, outgroup members in other situations, and even outgroups not involved in the contact" (Pettigrew and Tropp 2006:766). There is much support for this notion. Indeed, synthesizing the effects from 713 independent samples in 515 studies, Pettigrew and Tropp's (2006) meta-analysis revealed that attitudes toward an outgroup tend to be more favorable among ingroup members who have personal contact experiences with one or more of its members. These patterns hold even when Allport's (1954) optimal conditions[1] are not in place and across multiple geographic areas of research (Australia, Africa, Asia, Canada, Europe, Israel, New Zealand, Latin America, and the U.S.), suggesting a robust relationship between social contact and favorable attitudes toward a particular group. Indeed, Pettigrew and Tropp (2006) note that "although there is variability in the magnitude of contact–prejudice effects across different intergroup contexts, the relationships between contact and prejudice remain significant across samples involving different target groups, age groups, geographical areas, and contact settings" (766). Moreover, although intergroup contact theory's original focus was on prejudices among racial and ethnic groups, much research supports the extension of the contact hypothesis to a variety of intergroup contexts (Pettigrew and Tropp 2006).

Specific to sexual identity/orientation prejudices, several researchers (Basow and Johnson 2000; Herek and Capitanio 1996; Herek and Glunt 1993; Hinrichs and Rosenberg 2002; Loehr, Doan, and Miller 2015; Raja and Stokes 1998; Smith, Axelton, and Saucier 2009; Worthen et al. 2019) have found more positive attitudes toward gays and lesbians among heterosexuals who report that they know lesbian/gay people. Moreover, Pettigrew and Tropp's (2006) meta-analysis of intergroup contact theory indicates that among prejudices directed toward gays/lesbians, racial/ethnic minorities, physically disabled, mentally disabled, mentally ill, and elderly people, the largest effects for support of the contact-prejudice hypothesis emerge for samples involving contact between heterosexuals and gays/lesbians. Additionally, studies in the U.S. and Canada show that those who know bisexuals have more positive attitudes toward bisexual people (Eliason 1997; Herek 2002; Mohr and Rochlen 1999). Furthermore, research in Montréal, Canada (Hill and Willoughby 2005), Hong Kong, China (King, Winter, and Webster 2009), and Spain (Worthen et al. 2019) shows that those who have personal contact with a transgender person have more positive attitudes toward transgender people. In the U.S., both a nationally representative survey (Flores 2015) and convenience-based college samples (Walch et al. 2012; Worthen et al. 2019) find a positive relationship between support of transgender issues and interpersonal contact with transgender people. In particular, having personal contact with LGBT people can disrupt hetero-cis-normative expectations and in doing so, this can diminish LGBT stigma. Put another way, more exposure to norm violators (i.e., LGBT people) lessens the stigma associated with norm violations (LGBT stigma).

## LGBTQ Stigma and Religiosity

In a nationally representative survey, nearly 8 in 10 (78%) of more than ten thousand Americans who indicated that "homosexuality should be discouraged" also indicated that religion is "very important" to them (Pew Research Center 2014; see Table 4.1). While there are many ways to explore these relationships, including examinations of "belief, religious motivation, organizational religious activities (ORA), non-organizational activities (NORA), attachment to God, trust in God, religious experience, religious coping, religious maturity, and history of lifetime exposure to religion" (Koenig et al. 2015:530), patterns across multiple measurements of religiosity demonstrate that those that indicate that they are "religious" tend to support hetero-cis-normativity and consequently, stigmatize LGBT people. Overall, there are three broad and overlapping experiences with religiosity that relate to LGBT stigma: (1) generalized religiousness; (2) participation in religious practices and behaviors; and (3) specific religious beliefs. Taken together, these experiences with religiosity typically enhance both hetero-cis-normativity and LGBTQ

**TABLE 4.1** U.S. Views about "Homosexuality" by Religiosity

|  |  | Percentage answering affirmatively among those who believe "homosexuality should be accepted" (n = 21,589) | Percentage answering affirmatively among those who believe "homosexuality should be discouraged" (n = 10,872) |
|---|---|---|---|
| **Generalized religiousness** | Religion is "very important" in my life. | 39% | 78% |
|  | Look most to religion as a source of guidance on right and wrong | 20% | 58% |
| **Religious practices and behaviors** | Pray at least daily | 44% | 76% |
|  | Attend religious services at least once a week | 23% | 59% |
|  | Read scripture at least once a week | 22% | 60% |
|  | Participate in scripture study or religious education group at least once a week | 14% | 45% |
| **Specific religious beliefs** | Believe in "god" or a "universal spirit"; "absolutely certain" | 51% | 84% |
|  | Believe in heaven | 65% | 85% |
|  | Believe in hell | 48% | 77% |
|  | Holy scripture is word of god and "is to be taken literally, word for word" | 18% | 55% |

Data come from the Pew Research Center Religion & Public Life Religious Landscape Study (2014) which is a nationally representative dual-frame (cellphone and landline) random-digit dialing telephone survey conducted among Americans from all 50 states and Washington, D.C.

stigma among potential stigmatizers of LGBTQ people. In other words, religiosity upholds the importance of hetero-cis norm following and in turn, religiosity impacts the relationship between being LGBTQ (hetero-cis-normativity violations) and the stigmatization of LGBTQ people.

## *LGBT Stigma and Generalized Religiousness*

Many researchers that explore relationships between LGBT stigma and "religiosity" do not examine the multi-dimensionality of religious experiences. Instead, they often rely on measures of generalized religiousness which typically include Likert-type survey items such as "how religious are you?" or "how important is religion to you in your daily life?" As a result, for the most part, "religiosity" as a common explanation for LGBT stigma is highly overgeneralized and rather unspecific. Even so, studies in the U.S., China, and Europe show that negative attitudes toward LGBT individuals are correlated with higher levels of generalized religiousness (Herek 2002; Hinrichs and Rosenberg 2002; Kelly 2001; Lin, Button, Su, and Chen 2016; Lingiardi, Falanga, and D'Augelli 2005; Mohr and Rochlen 1999; Nagoshi et al. 2008; Sotelo 2000; Sherkat 2017; van de Meerendonk and Scheepers 2004; Worthen 2012; 2014; Worthen, Lingiardi, and Caristo 2017). Thus, across multiple geographic and socio-cultural experiences, "religiousness" tends to overlap with the maintenance of hetero-cis-normativity and LGBT negativity.

## LGBTQ Stigma and Participation in Religious Practices and Behaviors

Beyond generalized measures of "religiousness," researchers sometimes examine religious practices and behaviors, such as frequency of prayer and church/religious service attendance, as they relate to LGBT stigma. In particular, going to church/religious services socializes and reinforces religiousness. In other words, *feeling* religious is one type of religious experience, but *doing* religion with others in an organized setting can build on these religious feelings and become significantly impactful on a person's attitudes toward religiously embedded topics such as LGBT issues and people. As U.S. researcher Allport (1966) stated, "It is a well-established fact in social science that, on the average, churchgoers … harbor more … prejudice than do non-churchgoers" (447). While it has been more than fifty years since this work on the religious context of prejudice was published, the origins of this relationship may still have meaning. Indeed, studies suggest that religious experiences have strong effects on social and political attitudes (DiMaggio, Evans, and Bryson 1996; Guth et al. 1996; Jaspers, Lubbers, and De Graaf 2007; Manza and Brooks 1997). For example, researchers have found that those who attend church/religious services report more negative attitudes toward gay men and lesbian women (Hinrichs and Rosenberg 2002; Lin et al. 2016; Worthen 2012; 2014) and less support for marriage equality (Sherkat 2017). American public opinion polls show that those who believe "homosexuality should be discouraged" participate in significantly more frequent religious practices and behaviors as compared to those who believe "homosexuality should be accepted." For example, as seen in Table 4.1, 3 out of 4 (76%) Americans who discourage "homosexuality" pray at least daily as compared to about 4 in 10 (44%) who accept "homosexuality." Nearly three times as many who deject "homosexuality" as compared to those who accept "homosexuality" read scripture at least once a week (60% and 22% respectively) and participate in scripture study at least once a week (45% and 14% respectively) and more than twice as many attend religious services at least once a week (59% and 23% respectively) (Pew Research Center 2014).

Participation in organized religion may be particularly impactful on LGBTQ stigma because church and religious leaders can shape attendees' attitudes toward particular topics (Wald, Owen, and Hill 1988; Welch et al. 1993). In particular, researchers have found that religious practices (i.e., church attendance) are more strongly related to attitudes toward "homosexuality" than religious denomination (Lubbers, Jaspers, and Ultee 2009; van de Meerendonk, Eisinga, and Felling 2003). Furthermore, church/religious service attendance relates to other experiences that can reinforce LGBTQ stigma. For example, churches/places of worship are often spaces dominated by hetero-cis people and hetero-cis-normativity. Thus, participating in activities in religious establishments may reinforce the normative existence of hetero-cis people and the deviance of LGBTQ people. In addition, those who frequently attend church/religious services may also actively choose to separate themselves from LGBTQ individuals. Indeed, research shows that higher levels of church attendance are related to social distancing from lesbians and bisexuals (Hinrichs and Rosenberg 2002; Mohr and Rochlen 1999) and negative attitudes toward LGBT individuals (Worthen 2012; 2014). Thus, there are overlapping and mutually reinforcing experiences among generalized religiousness, religious practices/behaviors, and LGBTQ stigma. While we certainly see increasing LGBTQ diversity and LGBTQ acceptance in contemporary churches and religions (e.g., UUA.org), the robust relationship between church/religious service attendance and LGBTQ negativity indicates that the dominant religious experiences among those that participate in organized religion—especially Christianity—enforce both hetero-cis-normativity and LGBTQ stigma.

## LGBTQ Stigma and Specific Religious Beliefs

Other than *feeling* generally religious and *doing* religion, it stands to reason that *believing* in specific religious concepts or perspectives can impact LGBTQ stigma. For example, believing in "God or a universal spirit," "heaven," and "hell" are all significantly more common among Americans who discourage "homosexuality" (84%, 85%, and 77% respectively) as compared to those that accept "homosexuality" (51%, 65%, and 48% respectively) (see Table 4.1). In addition, while some religious groups, such as Unitarian Universalism, promote religious education that advocates for social justice for LGBTQ people (UUA. org), others actively condemn LGBTQ people. Indeed, scholars find that alignment with fundamentalist protestant religions and Catholicism relates to negative attitudes toward gays and lesbians (Hinrichs and Rosenberg 2002) and transgender people (Nagoshi et al. 2008). Similarly, biblical literalism has also been found to be strongly related to LGBT prejudices (Sherkat 2017; Worthen 2012, 2016). American public opinion polls show that over half of Jehovah's Witnesses (76%), Mormons (57%), and Evangelical Protestants (55%) as well as those that interpret the holy scripture as the literal word of God (55%, see

Table 4.1) believe that "homosexuality should be discouraged" (Pew Research Center 2014). Alignment with such religious perspectives relates to unsupportive LGBTQ attitudes because, generally, such religions utilize teachings that have been described as condemnatory of LGBTQ lives (although some interpret such teachings quite differently) (Boswell 1980). Furthermore, biblical literalists are typically strong supporters of "traditional" (i.e., cis man + cis woman) family values leaving little space for LGBTQ relationships and families (Burdette, Ellison, and Hill 2005; McDaniel and Ellison 2008; Sherkat 2017). Thus, interpreting scripture "literally" and adhering to religious denominations that do so both strongly relate to LGBT stigma and hetero-cis-normativity (McDaniel and Ellison 2008; Worthen 2012). Church/religious service attendance may also amplify such negative LGBTQ attitudes since more involvement in church may represent more intense involvement with religion, which may also be related to higher levels of emersion within biblical/scriptural literalism and generalized religiousness (van de Meerendonk, Eisinga, and Felling 2003), all of which amplify LGBTQ stigma and maintain hetero-cis-normativity.

## *LGBTQ Stigma, Race, Ethnicity, and Religiosity*

Experiences with religion, hetero-cis-normativity, and LGBTQ stigma can also be entwined with race and ethnicity (see also, Chapter 3). These patterns demonstrate the interlocking intricacies embedded within these relationships. For example, the Black church[2] has a complex relationship with LGBT issues and people (Harris 2010; Schulte and Battle 2004; Ward 2005). Indeed, participation in the Black church has historically been found to be related to less supportive attitudes towards gay men and lesbian women (Schulte and Battle 2004; see also Ward 2005) and the Black church has been historically damning of "homosexuality" as "wrong and sinful" (Battle et al. 2002:48) with a majority of Black LGBT people indicating negative experiences in churches or religious institutions (Battle et al. 2002) and a little over one-fourth (27%) of Black LGBT people remaining closeted in their religious communities (Battle, Pastrana, and Harris 2017b). Rigid beliefs about gender, especially regarding Black men and hyper heteromasculinity, have also been historically reinforced in Black churches creating a particularly hostile climate for Black GBT men (Ward 2005).

In addition, cultural norms rooted in Asian religions and philosophies such as Confucianism and Taoism can generate LGBTQ negativity. For example, Confucianism dictates gender norms whereby the wife must obey the husband and "homosexual relationships are problematic because they do not fit the Confucian order" (Liu and Chan 2003:91). LGBTQ people can also disrupt the Taoist philosophical belief of the marriage of the yin (female) and yang (male) as ultimate balance, rightful order, and happiness that is common especially in East Asian societies (Liu and Chan 2003). However, it is important to note that only 39% of Asian Americans say religion is very important in their lives (compared to 49% of Whites, 59% of Hispanics, and 75% of Blacks) and 26% of Asian Americans are not affiliated with any religion (Pew Research Center 2012). Even so, the cultural norms regarding family and gender embedded in these religious philosophical teachings are evident in some Asian communities and can uphold hetero-cis-normativity.

Furthermore, the importance of religiosity in some Latinx families can also mutually reinforce LGBTQ negativity and hetero-cis-normativity. For example, research shows that church attendance and the belief that religion plays an important role in guiding everyday life are significantly associated with anti-gay and anti-lesbian attitudes among Latinx people (Herek and Gonzalez-Rivera 2006). In addition, religiosity has been found to be related to internalized homonegativity among bisexual Latino men (Severson, Muñoz-Laboy, and Kaufman 2014) and may also encourage closeting behavior. Indeed, a 2010 survey found that a little over one-third (35%) of Latinx LGBT people are closeted in their religious communities (Pastrana, Battle, and Harris 2017). Religious practices and beliefs can also reinforce patriarchal gender expectations, hetero-cis-normativity, and more conservative attitudes toward sexuality among Latinx individuals (Severson, Muñoz-Laboy, and Kaufman 2014). For example, Latino Catholicism in particular has been linked to both *familismo* (familial closeness) and *machismo* (described further later in this chapter) (Ellison, Wolfinger, and Ramos-Wada 2013). Taken together, it is evident that religiosity and the overlapping familial and community scripts of hetero-cis-normativity and patriarchy play a role in the stigmatization of LGBTQ people among Latinx individuals.

Multiple measures of religiosity including *feeling* generally religious, *doing* religion, and *believing* in specific religious concepts or perspectives impact LGBTQ stigma across numerous geographic and socio-cultural explorations of these patterns. Much religiosity (and in turn, LGBTQ negativity) is actively reinforced through groups (e.g., families, friends, communities) and larger social systems (e.g., religious institutions, political platforms, media representations). Some racial and ethnic religious experiences can further impact LGBTQ stigma and strengthen the coupling of "Whiteness" and "gayness" as described in Chapter 3. There are numerous additional dynamics at work beyond those offered here (e.g., class experiences, investment in religion, religious sociocultural dynamics) but overall, both the generals and particulars of many religious experiences impact LGBTQ stigma largely because they promote LGBTQ negativity. For most, experiences with religion are also experiences with the maintenance of hetero-cis-normativity.

## LGBTQ Stigma and Political Beliefs

Perspectives about "LGBTQ issues" have become politically entrenched in recent years. Historian John D'Emilio's (2002) work shows that the role of gay men and lesbian women in marriage, the military, parenting, media/arts, hate crimes, politics, public school curricula, and religion became a part of predominant political and social discourse in the 1990s: "Gay issues in this period became a permanent part of the world of politics and public policy, and gay people became a regularly visible part of American cultural and social life" (91). Similarly, the political contexts of many parts of the world have been painted with debates about LGBTQ rights in recent decades, many of which continue to remain prominent (Kollman and Waites 2009; McCarthy 2019). Nearly all political candidates identify their stance on LGBTQ rights in today's political climate (Lewis 2005; Worthen, Lingiardi, and Caristo 2017). As a result, political discourse *is* LGBTQ discourse and vice versa.

## *LGBTQ Stigma and "Liberal vs. Conservative"*

Recent explorations of the relationships between political beliefs and LGBTQ stigma are often a two-sided, rather simplistic dialogue. Indeed, political alignment can function as a heuristic device that individuals use to organize their opinions and attitudes about important issues. For example, researchers have found that most people utilize "information short cuts" when making political decisions (Brody and Lawless 2003:54; see also Popkin 1994). Political parties themselves are organized in such a way to allow voters to be able to use these "information short cuts" to choose the political candidate they would like to support. Some even suggest that "voters need to know only what liberals and conservatives generally support" in order to choose who they will vote for in the next election (Brody and Lawless 2003:55).

In the U.S., this is typically organized into a "Republican vs. Democrat" battle. In Western Europe, it is "right wing vs. left wing." More generally, these arguments fall into politically "conservative vs. liberal." Although the operationalization of political beliefs as "conservative" to "liberal" and "right-wing" to "left-wing" may seem rather unsophisticated, interestingly, studies indicate that most people organize their political leanings in these simplistic ways. For example, American social psychological research shows that students overwhelmingly support policies if they align with their preferred party (Republican or Democrat). They need not even know the particulars of such policies, instead, they blindly support them because they have the seal of approval from their preferred party who embodies either a conservative or liberal political ideology (Cohen 2003).

In social science research, political beliefs are usually measured on a simple spectrum (typically a Likert-type index from liberal to conservative or left-wing to right-wing) with those identifying as more liberal or left wing usually being more supportive of LGBTQ individuals. Studies utilizing such measures in the U.S., China, and Europe indicate a strong relationship between self-reported conservative political ideology and negative attitudes toward "homosexuals" (Lin et al. 2016; Lingiardi, Falanga, and D'Augelli 2005; Lingiardi et al. 2016), bisexuals (Mohr and Rochlen 1999; Worthen et al. 2019), and transgender people (Flores 2015; Norton and Herek 2013; Worthen et al. 2019). American public opinion polls also reflect these patterns with 83% of Democrats and only 54% of Republicans agreeing that "homosexuality should be accepted by society" (Pew Research Center 2017). Thus, in today's political climate, "liberal vs. conservative" may be currently organized as "pro-LGBT vs. anti-LGBT."

## *LGBTQ Stigma and the Foundations of "Liberal vs. Conservative"*

The foundations of political liberalism reflect the importance of individualism, liberty, and freedom (Graham, Haidt, and Nosek 2009). Liberals tend to be open to new experiences and are vested in disrupting social injustices (Jost et al. 2003). Challenging the status quo, questioning inequalities, and advocating for social changes based on harm and fairness are all essential components of liberalism (Graham, Haidt, and Nosek 2009). Thus, politically liberal people are more likely to support LGBTQ people because LGBTQ people are often navigating severe social injustices based on their desire to express their own individualism as LGBTQ people. In other words, much of the foundation of political liberalism aligns with the fight for LGBTQ rights.

On the other hand, the foundational components of political conservatism include "avoidance of uncertainty and an intolerance of ambiguity as well as resistance to change and justification of inequality" (Norton and Herek 2013:741; see also Jost et al. 2003). Jost et al.'s (2003) meta-analysis with 88 samples from 12 countries and 22,818 cases identified a negative relationship between political conservativism and openness to experience. As a social cognition, aligning with political conservativism is connected to a desire to maintain the status quo, secure order and structure, and avoid the unknown (Jost et al. 2003). Indeed, overarching conservative perspectives may represent a general aversion toward anyone or anything that is perceived as a challenge to existing social and traditional values (Norton and Herek 2013). In this respect, negative attitudes toward LGBTQ people are collectively underscored by negativity toward outgroups, a perspective that has been historically linked to conservativism in both political and religious realms. Thus, politically conservative people are less likely to support LGBTQ people because LGBTQ people challenge core aspects imbued within conservative paradigms.

The relationships between LGBTQ stigma and political beliefs are so closely entwined in today's political climate that it is difficult to ascertain the precise constellation of complexities embedded within these relationships, including the ways race, ethnicity, class, and gender inform these patterns. In particular, because hetero-cis-normativity is the dominant system of norms in many parts of the world, disrupting hetero-cis-normativity (as LGBTQ people tend to do) challenges the status quo—a practice that feels relatively comfortable to most political liberals but categorically uncomfortable to most political conservatives. Through this lens, "liberal vs. conservative" can be conceptualized as a two-sided debate about the maintenance of hetero-cis-normativity: "oppose vs. support hetero-cis-normativity." Embedded in our allegiances to political belief systems is a deep relationship to hetero-cis-normativity that shapes our understandings of LGBTQ stigma.

## LGBTQ Stigma and Beliefs about Gender

Perspectives about LGBTQ people are closely connected to perspectives about gender. In particular, more traditional, conservative, and patriarchal cultural expectations about men and women including what types of "roles" they should (or should not) take on and behaviors they should (or should not) participate in relate to more negative attitudes toward LGBTQ people while more liberal, diverse, and equality/feminist-oriented expectations about men and women relate to more supportive attitudes toward LGBTQ people (e.g., Hill and Willoughby 2005; Worthen 2018). This is in part because LGBTQ people are stereotypically presumed to be in violation of such traditional, conservative, and patriarchal cultural expectations about men and women due to their existence as non-hetero-cis-normative people. Therefore, LGBTQ stigma is shaped by narrow social scripts regarding gender. Some common ways to better understand these perspectives include: (1) patriarchal gender norms; and (2) feminism.

### *LGBTQ Stigma and Patriarchal Gender Norms*

Simply put, patriarchy is a social system that upholds the power and privileges of masculine, man-identified males and secures dominance of this group over others. Adherence to and support of patriarchal gender norms reflect agreement with this social system. Also referred to as "traditional gender roles," patriarchal gender norms include specific concepts regarding (1) domestic behaviors (i.e., females should take care of the children, prepare all meals, clean the home) and (2) occupations (i.e., males' careers are most important, males should be political, social, and economic leaders). More generally, however, patriarchal gender norms are predicated on the maintenance of hetero-cis-normative relationships. This is perhaps why multiple studies have demonstrated a relationship between support of patriarchal gender norms and negative attitudes toward gays, lesbians, and "homosexuals" (Herek 1988; Whitley, Childs, and Collins 2011; Worthen 2018), bisexual men and women (Worthen 2018), and transgender people (Hill and Willoughby 2005; Worthen 2018). In other words, agreeing with patriarchal gender norms reflects not only support of patriarchy and hetero-cis-normativity, but also, the devaluation of LGBTQ people.

These relationships are further complicated by racial, ethnic, and family dynamics as described briefly in Chapter 3 (see also Worthen 2018). In particular, patriarchal familial expectations that are highly structured around strict gendered roles of father, mother, daughter, and son, can generate hostility toward LGBTQ people (Bridges, Selvidge, and Matthews 2003; Worthen 2018). For example, Asian American men are expected to be good family providers and to adhere to the "model minority" myth by being "highly self-reliant, economically successful, and politically non-resisting" (Chua and Fujino 1999:395; see also Battle, Pastrana, and Harris 2017a). The role of the "family man" in the Asian family is juxtaposed to the docile female marital partner. In addition, obedience and sexual repression are common themes in the traditional dynamics of Asian families and thus discourage gender and sexual exploration of any kind but especially non-heteronormative, non-cisgender experiences (Bridges, Selvidge, and Matthews 2003; Liu and Chan 2003). As a result, LGBTQ stigma relates to the maintenance of patriarchal gender norms, hetero-cis-normativity, and desire for family acceptance, all of which may be strongly enhanced in Asian families and communities (Han, Proctor, and Choi 2014). Indeed, research shows that less than half (41%) of Asian American/Pacific Islander LGBT Americans are out to all their family members and only a minority feel completely supported by their families (Battle, Pastrana, and Daniels 2012; Harrison-Quintana, De Guzman, Chaudhry, and Grant 2008).

Latinx family dynamics can also shape patriarchal gender norms, hetero-cis-normativity, and LGBT stigma. For example, a study of Latino gay and bisexual men revealed astonishingly high levels of childhood homophobia with nearly all (91%) indicating hearing that "gays are not normal" while growing up, over two thirds (70%) believing that being gay hurt and embarrassed their family, and well over half (64%) indicating they had to pretend to be straight (Diaz et al. 2001). Other research finds that less than half (45%) of Latinx LGBT people are out to all of their family members and only about one-third (38%) feel completely supported by their families (Battle, Pastrana, and Daniels 2012). This negativity can be further reinforced by Latinx family and community norms about gender, in particular, *machismo* and *marionismo*. *Machismo* has been described as a Latino gender construct related to hypermasculinity, patriarchy, and family dominance while its counterpart, *marionismo*, has been described as a Latina gender construct related to submissiveness, obedience, and self-sacrifice (Cauce and Melanie 2002). Herek and Gonzalez-Rivera's (2006) research with U.S. residents of Mexican descent found that those who supported more traditional patriarchal gender norms in line with *machismo* and *marionismo* (e.g., "Men should be in charge of the family," and "Latin women should obey their husbands," p. 135) were less supportive of gay men and lesbian women. Together, these findings demonstrate the complex nature of attitudes toward gay men and lesbian women among Latinx individuals and suggest such patterns may also be evident in attitudes toward bisexual, transgender, and non-binary people. For example, according to the National Transgender Discrimination Survey, less than half (47%) of Latinx transgender and gender non-conforming people are accepted by their families (Harrison-Quintana, Pérez, and Grant 2008). Latinx bisexuals also struggle with family acceptance and many note that heterosexuality and gender conformity are heavily enforced cultural scripts common in Latinx families (Yon-Leau and Miguel 2010). Thus, family dynamics as well as beliefs about patriarchy and gender inform relationships between race, ethnicity, and LGBT stigma.

Certainly additional racial, ethnic, class, and cultural dynamics are important to consider as they relate to the relationships among patriarchal gender norms, hetero-cis-normativity, and LGBT stigma. These examples only begin to illuminate some of these patterns. What is clear is that experiences with and the desired maintenance of the core system of hetero-cis-normativity that can be illustrated through restrictive beliefs about gender and the support of patriarchal gender norms strongly relate to the stigmatization of LGBT people.

## *LGBTQ Stigma and Feminism*

Perhaps the inverse of patriarchy, feminism is another important socio-cultural belief system that shapes LGBTQ stigma. By and large, feminist ideologies suggest that there should be political, economic, personal, and social equality between men and women and thus operate in diametric opposition to patriarchal ideologies (e.g., Millett 1970; Morgan 1996). Gender scholar Raewyn Connell (1990) further contextualizes gender and sexual politics in the realm of the slogan "the personal is political." Connell (1990) purports that this relationship between the personal and the political is a basic feature of both feminist and gay/lesbian politics and a link between personal experience and power relations (see also Taylor and Rupp 1993). Although certainly not ubiquitous among all feminists, LGBTQ issues are evident in feminist discourse. Generally speaking, both LGBTQ rights and feminism represent efforts to combat prejudices based on gender, sex, and sexuality (Scott-Dixon 2006; Serano 2007). In this way, both feminism and LGBTQ rights challenge hetero-cis-normativity. Indeed, some studies have shown that support of a basic tenet of feminism, "equality between men and women," is related to more positive attitudes toward gays and lesbians (Ojerholm and Rothblum 1999) and transgender individuals (Hill and Willoughby 2005; Norton and Herek 2013). Additional research indicates that self-identified "feminists" are more likely than non-feminists to report supportive attitudes toward LGBT individuals (Minnigerode 1976; Ojerholm and Rothblum 1999; Worthen 2012, 2016; Worthen, Lingiardi, and Caristo 2017).

Feminism is a multi-dimensional and evolving construct. What's more, identifying as a feminist is also an ever-changing process. Socio-cultural experiences including race, class, gender, and culture inform feminist politics (e.g., Black lesbian politics, trans-feminist politics, fourth-wave feminism) and thus embed strongly into perspectives about gender dynamics and hetero-cis-normativity. The overview of findings here suggests that both being a feminist and agreeing with feminist ideals relate to LGBTQ support and may also disrupt hetero-cis-normativity.

In sum, beliefs about gender are strongly encoded in our perspectives about LGBTQ people and issues. While there are numerous highly complex sociological constructs hidden within attitudes toward patriarchy and feminism, it is clear that the relatively simplistic operationalization of these concepts has a robust impact on LGBTQ stigmatization with the former related to LGBTQ stigma and the latter related to LGBTQ positivity. Furthermore, beliefs about gender are inherently connected to perspectives about hetero-cis-normativity (recall Figure 3.2 in Chapter 3). Strict, traditional, and conservative expectations about gender are embedded in the maintenance of hetero-cis-normativity and thus, work together to impact LGBTQ stigma.

## Relationships among the Four Common Explanations for LGBTQ Stigma

There is clear evidence to support the individual ways that (1) LGBT contact, (2) religiosity, (3) political perspectives, and (4) beliefs about gender relate to LGBTQ stigma; however, it is also important to recognize the relationships among these. For example, those who attend religious services frequently are significantly less likely to have contact with LGB people as compared to those who do not attend religious services frequently and they are more likely to socially distance themselves from LGB people (Herek and Capitanio 1996; Hinrichs and Rosenberg 2002; Mohr and Rochlen 1999). In addition, those who indicate conservative political ideologies are significantly less likely to indicate contact experiences with "homosexual" people as compared to political liberals and moderates (Herek and Glunt 1993). Furthermore, adherence to strict cultural expectations about gender are correlated with social distancing from transgender people (King, Winter, and Webster 2009). Thus, religiosity, political perspectives, and beliefs about gender shape the likelihood of social contact with LGBT people and all of these beliefs/experiences work together to impact LGBTQ stigma.

In addition, research indicates that there are important interrelationships between attitudes toward socio-politically motivated topics (such as LGBTQ rights) and religion, political conservatism, and beliefs about gender (Sherkat 2017; Worthen, Lingiardi, and Caristo 2017). For example, in the U.S., biblical literalists have aligned themselves with the Republican (conservative) Party and both promote explicitly anti-LGBTQ perspectives (McDaniel and Ellison 2008;

Sherkat 2017). Moreover, both religion and attitudes toward gender egalitarianism have been found to impact the degrees of public acceptance of "homosexuality" (Beckers 2010) and support of transgender people (Norton and Herek 2013). Furthermore, self-designated liberals have been found to be less likely to attend church and more likely than self-designated conservatives to support equality for women in social, economic, and political institutions (Brody and Lawless 2003). In the U.S., the Republican (conservative) Party has defined itself as "anti-feminist" and anti-feminist groups (many of which are religious in nature) have rallied to combat laws and policies directed toward feminist goals (Young and Cross 2003:207). Indeed, studies show that those who identify with feminism are less likely to have politically conservative beliefs compared to non-feminists (Jackson, Fleury, and Lewandowski 1996; Liss et al. 2001; Roy, Weibust, and Miller 2007). In these ways, religious, political, and feminist experiences and perspectives are intimately and interactively tied to the maintenance of both hetero-cis-normativity and LGBTQ stigma.

## Hetero-cis-normativity Underlies Common Explanations for LGBTQ Stigma

Overall, the four interconnected constructs that relate to LGBTQ stigma typically identified in past research can be described as symptoms of hetero-cis-normativity. In other words, the common underlying mechanism operating beneath and within each of these explanations of LGBTQ stigma is the desire to maintain a world dominated by hetero-cis people (whereby LGBTQ people are oppressed) and the belief that it is normative and expected to do so. Contact with LGBTQ people as well as religious, political, and feminist experiences and perspectives are all embedded and mutually reinforced in this system. LGBTQ stigma emerges from this system of hetero-cis-normativity. Put another way, LGBTQ stigma would not exist without hetero-cis-normativity.

Through this perspective, it becomes clear that a black and white façade is often placed onto an intensely complex set of emotionally driven and politically motivated ideas related to LGBTQ stigma. Claims such as "All religious people are anti-LGBTQ" or "I'm not anti-gay, I have a gay friend" are often suggested as "explanations" for or against LGBTQ stigma but underlying each of these is something more insidious and more deeply engrained. Hetero-cis-normativity is the tacitly taken-for-granted foundational core of LGBTQ stigma. Numerous cultural experiences shape it, reinforce it, and contribute to its permanence. But unlike its symptoms that most recognize their participation in (e.g., politics, religion), most are utterly unaware of its existence and its impact on daily interactions as well as the larger cultural dynamics and socio-political dialogues informed by hetero-cis-normativity.

## NCST, Hetero-cis-normativity, and Common Explanations for LGBTQ Stigma

NCST offers a theoretical model from which to explore the well-established relationships between LGBTQ stigma and its common correlates reviewed here (LGBT contact, religiosity, political perspectives, and beliefs about gender) which focuses on the *norm centrality* of hetero-cis-normativity and the social power dynamics that organize and justify LGBTQ stigma. Specifically, each of these common correlates can be conceptualized as related to an interest in and/or experiences with the maintenance of hetero-cis-normativity (i.e., uphold or disrupt) and perspectives toward norm violations/norm violators (i.e., stigmatize or support). For example, those interested in upholding the system of hetero-cis-normativity tend to be more stigmatizing toward violators of hetero-cis-normativity. In contrast, those interested in disrupting and challenging the power dynamics embedded in hetero-cis-normativity tend to be less stigmatizing toward violations of hetero-cis-normativity and more supportive of LGBTQ people. Axes of social power further shape these dynamics. Recall NCST's definition of social power as provided in Chapter 2:

> Social power is privilege based on access to and embodiment of social, cultural, economic, and political advantages afforded to certain beliefs, behaviors, and identities and not others.

Using this definition of social power, when experiences with LGBTQ contact, religiosity, political perspectives, and beliefs about gender uphold hetero-cis-normativity, they are likely to align with privilege, advantage, and social power. In contrast, when these experiences disrupt or challenge hetero-cis-normativity, they are likely to align with oppression and disadvantage. Those with more hetero-cis-normative social power themselves tend to have more of a vested interest in maintaining hetero-cis-normativity and stigmatizing LGBTQ people because these processes further secure their own social power as hetero-cis-normative people. Using the theoretical model of NCST and LGBTQ stigma outlined in Chapter 3, these are all interconnected experiences whereby these common "explanations" for LGBTQ stigma link to axes of social power and together, they inform both the desire for the maintenance of hetero-cis-normativity and the stigmatization of LGBTQ people.

For example, using NCST and the stigmatizer lens to explore these patterns, religious, politically conservative, and patriarchal/non-feminist individuals who avoid LGBTQ contact tend to have more social power and more vested interested in upholding hetero-cis-normativity and stigmatizing violators of it (i.e., LGBTQ people). In contrast, non-religious, politically liberal, feminist individuals who seek out LGBTQ contact tend to have less social power and are more interested in disrupting hetero-cis-normativity and supporting violators of it. In these ways, NCST provides a theoretical model from which to understand the common correlates of LGBTQ stigma reviewed throughout this chapter.

## Reviewing Common "Explanations"?

Certainly, the discussion of correlates of LGBT(Q) stigma provided here is not exhaustive. Quite the contrary, much of the discussion of "common explanations" for LGBT stigma remains underdeveloped. Often, racial and ethnic complexities are missing. Class issues, including access to school and social experiences with openly LGBTQ people, are neglected. Religiosity is frequently operationalized only as "church attendance" and rarely explored as a non-Christian-based concept. Political experiences are increasingly oversimplified. Even so, from Chapter 3's discussion of intersectionality and social power and the current chapter's emphasis on the frequently explored experiences and perspectives that contribute to LGBT(Q) stigma, it is evident that we can discern clear patterns in our understandings of LGBTQ stigma, especially when informed by NCST.

Much like Chapter 3's finale, "Hetero-cis-normativity Equals LGBTQ stigma," the conclusions of this chapter remain similar: "Hetero-cis-normativity Underlies Common Explanations for LGBT Stigma." The overarching theme of this chapter has been to demonstrate the ways the most frequently investigated explanations for LGBT(Q) stigma fit within the system of hetero-cis-normativity and how they can be better understood using NCST. As noted in the introduction, on the whole, existing explanations lack conceptual arguments that distinguish L, G, B, and T stigma and entirely neglect "Q" stigma and explorations from the stigmatized lens (i.e., LGBTQ people's experiences and perspectives). These more nuanced explorations will be provided throughout the remainder of this text. To conclude Part I, in Chapters 5 and 6, tools to measure hetero-cis-normativity and LGBTQ stigma are reviewed.

## Notes

1 Allport's (1954) theory purports that reduced prejudice will result when four features of the contact situation are present: equal status between the groups in the situation; common goals; intergroup cooperation; and the support or authorities, law, or custom.
2 Schulte and Battle (2004:130) define the "Black church" as "a cultural experience involving ethnicity (African American), region (having had some orientation to the South), socioeconomic status (working class), and sociopolitical ideology (conservative)."

## References

Allport, Gordon. 1954. *The Nature of Prejudice*. Reading, MA: Addison-Wesley.
Allport, Gordon. 1966. "The Religious Context of Prejudice." *Journal for the Scientific Study of Religion* 5:447–457.

Basow, Susan and Kelly Johnson. 2000. "Predictors of Homophobia in Female College Students." *Sex Roles* 42:391–404.
Battle, Juan, Cathy J. Cohen, Dorian Warren, Gerard Fergerson, and Suzette Audam. 2002. "Say It Loud I'm Black and I'm Proud: Black Pride Survey 2000." *New York: the Policy Institute of the National Gay and Lesbian Task Force.*
Battle, Juan, Antonio (Jay) Pastrana, and Jessie Daniels. 2012. *Social Justice Sexuality Project, 2010: Cumulative Codebook.* New York, NY: City University of New York–Graduate Center. Retrieved January 30, 2020 (http://socialjusticesexuality.com/files/2014/09/Codebook-Reformatted.pdf).
Battle, Juan, Antonio (Jay) Pastrana, and Angelique Harris. 2017a. *An Examination of Asian and Pacific Islander LGBT Populations across the United States.* New York, NY: Palgrave.
Battle, Juan, Antonio (Jay) Pastrana, and Angelique Harris. 2017b. *An Examination of Black LGBT Populations across the United States.* New York, NY: Palgrave.
Beckers, Tilo. 2010. "Islam and the Acceptance of Homosexuality: The Shortage of Socioeconomic Well-Being and Responsive Democracy." *Islam and Homosexuality* 1:57–98.
Boswell, John. 1980. *Christianity, Social Tolerance and Homosexuality.* Chicago, IL: University of Chicago Press.
Bridges, Sara K., Mary Selvidge, and Connie R. Matthews. 2003. "Lesbian Women of Color: Therapeutic Issues and Challenges." *Journal of Multicultural Counseling and Development* 31(2):113–130.
Brody, Richard A. and Jennifer L. Lawless. 2003. "Political Ideology in the United States: Conservatism and Liberalism in the 1980s and 1990s." Pp. 53–77 in *Conservative Parties and Right-Wing Politics in North America,* edited by Rainer-Olaf Schultze, Roland Sturm, and Dagmar Eberle. Wiesbaden: VS Verlag für Sozialwissenschaften.
Brown, Anna. 2017. "Transgender Issues Sharply Divide Republicans, Democrats." *Pew Research Center.* Retrieved June 26, 2019 (www.pewresearch.org/fact-tank/2017/11/08/transgender-issues-divide-republicans-and-democrats/).
Burdette, Amy M., Christopher G. Ellison, and Terrence D. Hill. 2005. "Conservative Protestantism and Tolerance toward Homosexuals: An Examination of Potential Mechanisms." *Sociological Inquiry* 75(2):177–196.
Cauce, Ana Mari and Domenech-Rodríguez. Melanie. 2002. "Latino Families: Myths and Realities." Pp. 3–25 in *Latino Children and Families in the United States,* edited by J. Contreras, K. Kerns, and A. Neal-Barnett. Westport, CT: Greenwood.
Chua, Peter and Dune Fujino. 1999. "Negotiating New Asian American Masculinities: Attitudes and Gender Expectations." *Journal of Men's Studies* 7:391–413.
Cohen, Geoffrey. 2003. "Party over Policy: The Dominating Impact of Group Influence on Political Beliefs." *Journal of Personality and Social Psychology* 85(5):808–822.
Connell, Raewyn. 1990. "The State, Gender, and Sexual Politics: Theory and Appraisal." *Theory and Society* 19(5):507–544.
Costa, Pedro Alexandre, Henrique Pereira, and Isabel Leal. 2015. "'The Contact Hypothesis' and Attitudes toward Same-Sex Parenting." *Sexuality Research and Social Policy* 12(2):125–136.
D'Emilio, John. 2002. *The World Turned.* Durham, NC: Duke University Press.
Diaz, Rafael M., George Ayala, Edward Bein, Jeff Henne, and Barbara V. Marin. 2001. "The Impact of Homophobia, Poverty, and Racism on the Mental Health of Gay and

Bisexual Latino Men: Findings from 3 US Cities." *American Journal of Public Health* 91 (6):927.

DiMaggio, Paul, John Evans, and Bethany Bryson. 1996. "Have Americans' Social Attitudes Become More Polarized?" *American Journal of Sociology* 102:690–755.

Eliason, Michele. 1997. "The Prevalence and Nature of Biphobia in Heterosexual Undergraduate Students." *Archives of Sexual Behavior* 26(3):317–326.

Ellison, Christopher G., Nicholas H. Wolfinger, and Aida I. Ramos-Wada. 2013. "Attitudes toward Marriage, Divorce, Cohabitation, and Casual Sex among Working-Age Latinos, Does Religion Matter?" *Journal of Family Issues* 34:295–322.

Flores, Andrew. 2015. "Attitudes toward Transgender Rights: Perceived Knowledge and Secondary Interpersonal Contact." *Politics, Groups, and Identities* 3:398–416.

Graham, Jesse, Jonathan Haidt, and Brian A. Nosek. 2009. "Liberals and Conservatives Rely on Different Sets of Moral Foundations." *Journal of Personality and Social Psychology* 96(5):1029–1046.

Guth, James L., John C. Green, Lyman A. Kellstedt, and Corwin E. Smidt. 1996. *Religion and the Culture Wars*. Lanham, MD: Rowman Littlefield.

Han, Chong-suk, Kristopher Proctor, and Kyung-Hee Choi. 2014. "We Pretend like Sexuality Doesn't Exist: Managing Homophobia in Gaysian America." *Journal of Men's Studies* 22:53–63.

Harris, Angelique. 2010. *AIDS, Sexuality, and the Black Church*. New York, NY: Peter Lang.

Harrison-Quintana, Jack, Ben De Guzman, Anj Chaudhry, and Jaime Grant. 2008. *Injustice at Every Turn: A Look at Asian American, South Asian, Southeast Asian, and Pacific Islander Respondents in the National Transgender Discrimination Survey*. New York, NY: National Gay and Lesbian Task Force Policy Institute.

Harrison-Quintana, Jack, David Pérez, and Jaime Grant. 2008. *Injustice at Every Turn: A Look at Latino/a Respondents in the National Transgender Discrimination Survey*. New York, NY: National Gay and Lesbian Task Force Policy Institute.

Herek, Gregory M. 1988. "Heterosexuals' Attitudes toward Lesbians and Gay Men: Correlates and Gender Differences." *Journal of Sex Research* 25(4):451–477.

Herek, Gregory M. 2002. "Heterosexuals' Attitudes toward Bisexual Men and Bisexual Women in the United States." *Journal of Sex Research* 39:264–274.

Herek, Gregory M. and John P. Capitanio. 1996. "Some of My Best Friends": Intergroup Contact, Concealable Stigma, and Heterosexuals' Attitudes toward Gay Men and Lesbians." *Personality and Social Psychology Bulletin* 22:412–424.

Herek, Gregory M. and Eric K. Glunt. 1993. "Interpersonal Contact and Heterosexuals' Attitudes toward Gay Men: Results from a National Survey." *Journal of Sex Research* 30(3):239–244.

Herek, Gregory M. and Milagritos Gonzalez-Rivera. 2006. "Attitudes toward Homosexuality among U.S. Residents of Mexican Descent." *Journal of Sex Research* 43:122–135.

Hill, Darryl and Brian Willoughby. 2005. "The Development and Validation of the Genderism and Transphobia Scale." *Sex Roles* 53:531–544.

Hinrichs, Donald W. and Pamela J. Rosenberg. 2002. "Attitudes toward Gay, Lesbian, and Bisexual Persons among Heterosexual Liberal Arts College Students." *Journal of Homosexuality* 43(1):61–84.

Jackson, Linda A., Ruth E. Fleury, and Donna A. Lewandowski. 1996. "Feminism: Definitions, Support, and Correlates of Support among Female and Male College Students." *Sex Roles* 34(9):687–693.

Jaspers, Eva, Marcel Lubbers, and Nan Dirk De Graaf. 2007. "'Horrors of Holland': Explaining Attitude Change Towards Euthanasia and Homosexuals in the Netherlands, 1970–1998." *International Journal of Public Opinion Research* 19(4):451–473.

Jost, John T., Jack Glaser, Arie W. Kruglanski, and Frank J. Sulloway. 2003. "Political Conservatism as Motivated Social Cognition." *Psychological Bulletin* 129(3):339–375.

Kelly, Jonathan. 2001. "Attitudes Towards Homosexuality in 29 Nations." *Australian Social Monitor* 4(1):15–22.

King, Mark E., Sam Winter, and Beverley Webster. 2009. "Contact Reduces Transprejudice: A Study on Attitudes Towards Transgenderism and Transgender Civil Rights in Hong Kong." *International Journal of Sexual Health* 21(1):17–34.

Koenig, Harold, Faten Al Zaben, Doaa Khalifa, and Saad Al Shohaib. 2015. "Chapter 19: Measures of Religiosity." Pp. 530–561 in *Measures of Personality and Social Psychological Constructs*, edited by Gregory Boyle, Donald Saklofske, and Gerald Matthews. San Diego, CA: Academic Press.

Kollman, Kelly and Matthew Waites. 2009. "The Global Politics of Lesbian, Gay, Bisexual and Transgender Human Rights: An Introduction." *Contemporary Politics* 15(1):1–17.

Lewis, Gregory B. 2005. "Same-Sex Marriage and the 2004 Presidential Election." *Political Science & Politics* 38(2):195–199.

Lin, Kai, Deeanna M. Button, Su Mingyue, and Sishi Chen. 2016. "Chinese College Students' Attitudes toward Homosexuality: Exploring the Effects of Traditional Culture and Modernizing Factors." *Sexuality Research and Social Policy* 13(2):158–172.

Lingiardi, Vittorio, Simona Falanga, and Anthony R. D'Augelli. 2005. "The Evaluation of Homophobia in an Italian Sample." *Archives of Sexual Behavior* 34(1):81–93.

Lingiardi, Vittorio, Nicola Nardelli, Salvatore Ioverno, Simona Falanga, Carlo Di Chiacchio, Annalisa Tanzilli, and Roberto Baiocco. 2016. "Homonegativity in Italy: Cultural Issues, Personality Characteristics, and Demographic Correlates with Negative Attitudes toward Lesbians and Gay Men." *Sexuality Research and Social Policy* 13(2):95–108.

Liss, Miriam, Christy O'Connor, Elena Morosky, and Mary Crawford. 2001. "What Makes a Feminist? Predictors and Correlates of Feminist Social Identity in College Women." *Psychology of Women Quarterly* 25(2):124–133.

Liu, Peter and Connie Chan. 2003. "Lesbian, Gay, and Bisexual Asian Americans and Their Families." Pp. 89–104 in *Asian Americans: Vulnerable Populations, Model Interventions, and Clarifying Agendas*, edited by L. Zhan. Sudbury, MA: Jones and Bartlett.

Loehr, Annalise, Long Doan, and Lisa R. Miller. 2015. "The Role of Selection Effects in the Contact Hypothesis: Results from a US National Survey on Sexual Prejudice." *Archives of Sexual Behavior* 44(8):2111–2123.

Lubbers, Marcel, Eva Jaspers, and Wout Ultee. 2009. "Primary and Secondary Socialization Impacts on Support for Same-Sex Marriage after Legalization in the Netherlands." *Journal of Family Issues* 30(12):1714–1745.

Manza, Jeff and Clem Brooks. 1997. "The Religious Factor in US Presidential Elections, 1960–1992." *American Journal of Sociology* 103(1):38–81.

McCarthy, Justin. 2019. "Gallup First Polled on Gay Issues in '77. What Has Changed?" *Gallup.Com*. Retrieved August 21, 2019 (https://news.gallup.com/poll/258065/gallup-first-polled-gay-issues-changed.aspx).

McDaniel, Eric and Christopher Ellison. 2008. "God's Party? Race, Religion, and Partisanship over Time." *Political Research Quarterly* 61:180–191.

Millett, Kate. 1970. *Sexual Politics*. New York, NY: Doubleday Press.

Minnigerode, Fred A. 1976. "Attitudes toward Homosexuality: Feminist Attitudes and Sexual Conservatism." *Sex Roles* 2(4):347–352.

Mohr, Jonathan J. and Aaron B. Rochlen. 1999. "Measuring Attitudes Regarding Bisexuality in Lesbian, Gay Male, and Heterosexual Populations." *Journal of Counseling Psychology* 46(3):353–369.

Morgan, Betsy Levonian. 1996. "Putting the Feminism into Feminism Scales: Introduction of a Liberal Feminist Attitude and Ideology Scale (LFAIS)." *Sex Roles* 34:359–390.

Nagoshi, Julie L., Katherine A. Adams, Heather K. Terrell, Eric D. Hill, Stephanie Brzuzy, and Craig T. Nagoshi. 2008. "Gender Differences in Correlates of Homophobia and Transphobia." *Sex Roles* 59:521–531.

Norton, Aaron T. and Gregory M. Herek. 2013. "Heterosexuals' Attitudes toward Transgender People: Findings from a National Probability Sample of US Adults." *Sex Roles* 68:738–753.

Ojerholm, Amy J. and Esther D. Rothblum. 1999. "The Relationships of Body Image, Feminism and Sexual Orientation in College Women." *Feminism & Psychology* 9(4):431–448.

Pastrana, Antonio (Jay), Juan Battle, and Angelique Harris. 2017. *An Examination of Latinx LGBT Populations across the United States*. New York, NY: Palgrave.

Pettigrew, Thomas F. and Linda R. Tropp. 2006. "A Meta-Analytic Test of Intergroup Contact Theory." *Journal of Personality and Social Psychology* 90(5):751–783.

Pew Research Center. 2012, June 19. "The Rise of Asian Americans." *Pew Research Center*. Retrieved January 30, 2020 (www.pewsocialtrends.org/2012/06/19/theriseof-asian-americans/).

Pew Research Center. 2014. "Views about Homosexuality." *Pew Research Center*. Retrieved January 30, 2020 (www.pewforum.org/religious-landscape-study/views-about-homosexuality/).

Pew Research Center. 2015. "Knowing Gays and Lesbians, Religious Conflicts, Beliefs about Homosexuality." *Pew Research Center*. Retrieved January 30, 2020 (www.people-press.org/2015/06/08/section-2-knowing-gays-and-lesbians-religious-conflicts-beliefs-about-homosexuality/).

Pew Research Center. 2017, October 4. "Majorities in Both Parties Now Say Homosexuality Should Be Accepted." *Pew Research Center*. Retrieved January 30, 2020 (www.people-press.org/2017/10/05/5-homosexuality-gender-and-religion/5_1-8/).

Popkin, Samuel. 1994. *The Reasoning Voter*. Chicago, IL: UC Press.

Raja, Sheela and Joseph P. Stokes. 1998. "Assessing Attitudes toward Lesbians and Gay Men: The Modern Homophobia Scale." *International Journal of Sexuality and Gender Studies* 3(2):113–134.

Roy, Robin E., Kristin S. Weibust, and Carol T. Miller. 2007. "Effects of Stereotypes about Feminists on Feminist Self-Identification." *Psychology of Women Quarterly* 31(2):146–156.

Schulte, Lisa J. and Juan Battle. 2004. "The Relative Importance of Ethnicity and Religion in Predicting Attitudes Towards Gays and Lesbians." *Journal of Homosexuality* 47(2):127–142.

Scott-Dixon, Krista. 2006. *Trans/Forming Feminisms: Transfeminist Voices Speak Out*. Toronto, Canada: Sumach Press.

Serano, Julia. 2007. *Whipping Girl: A Transsexual Woman on Sexism and the Scapegoating of Femininity*. Berkeley, CA: Seal Press.
Severson, Nicolette, Miguel Muñoz-Laboy, and Rebecca Kaufman. 2014. "'At Times, I Feel like I'm Sinning': The Paradoxical Role of Non-Lesbian, Gay, Bisexual and Transgender-Affirming Religion in the Lives of Behaviourally-Bisexual Latino Men." *Culture, Health & Sexuality* 16(2):136–148.
Sherkat, Darren E. 2017. "Intersecting Identities and Support for Same-Sex Marriage in the United States." *Social Currents* 4(4):380–400.
Smith, Sara J., Amber M. Axelton, and Donald A. Saucier. 2009. "The Effects of Contact on Sexual Prejudice: A Meta-Analysis." *Sex Roles* 61:178–191.
Sotelo, Maria Jose. 2000. "Political Tolerance among Adolescents Towards Homosexuals in Spain." *Journal of Homosexuality* 39:95–105.
Taylor, Verta and Leila J. Rupp. 1993. "Women's Culture and Lesbian Feminist Activism: A Reconsideration of Cultural Feminism." *Signs* 19(1):32–61.
UUA.org. "Lesbian, Gay, Bisexual, Transgender, and Queer Justice." *Unitarian Universalist Association*. Retrieved January 30, 2020 (www.uua.org/lgbtq).
van de Meerendonk, Bas, Rob Eisinga, and Albert Felling. 2003. "Application of Herek's Attitudes toward Lesbians and Gay Men Scale in the Netherlands." *Psychological Reports* 93(1):265–275.
van de Meerendonk, Bas and Peer Scheepers. 2004. "Denial of Equal Civil Rights for Lesbians and Gay Men in the Netherlands, 1980–1993." *Journal of Homosexuality* 47(2):63–80.
Walch, Susan E., Kimberly A. Sinkkanen, Elisabeth M. Swain, Jacquelyn Francisco, Cassi A. Breaux, and Marie D. Sjoberg. 2012. "Using Intergroup Contact Theory to Reduce Stigma against Transgender Individuals: Impact of a Transgender Speaker Panel Presentation." *Journal of Applied Social Psychology* 42(10):2583–2605.
Wald, Kenneth D., Dennis E. Owen, and Samuel S. Hill. 1988. "Churches as Political Communities." *American Political Science Review* 82(2):531–548.
Ward, Elijah G. 2005. "Homophobia, Hypermasculinity and the US Black Church." *Culture, Health, and Sexuality* 7:493–504.
Welch, Michael R., David C. Leege, Kenneth D. Wald, and Lyman A. Kellstedt. 1993. "Are the Sheep Hearing the Shepherds? Cue Perceptions, Congregational Responses, and Political Communication Processes." Pp. 235–254 in *Rediscovering the Religious Factor in American Politics*, edited by David Leege and Lyman Kellstedt. Armonk, NY: M.E. Sharpe.
Whitley, Bernard E., Christopher E. Childs, and Jena B. Collins. 2011. "Differences in Black and White American College Students' Attitudes toward Lesbians and Gay Men." *Sex Roles* 64:299–310.
Worthen, Meredith G. F. 2012. "Heterosexual College Student Sexual Experiences, Feminist Identity, and Attitudes toward LGBT Individuals." *Journal of LGBT Youth* 9(2):77–113.
Worthen, Meredith G. F. 2016. "Hetero-cis-normativity and the Gendering of Transphobia." *International Journal of Transgenderism* 17(1):31–57.
Worthen, Meredith G. F. 2018. "'Gay Equals White?' Racial, Ethnic, and Sexual Identities and Attitudes toward LGBT Individuals among College Students." *Journal of Sex Research* 55(8):995–1011.
Worthen, Meredith G. F., Vittorio Lingiardi, and Chiara Caristo. 2017. "The Roles of Politics, Feminism, and Religion in Attitudes toward LGBT Individuals: A

Cross-Cultural Study of College Students in the United States, Italy, and Spain." *Sexuality Research and Social Policy* 14(3):241–258.

Worthen, Meredith G. F., Annalisa Tanzilli, Chiara Caristo, and Vittorio Lingiardi. 2019. "Social Contact, Social Distancing, and Attitudes toward LGT Individuals: A Cross-Cultural Study of Heterosexual College Students in the United States, Italy, and Spain." *Journal of Homosexuality* 66(13):1882–1908.

Yon-Leau, Carmen and Muñoz-Laboy Miguel. 2010. "'I Don't like to Say that I'm Anything': Sexuality Politics and Cultural Critique among Sexual-Minority Latino Youth." *Sexuality Research and Social Policy* 7(2):105–117.

Young, Lisa and William Cross. 2003. "Women and Conservative Parties in Canada and the United States." Pp. 207–227 in *Conservative Parties and Right-Wing Politics in North America*, edited by Rainer-Olaf Schultze, Roland Sturm, and Dagmar Eberle. Wiesbaden: VS Verlag für Sozialwissenschaften.

# 5
# MEASURING LGBTQ STIGMA AND HETERO-CIS-NORMATIVITY IN NCST

The importance of examining hetero-cis-normativity and LGBTQ stigma using NCST has been demonstrated throughout this text. To continue to move these arguments forward, it is essential to discuss ways to measure these constructs. In this chapter, the socio-historical contexts of previously established tools that measure attitudes toward "homosexual," gay, lesbian, bisexual, trans, and queer people are reviewed (attitudes toward non-binary/genderqueer people have not been explored in these ways). Seven LGBTQ Measurement Principles that highlight the importance of the intersections between gender and sexuality are offered. In addition, hetero-cis-normativity measurement tools are detailed. Finally, these new ways to measure LGBTQ stigma and hetero-cis-normativity are situated in NCST. Overall, the current chapter both explains and establishes the measurement tools that are utilized in Part II's exploration of NCST and LGBTQ stigma.

## Measuring Attitudes toward "Homosexuals"

Although the psychological and medical fields had been examining "homosexuals" for decades prior, scholars began to explore the cultural stigma and negativity that these individuals experienced in depth alongside American psychologist George Weinberg's coining of the term "homophobia" in 1965 (Herek 2000). By defining "homophobia" as a socio-cultural experience of hostility directed toward "homosexuals," scholars identified the examination of negative attitudes toward this group as an important field of study. In 1971, one of the first scales of its kind was designed to measure homophobic attitudes, Kenneth Smith's (1971) Homophobia Scale. Most of the early research in this area of inquiry did not identify the specific target of prejudice but instead focused on "homosexuals" and/or "homophobia." Part of this has to do with the fact that up until the 1960s, both men and women with same-gender romantic and sexual attractions were most commonly identified as "homosexuals" and as a result, it was generally believed that there was not a need to specifically identify them by gender (i.e., as gay men and lesbian women) in most empirical work (Weinberg 1972).

However, four significant cultural shifts in the 1960s and 1970s diluted the effectiveness of measuring "homosexual" stigma. First, the term "gay" began to be appropriated and adopted by men with same-gender romantic and sexual attractions, while the term "lesbian" became associated with women with same-gender romantic and sexual attractions (for an historical review about the etymology and popularization of these identity terms see Stein 1997; Weinberg 1972). In doing so, the terms "homophile" and "homosexual" were less often used and the commonplace terms that replaced it carried gendered associations (i.e., gay man and lesbian woman). Today, we often still see this gender distinction in gay and lesbian identities in most English-speaking countries alongside an ever-expanding list of self-identity terms.

Second, as "homosexual" was dropping out of popular self-identity discourse, the associations of "homosexuality" with "criminality" were also changing. Up until the mid-twentieth century, acts of sodomy were illegal in most parts of the world and "homosexuals," who were presumably breaking the law by engaging in illegal sex acts, were frequently associated with criminality and deviance (recall Chapter 3's discussion of the sexualization of LGBTQ stigma). In particular, same-sex sex acts between men were targeted harshly under the sodomy laws in part because the "homosexual man" was perceived as a more violent sexual predator than the "homosexual woman" and in part because sex acts between men are viewed as more deviant and are more stigmatized than sex acts between women (Worthen 2016a). However, starting in 1961, Illinois repealed its sodomy law and nineteen states followed throughout the 1960s and 1970s, as did many countries in the West (Eskridge 2008). The stigma surrounding same-sex sex acts as "criminal" largely remained associated with those identified as "homosexuals" and not "gay" and "lesbian" people. In other words, the term "homosexual" was recognized as negative, criminal, and deviant while "gay" and "lesbian" were terms that were less culturally stigmatizing and more identity-focused.

Third, the Stonewall Uprising in 1969 triggered worldwide conversations about the rights of gay and lesbian people and sparked the founding of many activism groups and events, most of which used the terms "gay" and/or "lesbian" and not "homosexual" (e.g., the Gay Liberation Front had groups in Canada, the U.K., and the U.S.). This activism became collectively organized under an umbrella known as the "Gay Liberation" and "Gay and Lesbian Rights" Movements (Myers 2013). In doing so, the word "homosexual" was largely removed from the global dialogue about the surrounding activism for these groups. Thus, at both micro and macro levels, "homosexuality" was being washed out and "gay" and "lesbian" were the popularized and preferred terms.

Fourth, the medical and clinical associations of the term "homosexual" with "mentally ill" were also shifting in the early 1970s. The first edition of the *Diagnostic and Statistical Manual of Mental Disorders* (DSM) classified "homosexuality" as a "sociopathic personality disturbance" (American Psychiatric Association 1952) and in the second edition, "homosexuality" was classified as a "nonpsychotic mental disorder" under the category "sexual deviation" (American Psychiatric Association 1968). It was not until 1973 (and printed as such in 1974) that "homosexuality" was officially declassified as a "mental disorder" (American Psychiatric Association 1974). Alongside this landmark decision in the medical community, larger cultural norms were shifting away from using the term "homosexual" in order to avoid harkening back to the diseased, mentally ill, and/or psychologically/emotionally disordered connotations this word once held (Worthen 2016a).

Even so, decades later, two Homophobia Scales, created by Bouton et al. (1987) and Wright, Adams, and Bernat (1999), continued to identify "homosexuals" as the subject of prejudice and failed to use more specific gendered and socially acceptable terms of "gay" and "lesbian." Employing these scales (as well as others) generated a wealth of research that examined the negativity and stigma that a rather vaguely identified group of "homosexuals" experienced (e.g., Aguero, Bloch, and Byrne 1984; Altemeyer and Hunsberger 1992; Hudson and Ricketts 1980; Larsen, Reed, and Hoffman 1980; Riddle 1996; Van de Ven, Bornholt, and Bailey 1996). Although such studies are certainly informative and help us to understand part of the landscape of LGBTQ stigma (i.e., attitudes toward "homosexuals"), they leave us with an incomplete picture.

Today, *The Associated Press*, *The New York Times*, and *The Washington Post* restrict their use of the term "homosexual" opting for "gay" or "lesbian" instead (GLAAD Media Reference Guide 2016). Simply put, the "H word" has fallen out of favor (Worthen 2016a:76). But beyond the concerns about the political correctness of the term "homosexual," the current and historical connotations of the term "homosexual" with deviant and/or criminal sex (especially between men) and mental illness render the use of measurement tools designed to capture attitudes toward "homosexuals" to be particularly problematic. For example, it is likely that many of the studies that utilize measures of attitudes toward "homosexuals" are only (or mostly) measuring stigma directed toward "homosexual men" and not lesbian women or others. Indeed, twenty-first century research continues to demonstrate that people think of a *man* when they hear the term "homosexual" (Whitley, Childs, and Collins 2011). In addition, it is impossible to disentangle the socio-historical negativity that most people associate with the term "homosexual." As a result, measuring attitudes toward "homosexuals" should not be considered a proxy for measuring attitudes toward gay, lesbian, or other queer people. Indeed, unless specifically interested in how the term "homosexual" incites negativity, scholars interested in investigating LGBTQ stigma should consider avoiding measurement tools that inquire about attitudes toward "homosexuals" and instead utilize those that include more specific and less deviantized terms such as gay, lesbian, or others.

> **LGBTQ STIGMA MEASUREMENT PRINCIPLE #1**
>
> Scholars should avoid terms such as "homosexual" in their measurement tools unless they are specifically interested in identifying stigma associated with perspectives about "homosexuality" and its cultural associations with same-sex sex acts between men, deviant and/or criminal sex, and mental illness.

## Measuring Attitudes toward Bisexual Individuals

About a decade after the emergence of scales and other research designed to examine attitudes toward "homosexuals," A. P. MacDonald (1981) carved a much-needed niche into the conversation with his comments on bisexuality. Specifically, MacDonald alerted the field to a measurement issue in existing research by indicating that previous scholars have most likely mistakenly clustered "bisexuals" and "homosexuals" together in their studies of "homosexuality." In doing so, MacDonald squarely identified bisexual stigma as an important area of future inquiry. This occurred alongside the emerging bisexual rights movement that was beginning to gain some cultural presence in the 1980s (Weiss 2004). Even so, studies about bisexuals' experiences remained rather scarce until the 1990s (e.g., Eliason 1997; Mohr and Rochlen 1999; Mulick and Wright 2002; Ochs 1996; Rust 1992, 1995; Weinberg, Williams, and Pryor 1995).

In 1997, Michele Eliason published one of the first studies to use a scale to specifically measure attitudes toward bisexuals. Eliason designed a survey based on "common" stereotypes about bisexuals determined from a review of the scant (at that point in time) literature about bisexuality. These included statements regarding the association of bisexuality with confusion, privilege, identity legitimacy, multiple sexual partners, and flexible attitudes about sex. Many of these stereotypes also apply to perspectives about lesbian women and gay men. To account for this, most of the items included in the survey instrument were designed to allow respondents to compare their attitudes about "bisexuals" to their attitudes about "gays/lesbians" as well as "heterosexuals." For example, respondents were asked to indicate their level of agreement with these two statements: "Bisexuals tend to have more sexual partners than gays or lesbians"; and

"Bisexuals tend to have more sexual partners than heterosexuals." In doing so, Eliason's (1997) work clarified a distinction between gay/lesbian stigma and bisexual stigma that was juxtaposed with perspectives about heterosexuals. This is especially important because, for example, Herek's (2002) national study of randomly selected adults (N = 1,335) showed that heterosexuals reported significantly more negative attitudes toward bisexual men and women as compared to their attitudes toward gay men and lesbian women.

In addition, others have offered additional stereotypes that are relatively unique to bisexual stigma. These include perspectives that call into question the legitimacy and authenticity of bisexuality (e.g., "Bisexuals are just gay and lesbian people who are afraid to admit they are gay," Eliason 1997:322, "bisexuals haven't made up their minds," Weiss 2004:45, and "no one was *really* bisexual," Weinberg, Williams, and Pryor 1995:35) as well as perspectives that suggest that bisexual people have more social privileges than gay/lesbian people (e.g., "Bisexuals have the best of both worlds," Eliason 1997:322, or "bisexuals just want to have their cake and eat it too," Weiss 2004:45). There is also a common perspective that bisexuals experience invisibility in both gay and lesbian communities as well as within the larger predominantly heterosexual culture. This is sometimes described as "bi-invisibility" and "bi-erasure" (Yoshino 2000). Indeed, some research suggests that bisexual men and bisexual women experience a double-stigmatization in which they are rejected from both heterosexual and gay/lesbian communities (Brewster and Moradi 2010; Mulick and Wright 2002; Ochs 1996; Weinberg, Williams, and Pryor 2009). These concepts create a much-needed unique space for understanding bisexual stigma.

## LGBTQ STIGMA MEASUREMENT PRINCIPLE #2

Scholars should be careful to distinguish the experiences of bisexuals from others in the LGBTQ spectrum.

## Measuring Attitudes toward Trans Individuals

While the published history of measuring attitudes toward "homosexuals" dates back to 1971 and for bisexuality, 1981, one of the very first published reports measuring general attitudes toward trans individuals was conducted a few years later in 1983. Psychologists Harold Leitenberg and Lesley Slavin (1983) designed a study to compare attitudes toward "transsexuality" and "homosexuality." Interestingly, Leitenberg and Slavin (1983) found that "transsexuality" was more accepted than "homosexuality" in their small sample (N = 318) of undergraduate students at a New England state university. However, it is difficult to understand these findings in the context of contemporary society decades later. In particular, as seen in Leitenberg and Slavin's (1983) study and elsewhere, until the 1950s and 1960s, those who today might identify with the term "transgender" were classified as "homosexual" by most of society (Weiss 2004). In the 1990s, we continued to see this conflation of identities in discussions of Brandon Teena, the trans man murder victim who was often described as "gay" (even though he identified as heterosexual) and who was frequently a part of discussions involving violence against "gay" youth (Halberstam 2003). Thus, in part due to the sweeping of all trans people in with all LGB people, the literature exploring attitudes specifically toward trans people remained scarce until the early 2000s (e.g., Landen and Innala 2000; Weiss 2004).

Even today, some may still continue to conflate being trans with being gay. For example, an individual who sees someone perceived to be a male dressing as a woman may identify this person as "gay;" however, this may be a misalignment of terms. In fact, a male dressing as a woman (more than likely) has more to do with an individual's gender identity, and less to do with an individual's sexual identity. Even so, some people may perceive any/all gender nonconforming behavior as "gay." Scholarly work provides some support for this notion. For example, research finds that LGBT people are frequently perceived as violating gender norms and are often the subject of gender nonconformity prejudice (Gerhardstein and Anderson 2010; Gordon and Meyer 2007). Because "gay" people are the most well-known group within the LGBTQ community, those not conforming to normative gender presentations are often labeled as "gay" by those who are less culturally aware of trans people's lives and others in the LGBTQ spectrum.

However, in the 2010s, two significant cultural shifts occurred. First, the fifth edition of the *Diagnostic and Statistical Manual of Mental Disorders* (American Psychiatric Association 2013) removed "Gender Identity Disorder" from its list of mental disorders. A new diagnosis of "Gender Dysphoria" (GD) is now included and in accordance with many trans rights activists' recommendations, including the World Professional Association for Transgender Health, GD is now listed in its own section (separate from sexual dysfunctions and paraphilias) and the diagnostic criteria for GD is now distress based. In other words, incongruence between an individual's sex assigned at birth and gender identity is no longer viewed as pathological. Instead, the diagnostic criteria for GD is related to the distress and/or problems with functioning one may endure from sex assigned at birth/gender identity incongruence (Drescher 2015; Knudson, De Cuypere, and Bockting 2010). This signifies a cultural shift away from the categorical association of trans people with mental illness. Such changes have certainly impacted trans stigma in both the medical community and society at large.

Second, popular media has brought more visibility to trans people's lives. When Caitlyn Jenner and Laverne Cox became household names, the general public put a set of cultural scripts onto trans women (note that despite the media presence of Christine Jorgensen in the 1950s, dominant cultural narratives continued to conflate "homosexuality" and "transsexuality" for decades). But as described in Chapter 3, although we often look to pop culture for examples of marginalized groups still situated on the "denigrated" side of the spectrum of stigma (as seen in Figure 3.3), this frequently leads to sweeping stereotypes. Thus, the need to better understand trans people's lives was becoming clear to mainstream culture alongside the dozens of researchers who had been carving a place for trans scholarship for decades prior (e.g., James et al. 2016; Landen and Innala 2000; Meyer 2008; Schilt and Westbrook 2009; Serano 2007; Stryker 2008).

These scholars had recently developed measurement tools to explore stigma unique to trans people's experiences. For example, Hill (2002) offered three interrelated theoretical constructs to measure negative attitudes toward trans individuals: (1) transphobia—a revulsion to masculine women, feminine men, cross-dressers, and trans individuals; (2) genderism—an ideology that reinforces the negative evaluation of gender non-conformity or incongruence between sex assigned at birth and gender identity; and (3) gender-bashing—assault and/or harassment of persons who do not conform to gender norms. Testing Hill's (2002) conceptual framework, Hill and Willoughby's (2005) three-part study yielded the 32-item Genderism and Transphobia Scale (GTS), which consisted of the same three domains identified by Hill (2002). Items within the scale included non-gender-specific statements such as "If I found out that my best friend was changing their sex, I would freak out" as well as gender-specific statements such as "Men who act like women should be ashamed of themselves" and "I would avoid talking to a woman if I knew she had a surgically created penis and testicles" (Hill and Willoughby 2005). Exploring the GTS with undergraduate samples in China, Canada, and the Philippines revealed high levels of negativity toward trans individuals (Hill and Willoughby 2005; Willoughby et al. 2010; Winter, Webster, and Cheung 2008). A few years later, Nagoshi et al. (2008) developed a 9-item Transphobia Scale from Bornstein's (1998) work. None of the items in their scale were gender-specific. Statements included: "I believe that the male/female dichotomy is natural," "I believe that a person can never change their gender," and "I don't like it when someone is flirting with me, and I can't tell if they are a man or a woman." Exploring their Transphobia Scale using U.S. undergraduate samples also revealed evidence of transphobia among college students (Nagoshi et al. 2008; Tebbe and Moradi 2012). Overall, both cultural shifts in the recognition of trans people's lives as well as emerging research about transphobia carved out the importance of the exploration of trans-specific stigma.

## LGBTQ STIGMA MEASUREMENT PRINCIPLE #3

Scholars should be careful to distinguish the experiences of trans individuals from others in the LGBTQ spectrum.

## Measuring Attitudes toward Non-binary and Genderqueer Individuals

Non-binary individuals, including those with genderqueer identities (e.g., gender non-conforming, gender variant, gender fluid/fluid, agender, bigender, and androgynous) are becoming increasingly more visible. Indeed, in a U. S. nationwide study conducted by the National Center for Transgender Equality with nearly 28,000 trans respondents, many identify within the genderqueer spectrum. In particular, 31% identify as non-binary, 29% identify as genderqueer, 27% identify as gender non-conforming or gender variant, 20% identify as gender fluid/fluid, 18% identify as androgynous, 14% as agender, 6% as bi-gender, and 4% as multi-gender (James et al. 2016). Even so, scholarly work investigating the experiences of non-binary/genderqueer individuals remains limited (e.g., Nadal et al. 2016; Richards, Bouman, and Barker 2017; Wyss 2004). In fact, no studies to date could be located that utilized scales measuring non-binary/genderqueer-specific stigma and attitudes toward non-binary/genderqueer people.

There are at least two important reasons to address this gap in the literature. First, evidence exists that non-binary/genderqueer people's experiences differ from those with binary gender identities (i.e., men and women) (e.g., Elizabeth 2013). Indeed, research indicates that non-binary/genderqueer people endure significantly more psychological stressors than trans men and women endure (Warren, Smalley, and Barefoot 2016). Thus, it is important to specifically examine non-binary/genderqueer individuals' experiences with stigma and other forms of stress in comparison to other groups. Second, non-binary/genderqueer people's lives and experiences are likely misrepresented in most existing research (Richards, Bouman, and Barker 2017). Much like the historical sweeping of bisexuals in with "homosexuals" in early research as described previously in this chapter, non-binary/genderqueer people are likely swept into the category of "transgender" or "other gender" in the majority of studies (Elizabeth 2013; Tate, Ledbetter, and Youssef 2013). As a result, most scholarly work is both missing and misrepresenting non-binary/genderqueer people. Thus, it is essential to explore non-binary/genderqueer-specific stigma.

> **LGBTQ STIGMA MEASUREMENT PRINCIPLE #4**
>
> Scholars should be careful to distinguish the experiences of non-binary/genderqueer individuals from others in the LGBTQ spectrum.

## Measuring Attitudes toward Queer Individuals

Despite the documented scholarly work over the past several decades explicitly examining LGBT stigma and attitudes toward LGBT people, few studies have specifically utilized scales to measure attitudes toward queer-identified individuals. While scholars examine the lives and experiences of queer people (e.g., Meyer 2008; Rodríguez 2003), measurement tools to examine queer stigma are missing from most existing scholarship (see more in Chapters 15 and 16).

There are three important reasons to address this gap in the literature. First, the term "queer" has been utilized in the English language as a derogatory slang term for "homosexuals" since the 1890s and "queer" continues to occupy the English-speaking world as a negative term, especially among heterosexual teen boys in the U.S. who use the term as a tool to deride one another (Burn 2000; Pascoe 2007). Yet even though there is awareness that "queer" can be used pejoratively, existing research has yet to specifically ask individuals about their attitudes toward "queer" individuals and as a result, queer-specific stigma is severely understudied.

Second, it is certainly true that "queer" has been categorically reclaimed as a new empowering, inclusive identity since the 1990s. What is unclear, however, is how this shift has shaped queer-specific stigma. Some still believe that the negativity surrounding the term "queer" is entirely too substantial to be fully washed away. Thus, at the same time as we see newfound positivity associated with queer identities, the adoption of a queer identity remains contentious. As scholar Didi Khayatt (2002) notes:

> It has become a term of choice because it is understood as inclusive and flexible, unstable and fluid. The term 'queer', was reclaimed precisely to cover the spectrum of genders and sexualities that were not and could not be accommodated by naming all the variations of perverse and marginalized sexualities: gay, lesbian, bisexual, transgendered, transsexual, male-to-female, female-to-male, butch and femme, etc. It was meant as an umbrella term to expand the boundaries of these above-mentioned categories, while, at the same time, broadening the possibilities of recognizing all those who are marginalized because they transgress the norm. 'Queer', however, became no less controversial and, despite its mandate for inclusion, was noted by some (see, for instance, Biddy Martin 1996:74) as not entirely acceptable nor comprehensive enough to cover all differences it presumed to name
>
> *(497)*

Thus, amidst the cultural divide between "queer identity" as empowering and "queer" as insulting, it is essential to examine what people think about "queer" individuals.

Third, while queer theory is prevalent on college campuses and in scholarly conversations, it has not fully made its way into dominant social discourse (Gamson 1995; Halperin 2003). Even the placement of "Q" at the end of the popular "LGBTQ" acronym is controversial. Thus, while talking about "queer" issues and using "queer" language are commonplace in some circles, especially among those familiar with queer theory, in non-academic spaces in much of the English-speaking world, "queer" discourse may not be as welcomed. As a result, it is important to consider how individuals are responding to "queer" people and the language of "queerness."

> **LGBTQ STIGMA MEASUREMENT PRINCIPLE #5**
>
> Scholars should be careful to distinguish the experiences of queer individuals from others in the LGBTQ spectrum.

## The Intersections of Gender and Sexual Identity in Measuring LGBTQ Attitudes

Some researchers have made careful note of the different social power experiences of LGBTQ men and women (e.g., Eliason 1997; Herek 1998; Serano 2007; Worthen 2013, 2016b). Gender is significantly relevant to this conversation due to the socially privileged status of men and the relatively disadvantaged social status of women, which certainly differentially locates the power statuses of LBTQ women and GBTQ men within patriarchal cultures. In addition, because most cultures value the significance of the man–woman dichotomy, non-binary/genderqueer individuals experience significant social power disadvantages. Thus, the intersections between gender and sexuality are essential to clarify for both the target of prejudice (i.e., the stigmatized must be identified as a LBTQ woman, GBTQ man, or LGBTQ non-binary/genderqueer person) and the person who may be expressing negativity or passing judgement (i.e., the stigmatizer's own gender and sexuality must be identified) in empirical analyses of LGBTQ stigma.

Scholars since the 1970s have worked toward developing measures that underscore some of these important gender and sexuality intersections in understanding LGBTQ stigma. For example, Raja and Stokes' (1998) Modern Homophobia Scale (MHS) includes separate scales examining attitudes toward lesbian women and gay men (see also Herek 1984; MacDonald et al. 1973). In addition, Mohr and Rochlen's (1999) Attitudes Regarding Bisexuality Scale (ABRS) also contains measures designed to capture attitudes about bisexual men and women (see also Eliason 1997). Furthermore, Hill and Willoughby (2005) Transphobia Scale consists of gender-specific items that allow for separate tests of attitudes toward trans men and women (see also Worthen 2016b). The majority of existing work that utilizes these scales explores heterosexual men's and women's attitudes toward LGBT individuals. Scholars rarely examine non-heterosexuals' attitudes toward LGBT individuals (for exceptions, see

Mohr and Rochlen 1999; Worthen 2012, 2016b). In addition, studies that utilize scales to examine attitudes toward queer men and women and attitudes toward non-binary/genderqueer people are few and far between. As a result, although many researchers have been careful to clarify both the stigmatized's (target of prejudice's) and the stigmatizer's gender and sexual identities in their explorations of heterosexual men's and women's attitudes toward LGBTQ individuals, fewer scholars have examined non-heterosexual or trans men's and women's attitudes toward LGBTQ individuals (e.g., lesbian women's attitudes toward trans men). Furthermore, few have utilized scales to investigate attitudes toward queer men, queer women, or non-binary/genderqueer people or queer men's, queer women's, or non-binary/genderqueer peoples' attitudes toward LGBTQ people. As a result, there are significant gaps in the existing LGBTQ stigma literature that deserve careful attention.

In addition to the significance of the intersections between gender, sexuality, and social power as they relate to LGBTQ stigma, there are a variety of other cultural constructs and perspectives that are often associated with LGBTQ people that are important to consider. Some of these include eroticization, hypersexualization, HIV/AIDS, authenticity, and invisibility. Not only are these constructs and perspectives associated with LGBTQ people generally, but also, they are often linked to specific *types* of people within the LGBTQ community and held more strongly among certain stigmatizers as compared to others (e.g., heterosexual men tend to eroticize lesbian and bisexual women; see Kite and Whitley 1998; Louderback and Whitley 1997; Raja and Stokes 1998; Worthen 2013).

There are also other groups and identities within the LGBTQ community that should be considered as they relate to both the stigmatization of LGBTQ people (stigmatizers' lens) as well as LGBTQ people's experiences with stigma (stigmatized lens). For example, those in leather, bear, and twink communities can experience sexualization and objectification that certainly inform their experiences and attitudes (Filiault and Drummond 2007; Hennen 2008; Lahti 1998). Culturally-shaped identities such as SGL and Two-Spirit can also impact perspectives about LGBTQ people and individual experiences with discrimination and violence (Battle, Pastrana, and Daniels 2012; Walters et al. 2006). Thus, it is important to incorporate diverse and intersecting experiences with identities when exploring LGBTQ stigma.

## *Summarizing LGBTQ Stigma Measurement*

It is essential that researchers continue to differentiate between the stigma experiences of lesbian, gay, bisexual, trans, non-binary/genderqueer, and queer people. Beyond the importance of examining the gaps in existing work that have been underexplored (e.g., queer men's attitudes toward trans women), it is equally important to underscore the significance of how gender and social power shape LGBTQ stigma, especially within patriarchal, hetero-cis-normative societies. Overall, clarifying the gender and sexuality of both the target of prejudice as well as the identities and axes of social power of the respondent who is being asked about their prejudicial attitudes must be identified in empirical studies of LGBTQ stigma due to the overlapping and strongly influential cultural experiences of gender and sexuality.

> **LGBTQ STIGMA MEASUREMENT PRINCIPLE #6**
>
> Scholars should be careful to clarify both the stigmatized's (target of prejudice's) and the stigmatizer's gender and sexual identities.

## Measuring Hetero-cis-normativity

As described in Chapter 3, hetero-cis-normativity is a system of norms, privilege, and oppression built from culturally bound and socially enforced standards and expectations about gender and sexuality that situates heterosexual cisgender people above all others and thus, places LGBTQ people in a place of systemic disadvantage. In this system, hetero-cis-normative people (i.e., norm followers) experience social power and privilege while non-hetero-cis-normative people (i.e., norm violators) endure social disadvantage and stigma. In these ways, hetero-cis-normativity is the set of norms linked to LGBTQ stigma and social power. Thus, hetero-cis-normativity is essential to examine in explorations of LGBTQ stigma.

Measures of hetero-cis-normativity investigate the normalcy that goes along with being both heterosexual and cisgender as well as the expected disadvantages that go along with *not* being both heterosexual and cisgender. In particular, direct measures of hetero-cis-normativity inquire specifically about the expectation that "it is 'normal' to be both heterosexual and cisgender and it is not normal (and therefore it is acceptable to be prejudiced toward) non-heterosexual and non-cisgender individuals" (Worthen 2016b:31). For example, studies investigating hetero-cis-normativity may ask respondents how they feel about the following statements: "It is okay to think negatively about gay people because it is not normal to be gay" and "It is upsetting to me that transgender people experience violence, harassment, and discrimination just because they are transgender people." Table 5.1 includes additional examples of direct measures of hetero-cis-normativity.

Indirect measures of hetero-cis-normativity can include stigmatizing associations with LGBTQ people (e.g., "Gay men are hypersexual") and discomfort with LGBTQ contact (e.g., "I think it would negatively affect our relationship if I learned that one of my close relatives was a lesbian woman") as well as belief

**TABLE 5.1** Hetero-cis-normativity Scale (HCN Scale) Items

1. It is okay to think negatively about people who are gay or lesbian because it is not normal to be gay or lesbian.
2. It is okay to think negatively about people who are bisexual because it is not normal to be bisexual.
3. It is okay to think negatively about transgender people because it is not normal to be transgender.
4. It is okay to think negatively about people who are queer because it is not normal to be queer.
5. It is okay to think negatively about people who are non-binary or genderqueer because it is not normal to be non-binary or genderqueer.
6. I don't think anyone should be gay, lesbian, bisexual, transgender, queer, non-binary, or genderqueer.

*Notes:* Suggested response options are "Strongly Disagree" to "Strongly Agree;" Individual items added together create the HCN Scale.

systems that may enforce and validate hetero-cis-normativity such as religiosity, conservative political perspectives, and patriarchal, non-feminist beliefs about gender (see Chapter 4). Together, both direct and indirect measures of hetero-cis-normativity can help provide an in depth understanding of LGBTQ stigma.

> **LGBTQ STIGMA MEASUREMENT PRINCIPLE #7**
>
> Scholars should be careful to include measures of hetero-cis-normativity in explorations of LGBTQ stigma.

## Measuring LGBTQ Stigma and Hetero-cis-normativity in NCST

The seven LGBTQ Stigma Measurement Principles outlined in this chapter were utilized to create the nine LGBTQ Stigma Scales that are introduced in Chapter 6. These scales fit nicely into the three tenets of NCST. In particular, bringing the Principles offered here into the LGBTQ Stigma Scales and the theoretical model of NCST demonstrates the importance of *norm centrality* and social power as both *organizational* and *justification* for enduring negativity that stigmatized people experience. In addition, there are multiple ways to measure the relationships between hetero-cis-normativity, being LGBTQ, axes of social power, and LGBTQ stigma because these experiences are situated on the *spectrum of stigma* (recall Figures 2.1 and 3.3). For example, one way to explore these elements together would be to examine how agreement with hetero-cis-normativity (e.g., see Table 5.1) among gay, White, middle-class, religious men relates to stigmatizing attitudes directed toward bisexual women. By utilizing the nuances detailed among the LGBTQ Stigma Measurement Principles within NCST to explore the LGBTQ Stigma Scales, these intersectional and highly complex relationships can be analyzed with theoretical rigor. In Part II, these patterns and associations will be examined in depth. In particular, the nine LGBTQ Stigma Scales are investigated using NCST to understand LGBTQ stigma within an intersectional framework that highlights the importance of gender, sexual identity, and social power.

## References

Aguero, Joseph E., Laura Bloch, and Donn Byrne. 1984. "The Relationships among Sexual Beliefs, Attitudes, Experience, and Homophobia." *Journal of Homosexuality* 10(1/2):95–107.

Altemeyer, Bob and Bruce Hunsberger. 1992. "Authoritarianism, Religious Fundamentalism, Quest, and Prejudice." *The International Journal for the Psychology of Religion* 2(2):113–133.

American Psychiatric Association. 1952. *Diagnostic and Statistical Manual of Mental Disorders I*. Washington, DC: APA.

American Psychiatric Association. 1968. *Diagnostic and Statistical Manual of Mental Disorders II*. Washington, DC: APA.

American Psychiatric Association. 1974. *Diagnostic and Statistical Manual of Mental Disorders II-Seventh Printing*. Washington, DC: APA.

American Psychiatric Association. 2013. *Diagnostic and Statistical Manual of Mental Disorders V*. Washington, DC: APA.

Battle, Juan, Antonio (Jay) Pastrana, and Jessie Daniels. 2012. *Social Justice Sexuality Project 2010 Cumulative Codebook*. City University of New York – Graduate Center. Retrieved January 30, 2020 (http://socialjusticesexuality.com/files/2014/09/Codebook-Reformatted.pdf).

Bornstein, Kate. 1998. *My Gender Workbook*. New York: Routledge.

Bouton, Richard A., Peggy E. Gallaher, Paul Arthur Garlinghouse, Terri Leal, Leslie D. Rosenstein, and Robert K. Young. 1987. "Scales for Measuring Fear of AIDS and Homophobia." *Journal of Personality Assessment* 51(4):606–614.

Brewster, Melanie E. and Bonnie Moradi. 2010. "Perceived Experiences of Anti-Bisexual Prejudice: Instrument Development and Evaluation." *Journal of Counseling Psychology* 57(4):451–468.

Burn, Shawn Meghan. 2000. "Heterosexuals' Use of "Fag" and "Queer" to Deride One Another: A Contributor to Heterosexism and Stigma." *Journal of Homosexuality* 40(2):1–11.

Drescher, Jack. 2015. "Out of DSM: Depathologizing Homosexuality." *Behavioral Sciences* 5(4):565–575.

Eliason, Michele J. 1997. "The Prevalence and Nature of Biphobia in Heterosexual Undergraduate Students." *Archives of Sexual Behavior* 26:317–326.

Elizabeth, Autumn. 2013. "Challenging the Binary: Sexual Identity that is Not Duality." *Journal of Bisexuality* 13:329–337.

Eskridge, William N. 2008. *Dishonorable Passions: Sodomy Laws in America, 1861–2003*. New York, NY: Penguin.

Filiault, Shaun M. and Murray J. N. Drummond. 2007. "The Hegemonic Aesthetic." *Gay and Lesbian Issues and Psychology Review* 3:175–184.

Gamson, Joshua. 1995. "Must Identity Movements Self-Destruct? A Queer Dilemma." *Social Problems* 42(3):390–407.

Gerhardstein, Kelly R. and Veanne N. Anderson. 2010. "There's More than Meets the Eye: facial Appearance and Evaluations of Transsexual People." *Sex Roles* 62(5/6):361–373.

GLAAD Media Reference Guide, tenth edition. 2016. New York, NY: GLAAD. Retrieved January 30, 2020 (https://www.glaad.org/sites/default/files/GLAAD-Media-Reference-Guide-Tenth-Edition.pdf).

Gordon, Allegra and Ilan Meyer. "Gender Nonconformity as a Target of Prejudice, Discrimination and Violence against LGB Individuals." *Journal of LGBT Health Research* 3:55–71.

Halberstam, Judith. 2003. "Reflections on Queer Studies and Queer Pedagogy." *Journal of Homosexuality* 45(2/4):361–364.

Halperin, David M. 2003. "The Normalization of Queer Theory." *Journal of Homosexuality* 45(2/4):339–343.

Hennen, Peter. 2008. *Faeries, Bears, and Leathermen: Men in Community Queering the Masculine*. Chicago, IL: University of Chicago Press.

Herek, Gregory. 1984. "Beyond 'Homophobia': A Social Psychological Perspective on Attitudes Toward Lesbians and Gay Men." *Journal of Homosexuality* 10(1/2):1–21.

Herek, Gregory. 1988. "Heterosexuals' Attitudes toward Lesbians and Gay Men: Correlates and Gender Differences." *The Journal of Sex Research* 25:451–477.

Herek, Gregory. 2000. "The Psychology of Sexual Prejudice." *Current Directions in Psychological Science* 9:19–22.

Herek, Gregory 2002. "Heterosexuals' Attitudes toward Bisexual Men and Women in the United States." *The Journal of Sex Research* 39:264–274.

Hill, Darryl 2002. "Genderism, Transphobia, and Gender Bashing: A Framework for Interpreting Anti-Transgender Violence." Pp. 113–136 in *Understanding and Dealing with Violence: A Multicultural Approach*, edited by Barbara C. Wallace and Robert T. Carter. Thousand Oaks, CA: Sage Publications.

Hill, Darryl and Brian Willoughby. 2005. "The Development and Validation of the Genderism and Transphobia Scale." *Sex Roles* 53(7/8):531–544.

Hudson, Walter W. and Wendell A. Ricketts. 1980. "A Strategy for the Measurement of Homophobia." *Journal of Homosexuality* 3(4):357–372.

James, Sandy, Jody Herman, Susan Rankin, Mara Keisling, Lisa Mottet, and Ma'ayan Anafi. 2016. *The Report of the 2015 U.S. Transgender Survey*. Washington, DC: National Center for Transgender Equality.

Khayatt, Didi. 2002. "Toward a Queer Identity." *Sexualities* 5(4):487–501.

Kite, Mary and Bernard Whitley, Jr. 1998. "Do Heterosexual Women and Men Differ in Their Attitudes Toward Homosexuality? A Conceptual and Methodological Analysis." Pp. 39–61 in *Psychological Perspectives on Lesbians and Gay Issues: Vol 4. Stigma and Sexual Orientation*, edited by Gregory Herek. Thousand Oaks, CA: Sage.

Knudson, Gail, Griet De Cuypere, and Walter Bockting. 2010. "Recommendations for Revision of the DSM Diagnoses of Gender Identity Disorders: Consensus Statement of The World Professional Association for Transgender Health." *International Journal of Transgenderism* 12(2):115–118.

Lahti, Martti 1998. "Dressing Up in Power: Tom of Finland and Gay Male Body Politics." *Journal of Homosexuality* 35(3/4):185–205.

Landen, Mikeal and Sune Innala. 2000. "Attitudes toward Transsexualism in a Swedish National Survey." *Archives of Sexual Behavior* 29:375–388.

Larsen, Knud, Michael Reed, and Susan Hoffman. 1980. "Attitudes of Heterosexuals toward Homosexuality: A Likert-Type Scale and Construct Validity." *The Journal of Sex Research* 16(3):245–257.

Leitenberg, Harold and Lesley Slavin. 1983. "Comparison of Attitudes toward Transsexuality and Homosexuality." *Archives of Sexual Behavior* 12:337–346.

Louderback, Laura and Bernard Whitley, Jr. 1997. "Perceived Erotic Value of Homosexuality and Sex-Role Attitudes as Mediators of Sex Differences in Heterosexual College Students' Attitudes toward Lesbians and Gay Men." *Journal of Sex Research* 34:175–182.

MacDonald, A. P. 1981. "Bisexuality: Some Comments on Research and Theory." *Journal of Homosexuality* 6:21–35.

MacDonald, A. P., Jim Huggins, Susan Young, and Richard Swanson. 1973. "Attitudes toward Homosexuality: Preservation of Sex Morality or the Double Standard?" *Journal of Consulting and Clinical Psychology* 40:161.

Martin, Biddy. 1996. *Femininity Played Straight: The Significance of Being Lesbian*. London and New York: Routledge.

Meyer, Doug. 2008. "Interpreting and Experiencing Anti-Queer Violence: Race, Class, and Gender Differences Among LGBT Hate Crime Victims." *Race, Gender & Class* 15(3/4):262–282.

Mohr, Jonathan and Aaron Rochlen. 1999. "Measuring Attitudes Regarding Bisexuality in Lesbian, Gay Male, and Heterosexual Populations." *Journal of Counseling Psychology* 46:353–369.

Mulick, Patrick S. and Lester W. Wright, Jr. 2002. "Examining the Existence of Biphobia in the Heterosexual and Homosexual Populations." *Journal of Bisexuality* 2(4):45–64.

Myers, JoAnne. 2013. *Historical Dictionary of the Lesbian and Gay Liberation Movements*. Lanham, MD: Scarecrow Press, Inc.

Nadal, Kevin L., Chassitty N. Whitman, Lindsey S. Davis, Tanya Erazo, and Kristin C. Davidoff. 2016. "Microaggressions toward Lesbian, Gay, Bisexual, Transgender, Queer, and Genderqueer People: A Review of the Literature." *The Journal of Sex Research* 53(4/5):488–508.

Nagoshi, Julie L., Katherine A. Adams, Heather K. Terrell, Eric D. Hill, Stephanie Brzuzy, and Craig T. Nagoshi. 2008. "Gender Differences in Correlates of Homophobia and Transphobia." *Sex Roles* 59(7/8):521–531.

Ochs, Robyn. 1996. "Biphobia: It Goes More than Two Ways." Pp. 217–239 in *Bisexuality: The Psychology and Politics of an Invisible Minority*, edited by Beth A. Firestein. Thousand Oaks, CA: Sage Publications.

Pascoe, C. J. 2007. *Dude, You're a Fag: Masculinity and Sexuality in High School*. Los Angeles, CA: University of California Press.

Raja, Sheela and Joseph Stokes. 1998. "Assessing Attitudes toward Lesbians and Gay Men: The Modern Homophobia Scale." *Journal of Gay, Lesbian, and Bisexual Identity* 3:113–134.

Richards, Christina, Walter Pierre Bouman, and Meg-John Barker, (eds). 2017. *Genderqueer and Non-Binary Genders*. London, UK: Palgrave Macmillan.

Riddle, Dorothy. 1996. "Riddle Homophobia Scale." P. 31 in *Social Diversity and Social Justice: Gay, Lesbian and Bisexual Oppression*, edited by Maurianne Adams, Peg Brigham, Paulette Dalpes, and Linda Marchesani. Dubuque, IA: Kendall/Hunt Publishing.

Rodríguez, Juana Maria. 2003. *Queer Latinidad: Identity Practices, Discursive Spaces.* New York, NY: NYU Press.

Rust, Paula C. 1995. *Bisexuality and the Challenge to Lesbian Politics: Sex, Loyalty, and Revolution* New York, NY: NYU Press.

Rust, Paula. 1992. "The Politics of Sexual Identity: Sexual Attraction and Behavior Among Lesbian and Bisexual Women." *Social Problems* 39(4):366–386.

Schilt, Kristen and Laurel Westbrook. 2009. "Doing Gender, Doing Heteronormativity: 'Gender Normals', Transgender People, and the Social Maintenance of Heterosexuality." *Gender & Society* 23(4):440–464.

Serano, Julia. 2007. *Whipping Girl: A Transsexual Woman on Sexism and the Scapegoating of Femininity.* Berkeley, CA: Seal Press.

Smith, Kenneth T. 1971. "Homophobia: A Tentative Personality Profile." *Psychological Reports* 29(3):1091–1094.

Stein, Arlene. 1997. *Sex and Sensibility: Stories of a Lesbian Generation.* Los Angeles, CA: University of California Press.

Stryker, Susan. 2008. *Transgender History.* Berkeley, CA: Seal Press.

Tate, Charlotte Chuck, Jay N. Ledbetter, and Cris P. Youssef. 2013. "A Two-Question Method for Assessing Gender Categories in the Social and Medical Sciences." *Journal of Sex Research* 50:767–776.

Tebbe, Esther N. and Bonnie Moradi. "Anti-Transgender Prejudice: A Structural Equation Model of Associated Constructs." *Journal of Counseling Psychology* 59(2):251–261.

Van de Ven, Paul, Laurel Bornholt, and Michael Bailey. 1996. "Measuring Cognitive, Affective, and Behavioral Components of Homophobic Reaction." *Archives of Sexual Behavior* 25(2):155–179.

Walters, Karina, Teresa Evans-Campbell, Jane M. Simoni, Theresa Ronquillo, and Rupaleem Bhuyan. 2006. ""My Spirit in My Heart": Identity Experiences and Challenges Among American Indian Two-Spirit Women." *Journal of Lesbian Studies* 10:125–149.

Warren, Jacob C., K. Bryant Smalley, and K. Nikki Barefoot. 2016. "Psychological Well-Being among Transgender and Genderqueer Individuals." *International Journal of Transgenderism* 17(3/4):114–123.

Weinberg, George. 1972. *Society and the Healthy Homosexual.* New York: St. Martin's.

Weinberg, Martin, Colin Williams, and Douglas Pryor. 2009. "Becoming Bisexual." Pp. 262–272 in *Constructions of Deviance*, edited by Patricia and Peter Adler. Belmont, CA: Thomson Wadsworth.

Weinberg, Martin S., Colin J. Williams, and Douglas W. Pryor. 1995. *Dual Attraction: Understanding Bisexuality.* London: Oxford University Press.

Weiss, Jillian Todd. 2004. "GL vs. BT: the Archaeology of Biphobia and Transphobia within the U.S. Gay and Lesbian Community." *Journal of Bisexuality* 3(3/4):25–55.

Whitley, Bernard E., Christopher E. Childs, and Jena B. Collins. 2011. "Differences in Black and White American College Students' Attitudes toward Lesbians and Gay Men." *Sex Roles* 64(5/6):299–310.

Willoughby, Brian, Darryl B. Hill, Cesar A. Gonzalez, Alessandra Lacorazza, Raymond A. Macapagal, Michelle E. Barton, and Nathan D. Doty. 2010. "Who Hates Gender

Outlaws? A Multisite and Multinational Evaluation of the Genderism and Transphobia Scale." *International Journal of Transgenderism* 12(4):254–271.

Winter, Sam, Beverley Webster and Pui Kei Eleanor Cheung. 2008. "Measuring Hong Kong Undergraduate Students' Attitudes towards Transpeople." *Sex Roles* 59 (9/10):670–683.

Worthen, Meredith G. F. 2012. "Understanding College Student Attitudes toward LGBT Individuals." *Sociological Focus* 45(4):285–305.

Worthen, Meredith G. F. 2013. "An Argument for Separate Analyses of Attitudes toward Lesbian, Gay, Bisexual Men, Bisexual Women, MtF and FtM Transgender Individuals." *Sex Roles* 68(11/12):703–723.

Worthen, Meredith G. F. 2016a. *Sexual Deviance and Society: A Sociological Examination*. London: Routledge.

Worthen, Meredith G. F. 2016b. "Hetero-cis-normativity and the Gendering of Transphobia." *International Journal of Transgenderism* 17(1):31–57.

Wright, Lester W., Henry E. Adams, and Jeffery Bernat. 1999. "Development and Validation of the Homophobia Scale." *Journal of Psychopathology and Behavioral Assessment* 21 (4):337–347.

Wyss, Shannon E. 2004. "'This was my Hell': The Violence Experienced by Gender Non–conforming Youth in U.S. High Schools." *International Journal of Qualitative Studies in Education* 17:709–730.

Yoshino, Kenji. 2000. "The Epistemic Contract of Bisexual Erasure." *Stanford Law Review* 52:353–461.

# 6
# THE LGBTQ STIGMA SCALES

To best understand LGBTQ stigma, it is important to utilize measures that tap into its multiple dimensions. In this chapter, nine scales that speak to the LGBTQ Measurement Principles outlined in Chapter 5 are introduced. Specifically, the elements of the LGBTQ Stigma Scales cluster around six key areas of stigma: (1) social and familial relationships; (2) positions of importance and social significance; (3) basic human rights; (4) sex-related stigma; (5) LGBTQ permanency; and (6) the achievement of femininity or masculinity (see Table 6.1). These key areas are briefly discussed in this chapter as they relate to LGBTQ stigma (more generally) and will be further examined (more specifically) as related to each of the nine LGBTQ groups in Chapters 7–16.

## LGBTQ Stigma and Social and Familial Relationships

A relatively established way to understand stigma includes the investigation of desired "closeness" to stigmatized groups. This can include the interest in building (or the interest in avoiding) friendships and other close relationships with stigmatized people, as well as feelings about family members who are in stigmatized groups. This moves beyond simple reports of "knowing" stigmatized people (as discussed in Chapter 4's common explanations) and instead focuses on desired social contact with (and in contrast, desired social distancing from) stigmatized individuals.

The desire for social distancing or "feelings of unwillingness among members of a group to accept or approve a given degree of intimacy in interaction with a member of an out-group" (Williams 1964:29) has been found to be related to prejudicial attitudes. Indeed, Bogardus' Social Distance Scale (Bogardus 1925) has been utilized to examine attitudes toward LGT people (Hinrichs

**TABLE 6.1** LGBTQ Stigma Scale Items by Key Area of Stigma

*Social and Familial Relationships*
I welcome new friends who are _____. [R]
I don't think it would negatively affect our relationship if I learned that one of my close relatives was a _____. [R]
_____ are not capable of being good parents.

*Positions of Importance and Social Significance*
I would not vote for a political candidate who was an openly _____.
_____ should not be allowed to join the military.

*Basic Human Rights*
I believe _____ should have all of the same rights as other people do. [R]
It is upsetting to me that _____ experience violence, harassment, and discrimination just because they are _____. [R]

*Sex Act-Related*
_____ are unfaithful to their romantic partners.
_____ are too sexual (hypersexual).
_____ are mostly responsible for spreading HIV/AIDS.
I am comfortable with the thought of a _____ having sex with a woman. [R]
I am comfortable with the thought of a _____ having sex with a man. [R]

*LGBTQ Permanency*
Most women/men/people who call themselves _____ are just temporarily experimenting with their sexuality/gender.*

*Achievement of Femininity or Masculinity*
_____ are not feminine/masculine enough.*
Non-binary/genderqueer people should just pick one, either be masculine or feminine.**

*Notes*: Suggested response options are "Strongly Disagree" to "Strongly Agree". [R] item should be reverse coded so that the individual items added together create the individual LGBTQ stigma scales. For most items, the stigmatized group of interest (i.e., lesbian women, gay men, bisexual women, bisexual men, trans women, trans men, non-binary/genderqueer people, queer women, and queer men) should be inserted into the blank. For * items, only one of the underlined words should be included in the survey, this should be the word that overlaps with the stigmatized group of interest.
** This item is specific to the non-binary/genderqueer stigma scale. Each of the specific nine LGBTQ scales is provided in each of the nine corresponding chapters.

and Rosenberg 2002; Worthen et al. 2019). Researchers in the U.S., Italy, and Spain have found that negative attitudes toward gay, lesbian, and transgender people are related to an increased desire for social distancing from them (Worthen et al. 2019). In Italy, researchers determined that homophobia was strongly related to the desire to avoid social relationships with gay men and lesbian women (Lingiardi, Falanga, and D'Augelli 2005; Worthen et al. 2019) and that the urge to avoid personal contact with gay men and lesbian women due to discomfort caused by their presence was negatively related to actual contact with lesbian and gay people (Lingiardi et al. 2016). Furthermore, a Hong Kong study (N = 856) found that previous contact with transgender people was associated with less social distancing from them (King, Winter, and Webster 2009). Together, this research demonstrates a clear relationship between the stigmatizers' desired social relationships/distancing from LGBTQ people and their stigmatization of LGBTQ people.

It is especially important to consider desired social relationships and social distancing because this type of inquiry can tap into something that might be missed by simple measures of social contact with a particular group. While a person may, for example, "know" a transgender person, they may not actually want to interact with this transgender person and may in fact want to distance themselves from this transgender person in particular and transgender people as a group more generally. In other words, knowing someone is one thing, actually wanting to have continued contact and build relationships with said person is quite another. The motivating factors behind intergroup contact theory can be thought of as "familiarity" (i.e., contact) and "liking" (desired, enjoyable, pleasant contact and relationships) (Pettigrew and Tropp 2006). "Closeness" is an important aspect of these relationships. Choosing friends and wanting to build friendships with those in stigmatized groups are indicators of decreased stigmatization toward the stigmatized group. Similarly, maintaining close relationships with family members who occupy stigmatized statuses is also indicative of lower levels of stigmatization of the stigmatized group. Indeed, not surprisingly, studies show that those who actively seek out and maintain social and familial relationships with LGBTQ people are more supportive of (and less stigmatizing toward) LGBTQ people (Friedman and Morgan 2009; Paceley, Hwu, and Arizpe 2017). In addition, selection effects can play a pivotal role in linking desired social/familial contact and prejudice such that some may actively avoid knowing and/or building relationships with LGBTQ persons and thus, not wanting to be involved in social or familial relationships with LGBTQ people is a choice that is indicative of unsupportive LGBTQ attitudes (Loehr, Doan, and Miller 2015).

Another layer of the social and familial aspect of LGBTQ stigma involves perspectives about LGBTQ parents. Indeed, the outright rejection of LGBTQ people as "fit" parents is commonly found in politicized media (Crawford et al. 1999; Joos and Broad 2007) and this connects to larger conversations about LGBTQ stigma. For example, in studies conducted in the U.S., France, Italy, and Portugal, more supportive attitudes toward same-gender parenting were associated with lower levels of lesbian and gay prejudices (Costa and Salinas-Quiroz 2018; Crawford et al. 1999; Pistella et al. 2018; Vecho et al. 2019). In addition, LGBTQ parents are especially cognizant of the cultural stigma associated with their parental status and their parenting practices. Indeed, research in the U.S. finds that gay and lesbian parents actively prepare their children with coping methods to manage the prejudicial experiences they anticipate that their children may endure because their parents are gay/lesbian (Oakley, Farr, and Scherer 2017). Such scholarly work demonstrates that perspectives about LGBTQ people as parents are an important aspect a LGBTQ stigma.

In sum, desiring social/familial contact and close relationships with LGBTQ people as well as the generalized support of the capability of LGBTQ people to be "good" parents are all indicative of a comfort with moving outside of the realm of hetero-cis-normativity, disrupting the status quo (i.e., reconceptualizing being LGBTQ away from being identified as "norm violating") and decreasing LGBTQ stigma. In these ways, negative feelings about LGBTQ social and familial relationships and LGBTQ parents are significant dimensions of LGBTQ stigma. *In the LGBTQ Stigma Scales, this area of stigma is measured with 3 statements aimed at understanding feelings about LGBTQ friends, family members, and parents* (see Table 6.1).

## LGBTQ Stigma and Positions of Importance and Social Significance

Another dimension of stigma includes perspectives about stigmatized people occupying positions of importance and social significance. This is perhaps especially relevant for visible leaders, including politicians who are often elected by the majority vote, as well as military members, who are often thought to both symbolize and defend traditional cultural values (Caforio and Nuciari 2018). In a broad sense, both politicians and military members are meant to represent "the people" in some way (Allen 2018; Caforio and Nuciari 2018). As a result, feelings about those who occupy these positions are also representative of broader societal attitudes toward the groups/identities they belong to and the perspectives they hold.

Among elected leaders, there is often a distinctly hetero-cis-normative and culturally traditional pattern. For example, 44 out of the 45 U.S. Presidents to date have been White[1], married, and heterosexual[2] cisgender men, all but five are/were fathers[3], and nearly all are/were self-identified Christians[4] (Masci 2017; Matuz, Harris, and Craughwell 2016). This type of pattern is also seen across other types of elected political positions across the West whereby the "traditional mould of a political candidate [is] something like a professional white man, married with children" (Allen 2018:94). While there are rarely official policies in place to prevent non-hetero-cis-normative people from holding elected positions, the largely hetero-cis-normative identities of elected leaders in most nations sends a strong message that reinforces LGBTQ negativity and stigma.

Similarly, the armed forces of the world are predominantly comprised of hetero-cis-normative people (Caforio and Nuciari 2018). But unlike the largely open parameters for the majority of political positions, most countries do have (or have had) restrictions against LGBTQ military service. For example, in the U.S. military, non-hetero-cis-normative people have been explicitly barred from joining in various ways since 1916 (Sinclair 2009; see Worthen 2019 for a timeline of events related to U.S. LGBT military service). In 2020, there remains active legislation working to ban transgender people from serving in the U.S. military (Liptack 2019; Rasha 2020). These formalized restrictive policies stress the importance of traditionally and narrowly defined military cultural constructs which include strict norms about sexuality (i.e., heteronormativity) and gender (i.e., cisnormativity) as well as repercussions for going against such norms (Allsep 2013; Worthen 2019; Yerke and Mitchell 2013). This impacts not only military members' LGBTQ perspectives (which tend to be less supportive when compared to civilians' perspectives, see Ender, Rohall, and Matthews 2016) but also, conveys dominant and globally pervasive hetero-cis-normativity. With the U.S. Department of Defense being the largest employer of people in the world (over 3.2 million employees) and the People's Liberation Army (the Chinese military) being the second largest (over 2.3 million employees) (Taylor 2015), the cultural norms of the military can be far-reaching. Thus, it is important to investigate how feelings about LGBTQ military members impact LGBTQ stigma.

In sum, hetero-cis-normativity and LGBTQ negativity are reinforced when elected leaders and others who hold positions of social significance, such as military members, are predominately (or entirely) hetero-cis-normative people. As a result, perspectives about the support of LGBTQ political candidates and LGBTQ military members are valuable in the examination of LGBTQ stigma. *In the LGBTQ Stigma Scales, this area of stigma is measured with 2 statements aimed at understanding feelings about LGBTQ political leaders and military membership* (see Table 6.1).

## LGBTQ Stigma and Basic Human Rights

There are 30 articles in the United Nations' Universal Declaration of Human Rights that are designed to put forth common rights for all people (United Nations 2015). These include, for example, rights and freedoms without distinction of any kind, such a race, colour, sex, language, religion, political or other opinion, national or social origin, property, birth or other status (Article 2), equal protection of the law (Article 7), protection from interference with privacy, family, and home (Article 12), right to marry and to found a family (Article 16), right to own property (Article 17), right to equal access to public service in his country (Article 21), and the right to work (Article 23). Established in 1948 by representatives from across the globe and translated into more than 500 languages, this list demonstrates a shared set of beliefs about the basic rights that *all* people should have.

While basic human rights are afforded to people who are deemed to be "worthy" citizens, LGBTQ individuals are frequently classified as "unworthy" of basic human rights. For example, marriage is a right that is often given to hetero-cis-normative "man + woman" duos (Symonides 2017; United Nations 2015). LGBTQ people have only recently been given the right to same-gender marriage in the U.S. (in 2015) and globally, the vast majority of countries do not allow marriages involving same-gender couples (Kollman 2016). In the U.S. as of 2020, there are no federal laws explicitly prohibiting discrimination against LGBTQ people in the areas of housing, employment, and public accommodations and in more than half of the U.S. states, you can be terminated from your job just for being lesbian, gay, bisexual, transgender, and/or non-binary (Human Rights Campaign 2019). Across the globe, a minority of countries (only 33% of UN states) have specific prohibitions against employment discrimination based on sexual orientation/identity (Carroll and Mendos 2017). Thus, it is clear that the United Nations' Universal Declaration of Human Rights is not unambiguously applied. Quite the contrary, when it comes to LGBTQ people, many countries have explicit laws denying LGBTQ people access to the rights designated by the United Nations as "universal." As a result, one aspect of LGBTQ stigma can be understood as a lack of support for human rights for LGBTQ people.

Being able to walk through life free from harassment, discrimination, and violence is another layer of basic human rights. For example, three articles in the United Nations' Universal Declaration of Human Rights speak well to this: Article 1: "All human beings are born free and equal in dignity and rights;" Article 3: "Everyone has the right to life, liberty and security of person;" and Article 5: "No one shall be subjected to torture or to cruel, inhuman or degrading treatment or punishment" (United Nations 2015).

However, as noted previously, these rights are not always distributed equally. In particular, hetero-cis-normative individuals are sometimes able to avoid harassment, discrimination, and violence in ways that LGBTQ people are not. For example, LGBTQ people who are in same-gender romantic relationships can be easily identified as violators of hetero-cis-normativity, leaving them open to harassment, discrimination, and violence in ways that those involved in hetero-cis-normative relationships are not. In addition, unlike most hetero-cis-normative people, LGBTQ people are often perceived of as gender-nonconforming and this can also result in various forms of harassment, discrimination, and violence. Indeed, a Pew Research Center study (2013) of 1,197 LGBT U.S. adults determined that more than half (58%) had been the target of anti-LGBT slurs or jokes and nearly one-third (30%) had been physically attacked or threatened (Pew Research Center 2013). A more recent, smaller study (N = 489) conducted by the Harvard Opinion Research Program (2017) found similar results with a majority of LGBTQ Americans indicating hearing slurs (57%) or offensive remarks (53%) and over half reporting that they or an LGBTQ friend or family member had experienced violence (51%), threats and harassment (57%), and/or sexual harassment (51%) due to their LGBTQ identity (Harvard T. H. Chan School of Public Health 2017).

Globally, LGBTQ people face state-sponsored violence (e.g., in Chechnya[5]) and same-sex sexual activity is a designated as a crime in nearly half of the countries across the world (Carroll and Mendos 2017). In his assessment of the global state of LGBTQ violence in 2017, International Lesbian, Gay, Bisexual, Trans and Intersex Association (ILGA) representative Aengus Carroll reported that there was nowhere in the world where LGBTQ people (including himself) would feel completely safe (Taylor 2017). In addition, although only a small minority of the actual number of hate crimes that occur in the U.S. are reported to law enforcement and compiled by the FBI, of those that are, close to one in five (19%) are designated as anti-LGBT[6] hate crimes (FBI 2018). Globally, a minority of countries (only 23% of UN states) designate hate crimes based on sexual orientation as an aggravating circumstance (Carroll and Mendos 2017). Thus, although the UN may identify freedom from "degrading treatment" and the "right to security of person" as basic human rights for everyone, it is clear that LGBTQ people are less likely than hetero-cis-normative people to experience such freedoms and securities.

In addition, because LGBTQ people violate hetero-cis-normativity, they are sometimes deemed as *deserving* of negative treatment. Indeed, one study found that heterosexual men who assaulted gay men did so because their "victims violated unwritten codes of appropriate behavior and thus deserved punishment" (Franklin 1998:8). In other words, gay men's behaviors of same-gender attraction and/or gender nonconformity that are perceived of as "inappropriate" can serve as justification and motivation for anti-gay assaults. Victims of anti-LGBQ violence have also been described as *blameworthy* for their own assaults because they are "too open" or "too obvious" about their LGBQ identities (Meyer 2015:25). Though still in the context of victim-blaming, trans-motivated violence differs in that trans victims can be perceived of as deserving of violence because they "deceived others" into thinking they were something they were not (Meyer 2015; Schilt and Westbrook 2009; Wodda and Panfil 2014). The link between deception and trans violence is further compounded by the dehumanization of trans people into objects—as something nonhuman—which often manifests into referring to trans people as "it" (Meyer 2015:35; see also Wodda and Panfil 2014). These processes have even been used as legal tactics in the form of the "gay panic defense" and the closely related "trans panic defense" whereby the defendant (most often a hetero-cis male) argues that an LGBTQ person (most often a gay man or trans woman) made unwanted sexual advances that caused the defendant to panic and respond with violence (Wodda and Panfil 2014). Both in and out of the courtroom, this type of argument lends cultural credence to the justification of anti-LGBTQ violence. Together, this suggests that another way to understand LGBTQ stigma is to examine feelings about violence, harassment, and discrimination directed toward LGBTQ people because they are LGBTQ.

In sum, attitudes toward the differential treatment of LGBTQ people when it comes to basic human rights are indicators of LGBTQ stigma. While we have systems in place that suggest that all persons are deserving of basic human rights (e.g., the United Nations' Universal Declaration of Human Rights), there seems to be an underlying set of assumptions that these rights should be afforded to all *hetero-cis-normative* people (and *not* all LGBTQ people). In addition, when LGBTQ people endure experiences that violate basic human rights (such as harassment, discrimination, and violence), some cultural scripts suggest that they are somehow both deserving and blameworthy of these experiences. Thus, perspectives about basic human rights are essential to explore when understanding LGBTQ stigma. *In the LGBTQ Stigma Scales, this area of stigma is measured with 2 statements aimed at understanding feelings about LGBTQ basic rights and concerns about LGBTQ people's experiences with violence, harassment, and discrimination* (see Table 6.1).

## LGBTQ Sex Act-Related Stigma

As described in Chapter 3's discussion of "The Sexualization of LGBTQ Stigma," LGBTQ people are stigmatized because their sexualities and the sex acts they are believed to be involved in are deemed to be abnormal and culturally problematic. Indeed, LGBTQ people have been clustered under the umbrella of "sexual deviants." They have been labeled "mentally ill," "perverts," "pedophiles," and "predators." This stigma has shifted and lessened over time to some degree in most parts of the world; however, sex act-related stigma still remains a prominent fixture of LGBTQ negativity.

In the U.S., this form of LGBTQ negativity became quite noticeable during the Lavender Scare whereby hundreds of those suspected of engaging in "homosexual" sex acts were terminated from government employment in the early 1950s. Both State Department and FBI officials worked to "purge" suspected gay and lesbian employees from the government using details they kept in documents containing hundreds of thousands of pages of information they titled the "Second World War-era Perverts in Government Service File," the "Obscene File," and the "Sex Deviates File" (Charles 2015:71–72). The hunt to be rid LGBTQ people from government service organized under the guise of the FBI's Sex Deviates Program (which ran from the 1950s to the 1970s) solidified the larger cultural stigma of being LGBTQ.

The DSM reinforced this process. For example, as noted previously, in its first two editions, both "homosexuality" and "transvestism" were classified first as "sociopathic personality disturbances" in the DSM-I (1952) and then as "as nonpsychotic mental disorders," under the category "sexual deviation" in the DSM-II (1968) (American Psychiatric Association 1952, 1968). In other words, because of their non-hetero-cis-normative sexual acts, LGBTQ people were diagnosed as mentally ill sexual deviants. It was not until the 1974 edition that the DSM-II declassified "homosexuality" as a "mental disorder," though the DSM-III (1980) still categorized "transsexualism" and other incongruences between sex and gender identity as "gender identity disorders," and in the DSM IV (1994), "transsexualism" was still included under "paraphilias" (American Psychiatric Association 1974, 1980, 1994). It was not until 2013 that the DSM-V stated that "gender nonconformity is not in itself a mental disorder" and instead includes "gender dysphoria" which "is the presence of clinically significant distress associated with the condition of gender nonconformity" (American Psychiatric Association 2013). Because the DSM is widely recognized as the preeminent source of both language and criteria for the classification of mental disorders, the DSM labeling of LGBTQ people has had an impact not only on the "mentally ill" diagnoses of LGBTQ people (and the subsequent opportunities and experiences that were closed/limited to them as a result of such diagnoses, such as government employment during the Lavender Scare and military employment for LGB people prior to 2011), but also, the larger cultural stigma associated with being LGBTQ. Furthermore, because this "mental illness" was mostly based on self-disclosures of non-hetero-cis-normative sexual behaviors to mental health care professionals, social responses to sexual acts have largely been at the core of LGBTQ stigma and often remain so today.

Sex act-related stigma is inclusive of negativity directed toward certain sexual behaviors as well as the context in which such sexual behaviors occur. Put another way, sex act-related stigma "emerges from opinions about particular people in particular types of relationships engaging in particular behaviors" (Worthen 2016:134). Below four sex act-related stigma processes that impact LGBTQ negativity are briefly discussed: (1) the hypersexualization of LGBTQ people; (2) the association of LGBTQ people with unfaithfulness; (3) the perceptions about the types of sexual behaviors LGBTQ people are involved in; and (4) the association of LGBTQ people with HIV/AIDS.

## Hypersexuality

LGBTQ people are stereotyped as "too sexual," "hypersexual," or even "sex-obsessed." In this way, LGBTQ stigma is built from perceptions that LGBTQ people want *more* sex than the "normal" (read: hetero-cis) person. For example, qualitative work shows that gay and lesbian individuals indicate being described as "sexually insatiable" and "sexually uncontrollable" and this can have significantly negative effects on LGBTQ people's lives (Mennicke et al. 2018:7, 11). Indeed, the perceived hypersexuality of LGBTQ people has led not only to their devalued cultural status and their overall negative treatment, but also, to the criminalization of LGBTQ people (Mogul, Ritchie, and

Whitlock 2011). "Hypersexuality" as a diagnosis in the mental health community has been up for debate and is not included in the most recent edition of the DSM (Kafka 2010; Kraus, Voon, and Potenza 2016). However, the proposed (though not utilized) diagnostic criteria included "Repetitively engaging in sexual behaviors while disregarding the risk for physical or emotional harm to self or others" (Kafka 2010:379). This framing of hypersexuality is closely linked to "sex-crazed" stereotypes that have been historically associated with LGBTQ people.

In addition to the perceived high frequency of LGBTQ people's sex acts, LGBTQ people are stereotyped as "hypersexual" because they are seen as sex objects themselves (Lahti 1998; Rupp and Taylor 2010). As described in Chapter 3, hetero-cis-normativity legitimizes and justifies the sexualizing and fetishizing of non-hetero and non-cis people and this contributes to LGBTQ stigma in ways that lead to complex patterns of objectification informed by social power. For example, heterosexual men's hypersexualization of bisexual women shapes bisexual women's stigma experiences in ways that differ from upper/middle-class gay men's sexual objectification of working-class gay men (Han 2007; Hennen 2008; Lahti 1998; Rupp and Taylor 2010). These processes will be further discussed in Chapters 7–16 as they inform stigma toward the nine LGBTQ groups explored in this book. Overall, however, it is clear that the sexual objectification of LGBTQ people leads to their social marginalization and stigma experiences.

## *Unfaithfulness*

Related to the stereotype that LGBTQ people want "*a lot of sex*" is the idea that LGBTQ want so much sex, they do not (or cannot) remain faithful to their sexual partners. Generally, LGBTQ people are thought to be less faithful in their romantic relationships when compared to hetero-cis-normative people (Brewster and Moradi 2010; Frederick and Fales 2016; Spalding and Peplau 1997). Part of this is related to the closeting of LGBTQ people. Due to the myriad social consequences of being openly LGBTQ, many LGBTQ people have had to (or still have to) participate in sexual and romantic relationships in clandestine ways. For some, this has included LGBTQ relationships outside of their hetero-cis-normative commitments. For example, in the 1960s, sociologist Laud Humphreys' (1970) exposé of tearoom sex between men revealed that the majority (54%) were married to and currently living with their wives (Humphreys 1970). Consider also men today who participate in "the Down Low" lifestyle as discussed in Chapter 3, wherein they have sex with men and women (but do not identify as gay or bisexual) and often do not tell their women partners about the sex they are having with other men (Heath and Goggin 2009).

The links between unfaithfulness and LGB people are not confined solely to closeted gay and bisexual men, however. Indeed, additional research indicates that unfaithfulness is more generally associated with LGB people as compared to heterosexual people. For example, a large-scale U.S. study (N = 63,894) determined that gay men, lesbian women, and bisexual men and women were significantly more likely to indicate a history of both cheating on and being cheated on by their relationship partners when compared to heterosexual men and women (Frederick and Fales 2016). In contrast, heterosexual men and women were more likely to indicate that they have never been unfaithful to anyone nor have any of their partners been unfaithful to them (Frederick and Fales 2016). Furthermore, when compared to heterosexuals, bisexuals have been perceived as less likely to remain monogamous/faithful to their current relationship partners and more likely to cheat on a partner (and especially seen as more likely to cheat on a heterosexual partner than a lesbian or gay partner) (Spalding and Peplau 1997). Indeed, Brewster and Moradi (2010) identified "cheating" as significant element of their anti-bisexual prejudice scale. Together, these patterns drive larger cultural stereotypes associating LGB people with unfaithfulness.

## *LGBTQ Sexual Behaviors*

LGBTQ sexual behaviors have been clustered under the highly deviantized umbrella term "sodomy" which is inclusive of numerous types of sexual activities deemed to be socially problematic. However, most formal anti-sodomy laws across the globe tend to explicitly outlaw oral and anal sex between same-sex couplings. In the U.S., all acts of sodomy were illegal until Illinois became the first to strike down their existing sodomy laws in 1961 and many states followed in subsequent decades. However, federal statutes continued to uphold the rights of individual states to criminalize oral and anal sex between consenting adults until *Lawrence v. Texas* (*Lawrence v. Texas*, 539 U.S. 558 2003). In many ways, anti-sodomy laws socialized the general public to believe that some types of sexual behaviors are normative and acceptable (i.e., penile–vaginal intercourse between hetero-cis people) and other types of sexual behaviors are deviant and illegal (i.e., oral and anal sex). In turn, this process continues to inform LGBTQ stigma because many exclusively or predominately associate LGBTQ sexual behaviors with previously criminalized behaviors (oral and anal sex). Yet there are important differences in perceptions about LGBTQ sexual behaviors that relate to these processes. For example, sex between two men is generally perceived to be more socially problematic than sex between two women (Heflick 2010; Worthen 2013). Even the two U.S. Supreme Court cases that challenged the anti-sodomy laws (*Bowers v. Hardwick*, 478 U.S. 186 1986; *Lawrence v. Texas*, 539 U.S. 558, 2003) involved only men[7]. Thus, the perceived sexual behaviors involved in LGBTQ sex are driving LGBTQ stigma in complex ways informed by both gender and sexual identity as well as (sometimes) sexualized subcultural experiences (e.g., bear, twink, leather, see Filiault and Drummond 2007; Hennen 2008; Lahti 1998).

As noted previously, a more detailed discussion of these processes as related to each of the nine LGBTQ groups will be provided in Chapters 7–16.

## HIV/AIDS

HIV/AIDS has been associated with "deviant sexual behaviors" most generally and some LGBTQ people more specifically. For example, in the 1980s when nearly a quarter of a million Americans were diagnosed with HIV (Centers for Disease Control 2001), many held the erroneous belief that only gay men could contract HIV/AIDS. In particular, the virus was negatively referred to as "the gay plague" and even briefly labeled as "gay-related immune deficiency (GRID)" by medical professionals (Dowsett 2009:130, 136). In addition, bisexual and queer people (in most cases, bisexual and queer men) have been blamed for the transmission of HIV from the gay population to the heterosexual population (Herek and Capitanio 1999; McKirnan et al. 1995). Indeed, some research indicates that compared to heterosexuals, gay men, and lesbian women, *bisexuals* are described as being significantly more likely to give an STI to a partner (Spalding and Peplau 1997). The stigma that gay, bisexual, and queer men endure remains associated with HIV/AIDS (Dowsett 2009; Dowshen et al. 2017; Herek and Capitanio 1999). More generally, however, some perceive all LGBTQ individuals as "vectors" of disease (Morse et al. 1991) and this relates to the stigmatization of LGBTQ people. Despite the numerous advancements in the treatment of HIV/AIDS available today, HIV/AIDS-related stigma still lingers and is predominantly associated with those who are deemed to be involved in socially problematic sexual behaviors including gay, bisexual, and queer men specifically, and LGBTQ people more broadly.

Overall, the characteristics of the sexual behaviors of LGBTQ people have been the primary or sole determinant of their stigmatized status (e.g., the "mentally ill homosexual" and/or the "sexual deviant"). In this way, LGBTQ people are stigmatized because the sex acts they are thought to engage in are deemed to be deviant. The processes whereby LGBTQ people's sex acts have been stigmatized are evident across various informal and formal mechanisms (e.g., the Lavender Scare, anti-sodomy laws, the DSM). Thus, social responses to *sexual acts* have largely been at the core of LGBTQ stigma in the past and today, sex act-related stigma remains a fixture of LGBTQ negativity. *In the LGBTQ Stigma Scales, this area of stigma is measured with 5 statements aimed at understanding feelings about LGBTQ people as hypersexual and unfaithful, the association of LGBTQ people with HIV/AIDS, and attitudes toward LGBTQ people's sex acts* (see Table 6.1).

## LGBTQ Stigma and the Permanency of Being LGBTQ

LGBTQ identities are sometimes thought of as temporary, experimental, or even changeable. There are four processes that closely relate to this stigmatizing set of attitudes. First, when same-gender sexual behaviors and gender nonconforming behaviors were starting to become more visible in West in the nineteenth century, this coincided with the emergence of conversion "therapies." For example, in the late 1800s, German psychiatrist Albert von Schrenck-Notzing (1862–1929) claimed that he could change "homosexuals" into "heterosexuals" through hypnosis (Beachy 2010). Following this, aversion and conversion therapies were available to those who wanted to "become" hetero-cis. Although many began to reject these therapies in the 1970s (including the American Psychological Association) and they have largely fallen out of favor, save a handful of "ex-gay" movement faith-based groups (Erzen 2006; Waidzunas 2015), the historical past of "converting" LGBTQ people in to hetero-cis people remains a known social artifact. Related to the notion that LGBTQ identities are changeable, there is also a stereotype that participating in LGBTQ behaviors is "only a phase" that is temporary and thus, one can "change" from LGBTQ to hetero-cis quite easily. Despite the ample research that does not support the idea that being LGBTQ is an "experimental phase" (Diamond 2003:12; 2008), this stereotype remains prominent. Together these falsities about LGBTQ identities contribute to a culturally stigmatizing notion that LGBTQ people could be "turned" hetero-cis if they only had the "right" set of hetero-cis-normative experiences to get them there (e.g., conversion therapies and/or hetero-cis romantic relationships). This focus on the experimental and temporary nature of sexual/gender behaviors of LGBTQ people and the ability to "convert" someone from "gay" to "straight" (for example) continue to reinforce the idea that being LGBTQ is not an authentic identity but rather a set of behaviors that are changeable. Thus, the permanency of being LGBTQ is called into question through these stigmatizing perspectives in a process that simultaneously reinforces hetero-cis-normativity.

Second, LGBTQ identities are sometimes thought to lack permanency because LGBTQ people often participate in a coming out process that can be falsely interpreted as changing *from* hetero-cis *to* LGBTQ (D'Augelli 1994). Hetero-cis-normativity reinforces the need for a coming out process because the predominant presumption is that (nearly) all people are hetero-cis (Wandrey, Mosack, and Moore 2015). In this way, the process of coming out as LGBTQ can lead to the inaccurate perception that a person was once "straight" but is now "gay" (for example). The context of the coming out process, then, is another set of cultural experiences that contributes to the stigmatizing belief that LGBTQ identities are changeable and lack permanency.

Third, though people have always participated in same-gender sexual behaviors and gender nonconforming behaviors, the idea that LGBTQ people are something *more than* just their sexual/gender behaviors is relatively new in the modern West. For example, it was not until the Victorian era that a Western discourse emerged recognizing those attracted to others of the same sex as having their own identity that differed from heterosexual identities. Prior to this, there was no direct parallel to our modern understandings of gay and lesbian identities; yet in the 1800s, Victorian literature offered a means to communicate these ideas. Oscar Wilde (1854–1900) has been described as the "originator of the homosexual identity" (Cocks 2003:159) because of his unique ability to discuss gay identity in his Victorian literary creations. Transgender, non-binary, and queer identities are also recent cultural phenomena (Bornstein 1994; Khayatt 2002; Stryker 2008; Wilchins 1997). Because modern LGBTQ identities are relatively new, their authenticity as "real" identities is called into question in ways that relate back to cultural stereotypes about the legitimacy and permanency of being LGBTQ.

Fourth, LGBTQ people can seem culturally invisible in part because the stigmatization of LGBTQ people has led to closeting behaviors (Cocks 2003; Sedgwick 1990). Remaining "in the closet" has shaped an overall lack of awareness of LGBTQ people as well as a lack of understanding of their identities. In addition, because being LGBTQ can sometimes be less visible than other minority identity statuses such as race/ethnicity, LGBTQ people and their identities may also be under-recognized, disregarded, and ignored (Firestein 1996). Indeed, LGBTQ people have only started to become culturally recognized as a minority group in the past few decades (Hacker 1971). Together, these processes have contributed to LGBTQ cultural invisibility which in turn relates to the overall questioning of LGBTQ identities as authentic and permanent.

In sum, cultural stereotypes related to the notion that a person can change (or be changed) from hetero-cis to LGBTQ coupled with false interpretations about the coming out process, the relatively recent cultural recognition of LGBTQ identities, and the lack of visibility of LGBTQ people all contribute to the stigmatizing perspective that LGBTQ identities lack permanency. *In the LGBTQ Stigma Scales, this area of stigma is measured with 1 statement aimed at understanding feelings about the permanency of being LGBTQ* (see Table 6.1).

## LGBTQ Stigma and the Achievement of Femininity or Masculinity

Perspectives about femininity and masculinity are embedded in stigmatizing attitudes toward LGBTQ people. Indeed, the cultural stereotypes that men should be masculine and women should be feminine extend beyond perspectives about gender. Specifically, presumptions about gender are built from a larger system of hetero-cis-normative perspectives that intersect with both sex and sexuality. As noted in Chapter 3, the often dichotomous male/female genital labeling/sex marker identification processes that happen when a baby is born lead to presumptions about gender identity, gender performance, and heterosexuality. All of this flows as part of the larger system of hetero-cis-normativity that reinforces the norms of being both cisgender and being heterosexual (recall Figure 3.2). In doing so, those who were labeled as male at birth, who identify as boys and then as men, who perform gender in a masculine way, and identify as heterosexual are socially rewarded for following a hetero-cis-normative path. All LGBTQ people break the assumptions of hetero-cis-normativity in some way and can be stigmatized for doing so.

A key part of this process is the stigmatizing perspective that LGBTQ people are not (nor will they ever be) feminine/masculine "enough" because only hetero-cis people are able to aptly achieve femininity/masculinity.

The perceived inability of LGBTQ people to perform femininity and masculinity in culturally successful ways is evident across multiple processes involved in the stigmatization of LGBTQ people. For example, during times when "homosexuals" have been rejected from certain spaces (e.g., U.S. government employment during the 1950s' Lavender Scare; U.S. military service prior to the 2011 repeal of Don't Ask, Don't Tell, Charles 2015; Worthen 2019), accused "homosexuals" were targeted largely based on their performances of gender. Indeed, men who were not masculine enough or too feminine were suspected of (and labeled as) "homosexuals" and a similar process occurred for women who were not feminine enough or too masculine. In many ways (both then and now), an "unsuccessful" gender performance is a signal that leads to the questioning of hetero-cis-normativity and to the suspicion of being LGBTQ. Interestingly, in their (failed) attempts to change a person from LGBTQ to hetero-cis, conversion therapies often include activities designed to reinforce the links between being a man and behaving in a stereotypically masculine manner (e.g., playing sports, fixing cars, hunting) and being a woman and behaving in a stereotypically feminine manner (e.g., taking care of babies and children, sewing, and beautification rituals involving hair, make-up, nails, etc.) (Erzen 2006; Waidzunas 2015). Overall, however, violations of femininity/masculinity norms can lead to the presumptions that an individual is LGBTQ (e.g., a masculine woman is presumed to be a lesbian) and is thusly deserving of some form of denigration or degradation for inadequately performing femininity/masculinity, for being LGBTQ, or both. Indeed, a fundamental motive driving perpetrators of LGBTQ violent attacks is the desire to reinforce culturally "appropriate" notions of femininity/masculinity through punishing those who violate hetero-cis-normativity (Franklin 1998; Schilt and Westbrook 2009; Wodda and Panfil 2014).

Non-binary/genderqueer people who identify beyond the masculinity/femininity dichotomy are also stigmatized for their inability to achieve "appropriate" masculinity or femininity (Krieger 2017) but the process slightly differs because the cultural stereotype that women/men should be feminine/masculine does not apply well to those who do not identify as women/men in the first place. Instead, the stigmatizing attitudes toward non-binary/genderqueer individuals along this line of inquiry fall into a perspective that non-binary/genderqueer people should just "pick one" (either feminine or masculine) (Frohard-Dourlent et al. 2016; Krieger 2017). The underlying stigmatizing assumption here is also that this process should align with a hetero-cis-normative path as described above (recall also Figure 3.2).

In sum, the presumption that LGBTQ people are unable to suitably achieve femininity/masculinity drives stigmatizing attitudes toward LGBTQ people. These processes are reinforced by hetero-cis-normativity. *In the LGBTQ Stigma Scales, this area of stigma is measured with 1 statement aimed at understanding feelings about the achievement of femininity and masculinity among LGBTQ people. Because this process is slightly different for non-binary/genderqueer people, there is a different (but similar) statement for the Non-binary/Genderqueer Stigma Scale* (see Table 6.1).

## The LGBTQ Stigma Scales and NCST

All fourteen statements provided in Table 6.1 are included in each of the nine LGBTQ stigma scales. However, the six key areas of stigma outlined in this chapter impact LGBTQ people in different ways because attitudes and experiences of LGBTQ people are situated on the *spectrum of stigma* (recall Figure 3.3). In Part II of this book, the nine LGBTQ stigma scales are explored utilizing the theoretical model of NCST specified in Chapters 2 and 3 through both the stigmatizer and stigmatized lenses. In particular, the three tenets of NCST are reinforced through the importance of *norm centrality* (i.e., focus on hetero-cis-normativity) and social power as both *organizational* and *justification* for variations and similarities among the relationships between hetero-cis-normativity, LGBTQ stigma, and social power axes across the nine groups.

## Notes

1 The 44th U.S. President, Barack Obama, was America's first Black President.
2 The 15th U.S. President, James Buchanan, remained a bachelor for his entire life. Some have speculated that he may have been gay (Nikel 2014).
3 The five U.S. Presidents who did not have children were: George Washington, James Polk, Warren Harding, James Buchanan, and Andrew Jackson (Matuz, Harris, and Craughwell 2016).
4 John Adams, John Q. Adams, Millard Fillmore, and William Howard Taft were all affiliated with the Unitarian church which is not explicitly Christian. In addition, Thomas Jefferson, Abraham Lincoln, and Andrew Johnson never specified any formal Christian religious affiliation (Masci 2017).
5 For example, in Russia in 2017, Chechnyan officials reportedly abducted more than 100 gay and bisexual men and placed them into concentration camps where they were beaten and tortured (Mapp and Gabel 2017).
6 In 2018, the FBI indicated that there were 8,819 hate crime offenses reported to law enforcement in the U.S. Among these, 1,445 (16%) were designated as motivated by "sexual orientation" in the categories of "anti-gay (male)," "anti-lesbian," "anti-lesbian, gay, bisexual, or transgender (mixed group)," or "anti-bisexual." In addition, 189 (2%) were designated as motivated by "anti-transgender" or "gender identity-bias" in the categories of "anti-gender non-conforming" (FBI 2018).
7 Originally, Hardwick joined a heterosexual married couple known only as "John and Mary Doe" who were also plaintiffs in the suit. Both Hardwick and "John and Mary Doe" believed that the anti-sodomy laws violated their constitutional right to engage in

consensual sex acts (of oral and anal nature) in the privacy of their own homes (Cliett 2003). However, even though Georgia law prohibited acts of oral and anal sex between *any* persons (regardless of sex, gender, or sexual identity), the Supreme Court determined that "John and Mary Doe" lacked standing to sue because the Justices were interested in focusing squarely on acts of sodomy between people of the same sex, citing their belief that heterosexuals (and their sex acts) upheld the traditional view of family and sex acts between those of the same sex did not. Thus, *Bowers v. Hardwick* (1986) became a case about sodomy acts between persons of the same sex despite the fact that Georgia anti-sodomy statutes prohibited both heterosexual and same-sex acts of sodomy (Worthen 2016).

# References

Allen, Peter. 2018. *The Political Class: Why It Matters Who Our Politicians Are*. Oxford, UK: Oxford University Press.

Allsep, L. Michael. 2013. "The Myth of the Warrior: Martial Masculinity and the End of Don't Ask, Don't Tell." *Journal of Homosexuality* 60(2/3):381–400.

American Psychiatric Association. 1952. *Diagnostic and Statistical Manual of Mental Disorders I*. Washington, D.C.: American Psychiatric Association, Inc.

American Psychiatric Association. 1968. *Diagnostic and Statistical Manual of Mental Disorders II*. Washington, D.C.: American Psychiatric Association, Inc.

American Psychiatric Association. 1974. *Diagnostic and Statistical Manual of Mental Disorders II-Seventh Printing*. Washington, D.C.: American Psychiatric Association, Inc.

American Psychiatric Association. 1980. *Diagnostic and Statistical Manual of Mental Disorders III*. Washington, D.C.: American Psychiatric Association, Inc.

American Psychiatric Association. 1994. *Diagnostic and Statistical Manual of Mental Disorders IV*. Washington, D.C.: American Psychiatric Association, Inc.

American Psychiatric Association. 2013. *Diagnostic and Statistical Manual of Mental Disorders V*. Washington, D.C.: American Psychiatric Association, Inc.

Beachy, Robert. 2010. "The German Invention of Homosexuality." *The Journal of Modern History* 82(4):801–838.

Bogardus, Emory. 1925. "Measuring Social Distances." *Journal of Applied Sociology* 6:299–308.

Bornstein, Kate. 1994. *Gender Outlaw: On Men, Women and the Rest of Us* (1st Edition). New York, NY: Routledge.

*Bowers v. Hardwick*, 478 U.S. 186. 1986.

Brewster, Melanie and Bonnie Moradi. 2010. "Perceived Experiences of Anti-Bisexual Prejudice: Instrument Development and Evaluation." *Journal of Counseling Psychology* 57:451–468.

Caforio, Giuseppe and Marina Nuciari. 2018. *Handbook of the Sociology of the Military*. New York, NY: Springer.

Carroll, Aengus and Lucas Ramón Mendos. 2017. "A World Survey of Sexual Orientation Laws: Criminalisation, Protection, and Recognition." *International Lesbian, Gay, Bisexual, Trans and Intersex Association (ILGA)*.

Centers for Disease Control. 2001. "HIV and AIDS — United States, 1981-2000." *Morbidity and Mortality Weekly Report* 50(21):430–434.

Charles, Douglas. 2015. *Hoover's War on Gays*. Lawrence, KS: Kansas University Press.

Cliett, C. Ray. 2003. "How a Note or a Grope Can Be Justification for the Killing of a Homosexual-An Analysis of the Effects of the Supreme Court's Views on

Homosexuals, African-Americans and Women." *New England Journal on Criminal and Civil Confinement* 29:219–253.

Cocks, H. G. 2003. *Nameless Offences: Homosexual Desire in the 19th Century.* London, UK: I.B.Tauris.

Costa, Pedro Alexandre and Fernando Salinas-Quiroz. 2019. "A Comparative Study of Attitudes toward Same-Gender Parenting and Gay and Lesbian Rights in Portugal and in Mexico." *Journal of Homosexuality* 66(13):1909–1926.

Crawford, Isiaah, Andrew McLeod, Brian D. Zamboni, and Michael B. Jordan. 1999. "Psychologists' Attitudes toward Gay and Lesbian Parenting." *Professional Psychology: Research and Practice* 30(4):394–401.

D'Augelli, Anthony R. 1994. "Identity Development and Sexual Orientation: Toward a Model of Lesbian, Gay and Bisexual Development." Pp. 312–333 in *Human Diversity: Perspectives on People in Context*, edited by Edison J. Trickett, Roderick J. Watts, and Dina Birman. San Francisco, CA, US: Jossey-Bass.

Diamond, Lisa M. 2003. "Was It a Phase? Young Women's Relinquishment of Lesbian/Bisexual Identities over a 5-year Period." *Journal of Personality and Social Psychology* 84(2):352–364.

Diamond, Lisa M. 2008. "Female Bisexuality from Adolescence to Adulthood: Results from a 10-year Longitudinal Study." *Developmental Psychology* 44(1):5–14.

Dowsett, Gilbert. 2009. "The 'Gay Plague' Revisited: AIDS and its Enduring Moral Panic." Pp. 130–156 in *Moral Panics, Sex Panics: Fear and the Fight over Sexual Rights*, edited by Gilbert Herdt. New York, NY: NYU Press.

Dowshen, Nadia, Susan Lee, Joshua Franklin, Marné Castillo, and Frances Barg. 2017. "Access to Medical and Mental Health Services across the HIV Care Continuum among Young Transgender Women: A Qualitative Study." *Transgender Health* 2(1):81–90.

Ender, Morten G., David E. Rohall, and Michael D. Matthews. 2016. "Cadet and Civilian Undergraduate Attitudes toward Transgender People: A Research Note." *Armed Forces & Society* 42(2):427–435.

Erzen, Tanya. 2006. *Straight to Jesus: Sexual and Christian Conversions in the Ex-Gay Movement.* Berkeley, CA: University of California Press.

FBI. 2018. "Hate Crimes Statistics 2018." *FBI.* Retrieved January 8, 2020 (https://ucr.fbi.gov/hate-crime/2018/topic-pages/victims).

Filiault, Shaun M. and Murray J. N. Drummond. 2007. "The Hegemonic Asethetic." *Gay & Lesbian Issues and Psychology Review* 3(3):1–11.

Firestein, Beth A. 1996. *Bisexuality: The Psychology and Politics of an Invisible Minority.* Thousand Oaks, CA, US: Sage Publications, Inc.

Franklin, Karen. 1998. "Unassuming Motivations: Contextualizing the Narratives of Antigay Assailants." Pp. 1–23 in *Stigma and Sexual Orientation: Understanding Prejudice against Lesbians, Gay Men, and Bisexuals*, edited by Gregory M. Herek. Thousand Oaks, CA: Sage Publications.

Frederick, David A. and Melissa R. Fales. 2016. "Upset over Sexual versus Emotional Infidelity among Gay, Lesbian, Bisexual, and Heterosexual Adults." *Archives of Sexual Behavior* 45(1):175–191.

Friedman, Carly K. and Elizabeth M. Morgan. 2009. "Comparing Sexual-Minority and Heterosexual Young Women's Friends and Parents as Sources of Support for Sexual Issues." *Journal of Youth and Adolescence* 38(7):920–936.

Frohard-Dourlent, Hélène, Beth A. Sarah Dobson, Marion Doull Clark, and Elizabeth Saewyc. 2016. "'I Would Have Preferred More Options': Accounting for Non-Binary Youth in Health Research." *Nursing Inquiry* 24(1):e12150.

Hacker, Helen M. 1971. "Homosexuals: Deviant or Minority Group." Pp. 65–92 in *The Other Minorities: Non-ethnic Collectivities Conceptualized as Minority Groups*, edited by E. Sagarin. Waltham, MA: Ginn and Co.

Han, Chong-suk. 2007. "They Don't Want to Cruise Your Type: Gay Men of Color and the Racial Politics of Exclusion." *Social Identities* 13(1):51–67.

Harvard T. H. Chan School of Public Health. 2017. "Poll Finds a Majority of LGBTQ Americans Report Violence, Threats, or Sexual Harassment Related to Sexual Orientation or Gender Identity; One-Third Report Bathroom Harassment." *Harvard*. Retrieved August 26, 2019 (www.hsph.harvard.edu/news/press-releases/poll-lgbtq-americans-discrimination/).

Heath, Jessie and Kathy Goggin. 2009. "Attitudes Towards Male Homosexuality, Bisexuality, and the Down Low Lifestyle: Demographic Differences and HIV Implications." *Journal of Bisexuality* 9(1):17–31.

Heflick, Nathan. 2010. "EWWW. Anal Sex Is Icky!" *Psychology Today*. Retrieved April 1, 2019 (www.psychologytoday.com/us/blog/the-big-questions/201002/ewwwanal-sex-is-icky).

Hennen, Peter. 2008. *Faeries, Bears, and Leathermen: Men in Community Queering the Masculine*. Chicago, IL: University of Chicago Press.

Herek, Gregory M. and John Capitanio. 1999. "AIDS Stigma and Sexual Prejudice." *American Behavioral Scientist* 42(7):1130–1147.

Hinrichs, Donald W. and Pamela J. Rosenberg. 2002. "Attitudes toward Gay, Lesbian, and Bisexual Persons among Heterosexual Liberal Arts College Students." *Journal of Homosexuality* 43(1):61–84.

Human Rights Campaign. 2019. "State Maps of Laws & Policies." *Human Rights Campaign*. Retrieved January 7, 2019 (www.hrc.org/state-maps/).

Humphreys, Laud. 1970. *Tearoom Trade: Impersonal Sex in Public Places*. Piscataway, NJ: Transaction Publishers.

Joos, Kristin E. and K. L. Broad. 2007. "Coming Out of the Family Closet: Stories of Adult Women with LGBTQ Parent(s)." *Qualitative Sociology* 30(3):275–295.

Kafka, Martin. 2010. "Hypersexual Disorder: A Proposed Diagnosis for DSM-V." *Archives of Sexual Behavior* 39(2):377–400.

Khayatt, Didi. 2002. "Toward a Queer Identity." *Sexualities* 5(4):487–501.

King, Mark E., Sam Winter, and Beverley Webster. 2009. "Contact Reduces Transprejudice: A Study on Attitudes Towards Transgenderism and Transgender Civil Rights in Hong Kong." *International Journal of Sexual Health* 21(1):17–34.

Kollman, Kelly. 2016. *The Same-Sex Unions Revolution in Western Democracies*. Manchester, England: Manchester University Press.

Kraus, Shane W., Valerie Voon, and Marc N. Potenza. 2016. "Should Compulsive Sexual Behavior Be Considered an Addiction?: Compulsive Sexual Behavior." *Addiction* 111(12):2097–2106.

Krieger, Irwin. 2017. *Counseling Transgender and Non-Binary Youth: The Essential Guide*. London, UK: Jessica Kingsley Publishers.

Lahti, Martti. 1998. "Dressing Up in Power: Tom of Finland and Gay Male Body Politics." *Journal of Homosexuality* 35(3/4):185–205.

*Lawrence v. Texas*, 539 U.S. 558. 2003.

Lingiardi, Vittorio, Simona Falanga, and Anthony R. D'Augelli. 2005. "The Evaluation of Homophobia in an Italian Sample." *Archives of Sexual Behavior* 34(1):81–93.

Lingiardi, Vittorio, Nicola Nardelli, Salvatore Ioverno, Simona Falanga, Carlo Di Chiacchio, Annalisa Tanzilli, and Roberto Baiocco. 2016. "Homonegativity in Italy: Cultural Issues, Personality Characteristics, and Demographic Correlates with Negative Attitudes toward Lesbians and Gay Men." *Sexuality Research and Social Policy* 13(2):95–108.

Liptack, Adam. 2019. "Supreme Court Revives Transgender Ban for Military Service." *New York Times*, January 22. Retrieved January 28, 2020 (https://www.nytimes.com/2019/01/22/us/politics/transgender-ban-military-supreme-court.html).

Loehr, Annalise, Long Doan, and Lisa R. Miller. 2015. "The Role of Selection Effects in the Contact Hypothesis: Results from a US National Survey on Sexual Prejudice." *Archives of Sexual Behavior* 44(8):2111–2123.

Mapp, Susan and Shirley Gatenio Gabel. 2017. "Government Abuses of Human Rights." *Journal of Human Rights and Social Work* 2(1):1–2.

Masci, David. 2017. "Almost All U.S. Presidents Have Been Christians, Including Trump." *Pew Research Center*. Retrieved August 26, 2019 (www.pewresearch.org/fact-tank/2017/01/20/almost-all-presidents-have-been-christians/).

Matuz, Roger, Bill Harris, and Thomas J. Craughwell. 2016. *The Presidents Fact Book: The Achievements, Campaigns, Events, Triumphs, and Legacies of Every President*. Philadelphia, PA: Running Press Book Publishers.

McKirnan, David J., Joseph P. Stokes, Lynda Doll, and Rebecca G. Burzette. 1995. "Bisexually Active Men: Social Characteristics and Sexual Behavior." *Journal of Sex Research* 32(1):65–76.

Mennicke, Annelise, Jill Gromer, Karen Oehme, and Lindsey MacConnie. 2018. "Workplace Experiences of Gay and Lesbian Criminal Justice Officers in the United States: A Qualitative Investigation of Officers Attending A LGBT Law Enforcement Conference." *Policing and Society* 28(6):712–729.

Meyer, Doug. 2015. *Violence against Queer People: Race, Class, Gender, and the Persistence of Anti-LGBT Discrimination*. New Brunswick, NJ: Rutgers University Press.

Mogul, Joey L., Andrea J. Ritchie, and Kay Whitlock. 2011. *Queer (In)justice: The Criminalization of LGBT People in the United States*. Boston, MA: Beacon Press.

Morse, Edward V., Patricia M. Simon, Howard J. Osofsky, Paul M. Balson, and H. Richard Gaumer. 1991. "The Male Street Prostitute: A Vector for Transmission of HIV Infection into the Heterosexual World." *Social Science & Medicine* 32(5):535–539.

Nikel, Jim. 2014. *The First Gay President?: A Look into the Life and Sexuality of James Buchanan, Jr.* Scotts Valley, CA: Createspace Independent Pub.

Oakley, M. K., Rachel H. Farr, and David G. Scherer. 2017. "Same-Sex Parent Socialization: Understanding Gay and Lesbian Parenting Practices as Cultural Socialization." *Journal of GLBT Family Studies* 13(1):56–75.

Paceley, Megan S., Amanda Hwu, and H. Denise Arizpe. 2017. "Nonmetropolitan Sexual and Gender Minority Youths' Friendships: Perceptions of Social Support among SGM and Non-SGM Peers." *Journal of Gay & Lesbian Social Services* 29(4):399–414.

Pettigrew, Thomas F. and Linda R. Tropp. 2006. "A Meta-Analytic Test of Intergroup Contact Theory." *Journal of Personality and Social Psychology* 90(5):751–783.

Pew Research Center. 2013. "Chapter 2: Social Acceptance." Retrieved February 7, 2019 (www.pewsocialtrends.org/2013/06/13/chapter-2-social-acceptance/).

Pistella, Jessica, Annalisa Tanzilli, Salvatore Ioverno, Vittorio Lingiardi, and Roberto Baiocco. 2018. "Sexism and Attitudes toward Same-Sex Parenting in a Sample of Heterosexuals and Sexual Minorities: The Mediation Effect of Sexual Stigma." *Sexuality Research and Social Policy* 15(2):139–150.

Ali, Rasha. 2020. "Will there be a Draft? How to Answer your Kids' Questions about a Military Draft." *USA Today*, January 6. Retrieved January 30, 2020 (https://www.usatoday.com/story/life/parenting/2020/01/06/military-draft-how-answer-your-kids-questions-draft/2823826001/).

Rupp, Leila J. and Verta Taylor. 2010. "Straight Girls Kissing." *Contexts* 9(3):28–32.

Schilt, Kristen and Laurel Westbrook. 2009. "Doing Gender, Doing Heteronormativity: 'Gender Normals,' Transgender People, and the Social Maintenance of Heterosexuality." *Gender & Society* 23(4):440–464.

Sedgwick, Eve Kosofsky. 1990. *Epistemology of the Closet*. Berkeley, CA: University of California Press.

Sinclair, Dean. 2009. "Homosexuality and the Military: A Review of the Literature." *Journal of Homosexuality* 56(6):701–718.

Spalding, Leah R. and Letitia Anne Peplau. 1997. "The Unfaithful Lover." *Psychology of Women Quarterly* 21(4):611–624.

Stryker, Susan. 2008. *Transgender History*. Berkeley, CA: Seal Press.

Symonides, Janusz. 2017. *Human Rights: Concept and Standards*. New York, NY: Routledge.

Taylor, Henry. 2015. "Who Is the World's Biggest Employer? the Answer Might Not Be What You Expect." *World Economic Forum*. Retrieved August 26, 2019 (www.weforum.org/agenda/2015/06/worlds-10-biggest-employers/).

Taylor, Lin. 2017. "Fewer Countries Ban Same-Sex Relations, but Homophobic Violence Common." *Reuters*. Retrieved August 26, 2019 (www.reuters.com/article/global-lgbt-laws-idUSL8N1IE3J5).

United Nations. 2015. "Universal Declaration of Human Rights." Retrieved January 7, 2019 (www.un.org/en/universal-declaration-human-rights/).

Vecho, Olivier, Martine Gross, Emmanuel Gratton, Salvatore D'Amore, and Robert-Jay Green. 2019. "Attitudes toward Same-Sex Marriage and Parenting, Ideologies, and Social Contacts: The Mediation Role of Sexual Prejudice Moderated by Gender." *Sexuality Research and Social Policy* 16(1):44–57.

Waidzunas, Tom. 2015. *The Straight Line: How the Fringe Science of Ex-Gay Therapy Reoriented Sexuality*. Minneapolis, MN: University of Minnesota Press.

Wandrey, Rachael L., Katie E. Mosack, and Erin M. Moore. 2015. "Coming Out to Family and Friends as Bisexually Identified Young Adult Women: A Discussion of Homophobia, Biphobia, and Heteronormativity." *Journal of Bisexuality* 15(2):204–229.

Wilchins, Riki Anne. 1997. *Read My Lips: Sexual Subversion and the End of Gender*. Ithaca, NY: Firebrand Books.

Williams, Robin M. 1964. *Strangers Next Door: Ethnic Relations in American Communities*. Englewood Cliffs, NJ: Prentice-Hall.

Wodda, Aimee and Vanessa R. Panfil. 2014. "Don't Talk to Me about Deception: The Necessary Erosion of the Trans Panic Defense." *Albany Law Review* 78:927–972.

Worthen, Meredith G. F. 2013. "An Argument for Separate Analyses of Attitudes toward Lesbian, Gay, Bisexual Men, Bisexual Women, MtF and FtM Transgender Individuals." *Sex Roles* 68(11):703–723.

Worthen, Meredith G. F. 2016. *Sexual Deviance and Society: A Sociological Examination*. London, UK: Routledge.

Worthen, Meredith G. F. 2019. "Transgender under Fire: Hetero-cis-normativity and Military Students' Attitudes toward Trans Issues and Trans Service Members Post DADT." *Sexuality Research and Social Policy* 16(3):289–308.

Worthen, Meredith G. F., Annalisa Tanzilli, Chiara Caristo, and Vittorio Lingiardi. 2019. "Social Contact, Social Distancing, and Attitudes toward LGT Individuals: A Cross-Cultural Study of Heterosexual College Students in the United States, Italy, and Spain." *Journal of Homosexuality* 66(13):1882–1908.

Yerke, Adam and Vallory Mitchell. 2013. "Transgender People in the Military: Don't Ask? Don't Tell? Don't Enlist!" *Journal of Homosexuality* 60(2/3):436–457.

# PART II
# NCST and Understanding LGBTQ Stigma

# 7
# PART II OVERVIEW

Building from the arguments and tools provided throughout Part I of this book, Part II examines the stigmatization of LGBTQ people through one of the first-ever empirical investigations of NCST. Specifically, I utilize the theoretical model of NCST specified in Chapters 2 and 3 and the LGBTQ Stigma Scales described in Chapter 6 to investigate how hetero-cis-normativity and violations of hetero-cis-normativity, as well as multiple axes of social power (gender, sexuality, race, ethnicity, basic needs) and intersections among these, relate to stigma directed toward nine LGBTQ groups: lesbian women (Chapter 8), gay men (Chapter 9), bisexual women (Chapter 10), bisexual men (Chapter 11), transgender women (Chapter 12), transgender men (Chapter 13), non-binary/genderqueer people (Chapter 14), queer women (Chapter 15), and queer men (Chapter 16). In doing so, specific stereotypes that are particularly entwined with hetero-cis-normativity and LGBTQ stigma are highlighted as they relate to the stigmatizer lens and the stigmatizers' intersecting identities and experiences with social power. In addition, LGBTQ peoples' experiences with gender- and sexuality-based discrimination, harassment, and violence (DHV) are explored from the stigmatized lens with careful attention to LGBTQ peoples' intersecting identities. The overarching goal of Part II is to provide a nuanced investigation of LGBTQ stigma that is both theory driven and empirically based.

## Part II Data, Sample, and Survey

### Data and Recruitment

The data were collected by the University of Oklahoma Public Opinion Learning Laboratory (OU POLL) using panelists recruited from Research Now/Survey

Sampling International (SSI), an international survey research and survey sample provider with over 60 million global and 12 million U.S. online panel participants. For this study, only those residing in the U.S. were contacted to participate. Panel members are recruited from online communities, social networks, and other areas on the Internet. SSI profiles, authenticates, and verifies each panel member as a reliable respondent for rigorous research participation. SSI awards incentives to respondents in the form of gift cards, points programs, charitable contributions, and partner products or services upon survey completion.

For the current study, 166,467 total email invites were sent to respondents. It is unknown how many of these emails were actually received and read by the potential respondents so an exact response rate is also unknown. For example, junk mail filters could have prevented potential respondents from seeing the email invitation, some may have opened the email but decided not to click the link to access the survey, and some may have been deemed ineligible due to identity quotas being met as requested by the author and set by SSI (see below for more information about the identity quotas). In all, 4,583 surveys were started and a total of 3,104 surveys were fully completed which serve as the current study's data.

## *Sampling Frames and Sample Characteristics*

A nationally representative sample of U.S. adults aged 18–64 stratified by U.S. census categories of age, gender, race, ethnicity, and census region was obtained (see Appendix A for comparisons between the survey data and the U.S. census). For the first sampling frame, a total of 63,466 email invites were sent out to *only* heterosexual-cisgender potential respondents. A quota of 1,500 respondents (750 hetero-cis men and 750 hetero-cis women) was requested and met (n = 1,500). For the second sampling frame, a total of 103,001 email invites were sent out to *only* LGBT potential respondents. A quota of 1,520 respondents (330 each of lesbian women, gay men, bisexual women, bisexual men; 100 each of trans women and trans men) was requested and exceeded for lesbian women (n = 346), gay men (n = 345), and bisexual women (n = 358); however, quotas were not met for bisexual men (n = 314), trans women (n = 74), nor trans men (n = 55). The total LGBTQ sample, including those who identify as non-binary/genderqueer (n = 95), pansexual (n = 79), and asexual (n = 45) (no quotas were set for these groups) was n = 1,604. Throughout Part II, these two groups are referred to as the hetero-cis subsample (n = 1,500) and the LGBTQ subsample (n = 1,604).

## *Survey Design and Implementation*

The author created the survey instrument and OU POLL was responsible for programming and testing the questionnaire with Qualtrics (an online survey platform). OU POLL also managed data collection activities in collaboration with

SSI. The survey was live on the Internet from November 5, 2018 to November 23, 2018. Panelists could access the survey via desktops, laptops, tablets, and mobile phones. The survey included 184 closed-ended questions with both multiple- and single-response items. The average time to complete the survey was 25.8 minutes. The survey was held open for 19 days in efforts to meet the quotas set for the LGBT groups (described above). Five quotas were met as follows: gay men (5 days in), bisexual women (7 days in), lesbian women (8 days in), cis men and cis women (16 days in). The quotas for the remaining three groups (bisexual men, trans women, and trans men) were not met. The survey was closed because SSI believed it was not realistic to expect these quotas to fill in a reasonable amount of time.

## Part II Chapter Organization and Overview

Each chapter in Part II includes three methods to investigate LGBTQ stigma: (1) rank-ordering and *t*-test comparisons of the LGBTQ Stigma Scales and individual scale items; (2) Ordinary Least Squares (OLS) regression models of NCST, social power axes, and the LGBTQ Stigma Scales; and (3) logistic regression models of NCST and LGBTQ gender- and sexuality-based DHV. These methods are further described below. In addition, I also provide an overview of the overarching trends and patterns that are found throughout Part II using these three methods of investigation. Because they are reviewed here, they are not discussed in the individual chapters for each of the LGBTQ groups.

## The LGBTQ Stigma Scales

In each chapter, the key areas of each LGBTQ Stigma Scale are explored first. All fourteen items in each of the nine scales are rank-ordered from most to least stigmatizing to highlight the mechanisms that are contributing most and least to the stigmatization of each group. In addition, all fourteen items in each of the nine LGBTQ Stigma Scales are investigated using *t*-tests to compare hetero-cis and LGBTQ people's attitudes. Overall, there are six patterns found across the investigations of the LGBTQ Stigma Scales, which are discussed below.

### *LGBTQ Stigma Scales Pattern #1*

*The mean values for all items on all nine scales demonstrate low to moderate LGBTQ stigma with no items reflecting strong LGBTQ negativity (no means greater than 3.0 for any group) for either subsample.*

Overall, most do not harbor strongly adverse attitudes toward LGBTQ people in this study's sample. Such findings may indicate increasing support of LGBTQ people in the U.S., which is also reflected by more LGBTQ visibility and more rights for LGBTQ people (Gallup 2019; Pew Research Center 2017). Even so, the variation across the LGBTQ stigma scales indicates that there are important nuances among attitudes toward these nine groups that deserve further attention.

## LGBTQ Stigma Scales Pattern #2

*For both the hetero-cis and LGBTQ subsamples, the rank ordering (from most to least stigmatized) of the nine LGBTQ groups based on the LGBTQ Stigma Scale mean values is as follows: (1) non-binary/genderqueer people; (2) trans men; (3) queer men; (4) trans women; (5) queer women; (6) bisexual men; (7) gay men; (8) bisexual women; and (9) lesbian women (see Figure 7.1).*

It is noteworthy that both the hetero-cis and LGBTQ subsamples followed identical patterns in their stigmatization of LGBTQ people. For example, both groups express the most hostility toward non-binary/genderqueer people. This finding suggests that among these nine LGBTQ groups, non-binary/genderqueer people are perhaps the most misunderstood (see more in Chapter 14). Indeed, research on non-binary/genderqueer individuals and their experiences is lacking in comparison to the other LGBTQ groups identified in this book (for exceptions

| LGBTQ Group | LGBTQ Subsample | Hetero-cis Subsample |
|---|---|---|
| Non-binary/Genderqueer People | 27.66 | 36.85 |
| Trans Men | 26.69 | 36.42 |
| Queer Men | 26.57 | 36.28 |
| Trans Women | 26.25 | 35.91 |
| Queer Women | 26.13 | 35.70 |
| Bisexual Men | 24.97 | 34.74 |
| Gay Men | 24.89 | 34.19 |
| Bisexual Women | 24.82 | 34.08 |
| Lesbian Women | 24.27 | 33.25 |

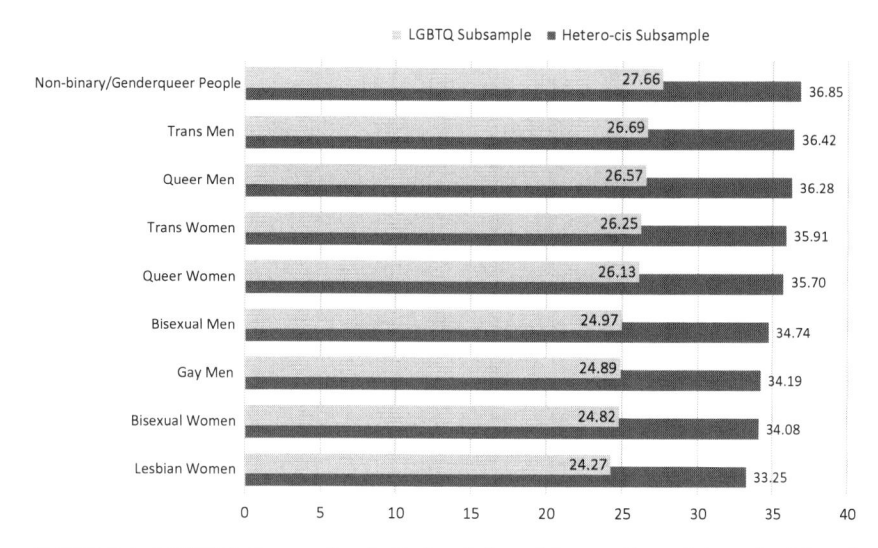

**FIGURE 7.1** LGBTQ Groups Rank Ordered from Most to Least Stigmatized based on the LGBTQ Stigma Scale Summed Total Mean Values for the Hetero-Cis (n = 1,500) and the LGBTQ (n = 1,604) Subsamples*

* *t*-test results comparing the hetero-cis and LGBTQ subsamples indicate that all means are significantly different from one another at the $p < .001$ level.

*Note:* see Tables 8.1, 9.1, 10.1, 11.1, 12.1, 13.1, 14.1, 15.1, and 16.1 for the items that comprise each of these scales and their mean values.

see Aparicio-García et al. 2018; Clarke 2018; Matsuno and Budge 2017; Richards, Bouman, and Barker 2017; Stachowiak 2017). In contrast, both hetero-cis and LGBTQ subsamples indicate the most support of lesbian women. Lesbian women may be perceived as most acceptable in comparison to the other groups due to overlapping stereotypes about their gender and sexual identities (see more in Chapter 8).

## LGBTQ Stigma Scales Pattern #3

*Hetero-cis individuals are significantly more stigmatizing toward LGBTQ people than LGBTQ people are as indicated by* t-*test comparisons in means for the LGBTQ Stigma Scale items for all nine groups (see note in Figure 7.1).*

Overall, such findings are not surprising because compared to heterosexual people, LGBTQ people have been found to be more interested in supporting other LGBTQ people. For example, a large-scale study (N = 3,519) of the American National Election Surveys found that LGB people were more than twenty times more likely than heterosexual people to participate in LGB social justice movements in their lifetimes (20.4% compared to .9%) (Swank 2018). In addition, due to their own (likely more frequent) experiences with sex act-related stigma, LGBTQ people tend to be less stigmatizing toward LGBTQ sex acts and sexualities than hetero-cis people are. Overall, because LGBTQ people's identities and gender expressions are called into question, invalidated, and perceived to be inauthentic much more often than hetero-cis people's identities and gender expressions are (Alegría 2018; Eliason 1996; Grossman et al. 2005; Weiss 2004), LGBTQ people may be more inclined to support other LGBTQ people who experience similar negativities and hostilities.

## LGBTQ Stigma Scales Pattern #4

*The Basic Human Rights key area has the lowest mean values across all nine LGBTQ Stigma Scales for both the hetero-cis and LGBTQ subsamples (see Figure 7.2).*

Most people in this study agree that LGBTQ people should have basic human rights. Generalized support of LGBTQ people and their rights is evident across other research as well. For example, Pew Research Center data (2013) indicate that the majority of LGBT adults believe there is "a lot" or "some" social acceptance of lesbian women (85%), bisexual women (78%), and gay men (71%). However, just over half believe that bisexual men (52%) are socially accepted and a minority (18%) believe that trans people experience social acceptance (Pew Research Center 2013). At the crux of generalized support of marginalized people is often the inclusion of those once viewed as "deviant others" in laws and policies involving basic human rights. Most in this sample support basic human rights for LGB people which reflects a small but growing trend

**130** NCST and Understanding LGBTQ Stigma

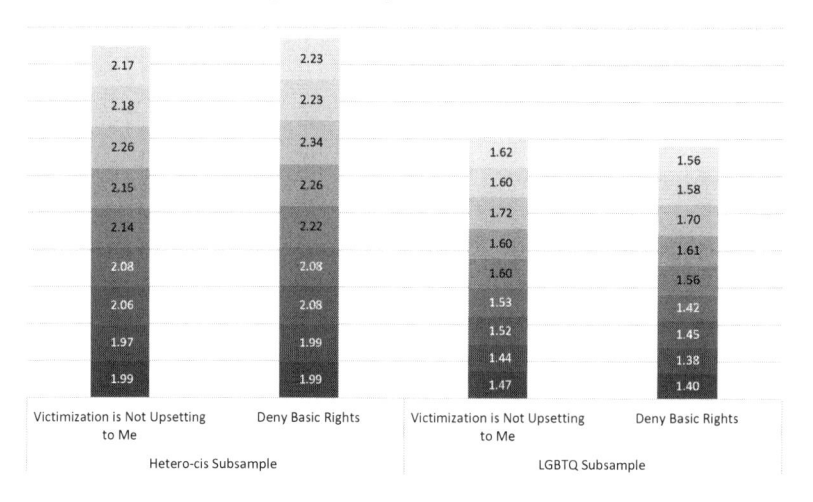

**FIGURE 7.2** Mean Values of the Two LGBTQ Stigma Scale Items in the Basic Human Rights Key Area for the Hetero-Cis (n = 1,500) and the LGBTQ (n = 1,604) Subsamples*

* *t*-test results comparing the hetero-cis and LGBTQ subsamples indicate that all means are significantly different from one another at the p < .001 level.

across the globe in the recognition of LGB people having the legal right to marry as well as legal protections from discrimination and the legal recognition of hate crimes based on sexual identity (Carroll and Mendos 2017). However, bisexuals are sometimes excluded from human rights discourse (Marcus 2015) and trans, non-binary/genderqueer, and queer individuals are often disregarded and underrepresented in these conversations (Clarke 2018; Human Rights Campaign 2018; Matsuno and Budge 2017). Indeed, compared to LGB people, trans, non-binary/genderqueer, and queer people experience the most stigma when it comes to basic human rights (see Figure 7.2).

## *LGBTQ Stigma Scales Pattern #5*

*Amongst the key areas with the highest mean values in LGBTQ Stigma Scales, sex act-related stigma is evident in the stigmatization of all nine LGBTQ groups for both the hetero-cis and LGBTQ subsamples (see Figure 7.3).*

Most LGBTQ people endure at least some negativity associated with their sexualities and/or sexual behaviors. For example, historically, the DSM-I (1952) and DSM-II (1968) diagnosis criteria for "homosexuality" as a "mental illness" focused nearly exclusively on a patient's report of same-sex desire and/or same-sex sexual behaviors (American Psychiatric Association 1952, 1968). Trans and non-binary/

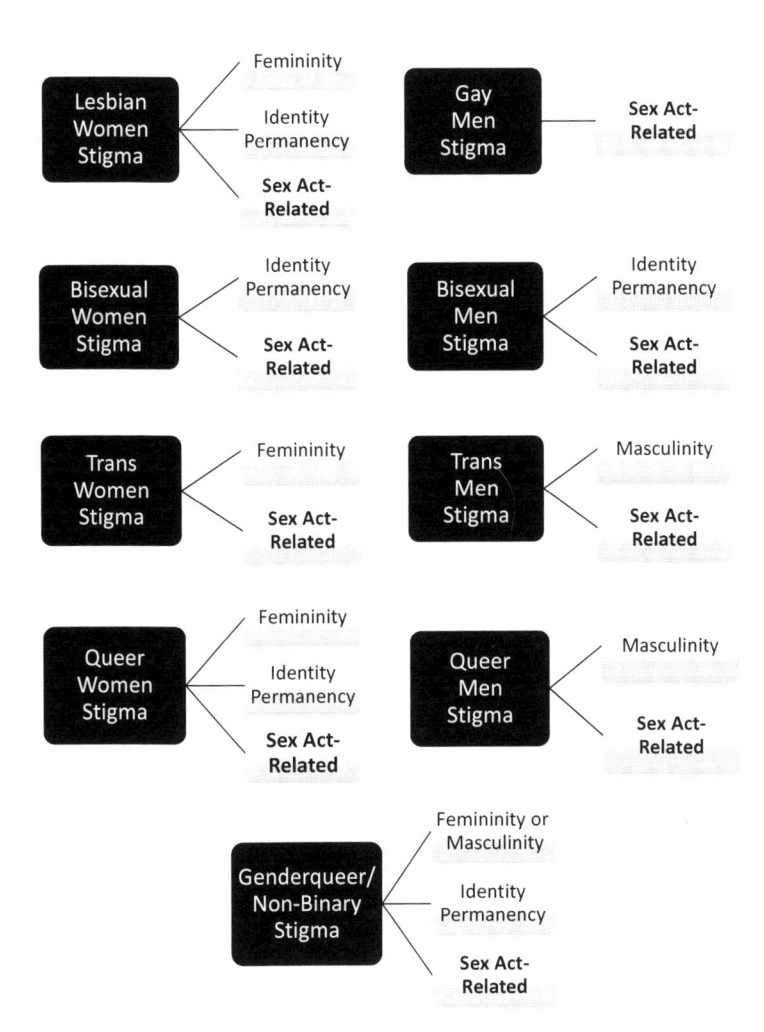

**FIGURE 7.3** Key Areas with the Highest Mean Values in LGBTQ Stigma Scales for Each LGBTQ Group

*Note*: for details about each of the LGBTQ Stigma Scales, see Tables 8.1–16.1 and Figures 8.2–16.2.

genderqueer people were often swept into the "homosexual" diagnosis as well (though "transvestism" was a potential diagnosis in the DSM-I and DSM-II). Largely, the diagnosis of "homosexuality" was due to the perceived "deviancy" of non-hetero-cis-normativity. Thus, attitudes toward same-sex sexual acts have largely been at the core of LGBTQ stigma (especially as related to being thought of as "mentally ill") and often remain so today (see more in Chapter 6).

**132** NCST and Understanding LGBTQ Stigma

### *LGBTQ Stigma Scales Pattern #6*

*The three groups with the highest means for the five items that comprise the sex act-related stigma key area are: (1) gay men (discomfort with sex with a man (for hetero-cis subsample), discomfort with sex with a woman (for both subsamples), and too hypersexual (for the LGBTQ subsample)); (2) bisexual men (unfaithful for both subsamples), and (3) queer men (too hypersexual (for the hetero-cis subsample) and responsible for HIV/AIDS (for both subsamples)) (see Figure 7.4).*

Sex act-related stigma is strongest for gay, bisexual, and queer men. These groups are stigmatized due to stereotypes and negative judgements about the sex acts they are believed to be involved in (i.e., penile–anal sex) as well as other culturally embedded stereotypes about sex, gender, and sexuality, such as the role of masculinity and insertive/receptive partners in sex acts. Indeed, problematic reactions to penile–anal sex between men, including discomfort and disgust, may be especially common (Heflick 2010). In addition, gay, bisexual, and queer men can be perceived as promiscuous, obsessed with sex (read: penile–anal sex), and unfaithful to their romantic partners (Frederick and Fales 2016; McDavitt and Mutchler 2014; Galupo, Lomash, and Mitchell 2017; Spalding and Peplau 1997). Furthermore, HIV/AIDS has also been most commonly associated with gay, bisexual, and queer men (Dowsett 2009; Herek and Capitanio 1999). As a result, sex act-related stigma directed toward gay, bisexual, and queer men involves responses to particular sexual behaviors believed to take place during sex acts between men, as well as stereotypes about hypersexuality, unfaithfulness, and HIV/AIDS (see more in Chapters 9, 11, and 16).

## NCST, Social Power Axes, and the LGBTQ Stigma Scales

In each chapter, the second method of investigation examines NCST to explore each LGBTQ Stigma Scale through the stigmatizer lens. Specifically, OLS regression is utilized to investigate the relationships among the HCN Scale, gender, sexuality, additional gender/sexuality, race/ethnicity, and basic needs as they relate to each LGBTQ Stigma Scale for the hetero-cis subsample and the LGBTQ subsample (see Appendix A for more details about why OLS regression was chosen).

### *Modeling Strategy*

In line with the theoretical model and hypotheses of NCST's stigmatizer lens, Model 1 includes the HCN Scale, social power axes, and controls. Specifically, all of the following social power axes are included for both subsamples: additional gender/sexual identity (queer, SGL, Two-Spirit, butch, femme, leather, bear, twink, Down Low), racial identity (Caucasian/White (reference category), African American/Black, Asian American/Pacific Islander, Native American/Alaskan Native, Multiracial, Latinx race, other race), ethnic identity (Latinx ethnicity), and basic needs (everything I need (reference category), mostly all I need, often needs not met, and

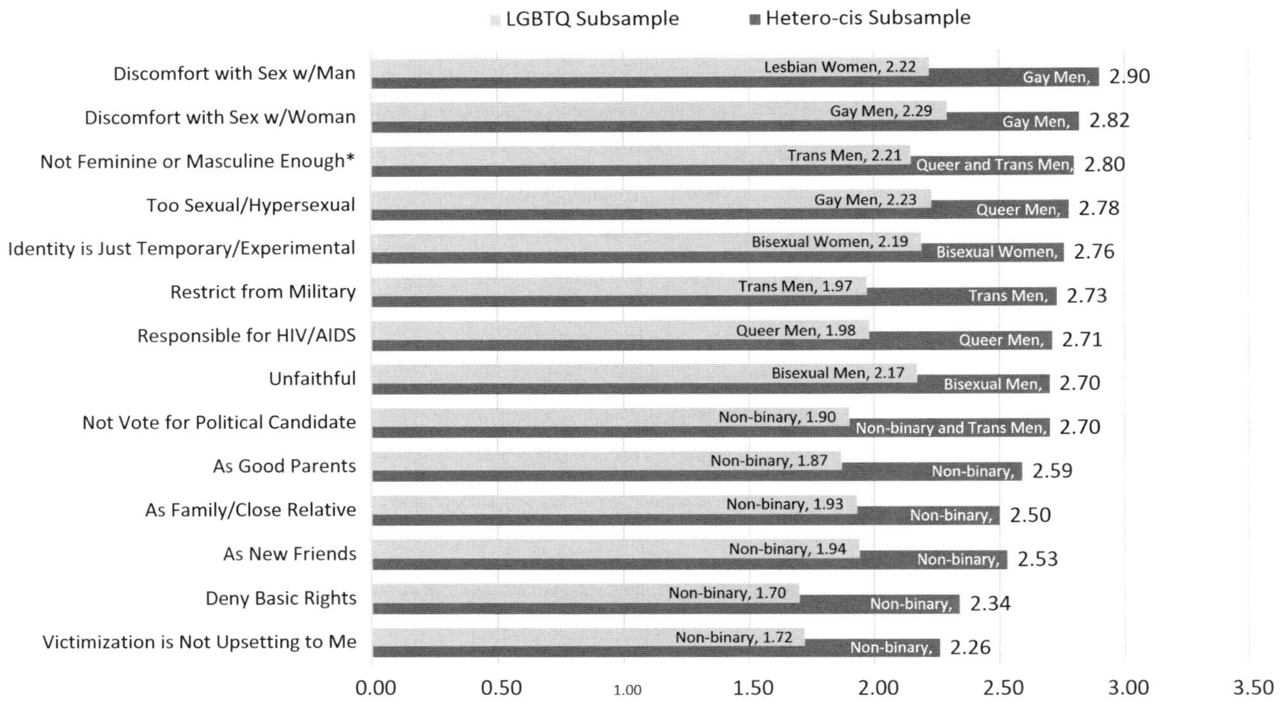

**FIGURE 7.4** LGBTQ Groups with the Highest Means for the Individual LGBTQ Stigma Scale Items for the Hetero-cis (n = 1,500) and LGBTQ (n = 1,604) Subsamples

* The similar item for the Non-binary/Genderqueer Stigma Scale was not included in this comparison.

few needs met). However, for the hetero-cis subsample, no sexual identity categories are explored (because everyone is heterosexual) and the gender identity categories are only cis man (reference category) and cis woman. For the LGBTQ subsample, sexual identities include gay/lesbian (reference category), bisexual, pansexual, and asexual, and gender identity includes cis man (reference category), cis woman, trans woman, trans man, and non-binary/genderqueer. See Table 7.1 for more information about the independent variables utilized in the models.

**TABLE 7.1** Description and Mean Values (Standard Deviations) for Independent Variables by the Hetero-Cis (n = 1,500) and LGBTQ (n = 1,604) Subsamples with *t*-test Results*

| Variable Name | Range | Survey Item/Description of Variable | Hetero-Cis Subsample Mean | LGBTQ Subsample Mean | |
|---|---|---|---|---|---|
| HCN Scale ($\alpha$ = .96; .96) | 6–30 | Sum of six items, see Table 5.1. | 15.10 (7.08) | 9.71 (5.85) | * |
| *Gender identity: what best describes your gender?* | | | | | |
| Cis man | 0–1 | I identify as a man and my assigned sex at birth was male. | .50 (.50) | .42 (.49) | * |
| Cis woman | 0–1 | I identify as a woman and my assigned sex at birth was female. | .50 (.50) | .44 (.50) | * |
| Trans woman | 0–1 | I am transgender: I identify as a woman and my assigned sex at birth was male. | — | .05 (.21) | |
| Trans man | 0–1 | I am transgender: I identify as a man and my assigned sex at birth was female. | — | .03 (.18) | |
| Non–binary/ genderqueer | 0–1 | I am gender non–binary, gender fluid, or genderqueer and my assigned sex at birth was male. Or I am gender non–binary, gender fluid, or genderqueer and my assigned sex at birth was female. | — | .06 (.24) | |
| *Sexual identity: how would you describe yourself?* | | | | | |
| Heterosexual | 0-1 | Heterosexual or straight | 1.0 | .03 (.17) | * |
| Gay or lesbian | 0-1 | Gay or lesbian | — | .45 (.50) | |
| Bisexual | 0-1 | Bisexual | — | .45 (.50) | |
| Pansexual | 0-1 | Pansexual | — | .05 (.22) | |
| Asexual | 0-1 | Asexual | — | .03 (.17) | |

(*Continued*)

**TABLE 7.1** (Cont.)

| Variable Name | Range | Survey Item/Description of Variable | Hetero-Cis Subsample Mean | LGBTQ Subsample Mean | |
|---|---|---|---|---|---|
| *Additional sexual/gender identity: "I identify as ..." (select all that apply).* | | | | | |
| Queer | 0–1 | Queer | .05 (.22) | .20 (.40) | * |
| SGL | 0–1 | Same–gender–loving (SGL) | .04 (.20) | .18 (.38) | * |
| Two–Spirit | 0–1 | Two–Spirit | .05 (.22) | .06 (.24) | |
| Butch | 0–1 | Butch | .02 (.14) | .08 (.27) | * |
| Femme | 0–1 | Femme | .05 (.22) | .14 (.35) | * |
| Leather | 0–1 | Leatherman/Leather | .02 (.15) | .02 (.15) | |
| Bear | 0–1 | Bear | .04 (.19) | .06 (.23) | * |
| Twink | 0–1 | Twink | .03 (.17) | .03 (.18) | |
| Down Low | 0–1 | Down Low | .03 (.14) | .06 (.24) | * |
| *Racial identity: please select the racial category with which you most closely identify.* | | | | | |
| Caucasian/White | 0–1 | Caucasian/White | .77 (.42) | .79 (.41) | |
| African American/Black | 0–1 | African American/Black | .10 (.30) | .09 (.29) | |
| Asian American/Pacific Islander | 0–1 | Asian American/Pacific Islander | .08 (.27) | .05 (.21) | * |
| Native American/Alaskan Native | 0–1 | Native American/Alaskan Native | .01 (.12) | .02 (.14) | |
| Multi–racial | 0–1 | Multi–racial | .02 (.14) | .03 (.18) | * |
| Other race | 0–1 | Other (please specify) Includes those who responded to "Please select the racial category with which you most closely identify" with "Other race" and wrote in responses that did not fit into any of the existing racial categories. In addition, those who responded with "Middle Eastern" were collapsed into the "Other race" category due to the small number of "Middle Eastern" respondents. See Appendix B, Table B.2. | .01 (.07) | .01 (.10) | |

(*Continued*)

**TABLE 7.1** (Cont.)

| Variable Name | Range | Survey Item/Description of Variable | Hetero-Cis Subsample Mean | LGBTQ Subsample Mean |
|---|---|---|---|---|
| Latinx race | 0–1 | Includes those who responded to "Please select the racial category with which you most closely identify" with "Other Race" and wrote in responses that were Latinx–oriented. See Appendix B, Table B.3. | .01 (.09) | .01 (.09) |

*Ethnic identity: are you Hispanic or Latino/a/x? (A person of Cuban, Mexican, Puerto Rican, South or Central American or other Spanish culture of origin regardless of race).*

| Latinx ethnicity | 0–1 | Response options: No/Yes | .14 (.35) | .13 (.34) |

*Basic Needs: How would you describe your life currently?*

| Everything I need | 0–1 | I have more than enough and everything I need, and so do the other family members in my household. | .33 (.47) | .25(.43)* |
| Mostly all I need | 0–1 | I have mostly everything I need for myself and so do the other family members in my household. | .47 (.50) | .53 (.50)* |
| Often basic needs not met | 0–1 | I often go without things I need and so do the other family members in my household. | .15 (.36) | .17 (.38) |
| Few needs met | 0–1 | Very few of my own and my household family members' basic needs are met. | .04 (.20) | .05 (.22) |

*Notes:* the two Cronbach alpha (α) scores reported for the HCN Scale listed in this table were computed for both the hetero-cis subsample (listed first) and LGBTQ subsample (listed second).

* *t*-test results allowing for unequal variances indicate that the hetero-cis and LGBTQ subsample means are significantly different from one another at the $p < .05$ level.

In Model 2, interaction terms between the HCN Scale and all social power axes are included as well as interaction terms between all social power axes. The HCN Scale interaction terms were created by multiplying the HCN Scale with all gender, sexual, additional gender/sexual, racial/ethnic, and basic needs identities. Because the HCN Scale is a continuous variable, the "c." prefix was utilized in STATA to construct the interaction terms between the HCN Scale and all social power axes. In addition, social power axes interaction terms were created by multiplying all gender, sexual, additional gender/sexual, racial/

ethnic, and basic needs identities together in dyads. However, to avoid extremely small cell sizes with inadequate power, only the interaction effects with n > 25 were included in these models (Van Voorhis and Morgan 2007). See Appendix B, Table B.1 for more details about the interaction effects.

## Controls

Aligning with the discussion provided in Chapter 4, all models for both subsamples include the following common explanations as controls: friends with LGBTQ group of interest, LGBTQ Friends Scales without the LGBTQ group of interest, religiousness, religious attendance, scriptural/biblical literalism, religious identities, liberal-conservative, openness to new experiences, support for laws/policies that help (1) those in poverty, (2) racial/ethnic minorities, (3) immigrants, (4) women, and (5) non-Christians, feminist identity, and the Patriarchal Gender Norms Scale. In addition, all models include the following sociodemographic controls: age, Northern U.S., Midwestern U.S., Western U.S., Southern U.S. (reference category), outside U.S., town type (rural–large city), education, and income. See Table 7.2 for more information about the control variables utilized in the models.

## Goodness of Fit and Post-Estimation Comparisons

Multicollinearity was examined using STATA command "collin" (Ender 2010) which provides collinearity diagnostics for all variables. The mean VIF values are reported for each model and suggest no problems with multicollinearity for any model (Allison 2012). To compare the findings between the two subsamples, Clogg et al.'s test was run using the post-estimation SUEST command in STATA (Clogg, Petkova, and Haritou 1995). The test of difference column in each table reports the comparisons of the significant findings in Model 2 between the hetero-cis subsample and the LGBTQ subsample.

Overall, there are sixteen patterns found across all of the investigations of NCST, the social power axes, and the LGBTQ Stigma Scales. These are organized and discussed below as they pertain to both subsamples, to the hetero-cis subsample (only), and to the LGBTQ subsample (only). Patterns related to common explanations and sociodemographic controls found in both subsamples are also provided. It is important to note that some of the overarching patterns discussed here also have corresponding significant effects in some models. For example, for the LGBTQ subsample, the individual effect of being SGL is *negatively* related to the Lesbian Women Stigma Scale but also, the interaction effects of being SGL and being gay/lesbian and of being SGL and bisexual are both *positively* related to the stigmatization of lesbian women (see Table 8.2). However, because the goal of this chapter is to review commonly found trends and patterns across all models, these less frequent corresponding significant effects are not discussed here. Even so, the patterns reviewed in this chapter should be considered as embedded within models that have distinct features.

**TABLE 7.2** Description and Mean Values (Standard Deviations) for Control Variables by the Hetero-Cis (n = 1,500) and LGBTQ (n = 1,604) Subsamples with t-test Results*

| Variable Name | Range | Survey Item/Description of Variable | Hetero-Cis Subsample Mean | LGBTQ Subsample Mean | |
|---|---|---|---|---|---|
| **Common explanations** | | | | | |
| *Friendships: I have friends who are (select all that apply):* | | | | | |
| Lesbian women friends | 0–1 | Lesbian women | .56 (.50) | .75 (.44) | * |
| Gay men friends | 0–1 | Gay men | .61 (.49) | .81 (.39) | * |
| Bisexual women friends | 0–1 | Bisexual women | .23 (.42) | .60 (.49) | * |
| Bisexual men friends | 0–1 | Bisexual men | .23 (.42) | .56 (.50) | * |
| Trans women friends | 0–1 | Transgender women | .09 (.28) | .29 (.46) | * |
| Trans men friends | 0–1 | Transgender men | .32 (.47) | .32 (.47) | |
| Non-binary friends | 0–1 | Non-binary people | .19 (.39) | .25 (.43) | * |
| Genderqueer friends | 0–1 | Genderqueer people | .04 (.21) | .19 (.39) | * |
| Queer women friends | 0–1 | Queer women | .07 (.26) | .25 (.43) | * |
| Queer men friends | 0–1 | Queer men | .09 (.29) | .27 (.44) | * |
| GBTQ Friends Scale w/o lesbian women friends ($\alpha$ = .62; $\alpha$ =.83) | 0–9 | All friendship items summed without lesbian women friends included. | 1.73 (1.60) | 3.54 (2.62) | * |
| LBTQ Friends Scale w/o gay men friends ($\alpha$ = .63; $\alpha$ =.83) | 0–9 | All friendship items summed without gay men friends included. | 1.68 (1.62) | 3.47 (2.66) | * |
| LGBTQ Friends Scale w/o bisexual women friends ($\alpha$ = .58; $\alpha$ =.82) | 0–9 | All friendship items summed without bisexual women friends included. | 1.97 (1.54) | 3.69 (2.54) | * |
| LGBTQ Friends Scale w/o bisexual men friends ($\alpha$ = .55; $\alpha$ =.83) | 0–9 | All friendship items summed without bisexual men friends included. | 2.07 (1.54) | 3.73 (2.55) | * |
| LGBTQ Friends Scale w/o trans women friends ($\alpha$ = .67; $\alpha$ =.81) | 0–9 | All friendship items summed without trans women friends included. | 2.21 (1.65) | 3.99 (2.53) | * |

| | | | | |
|---|---|---|---|---|
| LGBTQ Friends Scale w/o trans men friends ($\alpha$ =.67; $\alpha$ =.81) | 0–9 | All friendship items summed without trans men friends included. | 2.21 (1.64) | 3.96 (2.51) | * |
| LGBT Friends Scale w/o non-binary/genderqueer friends ($\alpha$ = .68; $\alpha$ =.79) | 0–8 | All friendship items summed without non-binary friends and genderqueer friends included. | 2.06 (1.72) | 3.84 (2.30) | * |
| LGBTQ Friends Scale w/o queer women friends ($\alpha$ = .66; $\alpha$ =.80) | 0–9 | All friendship items summed without queer women friends included. | 2.22 (1.63) | 4.03 (2.49) | * |
| LGBTQ Friends Scale w/o queer men friends ($\alpha$ = .67; $\alpha$ =.80) | 0–9 | All friendship items summed without queer men friends included. | 2.20 (1.64) | 4.01 (2.50) | * |
| *Religiosity* | | | | | |
| Religiousness | 1–4 | Would you consider yourself to be: 1–not at all religious, 2–somewhat religious, 3–religious, 4–very religious. | 2.23 (1.01) | 1.80 (.89) | * |
| Religious attendance | 1–5 | How often do you attend church? 1–never, 2–a few times a year, 3–about once a month, 4–several times a month/every week, 5–more than once a month. | 2.32 (1.35) | 1.78 (1.11) | * |
| Scripture/biblical literalism | 0–1 | Which of these statements comes closest to describing your current feelings about the Holy Scripture? 1–the Holy Scripture is the actual word of God and is to be taken literally, word for word, 0–the Holy Scripture is the inspired word of God but not everything in it should be taken literally, 0–the Holy Scripture is an ancient book of fables, legends, history, and moral precepts recorded by men, 0–none of these statements describe my feelings about the Holy Scripture. | .27 (.44) | .10 (.30) | * |

(*Continued*)

**TABLE 7.2** (Cont.)

| Variable Name | Range | Survey Item/Description of Variable | Hetero-Cis Subsample Mean | LGBTQ Subsample Mean |
|---|---|---|---|---|
| *Religious identity: Which religion do you identify with most?* | | | | |
| Protestant—mainline | 0–1 | Protestant—mainline | .14 (.35) | .14 (.35) |
| Protestant—evangelical | 0–1 | Includes those who responded with the response category of "Protestant—evangelical" or with "Other (please specify)" and wrote in some other evangelical-related term. See Appendix B, Table B.4. | .12 (.33) | .06 (.24) * |
| Protestant—historically Black | 0–1 | Protestant—historically Black | .03 (.17) | .02 (.14) * |
| Catholic | 0–1 | Catholic | .26 (.44) | .18 (.39) * |
| Mormon | 0–1 | Mormon | .01 (.12) | .01 (.12) |
| Christian/Other Christian | 0–1 | Includes those who responded with "Other (please specify)" and wrote in responses of "Christian" or some other Christian-related term or religion that resulted in total n values < 25. See Appendix B, Table B.5. | .06 (.24) | .03 (.18) * |
| Jewish | 0–1 | Jewish | .03 (.16) | .03 (.16) |
| Buddhist | 0–1 | Buddhist | .02 (.13) | .03 (.16) |
| Pagan/Wiccan | 0–1 | Includes those who responded with "Other (please specify)" and wrote in a response that included the words "pagan" or "wiccan" or some other pagan/wiccan-related term. See Appendix B, Table B.6. | .00 (.07) | .02 (.15) * |

| | | | | |
|---|---|---|---|---|
| Spiritual | 0–1 | Includes those who responded with "Other (please specify)" and wrote in a response that included the word "spiritual," or "spiritualist," or "spirituality." | .00 (.06) | .01 (.11) | * |
| Other non–Christian religion | 0–1 | Includes those who responded with "Other (please specify)" and wrote in a non-Christian or mixed-non-Christian/Christian response that resulted in total n values < 25. See Appendix B, Table B.7. | .02 (.14) | .03 (.16) | |
| Agnostic | 0–1 | Not religious—agnostic | .09 (.28) | .18 (.38) | * |
| Atheist | 0–1 | Not religious—atheist | .06 (.25) | .13 (.33) | * |
| None | 0–1 | None | .14 (.35) | .13 (.34) | |
| *Political perspectives* | | | | | |
| Liberal—conservative | 1–5 | Which of the following describes you best? 1-extremely liberal, 2-liberal, 3-moderate, 4-conservative, 5-extremely conservative. | 2.90 (1.11) | 2.36 (1.05) | * |
| Openness to new experiences | 1–5 | In general, I am open to new ideas and experiences. (Strongly Disagree—Strongly Agree) | 3.87 (.92) | 4.24 (.80) | * |
| *"In general, I support laws and policies that help …" (select all that apply):* | | | | | |
| Those in poverty | 0–1 | Those in poverty | .69 (.46) | .80 (.40) | * |
| Racial/ethnic minorities | 0–1 | Racial/ethnic minorities | .54 (.50) | .74 (.44) | * |
| Immigrants | 0–1 | Immigrants | .49 (.50) | .67 (.47) | * |

(*Continued*)

TABLE 7.2 (Cont.)

| Variable Name | Range | Survey Item/Description of Variable | Hetero-Cis Subsample Mean | LGBTQ Subsample Mean | |
|---|---|---|---|---|---|
| Women | 0–1 | | .62 (.49) | .79 (.41) | * |
| Non-Christians | 0–1 | | .36 (.48) | .60 (.49) | * |
| *Beliefs about gender* | | | | | |
| Feminist identity | 0–1 | Do you think of yourself as a feminist? 1-yes, I consider myself to be a strong feminist, 1-yes, I consider myself to be a feminist, 0-no, I do not consider myself to be a feminist, 0-no, I do not consider myself to be a feminist and I disagree with feminism. | 2.34 (.88) | 2.66 (.88) | * |
| Patriarchal Gender Norms Scale ($\alpha$ = .66; $\alpha$ = .75) | 5–25 | Sum of five items: 1-if my political party nominated a woman for President, I would vote for her if she was qualified for the job (reverse coded). 2-it is more important for a wife to help her husband's career than to have one herself. 3-the household tasks should be evenly divided between both partners in committed relationships (reverse coded). 4-all-in-all, family life suffers when both partners have full-time jobs. 5-it is much better for everyone involved if the man is the earner outside of the home and the woman takes care of the home and family. (Strongly Disagree—Strongly Agree) | 12.44 (3.66) | 9.95 (3.86) | * |

## Sociodemographic Controls

| | | | | | |
|---|---|---|---|---|---|
| Age | 18–64 | How old are you? | 39.65 (14.11) | 40.69 (14.51) | * |
| Region where from: Where would you say that you are from? | | | | | |
| Northeastern U.S. | 0–1 | Northeastern United States | .25 (.43) | .24 (.42) | * |
| Midwestern U.S. | 0–1 | Midwestern United States | .22 (.42) | .24 (.43) | |
| Western U.S. | 0–1 | Western United States | .19 (.38) | .23 (.42) | * |
| Southern U.S. | 0–1 | Southern United States | .30 (.46) | .28 (.45) | * |
| Outside U.S. | 0–1 | Outside of the United States | .04 (.18) | .02 (.15) | * |
| Town type | 1–4 | How would you describe the town/city where you spent the majority of your life? 1–rural, 2–small town, 3–suburb of a large city, 4–large city. | 2.53 (1.03) | 2.73 (.98) | |
| Education | 1–6 | Please indicate your highest level of education completed: 1–less than high school education, 2–high school education or GED, 3–some college, 4–college degree (Associate's), 5–college degree (Bachelor's), 6–college degree, higher than Bachelor's. | 3.67 (1.45) | 3.79 (1.47) | * |

*(Continued)*

**TABLE 7.2** (Cont.)

| Variable Name | Range | Survey Item/Description of Variable | Hetero-Cis Subsample Mean | LGBTQ Subsample Mean |
|---|---|---|---|---|
| Income | 1–5 | Which of these categories best describes your total combined family income for the past 12 months? This should include income (before taxes) from all sources, wages, rent from properties, social security, disability and/or veteran's benefits, unemployment benefits, worker's compensation, help from relatives (including child payments and alimony), and so on. 1-less than $5,000, 2-$5000–$24,999, 3-$25,000–$49,999, 4-$50,000–$99,999, 5-$100,000 and greater | 3.29 (2.88) | 3.30 (2.81) |

*Notes:* the two Cronbach alpha ($\alpha$) scores reported for each of the scales in this table were computed for both the hetero–cis (listed first) and LGBTQ (listed second) subsamples.

\* *t*-test results allowing for unequal variances indicate that the hetero–cis and LGBTQ subsample means are significantly different from one another at the $p < .05$ level.

## Patterns in Both Subsamples

### NCST, Social Power Axes, and the LGBTQ Stigma Scales Pattern #1

*The HCN Scale is positively related to the LGBTQ Stigma Scales (all nine groups) for both the hetero-cis and LGBTQ subsamples. (Hypothesis 1a)*

Overall, these findings strongly support Part I's conceptualization of hetero-cis-normativity as the centralized overarching concept that helps us to understand LGBTQ stigma and the cultural devaluation of LGBTQ people (see also Worthen 2016). As demonstrated across all models for all nine LGBTQ groups for both subsamples, even with the inclusion of a battery of common explanations and sociodemographic controls, hetero-cis-normativity remains a robust predictor of LGBTQ stigma. Specifically, these results support Chapter 3's argument that hetero-cis-normativity situates non-hetero and non-cis people in a place of social disadvantage whereby they are at risk for enduring negativity, stigma, and other social sanctions because they are violating the norms of hetero-cis-normativity. Confirming the first hypothesized relationship described in NCST (Hypothesis 1a), these findings show us that hetero-cis-normativity *is* the set of norms linked to LGBTQ stigma.

### NCST, Social Power Axes, and the LGBTQ Stigma Scales Pattern #2

*Individual social power axes are significantly related to the LGBTQ Stigma Scales (all nine groups) for both the hetero-cis and LGBTQ subsamples. (Hypothesis 1b)*

Consistent with Part I's discussion of the influences of multiple intersectional experiences built into hetero-cis-normativity which inform privilege and oppression as well as power and stigma, the findings here show that individual social power axes (gender, sexuality, race, ethnicity, basic needs) are strongly related to LGBTQ stigma across all models for all nine LGBTQ groups for both subsamples alongside the inclusion of numerous common explanations and sociodemographic controls. As discussed in Chapter 3, these results demonstrate that social power and LGBTQ stigma are strongly linked. Overall, these findings confirm the second hypothesized relationship described in NCST (Hypothesis 1b).

### NCST, Social Power Axes, and the LGBTQ Stigma Scales Pattern #3

*The interaction effects between the HCN Scale and social power axes as well as the interaction effects between the social power axes moderate the relationships between the HCN Scale and the LGBTQ Stigma Scales (all nine groups) but the significant interaction effects largely differ for the hetero-cis and LGBTQ subsamples. (Hypotheses 2a and 2b)*

As suggested in Part I, the intersecting layers of advantage and disadvantage involved in hetero-cis-normativity and in social power experiences emerged as significant in all models for all nine groups for both subsamples. Confirming the relationships described in NCST, these findings contribute to Chapter 3's arguments that social power both *organizes* and *justifies* the relationships between hetero-cis-normativity and LGBTQ stigma (Hypotheses 2a and 2b). However, interestingly, the specific interaction effects differ for the hetero-cis and LGBTQ subsamples. Thus, as demonstrated in previous work that has found different predictors of LGBT prejudices among heterosexual and LGB populations (Worthen 2016, 2018), the findings here show that the intersecting experiences with social power that shape hetero-cis people's attitudes toward LGBTQ people largely differ from the intersecting experiences with social power that inform LGBTQ people's attitudes toward other LGBTQ people.

### NCST, Social Power Axes, and the LGBTQ Stigma Scales Pattern #4

*There is only one significant interaction term that is found across several models for both subsamples. The interaction term between the HCN Scale and indicating "mostly all I need" is positive in models stigmatizing bisexual men, trans women, and trans men (for the hetero-cis subsample) and trans women, trans men, non-binary /genderqueer people, queer women, and queer men (for the LGBTQ subsample) (see Figure 7.5a).*

This finding indicates that hetero-cis-normativity is more powerfully related to BTQ stigma among those who have "mostly all" their basic needs met than among those with other experiences with basic needs. Specifically, supporting hetero-cis-normative perspectives conditions the effect of having "mostly all I need" on stigmatizing attitudes toward BTQ people such that higher values on the HCN Scale have a more robust impact on the stigmatization of BTQ people among those who have "mostly all" their basic needs met as compared to the stigmatization of BTQ people among those with other basic needs experiences. Complementing other work that highlights the ways class informs LGBTQ stigma (Appleby 2001; Balay 2014; Embrick, Walther, and Wickens 2007; Meyer 2015), these results demonstrate how the intersecting experiences of basic needs, class experiences, and the support of hetero-cis-normativity interact to shape hostilities toward bisexual, trans, non-binary/genderqueer, and queer people.

## Patterns in the Hetero-cis Subsample

### NCST, Social Power Axes, and the LGBTQ Stigma Scales Pattern #5

*There is a negative relationship between being a cis woman and the stigmatization of lesbian women, trans men, non-binary/genderqueer people, queer women, and queer men among the hetero-cis subsample (see Figure 7.5a).*

The negative relationship between being a cis woman and LTQ stigma supports some previous work that has documented a "gender gap" (men as compared to women) in attitudes toward LGBT people (Herek 1988, 2000, 2002; Norton and Herek 2013; Worthen 2013, 2016; Worthen, Lingiardi, and Caristo 2017). However, because this study separated hetero-cis people from LGBTQ people to explore these patterns unlike most past research, these results further clarify the parameters of this so-called "gender gap" in LGBTQ attitudes. Specifically, these findings indicate a hetero-cis man/hetero-cis woman "gender gap" in LTQ stigmatization but do not support other "gender gaps" (e.g., GBTQ man/LGBTQ woman). Thus, the relationship between being a cis woman and LGBTQ supportive perspectives may be more meaningful when exploring hetero-cis people's attitudes.

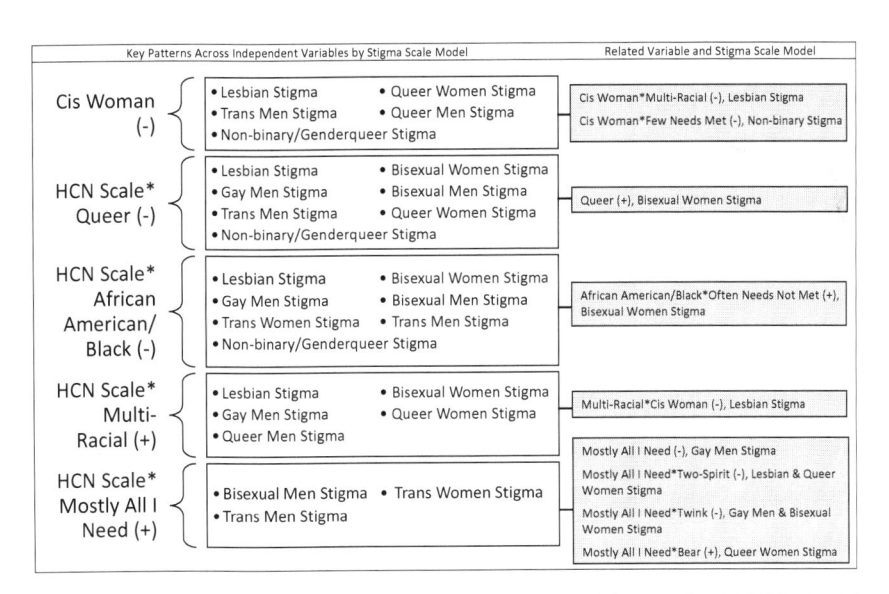

| Key Patterns Across Independent Variables by Stigma Scale Model | | Related Variable and Stigma Scale Model |
|---|---|---|
| **Cis Woman (-)** | • Lesbian Stigma • Queer Women Stigma<br>• Trans Men Stigma • Queer Men Stigma<br>• Non-binary/Genderqueer Stigma | Cis Woman*Multi-Racial (-), Lesbian Stigma<br>Cis Woman*Few Needs Met (-), Non-binary Stigma |
| **HCN Scale*<br>Queer (-)** | • Lesbian Stigma • Bisexual Women Stigma<br>• Gay Men Stigma • Bisexual Men Stigma<br>• Trans Men Stigma • Queer Women Stigma<br>• Non-binary/Genderqueer Stigma | Queer (+), Bisexual Women Stigma |
| **HCN Scale*<br>African American/<br>Black (-)** | • Lesbian Stigma • Bisexual Women Stigma<br>• Gay Men Stigma • Bisexual Men Stigma<br>• Trans Women Stigma • Trans Men Stigma<br>• Non-binary/Genderqueer Stigma | African American/Black*Often Needs Not Met (+), Bisexual Women Stigma |
| **HCN Scale*<br>Multi-Racial (+)** | • Lesbian Stigma • Bisexual Women Stigma<br>• Gay Men Stigma • Queer Women Stigma<br>• Queer Men Stigma | Multi-Racial*Cis Woman (-), Lesbian Stigma |
| **HCN Scale*<br>Mostly All I Need (+)** | • Bisexual Men Stigma • Trans Women Stigma<br>• Trans Men Stigma | Mostly All I Need (-), Gay Men Stigma<br>Mostly All I Need*Two-Spirit (-), Lesbian & Queer Women Stigma<br>Mostly All I Need*Twink (-), Gay Men & Bisexual Women Stigma<br>Mostly All I Need*Bear (+), Queer Women Stigma |

**FIGURE 7.5A** Key Patterns Across the Independent Variables in the NCST, Social Power Axes, and LGBTQ Stigma Scales Models for the Hetero-cis Subsample (n = 1,500)

*Note:* the * indicates an interaction. The (+) indicates a positive relationship to the LGBTQ Stigma Scale and the (-) indicates a negative relationship.

## NCST, Social Power Axes, and the LGBTQ Stigma Scales Pattern #6

*The interaction between the HCN Scale and queer identity is negatively related to the stigmatization of lesbian women, gay men, bisexual women, bisexual men, trans men, non-binary/genderqueer people, and queer women for the hetero-cis subsample (see Figure 7.5a).*

Because the relationship between the HCN Scale and queer identity is negative in nearly all models for the hetero-cis subsample, this tells us that support of hetero-cis-normativity has a greater impact on shaping non-queer-identified hetero-cis individuals' attitudes toward LGBTQ people than it does on queer-identified hetero-cis individuals' attitudes. In other words, opting into hetero-cis-normative ways of thinking conditions the effect of queer identity on stigmatizing attitudes toward LGBTQ people such that higher values on the HCN Scale have a more robust impact on non-queer-identified individuals' stigmatization of LGBTQ people as compared to queer-identified individuals' stigmatization of LGBTQ people. Such findings demonstrate that being queer (or not) is important in our understandings of the relationships between hetero-cis-normativity and LGBTQ stigma. These results complement other work that highlights the significance of identifying as queer as it shapes experiences and attitudes (Mereish, Katz-Wise, and Woulfe 2017; Morandini, Blaszczynski, and Dar-Nimrod. 2017).

## NCST, Social Power Axes, and the LGBTQ Stigma Scales Pattern #7

*The interaction between the HCN Scale and African American/Black identity is negatively related to the stigmatization of lesbian women, gay men, bisexual women, bisexual men, trans women, trans men, and non-binary/genderqueer people among the hetero-cis subsample (see Figure 7.5a).*

The negative relationship between the HCN Scale and being African American/Black demonstrates that support of hetero-cis-normativity has a greater impact on non-African American/Black individuals' stigmatization of LGBTQ people than it does on African American/Black stigmatization of LGBTQ people among the hetero-cis subsample. Specifically, hetero-cis-normativity conditions the effect of African American/Black identity on stigmatizing attitudes toward LGBTQ people such that higher levels of agreement with the HCN Scale have a more robust impact on non-African American/Black individuals' LGBTQ attitudes as compared to African American/Black individuals' LGBTQ attitudes. In particular, because African American/Black hetero-cis individuals report significantly higher means on the HCN Scale than non-African American/Black hetero-cis individuals report (17.75 vs. 14.79, respectively, $p < .001$), hetero-cis-normativity has a more powerful relationship to LGBTQ attitudes among those with lower levels of hetero-cis-normativity (non-African American/Black individuals) while other factors (e.g., religiosity) may help to better explain LGBTQ attitudes among African American/Black individuals. As demonstrated in previous work (Bowleg 2013; Lemelle and Battle 2004; Worthen 2018), these results support the continued need to explore additional complexities among the relationships between African American/Black and other racial/ethnic identities, hetero-cis-normativity, and LGBTQ stigma.

### NCST, Social Power Axes, and the LGBTQ Stigma Scales Pattern #8

*The interaction between the HCN Scale and Multi-racial identity is positively related to the stigmatization of lesbian women, gay men, bisexual women, queer women, and queer men among the hetero-cis subsample (see Figure 7.5a).*

The positive relationship between the HCN Scale and being Multi-racial indicates that hetero-cis-normativity has a more robust impact on Multi-racial individuals' stigmatization of LGBQ people than it does on non-Multi-racial individuals' stigmatization of LGBQ people among the hetero-cis subsample. Specifically, hetero-cis-normativity conditions the effect of Multi-racial identity on stigmatizing attitudes toward LGBQ people such that higher levels of agreement with the HCN Scale have a more robust impact on Multi-racial hetero-cis individuals' LGBQ attitudes as compared to non-Multi-racial hetero-cis individuals' LGBQ attitudes. In particular, there is relatively low support of hetero-cis-normativity among Multi-racial hetero-cis individuals (mean on the HCN Scale = 11.52); however, hetero-cis-normative thinking shapes LGBQ stigmatization among Multi-racial individuals in a more powerful way as compared to non-Multi-racial individuals, who indicate significantly ($p < .01$) higher levels of agreement with the HCN Scale (mean = 15.17). Other have underscored the unique experiences of Multi-racial individuals (Fisher et al. 2014; Grier, Rambo, and Taylor 2014; Herman 2004). These findings demonstrate the significance of examining intersecting experiences with Multi-racial identity and hetero-cis-normativity as they inform the stigmatization of LGBQ people.

## Patterns in the LGBTQ Subsample

### NCST, Social Power Axes, and the LGBTQ Stigma Scales Pattern #9

*There is a negative relationship between SGL identity and the stigmatization of lesbian women, gay men, bisexual men, trans women, and trans men among the LGBTQ subsample (see Figure 7.5b).*

The negative relationship between SGL identity and LGBT stigma supports some previous work that suggests that SGL identities can be inclusive of those in the LGBTQ spectrum (Lewis 2017; Truong et al. 2016). For example, in the current study, about 1 in 5 (18%, 282/1604) LGBTQ people identified as

**150** NCST and Understanding LGBTQ Stigma

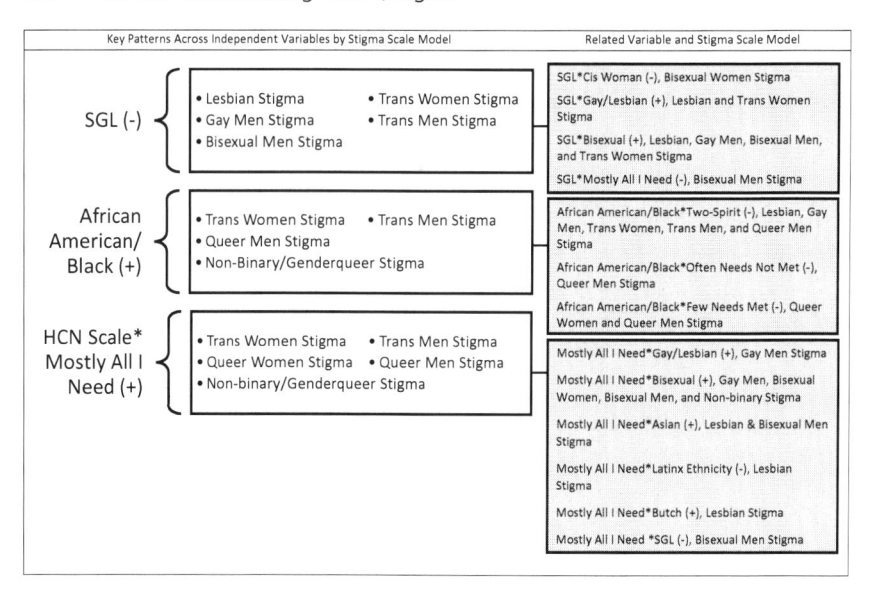

| Key Patterns Across Independent Variables by Stigma Scale Model | | | Related Variable and Stigma Scale Model |
|---|---|---|---|
| SGL (-) | • Lesbian Stigma<br>• Gay Men Stigma<br>• Bisexual Men Stigma | • Trans Women Stigma<br>• Trans Men Stigma | SGL*Cis Woman (-), Bisexual Women Stigma |
| | | | SGL*Gay/Lesbian (+), Lesbian and Trans Women Stigma |
| | | | SGL*Bisexual (+), Lesbian, Gay Men, Bisexual Men, and Trans Women Stigma |
| | | | SGL*Mostly All I Need (-), Bisexual Men Stigma |
| African American/ Black (+) | • Trans Women Stigma<br>• Queer Men Stigma<br>• Non-Binary/Genderqueer Stigma | • Trans Men Stigma | African American/Black*Two-Spirit (-), Lesbian, Gay Men, Trans Women, Trans Men, and Queer Men Stigma |
| | | | African American/Black*Often Needs Not Met (-), Queer Men Stigma |
| | | | African American/Black*Few Needs Met (-), Queer Women and Queer Men Stigma |
| HCN Scale*<br>Mostly All I<br>Need (+) | • Trans Women Stigma<br>• Queer Women Stigma<br>• Non-binary/Genderqueer Stigma | • Trans Men Stigma<br>• Queer Men Stigma | Mostly All I Need*Gay/Lesbian (+), Gay Men Stigma |
| | | | Mostly All I Need*Bisexual (+), Gay Men, Bisexual Women, Bisexual Men, and Non-binary Stigma |
| | | | Mostly All I Need*Asian (+), Lesbian & Bisexual Men Stigma |
| | | | Mostly All I Need*Latinx Ethnicity (-), Lesbian Stigma |
| | | | Mostly All I Need*Butch (+), Lesbian Stigma |
| | | | Mostly All I Need *SGL (-), Bisexual Men Stigma |

**FIGURE 7.5B** Key Patterns Across the Independent Variables in the NCST, Social Power Axes, and LGBTQ Stigma Scales Models for the LGBTQ Subsample (n = 1,604)
*Note:* The * indicates an interaction. The (+) indicates a positive relationship to the LGBTQ Stigma Scale and the (-) indicates a negative relationship.

SGL. Overall, as a culturally affirming identity that works against oppressive experiences, this prominence/preference of SGL identities in the LGBTQ community may impact supportive perspectives toward LGBT people among those who identify as SGL.

## NCST, Social Power Axes, and the LGBTQ Stigma Scales Pattern #10

*There is a positive relationship between being African American/Black and the stigmatization of trans women, trans men, non-binary/genderqueer people, and queer men among the LGBTQ subsample (see Figure 7.5b).*

Somewhat surprisingly, this finding demonstrates trans, non-binary/genderqueer, and queer hostility among African American/Black individuals in the LGBTQ subsample. Other research has found that African American/Black LGBTQ people experience racism, exclusion, and hostility from hetero-cis individuals and in White LGBT communities (Bowleg 2013; Han 2007; Lemelle and Battle 2004). However, these findings demonstrate that there may be some palpable TQ negativities among African American/Black LGBTQ individuals. Perhaps because identities such as "queer" have been associated with both privilege and "whiteness" (Alimahomed 2010; Brontsema 2004; Logie and Rwigema 2014), trans, non-binary/genderqueer, and queer people may be stigmatized by African American/Black LGBTQ individuals. These findings highlight important differences in African American/Black LGBTQ people's experiences and demonstrate the need for continued investigation of these complexities.

## Patterns in the Common Explanations and Sociodemographic Controls

### NCST, Social Power Axes, and the LGBTQ Stigma Scales Pattern #11

*Having friends in the LGBTQ group of interest is negatively related to the stigmatization of lesbian women, gay men, bisexual women, trans women, non-binary/genderqueer people and queer men for both the hetero-cis and LGBTQ subsamples and queer women for the LGBTQ subsample only (see Figure 7.5c).*

**Friends with LGBTQ Group of Interest (-)**
- Lesbian Stigma
- Gay Men Stigma
- Bisexual Women Stigma
- Trans Women Stigma
- Queer Women Stigma**
- Queer Men Stigma
- Non-binary/Genderqueer Stigma (genderqueer friends only)

**LGBTQ Friends Scales w/o Group of Interest(-)**
- Lesbian Stigma
- Gay Men Stigma
- Bisexual Women Stigma*
- Bisexual Men Stigma**
- Non-binary/Genderqueer Stigma
- Trans Women Stigma
- Trans Men Stigma
- Queer Women Stigma*
- Queer Men Stigma*

**Openness to New Experiences (-)**
- Lesbian Stigma
- Gay Men Stigma
- Bisexual Women Stigma
- Bisexual Men Stigma
- Non-binary/Genderqueer Stigma
- Trans Women Stigma
- Trans Men Stigma
- Queer Women Stigma
- Queer Men Stigma

**Support those in Poverty (-)**
- Lesbian Stigma
- Gay Men Stigma*
- Bisexual Women Stigma*
- Bisexual Men Stigma*
- Trans Women Stigma*
- Queer Women*
- Queer Men Stigma

**Patriarchal Gender Norms Scale (+)**
- Lesbian Stigma
- Gay Men Stigma
- Bisexual Women Stigma
- Bisexual Men Stigma
- Non-binary/Genderqueer Stigma
- Trans Women Stigma
- Trans Men Stigma
- Queer Women
- Queer Men

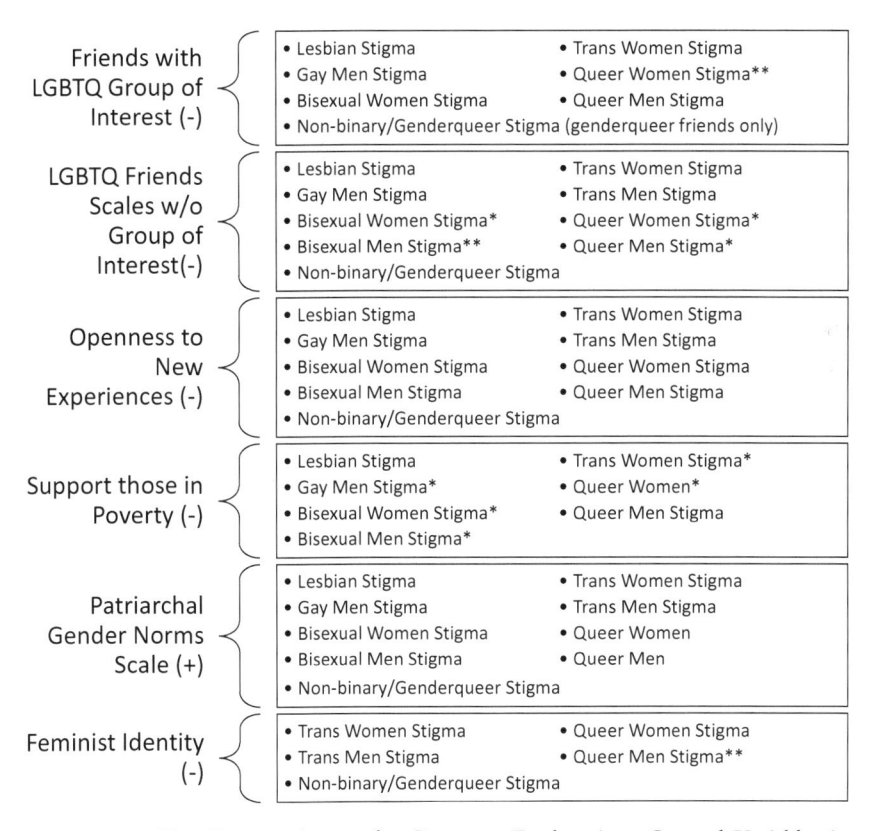

**Feminist Identity (-)**
- Trans Women Stigma
- Trans Men Stigma
- Non-binary/Genderqueer Stigma
- Queer Women Stigma
- Queer Men Stigma**

**FIGURE 7.5C** Key Patterns Across the Common Explanations Control Variables in the NCST, Social Power Axes, and LGBTQ Stigma Scales Models for Both Subsamples (N = 3,104)

\* only significant for the hetero-cis subsample; ** only significant for the LGBTQ subsample.

### NCST, Social Power Axes, and the LGBTQ Stigma Scales Pattern #12

The LGBTQ Friend Scales (without the group of interest) are negatively related to the stigmatization of lesbian women, gay men, trans women, trans men, and non-binary/genderqueer people for both the hetero-cis and LGBTQ subsamples, for bisexual women, queer women, and queer men for the hetero-cis subsample only and bisexual men for the LGBTQ subsample only (see Figure 7.5c).

### NCST, Social Power Axes, and the LGBTQ Stigma Scales Pattern #13

Openness to new experiences is negatively related to the stigmatization of lesbian women, gay men, bisexual women, bisexual men, trans women, trans men, non-binary/genderqueer people, queer women, and queer men (all nine groups) for both the hetero-cis and LGBTQ subsamples (see Figure 7.5c).

### NCST, Social Power Axes, and the LGBTQ Stigma Scales Pattern #14

Supporting those in poverty is negatively related to the stigmatization of lesbian women and queer men for both the hetero-cis and LGBTQ subsamples and gay men, bisexual women, bisexual men, trans women, and queer women for the hetero-cis subsample only (see Figure 7.5c).

### NCST, Social Power Axes, and the LGBTQ Stigma Scales Pattern #15

The Patriarchal Gender Norms Scale is positively related to the stigmatization of lesbian women, gay men, bisexual women, bisexual men, trans women, trans men, non-binary/genderqueer people, queer women, and queer men (all nine groups) for both the hetero-cis and LGBTQ subsamples (see Figure 7.5c).

### NCST, Social Power Axes, and the LGBTQ Stigma Scales Pattern #16

Feminist identity is negatively related to the stigmatization of trans women, trans men, non-binary/genderqueer people, and queer women for both the hetero-cis and LGBTQ subsamples and queer men for the LGBTQ subsample only (see Figure 7.5c).

Figure 7.5c summarizes these patterns. Both measures of LGBTQ social contact (having friends in the LGBTQ group of interest and the LGBTQ Friend Scales without the LGBTQ group of interest) are negatively related to the

LGBTQ Stigma Scales in nearly all models for both subsamples as found in previous work (Basow and Johnson 2000; Herek and Capitanio 1996; Hinrichs and Rosenberg 2002; Pettigrew and Tropp 2006; Worthen, Lingiardi, and Caristo 2017). In addition, openness to new experiences is negatively related to the stigmatization of LGBTQ people in all models, as demonstrated in some past studies (Cramer et al. 2013; Cullen, Wright, and Alessandri 2002; Shackelford and Besser 2007). Supporting laws/policies helping those in poverty is significantly negatively related to the LGBTQ Stigma Scales. Although the particulars of liberal political perspectives in the form of supporting laws/policies helping those in poverty have not been previously investigated as they relate to LGBTQ stigmatization (though supporting policies to aid those in poverty has been found to be related to liberal ideology, see Applebaum 2001), this study shows that this tenet of liberal perspectives is rather strongly related to attitudes toward LGBTQ people. It is also important to note that among the five measures of laws/policies, supporting those in poverty had the highest mean value for both groups (.69 for the hetero-cis subsample and .80 for the LGBTQ subsample). The social and economic justice framework that welfare laws/policies exist within coupled the documented importance of and barriers to including LGBTQ people in the welfare system (Lind 2004) likely shape these relationships between helping those in poverty and LGBTQ support. The Patriarchal Gender Norms Scale is positively related to LGBTQ stigmatization of all nine groups in all models. This also aligns with past research that has demonstrated that more traditional, conservative, and patriarchal cultural expectations about men and women relate to more negative attitudes toward LGBTQ people (Hill and Willoughby 2005; Worthen 2018). Feminist identity is negatively related to trans, non-binary/genderqueer, and queer stigma. Previous studies have also found that self-identified feminists are more likely to support LGBTQ people as compared to those who do not agree with feminism and those who do not identify as feminists (Hill and Willoughby 2005; Ojerholm and Rothblum 1999; Worthen 2012; Worthen, Lingiardi, and Caristo 2017).

## NCST and LGBTQ Gender- and Sexuality-Based DHV

In each chapter, the third and final method of investigation shifts our focus to LGBTQ people's own experiences. In particular, due to their intersecting marginalized identities, LGBTQ people's experiences with gender- and sexuality-based DHV are critical to explore. Specifically, logistic regression is utilized to investigate the relationships among being LGBTQ and intersecting experiences of being LGBTQ and gender, sexuality, additional gender/sexuality, race/ethnicity, and basic needs as they relate to the likelihood of experiencing gender- and sexuality-based DHV. This exploration of LGBTQ people's actual experiences with stigma (i.e., the stigmatized lens) complements earlier examinations of the nuances of social stigma and hostilities directed toward LGBTQ people (i.e., the stigmatizer lens).

## Dependent Variables

Gender- and sexuality-based DHV were measured using six responses to three items. Specifically, respondents were asked to respond to the following statement, "I have experienced discrimination because of my (select all that apply)." The respondent could mark "gender" and/or "sexual identity/orientation" for this survey item. Respondents were also asked to respond to two similar statements: "I have experienced harassment because of my (select all that apply)" and "I have experienced violence because of my (select all that apply)." Again, respondents could indicate "gender" and/or "sexual identity/orientation." For the logistic regression models, these responses were collapsed into dichotomous variables. Those that indicated "gender" as a response to any of these three items (discrimination, harassment, and/or violence) were coded as (1) for gender-based DHV and (0) for others. Those that indicated "sexual identity/orientation" as a response to any of these three items (discrimination, harassment, and/or violence) were coded as (1) for sexuality-based DHV and (0) for others.

## Modeling Strategy

To best understand LGBTQ people's DHV experiences, the LGBTQ subsample (n = 1,604) was utilized for these models. This strategy allows for comparisons whereby being a lesbian woman is compared to all other GBTQ people (for example). In line with the theoretical model and the hypotheses of NCST's stigmatized lens, Model 1 includes being a lesbian woman, gay man, bisexual woman, bisexual man, trans woman, trans man, non-binary/genderqueer person, queer woman, or queer man (henceforth, "the LGBTQ group of interest") as related to gender-based DHV in the first set of models and sexuality-based DHV in the second set of models. In addition, the individual social power axes that are relevant to the LGBTQ group of interest are also included in Model 1. However, to avoid extremely small cell sizes with inadequate power, only the individual social power axes variables that were experienced by the LGBTQ group of interest and had cell sizes with adequate power (n > 25) were included in the models (Van Voorhis and Morgan 2007) (see Appendix B Table B.1 for more details about the cell sizes). In Model 2, intersections among the LGBTQ group of interest and all relevant axes of social power with adequate cell sizes are included.

## Controls and Goodness of Fit

Unlike the extensive work reviewed in Chapter 4 that has uncovered a host of common explanations and sociodemographics that relate to attitudes toward LGBTQ people, there is less research that has identified how these types of experiences are associated with LGBTQ people's DHV. However, four sociodemographic variables are utilized as controls in these models (age, town type (rural–large city), education, and income) because they have been found to be related to experiences with violence (Alden and Parker 2005; Birkett, Newcomb, and Mustanski 2015; Bonomi et al. 2014; Crouch et al. 2000; Decker et al. 2015; DeKeseredy and Schwartz 2009; Grossman et al. 2005; Herek, Gillis, and Cogan 1999; Li et al. 2010; Stacey, Averett, and Knox 2018). As done before, multicollinearity was examined using STATA command "collin" (Ender 2010), which provides collinearity diagnostics for all variables. The mean VIF values are reported for each model and suggest no problems with multi-collinearity for any model (Allison 2012).

Overall, as summarized in Figure 7.6, there are no strongly overlapping patterns found across the investigations of NCST and LGBTQ experiences with DHV as related to being the LGBTQ group of interest. In fact, while there is some support for the NCST theoretical model and both corresponding hypotheses (e.g., being a lesbian woman increases the likelihood of experiencing gender-based DHV; the intersections of being a gay man and being butch increase the likelihood of experiencing sexuality-based DHV), no identical patterns as related to being the LGBTQ group of interest cut across all or even a majority of the models. However, there are eight patterns related to the DHV experiences of LGBTQ people that are essential to acknowledge. It is also important to note that some of the patterns discussed below also have corresponding significant effects in some models. For example, the interaction effect of being a bisexual man is *positively* related to

| Summary of the Key Independent Variables by DHV Model | Significant Interaction Terms in DHV Models |
|---|---|
| **Gender-Based DHV** | |
| Being L,G,B,T or Q** • Lesbian DHV (+) • Gay Man DHV (–) • Trans Man DHV (+) | Gay Man*SGL (–) Bisexual Woman*Trans (+) Bisexual Woman*SGL (+) Bisexual Woman*Femme (+) Bisexual Woman*African American/Black (–) Bisexual Woman*Latinx Ethnicity (+) Queer Woman*White (–) Queer Man*Gay (+) Queer Man*SGL (–) Queer Man*White (+) |
| **Sexuality-Based DHV** | |
| Being L,G,B,T or Q** • Bisexual Man DHV (+) • Non-binary/Genderqueer DHV (–) | Lesbian Woman*Butch (–) Gay Man*Butch (+) Bisexual Man*Queer (–) Bisexual Man*White (+) Trans Woman*White (–) Non-binary/Genderqueer*Bisexual (–) |

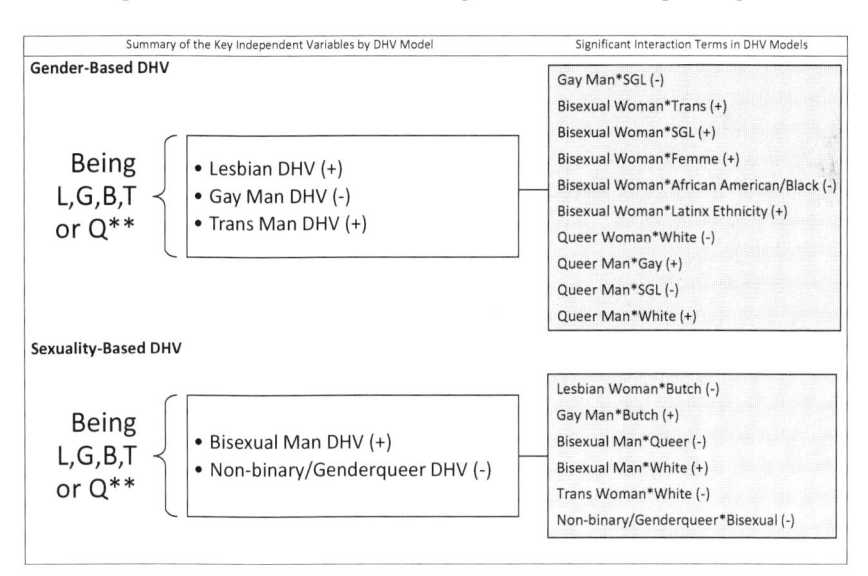

**FIGURE 7.6** Summary of the Key Independent Variables in the NCST, Social Power Axes, and DHV Models for the LGBTQ Subsample (n = 1,604)

** Refers to nine separate models estimating the effects of being a lesbian woman, gay man, bisexual woman, bisexual man, trans woman, trans man, nonbinary/genderqueer person, queer woman, or queer man on DHV.

*Notes:* The * indicates an interaction. The (+) indicates an increased likelihood of DHV and the (–) indicates a decreased likelihood.

sexuality-based DHV but also, the individual effect of being a bisexual man is *negatively* related to sexuality-based DHV (see Table 11.5). However, as noted above, because the goal of this chapter is to review commonly found trends and patterns across all models, these less frequent corresponding significant effects are not discussed here and all patterns reviewed below should be understood as embedded within models that have distinct features.

### NCST and LGBTQ DHV Pattern #1

*Among all nine groups, queer women and queer men in the LGBTQ subsample are at the highest risk for nearly all types of gender- and sexuality-based DHV (with the exception of gender-based violence) (see Figure 7.7).*

It is striking that queer women and queer men in the LGBTQ subsample experience such extreme DHV. As seen in Table 7.1, 1 in 5 LGBTQ people (20%, n = 313/1,604) identified as "queer." By examining all those that identify as both LGBT and queer, the findings here indicate that that being "queer" is associated with an increased risk for nearly all types of gender- and sexuality-based DHV for both women and men. Though some small-scale research has found that queer-identified women and men may be at risk for stigma (Alimahomed 2010; Friedman and Leaper 2010; Jones 2015; Logie and

**Discrimination**
- Sexuality-Based: Queer Women 64%
- Gender-Based: Queer Women 61%

**Harassment**
- Sexuality-Based: Queer Men 59%
- Gender-Based: Queer Women 62%

**Violence**
- Sexuality-Based: Queer Men 37%
- Gender-Based: Bisexual Women and Non-binary 25%

**Any DHV Experience**
- Sexuality-Based: Queer Women and Queer Men 72%
- Gender-Based: Queer Women 78%

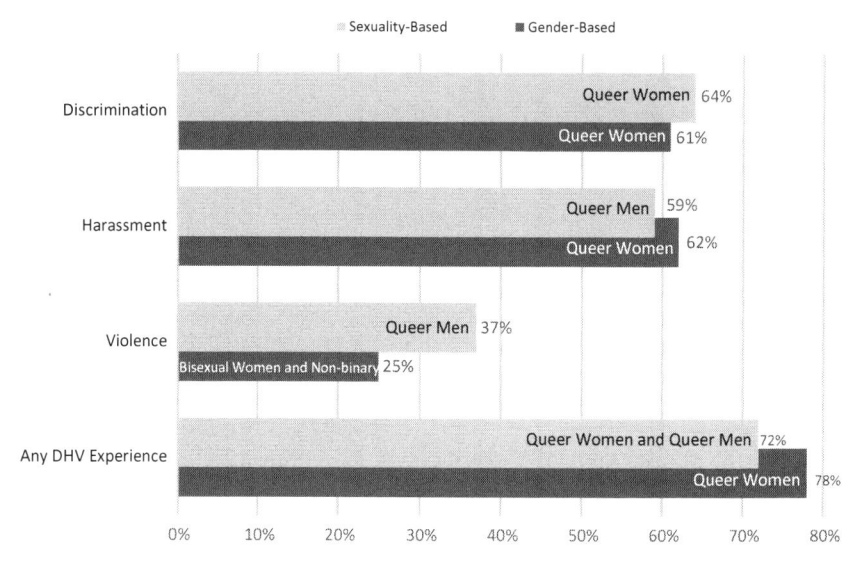

**FIGURE 7.7** LGBTQ Groups with the Highest Gender- and Sexuality-Based DHV Experiences

*Notes:* queer-identified heterosexuals were not included in these comparisons. See Tables and Figures 8.3, 9.3, 10.3, 11.3, 12.3, 13.3, 14.3, 15.3, and 16.3 for further information about LGBTQ people's DHV experiences.

Earnshaw 2015; Meyer 2015; Morandini, Blaszczynski, and Dar-Nimrod. 2017; Galupo et al. 2017), queer identity is not often clearly identified as a risk factor for gender- and sexuality-based DHV (for an exception see Meyer 2015). These findings demonstrate the importance of continuing to explore how queer identity shapes LGBT people's experiences with DHV (see more in Chapters 15 and 16).

## NCST and LGBTQ DHV Pattern #2

*Being a woman (individual social power axis non-interaction term) significantly increases the likelihood of experiencing gender-based DHV in the models examining the experiences of lesbian women, bisexual women, and queer women but being a man significantly decreases the likelihood of experiencing gender-based DHV in the models for gay men, bisexual men, and queer men (see Figure 7.8).*

## NCST and LGBTQ DHV Pattern #3

*Being lesbian/gay (individual social power axis non-interaction term) significantly increases the likelihood of experiencing sexuality-based DHV in the models examining lesbian women, gay*

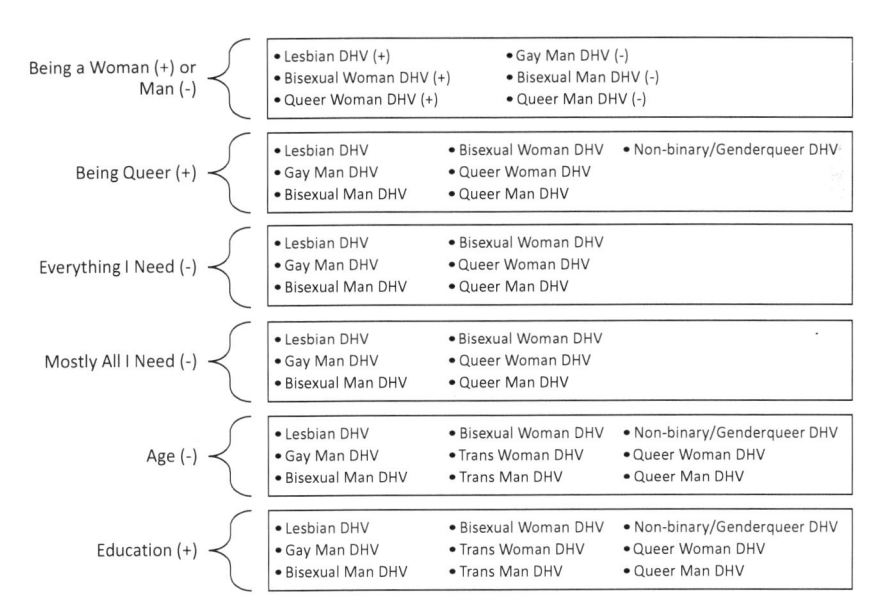

| Axis | Groups |
|---|---|
| Being a Woman (+) or Man (-) | • Lesbian DHV (+) • Gay Man DHV (-) <br> • Bisexual Woman DHV (+) • Bisexual Man DHV (-) <br> • Queer Woman DHV (+) • Queer Man DHV (-) |
| Being Queer (+) | • Lesbian DHV • Bisexual Woman DHV • Non-binary/Genderqueer DHV <br> • Gay Man DHV • Queer Woman DHV <br> • Bisexual Man DHV • Queer Man DHV |
| Everything I Need (-) | • Lesbian DHV • Bisexual Woman DHV <br> • Gay Man DHV • Queer Woman DHV <br> • Bisexual Man DHV • Queer Man DHV |
| Mostly All I Need (-) | • Lesbian DHV • Bisexual Woman DHV <br> • Gay Man DHV • Queer Woman DHV <br> • Bisexual Man DHV • Queer Man DHV |
| Age (-) | • Lesbian DHV • Bisexual Woman DHV • Non-binary/Genderqueer DHV <br> • Gay Man DHV • Trans Woman DHV • Queer Woman DHV <br> • Bisexual Man DHV • Trans Man DHV • Queer Man DHV |
| Education (+) | • Lesbian DHV • Bisexual Woman DHV • Non-binary/Genderqueer DHV <br> • Gay Man DHV • Trans Woman DHV • Queer Woman DHV <br> • Bisexual Man DHV • Trans Man DHV • Queer Man DHV |

**FIGURE 7.8** Patterns Across the Individual Social Power Axes (Non-Interaction Terms) and the Socio-demographic Controls in the NCST, Social Power Axes, and Gender-Based DHV Models for the LGBTQ Subsample (n = 1,604)

*Note:* The (+) indicates an increased likelihood of DHV and the (-) indicates a decreased likelihood.

**158** NCST and Understanding LGBTQ Stigma

*men, queer men, and queer women while being bisexual significantly decreases the likelihood of experiencing sexuality-based DHV in the models for bisexual women, bisexual men, trans women, and non-binary/genderqueer people (see Figure 7.9).*

## NCST and LGBTQ DHV Pattern #4

*Being queer (individual social power axis non-interaction term) significantly increases the likelihood of both gender- and sexuality-based DHV in the models examining the experiences of lesbian women, gay men, bisexual women, bisexual men, non-binary /genderqueer people, queer women, and queer men (see Figures 7.8 and 7.9).*

## NCST and LGBTQ DHV Pattern #5

*Indicating "I have everything I need" (individual social power axis non-interaction term) significantly decreases the likelihood of gender- or sexuality-based DHV in the models examining the experiences of lesbian women, gay men, bisexual women, bisexual men, queer women, and queer men (see Figures 7.8 and 7.9).*

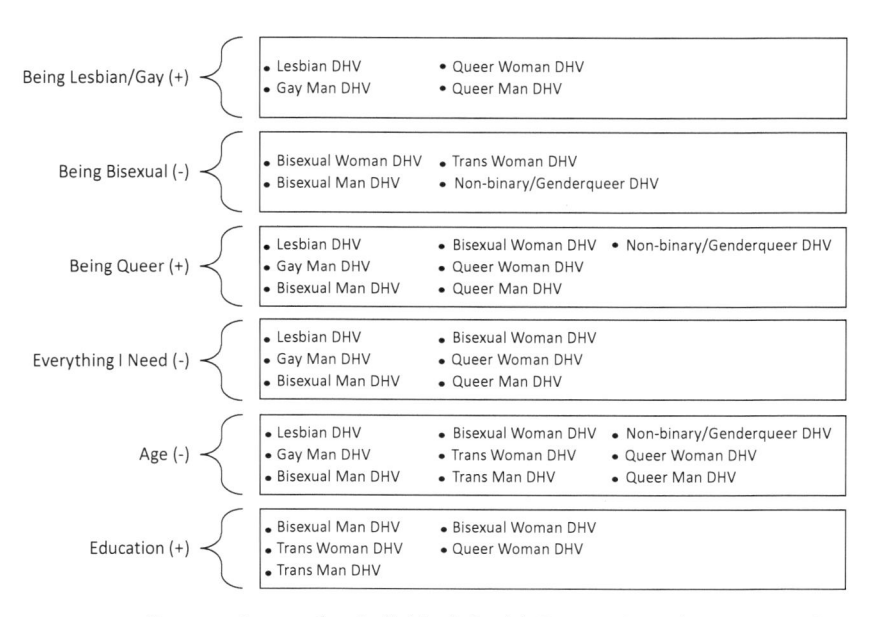

| Axis | Models |
|---|---|
| Being Lesbian/Gay (+) | • Lesbian DHV • Queer Woman DHV • Gay Man DHV • Queer Man DHV |
| Being Bisexual (-) | • Bisexual Woman DHV • Trans Woman DHV • Bisexual Man DHV • Non-binary/Genderqueer DHV |
| Being Queer (+) | • Lesbian DHV • Bisexual Woman DHV • Non-binary/Genderqueer DHV • Gay Man DHV • Queer Woman DHV • Bisexual Man DHV • Queer Man DHV |
| Everything I Need (-) | • Lesbian DHV • Bisexual Woman DHV • Gay Man DHV • Queer Woman DHV • Bisexual Man DHV • Queer Man DHV |
| Age (-) | • Lesbian DHV • Bisexual Woman DHV • Non-binary/Genderqueer DHV • Gay Man DHV • Trans Woman DHV • Queer Woman DHV • Bisexual Man DHV • Trans Man DHV • Queer Man DHV |
| Education (+) | • Bisexual Man DHV • Bisexual Woman DHV • Trans Woman DHV • Queer Woman DHV • Trans Man DHV |

**FIGURE 7.9** Patterns Across the Individual Social Power Axes (Non-Interaction Terms) and the Socio-demographic Controls in the NCST, Social Power Axes, and Sexuality-Based DHV Models for the LGBTQ Subsample (n = 1,604)

*Note:* The (+) indicates an increased likelihood of DHV and the (-) indicates a decreased likelihood.

### NCST and LGBTQ DHV Pattern #6

*Indicating "I have mostly all I need" (individual social power axis non-interaction term) significantly decreases the likelihood of gender-based DHV in the models examining the experiences of lesbian women, gay men, bisexual women, bisexual men, queer women, and queer men (see Figure 7.8).*

### NCST and LGBTQ DHV Pattern #7

*Older age significantly decreases the likelihood of experiencing gender- or sexuality-based DHV in the models examining all nine groups (see Figures 7.8 and 7.9).*

### NCST and LGBTQ DHV Pattern #8

*Greater levels of education significantly increase the likelihood of experiencing gender-based DHV in the models examining all nine groups and experiencing sexuality-based DHV in the models examining bisexual women, bisexual men, trans women, trans men, and queer women (see Figures 7.8 and 7.9).*

Overall, the patterns among the individual social power axes (non-interaction terms) and socio-demographics both align and contrast with existing research. For example, findings here indicate that being a woman increases the likelihood of experiencing gender-based DHV while being a man decreases the likelihood of experiencing gender-based DHV in some models. This is similar to other research that has found that compared to men, women are more likely to be targeted for gender-based DHV (Jagsi et al. 2016; Katz-Wise and Hyde 2012). In addition, while the finding that being lesbian/gay increases the likelihood of experiencing sexuality-based DHV aligns with existing work (Badgett 1994; Huebner, Rebchook, and Kegeles 2004; Kalichman et al. 2001; Katz-Wise and Hyde 2012; Mays and Cochran 2001), the results also demonstrated that being bisexual *decreases* the likelihood of experiencing sexuality-based DHV (in some models). These findings do not align with existing work that has found that being bisexual is related to an increased risk of DHV (Badgett 1994; Balsam, Rothblum, and Beauchaine 2005; Coston 2017; Huebner, Rebchook, and Kegeles 2004; Kalichman et al. 2001; Katz-Wise and Hyde 2012; Mays and Cochran 2001; Meyer 2015; Stephenson and Finneran 2017).

Results also show that being queer increases the likelihood of both gender- and sexuality-based DHV which is consistent with some past research (Alimahomed 2010; Friedman and Leaper 2010; Jones 2015; Logie and Earnshaw 2015; Meyer 2015; Morandini, Blaszczynski, and Dar-Nimrod. 2017; Galupo, Lomash, and Mitchell 2017). Also, two indicators of basic needs security ("everything I need" and "mostly all I need") decrease the likelihood of both gender- and sexuality-based DHV in some models, which is in line with previous work that demonstrates lower risk of violence among those with higher socioeconomic status life experiences (Crouch et al. 2000; Decker et al. 2015). Age also slightly decreases the likelihood of gender- and sexuality-based DHV, as indicated in some past studies (Birkett, Newcomb, and Mustanski 2015; Stacey, Averett, and Knox 2018). Finally, education increases the likelihood of gender- and sexuality-based DHV, which runs counter to previous research at the individual level (Herek, Gillis, and Cogan 1999) but supports other macro-level findings (Alden and Parker 2005).

## Summary of Part II

In Part II, the three methods of investigation reviewed here are utilized to explore nine LGBTQ groups. Both the stigmatization of LGBTQ people (stigmatizer lens) as well as LGBTQ people's own experiences with stigma (stigmatized lens) are examined through one of the first ever empirical explorations of NCST. Overall, by utilizing the three tenets of NCST, Part II extends upon existing work and highlights the significance of hetero-cis-normativity (*norm centrality*), social power (as *organizational* and *justification* for enduring negativity), and intersectionality (as related to the *spectrum of stigma*) in understanding the mechanisms and processes of LGBTQ stigmatization.

## References

Alden, Helena L. and Karen F. Parker. 2005. "Gender Role Ideology, Homophobia and Hate Crime: Linking Attitudes to Macro-Level Anti-Gay and Lesbian Hate Crimes." *Deviant Behavior* 26(4):321–343.

Alegría, Christine 2018. "Supporting Families of Transgender Children/Youth: Parents Speak on Their Experiences, Identity, and Views." *International Journal of Transgenderism* 19(2):132–143.

Alimahomed, Sabrina. 2010. "Thinking Outside the Rainbow: Women of Color Redefining Queer Politics and Identity." *Social Identities* 16(2):151–168.

Allison, Paul. 2012. "When Can You Safely Ignore Multicollinearity?" Retrieved January 7, 2019 (https://statisticalhorizons.com/multicollinearity).

American Psychiatric Association. 1952. *Diagnostic and Statistical Manual of Mental Disorders I*. Washington D.C.: American Psychiatric Association, Inc.

American Psychiatric Association. 1968. *Diagnostic and Statistical Manual of Mental Disorders II*. Washington D.C.: American Psychiatric Association, Inc.

Aparicio-García, Marta Evelia, Eva María Díaz-Ramiro, Susana Rubio-Valdehita, María Inmaculada López-Núñez, and Isidro García-Nieto. 2018. "Health and Well-Being of Cisgender, Transgender and Non-binary Young People." *International Journal of Environmental Research and Public Health* 15(10):2133.

Applebaum, Lauren D. 2001. "The Influence of Perceived Deservingness on Policy Decisions Regarding Aid to the Poor." *Political Psychology* 22(3):419–442.

Appleby, George A. 2001. "Ethnographic Study of Gay and Bisexual Working-Class Men in the United States." *Journal of Gay & Lesbian Social Services* 12(3/4):51–62.

Badget, M. V. Lee. 1994. "The Wage Effects of Sexual Orientation Discrimination." *Industrial and Labor Relations Review* 48:726–739.

Balay, Anne. 2014. *Steel Closets: Voices of Gay, Lesbian, and Transgender Steelworkers.* Chapel Hill, NC: UNC Press Books.

Balsam, Kimberly F., Esther D. Rothblum, and Theodore P. Beauchaine. 2005. "Victimization Over the Life Span: A Comparison of Lesbian, Gay, Bisexual, and Heterosexual Siblings." *Journal of Consulting and Clinical Psychology* 73(3):477–487.

Basow, Susan A. and Kelly Johnson. 2000. "Predictors of Homophobia in Female College Students." *Sex Roles* 42(5/6):391–404.

Birkett, Michelle, Michael E. Newcomb, and Brian Mustanski. 2015. "Does It Get Better? A Longitudinal Analysis of Psychological Distress and Victimization in Lesbian, Gay, Bisexual, Transgender, and Questioning Youth." *Journal of Adolescent Health* 56(3):280–285.

Bonomi, Amy E., Britton Trabert, Melissa L. Anderson, Mary A. Kernic, and Victoria L. Holt. 2014. "Intimate Partner Violence and Neighborhood Income: A Longitudinal Analysis." *Violence Against Women* 20(1):42–58.

Bowleg, Lisa. 2013. "'Once You've Blended the Cake, You Can't Take the Parts Back to the Main Ingredients': Black Gay and Bisexual Men's Descriptions and Experiences of Intersectionality." *Sex Roles* 68(11):754–767.

Brontsema, Robin. 2004. "A Queer Revolution: Reconceptualizing the Debate Over Linguistic Reclamation." *Colorado Research in Linguistics* 17(1):1–17.

Carroll, Aengus and Lucas Ramón Mendos. 2017. "A World Survey of Sexual Orientation Laws: Criminalisation, Protection, and Recognition." *International Lesbian, Gay, Bisexual, Trans and Intersex Association (ILGA)*.

Clarke, Jessica A. 2018. "They, Them, and Theirs." *Harvard Law Review* 132:894.

Clogg, Clifford C., Eva Petkova, and Adamantios Haritou. 1995. "Statistical Methods for Comparing Regression Coefficients Between Models." *American Journal of Sociology* 100(5):1261–1293.

Coston, Bethany M. 2017. "Power and Inequality: Intimate Partner Violence Against Bisexual and Non-Monosexual Women in the United States." *Journal of Interpersonal Violence* DOI: 088626051772641.

Cramer, Robert J., Audrey K. Miller, Amanda M. Amacker, and Alixandra C. Burks. 2013. "Openness, Right-Wing Authoritarianism, and Antigay Prejudice in College Students: A Mediational Model." *Journal of Counseling Psychology* 60(1):64–71.

Crouch, Julie L., Rochelle F. Hanson, Benjamin E. Saunders, Dean G. Kilpatrick, and Heidi S. Resnick. 2000. "Income, Race/Ethnicity, and Exposure to Violence in Youth: Results from the National Survey of Adolescents." *Journal of Community Psychology* 28(6):625–641.

Cullen, Jenifer, Lester Wright, and Michael Alessandri. 2002. "The Personality Variable Openness to Experience as It Relates to Homophobia." *Journal of Homosexuality* 42(4):119–134.

Decker, Michele R., Amanda D. Latimore, Suzumi Yasutake, Miriam Haviland, Saifuddin Ahmed, Robert W. Blum, Freya Sonenstein, and Nan Marie Astone. 2015. "Gender-Based Violence Against Adolescent and Young Adult Women in Low- and Middle-Income Countries." *Journal of Adolescent Health* 56(2):188–196.

DeKeseredy, Walter and Martin Schwartz. 2009. *Dangerous Exits: Escaping Abusive Relationships in Rural America.* New Brunswick, New Jersey: Rutgers University Press.

Dowsett, Gilbert. 2009. "The 'Gay Plague' Revisited: AIDS and its Enduring Moral Panic." Pp. 130–56 in *Moral Panics, Sex Panics: Fear and the Fight Over Sexual Rights*, edited by Gilbert Herdt New York, NY: NYU Press.

Eliason, Michele J. 1996. "Identity Formation for Lesbian, Bisexual, and Gay Persons: Beyond a 'Minoritizing' View." *Journal of Homosexuality* 30(3):31–58.

Embrick, David G., Carol S. Walther, and Corrine M. Wickens. 2007. "Working Class Masculinity: Keeping Gay Men and Lesbians out of the Workplace." *Sex Roles* 56(11):757–766.

Ender, Phil. 2010. "Collinearity Issues." Retrieved January 7, 2019 (www.philender.com/courses/categorical/notes2/collin.html).

Fisher, Sycarah, Jennifer L. Reynolds, Wei-Wen Hsu, Jessica Barnes, and Kenneth Tyler. 2014. "Examining Multiracial Youth in Context: Ethnic Identity Development and Mental Health Outcomes." *Journal of Youth and Adolescence* 43(10):1688–1699.

Frederick, David A. and Melissa R. Fales. 2016. "Upset Over Sexual versus Emotional Infidelity Among Gay, Lesbian, Bisexual, and Heterosexual Adults." *Archives of Sexual Behavior* 45(1):175–191.

Friedman, Carly and Campbell Leaper. 2010. "Sexual-Minority College Women's Experiences with Discrimination: Relations with Identity and Collective Action." *Psychology of Women Quarterly* 34(2):152–164.

Gallup. 2019. "Gay and Lesbian Rights: In Depth Topics A to Z." *Gallup*. Retrieved February 6, 2019 (https://news.gallup.com/poll/1651/Gay-Lesbian-Rights.aspx).

Galupo, M. Paz, Edward Lomash, and Renae C. Mitchell. 2017. "All of My Lovers Fit into this Scale": Sexual Minority Individuals' Responses to Two Novel Measures of Sexual Orientation." *Journal of Homosexuality* 64(2):145–165.

Grier, Tiffanie, Carol Rambo, and Marshall A. Taylor. 2014. "'What Are You?': Racial Ambiguity, Stigma, and the Racial Formation Project." *Deviant Behavior* 35(12):1006–1022.

Grossman, Arnold H., Anthony R. D'Augelli, Tamika Jarrett Howell, and Steven Hubbard. 2005a. "Parents' Reactions to Transgender Youths' Gender Nonconforming Expression and Identity." *Journal of Gay & Lesbian Social Services* 18(1):3–16.

Grossman, Susan F., Sarah Hinkley, Annie Kawalski, and Carolyn Margrave. 2005b. "Rural Versus Urban Victims of Violence: The Interplay of Race and Region." *Journal of Family Violence* 20(2):71–81.

Han, Chong-suk. 2007. "They Don't Want To Cruise Your Type: Gay Men of Color and the Racial Politics of Exclusion." *Social Identities* 13(1):51–67.

Heflick, Nathan. 2010. "EWWW … Anal Sex Is Icky!" *Psychology Today*. Retrieved April 1, 2019 (www.psychologytoday.com/us/blog/the-big-questions/201002/ewwwanal-sex-is-icky).

Herek, Gregory M. 1988. "Heterosexuals' Attitudes toward Lesbians and Gay Men: Correlates and Gender Differences." *Journal of Sex Research* 25(4):451–477.

Herek, Gregory M. 2000. "Sexual Prejudice and Gender: Do Heterosexuals' Attitudes Toward Lesbians and Gay Men Differ?" *Journal of Social Issues* 56(2):251–266.

Herek, Gregory M. 2002. "Gender Gaps in Public Opinion about Lesbians and Gay Men." *Public Opinion Quarterly* 66(1):40–66.

Herek, Gregory M. and John Capitanio. 1996. "'Some of My Best Friends' Intergroup Contact, Concealable Stigma, and Heterosexuals' Attitudes Toward Gay Men and Lesbians." *Personality and Social Psychology Bulletin* 22(4):412–424.

Herek, Gregory M. and John Capitanio. 1999. "AIDS Stigma and Sexual Prejudice." *American Behavioral Scientist* 42(7):1130–1147.

Herek, Gregory M., J. Roy Gillis, and Jeanine C. Cogan. 1999. "Psychological Sequelae of Hate-Crime Victimization among Lesbian, Gay, and Bisexual Adults." *Journal of Consulting and Clinical Psychology* 67(6):945–951.

Herman, Melissa. 2004. "Forced to Choose: Some Determinants of Racial Identification in Multiracial Adolescents." *Child Development* 75(3):730–748.

Hill, Darryl B. and Brian L. B. Willoughby. 2005. "The Development and Validation of the Genderism and Transphobia Scale." *Sex Roles* 53(7/8):531–544.

Hinrichs, Donald W. and Pamela J. Rosenberg. 2002. "Attitudes Toward Gay, Lesbian, and Bisexual Persons Among Heterosexual Liberal Arts College Students." *Journal of Homosexuality* 43(1):61–84.

Huebner, David M., Gregory M. Rebchook, and Susan M. Kegeles. 2004. "Experiences of Harassment, Discrimination, and Physical Violence Among Young Gay and Bisexual Men." *American Journal of Public Health* 94(7):1200–1203.

Human Rights Campaign. 2018. *Dismantling a Culture of Violence: Understanding Anti-Transgender Violence and Ending the Crisis*. Washington, D.C: Human Rights Campaign Foundation.

Jagsi, Reshma, Kent A. Griffith, Rochelle Jones, Chithra R. Perumalswami, Peter Ubel, and Abigail Stewart. 2016. "Sexual Harassment and Discrimination Experiences of Academic Medical Faculty." *JAMA* 315(19):2120–2121.

Jones, Richard G. 2015. "Queering the Body Politic: Intersectional Reflexivity in the Body Narratives of Queer Men." *Qualitative Inquiry* 21(9):766–775.

Kalichman, Seth C., Eric Benotsch, David Rompa, Cheryl Gore-Felton, James Austin, Webster Luke, Kari DiFonzo, Jeff Buckles, Florence Kyomugisha, and Dolores Simpson. 2001. "Unwanted Sexual Experiences and Sexual Risks in Gay and Bisexual Men: Associations among Revictimization, Substance Use, and Psychiatric Symptoms." *The Journal of Sex Research* 38(1):1–9.

Katz-Wise, Sabra L. and Janet S. Hyde. 2012. "Victimization Experiences of Lesbian, Gay, and Bisexual Individuals: A Meta-Analysis." *The Journal of Sex Research* 49(2/3):142–167.

Lemelle, Anthony and Juan Battle. 2004. "Black Masculinity Matters in Attitudes Toward Gay Males." *Journal of Homosexuality* 47(1):39–51.

Lewis, Mel. 2017. "A Genuine Article: Intersectionality, Black Lesbian Gender Expression, and the Feminist Pedagogical Project." *Journal of Lesbian Studies* 21(4):420–431.

Li, Qing, Russell S. Kirby, Robert T. Sigler, Sean-Shong Hwang, Mark E. LaGory, and Robert L. Goldenberg. 2010. "A Multilevel Analysis of Individual, Household, and Neighborhood Correlates of Intimate Partner Violence Among Low-Income Pregnant Women in Jefferson County, Alabama." *American Journal of Public Health* 100(3):531–539.

Lind, Amy. 2004. "Legislating the Family: Heterosexual Bias in Social Welfare Policy Frameworks." *Journal of Sociology and Social Welfare* 31:21–36.

Logie, Carmen H. and Valerie Earnshaw. 2015. "Adapting and Validating a Scale to Measure Sexual Stigma among Lesbian, Bisexual and Queer Women." *Plos One* 10(2): e0116198.

Logie, Carmen H. and Marie-Jolie Rwigema. 2014. "'The Normative Idea of Queer Is a White Person': Understanding Perceptions of White Privilege Among Lesbian, Bisexual, and Queer Women of Color in Toronto, Canada." *Journal of Lesbian Studies* 18(2):174–191.

Marcus, Nancy C. 2015. "Bridging Bisexual Erasure in LGBT-Rights Discourse and Litigation." *Michigan Journal of Gender & Law* 22(2):291–344.

Matsuno, Emmie and Stephanie L. Budge. 2017. "Non-binary/Genderqueer Identities: A Critical Review of the Literature." *Current Sexual Health Reports* 9(3):116–120.

Mays, Vickie M. and Susan D. Cochran. 2001. "Mental Health Correlates of Perceived Discrimination Among Lesbian, Gay, and Bisexual Adults in the United States." *American Journal of Public Health* 91(11):1869–1876.

McDavitt, Bryce and Matt G. Mutchler. 2014. "'Dude, You're Such a Slut!' Barriers and Facilitators of Sexual Communication Among Young Gay Men and Their Best Friends." *Journal of Adolescent Research* 29(4):464–498.

Mereish, Ethan H., Sabra L. Katz-Wise and Julie Woulfe. 2017. "We're Here and We're Queer: Sexual Orientation and Sexual Fluidity Differences Between Bisexual and Queer Women." *Journal of Bisexuality* 17(1):125–139.

Meyer, Doug. 2015. *Violence Against Queer People: Race, Class, Gender, and the Persistence of Anti-LGBT Discrimination*. New Brunswick, NJ: Rutgers University Press.

Morandini, James S., Alexander Blaszczynski, and Ilan Dar-Nimrod. 2017. "Who Adopts Queer and Pansexual Sexual Identities?." *The Journal of Sex Research* 54(7):911–922.

Norton, Aaron T. and Gregory M. Herek. 2013. "Heterosexuals' Attitudes Toward Transgender People: Findings from a National Probability Sample of U.S. Adults." *Sex Roles* 68(11–12):738–753.

Ojerholm, Amy and Esther Rothblum. 1999. "The Relationships of Body Image, Feminism and Sexual Orientation in College Women." *Feminism & Psychology* 9:431–448.

Pettigrew, Thomas F. and Linda R. Tropp. 2006. "A Meta-Analytic Test of Intergroup Contact Theory." *Journal of Personality and Social Psychology* 90(5):751–783.

Pew Research Center 2013. "Chapter 2: Social Acceptance." Retrieved February 7, 2019 (www.pewsocialtrends.org/2013/06/13/chapter-2-social-acceptance/).

Pew Research Center 2017. "Majorities in Both Parties Now Say Homosexuality Should Be Accepted." Retrieved January 7, 2019 (www.people-press.org/2017/10/05/5-homosexuality-gender-and-religion/5_1-8/).

Richards, Christina, Walter Pierre Bouman and Meg-John Barker, (eds). 2017. *Genderqueer and Non-binary Genders*. London, UK: Palgrave Macmillan.

Shackelford, Todd K. and Avi Besser. 2007. "Predicting Attitudes toward Homosexuality: Insights from Personality Psychology." *Individual Differences Research* 5(2):9.

Spalding, Leah R. and Letitia Anne Peplau. 1997. "The Unfaithful Lover: Heterosexuals' Perceptions of Bisexuals and their Relationships." *Psychology of Women Quarterly* 21(4):611–625.

Stacey, Michele, Paige Averett, and Brianna Knox. 2018. "An Exploration of Victimization in the Older Lesbian Population." *Victims & Offenders* 13(5):693–710.

Stachowiak, Dana M. 2017. "Queering It up, Strutting Our Threads, and Baring Our Souls: Genderqueer Individuals Negotiating Social and Felt Sense of Gender." *Journal of Gender Studies* 26(5):532–543.

Stephenson, Rob and Catherine Finneran. 2017. "Minority Stress and Intimate Partner Violence Among Gay and Bisexual Men in Atlanta." *American Journal of Men's Health* 11(4):952–961.

Swank, Eric. 2018. "Sexual Identities and Participation in Liberal and Conservative Social Movements." *Social Science Research* 74:176–186.

Truong, Nhan, Amaya Perez-Brumer, Melissa Burton, June Gipson, and DeMarc Hickson. 2016. "What's in a Label?: Multiple Meanings of 'MSM' among Same-Gender-Loving Black Men in Mississippi." *Global Public Health* 11(7/8):937–952.

Van Voorhis, Carmen R. Wilson, and Betsy L. Morgan. 2007. "Understanding Power and Rules of Thumb for Determining Sample Sizes." *Tutorials in Quantitative Methods for Psychology* 3(2):43–50.

Weiss, Jillian Todd. 2004. "GL vs. BT: The Archaeology of Biphobia and Transphobia within the US Gay and Lesbian Community." *Journal of Bisexuality* 3(3/4):25–55.

Worthen, Meredith G. F. 2012. "Heterosexual College Student Sexual Experiences, Feminist Identity, and Attitudes Toward LGBT Individuals." *Journal of LGBT Youth* 9:77–113.

Worthen, Meredith G. F. 2013. "An Argument for Separate Analyses of Attitudes Toward Lesbian, Gay, Bisexual Men, Bisexual Women, MtF and FtM Transgender Individuals." *Sex Roles* 68(11):703–723.

Worthen, Meredith G. F. 2016. "Hetero-cis–normativity and the Gendering of Transphobia." *International Journal of Transgenderism* 17(1):31–57.

Worthen, Meredith G. F. 2018. "'Gay Equals White'? Racial, Ethnic, and Sexual Identities and Attitudes Toward LGBT Individuals Among College Students at a Bible Belt University." *The Journal of Sex Research* 55(8):995–1011.

Worthen, Meredith G. F., Vittorio Lingiardi, and Chiara Caristo. 2017. "The Roles of Politics, Feminism, and Religion in Attitudes Toward LGBT Individuals: A Cross-Cultural Study of College Students in the USA, Italy, and Spain." *Sexuality Research and Social Policy* 14(3):241–258.

# 8
# LESBIAN WOMEN STIGMA

*The Lesbian has been downtrodden, but doubly so: first, because she is a woman, and second, because she is a Lesbian.*
  Del Martin and Phyllis Lyon (1972:7), co-founders[1] of the Daughters of Bilitis

**IMAGE 8.1** Published from 1956 to 1972, *The Ladder* was the first lesbian-focused publication to be distributed nationally. It was produced by the Daughters of Bilitis which was the first lesbian civil and political rights organization in the United States. This cover image from the October 1957 issue reflects the difficulties that many closeted lesbian women experienced in hiding behind "masks" and advocated for a time when lesbian women could be more open about their identities.

## The Stigmatization of Lesbian Women

In the survey instrument, the section focusing on attitudes toward lesbian women was preceded by the following statement:

> *Next, please let us know your thoughts, feelings, and predicted behaviors about lesbian women (women who have romantic and sexual attractions to women).*

### The Lesbian Women Stigma Scale

Based on comparisons of all nine of the summed LGBTQ Stigma Scales, lesbian women are the least stigmatized group examined in this book (recall Figure 7.1). Even so, it is important to understand the particulars of lesbian stigmatization. The 14 items in the Lesbian Women Stigma Scale are included in Figure 8.1 and Table 8.1 and are further discussed below by key area.

### Lesbian Women and Social and Familial Relationships

Overall, lesbian stigma in this key area is low with means ranging from 1.55 to 2.24. Such results indicate that there is not pervasive negativity toward having lesbian women friends and family members among this sample. These

| Item | LGBTQ Subsample | Hetero-cis Subsample |
|---|---|---|
| Not Feminine Enough | 1.99 | 2.60 |
| Too Sexual/Hypersexual | 1.98 | 2.59 |
| Identity is Just Temporary/Experimental | 1.96 | 2.59 |
| Discomfort with Sex w/Man | 2.22 | 2.57 |
| Unfaithful | 1.96 | 2.56 |
| Discomfort with Sex w/Woman | 1.60 | 2.56 |
| Not Vote for Political Candidate | 1.62 | 2.46 |
| Restrict from Military | 1.67 | 2.43 |
| Responsible for HIV/AIDS | 1.60 | 2.40 |
| As Good Parents | 1.58 | 2.24 |
| As New Friends | 1.65 | 2.16 |
| As Family/Close Relative | 1.55 | 2.11 |
| Deny Basic Rights | 1.40 | 1.99 |
| Victimization is Not Upsetting to Me | 1.47 | 1.99 |

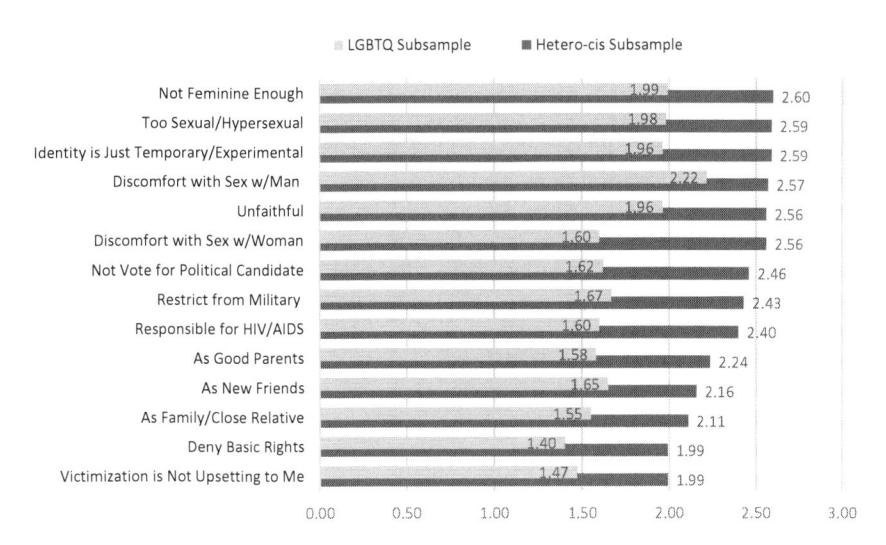

**FIGURE 8.1** Lesbian Women Stigma Scale Item Mean Values Rank-Ordered from Most to Least Stigmatizing for the Hetero-cis (n = 1,500) and the LGBTQ (n = 1,604) Subsamples

*Notes:* see Table 8.1 for the exact wording for each item. *t*-test results comparing the hetero-cis and LGBTQ subsamples indicate that all means are significantly different from one another at the p < .001 level.

**TABLE 8.1** Lesbian Women Stigma Scale Item Mean Values (Standard Deviations) and t-test Results Comparing the Means for the Hetero-cis Subsample and the LGBTQ Subsample

|  | Hetero-cis Subsample | LGBTQ Subsample | t-test Results |
|---|---|---|---|
|  | n = 1,500 | n = 1,604 |  |
| *Social and familial relationships* |  |  |  |
| I welcome new friends who are lesbian women. [R] | 2.16 (1.11) | 1.65 (0.96) | t = 13.61* |
| I don't think it would negatively affect our relationship if I learned that one of my close relatives was a lesbian woman. [R] | 2.11 (1.13) | 1.55 (0.97) | t = 14.59* |
| Lesbian women are not capable of being good parents. | 2.24 (1.29) | 1.58 (1.08) | t = 15.48* |
| *Positions of importance and social significance* |  |  |  |
| I would not vote for a political candidate who was an openly lesbian woman. | 2.46 (1.37) | 1.62 (1.13) | t = 18.46* |
| Lesbian women should not be allowed to join the military. | 2.43 (1.38) | 1.67 (1.20) | t = 16.18* |
| *Basic human rights* |  |  |  |
| I believe lesbian women should have all of the same rights as other people do. [R] | 1.99 (1.13) | 1.40 (0.86) | t = 16.32* |
| It is upsetting to me that lesbian women experience violence, harassment, and discrimination just because they are lesbian women. [R] | 1.99 (1.11) | 1.47 (0.93) | t = 13.91* |
| *Sex act-related stigma* |  |  |  |
| Lesbian women are unfaithful to their romantic partners. | 2.56 (1.18) | 1.96 (1.11) | t = 14.63* |
| Lesbian women are too sexual (hypersexual). | 2.59 (1.18) | 1.98 (1.11) | t = 14.79* |
| Lesbian women are mostly responsible for spreading HIV/AIDS. | 2.40 (1.21) | 1.60 (1.01) | t = 19.90* |
| I am comfortable with the thought of a lesbian woman having sex with a woman. [R] | 2.56 (1.24) | 1.60 (0.99) | t = 23.77* |
| I am comfortable with the thought of a lesbian woman having sex with a man. | 2.57 (1.13) | 2.22 (1.20) | t = 8.45* |
| *Lesbian identity permanency* |  |  |  |
| Most women who call themselves lesbians are just temporarily experimenting with their sexuality. | 2.59 (1.16) | 1.96 (1.13) | t = 15.32* |
| *Achievement of femininity* |  |  |  |
| Lesbian women are not feminine enough. | 2.60 (1.16) | 1.99 (1.14) | t = 14.77* |
| α | .90 | .90 |  |
| Summed scale actual range | 14-68 | 14-58 |  |
| Summed scale mean | 33.25 (11.10) | 24.27 (9.87) | t = 23.76* |

*Notes:* response options were Strongly Disagree–Strongly Agree (range: 1–5). [R] This item is reverse coded.
* t-test results allowing for unequal variances indicate that the hetero-cis subsample and LGBTQ subsample means are significantly different from one another at the $p < .001$ level.

findings reflect shifts in the visibility of lesbian women in social and familial networks. For example, U.S. Gallup Poll (1985–2013) trends demonstrate that while only 24% of people in 1985 indicated having a gay or lesbian friend, relative, or co-worker, this number tripled to 75% by 2013 (Gallup 2019). In addition, U.S. Pew Research Center Data show that lesbian women are between two and nearly six times more likely than bisexual individuals to have told all or most of their family and friends about their sexual identity (71% of lesbian women compared to 33% of bisexual women and 12% of bisexual men) (Pew Research Center 2013a). Thus, as more lesbian women are out amongst their social and familial networks (alongside myriad other social climate shifts), there is more support of lesbian women as friends and family members.

The item in this key area with the lowest mean values for both groups is: "I don't think it would negatively affect our relationship if I learned that one of my close relatives was a lesbian woman," which was reverse coded. Lesbian women are sometimes stereotyped as both relationship- and family-oriented (Eliason 2010) and there is some research to support these perspectives. Indeed, U.S. Pew Research Center data (2013b) indicate that 66% of lesbian women are in committed relationships which closely approximates the 70% of the general public who are in committed relationships (but is significantly more than the 40% of gay men in committed relationships). In addition, lesbian women are twice as likely to have children when compared to gay men (31% of lesbian women vs. 16% of gay men) (Pew Research Center 2013c). Overall, these patterns contribute to support of and comfort with having a lesbian woman relative.

The item in this key area with the highest mean value for the hetero-cis subsample (2.24) is: "Lesbian women are not capable of being good parents." There has been heated debate about the "fitness" of lesbian parents in politicized media (Crawford et al. 1999; Gander 2018; Joos and Broad 2007). The cultural stigmatization of lesbian parents can be seen in problematic stereotypes about "family" (e.g., a child with two mothers will be too emotional; a good family needs both a mother and a father), false beliefs about children in lesbian-parent households (e.g., they fare worse than those in heterosexual-parent households), and religion (e.g., the holy scripture dictates that being a lesbian is a sin) (Clarke 2001; Wall 2013). However, these negative perspectives about lesbian parents have shifted somewhat over time. For example, U.S. public opinion data indicate that support for the legal adoption of children among same-sex couples close to tripled in recent decades with only 29% supporting same-sex adoption in 1992 compared to 75% in 2019 (Gallup 2014; McCarthy 2019). In addition, there is some evidence that lesbian mothers are more socially accepted than gay fathers. In a small study conducted in Italy with older, heterosexual adults (N = 280), lesbian women parents were rated significantly better than gay men parents in terms of emotional stability, competence, nurturance, sensitivity, and affection. In addition, participants perceived fewer problematic negative outcomes for the children of lesbian women as compared to children of gay men parents (Baiocco et al. 2013). Even so, there remains a palpable stigma directed toward lesbian women as "capable" parents and they continue to face barriers with becoming and being parents (Brown et al. 2009; Wall 2013).

The item in this key area with the highest mean value (1.65) for the LGBTQ subsample is: "I welcome new friends who are lesbian women," which was reverse coded. This finding suggests that within the LGBTQ community, there is slightly stronger disagreement with the welcoming of lesbian friends as compared to the support of lesbian relatives (1.55) and parents (1.58). There is an historical basis for this finding. Indeed, due to both the general association of "gay" with "man" and the patriarchal domination of White gay cis men in the Gay Liberation Movement of the 1970s onward, lesbian women have been marginalized. As a result, many lesbian women retreated from the larger "gay" movement starting in the 1970s (Stein 1997; Weiss 2004). While out gay men frequently adopted an assimilationist strategy (i.e., "Gay people are just like you"), many lesbian women opted for more separatist, radical strategies splitting themselves from gay men as well as bisexual and trans women (Rust 1995; Weiss 2004). More recently, lesbian friendship patterns reflect this trend. For example, lesbian women have been found to have a more exclusive preference for friendships with other lesbian women as compared to gay men's, bisexual men's, and bisexual women's friendship preferences (Galupo 2007). In addition, lesbian friendships have different cultural meanings than other types of friendships within the LGBTQ community (Weinstock and Rothblum 2018). Overall, the historical schisms between lesbian women and others in the LGBTQ community likely shape the stigmatization toward lesbian friendships found within this LGBTQ subsample.

## *Lesbian Women and Positions of Importance and Social Significance*

Overall, there was low stigmatization of lesbian women in positions of importance and social significance with means ranging from 1.62 to 2.46. The two items in this key area are: "I would not vote for a political candidate who was an openly lesbian woman" and "Lesbian women should not be allowed to join the military." The means were quite similar for the hetero-cis subsample for these two items. However, for the LGBTQ subsample, there was just slightly higher stigmatization toward lesbian women in the military (1.67) as compared to lesbian women political candidates (1.62). Most LGBTQ people are especially cognizant of the palpable LGBTQ negativity in the Armed Forces (Burks 2011). For example, Pew Research Center Data indicates that over half (51%) of lesbian women and 39% of gay men view the military as especially un-LGBTQ-friendly (Pew Research Center 2013a). In addition, according to the RAND Corporation, lesbian and bisexual women serve in the military at significantly higher rates than gay and bisexual men. Specifically, 2011 estimates indicate that lesbian and bisexual women comprised 10.7% of women in the military but only 4.2% in the general population while gay and bisexual men comprised 2.2% of men in the military and 3.2% in the general population (Rostker, Hosek, and Vaiana 2011). Thus, lesbian and bisexual women are particularly vulnerable in the military and LGBTQ people are likely to be keenly aware of this. For example, in 2008 during the ban on openly LGB people from serving in the U.S. military (DADT)[2], women comprised 15% of the U.S. Armed Forces but more than one-third of those discharged due to their sexual identity (Associated Press 2009). Furthermore, the military's overt preference for masculine hetero-cis men and the denigration and exclusion of women and LGBTQ people are well-recognized among LGBTQ people (Allsep 2013; Worthen 2019b). Due to their increased awareness of both specific lesbian negativity and more generalized LGBTQ hostility in the Armed Forces, LGBTQ people may harbor some hesitancy toward LGBTQ military inclusion. In addition, the awareness of the difficulties lesbian women might endure in the military (due to both their gender and sexuality) likely contributes to some LGBTQ people's caution toward supporting the inclusion of lesbian women in the military.

## Lesbian Women and Sex Act-Related Stigma

Overall, there was more support for lesbian sex act-related stigma as compared to many of the other key areas with most means for the five items in this key area close to 2.50 or higher among the hetero-cis subsample. As seen in Figure 8.1, four of the top six most stigmatizing attitudes toward lesbian women are found among the sex act-related stigma items (hypersexuality, discomfort with sex with men and women, and unfaithful). As noted in Chapters 3 and 6 especially, LGBTQ people are stigmatized because their sexualities and the sex acts they are believed to be involved in are deemed to be abnormal and culturally problematic. Described as "sexual deviants," "perverts," "pedophiles," LGBTQ people's experiences with negativity are closely entwined with sex act-related stigma. For lesbian women, sex act-related stigma is embedded in additional cultural processes that eroticize them as well as objectify and diminish their value both as women and as lesbians (Rupp and Taylor 2010). As a result, lesbian sex act-related stigma involves overlapping stereotypes about gender, sexuality, and sexual behavior.

In Table 8.1, the item with the lowest mean value in the sex act-related stigma key area for both groups is: "Lesbian women are mostly responsible for spreading HIV/AIDS." Generally, HIV/AIDS-related stigma has been associated with gay, bisexual, and queer men (Dowsett 2009; Herek and Capitanio

1999; McKirnan et al. 1995). Even so, due to stereotypes about lesbian women and their sexual behaviors, lesbian women who are HIV-positive tend to be ignored and marginalized (Logie et al. 2012). Such processes shape stigmatizing perspectives about HIV/AIDS that relate to problematic stereotypes about lesbian women.

The item with the highest mean value in the sex act-related stigma key area for the hetero-cis subsample (2.59) is: "Lesbian women are too sexual (hypersexual)" (the mean was also relatively high for the LGBTQ subsample at 1.98). In many Western cultures, lesbian women are both sexualized and eroticized, especially by heterosexual men (LaMar and Kite 1998; Louderback and Whitley 1997; Raja and Stokes 1998; Worthen 2013). In particular, certain types of lesbian women, sometimes described as "lipstick" or "femme," embody heteronormative conceptualizations of attractiveness. Because they stereotypically look like the heterosexual women who are also frequently eroticized, they can be perceived of as sexual objects to heterosexual men. In addition, numerous media outlets designed to appeal to heterosexual men—including pornography—feature highly sexualized lipstick/femme lesbian women. Together, these processes contribute to the cultural perspective that lesbian women are "too sexual" and these attitudes are strongest among heterosexual men (the mean for this item was 2.84 for heterosexual men).

The two items, "I am comfortable with the thought of a lesbian woman having sex with a woman" and "I am comfortable with the thought of a lesbian woman having sex with a man," (which were both reverse coded because *dis*comfort with lesbian women engaging in sex acts reflects a stigmatizing attitude toward lesbian women) yielded some interesting patterns. While hetero-cis people's negative attitudes toward lesbian sex acts with women and men are significantly higher than LGBTQ people's perspectives (2.56/2.57 compared to 1.60/2.22 respectively), there are gendered processes at work here that deserve further attention. For heterosexual men in particular, both comfort with lesbian women having sex with women and comfort with lesbian women having sex with men reflect erotic fantasies of participating in group sex with lesbian women, "turning" lesbian women straight via their own sexual prowess, and/or a generalized affinity toward lesbians (especially if they themselves, specifically, or men, generally, may be able to have sex with them) (Louderback and Whitley 1997; Rupp and Taylor 2010; Worthen 2013). Indeed, compared to heterosexual women, heterosexual men indicated *less discomfort* with lesbian women having sex with women (mean values for this item were 2.64 for heterosexual women compared to 2.49 for heterosexual men) and lesbian women having sex with men (mean values for this item were 2.71 for heterosexual women compared to 2.45 for heterosexual men).

In contrast, compared to all other items in the Lesbian Women Stigma Scale, LGBTQ people indicated their highest levels of stigmatization toward lesbian women having sex with men (2.22). In fact, for the LGBTQ sample only, lesbian women are the most likely of all nine LGBTQ groups to experience stigma associated with their potential sex acts with men (recall Figure 7.4). Due to their own experiences with being disregarded in their sexual preferences, LGBTQ people may feel that being comfortable with lesbian women having sex with men reinforces negativity toward lesbian women's preferred/desired sex acts with women. In addition, this may also reflect a delegitimizing perspective that lesbian identities are temporary, experimental, or even changeable (see more about this below), which is particularly distressing for LGBTQ people who must regularly defend their identities.

## Lesbian Identity Permanency

There is support for stigma associated with lesbian identity permanency. As seen in Figure 8.1, the means for this item were amongst the top five most stigmatizing attitudes for both the hetero-cis and LGBTQ subsamples (2.59 and 1.96, respectively). Thus, there is some agreement across the entire sample that "Most women who call themselves lesbians are just temporarily experimenting with their sexuality." The stereotype that lesbian women are going through an "experimental phase" is amplified by the "straight girls kissing" phenomenon whereby women, especially college-aged women, kiss other young women in public social/drinking settings (e.g., at parties and bars/clubs/pubs) to garner attention from heterosexual men (Rupp and Taylor 2010). Indeed, as demonstrated by the $t$-test results, the mean value on this item was significantly higher for the hetero-cis subsample as compared to the LGBTQ subsample perhaps because heterosexual men and women are more likely to participate in these straight girls kissing/hetero-male gaze experiences. Overall, despite the ample research that confirms lesbian identity permanence (Diamond 2003, 2008), the erotic value placed on women kissing other women (in social settings and in media/pornography) coupled with the titillating notion that this is "just for fun" continue to contribute to the problematic belief that lesbian women are just temporarily experimenting with their sexuality.

## Lesbian Women and the Achievement of Femininity

There is moderate support for stigma associated with lesbian women and the achievement of femininity. In particular, across all 14 items in the Lesbian Women Stigma Scale, this item has the highest mean value for the hetero-cis subsample (2.60) and has the second highest mean value for the LGBTQ subsample (1.99) (see Figure 8.1). Thus, there is agreement across the entire sample that "Lesbian women are not feminine enough." Perceptions of masculinity and femininity are rooted in a hetero-cis-normative process that dictates being "feminine" as necessarily entwined with being involved in relationships with men. Because lesbian women are not in relationships with men, they are stereotyped as unable to achieve this idealized form of femininity.

In addition, research suggests that lesbian women's femininities are often critiqued and some lesbian women are stereotyped as masculine (Eliason 2010; Eliason, Donelan, and Randall 1992; Geiger, Harwood, and Hummert 2006). For example, there are a host of terms/slurs associated with lesbian women and masculinity including "butch," "dyke," "bull dyke," "boi," "stud," "ag/aggressive." However, these are not universal for all lesbian women. In particular, "butch" lesbian women are more likely to be deemed by heterosexual men and women to be "not feminine enough" and as a result, they are not afforded the same social value as feminine "lipstick" lesbian women (Blair and Hoskin 2015). In contrast, LGBTQ people and lesbian women in particular are much more open to diverse gender expressions among lesbian women. For example, one study found that lesbian women regularly described themselves and their preferred partners as "androgynous" and they were equally likely to be interested in lesbian women with feminine or masculine leanings (Bailey et al. 1997). The findings reflect this pattern in the *t*-test results whereby the mean for the stereotype that "Lesbian women are not feminine enough" for the LGBTQ subsample was significantly lower than the mean value for the hetero-cis subsample. Even so, the (in)ability of lesbian women to achieve idealized femininity is a significant layer of lesbian stigmatization for both hetero-cis and LGBTQ people.

## *Lesbian Women Stigma Summed Scale*

As seen in Table 8.1, all 14 items were summed together to create the Lesbian Women Stigma Scale and Cronbach's alphas were quite high (.90) for both subsamples. The actual range in values differed between the two subsamples with the highest value for the hetero-cis subsample (68) 10 points higher than the highest value for the LGBTQ subsample (58). Mean values for the summed Lesbian Women Stigma Scale also differed substantially and significantly with the hetero-cis subsample mean (33.25) 8.98 points higher than the LGBTQ subsample mean (24.27). In addition, the key area with the highest individual mean values differed. For the hetero-cis subsample, the highest mean value was related to lesbian women's achievement of femininity (2.60) while for the LGBTQ subsample, the highest mean value was related to lesbian sex act-related stigma (2.22). However, it is important to note that for the hetero-cis subsample, lesbian women's identity permanency (2.59) and lesbian sex act-related stigma related to hypersexuality (2.59) were only .01 points less than the highest item. Similarly, for the LGBTQ subsample, lesbian women's identity permanency (1.96) and lesbian women's achievement of femininity (1.99) were also relatively high. Thus, it is fair to say that lesbian sex act-related stigma, lesbian women's identity permanency, and lesbian women's achievement of femininity are the driving forces behind the stigmatization of lesbian women (recall Figure 7.3).

## NCST, Hetero-cis-normativity, Social Power Axes, and the Lesbian Women Stigma Scale

The first set of regression models examine the Lesbian Women Stigma Scale using NCST. The hypotheses are as follows:

- *Hypothesis 1a*: there is a significant positive relationship between the HCN Scale and the Lesbian Women Stigma Scale.
- *Hypothesis 1b*: there are significant relationships between individual social power axes (gender identity, sexual identity, additional gender/sexuality, racial/ethnic identity, basic needs) and the Lesbian Women Stigma Scale.
- *Hypothesis 2a*: the relationship between the HCN Scale and the Lesbian Women Stigma Scale is moderated by interactions between the HCN Scale and axes of social power.
- *Hypothesis 2b*: the relationships between individual social power axes and the Lesbian Women Stigma Scale are moderated by interactions between axes of social power.

Figure 8.2 outlines these relationships and the two models of NCST to be estimated. Specifically, Table 8.2 utilizes OLS regression to examine NCST and the relationships among hetero-cis-normativity, axes of social power (gender, sexuality, additional gender/sexuality, race/ethnicity, and basic needs), and the Lesbian Women Stigma Scale for the hetero-cis subsample and the LGBTQ subsample. See Chapter 7 for a more complete description of the models. Regarding model fit statistics, the adjusted $R^2$ values ranged from .68 to .71.

## NCST, HCN, Social Power Axes, and the Lesbian Women Stigma Scale: Model 1

In Table 8.2, Model 1 estimates the HCN Scale and axes of social power as they relate to the Lesbian Women Stigma Scale. For both groups, there is a positive relationship between the HCN Scale and the Lesbian Women Stigma Scale in Model 1. Thus, *Hypothesis 1a* is well supported: hetero-cis-normativity is positively related to lesbian stigmatization for both subsamples. In addition, individual axes of social power are significantly related to lesbian stigmatization for the hetero-cis subsample (cis woman, Asian American/Pacific Islander, mostly all I need, and often basic needs not met) and for the LGBTQ subsample (cis woman, trans woman, leather, other race, and few needs met). Thus, *Hypothesis 1b* is well supported: individual social power axes are related to lesbian stigmatization for both subsamples. These relationships are notably robust because they emerge as significant even when a battery of established common explanations and sociodemographics are utilized as controls.

**176** NCST and Understanding LGBTQ Stigma

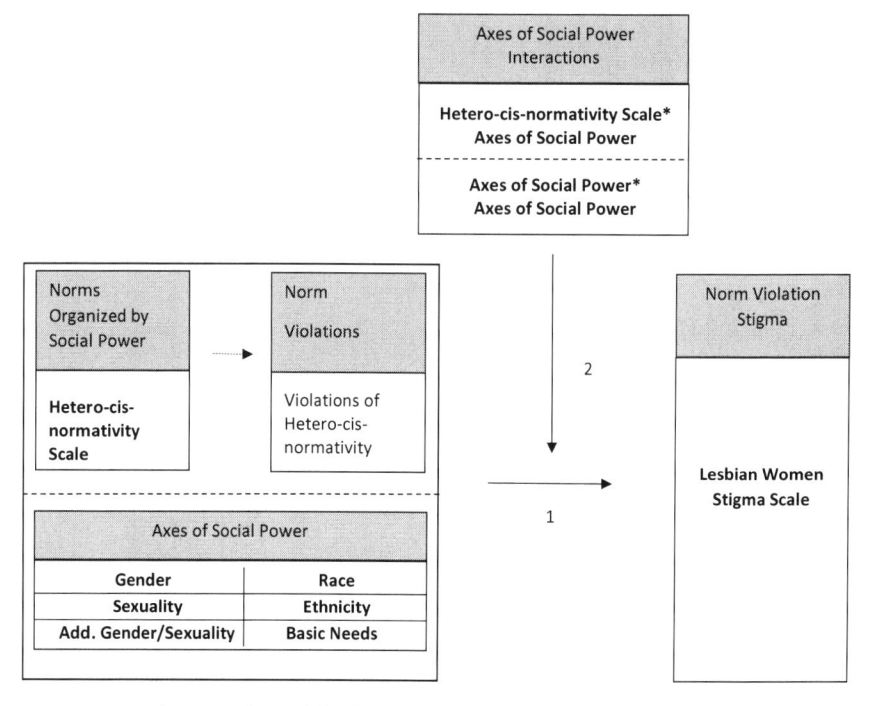

**FIGURE 8.2** Theoretical Model of NCST and Lesbian Stigma using the Stigmatizer Lens with Model Numbers to be Examined in Table 8.2

*Notes:* Model 1 estimates the HCN Scale and axes of social power (gender, sexuality, additional gender/sexuality, race, ethnicity, and basic needs) as they relate to the Lesbian Women Stigma Scale. Model 2 estimates interactions among axes of social power and the HCN Scale as they moderate the relationships between the HCN Scale and the Lesbian Women Stigma Scale as well as interactions among axes of social power as they moderate the relationships between the HCN Scale and the Lesbian Women Stigma Scale. The * indicates an interaction.

## NCST, HCN, Social Power Axes, and the Lesbian Women Stigma Scale: Model 2

Model 2 includes the addition of interaction effects among axes of social power and the HCN Scale as well as interaction effects among axes of social power. Even when including these interactions, the HCN Scale remains significantly positively related to the Lesbian Women Stigma Scale for both groups. In addition, HCN Scale and social power axes interaction effects are significant in Model 2 among both subsamples. For the hetero-cis subsample, interactions between the HCN Scale, queer, African American/Black, and Multi-racial are all significant (see Chapter 7 for a discussion of these). Among the LGBTQ subsample, interactions between the HCN Scale, asexual, Latinx (ethnicity), and Latinx (race) are also significant. While the individual effect of asexual is significantly negatively related to

**TABLE 8.2** OLS Regression Results Estimating NCST and the Lesbian Women Stigma Scale for the Hetero-cis Subsample (n = 1,500) and the LGBTQ Subsample (n = 1,604)

|  | Hetero-cis Subsample | | LGBTQ Subsample | | Test of Difference |
|---|---|---|---|---|---|
|  | *Model 1* | *Model 2* | *Model 1* | *Model 2* |  |
| HCN Scale | .71* | .74* | .72* | .55* | . |
| *Gender identity* | | | | | |
| Cis woman | -.95* | -2.11* | -1.11* | . | ** |
| Trans woman | — | — | 1.76* | . | |
| *Sexual identity* | | | | | |
| Pansexual | — | — | . | -10.78* | |
| Asexual | — | — | . | -6.91* | |
| *Additional sexual/gender identity* | | | | | |
| SGL | . | . | . | -7.21* | ** |
| Leather | . | . | 2.80* | . | |
| *Racial/ethnic identity* | | | | | |
| Asian American/Pacific Islander | 1.51* | . | . | . | |
| Other race | . | . | 4.23* | 5.86* | . |
| *Basic needs* | | | | | |
| Mostly all I need | -1.21* | . | . | . | |
| Often basic needs not met | -1.84* | . | . | -11.07* | . |
| Few needs met | . | . | 1.61* | . | |
| *HCN Scale\*Social power axes interactions* | | | | | |
| HCN Scale*asexual | — | — | — | .40* | |
| HCN Scale*queer | — | -.32* | — | . | ** |
| HCN Scale*African American/Black | — | -.26* | — | . | . |
| HCN Scale*Multi-racial | — | .66* | — | . | ** |
| HCN Scale*Latinx race | — | . | — | -.65* | . |
| HCN Scale*Latinx ethnicity | — | . | — | .14* | . |
| *Social power axes interactions* | | | | | |
| Cis woman*pansexual | — | — | — | 7.02* | |
| Cis woman*Multi-racial | — | -7.19* | — | . | ** |
| Cis woman*few needs met | — | . | — | 3.96* | ** |
| Trans woman*bisexual | — | — | — | -3.39* | |
| Gay/lesbian*SGL | — | — | — | 4.48* | |
| Bisexual*SGL | — | — | — | 5.77* | |
| Bisexual*often needs not met | — | — | — | 4.17* | |
| African American/Black*Two-Spirit | — | . | — | -5.71* | . |
| Asian American/Pacific Islander*mostly all I need | — | . | — | 3.17* | . |

*(Continued)*

**TABLE 8.2** (Cont.)

|  | Hetero-cis Subsample | | LGBTQ Subsample | | Test of Difference |
|---|---|---|---|---|---|
|  | Model 1 | Model 2 | Model 1 | Model 2 |  |
| Asian American/Pacific Islander* often needs not met | — | . | — | 6.12* | ** |
| Latinx ethnicity*SGL | — | 5.96* | — | . | ** |
| Latinx ethnicity*mostly all I need | — | . | — | -3.14* | ** |
| Mostly all I need*butch | — | . | — | 2.27* | ** |
| Mostly all I need*Two-Spirit | — | -4.76* | — | . | . |
| *Controls: common explanations* | | | | | |
| *LGBTQ contact* | | | | | |
| Lesbian friends | -.76* | -.77* | -1.61* | -1.53* | . |
| GBTQ Friends Scale | -.33* | -.36* | -.14* | . | . |
| *Religiosity* | | | | | |
| Church attendance | .36* | .40* | . | . | . |
| *Religious identity* | | | | | |
| Protestant—evangelical | 1.43* | . | 1.70* | 1.66* | . |
| *Political perspectives* | | | | | |
| Liberal—conservative | .36* | . | . | . | . |
| Openness to new experiences | -1.72* | -1.52* | -1.51* | -1.56* | . |
| *Support laws/policies helping:* | | | | | |
| Those in poverty | -2.39* | -2.31* | -1.36* | . | ** |
| Women | -1.46* | -1.60* | . | . | ** |
| *Beliefs about gender* | | | | | |
| Patriarchal Gender Norms Scale | .60* | .59* | .56* | .59* | . |
| *Sociodemographic controls* | | | | | |
| Age | .03* | .03* | .03* | .02* | . |
| Adjusted $R^2$ | .68 | .68 | .70 | .71 |  |
| Mean VIF | 1.50 | 1.50 | 1.92 | 1.92 |  |

*Notes:* unstandardized regression coefficients are presented. Only the rows with significant results are displayed here. See Table 8.1 for detailed information about the Lesbian Women Stigma Scale. See Tables 7.1 and 7.2 for details about all other variables and Appendix B Table B.1 for details about the interaction effects.

* $p < .05$; a dot (.) indicates non-statistically significant results. A dash (—) indicates this was not included in the model.

** $p < .05$ for Clogg et al.'s (1995) test of equality of regression coefficients comparing Model 2 for the hetero-cis subsample and Model 2 for the LGBTQ subsample.

lesbian stigmatization, the interaction term between asexual and the HCN Scale is positive. The positive HCN Scale and asexual interaction term indicates that the endorsement of hetero-cis-normativity has a larger effect on asexual individuals' lesbian attitudes as compared to non-asexual individuals' lesbian attitudes. Asexual people who support hetero-cis-normativity may indicate negativity toward lesbian women/LGBTQ people because there is some tension in regards to the inclusion of asexual people in the LGBTQ(A) community (despite efforts that attempt to appeal to potential commonalities of both asexual and LGBTQ people as stigmatized sexual minorities) (Colborne 2018; Pinto 2014). Indeed, asexuals and their experiences differ from those who express sexual interests in others (Carrigan 2011; Hoffarth et al. 2016). In particular, asexual women navigate a process of actively differentiating themselves from lesbian and bisexual individuals (Houdenhove et al. 2015) and these practices may reinforce hetero-cis-normativity in various ways. Embedded in these dynamics, there are relationships between lesbian negativity, hetero-cis-normativity, and asexuality.

Similarly, more support of the HCN Scale has a larger impact on Latinx (ethnicity) LGBTQ individuals' lesbian attitudes as compared to non-Latinx (ethnicity) LGBTQ individuals' lesbian attitudes. However, the reverse is true for Latinx (race) individuals and it is non-Latinx (race) LGBTQ individuals who are impacted by hetero-cis-normativity in more powerful ways as compared to Latinx (race) LGBTQ individuals when it comes to their attitudes toward lesbians. These results complement previous work that has found evidence of Latinx lesbian negativity (Herek and Gonzalez-Rivera 2006; Hirai, Winkel, and Popan 2014). Overall, *Hypothesis 2a* is supported: interactions between the HCN Scale and axes of social power moderate the relationship between the HCN Scale and the Lesbian Women Stigma Scale for both subsamples. Such findings suggest that there are intersecting relationships between sexual identities, racial/ethnic identities, hetero-cis-normativity, and lesbian stigmatization that deserve further attention, as demonstrated in some previous work (e.g., Bowleg 2013; Lemelle and Battle 2004; Worthen 2018b). In particular, hetero-cis-normativity may have qualitatively different meanings among these groups in ways that contribute to their perspectives about lesbian women. Thus, hetero-cis-normativity, though clearly antithetical to lesbian support, informs attitudes toward lesbians in complex ways when considering intersecting identities such as race and ethnicity.

Looking at the individual social power axes, for the hetero-cis subsample, only one remains significant in Model 2: being a cis woman (wherein the reference category is being a cis man) is negatively related to lesbian stigmatization. In addition, among the associated social power axes interactions, being a Multi-racial hetero-cis woman is negatively related to lesbian stigmatization. Lesbian support among Multi-racial hetero-cis women is shaped by their intersecting experiences. While most people of color experience some level of marginalization in the West, Multi-racial women have a unique positionality that can impact their support of lesbian women. In particular, Multi-racial women can regularly experience oppressive circumstances whereby their identities are called into question, mislabeled, ignored, and/or stigmatized (Grier, Rambo, and Taylor 2014; Herman 2010). Lesbian women may also experience rejection from multiple groups because they occupy (at least) two marginalized statuses as both gender and sexual minorities. As I have demonstrated elsewhere, liberal social justice perspectives (including support of lesbian women) may be particularly common among those with multiple oppressed identities and unique experiences with stigma and discrimination (Worthen 2018a; Worthen 2019a). Because both Multi-racial individuals and lesbian women have multiple oppressed identities, these commonalities may contribute to the support of lesbian women among Multi-racial hetero-cis women.

For the hetero-cis subsample, there are two more significant social power axes interaction terms with no significant individual effects. Being Latinx (ethnicity) and SGL is positively related to lesbian stigmatization. Though some research has demonstrated links between traditional Latinx cultural scripts and lesbian negativity (Herek and Gonzalez-Rivera 2006; see also, Chapter 4), findings here show that it is the intersecting experiences of being Latinx (ethnicity) and being SGL that most strongly relate to attitudes toward lesbian women. Such findings are notable because despite the common association of SGL identities with African American/Black communities, about 1 in 6 Latinx (ethnicity) individuals (16%, n = 54/342) in this study's sample identified as SGL. Negativity toward lesbian women among Latinx (ethnicity) SGL hetero-cis individuals may reflect both anti-lesbian Latinx cultural scripts (Herek and Gonzalez-Rivera 2006; Hirai, Winkel, and Popan 2014) as well as a preference for more culturally-specific identities such as SGL as opposed to the largely White-washed "lesbian" identity. In contrast, being a Two-Spirit individual with "mostly all" basic needs met is negatively related to lesbian stigmatization among the hetero-cis subsample. Close to half of Two-Spirit individuals (43%, n = 76/177) in this study's sample identified as hetero-cis. While there is existing research that has explored Two-Spirit individuals' lives (Gilley 2006, 2010; Walters et al. 2006), here, it is clear that the intersecting experiences of Two-Spirit, hetero-cis, and basic needs experiences work together to shape lesbian support.

In contrast to the hetero-cis subsample which only has a handful of significant results among the social power axes in Model 2, there are many more significant results for the LGBTQ subsample in Model 2. Additional tests to compare the regression coefficients of the two subsamples also reveal numerous significant differences (see final column of Table 8.1) (Clogg, Petkova, and Haritou 1995). Thus, the social power axes that relate to hetero-cis people's lesbian stigmatization largely differ from the social power axes that inform LGBTQ people's lesbian stigmatization.

In particular, with the exception of gender identity, there are significant findings across all of the other dimensions of social power as related to the Lesbian Women Stigma Scale for the LGBTQ subsample in Model 2. For example, among the sexual identities (wherein being heterosexual[3] is the reference category), being pansexual is negatively related to lesbian stigmatization. The "LGBTQ umbrella" can sometimes unite pansexuals with lesbians and others (Flanders 2017). In this way, the relationships between identifying as pansexual and supporting lesbian women may be indicative of an overlap between similarities, sympathies, and empathies among these groups.

However, while the baseline relationship between being pansexual and the Lesbian Women Stigma Scale is negative, among the social power axes interaction effects, being a pansexual cis woman is positively related to lesbian stigmatization. This lesbian negativity among pansexual cis women may be a reflection of the documented schism between lesbian women and others in the LGBTQ community and in particular, bisexual (and perhaps other non-monosexual) women (Brewster and Moradi 2010; Rust 1995; Weiss 2004; Worthen 2013). Indeed, the historical/current separatism of lesbian women may be driving a particular rift between pansexual and lesbian women that is evidenced by the findings here. Interestingly, however, some research indicates that cis women are more likely to adopt pansexual identities as compared to cis men and that younger people are increasingly likely to identify as pansexual (Morandini, Blaszczynski, and Dar-Nimrod 2017). In particular, over half (57%) of those who identified as pansexual in this study's sample were cis or trans women while only 25% were cis or trans men and 19% of pansexuals identified as non-binary. In addition, the average age of pansexual women respondents (30.58 years) was more than twelve years younger in comparison to lesbian women (43.06 years). Thus, amidst an emerging group of young women identifying as pansexual, it is important to continue to carefully consider the ways intersectionality informs lesbian stigmatization.

Among the additional sexual/gender identities, being SGL (individual effect) is negatively related to the Lesbian Women Stigma Scale for the LGBTQ subsample but the interaction terms of being SGL and gay/lesbian and of being SGL and bisexual are both positively related to lesbian stigmatization. Thus, SGL identity is associated with LGBTQ stigma in contrasting ways informed by identity experiences (see Chapter 7 for further discussion).

Moving to the racial/ethnic identities, identifying as "other race" is positively related to the Lesbian Women Stigma Scale for the LGBTQ subsample. About half (46%) of those in the "other race" group identified as Middle Eastern (see Appendix B Table B.2). Lesbian stigmatization is strong in Middle Eastern cultures due to overlapping religious and social norms as well as official laws and policies about gender and sexuality. Indeed, in at least five Middle Eastern countries (Iran, Qatar, Saudi Arabia, United Arab Emirates, and Yemen) "homosexuality" can be punishable by death (Human Rights Campaign 2019). In addition, women are particularly disadvantaged in the Middle East. Among 160 countries across the globe, Arab countries collectively rank among the worst in terms of women's reproductive health, empowerment, and labour market participation (United Nations Development Programme 2017). Thus, the stigmatization of lesbian women among those who identify as "other race" is shaped by these sociocultural norms about both gender and sexuality.

Among the basic needs measures, indicating "often basic needs not met" (wherein the reference category is "everything I need") is negatively related to the Lesbian Women Stigma Scale for the LGBTQ subsample. These findings are evidenced in previous work that demonstrates relationships between higher social standing, income, educational attainment, occupational status, and conservative politics which tend to devalue both women and sexual minorities (Balay 2014; Horowitz, Parker, and Stepler 2017; Worthen, Lingiardi, and Caristo 2017). However, while the baseline relationship between "often basic needs not met" and lesbian stigmatization is negative, among the social power axes interaction effects, there is a positive relationship between bisexual individuals who indicate "often needs not met" as well as Asian American/Pacific Islander individuals who indicate "often needs not met" and the Lesbian Women Stigma Scale. There are overlapping scripts that shape these patterns. In particular, the traditional Asian family is highly structured around strict gendered roles whereby the docile female marital partner is contrasted with the "family man" in a process that reinforces both heteronormativity and the control of women's sexualities (Bridges, Selvidge, and Matthews 2003). Among Asian families, these types of hetero-cis-normative gender roles are more strongly reinforced among those with lower levels of parental education and lower financial stability, while in contrast, those with higher levels of education and more financial stability are more likely to support gender equality and sexual diversity (Kulik 2002). Thus, familial, gender, and sexuality norms among Asian American/Pacific Islander individuals who experience less basic needs stability shape lesbian negativity.

Among the other significant interaction terms, all five possible axes of social power are significant: gender identity (cis woman, trans woman), sexual identity (gay/lesbian, bisexual, pansexual), additional gender/sexual identity (SGL, Two-Spirit, butch), racial/ethnic identity (African American/Black, Asian American/Pacific Islander, Latinx ethnicity), and basic needs (mostly all I need, often needs not met, few needs met). However, for some significant interaction terms, there are no corresponding individual effects. For example, there is a negative relationship between being a trans bisexual woman and lesbian stigma. Trans bisexual women may support lesbian women due to their intersecting experiences as marginalized women who experience both gender- and sexuality-based oppressive circumstances (Serano 2007). In particular, the unique positionality of trans bisexual women who have (at least) three identities that can be denigrated may make them especially aware of and sympathetic to lesbian stigmatization.

Overall, the numerous significant social power axes interaction effects in Model 2 support *Hypothesis 2b*: interactions between axes of social power moderate the relationship between the individual axes of social power and the Lesbian Women Stigma Scale for both subsamples. However, among the social power axes, there are no overlapping findings between the two subsamples. Thus, the particular axes of social power that inform lesbian stigmatization are entirely different for the hetero-cis and LGBTQ subsamples. This is similar to other research (e.g., Worthen 2018b) that has found different patterns in lesbian stigmatization among heterosexual and LGB subsamples that vary by axes of social power.

## Summarizing NCST, HCN, Social Power Axes, and the Lesbian Women Stigma Scale

In sum, the findings in Table 8.2 demonstrate that lesbian stigmatization is shaped by axes of social power in complex, intersecting ways. However, there are numerous differences between the two subsamples. By utilizing NCST to explore the Lesbian Women Stigma Scale and centering the importance of hetero-cis-normativity and social power axes, these dynamics are highlighted in powerful manners that support the continued intersectional exploration of the processes motivating both lesbian negativity and support.

## Lesbian Women's Experiences

### The Lesbian Women Subsample

The recruitment of lesbian women to participate in this study was successful and the requested quota (n = 330) from Survey Sampling International was met and exceeded. The study sample included 346 lesbian women (learn more about the data and sampling procedures in Chapter 7 and Appendix A). At the beginning of the survey, respondents were asked two questions: (1) "How would you describe yourself?" and (2) "What best describes your gender?" Lesbian women were those who selected "gay or lesbian" for the first question and either "I identify as a woman and my assigned sex at birth was female" or "I am transgender: I identify as a woman and my assigned sex at birth was male" for the second question. See Table 8.3 for more details about the lesbian women in this study.

### Lesbian Women's Experiences with Gender- and Sexuality-Based DHV

Research indicates that the prevalence of DHV is quite high for lesbian women (Balsam, Rothblum, and Beauchaine 2005; Bartle 2000; Katz-Wise and Hyde 2012; Meyer 2015), though, sometimes the motivations (gender- or sexuality-based, both, or neither) are not made clear. As seen in Figure 8.3, over half (57%) of lesbian women in this study have had one or more experiences of gender-based DHV and nearly 7 in 10 (69%) have had one or more experiences of sexuality-based DHV. Sexuality-based discrimination is the most common form (61%) while gender-based violence is the least common (14%). To better understand lesbian women's gender- and sexuality-based DHV, lesbian women's experiences were compared to the LGBTQ subsample and the

**TABLE 8.3** Lesbian Women Characteristics (n = 346)

|  | % | n |
|---|---|---|
| *Gender identity* | | |
| Cis woman | 95.7% | 331 |
| Trans woman | 4.3% | 15 |
| *Additional gender/sexual identity* | | |
| Queer** | 17.6% | 61 |
| SGL** | 27.5% | 95 |
| Two-Spirit | 2.3% | 8 |
| Butch** | 15.0% | 52 |
| Femme** | 21.4% | 74 |
| Leather | 0.3% | 1 |
| Bear | 0.6% | 2 |
| Twink | 0.3% | 1 |
| Down Low | 1.2% | 4 |
| *Race/ethnicity* | | |
| Caucasian/White* | 79.5% | 275 |
| African American/Black** | 10.7% | 37 |
| Asian American/Pacific Islander* | 4.6% | 16 |
| Native American/Alaskan Native* | 0.6% | 2 |
| Multi-racial* | 2.6% | 9 |
| Other race* | 0.9% | 3 |
| Latinx race* | 0.9% | 3 |
| Latinx ethnicity** | 10.4% | 36 |
| *Basic needs* | | |
| Everything I need** | 30.6% | 106 |
| Mostly all I need** | 54.9% | 190 |
| Often needs not met* | 10.7% | 37 |
| Few needs met* | 3.8% | 13 |

* Reference category in analyses in Table 8.5.
** Included in analyses shown in Table 8.5.

women subsample using *t*-tests. As seen in Table 8.4, as compared to all LGBTQ people and all women, lesbian women report significantly more experiences with both gender- and sexuality-based DHV of all types with the three exceptions. When it comes to gender-based violence, there are no significant differences between the lesbian, LGBTQ, and women subsamples and for sexuality-based violence, lesbian women are only significantly different from the women subsample (not the LGBTQ subsample). In addition, the lesbian women and women subsamples do not significantly differ in their gender-based harassment experiences. Overall, however, lesbian women are at particular risk for DHV. To better understand these dynamics, it is important to consider multiple, intersecting axes of social power as they shape the relationships between being a lesbian woman and experiencing gender- and sexuality-based DHV.

■ Gender-Based　　Sexuality-Based

| | DISCRIMINATION | HARASSMENT | VIOLENCE | ANY DHV EXPERIENCE (0/1) |
|---|---|---|---|---|
| Gender-Based | 45% | 39% | 14% | 57% |
| Sexuality-Based | 61% | 56% | 22% | 69% |

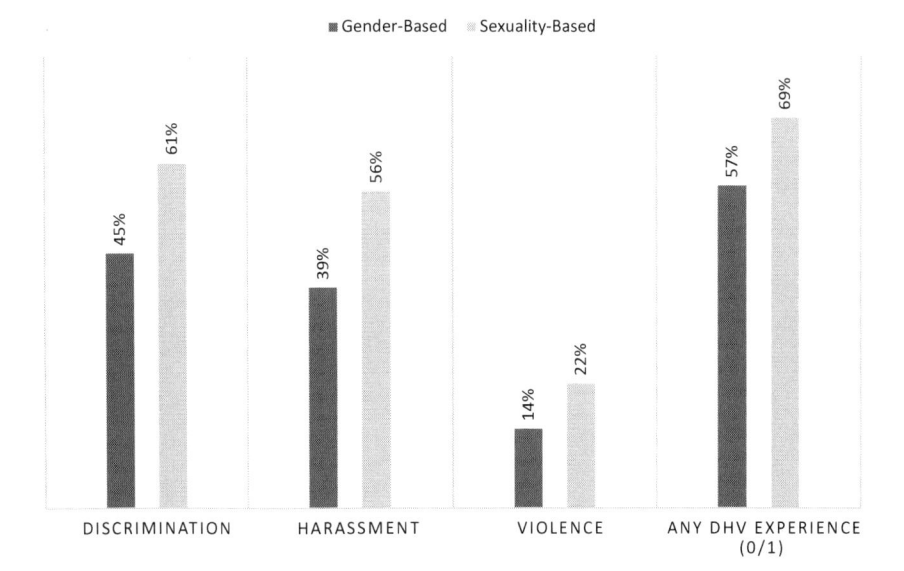

**FIGURE 8.3** Lesbian Women's (n = 346) Experiences with Gender- and Sexuality-Based DHV

*Note:* See Table 8.4 for comparisons of lesbian women's experiences to the LGBTQ subsample and the women subsample.

**TABLE 8.4** Gender- and Sexuality-Based DHV Mean Values (Standard Deviations) among Lesbian Women, the LGBTQ Subsample, and the Women Subsample with *t*-test Results

| | | Lesbian Women | LGBTQ Subsample | Women Subsample |
|---|---|---|---|---|
| | n | 346 | 1604 | 1535 |
| *Gender-based* | | | | |
| Discrimination | | .45 (.50) *** | .32 (.47) | .36 (.48) |
| Harassment | | .39 (.49) ** | .28 (.45) | .34 (.47) |
| Violence | | .14 (.35) | .14 (.34) | .16 (.37) |
| Any gender DHV experience (0/1) | | .57 (.50) *** | .40 (.49) | .46 (.50) |
| *Sexuality-based* | | | | |
| Discrimination | | .61 (.49) *** | .44 (.50) | .26 (.44) |
| Harassment | | .56 (.50) *** | .41 (.49) | .23 (.42) |
| Violence | | .22 (.41) * | .20 (.40) | .10 (.31) |
| Any sexuality DHV experience (0/1) | | .69 (.46) *** | .53 (.50) | .32 (.47) |

\* Lesbian women are significantly different from the women subsample (only) at p < .05 level.
\*\* Lesbian women are significantly different from the LGBTQ subsample (only) at p < .05 level.
\*\*\* Lesbian women are significantly different from both the LGBTQ and women subsamples at p < .05 level.

## NCST and Lesbian Women's Experiences with Gender- and Sexuality-Based DHV

The second set of regression models examines lesbian women's experiences with gender- and sexuality-based DHV using NCST with special attention to lesbian women's axes of social power. The hypotheses are as follows:

- *Hypothesis 1*: being a lesbian woman (violating hetero-cis-normativity) increases the likelihood of experiencing gender- and sexuality-based DHV (lesbian stigma).
- *Hypothesis 2*: the relationship between being a lesbian woman and gender- and sexuality-based DHV is moderated by interactions among being a lesbian woman and axes of social power.

Figure 8.4 outlines these relationships and Table 8.5 displays logistic regression results that examine NCST and the relationships among being a lesbian woman, intersections among lesbian women's axes of social power, and any experiences of gender-based DHV (dichotomized as 0/1) or sexuality-based DHV (dichotomized as 0/1) utilizing the LGBTQ subsample (n = 1,604; whereby being a lesbian woman is compared to all other GBTQ people). Because lesbian women's experiences are the focus of this exploration (i.e., the stigmatized lens

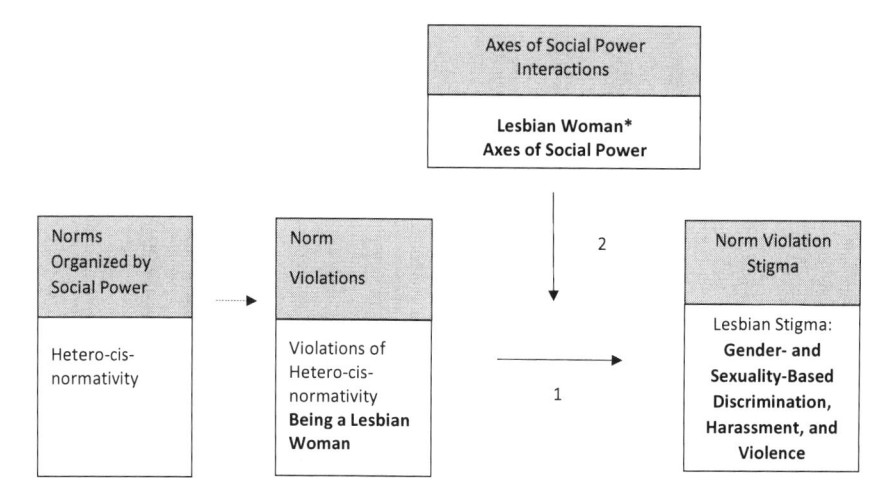

**FIGURE 8.4** Theoretical Model of NCST and Lesbian Stigma among Lesbian Women using the Stigmatized Lens with Model Numbers to be Examined in Table 8.5

*Notes:* Model 1 estimates being a lesbian woman as related to gender- and sexuality-based DHV. Model 2 estimates interactions among lesbian women's axes of social power as they moderate the relationships between being a lesbian woman and gender- and sexuality-based DHV. The * indicates an interaction.

of NCST is being utilized), the lesbian woman and social power axes interaction terms are listed at the top of the table and will be the focus of the discussion here. However, there are significant corresponding individual effects related to being lesbian/gay and being a woman (for example) that are important to recognize. See Chapter 7 for a more complete description of the models and a discussion of overarching trends and patterns. Regarding model fit statistics, the pseudo $R^2$ values ranged from .09 to .16.

## NCST, Lesbian Women, and Gender- and Sexuality-Based DHV: Model 1

In Table 8.5, both Model 1s estimate the relationships between violations of hetero-cis-normativity conceptualized as being a lesbian woman and lesbian stigma conceptualized as gender- and sexuality-based DHV along with sociodemographic controls. Findings show that being a lesbian woman significantly increases the likelihood of gender-based DHV by 1.45 but being a lesbian woman is *not* significantly related to sexuality-based DHV. These results both align and contrast with previous work that demonstrates that lesbian women are at a high risk for DHV (Bartle 2000; Katz-Wise and Hyde 2012; Meyer 2015). In particular, findings here expand upon past studies to draw specific comparisons between lesbian women and others GBTQ people while also highlighting the significance of DHV based on two marginalized identities of lesbian women (gender and sexuality). In doing so, it becomes clear that lesbian women's gender-based DHV experiences and sexuality-based DHV experiences may be shaped by different processes. This is perhaps due to the overall differing DHV experiences of LGBTQ men and women. For example, studies indicate that compared to men, women are more likely to be targeted for gender-based DHV (e.g., Jagsi et al. 2016; Katz-Wise and Hyde 2012), and thus, it follows that similarly, LGBTQ women are more likely to experience gender-based DHV when compared to GBTQ men. However, when it comes to sexuality-based DHV among LGB people, a large-scale meta-analysis with over 500,000 cases shows that gay and bisexual men report significantly greater rates of physical assault, weapon assault, robbery, and sexual harassment when compared to lesbian and bisexual women (Katz-Wise and Hyde 2012). U.S. FBI statistics also indicate that among those crimes reported and coded as sexual-orientation bias motivated crimes, over half (59.7%) are classified as "anti-gay (male)" while only 12.2% are classified as "anti-lesbian" (FBI 2018). Thus, the processes motivating gender- and sexuality-based DHV differ among LGBTQ people. Overall, *Hypothesis 1* is only partially supported: being a lesbian woman increases the likelihood of experiencing gender-based DHV but not sexuality-based DHV.

**TABLE 8.5** Logistic Regression Results with Odds Ratios and (Standard Errors) Estimating NCST and Gender- and Sexuality-Based DHV as Related to Being a Lesbian Woman for the LGBTQ Subsample (n = 1,604)

|  | Gender-Based DHV |  |  |  | Sexuality-Based DHV |  |  |  |
|---|---|---|---|---|---|---|---|---|
|  | Model 1 |  | Model 2 |  | Model 1 |  | Model 2 |  |
|  | OR | SE | OR | SE | OR | SE | OR | SE |
| Lesbian woman | 2.45* | (.59) | 3.06* | (1.03) | . | . | . | . |
| *Lesbian woman social power axes interactions* | | | | | | | | |
|   Lesbian woman*queer | — | — | . | . | — | — | . | . |
|   Lesbian woman*SGL | — | — | . | . | — | — | . | . |
|   Lesbian woman*butch | — | — | . | . | — | — | .36* | (.18) |
|   Lesbian woman*femme | — | — | . | . | — | — | . | . |
|   Lesbian woman*African American/Black | — | — | . | . | — | — | . | . |
|   Lesbian woman*Latinx (ethnicity) | — | — | . | . | — | — | . | . |
|   Lesbian woman*everything I need | — | — | . | . | — | — | . | . |
|   Lesbian woman*mostly all I need | — | — | . | . | — | — | . | . |
| *Lesbian woman social power axes* | | | | | | | | |
|   Lesbian/gay | .50* | (.09) | .50* | (.09) | 3.26* | (.51) | 3.29* | (.52) |
|   Woman | 2.72* | (.43) | 2.68* | (.42) | . | . | . | . |
|   Queer | 2.82* | (.43) | 2.46* | (.84) | 2.12* | (.31) | . | . |
|   SGL | . | . | . | . | . | . | . | . |
|   Butch | 1.61* | (.34) | 2.10* | (.75) | . | . | 2.25* | (.91) |
|   Femme | . | . | . | . | . | . | . | . |
|   African American/Black | . | . | . | . | . | . | . | . |
|   Latinx (ethnicity) | . | . | . | . | . | . | . | . |
|   Everything I need | .62* | (.11) | .58* | (.11) | .64* | (.11) | . | . |
|   Mostly all I need | .71* | (.10) | .52* | (.14) | . | . | . | . |
| *Socio-demographic controls* | | | | | | | | |
|   Age | .97* | (.00) | .97* | (.00) | .98* | (.00) | .98* | (.00) |
|   Town type (rural–large city) | . | . | . | . | . | . | . | . |
|   Education | 1.17* | (.05) | 1.18* | (.05) | . | . | . | . |
|   Income | . | . | . | . | . | . | . | . |
| Pseudo $R^2$ | .15 | | .16 | | .09 | | .10 | |
| Mean VIF | 1.43 | | 1.43 | | 1.42 | | 1.39 | |

* $p < .05$; a dot (.) indicates non-statistically significant results. A dash (—) indicates this was not included in the model.

*Notes:* all rows are displayed, including those without significant results. See Table 8.3 for more details about the lesbian women in the study.

## NCST, Lesbian Women, and Gender- and Sexuality-Based DHV: Model 2

Both Model 2s include intersections among axes of social power and being a lesbian woman as they moderate the relationship between being a lesbian woman and gender- and sexuality-based DHV. Being a lesbian woman remains significantly related to the likelihood of gender-based DHV in Model 2. Specifically, being a lesbian woman increases the likelihood of gender-based DHV by 2.06. However, being a lesbian woman is not significantly related to the likelihood of sexuality-based DHV in Model 2. As discussed above, these findings continue to suggest that being a lesbian woman shapes the likelihood of gender- and sexuality-based DHV in different ways.

In addition, there is only one significant interaction effect in Model 2: being a lesbian butch woman decreases the likelihood of sexuality-based DHV by .64. Thus, *Hypothesis 2* is supported in the sexuality-based DHV models but not in the gender-based DHV models. Others have found that compared to femmes especially, butches are generally less sexualized and more masculinized (Bailey et al. 1997; Blair and Hoskin 2015; Levitt and Horne 2002) and thus, may be less vulnerable to sexuality-based DHV. Indeed, unlike other lesbian identities (e.g., femme, lipstick), being "butch" is not commonly associated with eroticization and objectification by heterosexual men (LaMar and Kite 1998; Louderback and Whitley 1997; Raja and Stokes 1998; Worthen 2013). These processes and stereotypes may contribute to lesbian butch women's decreased likelihood of experiencing sexuality-based DHV.

## Summarizing NCST, Lesbian Women, and Gender- and Sexuality-Based DHV

In sum, the findings in Table 8.5 indicate that being a lesbian woman increases the likelihood of experiencing gender-based DHV; however, the intersecting experiences of being butch and lesbian decrease the likelihood of experiencing sexuality-based DHV. Overall, the use of NCST to explore lesbian women's gender- and sexuality-based DHV highlights the importance of social power axes as related to these experiences while also supporting the continued intersectional investigation of the mechanisms that contribute to DHV among lesbian women.

## Summary of Patterns of Lesbian Women Stigma

In line with the three tenets and hypotheses derived from NCST, there are six patterns related to the stigmatization of lesbian women reviewed in this chapter:

1. Discomfort with lesbian women's sex acts are a driving force in the stigmatization of lesbian women for both hetero-cis and LGBTQ people.

2. For both hetero-cis and LGBTQ people, there is also strong overlap among the top most stigmatizing beliefs about lesbian women which include: lesbian women are not feminine enough, lesbian women's identity permanency, and sex-act related perspectives (hypersexuality, unfaithfulness, and discomfort with lesbian women having sex with men and women).
3. Hetero-cis-normativity is positively related to lesbian women stigma for both subsamples; however, the interaction effects between the HCN Scale and social power axes that moderate this relationship differ for the hetero-cis and LGBTQ subsamples.
4. Individual social power axes are significantly related to lesbian women stigma for both subsamples; however, the interaction effects between the social power axes that moderate these relationships differ for the hetero-cis and LGBTQ subsamples. In addition, there are more significant interaction effects between the social power axes for the LGBTQ subsample than there are for the hetero-cis subsample.
5. Lesbian women experience high levels of both gender- and sexuality-based DHV in comparison to both the LGBTQ and all women subsamples with few exceptions.
6. The individual effect of being a lesbian woman increases the likelihood of gender-based DHV while butch lesbian women have a decreased likelihood of sexuality-based DHV.

## Notes

1 Dorothy Louise Taliaferro "Del" Martin (1921–2008) and Phyllis Lyon (1924–) are often described as two of eight co-founders of the Daughters of Bilitis. However, in a 2012 article, Lyon disputes this claim as follows:

> WE ARE erroneously given credit as the founders of the Daughters of Bilitis in San Francisco in 1955. It wasn't even our idea. A young Filipina immigrant envisioned a club for lesbians here in the States that would give us an opportunity to meet and socialize (and especially to dance) outside of the gay bars that were frequently raided by police. Meeting in each others' homes provided us with privacy and a sense of safety from the police and gawking tourists in the bars. Personally, our motivation was simply to meet other lesbians. There were eight of us in the beginning: four couples, four blue-collar and four white-collar workers, two lesbian mothers, and two women of color.
>
> *(Lyon 2012)*

On June 16, 2008, Martin and Lyon become the first same-sex couple to be legally married in the state of California and only two months later, Martin passed away on August 27, 2008. On the 50th anniversary of the Stonewall Uprising in June 2019, Martin was one of fifty inaugural activists inducted into the National LGBTQ Wall of Honor located in the Stonewall Inn (National LGBTQ Task Force 2019). Still thriving, Lyon celebrated her 95th birthday in 2019.

2 U.S. Public Law 103–160 (10 U.S.C. § 654, 1993), colloquially known as "Don't Ask, Don't Tell, Don't Pursue," or in short DADT, restricted lesbian, gay, and bisexual people from openly serving in the U.S. military from 1993–2011.
3 For the LGBTQ subsample, both trans and non-binary individuals could identify as heterosexual.

## References

Allsep, L. Michael. 2013. "The Myth of the Warrior: Martial Masculinity and the End of Don't Ask, Don't Tell." *Journal of Homosexuality* 60(2/3):381–400.

Associated Press. 2009. "Lesbians More Likely to Be Kicked Out of Military." *MSNBC.Com*. Retrieved February 8, 2019 (www.nbcnews.com/id/33230836/ns/us_news-military/t/lesbians-more-likely-be-kicked-out-military/).

Bailey, Michael, Peggy Kim, Alex Hills, and Joan Linsenmeier. 1997. "Butch, Femme, or Straight Acting? Partner Preferences of Gay Men and Lesbians." *Journal of Personality & Social Psychology* 73(5):960–973.

Baiocco, Roberto, Nicola Nardelli, Lina Pezzuti, and Vittorio Lingiardi. 2013. "Attitudes of Italian Heterosexual Older Adults Towards Lesbian and Gay Parenting." *Sexuality Research and Social Policy* 10(4):285–292.

Balay, Anne. 2014. *Steel Closets: Voices of Gay, Lesbian, and Transgender Steelworkers*. Chapel Hill, NC: University of North Carolina Press.

Balsam, Kimberly F., Esther D. Rothblum, and Theodore P. Beauchaine. 2005. "Victimization over the Life Span: A Comparison of Lesbian, Gay, Bisexual, and Heterosexual Siblings." *Journal of Consulting and Clinical Psychology* 73(3):477–487.

Bartle, Elizabeth E. 2000. "Lesbians and Hate Crimes." *Journal of Poverty* 4(4):23–43.

Blair, Karen L. and Rhea Ashley Hoskin. 2015. "Experiences of Femme Identity: Coming Out, Invisibility and Femmephobia." *Psychology & Sexuality* 6(3):229–244.

Bowleg, Lisa. 2013. "'Once You've Blended the Cake, You Can't Take the Parts Back to the Main Ingredients': Black Gay and Bisexual Men's Descriptions and Experiences of Intersectionality." *Sex Roles* 68(11):754–767.

Brewster, Melanie and Bonnie Moradi. 2010. "Perceived Experiences of Anti-Bisexual Prejudice: Instrument Development and Evaluation." *Journal of Counseling Psychology* 57:451–468.

Bridges, Sara K. Mary M. D. Selvidge, and Connie R. Matthews. 2003. "Lesbian Women of Color: Therapeutic Issues and Challenges." *Journal of Multicultural Counseling and Development* 31(2):113–130.

Brown, Suzanne, Susan Smalling, Victor Groza, and Scott Ryan. 2009. "The Experiences of Gay Men and Lesbians in Becoming and Being Adoptive Parents." *Adoption Quarterly* 12(3/4):229–246.

Burks, Derek J. 2011. "Lesbian, Gay, and Bisexual Victimization in the Military: An Unintended Consequence of 'Don't Ask, Don't Tell'?" *American Psychologist* 66(7):604–613.

Carrigan, Mark. 2011. "There's More to Life than Sex? Difference and Commonality within the Asexual Community." *Sexualities* 14(4):462–478.

Clarke, Victoria. 2001. "What about the Children? Arguments against Lesbian and Gay Parenting." *Women's Studies International Forum* 24(5):555–570.

Clogg, Clifford C., Eva Petkova, and Adamantios Haritou. 1995. "Statistical Methods for Comparing Regression Coefficients between Models." *American Journal of Sociology* 100 (5):1261–1293.

Colborne, Adrienne. 2018. "Chasing Aces: Asexuality, Misinformation and the Challenges of Identity." *Dalhousie Journal of Interdisciplinary Management* 14:1–13.

Crawford, Isiaah, Andrew McLeod, Brian D. Zamboni, and Michael B. Jordan. 1999. "Psychologists' Attitudes toward Gay and Lesbian Parenting." *Professional Psychology: Research and Practice* 30(4):394–401.

Diamond, Lisa M. 2003. "Was It a Phase? Young Women's Relinquishment of Lesbian/Bisexual Identities over a 5-year Period." *Journal of Personality and Social Psychology* 84(2):352–364.

Diamond, Lisa M. 2008. "Female Bisexuality from Adolescence to Adulthood: Results from a 10-year Longitudinal Study." *Developmental Psychology* 44(1):5–14.

Dowsett, Gilbert. 2009. "The 'Gay Plague' Revisited: AIDS and its Enduring Moral Panic." Pp. 130–156 in *Moral Panics, Sex Panics: Fear and the Fight over Sexual Rights*, edited by Gilbert Herdt. New York, NY: NYU Press.

Eliason, Michele, Carol Donelan, and Carla Randall. 1992. "Lesbian Stereotypes." *Health Care for Women International* 13(2):131–144.

Eliason, Michele J. 2010. "A New Classification System for Lesbians: The Dyke Diagnostic Manual." *Journal of Lesbian Studies* 14(4):401–414.

FBI. 2018. "2018 Hate Crimes Statistics." *FBI*. Retrieved January 9, 2020 (https://ucr.fbi.gov/hate-crime/2018/topic-pages/victims).

Flanders, Corey E. 2017. "Under the Bisexual Umbrella: Diversity of Identity and Experience." *Journal of Bisexuality* 17(1):1–6.

Gallup. 2014. "Most Americans Say Same-Sex Couples Entitled to Adopt." *Gallup*. Retrieved February 7, 2019 (https://news.gallup.com/poll/170801/americans-say-sex-couples-entitled-adopt.aspx).

Gallup. 2019. "Gay and Lesbian Rights: In Depth Topics A to Z." *Gallup*. Retrieved February 6, 2019 (https://news.gallup.com/poll/1651/Gay-Lesbian-Rights.aspx).

Galupo, M. Paz. 2007. "Friendship Patterns of Sexual Minority Individuals in Adulthood." *Journal of Social and Personal Relationships* 24(1):139–151.

Gander, Kashmira. 2018. "Children Raised by Gay and Lesbian Parents Develop as Well as Kids of Heterosexual Couples, Study Suggests." *Newsweek*. Retrieved January 30, 2020 (https://www.newsweek.com/children-raised-gay-and-lesbian-parents-develop-well-kids-heterosexual-1001515).

Geiger, Wendy, Jake Harwood, and Mary Lee Hummert. 2006. "College Students' Multiple Stereotypes of Lesbians: A Cognitive Perspective." *Journal of Homosexuality* 51(3):165–182.

Gilley, Brian Joseph. 2006. *Becoming Two-Spirit: Gay Identity and Social Acceptance in Indian Country* Lincoln, NE: University of Nebraska Press.

Gilley, Brian Joseph. 2010. "Native Sexual Inequalities: American Indian Cultural Conservative Homophobia and the Problem of Tradition." *Sexualities* 13(1):47–68.

Grier, Tiffanie, Carol Rambo, and Marshall A. Taylor. 2014. "'What are You?': Racial Ambiguity, Stigma, and the Racial Formation Project." *Deviant Behavior* 35 (12):1006–1022.

Herek, Gregory M. and John Capitanio. 1999. "AIDS Stigma and Sexual Prejudice." *American Behavioral Scientist* 42(7):1130–1147.

Herek, Gregory M. and Milagritos Gonzalez-Rivera. 2006. "Attitudes toward Homosexuality among U.S. Residents of Mexican Descent." *The Journal of Sex Research* 43(2):122–135.

Herman, Melissa R. 2010. "Do You See What I Am?: How Observers' Backgrounds Affect Their Perceptions of Multiracial Faces." *Social Psychology Quarterly* 73(1):58–78.

Hirai, Michiyo, Mark H. Winkel, and Jason R. Popan. 2014. "The Role of Machismo in Prejudice toward Lesbians and Gay Men: Personality Traits as Moderators." *Personality and Individual Differences* 70:105–110.

Hoffarth, Mark R., Caroline E. Drolet, Gordon Hodson, and Carolyn L. Hafer. 2016. "Development and Validation of the Attitudes Towards Asexuals (ATA) Scale." *Psychology & Sexuality* 7(2):88–100.

Horowitz, Juliana, Kim Parker, and Renee Stepler. 2017. "Wide Partisan Gaps in U.S. Over How Far the Country Has Come on Gender Equality." *Pew Research Center*. Retrieved February 25, 2019 (www.pewresearch.org/fact-tank/2017/12/28/10-things-we-learned-about-gender-issues-in-the-u-s-in-2017/).

Houdenhove, Ellen Van, Luk Gijs, Guy T'Sjoen, and Paul Enzlin. 2015. "Stories about Asexuality: A Qualitative Study on Asexual Women." *Journal of Sex & Marital Therapy* 41(3):262–281.

Human Rights Campaign. 2019. "Criminalization around the World." *Human Rights Campaign*. Retrieved August 21, 2019 (http://assets2.hrc.org/files/assets/resources/Criminalization-Map-042315.pdf).

Jagsi, Reshma, Kent A. Griffith, Rochelle Jones, Chithra R. Perumalswami, Peter Ubel, and Abigail Stewart. 2016. "Sexual Harassment and Discrimination Experiences of Academic Medical Faculty." *JAMA* 315(19):2120–2121.

Joos, Kristin E. and K. L. Broad. 2007. "Coming Out of the Family Closet: Stories of Adult Women with LGBTQ Parent(s)." *Qualitative Sociology* 30(3):275–295.

Katz-Wise, Sabra L. and Janet S. Hyde. 2012. "Victimization Experiences of Lesbian, Gay, and Bisexual Individuals: A Meta-Analysis." *The Journal of Sex Research* 49(2/3):142–167.

Kulik, Liat. 2002. "The Impact of Social Background on Gender-Role Ideology: Parents' versus Children's Attitudes." *Journal of Family Issues* 23(1):53–73.

LaMar, Lisa and Mary Kite. 1998. "Sex Differences in Attitudes toward Gay Men and Lesbians: A Multidimensional Perspective." *The Journal of Sex Research* 35(2):189–196.

Lemelle, Anthony and Juan Battle. 2004. "Black Masculinity Matters in Attitudes toward Gay Males." *Journal of Homosexuality* 47(1):39–51.

Levitt, Heidi M. and Sharon G. Horne. 2002. "Explorations of Lesbian-Queer Genders: Butch, Femme, Androgynous or 'Other'." *Journal of Lesbian Studies* 6(2):25–39.

Logie, Carmen H., LLana James, Wangari Tharao, and Mona R. Loutfy. 2012. "'We Don't Exist': A Qualitative Study of Marginalization Experienced by HIV-positive Lesbian, Bisexual, Queer and Transgender Women in Toronto, Canada." *Journal of the International AIDS Society* 15(2): 10.7448/IAS.15.2.17392.

Louderback, Laura A. and Bernard E. Whitley. 1997. "Perceived Erotic Value of Homosexuality and Sex-Role Attitudes as Mediators of Sex Differences in Heterosexual College Students' Attitudes toward Lesbians and Gay Men." *The Journal of Sex Research* 34(2):175–182.

Lyon, Phyllis. 2012. "Lesbian Liberation Begins." *The Gay & Lesbian Review*. Retrieved August 4, 2019 (https://glreview.org/article/lesbian-liberation-begins/).

Martin, Del and Phyllis Lyon. 1972. *Lesbian Woman*. San Francisco, CA: Bantam.

McCarthy, Justin. 2019. "Gallup First Polled on Gay Issues in '77. What Has Changed?" *Gallup*. Retrieved August 21, 2019 (https://news.gallup.com/poll/258065/gallup-first-polled-gay-issues-changed.aspx).

McKirnan, David J., Joseph P. Stokes, Lynda Doll, and Rebecca G. Burzette. 1995. "Bisexually Active Men: Social Characteristics and Sexual Behavior." *Journal of Sex Research* 32(1):65–76.

Meyer, Doug. 2015. *Violence against Queer People: Race, Class, Gender, and the Persistence of Anti-LGBT Discrimination*. New Brunswick, NJ: Rutgers University Press.

Morandini, James S., Alexander Blaszczynski, and Ilan Dar-Nimrod. 2017. "Who Adopts Queer and Pansexual Sexual Identities?" *The Journal of Sex Research* 54(7):911–922.

National LGBTQ Task Force. 2019. "National LGBTQ Wall of Honor Unveiled at Historic Stonewall Inn." *National LGBTQ Task Force*. Retrieved August 4, 2019 (www.thetaskforce.org/nationallgbtqwallofhonortobeunveiled/).

Pew Research Center. 2013a. "Chapter 2: Social Acceptance." Retrieved February 7, 2019 (www.pewsocialtrends.org/2013/06/13/chapter-2-social-acceptance/).

Pew Research Center. 2013b. "Chapter 3: The Coming Out Experience." Retrieved February 6, 2019 (www.pewsocialtrends.org/2013/06/13/chapter-3-the-coming-out-experience/).

Pew Research Center. 2013c. "Chapter 4: Marriage and Parenting." Retrieved February 7, 2019 (www.pewsocialtrends.org/2013/06/13/chapter-4-marriage-and-parenting/).

Pinto, Stacy Anne. 2014. "ASEXUally: On Being an Ally to the Asexual Community." *Journal of LGBT Issues in Counseling* 8(4):331–343.

Raja, Sheela and Joseph P. Stokes. 1998. "Assessing Attitudes toward Lesbians and Gay Men: The Modern Homophobia Scale." *International Journal of Sexuality and Gender Studies* 3(2):113–134.

Rostker, Bernard, Susan Hosek, and Mary Vaiana. 2011. "Sexual Orientation and U.S. Personnel Policy Revisited." RAND Corporation. Retrieved February 8, 2019 (www.rand.org/pubs/research_briefs/RB9565/index1.html).

Rupp, Leila J. and Verta Taylor. 2010. "Straight Girls Kissing." *Contexts* 9(3):28–32.

Rust, Paula C. 1995. *Bisexuality and the Challenge to Lesbian Politics: Sex, Loyalty, and Revolution*. New York, NY: NYU Press.

Serano, Julia. 2007. *Whipping Girl: A Transsexual Woman on Sexism and the Scapegoating of Femininity*. Berkeley, CA: Seal Press.

Stein, Arlene. 1997. *Sex and Sensibility: Stories of a Lesbian Generation*. Berkeley, CA: University of California Press.

United Nations Development Programme. 2017. "Human Development Reports: Gender Inequality Index." Retrieved February 15, 2019 (http://hdr.undp.org/en/composite/GII).

Wall, Misty L. 2013. "Lesbians' Perceived Readiness to Parent." *Affilia* 28(4):391–400.

Walters, Karina L., Jane M. Teresa Evans-Campbell, Theresa Ronquillo Simoni, and Rupaleem Bhuyan. 2006. "'My Spirit in My Heart': Identity Experiences and Challenges among American Indian Two-Spirit Women." *Journal of Lesbian Studies* 10(1/2):125–149.

Weinstock, Jacqueline S. and Esther D. Rothblum. 2018. "Just Friends: The Role of Friendship in Lesbians' Lives." *Journal of Lesbian Studies* 22(1):1–3.

Weiss, Jillian Todd. 2004. "GL vs. BT: The Archaeology of Biphobia and Transphobia within the US Gay and Lesbian Community." *Journal of Bisexuality* 3(3/4):25–55.

Worthen, Meredith G. F. 2013. "An Argument for Separate Analyses of Attitudes toward Lesbian, Gay, Bisexual Men, Bisexual Women, MtF and FtM Transgender Individuals." *Sex Roles* 68(11):703–723.

Worthen, Meredith G. F. 2018a. "'All the Gays are Liberal?' Sexuality and Gender Gaps in Political Perspectives among Lesbian, Gay, Bisexual, Mostly Heterosexual, and Heterosexual College Students in the Southern USA." *Sexuality Research and Social Policy* DOI: 10.1007/s13178-018-0365-6.

Worthen, Meredith G. F. 2018b. "'Gay Equals White'? Racial, Ethnic, and Sexual Identities and Attitudes toward LGBT Individuals among College Students at a Bible Belt University." *The Journal of Sex Research* 55(8):995–1011.

Worthen, Meredith G. F. 2019a. "A Rainbow Wave? LGBTQ Liberal Political Perspectives during Trump's Presidency: An Exploration of Sexual, Gender, and Queer Identity Gaps." *Sexuality Research and Social Policy* DOI: 10.1007/s13178-019-00393-1.

Worthen, Meredith G. F. 2019b. "Transgender under Fire: Hetero-cis-normativity and Military Students' Attitudes toward Trans Issues and Trans Service Members Post DADT." *Sexuality Research and Social Policy* 16(3):289–308.

Worthen, Meredith G. F., Vittorio Lingiardi, and Chiara Caristo. 2017. "The Roles of Politics, Feminism, and Religion in Attitudes toward LGBT Individuals: A Cross-Cultural Study of College Students in the USA, Italy, and Spain." *Sexuality Research and Social Policy* 14(3):241–258.

# 9
# GAY MEN STIGMA

*I always say to people, "If you share my dream, why don't we walk together?" And that's my only organizing tool.*

(Cusac [1998] 2016)
Harry Hay, founder of the Mattachine Society

**IMAGE 9.1** The Mattachine Steps.[1] This outdoor staircase in Silver Lake, Los Angeles, California was renamed "The Mattachine Steps" in 2012. The sign reads, "Harry Hay founded The Mattachine Society on this hillside on November 11, 1950." Hay lived in a house adjacent to the stairs when he founded the Mattachine Society. It is one of the oldest American national gay rights organizations and is recognized as one of the first organized collectives of the gay and lesbian movement.

## The Stigmatization of Gay Men

In the survey instrument, the section focusing on attitudes toward gay men was preceded by the following statement:

> *Below, please let us know your thoughts, feelings, and predicted behaviors about gay men (men who have romantic and sexual attractions to men).*

### The Gay Men Stigma Scale

In comparison to the eight other LBTQ groups explored in this book, gay men are the third least stigmatized behind bisexual women and lesbian women (recall Figure 7.1). The mechanisms that shape the stigmatization of gay men can be better understood by exploring the 14 items in the Gay Men Stigma Scale as seen in Figure 9.1 and Table 9.1 and discussed below.

### Gay Men and Social and Familial Relationships

The stigmatization of gay men is low with means ranging from 1.53 to 2.27. These findings indicate that the majority of respondents in this nationally

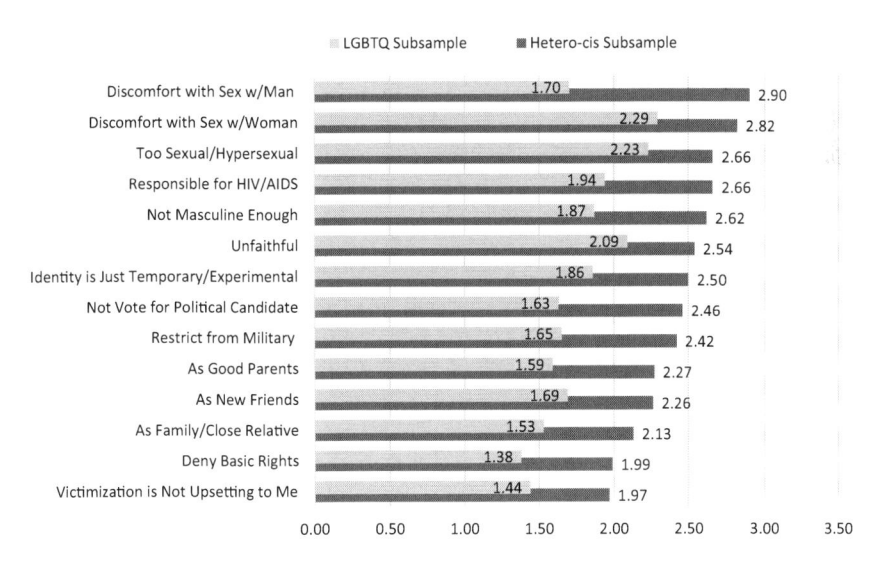

| Item | LGBTQ Subsample | Hetero-cis Subsample |
|---|---|---|
| Discomfort with Sex w/Man | 1.70 | 2.90 |
| Discomfort with Sex w/Woman | 2.29 | 2.82 |
| Too Sexual/Hypersexual | 2.23 | 2.66 |
| Responsible for HIV/AIDS | 1.94 | 2.66 |
| Not Masculine Enough | 1.87 | 2.62 |
| Unfaithful | 2.09 | 2.54 |
| Identity is Just Temporary/Experimental | 1.86 | 2.50 |
| Not Vote for Political Candidate | 1.63 | 2.46 |
| Restrict from Military | 1.65 | 2.42 |
| As Good Parents | 1.59 | 2.27 |
| As New Friends | 1.69 | 2.26 |
| As Family/Close Relative | 1.53 | 2.13 |
| Deny Basic Rights | 1.38 | 1.99 |
| Victimization is Not Upsetting to Me | 1.44 | 1.97 |

**FIGURE 9.1** Gay Men Stigma Scale Item Mean Values Rank-Ordered from Most to Least Stigmatizing for the Hetero-cis (n = 1,500) and the LGBTQ (n = 1,604) Subsamples

*Notes:* see Table 9.1 for the exact wording for each item. *t*-test results comparing the hetero-cis and LGBTQ subsamples indicate that all means are significantly different from one another at the p < .001 level.

**TABLE 9.1** Gay Men Stigma Scale Item Mean Values (Standard Deviations) and *t*-test Results Comparing the Means for the Hetero-cis Subsample and the LGBTQ Subsample

|  | Hetero-cis Subsample | LGBTQ Subsample | t-test Results |
|---|---|---|---|
|  | n = 1,500 | n = 1,604 |  |
| *Social and familial relationships* |  |  |  |
| I welcome new friends who are gay men. [R] | 2.26 (1.14) | 1.69 (0.92) | t = 15.39* |
| I don't think it would negatively affect our relationship if I learned that one of my close relatives was a gay man. [R] | 2.13 (1.12) | 1.53 (0.95) | t = 16.01* |
| Gay men are not capable of being good parents. | 2.27 (1.30) | 1.59 (1.08) | t = 15.83* |
| *Positions of importance and social significance* |  |  |  |
| I would not vote for a political candidate who was an openly gay man. | 2.46 (1.39) | 1.63 (1.14) | t = 18.33* |
| Gay men should not be allowed to join the military. | 2.42 (1.40) | 1.65 (1.19) | t = 16.34* |
| *Basic human rights* |  |  |  |
| I believe gay men should have all of the same rights as other people do. [R] | 1.99 (1.16) | 1.38 (0.85) | t = 16.83* |
| It is upsetting to me that gay men experience violence, harassment, and discrimination just because they are gay men. [R] | 1.97 (1.10) | 1.44 (0.89) | t = 14.52* |
| *Sex act-related stigma* |  |  |  |
| Gay men are unfaithful to their romantic partners. | 2.54 (1.19) | 2.09 (1.15) | t = 10.60* |
| Gay men are too sexual (hypersexual). | 2.66 (1.19) | 2.23 (1.19) | t = 10.10* |
| Gay men are mostly responsible for spreading HIV/AIDS. | 2.66 (1.21) | 1.94 (1.16) | t = 16.80* |
| I am comfortable with the thought of a gay man having sex with a man. [R] | 2.90 (1.30) | 1.70 (1.01) | t = 28.56* |
| I am comfortable with the thought of a gay man having sex with a woman. [R] | 2.82 (1.18) | 2.29 (1.19) | t = 12.24* |
| *Gay identity permanency* |  |  |  |
| Most men who call themselves gay are just temporarily experimenting with their sexuality. | 2.50 (1.15) | 1.86 (1.09) | t = 15.69* |
| *Achievement of masculinity* |  |  |  |
| Gay men are not masculine enough. | 2.62 (1.18) | 1.87 (1.07) | t = 18.30* |
| α | .89 | .88 |  |
| Summed scale actual range | 14–70 | 14–53 |  |
| Summed scale mean | 34.19 (10.98) | 24.89 (9.33) | t = 25.35* |

Notes: response options were Strongly Disagree–Strongly Agree (range: 1–5). [R] This item is reverse coded.
* *t*-test results allowing for unequal variances indicate that the hetero-cis subsample and LGBTQ subsample means are significantly different from one another at the $p < .001$ level.

representative U.S. sample are comfortable with having gay men as friends and family members. As noted in Chapter 8, this is consistent with changes in the visibility of gay men in friendship and family networks (i.e., 75% of Americans indicated they have gay or lesbian friend, relative, or co-worker in a recent Gallup Poll, Gallup 2019). Furthermore, among LGB individuals, gay men are *most* likely to have told all or most of their family and friends about their sexual identity (77% of gay men when compared to 71% of lesbian women, 33% of bisexual women, and 12% of bisexual men) (Pew Research Center 2013a). Thus, as gay men are more visible in their social and familial networks, there is also more support of gay men as friends and family members.

The item in this key area with the lowest mean values for both groups is: "I don't think it would negatively affect our relationship if I learned that one of my close relatives was a gay man," which was reverse coded. With nearly 8 in 10 (77%) gay men indicating that they have told all or most of their family about their sexual identity (Pew Research Center 2013), the experience of having a "gay relative" is relatively common and perhaps, least troublesome to potentially-objecting family members. Indeed, though there are generational differences in support of gay men relatives (Nordqvist and Smart 2014) and some evidence of ambivalence between adult gay children and their parents (Reczek 2016), research suggests that many gay men do not have great difficulties with coming out to their families. For example, Pew Research Center data (N = 1,083) show that only 12% of gay men indicate that coming out to their mother and/or father weakened their relationship with them (Pew Research Center 2013). Having gay men family members, then, does not appear to be highly stigmatizing for either hetero-cis or LGBTQ people.

The item in this key area with the highest mean values for the hetero-cis subsample (though only by a difference of .01) is: "Gay men are not capable of being good parents." Politicized media has certainly grabbed onto the heated debate about the "fitness" of gay and lesbian parents (Crawford et al. 1999; Joos and Broad 2007; Lee 2019; Rapaport 2019). Yet gay fathers face unique stigmatization experiences. As men, gay dads face hostilities because they challenge both the traditional conventional definitions of family (mother + father) as well as norms about masculinity and fatherhood (Murphy 2013; Schacher, Auerbach, and Silverstein 2005). In particular, the cultural stigmatization of gay men parents can be seen in problematic stereotypes about childhood outcomes (e.g., a child of two gay men will not be masculine enough) as well as a generalized fear of gay men as "sexual deviants" (e.g., that gay men are "pedophiles" and "perverts," Clarke 2001; Worthen 2016). However, there have been some shifts in the negativity surrounding gay parenting in the past few decades. For example, as noted in Chapter 8, public support for the legal adoption of children among same-sex couples close to tripled from 1992 (29%) to 2019 (75%) (Gallup 2014; McCarthy 2019). In addition, in February 2019, *Parents* magazine featured their first-ever cover profile of a same sex couple, gay fathers Shaun T (American fitness mogul) and Scott Blokker (Bried 2019). Even so, a palpable stigma *specifically* directed toward gay men as "capable" parents remains. For example, some small-scale research indicates that gay fathers are thought to be less emotionally stable, less nurturing, and less affectionate than both lesbian mothers and heterosexual parents (Baiocco et al. 2013). In addition, heterosexual people's social concerns about the potentially negative life outcomes of the children of gay men parents are more prominent as compared to their concerns about the children of lesbian women and heterosexual parents (Baiocco et al. 2013; Biblarz and Stacey 2010). Thus, it is perhaps not surprising that means for this item are highest among the hetero-cis subsample.

The item in this key area with the highest mean value (1.69) for the LGBTQ subsample is: "I welcome new friends who are gay men," which was reverse coded. As compared to the support of gay men relatives (1.53) and parents (1.59), there is greater negativity toward gay men friends. As discussed previously, there is an historical basis for this divisiveness. As the Gay Liberation Movement began to solidify in the 1970s, White gay cis men were largely at the forefront while others in the LGBTQ spectrum were marginalized. As a result, the larger "gay" movement became fractured, with gay men divided from lesbian women (especially) who opted into separatist, radical strategies (Stein 1997; Weiss 2004). These historical happenings may also reflect current gay men's friendship patterns which are characterized by a particular preference for friendships with other gay men (Galupo 2007; Nardi 1999; Nardi and Sherrod 1994). In addition, gay men's friendships have been found to serve specific familial support functions which can contribute to a sense of exclusivity among gay men and within gay men's friendships (Nardi 1999; Nardi and Sherrod 1994). Overall, both the historical divisiveness between gay men and others in the LGBTQ community as well as the close, familial (and sometimes exclusive) dynamics of gay men's friendships contribute to the somewhat heightened stigmatization toward gay men's friendships found among the LGBTQ subsample.

## *Gay Men and Positions of Importance and Social Significance*

Means in this key area ranged from 1.63 to 2.46 indicating low stigmatization of gay men in positions of importance and social significance. The two items in this key area are: "I would not vote for a political candidate who was an openly gay man" and "Gay men should not be allowed to join the military." Interestingly, stigmatizing perspectives about gay men as political candidates and as military members were very similar within each group, separated by only .04 for the hetero-cis subsample and .02 for the LGBTQ subsample. Thus, when it comes to gay men in these specific positions of importance and social significance, attitudes do not differ very much. This may also reflect a slow but changing landscape of gay men in high-ranking leadership positions such as Jared Polis, who became the first-ever openly gay U.S. governor in 2019 (in Colorado) and Eric Fanning, the highest ranked and first-ever openly gay leader of any service in the U.S. Military who served as the 22nd Secretary of the U.S. Army from 2016–2017 (Caron 2018; Koren 2016; Lubold 2015).

## Gay Men and Sex Act-Related Stigma

As compared to all other key areas, gay men sex act-related stigma was highest for both subsamples with most mean values for the five items close to 2.0 or higher and some values reaching nearly 3.0 for the hetero-cis subsample. In addition, of all nine LGBTQ groups, gay men are the most likely to experience stigma associated with having sex with a woman among both samples (recall Figure 7.4). Thus, there is discomfort across the entire sample with the thought of a gay man having sex with a woman. Furthermore, for the hetero-cis sample only, of all nine LGBTQ groups, gay men are the most likely to experience stigma associated with having sex with a man. Hostilities directed toward sex between men are at the center of negative attitudes toward gay men among hetero-cis individuals. In particular, both gay and bisexual men are stigmatized due to stereotypes and negative judgements about the sex acts they are believed to be involved in. See Chapter 7 for a discussion of these overlapping patterns associated with negativities toward sex between men.

Gay men are also stigmatized based on other sex-related stereotypes. For example, for the LGBTQ sample only, gay men are the most likely of all nine LGBTQ groups to experience stigma associated with being too sexual/hypersexual (recall Figure 7.4). HIV/AIDS-related stigma is also quite strong among gay men. Indeed, as seen in Figure 9.1, these are amongst the top most stigmatizing perspectives directed toward gay men for both subsamples. Originally described as "the gay plague," HIV/AIDS-related stigma has largely been associated with gay, bisexual, and queer men and their (perceived as) "risky" hypersexuality in part because much of the conversation about the so-called "AIDS Epidemic" in the 1980s centered on the (perceived as) numerous sex partners of gay men and their (perceived as) unsafe sexual practices (Dowsett 2009; Herek and Capitanio 1999). There is also evidence of similar problematic discourse among teens found more recently (Mutchler and McDavitt 2011). In addition, research indicates that there are more generalized implicit associations with gay men and "promiscuity" (Javaid 2018; Pinsof and Haselton 2016). These interconnected sex act-related stereotypes remain associated with the stigmatization of gay men among both hetero-cis and LGBTQ people.

## Gay Men Identity Permanency

Reactions to the statement "Most men who call themselves gay are just temporarily experimenting with their sexuality" are split. For the hetero-cis subsample, there is moderate support for stigma associated with gay men identity permanency (2.50); however, for LGBTQ subsample, there is much lower support for this type of stigmatization (1.86). While the authenticity of gay identity is being questioned less and less over time, there may still be a sentiment among some hetero-cis individuals that gay men just need to "find the right girl" to "help" them realize they are not actually gay. Indeed, as described in Chapter 6, the "conversion" of a "homosexual" into a "heterosexual" has been claimed to be possible through everything from hypnosis to aversion therapy to forced heterosexual encounters (Beachy 2010; Erzen 2006). The very existence of these processes (even though they are not supported by the American Psychological Association) may be enough for some to support the stigmatizing perspective that gay identity is just temporary and/or experimental.

## Gay Men and the Achievement of Masculinity

There is support for the statement "Gay men are not masculine enough" among the LGBTQ (1.87) and hetero-cis (2.62) subsamples. This sentiment is among the top five most stigmatizing perspectives toward gay men for both groups (see Figure 9.1). As noted previously, perceptions of masculinity and femininity are rooted in a hetero-cis-normative process that entwines being masculine with being involved in relationships with women. Because gay men are not in relationships with women, they are viewed as unable to successfully achieve masculinity. In addition, some of the sex acts gay men are perceived to be participating in are also deemed to be un-masculine. Specifically, the receptive anal and oral sex partners of those with penises are viewed as submissive, feminine, and inferior to the insertive partners who are deemed to be dominant, masculine, and superior (see Chapter 7 for a further discussion of these stereotypes). There is also evidence of anti-effeminacy prejudice among both heterosexual and gay men who prefer to distance themselves from feminine gay men (Glick et al. 2007; Taywaditep 2002). Together these hetero-cis-normative and misogynistic processes shape the stigma that some gay men endure as associated with being stereotyped as too feminine and not masculine enough by both hetero-cis and LGBTQ people (Glick et al. 2007; Hunt et al. 2016).

## Gay Men Stigma Summed Scale

As seen in Table 9.1, the Gay Men Stigma Scale was created by summing all 14 items together. Cronbach's alphas were quite high for the hetero-cis (.89) and LGBTQ (.88) subsamples. However, the actual ranges in the summed scale values were very different between the two subsamples with the highest value for the hetero-cis subsample (70) 17 points higher than the highest value for the LGBTQ subsample (53). It is important to note that a value of 70 on the Gay Men Stigma Scale indicates that a single hetero-cis respondent reported the highest level of stigma on all 14 items in the scale. Mean values for the summed Gay Men Stigma Scale also differed substantially and significantly with the hetero-cis subsample mean (34.19) 9.30 points higher than the LGBTQ subsample mean (24.89). Despite these differences, there was strong overlap among each subsample's top most stigmatizing beliefs about gay men (discomfort with sex with women, too sexual/hypersexual, HIV/AIDS, and masculinity, see Figure 9.1) and the key area with the highest means was the same for both groups: gay sex act-related stigma. Thus, the stigmatization of gay men is largely driven by negativity associated with sex between men (recall Figure 7.3).

## NCST, Hetero-cis-normativity, Social Power Axes, and the Gay Men Stigma Scale

The first set of regression models examine the Gay Men Stigma Scale using NCST. The hypotheses are as follows:

- *Hypothesis 1a*: there is a significant positive relationship between the HCN Scale and the Gay Men Stigma Scale.
- *Hypothesis 1b*: there are significant relationships between individual social power axes (gender identity, sexual identity, additional gender/sexuality, racial/ethnic identity, basic needs) and the Gay Men Stigma Scale.
- *Hypothesis 2a*: the relationship between the HCN Scale and the Gay Men Stigma Scale is moderated by interactions between the HCN Scale and axes of social power.
- *Hypothesis 2b*: the relationships between individual social power axes and the Gay Men Stigma Scale are moderated by interactions between axes of social power.

Figure 9.2 outlines these relationships and the two models of NCST to be estimated. Specifically, Table 9.2 utilizes OLS regression to examine NCST and the relationships among hetero-cis-normativity, axes of social power (gender, sexuality, additional gender/sexuality, race/ethnicity, and basic needs), and the Gay Men Stigma Scale for the hetero-cis subsample and the LGBTQ subsample. See Chapter 7 for a more complete description of the models. Regarding model fit statistics, the adjusted $R^2$ values ranged from .68 to .70.

**204** NCST and Understanding LGBTQ Stigma

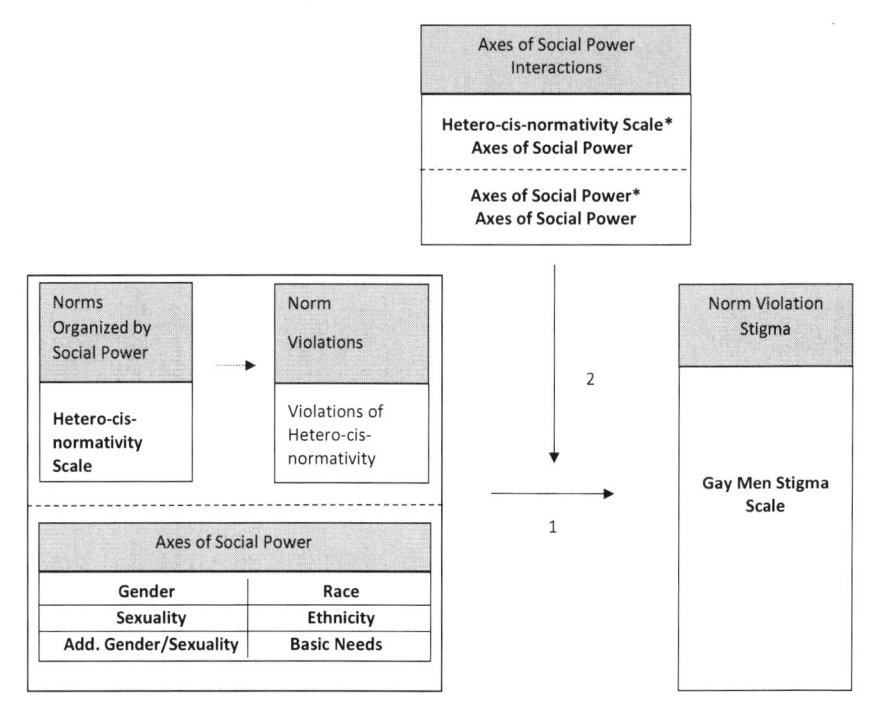

**FIGURE 9.2** Theoretical Model of NCST and Gay Men Stigma using the Stigmatizer Lens with Model Numbers to be Examined in Table 9.2

*Notes:* Model 1 estimates the HCN Scale and axes of social power (gender, sexuality, additional gender/sexuality, race, ethnicity, and basic needs) as they relate to the Gay Men Stigma Scale. Model 2 estimates interactions among axes of social power and the HCN Scale as they moderate the relationships between the HCN Scale and the Gay Men Stigma Scale as well as interactions among axes of social power as they moderate the relationships between the HCN Scale and the Gay Men Stigma Scale. The * indicates an interaction.

## NCST, HCN, Social Power Axes, and the Gay Men Stigma Scale: Model 1

Table 9.2 Model 1 estimates the HCN Scale and axes of social power as they relate to the Gay Men Stigma Scale. There is a positive relationship between the HCN Scale and the Gay Men Stigma Scale in Model 1 for both subsamples. Thus, *Hypothesis 1a* is well supported: hetero-cis-normativity is positively related to gay men stigmatization for both groups. In addition, individual axes of social power are significantly related to gay men stigmatization for the hetero-cis subsample (cis woman, mostly all I need, and often basic needs not met) and for the LGBTQ subsample (trans woman, trans man, African American/Black, Asian American/Pacific Islander, other race, and often basic needs not met). Thus, *Hypothesis 1b* is well supported: individual social power axes are related to gay men stigmatization for both subsamples.

**TABLE 9.2** OLS Regression Results Estimating NCST and the Gay Men Stigma Scale for the Hetero-cis Subsample (n = 1,500) and the LGBTQ Subsample (n = 1,604)

|  | Hetero-cis Subsample | | LGBTQ Subsample | | Test of Difference |
|---|---|---|---|---|---|
|  | Model 1 | Model 2 | Model 1 | Model 2 |  |
| HCN Scale | .69* | .74* | .67* | .45* | . |
| *Gender identity* | | | | | |
| Cis woman | -1.99* | . | . | . | |
| Trans woman | — | — | 2.40* | . | |
| Trans man | — | — | 2.24* | . | |
| *Additional sexual/gender identity* | | | | | |
| SGL | . | 9.44* | . | -5.23* | ** |
| Femme | . | 7.17* | . | . | . |
| *Racial/ethnic identity* | | | | | |
| African American/Black | . | . | 1.15* | . | |
| Asian American/Pacific Islander | . | . | 1.72* | 4.37* | ** |
| Other race | . | . | 4.43* | . | |
| *Basic needs* | | | | | |
| Mostly all I need | -.89* | -15.58* | . | . | . |
| Often basic needs not met | -1.31* | . | -.92* | -11.07* | . |
| *HCN Scale\*social power axes interactions* | | | | | |
| HCN Scale*asexual | — | — | — | .44* | |
| HCN Scale*queer | — | -.30* | — | . | ** |
| HCN Scale*African American/Black | — | -.19* | — | . | . |
| HCN Scale*Multi-racial | — | .57* | — | . | ** |
| *Social power axes interactions* | | | | | |
| Cis woman*few needs met | — | . | — | 3.29* | ** |
| Gay/lesbian*mostly all I need | — | — | — | 3.87* | |
| Bisexual*SGL | — | — | — | 3.15* | |
| Bisexual*mostly all I need | — | — | — | 4.95* | |
| African American/Black*Two-Spirit | — | . | — | -6.39* | . |
| SGL*mostly all I need | — | . | — | -2.08* | ** |
| Twink*mostly all I need | — | -7.94* | — | . | ** |
| *Controls: common explanations* | | | | | |
| *LGBTQ contact* | | | | | |
| Gay friends | -2.57* | -2.50* | -1.95* | -1.89* | . |

*(Continued)*

**TABLE 9.2** (Cont.)

|  | Hetero-cis Subsample | | LGBTQ Subsample | | Test of Difference |
| --- | --- | --- | --- | --- | --- |
|  | Model 1 | Model 2 | Model 1 | Model 2 |  |
| LBTQ Friends Scale | -.32* | -.35* | -.16* | -.14* | . |
| *Religiosity* |  |  |  |  |  |
| Church attendance | .38* | .38* | . | . | . |
| Scripture/biblical literalism | .83* | .97* | . | . | ** |
| *Religious identity* |  |  |  |  |  |
| Protestant—evangelical | 1.43* | . | 1.76* | 2.01* | . |
| *Political perspectives* |  |  |  |  |  |
| Liberal—conservative | .67* | .66* | . | . | ** |
| Openness to new experiences | -1.63* | -1.47* | -1.14* | -1.20* | . |
| *Support laws/policies helping:* |  |  |  |  |  |
| Those in poverty | -1.40* | -1.35* | . | . | . |
| Racial/ethnic minorities | . | . | -1.60* | -1.60* | . |
| Women | -1.11* | -1.10* | 1.04* | 1.05* | ** |
| *Beliefs about gender* |  |  |  |  |  |
| Patriarchal Gender Norms Scale | .52* | .51* | .53* | .55* | . |
| *Sociodemographic controls* |  |  |  |  |  |
| Age | .05* | .05* | .04* | .04* | . |
| Outside U.S. | . | . | 2.33* | 2.45* | . |
| Adjusted $R^2$ | .70 | .70 | .68 | .68 |  |
| Mean VIF | 1.50 | 1.50 | 1.92 | 1.92 |  |

*Notes:* unstandardized regression coefficients are presented. Only the rows with significant results are displayed here. See Table 9.1 for detailed information about the Gay Men Stigma Scale. See Tables 7.1 and 7.2 for details about all other variables and Appendix B Table B.1 for details about the interaction effects.

* $p < .05$; a dot (.) indicates non-statistically significant results. A dash (—) indicates this was not included in the model.

** $p < .05$ for Clogg et al.'s (1995) test of equality of regression coefficients comparing Model 2 for the hetero-cis subsample and Model 2 for the LGBTQ subsample.

## NCST, HCN, Social Power Axes, and the Gay Men Stigma Scale: Model 2

Interaction effects among axes of social power and the HCN Scale as well as interaction effects among axes of social power are included in Model 2. The HCN Scale remains significantly positively related to the Gay Men Stigma Scale for both groups even when including these interaction effects. In addition, interactions among the HCN Scale and social power axes are significant in Model 2 among both subsamples. All significant findings for the Gay Men

Stigma Scale in this area overlap with those found for the Lesbian Women Stigma Scale. Three of these are discussed in Chapter 7 (for the hetero-cis-subsample: interactions between the HCN Scale, queer, African American/Black, and Multi-racial). For the LGBTQ subsample, the positive HCN Scale and asexual interaction term indicates that support of hetero-cis-normativity has a more robust effect on asexual individuals' attitudes toward gay men as compared to non-asexual individuals' attitudes toward gay men. As noted in Chapter 8, there is some strain in the LGBTQ(A) community when it comes to the inclusion of asexual people (Colborne 2018; Pinto 2014) and this may reinforce relationships between gay men negativity, hetero-cis-normativity, and asexuality. Overall, *Hypothesis 2a* is supported: interactions between the HCN Scale and axes of social power moderate the relationship between the HCN Scale and the Gay Men Stigma Scale for both subsamples.

Among the individual social power axes, for the hetero-cis subsample, there are three that are significantly related to the Gay Men Stigma Scale in Model 2. First, as compared to indicating they have everything they need and more (reference category), indicating "mostly all I need" is negatively related to gay men stigmatization. As others have found (Appleby 2001; Connell, Davis, and Dowsett 1993; Embrick, Walther, and Wickens 2007), these patterns suggest that there are important basic needs and class experiences that shape the stigmatization of gay men. In addition, being SGL is positively related to gay men stigmatization. Thus, the intersections of SGL identity and hetero-cis identity contribute to stigmatizing attitudes toward gay men. Though SGL identity is often not described as an identity among hetero-cis individuals, about 1 in 5 SGL individuals (18%, n = 60/342) in this study's sample identified as hetero-cis. Such findings suggest that it is important to consider how SGL hetero-cis identities may be constructed, what their "multiple meanings" may be (Truong et al. 2016:937), and how they may impact the stigmatization of gay men. However, interestingly and in direct contrast to these findings, being SGL is *negatively* related to the Gay Men Stigma Scale among the LGBTQ subsample, which is discussed in Chapter 7.

Another axis of social power that is significantly related to the Gay Men Stigma Scale for hetero-cis subsample in Model 2 is also among the additional sexual/gender identities: being femme is positively related to the stigmatization of gay men. Though femme identity is often associated with the LGBTQ community, about 1 in 4 femmes (24%, n = 74/303) in this study's sample identified as hetero-cis. As seen in other research (Blair and Hoskin 2015), the connections between femme and hetero-cis identities are important to consider because they shape experiences with stigma and perspectives about various issues, including anti-gay sentiments. The results here demonstrate that femme hetero-cis people may be especially likely to harbor hostilities toward gay men.

In addition to the individual social power axes, there is one social power interaction term that is significantly related to the Gay Men Stigma Scale for hetero-cis subsample in Model 2: identifying as "twink" and indicating "mostly all I need" is negatively related to gay men stigmatization. Here, the interacting experiences of having one's basic needs mostly met and twink identity among hetero-cis individuals relate to more supportive attitudes toward gay men. About half (44%, n = 43/98) of twinks in this study's sample identified as hetero-cis. Though twink identities have been explored in gay communities (Ravenhill and de Visser 2019; Rodriguez, Huemmer, and Blumell 2016), the findings here indicate that twink hetero-cis people may occupy a unique space of empathic concern for gay men perhaps due to their own experiences with marginalization associated with being feminized and stigmatized.

Contrasting with the hetero-cis subsample, there are many more significant results among the social power axes for the LGBTQ subsample in Model 2. Additional tests to compare the regression coefficients of the two subsamples also reveal numerous significant differences (Clogg, Petkova, and Haritou 1995). Thus, the social power axes that relate to hetero-cis people's attitudes toward gay men largely differ from the social power axes that inform LGBTQ people's gay men stigmatization.

Moving to the significant individual social power axes for the LGBTQ subsample, being Asian American/Pacific Islander is positively related to gay men stigma for the LGBTQ subsample. Such findings align with previous work that demonstrates that being Asian American/Pacific Islander and being LGBTQ intersect in ways that impact perspectives about gay men (Battle, Pastrana, and Harris 2017; Han, Proctor, and Choi 2014; Worthen 2018). In addition, among the basic needs measures, indicating "often basic needs not met" (wherein the reference category is "everything I need") is negatively related to the Gay Men Stigma Scale for the LGBTQ subsample. Interestingly, these results contrast with past research that finds ample evidence of anti-gay sentiments in working-class environments (Balay 2014; Connell, Davis, and Dowsett 1993; Embrick, Walther, and Wickens 2007).

Among the significant social power axes interaction terms in Model 2 for the LGBTQ subsample, all five possible axes of social power are significant: gender identity (cis woman), sexual identity (gay/lesbian, bisexual), additional gender/sexual identity (SGL, Two-Spirit), racial/ethnic identity (African American/Black), and basic needs (mostly all I need, few needs met). However, for all except one of the significant interaction terms (SGL bisexual individuals), there are no corresponding individual effects. In addition, only two of the six significant social power axes interaction terms (African American/Black Two-Spirit individuals and SGL individuals who indicate "mostly all I need") are negatively related to the Gay Men Stigma Scale while the rest are positive. Interestingly, one of these includes gay/lesbian identity: being a gay/lesbian individual who indicates "mostly all I need" is positively related to the stigmatization of gay men. Thus, gay/lesbian identity and adequate basic needs experiences interact to shape disapproving attitudes toward gay men. In all, the six significant social power axes interaction terms that relate to the stigmatization of gay men among the LGBTQ subsample indicate that the intersecting experiences of numerous elements of social power (gender, sexuality, race, and class) impact attitudes toward gay men.

Overall, social power axes interactions emerge as significantly related to the Gay Men Stigma Scale in Model 2 for both the hetero-cis and LGBTQ subsamples. Thus, *Hypothesis 2b* is supported: interactions between axes of social power moderate the relationship between the individual axes of social power and the Gay Men Stigma Scale for both subsamples. However, there are no overlapping similarities between the two subsamples in terms of significant relationships between axes of social power and the stigmatization of gay men. In fact, the single common predictor (being SGL) has opposite effects for the hetero-cis and LGBTQ subsamples. Thus, as found among the Lesbian Woman Stigma Scale regression models, the specific axes of social power that shape the stigmatization of gay men differ for the hetero-cis and LGBTQ subsamples. This set of findings continues to reflect previous work (e.g., Worthen 2018) that has found different patterns among heterosexual and LGB subsamples in the stigmatization of gay men.

## Summarizing NCST, HCN, Social Power Axes, and the Gay Men Stigma Scale

The findings in Table 9.2 show that both individual and intersecting axes of social power impact the stigmatization of gay men, though the only overlapping finding between the hetero-cis and LGBTQ subsamples is the robust effect of the hetero-cis-normativity scale on the Gay Men Stigma Scale which is significant in all models. In particular, the significant social power interaction effects found among the hetero-cis subsample differ from those found among the LGBTQ subsample. However, across all models, experiences related to gender, sexuality, race, and basic needs emerge as significantly related to the stigmatization of gay men. Such findings contribute to better understandings of the complexities in our understandings of gay men stigma.

## Gay Men's Experiences

### The Gay Men Subsample

The recruitment of gay men to participate in this study was successful and the requested quota (n = 330) from Survey Sampling International was met and exceeded (learn more about the data and sampling procedures in Chapter 7 and Appendix A). The study sample included 345 gay men. At the beginning of the survey, respondents were asked two questions: (1) "How would you describe yourself?" and (2) "What best describes your gender?" Gay men were those who selected "gay or lesbian" for the first question and either "I identify as a man and my assigned sex at birth was male" or "I am transgender: I identify as a man and my assigned sex at birth was female" for the second question. See Table 9.3 for more details about the gay men in this study.

**TABLE 9.3** Gay Men Characteristics (n = 345)

|  | % | n |
|---|---|---|
| *Gender identity* | | |
| Cis man | 95.7% | 330 |
| Trans man | 4.3% | 15 |
| *Additional gender/sexual identity* | | |
| Queer** | 27.5% | 95 |
| SGL** | 22.9% | 79 |
| Two-Spirit | 3.2% | 11 |
| Butch** | 7.8% | 27 |
| Femme | 4.1% | 14 |
| Leather | 4.6% | 16 |
| Bear** | 12.8% | 44 |
| Twink | 6.4% | 22 |
| Down Low | 4.9% | 17 |
| *Race/ethnicity* | | |
| Caucasian/White* | 83.5% | 288 |
| African American/Black** | 7.2% | 25 |
| Asian American/Pacific Islander* | 5.2% | 18 |
| Native American/Alaskan Native* | 1.2% | 4 |
| Multi-racial* | 1.2% | 4 |
| Other race* | 0.6% | 2 |
| Latinx race* | 1.2% | 4 |
| Latinx ethnicity** | 14.2% | 49 |
| *Basic needs* | | |
| Everything I need** | 29.3% | 101 |
| Mostly all I need** | 55.7% | 192 |
| Often needs not met* | 10.7% | 37 |
| Few needs met* | 4.3% | 15 |

* Reference category in analyses in Table 9.5.
** Included in analyses shown in Table 9.5.

## Gay Men's Experiences with Gender- and Sexuality-Based DHV

Gay men are at high risk for DHV. For example, a meta-analysis with over 500,000 participants across 386 studies from the years 1992 to 2009 found that gay/bisexual men are significantly more likely than lesbian/bisexual women to experience certain types of victimization (i.e., weapon assault, robbery, physical assault, and sexual harassment) (Katz-Wise and Hyde 2012). Additional research finds abundant evidence of discrimination experiences among gay men in the workplace and elsewhere (Hendren and Blank 2009; Lim, Trau, and Foo 2018; Tilcsik 2011). However, it is often unclear if these experiences are interpreted as motivated by gender, sexuality, both, or neither.

As demonstrated in Figure 9.3, a majority (65%) of gay men in this study indicate that they have had one or more sexuality-based DHV experiences and more specifically, half (54%) have had one or more experiences of sexuality-based discrimination and/or harassment. In particular, gay men are between 3.6 and 5.4 times more likely to experience sexuality-based DHV than gender-based DHV. Sexuality-based discrimination and harassment experiences are most common (54%) and gender-based violence is the least

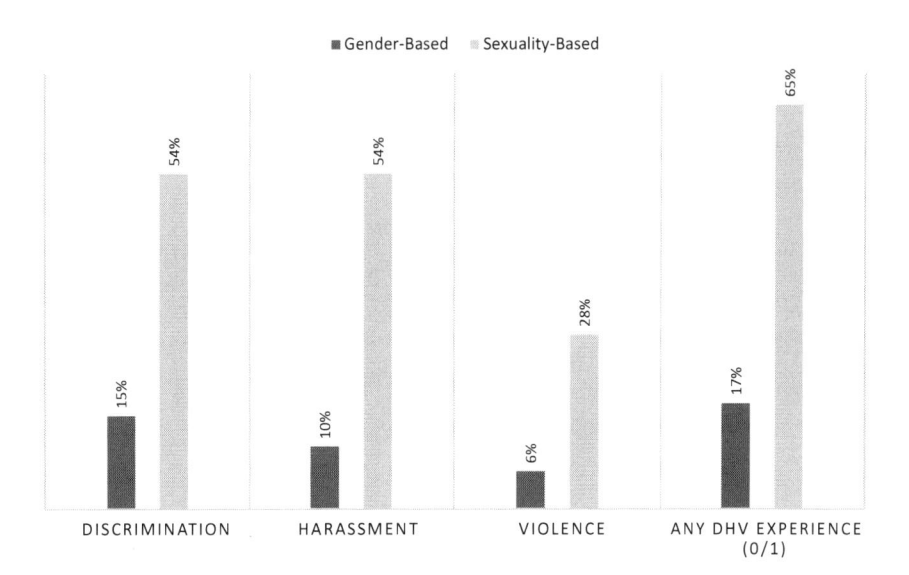

**FIGURE 9.3** Gay Men's (n = 345) Experiences with Gender- and Sexuality-Based DHV

*Note*: See Table 9.4 for comparisons of gay men's experiences to the LGBTQ subsample and the men subsample.

**TABLE 9.4** Gender- and Sexuality-Based DHV Mean Values (Standard Deviations) among Gay Men, the LGBTQ Subsample, and the Men Subsample with *t*-test Results

|  | Gay Men | LGBTQ Subsample | Men Subsample |
|---|---|---|---|
| *n* | 345 | 1604 | 1474 |
| *Gender-based* | | | |
| Discrimination | .15 (.36)** | .32 (.47) | .17 (.38) |
| Harassment | .10 (.29)** | .28 (.45) | .09 (.29) |
| Violence | .06 (.23)** | .14 (.34) | .07 (.26) |
| Any gender DHV experience (0/1) | .17 (.38)** | .40 (.49) | .21 (.41) |
| *Sexuality-based* | | | |
| Discrimination | .54 (.50)*** | .44 (.50) | .23 (.42) |
| Harassment | .54 (.50)*** | .41 (.49) | .24 (.43) |
| Violence | .28 (.45)*** | .20 (.40) | .13 (.34) |
| Any sexuality DHV experience (0/1) | .65 (.48)*** | .53 (.50) | .33 (.47) |

\*\* Gay men are significantly different from the LGBTQ subsample (only) at p < .001 level.
\*\*\* Gay men are significantly different from both the LGBTQ and men subsamples at p < .001 level.

common (6%). To better understand gay men's gender- and sexuality-based DHV, gay men's experiences were compared to the LGBTQ subsample and the men subsample using *t*-tests. As seen in Table 9.4, compared to all men (33%) and all LGBTQ people (53%), gay men (64%) are significantly more likely to experience any sexuality-based DHV. In contrast, as compared to all LGBTQ people, gay men are significantly less likely to experience any gender-based DHV (40% vs. 17% respectively) and do not significantly differ from all men in these experiences. Thus, as shown in both Figure 9.3 and Table 9.4, gay men are at particular risk for sexuality-based DHV but not gender-based DHV.

## NCST and Gay Men's Experiences with Gender- and Sexuality-Based DHV

The second set of regression models examines gay men and their experiences with gender- and sexuality-based DHV using NCST with special attention to gay men's axes of social power. The hypotheses are as follows:

- *Hypothesis 1*: being a gay man (violating hetero-cis-normativity) increases the likelihood of experiencing gender- and sexuality-based DHV (gay stigma).

- *Hypothesis 2*: the relationship between being a gay man and gender- and sexuality-based DHV is moderated by interactions among being a gay man and axes of social power.

Figure 9.4 displays these relationships and Table 9.5 provides logistic regression results that examine NCST and the relationships among being a gay man, intersections among gay men's axes of social power, and any experiences of gender-based DHV (dichotomized as 0/1) or sexuality-based DHV (dichotomized as 0/1) utilizing the LGBTQ subsample (n = 1,604; whereby being a gay man is compared to all other LBTQ people). Because gay men's experiences are the focus of this investigation (i.e., the stigmatized lens of NCST is being utilized), the gay man and social power axes interaction terms are listed first in Table 9.5 and the discussion below focuses on these variables. However, there are significant corresponding individual effects related to being lesbian/gay and being a man (for example) that are important to recognize. See Chapter 7 for a more complete description of the models and a discussion of overarching trends and patterns. Regarding model fit statistics, the pseudo $R^2$ values ranged from .09 to .17.

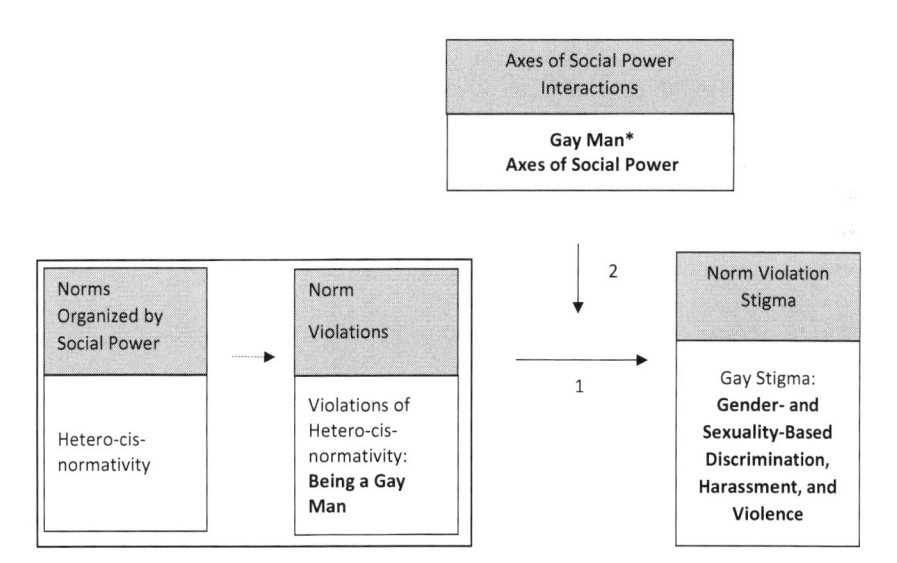

**FIGURE 9.4** Theoretical Model of NCST and Gay Stigma among Gay Men using the Stigmatized Lens with Model Numbers to be Examined in Table 9.5

*Notes:* Model 1 estimates being a gay man as related to gender- and sexuality-based DHV. Model 2 estimates interactions among gay men's axes of social power as they moderate the relationships between being a gay man and gender- and sexuality-based DHV. The * indicates an interaction.

## NCST, Gay Men, and Gender- and Sexuality-Based DHV: Model 1

Model 1 in Table 9.5 estimates the relationships between violations of hetero-cis-normativity (conceptualized as being a gay man) and gay stigma (conceptualized as gender-based DHV in the first set of models and sexuality-based DHV in the second set of models). Interestingly, results for Model 1 show that being a gay man significantly decreases the likelihood of gender-based DHV by .48; however, being a gay man is *not* significantly related to sexuality-based DHV. These findings strongly contrast with previous research that shows that gay men are at a high risk for DHV (FBI 2018; Katz-Wise and Hyde 2012; Meyer 2015). However, it is important to note that Table 9.5 utilizes other LBTQ people as the comparison group, and thus, may be illuminating different patterns than other research that has examined DHV experiences among gay men. In particular, findings here provide a unique vantage point that demonstrates differences between gay men's gender- and sexuality-based DHV experiences from others' experiences in the LBTQ community. In doing so, it becomes clear that being a gay man does not significantly increase the likelihood of gender- or sexuality-based DHV when the comparison group is other LBTQ people.

TABLE 9.5 Logistic Regression Results with Odds Ratios and (Standard Errors) Estimating NCST and Gender- and Sexuality-Based DHV as Related to Being a Gay Man for the LGBTQ Subsample (n = 1,604)

|  | Gender-Based DHV || | Sexuality-Based DHV ||||
|---|---|---|---|---|---|---|---|---|
|  | Model 1 || Model 2 || Model 1 || Model 2 ||
|  | OR | SE | OR | SE | OR | SE | OR | SE |
| Gay man | .52* | (.13) | . | . | . | . | . | . |
| *Gay man social power axes interactions* | | | | | | | | |
| Gay man*queer | — | — | . | . | — | — | . | . |
| Gay man*SGL | — | — | .31* | (.12) | — | — | . | . |
| Gay man*butch | — | — | . | . | — | — | 3.15* | (1.57) |
| Gay man*bear | — | — | . | . | — | — | . | . |
| Gay man*African American/Black | — | — | . | . | — | — | . | . |
| Gay man*Latinx (ethnicity) | — | — | . | . | — | — | . | . |
| Gay man*everything I need | — | — | 2.81* | (1.38) | — | — | . | . |
| Gay man*mostly all I need | — | — | 2.90* | (1.24) | — | — | . | . |

(*Continued*)

**TABLE 9.5** (Cont.)

|  | Gender-Based DHV | | | | Sexuality-Based DHV | | | |
|---|---|---|---|---|---|---|---|---|
|  | Model 1 | | Model 2 | | Model 1 | | Model 2 | |
|  | OR | SE | OR | SE | OR | SE | OR | SE |
| *Gay man social power axes* | | | | | | | | |
| Gay/lesbian | . | . | . | . | 3.61* | (.58) | 3.48* | (.57) |
| Man | .27* | (.04) | .26* | (.04) | . | . | . | . |
| Queer | 2.51* | (.38) | . | . | 2.11* | (.30) | 1.97* | (.56) |
| SGL | . | . | 3.21* | (1.06) | . | . | . | . |
| Butch | 1.58* | (.33) | . | . | . | . | . | . |
| Bear | . | . | . | . | . | . | . | . |
| African American/Black | . | . | . | . | . | . | . | . |
| Latinx (ethnicity) | . | . | . | . | . | . | . | . |
| Everything I need | .67* | (.12) | .28* | (.13) | .64* | (.10) | . | . |
| Mostly all I need | . | . | .31* | (.12) | .77* | (.11) | . | . |
| *Socio-demographic controls* | | | | | | | | |
| Age | .98* | (.00) | .98* | (.00) | .98* | (.00) | .98* | (.00) |
| Town type (rural–large city) | . | . | . | . | . | . | . | . |
| Education | 1.19* | (.05) | 1.19* | (.05) | . | . | . | . |
| Income | . | . | . | . | . | . | . | . |
| Pseudo $R^2$ | .16 | | .17 | | .09 | | .10 | |
| Mean VIF | 1.44 | | 1.44 | | 1.43 | | 1.43 | |

*Notes:* all rows are displayed, including those without significant results. See Table 9.3 for more details about gay men.

* $p < .05$; a dot (.) indicates non-statistically significant results. A dash (—) indicates this was not included in the model.

Such findings are partially consistent with research that demonstrates that men are less likely to be targeted for gender-based DHV than women are (Jagsi et al. 2016; Katz-Wise and Hyde 2012); however, when it comes to sexuality-based DHV among gay men, these results do not align with previous work. As noted above, gay and bisexual men report significantly greater rates of certain types of victimization when compared to lesbian and bisexual women (Katz-Wise and Hyde 2012). In addition, among crimes reported to the FBI and coded as sexual-orientation bias motivated crimes, over half (59.7%) are classified as "anti-gay(male)" (FBI 2018). Thus, it is at least somewhat surprising that there is no significant relationship between being a gay man and sexuality-based DHV found when the comparison group is LBTQ people. Overall, *Hypothesis 1* is not supported: being a gay man does not increase the likelihood of gender- or sexuality-based DHV.

## NCST, Gay Men, and Gender- and Sexuality-Based DHV: Model 2

The next set of models include intersections among being a gay man and axes of social power as they moderate the relationship between being a gay man and gender- and sexuality-based DHV. In both Model 2s, the individual effect of being a gay man is not significantly related to gender- or sexuality-based DHV. However, there are significant interaction effects in both models. For gender-based DHV, three interaction terms are significant. First, being a SGL gay man decreases the likelihood of gender-based DHV by .69. Thus, SGL identity among gay men may serve as protective factor against certain types of victimization. Other research also finds that SGL-identified men have different experiences from other non-heterosexual men in ways that intersect with masculinity, race/ethnicity, and religiosity (Moore 2008; Truong et al. 2016; Wilson and Miyashita 2016). Second and third, in comparison to gay men who do not have their basic needs met, gay men who have everything they need and more have a 1.81 increased likelihood of experiencing gender-based DHV and gay men who have mostly all they need have a 1.90 increased likelihood of experiencing gender-based DHV. Thus, the luxury and security of having one's basic needs met (or mostly met) among gay men are not protective factors for DHV, in fact, these experiences have the opposite effect on gay men's likelihood of experiencing DHV. Though previous studies have found evidence of anti-gay sentiments in working-class settings (Balay 2014; Connell, Davis, and Dowsett 1993; Embrick, Walther, and Wickens 2007), gender-based DHV among gay men remains relatively under-examined as it relates to basic needs experiences. These results suggest there may be something unique about gay men's basic needs being fully or mostly met that impacts their victimization. Gay men who have basic needs security may be more open about their gay identities and this may put them at risk for DHV in ways that gay men who are struggling to meet their basic needs are not.

Among the sexuality-based DHV models, there is one significant interaction term: being a butch gay man increases the likelihood of sexuality-based DHV by 2.15. Interestingly, this is in opposition to the butch-top/dominant/masculine and femme-bottom/submissive/feminine dynamic sometimes described in gay men's relationships (Johns et al. 2012) wherein it could be presumed that butches are less likely to be victimized due to their (perceived as) dominant relational position (McKenry et al. 2006) (this type of dynamic is somewhat in line with the findings among lesbian women wherein lesbian butch women experienced a decreased odds of sexuality-based DHV, see Table 8.5). However, butches can also represent a sexualized/fetishized subculture within gay men's communities. As discussed in Chapter 3, the gay and "beefy" lumberjack, leatherman, military man, construction worker, mechanic, sailor, and biker are all classed sex objects (Han 2007; Lahti 1998). In these ways, butch gay men may be targeted for sexuality-based

DHV in ways that non-butch gay men are not. Overall, the gay identity and social power axes interaction terms that are significantly related to both gender- and sexuality-based DHV support *Hypothesis 2*.

### Summarizing NCST, Gay Men, and Gender- and Sexuality-Based DHV

In sum, Table 9.5 demonstrates that the individual effect of being a gay man decreases the likelihood of gender-based DHV and is not directly related to sexuality-based DHV; however, gay men's intersecting social power experiences effect the likelihood of gender- and sexuality-based DHV in different ways. In particular, the intersections of gay and SGL identities decreased the likelihood of gender-based DHV while gay men's intersecting experiences with basic needs security (everything I need and mostly all I need) increased the likelihood of gender-based DHV. In addition, being a butch gay man had a more than two-fold increase on the likelihood of sexuality-based DHV. These findings demonstrate the importance of utilizing an intersectional approach to NCST to examine gay men's experiences with victimization.

## Summary of Patterns of Gay Men Stigma

In line with the three tenets and hypotheses derived from NCST, there are six patterns related to the stigmatization of gay men reviewed in this chapter:

1. Discomfort with gay men's sex acts are a driving force in the stigmatization of gay men for both hetero-cis and LGBTQ people.
2. For both hetero-cis and LGBTQ people, there is also strong overlap among the top most stigmatizing beliefs about gay men which include sex act-related perspectives (discomfort with gay men having sex with women, gay men are too sexual/hypersexual, gay men are responsible for HIV/AIDS,) and gay men are not masculine enough.
3. Hetero-cis-normativity is positively related to gay men stigma for both subsamples; however, the interaction effects between the HCN Scale and social power axes that moderate this relationship differ for the hetero-cis and LGBTQ subsamples. In addition, there are more significant interaction effects between the HCN Scale and social power axes for the hetero-cis subsample than there are for the LGBTQ subsample.
4. Individual social power axes are significantly related to gay men stigma for both subsamples; however, the interaction effects between the social power axes that moderate these relationships differ for the hetero-cis and LGBTQ subsamples. In addition, there are more significant interaction

effects between the social power axes for the LGBTQ subsample than there are for the hetero-cis subsample.
5. Gay men experience high levels of sexuality-based DHV in comparison to both the LGBTQ and all men subsamples but relatively low levels of gender-based DHV in comparison to the LGBTQ subsample.
6. The individual effect of being a gay man and gay men's intersecting experiences with SGL identity decrease the likelihood of gender-based DHV; however, gay men with adequate basic needs experiences have an increased likelihood of gender-based DHV and butch gay men have an increased likelihood of sexuality-based DHV.

## Note

1 Harry Hay (1912–2002) founded the Mattachine Society in Los Angeles, California in 1950. On the 50th anniversary of the Stonewall Uprising in June 2019, Harry Hay was one of fifty inaugural activists inducted into the National LGBTQ Wall of Honor located in the Stonewall Inn (National LGBTQ Task Force 2019).

## References

Appleby, George A. 2001. "Ethnographic Study of Gay and Bisexual Working-Class Men in the United States." *Journal of Gay & Lesbian Social Services* 12(3/4):51–62.

Baiocco, Roberto, Nicola Nardelli, Lina Pezzuti, and Vittorio Lingiardi. 2013. "Attitudes of Italian Heterosexual Older Adults Towards Lesbian and Gay Parenting." *Sexuality Research and Social Policy* 10(4):285–292.

Balay, Anne. 2014. *Steel Closets: Voices of Gay, Lesbian, and Transgender Steelworkers*. Chapel Hill, NC: University of North Carolina Press.

Battle, Juan, Antonio Pastrana and Angelique Harris. 2017. *An Examination of Asian and Pacific Islander LGBT Populations across the United States*. New York, NY: Palgrave Macmillan.

Beachy, Robert. 2010. "The German Invention of Homosexuality." *The Journal of Modern History* 82(4):801–838.

Biblarz, Timothy J. and Judith Stacey. 2010. "How Does the Gender of Parents Matter?" *Journal of Marriage and Family* 72(1):3–22.

Blair, Karen L. and Rhea Ashley Hoskin. 2015. "Experiences of Femme Identity: Coming Out, Invisibility and Femmephobia." *Psychology & Sexuality* 6(3):229–244.

Bried, Erin. 2019. "Insanity Founder Shaun T Opens up about Twin Life after 12 Pregnancy Attempts with 5 Surrogates." *Parents*. Retrieved March 29, 2019 (www.parents.com/parenting/celebrity-parents/shaun-t-insanity-life-with-twins/).

Caron, Christina. 2018. "In 'Rainbow Wave,' L.G.B.T. Candidates are Elected in Record Numbers." *The New York Times*, November 8. Retrieved January 30, 2020 (https://www.nytimes.com/2018/11/07/us/politics/lgbt-election-winners-midterms.html).

Clarke, Victoria. 2001. "What about the Children? Arguments against Lesbian and Gay Parenting." *Women's Studies International Forum* 24(5):555–570.

Clogg, Clifford C., Eva Petkova, and Adamantios Haritou. 1995. "Statistical Methods for Comparing Regression Coefficients between Models." *American Journal of Sociology* 100(5):1261–1293.

Colborne, Adrienne. 2018. "Chasing Aces: Asexuality, Misinformation and the Challenges of Identity." *Dalhousie Journal of Interdisciplinary Management* 14:1–13.

Connell, R. W., M. D. Davis, and G. W. Dowsett. 1993. "A Bastard of A Life: Homosexual Desire and Practice among Men in Working-Class Milieux." *The Australian and New Zealand Journal of Sociology* 29(1):112–135.

Crawford, Isiaah, Andrew McLeod, Brian D. Zamboni, and Michael B. Jordan. 1999. "Psychologists' Attitudes toward Gay and Lesbian Parenting." *Professional Psychology: Research and Practice* 30(4):394–401.

Cusac, Anne-Marie. [1998] 2016. "Meet Pioneer of Gay Rights, Harry Hay." *The Progressive* Retreived January 30, 2020 (https://progressive.org/magazine/meet-pioneer-gay-rights-harry-hay/).

Dowsett, Gilbert. 2009. "The 'Gay Plague' Revisited: AIDS and its Enduring Moral Panic." Pp. 130–156 in *Moral Panics, Sex Panics: Fear and the Fight over Sexual Rights* edited by Gilbert Herdt. New York, NY: NYU Press.

Embrick, David G., Carol S. Walther, and Corrine M. Wickens. 2007. "Working Class Masculinity: Keeping Gay Men and Lesbians Out of the Workplace." *Sex Roles* 56(11):757–766.

Erzen, Tanya. 2006. *Straight to Jesus: Sexual and Christian Conversions in the Ex-Gay Movement*. Berkeley, CA: University of California Press.

FBI. 2018. "2018 Hate Crimes Statistics." *FBI*. Retrieved January 9, 2020 (https://ucr.fbi.gov/hate-crime/2018/topic-pages/victims).

Gallup. 2014. "Most Americans Say Same-Sex Couples Entitled to Adopt." *Gallup*. Retrieved February 7, 2019 (https://news.gallup.com/poll/170801/americans-say-sex-couples-entitled-adopt.aspx).

Gallup. 2019. "Gay and Lesbian Rights: In Depth Topics A to Z." *Gallup*. Retrieved February 6, 2019 (https://news.gallup.com/poll/1651/Gay-Lesbian-Rights.aspx).

Galupo, M. Paz. 2007. "Friendship Patterns of Sexual Minority Individuals in Adulthood." *Journal of Social and Personal Relationships* 24(1):139–151.

Glick, Peter, Candice Gangl, Samantha Gibb, Susan Klumpner, and Emily Weinberg. 2007. "Defensive Reactions to Masculinity Threat: More Negative Affect toward Effeminate (But not Masculine) Gay Men." *Sex Roles* 57(1):55–59.

Han, Chong-suk. 2007. "They Don't Want to Cruise Your Type: Gay Men of Color and the Racial Politics of Exclusion." *Social Identities* 13(1):51–67.

Han, Chong-Suk, Kristopher Proctor, and Kyung-Hee Choi. 2014. "We Pretend like Sexuality Doesn't Exist: Managing Homophobia in Gaysian America." *The Journal of Men's Studies* 22(1):53–63.

Hendren, Amy and Hartmut Blank. 2009. "Prejudiced Behavior toward Lesbians and Gay Men." *Social Psychology* 40(4):234–238.

Herek, Gregory M. and John Capitanio. 1999. "AIDS Stigma and Sexual Prejudice." *American Behavioral Scientist* 42(7):1130–1147.

Hunt, Christopher John, Fabio Fasoli, Andrea Carnaghi, and Mara Cadinu. 2016. "Masculine Self-Presentation and Distancing from Femininity in Gay Men: An Experimental Examination of the Role of Masculinity Threat." *Psychology of Men & Masculinity* 17(1):108–112.

Jagsi, Reshma, Kent A. Griffith, Chithra R. Rochelle Jones, Peter Ubel Perumalswami, and Abigail Stewart. 2016. "Sexual Harassment and Discrimination Experiences of Academic Medical Faculty." *JAMA* 315(19):2120–2121.

Javaid, Aliraza. 2018. "'Poison Ivy': Queer Masculinities, Sexualities, Homophobia and Sexual Violence." *European Journal of Criminology* 15(6):748–766.

Johns, Michelle Marie, Emily Pingel, Anna Eisenberg, Matthew Leslie Santana, and José Bauermeister. 2012. "Butch Tops and Femme Bottoms? Sexual Positioning, Sexual Decision Making, and Gender Roles among Young Gay Men." *American Journal of Men's Health* 6(6):505–518.

Joos, Kristin E. and K. L. Broad. 2007. "Coming Out of the Family Closet: Stories of Adult Women with LGBTQ Parent(s)." *Qualitative Sociology* 30(3):275–295.

Katz-Wise, Sabra L. and Janet S. Hyde. 2012. "Victimization Experiences of Lesbian, Gay, and Bisexual Individuals: A Meta-Analysis." *The Journal of Sex Research* 49(2/3):142–167.

Koren, Marina. 2016. "Meet the Highest-Ranking Openly Gay Military Official in U.S. History." *The Atlantic*. Retrieved April 1, 2019 (www.theatlantic.com/politics/archive/2016/05/eric-fanning-army-secretary/483291/).

Lahti, Martti. 1998. "Dressing Up in Power: Tom of Finland and Gay Male Body Politics." *Journal of Homosexuality* 35(3/4):185–205.

Lee, Kendra. 2019. "It's Easier Now for Gay Men to Adopt. But They Still Face Lots of Pushback, and Weird Questions." *Washington Post*, January 25. Retrieved January 20, 2020 (https://www.washingtonpost.com/lifestyle/2019/01/25/its-easier-now-gay-men-adopt-they-still-face-lots-pushback-weird-questions/).

Lim, Angeline Cuifang, Raymond Nam Cam Trau, and Maw-Der Foo. 2018. "Task Interdependence and the Discrimination of Gay Men and Lesbians in the Workplace." *Human Resource Management* 57(6):1385–1397.

Lubold, Gordon. 2015. "Obama Appoints Eric Fanning as First Openly Gay U.S. Army Secretary." *Wall Street Journal*, September 18. Retrieved January 20, 2020 (https://www.wsj.com/articles/obama-appoints-eric-fanning-as-first-openly-gay-u-s-army-secretary-1442613600).

McCarthy, Justin. 2019. "Gallup First Polled on Gay Issues in '77. What Has Changed?" *Gallup*. Retrieved August 21, 2019 (https://news.gallup.com/poll/258065/gallup-first-polled-gay-issues-changed.aspx).

McKenry, Patrick C., Julianne M. Serovich, Tina L. Mason, and Katie Mosack. 2006. "Perpetration of Gay and Lesbian Partner Violence: A Disempowerment Perspective." *Journal of Family Violence* 21(4):233–243.

Meyer, Doug. 2015. *Violence against Queer People: Race, Class, Gender, and the Persistence of Anti-LGBT Discrimination*. New Brunswick, NJ: Rutgers University Press.

Moore, Darnell. 2008. "Guilty of Sin: African-American Denominational Churches and Their Exclusion of SGL Sisters and Brothers." *Black Theology* 6(1):83–97.

Murphy, Dean A. 2013. "The Desire for Parenthood: Gay Men Choosing to Become Parents through Surrogacy." *Journal of Family Issues* 34(8):1104–1124.

Mutchler, Matt G. and Bryce McDavitt. 2011. "'Gay Boy Talk' Meets 'Girl Talk': HIV Risk Assessment Assumptions in Young Gay Men's Sexual Health Communication with Best Friends." *Health Education Research* 26(3):489–505.

Myers, JoAnne. 2013. *Historical Dictionary of the Lesbian and Gay Liberation Movements*. Lanham, MD: Scarecrow Press.

Nardi, Peter M. and Drury Sherrod. 1994. "Friendship in the Lives of Gay Men and Lesbians." *Journal of Social and Personal Relationships* 11:185–199.

Nardi, Peter M. 1999. *Gay Men's Friendships: Invincible Communities.* Chicago, IL: University of Chicago Press.

National LGBTQ Task Force. 2019. "National LGBTQ Wall of Honor Unveiled at Historic Stonewall Inn." *National LGBTQ Task Force.* Retrieved August 4, 2019 (www.thetaskforce.org/nationallgbtqwallofhonortobeunveiled/).

Nordqvist, Petra and Carol Smart. 2014. "Troubling the Family: Ongoing Problems of Coming Out as Lesbian or Gay to Families of Origin." *Families, Relationships and Societies* 3(1):97–112.

Pew Research Center. 2013. "Chapter 3: The Coming Out Experience." Retrieved February 6, 2019 (www.pewsocialtrends.org/2013/06/13/chapter-3-the-coming-out-experience/).

Pinsof, David and Martie Haselton. 2016. "The Political Divide over Same-Sex Marriage: Mating Strategies in Conflict?" *Psychological Science* 27(4):435–442.

Pinto, Stacy Anne. 2014. "ASEXUally: On Being an Ally to the Asexual Community." *Journal of LGBT Issues in Counseling* 8(4):331–343.

Rapaport, Lisa. 2019. "Gay Fathers Face Stigma as Parents." *Reuters.* Retrieved March 29, 2019 (www.reuters.com/article/us-health-lgbt-gay-dads/gay-fathers-face-stigma-as-parents-idUSKCN1P92TS).

Ravenhill, James P. and Richard O. de Visser. 2019. "'I Don't Want to Be Seen as a Screaming Queen': An Interpretative Phenomenological Analysis of Gay Men's Masculine Identities." *Psychology of Men and Masculinity* 20(3):324–336.

Reczek, Corinne. 2016. "Ambivalence in Gay and Lesbian Family Relationships: Ambivalence in Gay & Lesbian Family Relationships." *Journal of Marriage and Family* 78:644–659.

Rodriguez, Nathian Shae, Jennifer Huemmer, and Lindsey Erin Blumell. 2016. "Mobile Masculinities: An Investigation of Networked Masculinities in Gay Dating Apps." *Masculinities & Social Change* 5(3):241–267.

Schacher, Stephanie Jill, Carl F. Auerbach, and Louise Bordeaux Silverstein. 2005. "Gay Fathers Expanding the Possibilities for Us All." *Journal of GLBT Family Studies* 1(3):31–52.

Stein, Arlene. 1997. *Sex and Sensibility: Stories of a Lesbian Generation* Berkeley, CA: University of California Press.

Taywaditep, Kittiwut Jod. 2002. "Marginalization among the Marginalized: Gay Men's Anti-Effeminacy Attitudes." *Journal of Homosexuality* 42(1):1–28.

Tilcsik, András. 2011. "Pride and Prejudice: Employment Discrimination against Openly Gay Men in the United States." *American Journal of Sociology* 117(2):586–626.

Truong, Nhan, Amaya Perez-Brumer, Melissa Burton, June Gipson, and DeMarc Hickson. 2016. "What's in a Label?: Multiple Meanings of 'MSM' among Same-Gender-Loving Black Men in Mississippi." *Global Public Health* 11(7/8):937–952.

Weiss, Jillian Todd. 2004. "GL vs. BT: The Archaeology of Biphobia and Transphobia within the US Gay and Lesbian Community." *Journal of Bisexuality* 3(3/4):25–55.

Wilson, Bianca D. M. and Ayako Miyashita. 2016. "Sexual and Gender Diversity within the Black Men Who Have Sex with Men HIV Epidemiological Category." *Sexuality Research and Social Policy* 13(3):202–214.

Worthen, Meredith G. F. 2016. *Sexual Deviance and Society: A Sociological Examination.* London, UK: Routledge.

Worthen, Meredith G. F. 2018. "'Gay Equals White'? Racial, Ethnic, and Sexual Identities and Attitudes toward LGBT Individuals among College Students at a Bible Belt University." *The Journal of Sex Research* 55(8):995–1011.

# 10
# BISEXUAL WOMEN STIGMA

*Some folks say that bisexuals do not experience oppression because at least we are accepted by mainstream society when we are in mixed-gender relationships. Agreed, society may like us when we show only that aspect of who we are. But conditional acceptance is not really acceptance at all. When we show our whole selves, including our same-gender loving side, we suffer the discrimination similar to that of lesbians and gay men.*

*Robyn Ochs, bisexual activist*[1]

**IMAGE 10.1** Robyn Ochs with a bisexual pride flag draped around her shoulders at the North Shore Pride Parade and Festival in Salem, Massachusetts on June 25, 2016. Photo by Marilyn Humphries used with permission from Robyn Ochs.

## The Stigmatization of Bisexual Women

In the survey instrument, the section focusing on attitudes toward bisexual women was preceded by the following statement:

> *Next, we're interested in your thoughts, feelings, and predicted behaviors about bisexual women (women who have romantic and sexual attractions to both men and women).*

### The Bisexual Women Stigma Scale

Among all nine groups explored in this book, bisexual women are the second least stigmatized, just slightly less stigmatized than lesbian women (recall Figure 7.1). However, the particulars driving the stigmatization of bisexual women are relatively unique from the other LGBTQ groups. To best understand these complexities, the 14 items in the Bisexual Women Stigma Scale are explored in Figure 10.1 and Table 10.1 and discussed below.

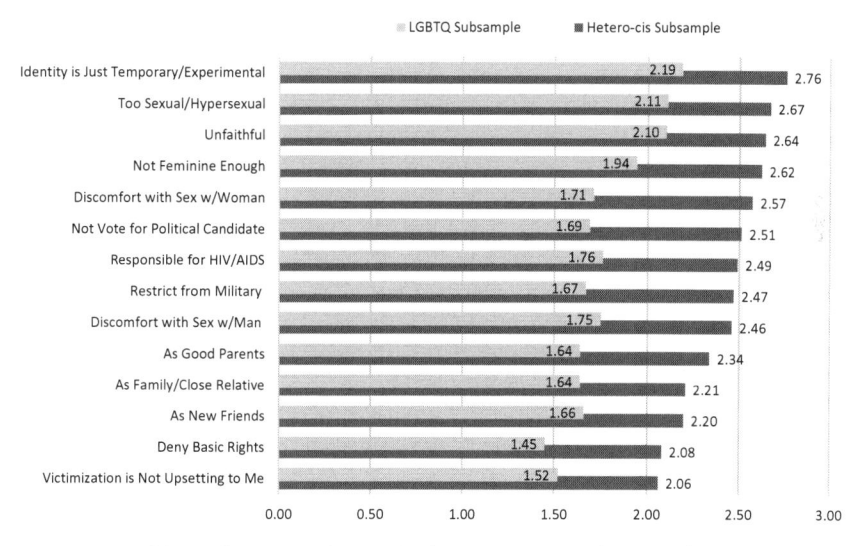

| Item | LGBTQ Subsample | Hetero-cis Subsample |
|---|---|---|
| Identity is Just Temporary/Experimental | 2.19 | 2.76 |
| Too Sexual/Hypersexual | 2.11 | 2.67 |
| Unfaithful | 2.10 | 2.64 |
| Not Feminine Enough | 1.94 | 2.62 |
| Discomfort with Sex w/Woman | 1.71 | 2.57 |
| Not Vote for Political Candidate | 1.69 | 2.51 |
| Responsible for HIV/AIDS | 1.76 | 2.49 |
| Restrict from Military | 1.67 | 2.47 |
| Discomfort with Sex w/Man | 1.75 | 2.46 |
| As Good Parents | 1.64 | 2.34 |
| As Family/Close Relative | 1.64 | 2.21 |
| As New Friends | 1.66 | 2.20 |
| Deny Basic Rights | 1.45 | 2.08 |
| Victimization is Not Upsetting to Me | 1.52 | 2.06 |

**FIGURE 10.1** Bisexual Women Stigma Scale Item Mean Values Rank-Ordered from Most to Least Stigmatizing for the Hetero-cis (n = 1,500) and the LGBTQ (n = 1,604) Subsamples

*Notes:* see Table 10.1 for the exact wording for each item. *t*-test results comparing the hetero-cis and LGBTQ subsamples indicate that all means are significantly different from one another at the p < .001 level.

**TABLE 10.1** Bisexual Women Stigma Scale Item Mean Values (Standard Deviations) and *t*-test Results Comparing the Means for the Hetero-cis Subsample and the LGBTQ Subsample

|  | Hetero-cis Subsample | LGBTQ Subsample | t-test Results |
|---|---|---|---|
|  | n = 1,500 | n = 1,604 |  |
| *Social and familial relationships* |  |  |  |
| I welcome new friends who are bisexual women. R | 2.20 (1.10) | 1.66 (0.99) | t = 14.40* |
| I don't think it would negatively affect our relationship if I learned that one of my close relatives was a bisexual woman. R | 2.21 (1.13) | 1.64 (1.04) | t = 14.66* |
| Bisexual women are not capable of being good parents. | 2.34 (1.27) | 1.64 (1.08) | t = 16.48* |
| *Positions of importance and social significance* |  |  |  |
| I would not vote for a political candidate who was an openly bisexual woman. | 2.51 (1.34) | 1.69 (1.16) | t = 18.27* |
| Bisexual women should not be allowed to join the military. | 2.47 (1.35) | 1.67 (1.16) | t = 17.61* |
| *Basic human rights* |  |  |  |
| I believe bisexual women should have all of the same rights as other people do. R | 2.08 (1.14) | 1.45 (0.91) | t = 16.94* |
| It is upsetting to me that bisexual women experience violence, harassment, and discrimination just because they are bisexual women. R | 2.06 (1.11) | 1.52 (0.96) | t = 14.62* |
| *Sex act-related stigma* |  |  |  |
| Bisexual women are unfaithful to their romantic partners. | 2.64 (1.16) | 2.10 (1.13) | t = 13.23* |
| Bisexual women are too sexual (hypersexual). | 2.67 (1.19) | 2.11 (1.14) | t = 13.56* |
| Bisexual women are mostly responsible for spreading HIV/AIDS. | 2.49 (1.18) | 1.76 (1.09) | t = 17.75* |
| I am comfortable with the thought of a bisexual woman having sex with a woman. R | 2.57 (1.21) | 1.71 (1.01) | t = 21.47* |
| I am comfortable with the thought of a bisexual woman having sex with a man. R | 2.46 (1.11) | 1.75 (1.00) | t = 18.58* |
| *Bisexual identity permanency* |  |  |  |
| Most women who call themselves bisexual are just temporarily experimenting with their sexuality. | 2.76 (1.15) | 2.19 (1.18) | t = 13.60* |

(Continued)

**TABLE 10.1** (Cont.)

|  | Hetero-cis Subsample | LGBTQ Subsample | t-test Results |
|---|---|---|---|
| *Achievement of femininity* |  |  |  |
| Bisexual women are not feminine enough. | 2.62 (1.15) | 1.94 (1.10) | $t = 16.85^*$ |
| α | .91 | .92 |  |
| Summed scale actual range | 14–68 | 14–63 |  |
| Summed scale mean | 34.08 (11.17) | 24.82 (10.65) | $t = 23.61^*$ |

Notes: response options were Strongly Disagree–Strongly Agree (range: 1–5). [R] This item is reverse coded.*

*t*-test results allowing for unequal variances indicate that the hetero-cis subsample and LGBTQ subsample means are significantly different from one another at the $p < .001$ level.

## Bisexual Women and Social and Familial Relationships

Looking at Table 10.1, there is not pervasive negativity toward bisexual women friends and family members. The items in this key area with the lowest mean values for the hetero-cis subsample (2.20 and 2.21) are: "I welcome new friends who are bisexual women" and "I don't think it would negatively affect our relationship if I learned that one of my close relatives was a bisexual woman," both of which were reverse coded. In addition, all three items in this key area had nearly identical (low) means for the LGBTQ subsample (1.64, 1.64, and 1.66). This is somewhat surprising because U.S. Pew Research Center data (N = 1,197) show that only one third (33%) of bisexual women and about 1 in 8 (12%) bisexual men have told all or most of their family and friends about their sexual identity as compared to nearly three fourths of gay men and lesbian women (77% and 71%, respectively) (Pew Research Center 2013). In particular, some (34%) bisexuals chose not to tell their parents about their sexual identity because these issues "never came up" or that "raising the subject was not important to them" (Pew Research Center 2013a). This may be especially true when bisexual individuals are in long term/married opposite gender relationships (Scherrer, Kazyak, and Schmitz 2015). The findings here suggest that even though only a minority of bisexual women are out amongst their social and familial networks, there is still relatively high support of bisexual women as friends and family members.

The item in this key area with the highest mean value for the hetero-cis subsample (2.34) is: "Bisexual women are not capable of being good parents." Though hostility toward gay and lesbian parents in politicized media is palpable (Crawford et al. 1999; Gander 2018; Joos and Broad 2007), there has been less focus on bisexual parents. It is likely that the cultural stigmatization of a bisexual woman who is co-parenting with another woman has some overlap with the stigmatization of lesbian parents (e.g., a child with two mothers will be too emotional; a good family needs both a mother and a father) (Clarke 2001). However, there may also be some specific negativities toward bisexual moms who are coupled with women related to hetero-cis-normative cultural biases and bi-negativity, such as "she should just pick a man to be with if she is going to raise a child" or "she should stop experimenting with women and just settle down with a man if she's going to have a baby." Indeed, Ross et al.'s (2012) study of bisexual mothers (n = 14) found that compared to other sexual minority (non-heterosexual) mothers (n = 50), bisexual mothers experienced more mental health distress and anxiety. Bisexual mothers also reported a particular discomfort with feeling "invisible" "due to deeply embedded cultural assumptions about mothers as exclusively heterosexual" (Ross et al. 2012:150). These negative perspectives demonstrate the unique complexities of the stigma that bisexual mothers can endure.

## Bisexual Women and Positions of Importance and Social Significance

There was relatively low stigmatization toward bisexual women in positions of importance and social significance with means ranging from 1.67 to 2.51. The two items in this key area are: "I would not vote for a political candidate who was an openly bisexual woman" and "Bisexual women should not be allowed to join the military." Those who agree with these statements may express negativity toward bisexual women in leadership positions because they have a preference for hetero-cis men leaders. This is especially significant because bisexual women have only recently become high-ranking visible political leaders (e.g., Kate Brown became the first openly bisexual U.S. state governor in 2015 (in Oregon) and Kyrsten Sinema was the first openly bisexual person elected to the U.S. Senate in 2018, Allen 2018) and there have been no visible bisexual women in high-ranking positions in the U.S. military to date. Thus, there are still notable barriers associated with bisexual women in these specific positions of importance and social significance that contribute to bisexual women stigma.

## Bisexual Women and Sex Act-Related Stigma

As seen in Table 10.1, there was support for sex act-related stigma among bisexual women. These perspectives continue to reflect generalized negativity toward LGBTQ peoples' sexualities and the sex acts they are believed to be involved in (as described in Chapters 3 and 6 especially). For bisexual women, sex act-related stigma is embedded in a specific set of cultural dynamics that eroticize and objectify them in a process that diminishes their value both as women and as bisexuals while simultaneously reinforcing their sexual worth as the ultimate "prize" for the heterosexual man (Rupp and Taylor 2010). Thus, sex act-related stigma for bisexual women includes intersecting negativities built from stereotypes about women and about bisexuality.

The item with the lowest mean value in the sex act-related stigma key area for the hetero-cis subsample (2.46) is: "I am comfortable with the thought of a bisexual woman having sex with a man" (which was reverse coded because *discomfort* with bisexual women engaging in sex acts reflects a stigmatizing attitude toward bisexual women). This is not surprising because a bisexual woman having sex with a man reflects hetero-cis-normativity and resembles cultural expectations of man + woman duos. Interestingly, however, for the LGBTQ subsample, the mean value for this item was slightly higher than the mean value for the item, "I am comfortable with the thought of a bisexual woman having sex with a woman" (which was also reverse coded) (1.75 vs. 1.71). Thus, while bisexual woman + man duos are least stigmatized among the hetero-cis subsample, it is bisexual woman + woman duos that are most acceptable among LGBTQ people. However, there are additional dynamics that inform this process.

For example, the item with the highest mean value in the sex act-related stigma key area for both the hetero-cis (2.67) and LGBTQ subsamples (2.11) is: "Bisexual women are too sexual (hypersexual)." It is also important to note that this item has the second highest mean values for both subsamples among all 14 items in the Bisexual Women Stigma Scale, as seen in Figure 10.1. The cultural sexualization and eroticization of bisexual women strongly contributes to this stigmatizing attitude (Chmielewski 2017; Eliason 1997; Mohr and Rochlen 1999; Raja and Stokes 1998; Rupp and Taylor 2010; Worthen 2013). In particular, bisexual women who are described as "lipstick" or "femme" are most frequently eroticized because while they may enjoy sex acts with women, heterosexual men can perceive their potential or actual sexual experiences with bisexual women as "victories" in their sexual conquests. At the same time, potential women partners of bisexual women may perceive heterosexual men's erotization of bisexual women as evidence that it is bisexual women (not the men who are objectifying them) who are "too sexual" or "hypersexual." In addition, the very fact that bisexual women can have sexual interests in both women and men may also oversexualize them as "up for anything" or even "sexually insatiable" because of the perception that they cannot be satisfied by a monogamous relationship with a single man or a woman (this also ties into the belief that bisexual women are unfaithful to their romantic partners, see Spalding and Peplau 1997, which is the third most stigmatizing attitude toward bisexual women for both subsamples, see Figure 10.1). This coupled with the numerous media representations of highly sexualized lipstick/femme bisexual women in pornography and elsewhere as well as the social rewards of girls kissing girls in public (discussed below) contribute to these processes and are a significant force in the stigmatization of bisexual women.

## Bisexual Woman Identity Permanency

There is support for stigma associated with bisexual woman identity permanency. In fact, across all 14 items in the Bisexual Women Stigma Scale, this item had the highest mean values for both groups as seen in Figure 10.1 (2.76 and 2.19 respectively). In addition, of all nine LGBTQ groups, bisexual women are most likely to endure stigma associated with identity permanency (recall Figure 7.4). Thus, there is agreement across the entire sample that "Most women who call themselves bisexual are just temporarily experimenting with their sexuality." Among both hetero-cis and LGBTQ populations, bisexual women are stereotyped as inauthentic. This false set of beliefs is squarely situated in the "straight girls kissing" phenomenon (Rupp and Taylor 2010). When stereotypically attractive "hetero-looking" women kiss other women in public social/drinking settings (e.g., at parties and bars/clubs/pubs), they are often socially rewarded by heterosexual men especially. As I have argued elsewhere, for heterosexual men, "bisexual women might be the epitome of 'sexy' because not only will they kiss girls, they may also kiss guys" (Worthen 2013:709). Ultimately, however, heterosexual men hope to enjoy watching these behaviors as a prelude to their own sexual trysts with these women. In fact, both hetero-cis and LGBTQ onlookers may believe that these girls are only kissing other girls to "get attention" (i.e., to attract heterosexual men) and that given the choice, these women would prefer to be with heterosexual men as opposed to another woman (Weiss 2004). This is calls into question the authenticity and permanency of bisexual woman identities because girl-on-girl sexualized behaviors are coded (though sometimes erroneously, see Rupp et al. 2014) purely as enticement for heterosexual men and not as genuine attraction between women (Hamilton 2007).

Additional negative stereotypes about the temporary/experimental nature of bisexuality such as "bisexual people just haven't made up their minds yet," "bisexuals are just confused," "bisexuality is just a phase," and "eventually, he/she/they will just pick one" (Hayfield, Clarke, and Halliwell 2014; Weiss 2004) are further amplified as they pertain to bisexual women because of their heightened sexualization by both hetero-cis and LGBTQ people. Within the LGBTQ community, there are also specific harmful stereotypes about bisexual identity permanency. For example, the slang phrase "switchhitter" is sometimes applied to bisexuals who are stereotyped as only briefly and temporarily "switching" over to same-sex relationships (also "AC/DC" and "fence-sitter" are similar slang terms, see Weiss 2004). Related is the notion that bisexuals "just want to have their cake and eat it too" (i.e., bisexuals want to reap the benefits of both heterosexual and gay/lesbian relationships). Notably, lesbian women have been especially critical of bisexual women due to these stereotypes (Hayfield, Clarke, and Halliwell 2014; Rust

1995; Weiss 2004). Thus, bisexual women's identities in particular have been targeted as temporary/experimental by both hetero-cis and LGBTQ people for both unique and overlapping reasons.

## Bisexual Women and the Achievement of Femininity

There is some support for stigma associated with the achievement of femininity among bisexual women, particularly among the hetero-cis subsample, as related to the statement "Bisexual women are not feminine enough." As noted previously, being "feminine" is often associated with being the complementary partner of a masculine man. Because some bisexual women have relationships with women, they are not able to achieve this idealized hetero-femininity in the same ways that straight women can. However, the achievement of a feminine appearance/presentation has been found to vary for bisexual women, especially in regards to their relationships. For example, Taub's (1999) study of bisexual women (N = 74) revealed that a majority (71%) felt their beauty ideas and practices changed based on the gender of their partners. In particular, when in relationships with men, bisexual women felt more compelled to embody a traditionally hetero-feminine "sexy" and "pretty" appearance as compared to when they were in relationships with women. In other words, the achievement of femininity may be especially important for bisexual women when in relationships with men. Thus, the idea that bisexual women are (or are not) feminine "enough" relates closely to their compatibility as partners for heterosexual men. Within the LGBTQ community, however, femme bisexual women can experience negativity and some feel that they will be miscoded as "straight" if they look too feminine (Blair and Hoskin 2015; Hayfield et al. 2013; Huxley, Clarke, and Halliwell 2014). Indeed, as indicated by the significant $t$-test results in Table 10.1, concerns about bisexual women achieving femininity and looking "feminine enough" are more pervasive among hetero-cis people than LGBTQ people. However, for both groups, this is the fourth most stigmatizing attitude among the 14 items (see Figure 10.1) indicating that there is some stigma associated with bisexual women and their ability to appropriately achieve femininity.

## Bisexual Women Stigma Summed Scale

As seen in Table 10.1, the Bisexual Women Stigma Scale was created by summing together all 14 items. Cronbach's alphas were quite high: .91 for the hetero-cis subsample and .92 for the LGBTQ subsample. The actual range in values was slightly different between the two subsamples with the highest value for the hetero-cis subsample (68) 5 points higher than the highest value for the LGBTQ subsample (63). In addition, the summed Bisexual Women Stigma Scale mean values differed quite substantially with the hetero-cis subsample mean (34.08) 9.26 points higher than the

LGBTQ subsample mean (24.82). However, the top four most stigmatizing beliefs about bisexual women were the same for both groups (identity permanency, hypersexuality, unfaithfulness, and femininity, see Figure 10.1) and the key area with the highest individual mean values was also the same (bisexual woman identity permanency). Thus, overall, questioning bisexual women's identity permanency and sex act-related stigma have the largest impact on the stigmatization of bisexual women among both hetero-cis and LGBTQ populations (recall Figure 7.3).

## NCST, Hetero-cis-normativity, Social Power Axes, and the Bisexual Women Stigma Scale

The first set of regression models examine the Bisexual Women Stigma Scale using NCST. The hypotheses are as follows:

- *Hypothesis 1a*: there is a significant positive relationship between the HCN Scale and the Bisexual Women Stigma Scale.
- *Hypothesis 1b*: there are significant relationships between individual social power axes (gender identity, sexual identity, additional gender/sexuality, racial/ethnic identity, basic needs) and the Bisexual Women Stigma Scale.
- *Hypothesis 2a*: the relationship between the HCN Scale and the Bisexual Women Stigma Scale is moderated by interactions between the HCN Scale and axes of social power.
- *Hypothesis 2b*: the relationships between individual social power axes and the Bisexual Women Stigma Scale are moderated by interactions between axes of social power.

Figure 10.2 outlines these relationships and the two models of NCST to be estimated. Specifically, OLS regression is utilized in Table 10.2 to examine NCST and the relationships among hetero-cis-normativity, axes of social power (gender, sexuality, additional gender/sexuality, race/ethnicity, and basic needs), and the Bisexual Women Stigma Scale for the hetero-cis subsample and the LGBTQ subsample. See Chapter 7 for a more complete description of the models. Regarding model fit statistics, the adjusted $R^2$ values ranged from .68 to .69.

### *NCST, HCN, Social Power Axes, and the Bisexual Women Stigma Scale: Model 1*

In Table 10.2 Model 1, the relationships between the HCN Scale, axes of social power, and the Bisexual Women Stigma Scale are examined. The HCN Scale is positively related to the Bisexual Women Stigma Scale in Model 1 for both groups, fully supporting *Hypothesis 1a*. In addition, individual axes of social power are significantly related to bisexual women stigmatization for the

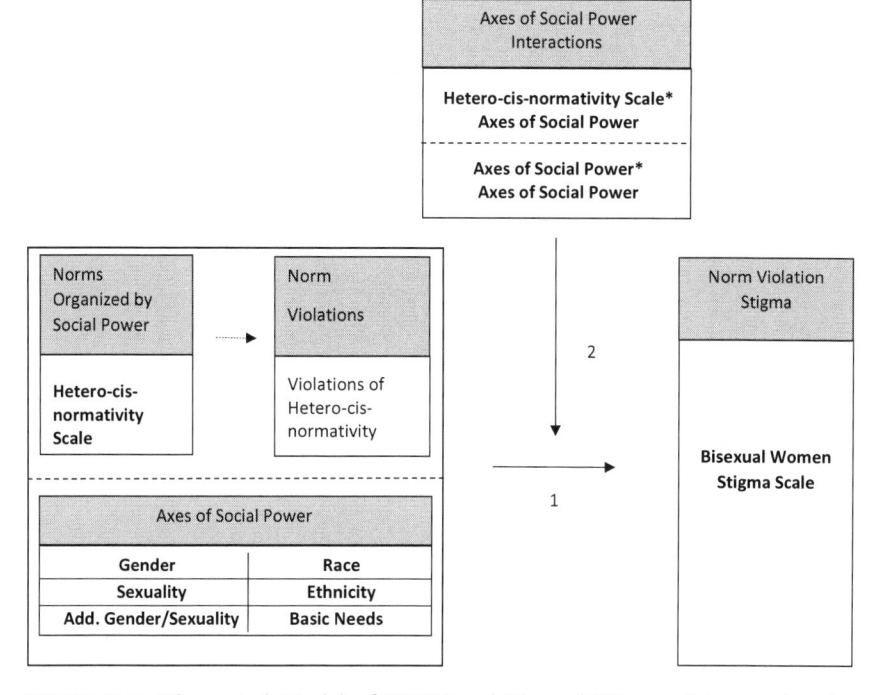

**FIGURE 10.2** Theoretical Model of NCST and Bisexual Women Stigma using the Stigmatizer Lens with Model Numbers to be Examined in Table 10.2

*Notes:* Model 1 estimates the HCN Scale and axes of social power (gender, sexuality, additional gender/sexuality, race, ethnicity, and basic needs) as they relate to the Bisexual Women Stigma Scale. Model 2 estimates interactions among axes of social power and the HCN Scale as they moderate the relationships between the HCN Scale and the Bisexual Women Stigma Scale as well as interactions among axes of social power as they moderate the relationships between the HCN Scale and the Bisexual Women Stigma Scale. The * indicates an interaction.

hetero-cis subsample (Multi-racial, mostly all I need, and often needs not met) and for the LGBTQ subsample (trans woman, leather, and other race), supporting *Hypothesis 1b*.

## NCST, HCN, Social Power Axes, and the Bisexual Women Stigma Scale: Model 2

In Model 2, intersections among axes of social power and the HCN Scale as well as interaction effects among axes of social power are examined. For both groups, the HCN Scale continues to be positively related to the Bisexual Women Stigma Scale in Model 2. In addition, there are significant HCN Scale and social power

**TABLE 10.2** OLS Regression Results Estimating NCST and the Bisexual Women Stigma Scale for the Hetero-cis Subsample (n = 1,500) and the LGBTQ Subsample (n = 1,604)

|  | Hetero-cis Subsample | | LGBTQ Subsample | | Test of Difference |
|---|---|---|---|---|---|
|  | Model 1 | Model 2 | Model 1 | Model 2 |  |
| HCN Scale | .75* | .75* | .79* | .58* | . |
| *Gender identity* | | | | | |
| Trans woman | — | — | 2.06* | . | |
| *Additional sexual/gender identity* | | | | | |
| Queer | . | 9.77* | . | . | . |
| Leather | . | . | 2.41* | . | . |
| Bear | . | 6.64* | . | . | . |
| *Racial/ethnic identity* | | | | | |
| Other race | . | . | 3.28* | . | . |
| Multi-racial | 2.50* | . | . | . | . |
| *Basic needs* | | | | | |
| Mostly all I need | -1.11* | . | . | . | . |
| Often needs not met | -1.82* | . | . | . | . |
| *HCN Scale\*social power axes Interactions* | | | | | |
| HCN Scale*queer | — | -.37* | — | . | ** |
| HCN Scale*bear | — | -.30* | — | . | . |
| HCN Scale*African American/Black | — | -.26* | — | . | ** |
| HCN Scale*Multi-racial | — | .67* | — | . | . |
| HCN Scale*few needs met | — | .30* | — | . | . |
| *Social power axes interactions* | | | | | |
| Cis woman*pansexual | — | — | — | 5.85* | . |
| Cis woman*SGL | — | . | — | -1.82* | . |
| Trans woman*bisexual | — | — | — | -3.90* | . |
| Gay/lesbian*Asian American/Pacific Islander | — | — | — | 3.92* | . |
| Bisexual*mostly all I need | — | — | — | 4.44* | . |
| Bisexual*often needs not met | — | — | — | 3.79* | . |
| Bisexual*few needs met | — | — | — | -5.63* | . |
| African American/Black*often needs not met | — | 5.13* | — | . | ** |
| Mostly all I need*twink | — | -6.03* | — | . | ** |

*(Continued)*

**TABLE 10.2** (Cont.)

|  | Hetero-cis Subsample | | LGBTQ Subsample | | Test of Difference |
|---|---|---|---|---|---|
|  | Model 1 | Model 2 | Model 1 | Model 2 |  |
| *Controls: common explanations* | | | | | |
| LGBTQ contact | | | | | |
| Bisexual women friends | -.90* | -.89* | -1.30* | -1.27* | . |
| LGBTQ Friends Scale (w/o bisexual women) | -.28* | -.33* | . | . | ** |
| *Religiosity* | | | | | |
| Church attendance | .38* | .38* | .34* | . | . |
| *Religious identity* | | | | | |
| Protestant—evangelical | 1.73* | 1.54* | . | . | . |
| Mormon | . | . | 3.47* | 3.75* | ** |
| *Political perspectives* | | | | | |
| Liberal—conservative | .43* | .41* | . | . | ** |
| Openness to New Experiences | -1.55* | -1.27* | -1.52* | -1.53* | . |
| *Support laws/policies helping:* | | | | | |
| Those in poverty | -1.99* | -1.86* | . | . | ** |
| Racial/ethnic minorities | . | . | -1.26* | . | . |
| *Beliefs about gender* | | | | | |
| Patriarchal Gender Norms Scale | .67* | .66* | .72* | .73* | . |
| *Sociodemographic controls* | | | | | |
| Western U.S. | . | . | -.89* | -1.00 | . |
| Adjusted R² | .68 | .69 | .68 | .69 |  |
| Mean VIF | 1.50 | 1.50 | 1.92 | 1.92 |  |

*Notes:* unstandardized regression coefficients are presented. Only the rows with significant results are displayed here. See Table 10.1 for detailed information about the Bisexual Women Stigma Scale. See Tables 7.1 and 7.2 for details about all other variables and Appendix B Table B.1 for details about the interaction effects.

* p < .05; a dot (.) indicates non-statistically significant results. A dash (—) indicates this was not included in the model.
** p < .05 for Clogg et al.'s (1995) test of equality of regression coefficients comparing Model 2 for the hetero-cis subsample and Model 2 for the LGBTQ subsample.

interaction effects, but only for the hetero-cis subsample. Three are discussed in Chapter 7: the interaction terms between the HCN Scale and queer, the HCN Scale and African American/Black, and the HCN Scale and Multi-racial. There are two additional HCN Scale interaction terms that are significantly related to the stigmatization of bisexual women. The negative interaction term between the HCN Scale and bear identity indicates that support of hetero-cis-normativity has a greater impact on shaping non-bear-identified hetero-cis individuals' attitudes toward bisexual women than it does on bear-identified hetero-cis individuals' attitudes. However, it is important to recall that the individual effect of bear identity is positive, indicating that without considering the interactive effects of hetero-cis-normativity, bear identity is positively related to the Bisexual Women Stigma Scale. Bear identities are most often explored among LGBT people (e.g., Edmonds and Zieff 2015; Hennen 2008), as a result, we know little about these relationships. Findings here suggest there may be specific relationships between bear identity and attitudes toward bisexual women (see more below).

In addition, the positive interaction between the HCN Scale and indicating that few basic needs are met demonstrates that hetero-cis-normativity has a greater impact on attitudes toward bisexual women among hetero-cis individuals who are struggling to have their basic needs met in comparison to others with more basic needs stability in the hetero-cis subsample. These results support other research that finds evidence of anti-LGBTQ sentiments in working-class environments (Balay 2014; Connell, Davis, and Dowsett 1993; Embrick, Walther, and Wickens 2007). In contrast to these findings, there are no significant HCN Scale and social power interaction effects for the LGBTQ subsample. Thus, *Hypothesis 2a* is only partially supported: interactions between the HCN Scale and axes of social power moderate the relationship between the HCN Scale and the Bisexual Women Stigma Scale for the hetero-cis subsample (only).

For the hetero-cis subsample, there are only two individual axes of social power that are significantly related to the Bisexual Women Stigma Scale in Model 2: queer and bear identities are both positively related to the stigmatization of bisexual women among the hetero-cis subsample. These findings are unique in that neither were found to be significantly related to any other LGBTQ stigma scales for either subsample in Model 2. Furthermore, in analyses not shown, the Bisexual Women Stigma Scale was positively correlated with queer identity ($r = .19$, $p < .001$) and bear identity ($r = .14$, $p < .001$) for the hetero-cis subsample. Because nearly all existing research explores queer and bear identities among LGBT people (e.g., Edmonds and Zieff 2015; Hennen 2008; Rollins and Hirsch 2003), there is a false underlying assumption that *all* queer and bear individuals are LGBT. However, in this study's sample, close to half of bears (39%, n = 59/153) and 1 in 5 queers (20%, n = 80/393) identified as hetero-cis. Together, these findings reveal that queer and bear hetero-cis individuals' hostilities toward bisexual women may be reflected in their own unique cultural dynamics. For example, some research indicates that bear culture can be quite exclusionary to women due to its focus on masculinity (Hennen 2005) and this may enhance bears' negativity toward women, including bisexual women.

There are two intersecting axes of social power that are significantly related to the Bisexual Women Stigma Scale for hetero-cis subsample in Model 2. Both are among the basic needs interaction effects. First, being an African American/Black individual who indicates that their needs are often not met is positively related to bisexual women stigmatization. These results align with past research that has identified LGBT negativity in some Black community experiences (Bowleg 2013; Greene 2000; Lemelle and Battle 2004; Worthen 2018) and in working-class environments (Balay 2014; Connell, Davis, and Dowsett 1993; Embrick, Walther, and Wickens 2007). Second, identifying as twink and indicating "mostly all need" is negatively related to bisexual women stigmatization. Thus, there is something unique among twinks who have their basic needs met that contributes to positive attitudes toward bisexual women. These supportive perspectives may relate to shared difficulties that bisexual women and twinks can experience as both feminized and sexualized groups (Ravenhill and de Visser 2019; Rodriguez, Huemmer, and Blumell 2016; Rupp and Taylor 2010). Though "twink" is often an identity that is discussed in relationship to gay and bisexual men (Ravenhill and de Visser 2019; Rodriguez, Huemmer, and Blumell 2016), with close to half of twinks in this study identifying as hetero-cis (44%, 43/98), it is clear that this group deserves further investigation. Together, these findings demonstrate that the intersecting experiences of identity (racial and gender/sexuality) and basic needs impact attitudes toward bisexual women.

In comparison to the hetero-cis subsample, there are many more significant social power axes among the LGBTQ subsample in Model 2. Additional tests to compare the regression coefficients of the two subsamples also reveal numerous significant differences (Clogg, Petkova, and Haritou 1995). Because there are no overlaps between the two subsamples among the significant relationships between axes of social power and bisexual women stigmatization, this tells us that the particular axes of social power that inform bisexual women stigmatization are entirely different for the hetero-cis and LGBTQ subsamples. As noted previously, these findings parallel other research (e.g., Worthen 2018) that has also found different patterns in the stigmatization of bisexual women among heterosexual and LGB subsamples that vary by axes of social power. Overall, however, *Hypothesis 2b* is supported: interactions between axes of social power moderate the relationship between the individual axes of social power and the Bisexual Women Stigma Scale for both subsamples.

Although there are no individual social power axes that are significantly related to the Bisexual Women Stigma Scale among the LGBTQ subsample, there are seven significant social power axes interaction terms in Model 2 and all of them include sexual identity. Specifically, being a pansexual cis woman, a gay/lesbian Asian American/Pacific Islander individual, a bisexual person who indicates mostly all I need, and a bisexual person who indicates that their needs are not often met are all positively related to the stigmatization of bisexual women. In contrast, being a SGL cis woman, a bisexual trans woman, and a bisexual individual who indicates that few of their basic needs are met are all negatively related to bisexual women stigma. Interestingly, three intersecting experiences of bisexual identity and basic needs experiences emerged as significantly related to the stigmatization of bisexual women. Thus, being bisexual can impact both positive and negative attitudes toward bisexual women when considering intersecting basic needs experiences. Such findings complement existing research that has drawn links between class and LGBTQ perspectives and experiences (Appleby 2001; Balay 2014).

It is also interesting that three of these findings are similar to those found among the regression models examining NCST and the Lesbian Women Stigma Scale (Table 8.2). Specifically, being a pansexual cis woman, a bisexual person who indicates that their needs are not often met, and a bisexual trans woman have similar effects on the stigmatization of both lesbian women and bisexual women. Thus, there may be some underlying overlapping patterns shaping lesbian and bisexual women stigma, as suggested in Chapter 7. Overall, the lack of significant individual social power axes terms in Model 2 demonstrates the robust influence that interacting social power experiences have on the stigmatization of bisexual women among the LGBTQ subsample.

## *Summarizing NCST, HCN, Social Power Axes, and the Bisexual Women Stigma Scale*

The findings in Table 10.2 demonstrate that the stigmatization of bisexual women is shaped by axes of social power in complex, intersecting ways that differ for hetero-cis and LGBTQ people. In particular, there are no commonalities among the ways that social power mechanisms impact attitudes toward bisexual women found among the hetero-cis and LGBTQ subsamples. Overall, the utilization of NCST to explore the Bisexual Women Stigma Scale allows us to see the importance of centering hetero-cis-normativity and intersecting social power experiences as they contribute to processes that shape the stigmatization of bisexual women.

## Bisexual Women's Experiences

### *The Bisexual Women Subsample*

The recruitment of bisexual women to participate in this study was successful and the requested quota (n = 330) from Survey Sampling International was met and exceeded. The study sample included 358 bisexual women (learn more about the

**TABLE 10.3** Bisexual Women Characteristics (n = 358)

|  | % | n |
|---|---|---|
| *Gender identity* | | |
| Cis women* | 92.2% | 330 |
| Trans women** | 7.8% | 28 |
| *Additional gender/sexual identity* | | |
| Queer** | 15.4% | 55 |
| SGL** | 13.1% | 47 |
| Two-Spirit** | 8.4% | 30 |
| Butch | 3.6% | 13 |
| Femme** | 23.5% | 84 |
| Leather | 0.3% | 1 |
| Bear | 0.6% | 2 |
| Twink | 0.8% | 3 |
| Down Low | 2.2% | 8 |
| *Race/ethnicity* | | |
| Caucasian/White* | 80.4% | 288 |
| African American/Black** | 8.1% | 29 |
| Asian American/Pacific Islander* | 2.8% | 10 |
| Native American/Alaskan Native* | 2.2% | 8 |
| Multi-racial* | 4.7% | 17 |
| Other race* | 0.8% | 3 |
| Latinx race* | 0.8% | 3 |
| Latinx ethnicity** | 13.4% | 48 |
| *Basic Needs* | | |
| Everything I need** | 29.3% | 58 |
| Mostly all I need** | 55.7% | 191 |
| Often needs not met* | 10.7% | 87 |
| Few needs met* | 4.3% | 22 |

\* Reference category in analyses in Table 10.5.
\*\* Included in analyses shown in Table 10.5.

data and sampling procedures in Chapter 7 and Appendix A). At the beginning of the survey, respondents were asked two questions: (1) "How would you describe yourself?" and (2) "What best describes your gender?" Bisexual women were those who selected "bisexual" for the first question and either "I identify as a woman and my assigned sex at birth was female" or "I am transgender: I identify as a woman and my assigned sex at birth was male" for the second question. See Table 10.3 for more details about the bisexual women in this study.

**FIGURE 10.3** Bisexual Women's (n = 358) Experiences with Gender- and Sexuality-Based DHV

*Notes*: See Table 10.4 for comparisons of bisexual women's experiences to the LGBTQ subsample and the women subsample.

## Bisexual Women's Experiences with Gender- and Sexuality-Based DHV

Numerous studies show that bisexual women are at a heightened risk for many types of victimization (Balsam, Rothblum, and Beauchaine 2005; Coston 2017; Katz-Wise and Hyde 2012; Meyer 2015) and discrimination (Badgett 1994; Friedman and Leaper 2010; Mays and Cochran 2001; McCabe et al. 2010). In Figure 10.3, it is clear that bisexual women are more likely to experience gender-based DHV than sexuality-based DHV. Specifically, more than half (57%) of bisexual women have had one or more experiences of gender-based DHV and close to half (43%) have had one or more experiences of sexuality-based DHV. Gender-based harassment is most common (45%) and sexuality-based violence is least common (13%). However, bisexual women (and non-binary individuals) are most likely of all LGBTQ groups to experience gender-based violence (25%) (recall Figure 7.7). To better understand bisexual women's gender- and sexuality-based DHV, bisexual women's experiences were compared to the LGBTQ subsample and the women subsample using *t*-tests. Table 10.4 demonstrates that bisexual women report significantly more gender-based DHV experiences of all types when compared to all LGBTQ people and all women. However, although bisexual women report significantly more sexuality-based DHV experiences of nearly all types when compared to all women

**TABLE 10.4** Gender- and Sexuality-Based DHV Mean Values (Standard Deviations) among Bisexual Women, the LGBTQ Subsample, and the Women Subsample with *t*-test Results

|  |  | *Bisexual Women* | *LGBTQ Subsample* | *Women Subsample* |
|---|---|---|---|---|
|  | n | 358 | 1604 | 1535 |
| *Gender-based* |  |  |  |  |
| Discrimination |  | .44 (.50)*** | .32 (.47) | .36 (.48) |
| Harassment |  | .45 (.50)*** | .28 (.45) | .34 (.47) |
| Violence |  | .25 (.43)*** | .14 (.34) | .16 (.37) |
| Any gender DHV experience (0/1) |  | .57 (.50)*** | .40 (.49) | .46 (.50) |
| *Sexuality-based* |  |  |  |  |
| Discrimination |  | .35 (.48)*** | .44 (.50) | .26 (.44) |
| Harassment |  | .30 (.46)*** | .41 (.49) | .23 (.42) |
| Violence |  | .13 (.34)** | .20 (.40) | .10 (.31) |
| Any sexuality DHV experience (0/1) |  | .43 (.50)*** | .53 (.50) | .32 (.47) |

** Bisexual women are significantly different from the LGBTQ subsample (only) at $p < .05$ level.
*** Bisexual women are significantly different from both the LGBTQ and women subsamples at $p < .05$ level.

(43% vs. 32% respectively) bisexual women report significantly fewer sexuality-based DHV experiences of all types when compared to LGBTQ people (43% vs. 53% respectively). Thus, compared to all women, bisexual women are at particular risk for both gender- and sexuality-based DHV but they are at a lower risk of sexuality-based DHV in comparison to the LGBTQ subsample. This suggests that there are multiple, intersecting experiences that relate to bisexual women's victimization.

## NCST and Bisexual Women's Experiences with Gender- and Sexuality-Based DHV

Below, bisexual women and their experiences with gender- and sexuality-based DHV are examined using NCST with a focus on bisexual women's axes of social power. The hypotheses are as follows:

- *Hypothesis 1*: being a bisexual woman (violating hetero-cis-normativity) increases the likelihood of experiencing gender- and sexuality-based DHV (bisexual women stigma).
- *Hypothesis 2*: the relationship between being a bisexual woman and gender- and sexuality-based DHV is moderated by interactions among being a bisexual woman and axes of social power.

**240** NCST and Understanding LGBTQ Stigma

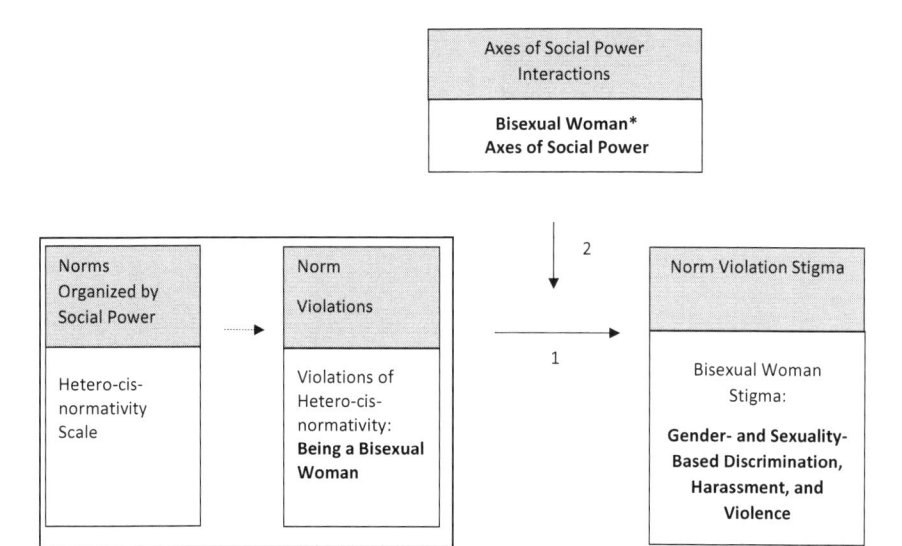

**FIGURE 10.4** Theoretical Model of NCST and Bisexual Women Stigma using the Stigmatized Lens with Model Numbers to be Examined in Table 10.5

*Notes:* Model 1 estimates being a bisexual woman as related to gender- and sexuality-based DHV. Model 2 estimates interactions among bisexual women's axes of social power as they moderate the relationships between being a bisexual woman and gender- and sexuality-based DHV. The * indicates an interaction.

Figure 10.4 outlines these relationships and Table 10.5 displays logistic regression results that examine NCST and the relationships among being a bisexual woman, intersections among bisexual women's axes of social power, and any experiences of gender-based DHV (dichotomized as 0/1) or sexuality-based DHV (dichotomized as 0/1) utilizing the LGBTQ sub-sample (n = 1,604; whereby being a bisexual woman is compared to all other LGBTQ people). Because bisexual women's experiences are the focus of this exploration (i.e., the stigmatized lens of NCST is being utilized), the bisexual woman and social power axes interaction terms are listed at the top of the table and the discussion below only focuses on these variables. However, there are significant corresponding individual effects related to being bisexual and being a woman (for example) that are important to recognize. See Chapter 7 for a more complete description of the models and a discussion of overarching trends and patterns. Regarding model fit statistics, the pseudo $R^2$ values ranged from .08 to .17.

**TABLE 10.5** Logistic Regression Results with Odds Ratios and (Standard Errors) Estimating NCST and Gender- and Sexuality-Based DHV as Related to Being a Bisexual Woman for the LGBTQ Subsample (n = 1,604)

|  | Gender-Based DHV | | | | Sexuality-Based DHV | | | |
|---|---|---|---|---|---|---|---|---|
|  | Model 1 | | Model 2 | | Model 1 | | Model 2 | |
|  | OR | SE | OR | SE | OR | SE | OR | SE |
| Bisexual woman | . | . | . | . | . | . | . | . |
| *Bisexual woman social power axes interactions* | | | | | | | | |
| Bisexual woman*trans | — | — | 5.99* | (3.24) | — | — | . | . |
| Bisexual woman*queer | — | — | . | . | — | — | . | . |
| Bisexual woman*SGL | — | — | 2.88* | (1.09) | — | — | . | . |
| Bisexual woman*Two-Spirit | — | — | . | . | — | — | . | . |
| Bisexual woman*femme | — | — | 2.02* | (.69) | — | — | . | . |
| Bisexual woman*African American/Black | — | — | .38* | (.19) | — | — | . | . |
| Bisexual woman*Latinx ethnicity | — | — | 3.46* | (1.36) | — | — | . | . |
| Bisexual woman*everything I need | — | — | . | . | — | — | . | . |
| Bisexual woman*mostly all I need | — | — | . | . | — | — | . | . |
| *Bisexual woman social power axes* | | | | | | | | |
| Bisexual | . | . | . | . | .42* | (.06) | .41* | (.06) |
| Woman | 4.34* | (.69) | 4.33* | (.70) | 1.40* | (.21) | 1.39* | (.21) |
| Trans | . | . | .25* | (.12) | . | . | . | . |
| Queer | 2.62* | (.39) | 2.52* | (.91) | 2.18* | (.31) | 3.42* | (1.11) |
| SGL | . | . | . | . | . | . | . | . |
| Two-Spirit | 1.71* | (.39) | . | . | . | . | 2.67* | (1.09) |
| Femme | . | . | . | . | . | . | . | . |
| African American/Black | . | . | . | . | . | . | . | . |
| Latinx ethnicity | . | . | .38* | (.13) | . | . | . | . |
| Everything I need | .60* | (.11) | .32* | (.12) | .68* | (.11) | . | . |
| Mostly all I need | .69* | (.10) | . | . | . | . | . | . |

*(Continued)*

**TABLE 10.5** (Cont.)

|  | Gender-Based DHV |  |  |  | Sexuality-Based DHV |  |  |  |
|---|---|---|---|---|---|---|---|---|
|  | Model 1 |  | Model 2 |  | Model 1 |  | Model 2 |  |
|  | OR | SE | OR | SE | OR | SE | OR | SE |
| *Socio-demographic controls* |  |  |  |  |  |  |  |  |
| Age | .97* | (.00) | .97* | (.00) | .98* | (.00) | .98* | (.00) |
| Town type (rural–large city) | . | . | . | . | . | . | . | . |
| Education | 1.16* | (.05) | 1.16* | (.05) | 1.10* | (.04) | 1.09* | (.04) |
| Income | . | . | . | . | . | . | . | . |
| Pseudo $R^2$ | .15 |  | .17 |  | .08 |  | .08 |  |
| Mean VIF | 1.41 |  | 1.41 |  | 1.40 |  | 1.40 |  |

*Notes:* all rows are displayed, including those without significant results. See Table 10.3 for more details about bisexual women.

* p < .05; a dot (.) indicates non-statistically significant results. A dash (—) indicates this was not included in the model.

## NCST, Bisexual Women, and Gender- and Sexuality-Based DHV: Model 1

Both Model 1s in Table 10.5 estimate the relationships between violations of hetero-cis-normativity conceptualized as being a bisexual woman and bisexual stigma conceptualized as gender- and sexuality-based DHV. Surprisingly, being a bisexual woman is *not* significantly related to gender- or sexuality-based DHV. This directly contrasts with previous work that demonstrates that bisexual women are at a high risk for DHV (Badgett 1994; Balsam, Rothblum, and Beauchaine 2005; Coston 2017; Katz-Wise and Hyde 2012; Meyer 2015). Overall, *Hypothesis 1* is not supported.

## NCST, Bisexual Women, and Gender- and Sexuality-Based DHV: Model 2

In Model 2, intersections among axes of social power and being a bisexual woman are included as they relate to gender- and sexuality-based DHV. Being a bisexual woman remains statistically non-significant in Model 2 as seen in Model 1. However, for gender-based DHV, five interaction terms emerge as significant. First, being a trans bisexual woman increases the likelihood of gender-based DHV by 4.99. As other research has demonstrated (Human Rights Campaign 2018; James et al. 2016; Schilt and Westbrook 2009), trans women can experience extreme hardships. Findings here further demonstrate that the intersections between bisexual and trans woman identities contribute to an especially high risk of gender-based DHV.

Second, being a SGL bisexual woman increases the likelihood of gender-based DHV by 1.88. This is interesting because the opposite pattern was found for SGL gay men in Chapter 9. For bisexual women, SGL identity serves as a risk factor for gender-based DHV. Such findings complement existing research that highlights the significance of SGL identity among women survivors of abuse (Parks et al. 2002) and demonstrate that bisexual SGL women's victimization should be understood from an intersectional lens.

Third, being a femme bisexual woman increases the likelihood of gender-based DHV by 1.02. There is some evidence that femme identity (as compared to butch identity) among bisexual and other sexual minority women is associated with more verbal victimization in intimate relationships (Balsam and Szymanski 2005) and a greater likelihood of experiencing sexual assault (Lehavot, Molina, and Simoni 2012). The findings here support the association between femme identity and increased risk for gender-based DHV (Hoskin 2017).

Fourth, being an African American/Black bisexual woman *de*creases the likelihood of gender-based DHV by .62. This is surprising because existing research highlights the multiple, intersecting oppressive experiences that African American/Black bisexual woman can endure that shape their experiences with discrimination and hostility (Calabrese et al. 2015; Greene 2000; Wilson, Okwu, and Mills 2011). For example, one study found that Black bisexual women endured significantly higher rates of adult victimization (75.4%) in comparison to White bisexual (51.9%) and lesbian (58.5%) women as well as Black lesbian women (64%) (Bostwick et al. 2019). The findings here suggest that bisexuality among African American/Black women may not be as strongly associated with DHV as compared to bisexuality among White women. This may be because White women's bisexuality is commercialized and objectified in ways that differ from African American/Black women's bisexuality and this may impact their DHV experiences in complex ways.

Fifth, being a Latinx (ethnicity) bisexual woman increases the likelihood of gender-based DHV by 2.46. This is especially significant because even though others have found that Latinx LGBTQ people are at high risk for discrimination and violence (Cerezo 2016; Coston 2019; Yon-Leau and Muñoz-Laboy 2010), there is still a surprising lack of research in this area. One study did find that Latina bisexual women experienced significantly higher rates of violence (45%) in comparison to White bisexual (17.3%) and lesbian (18%) women as well as Latina lesbian women (29%) (Bostwick et al. 2019). Especially in light of the horrific tragedy of the 2016 mass shooting at Pulse nightclub's Latin Pride Night in Orlando, Florida which resulted in 49 deaths and 53 casualties of mostly LGBTQ Latinx people (Ramirez, Gonzalez, and Galupo 2018), these findings emphasize how the intersectional experiences of Latinx bisexual women can relate to experiences with violence and discrimination.

Overall, although the individual effect of being a bisexual woman is not significantly related to gender-based DHV, numerous additional intersecting experiences of social power (i.e., gender, sexuality, race, ethnicity) increase the likelihood of experiencing gender-based DHV among bisexual women. However, in extreme contrast, there are no statistically significant results related to being a bisexual woman among the sexuality-based DHV models. Thus, *Hypothesis 2* is supported in the gender-based DHV models but not in the sexuality-based DHV models. Even so, the findings here demonstrate the importance of centering social power intersectional experiences to best understand the overlapping complexities of bisexual women's victimization experiences.

## Summarizing NCST, Bisexual Women, and Gender- and Sexuality-Based DHV

In sum, Table 10.5 indicates that being a bisexual woman is not directly related to the likelihood of experiencing gender- or sexuality-based DHV; however, additional intersecting axes of social power among bisexual women do increase the likelihood of gender-based DHV. In contrast, no experiences of bisexual woman identity are significantly related to sexuality-based DHV. These results appear to both align and contrast with existing research and suggest that more intersectional work is needed to better understand the complexities surrounding gender- and sexuality-based DHV among bisexual women.

## Summary of Patterns of Bisexual Women Stigma

In line with the three tenets and hypotheses derived from NCST, there are six patterns related to the stigmatization of bisexual women illustrated in this chapter:

1. Bisexual women are largely stigmatized by both hetero-cis and LGBTQ people due to the stereotype that their identities are temporary and/or experimental.
2. The stigmatization of bisexual women by both hetero-cis and LGBTQ people is also situated within sex act-related stigma (i.e., that bisexual women are too sexual/hypersexual, that they are unfaithful to their romantic partners) and that they are not feminine enough.
3. Hetero-cis-normativity is positively related to bisexual women stigma for both subsamples; however, the interaction effects between the HCN scale and social power axes only moderate these relationships for the hetero-cis subsample.
4. Individual social power axes are significantly related to bisexual women stigma for both subsamples; however, the interaction effects between the social power axes that moderate these relationships differ for the hetero-cis

and LGBTQ subsamples. In addition, there are more significant interaction effects between the social power axes for the LGBTQ subsample than there are for the hetero-cis subsample.
5. Bisexual women experience high levels of gender- and sexuality-based DHV (about half indicate DHV); however, in comparison to the LGBTQ subsample, bisexual women experience significantly less sexuality-based DHV.
6. Being a bisexual woman is not in and of itself related to the likelihood of gender- or sexuality-based DHV; however, bisexual women's intersecting experiences with trans identity, SGL identity, femme identity, and Latinx ethnicity do increase the likelihood of gender-based DHV while African American/Black identity among bisexual women decreases the likelihood of gender-based DHV.

## Note

1 Robyn Ochs (born in 1958) is an American bisexual rights activist. As stated on her website, "Robyn Ochs is an educator, speaker, grassroots activist, and editor of *Bi Women Quarterly* and two anthologies: the 42-country collection *Getting Bi: Voices of Bisexuals Around the World* and *RECOGNIZE: The Voices of Bisexual Men*. An advocate for the rights of people of ALL orientations and genders to live safely, openly and with full access and opportunity, Robyn's work focuses on increasing awareness and understanding of complex identities and mobilizing people to be powerful allies to one another within and across identities and social movements" (Ochs, n.d.).

## References

Allen, Samantha. 2018. "Kyrsten Sinema's Election Win in Arizona Is a Big, Bisexual Leap Forward." *The Daily Beast*, November 13. Retrieved January 30, 2020 (https://www.thedailybeast.com/kyrsten-sinemas-election-win-in-arizona-is-a-big-bisexual-leap-forward).

Appleby, George A. 2001. "Ethnographic Study of Gay and Bisexual Working-Class Men in the United States." *Journal of Gay & Lesbian Social Services* 12(3/4):51–62.

Badgett, M. V. Lee. 1994. "The Wage Effects of Sexual Orientation Discrimination." *Industrial and Labor Relations Review* 48:726–739.

Balay, Anne. 2014. *Steel Closets: Voices of Gay, Lesbian, and Transgender Steelworkers*. Chapel Hill, NC: University of North Carolina Press.

Balsam, Kimberly F., Esther D. Rothblum, and Theodore P. Beauchaine. 2005. "Victimization over the Life Span: A Comparison of Lesbian, Gay, Bisexual, and Heterosexual Siblings." *Journal of Consulting and Clinical Psychology* 73(3):477–487.

Balsam, Kimberly F. and Dawn M. Szymanski. 2005. "Relationship Quality and Domestic Violence in Women's Same-Sex Relationships: The Role of Minority Stress." *Psychology of Women Quarterly* 29(3):258–269.

Blair, Karen L. and Rhea Ashley Hoskin. 2015. "Experiences of Femme Identity: Coming Out, Invisibility and Femmephobia." *Psychology & Sexuality* 6(3):229–244.

Bostwick, Wendy B., Tonda L. Hughes, Alana Steffen, Cindy B. Veldhuis, and Sharon C. Wilsnack. 2019. "Depression and Victimization in a Community Sample of

Bisexual and Lesbian Women: An Intersectional Approach." *Archives of Sexual Behavior* 48(1):131–141.
Bowleg, Lisa. 2013. "'Once You've Blended the Cake, You Can't Take the Parts Back to the Main Ingredients': Black Gay and Bisexual Men's Descriptions and Experiences of Intersectionality." *Sex Roles* 68(11):754–767.
Calabrese, Sarah K., Ilan H. Meyer, Nicole M. Overstreet, Rahwa Haile, and Nathan B. Hansen. 2015. "Exploring Discrimination and Mental Health Disparities Faced by Black Sexual Minority Women Using a Minority Stress Framework." *Psychology of Women Quarterly* 39(3):287–304.
Cerezo, Alison. 2016. "The Impact of Discrimination on Mental Health Symptomatology in Sexual Minority Immigrant Latinas." *Psychology of Sexual Orientation and Gender Diversity* 3(3):283–292.
Chmielewski, Jennifer F. 2017. "A Listening Guide Analysis of Lesbian and Bisexual Young Women of Color's Experiences of Sexual Objectification." *Sex Roles* 77(7/8):533–549.
Clarke, Victoria. 2001. "What about the Children? Arguments against Lesbian and Gay Parenting." *Women's Studies International Forum* 24(5):555–570.
Clogg, Clifford C., Eva Petkova, and Adamantios Haritou. 1995. "Statistical Methods for Comparing Regression Coefficients between Models." *American Journal of Sociology* 100(5):1261–1293.
Connell, R. W., M. D. Davis, and G. W. Dowsett. 1993. "A Bastard of A Life: Homosexual Desire and Practice among Men in Working-Class Milieux." *The Australian and New Zealand Journal of Sociology* 29(1):112–135.
Coston, Bethany M. 2017. "Power and Inequality: Intimate Partner Violence against Bisexual and Non-Monosexual Women in the United States." *Journal of Interpersonal Violence* DOI:088626051772641.
Coston, Bethany M. 2019. "We Need More Resources: Stories of QTPOC* Survival in the South." *Journal of Gay & Lesbian Social Services* 31(1):35–52.
Crawford, Isiaah, Andrew McLeod, Brian D. Zamboni, and Michael B. Jordan. 1999. "Psychologists' Attitudes toward Gay and Lesbian Parenting." *Professional Psychology: Research and Practice* 30(4):394–401.
Edmonds, Shaun E. and Susan G. Zieff. 2015. "Bearing Bodies: Physical Activity, Obesity Stigma, and Sexuality in the Bear Community." *Sociology of Sport Journal* 32(4):415–435.
Eliason, Michele J. 1997. "The Prevalence and Nature of Biphobia in Heterosexual Undergraduate Students." *Archives of Sexual Behavior* 26(3):317–326.
Embrick, David G., Carol S. Walther, and Corrine M. Wickens. 2007. "Working Class Masculinity: Keeping Gay Men and Lesbians Out of the Workplace." *Sex Roles* 56(11):757–766.
Friedman, Carly and Campbell Leaper. 2010. "Sexual-Minority College Women's Experiences with Discrimination: Relations with Identity and Collective Action." *Psychology of Women Quarterly* 34(2):152–164.
Gander, Kashmira. 2018. "Children Raised by Gay and Lesbian Parents Develop as Well as Kids of Heterosexual Couples, Study Suggests." *Newsweek*, June 28. Retrieved January 30, 2020 (https://www.newsweek.com/children-raised-gay-and-lesbian-parents-develop-well-kids-heterosexual-1001515).
Greene, Beverly. 2000. "African American Lesbian and Bisexual Women." *Journal of Social Issues* 56(2):239–249.

Hamilton, Laura. 2007. "Trading on Heterosexuality: College Women's Gender Strategies and Homophobia." *Gender & Society* 21(2):145–172.

Hayfield, Nikki, Victoria Clarke, and Emma Halliwell. 2014. "Bisexual Women's Understandings of Social Marginalisation: 'The Heterosexuals Don't Understand Us but nor Do the Lesbians'." *Feminism & Psychology* 24(3):352–372.

Hayfield, Nikki, Victoria Clarke, Emma Halliwell, and Helen Malson. 2013. "Visible Lesbians and Invisible Bisexuals: Appearance and Visual Identities among Bisexual Women." *Women's Studies International Forum* 40:172–182.

Hennen, Peter. 2005. "Bear Bodies, Bear Masculinity: Recuperation, Resistance, or Retreat?" *Gender & Society* 19(1):25–43.

Hennen, Peter. 2008. *Faeries, Bears, and Leathermen: Men in Community Queering the Masculine*. Chicago, IL: University of Chicago Press.

Hoskin, Rhea Ashley. 2017. "Femme Theory: Refocusing the Intersectional Lens." *Atlantis: Critical Studies in Gender, Culture & Social Justice* 38(1):95–109.

Human Rights Campaign. 2018. *Dismantling a Culture of Violence: Understanding Anti-Transgender Violence and Ending the Crisis*. Washington, D.C.: Human Rights Campaign Foundation.

Huxley, Caroline, Victoria Clarke, and Emma Halliwell. 2014. "Resisting and Conforming to the 'Lesbian Look': The Importance of Appearance Norms for Lesbian and Bisexual Women: Lesbian and Bisexual Women Discuss Their Appearance." *Journal of Community & Applied Social Psychology* 24(3):205–219.

James, Sandy, Jody L. Herman, Sue Rankin, Mara Keisling, Lisa Mottet, and Ma'ayan Anafi. 2016. *The Report of the 2015 U.S. Transgender Survey*. Washington, D.C.: National Center for Transgender Equality.

Joos, Kristin E. and K. L. Broad. 2007. "Coming Out of the Family Closet: Stories of Adult Women with LGBTQ Parent(s)." *Qualitative Sociology* 30(3):275–295.

Katz-Wise, Sabra L. and Janet S. Hyde. 2012. "Victimization Experiences of Lesbian, Gay, and Bisexual Individuals: A Meta-Analysis." *The Journal of Sex Research* 49(2/3):142–167.

Lehavot, Keren, Yamile Molina, and Jane M. Simoni. 2012. "Childhood Trauma, Adult Sexual Assault, and Adult Gender Expression among Lesbian and Bisexual Women." *Sex Roles* 67(5):272–284.

Lemelle, Anthony and Juan Battle. 2004. "Black Masculinity Matters in Attitudes toward Gay Males." *Journal of Homosexuality* 47(1):39–51.

Mays, Vickie M. and Susan D. Cochran. 2001. "Mental Health Correlates of Perceived Discrimination among Lesbian, Gay, and Bisexual Adults in the United States." *American Journal of Public Health* 91(11):1869–1876.

McCabe, Sean Esteban, Wendy B. Bostwick, Tonda L. Hughes, Brady T. West, and Carol J. Boyd. 2010. "The Relationship between Discrimination and Substance Use Disorders among Lesbian, Gay, and Bisexual Adults in the United States." *American Journal of Public Health* 100(10):1946–1952.

Meyer, Doug. 2015. *Violence against Queer People: Race, Class, Gender, and the Persistence of Anti-LGBT Discrimination*. New Brunswick, NJ: Rutgers University Press.

Mohr, Jonathan J. and Aaron B. Rochlen. 1999. "Measuring Attitudes regarding Bisexuality in Lesbian, Gay Male, and Heterosexual Populations." *Journal of Counseling Psychology* 46(3):353–369.

Ochs, Robyn. n.d. "Robyn Ochs/Biography." *RobynOchs.com*. Retrieved January 30, 2020 (https://robynochs.com/biography/).

Parks, Carlton W., Rhona Nicole Cutts, Kamilah M. Woodson, and Laurie Flarity-White. 2002. "Issues Inherent in the Multicultural Feminist Couple Treatment of African-American, Same-Gender Loving Female Adult Survivors of Child Sexual Abuse." *Journal of Child Sexual Abuse* 10(3):17–34.

Pew Research Center. 2013. "Chapter 3: The Coming Out Experience." Retrieved February 6, 2019 (www.pewsocialtrends.org/2013/06/13/chapter-3-the-coming-out-experience/).

Raja, Sheela and Joseph P. Stokes. 1998. "Assessing Attitudes toward Lesbians and Gay Men: The Modern Homophobia Scale." *International Journal of Sexuality and Gender Studies* 3(2):113–134.

Ramirez, Johanna L., Kirsten A. Gonzalez, and M. Paz Galupo. 2018. "'Invisible during My Own Crisis': Responses of LGBT People of Color to the Orlando Shooting." *Journal of Homosexuality* 65(5):579–599.

Ravenhill, James P. and Richard O. de Visser. 2019. "'I Don't Want to Be Seen as a Screaming Queen': An Interpretative Phenomenological Analysis of Gay Men's Masculine Identities." *Psychology of Men and Masculinity* 20(3):324–336.

Rodriguez, Nathian Shae, Jennifer Huemmer, and Lindsey Erin Blumell. 2016. "Mobile Masculinities: An Investigation of Networked Masculinities in Gay Dating Apps." *Masculinities & Social Change* 5(3):241–267.

Rollins, Joe and H. N. Hirsch. 2003. "Sexual Identities and Political Engagements: A Queer Survey." *Social Politics* 10(3):290–313.

Ross, Lori E., Amy Siegel, Cheryl Dobinson, Rachel Epstein, and Leah S. Steele. 2012. "'I Don't Want to Turn Totally Invisible': Mental Health, Stressors, and Supports among Bisexual Women during the Perinatal Period." *Journal of GLBT Family Studies* 8(2):137–154.

Rupp, Leila J. and Verta Taylor. 2010. "Straight Girls Kissing." *Contexts* 9(3):28–32.

Rupp, Leila J., Verta Taylor, Alison C. Shiri Regev-Messalem, K. Fogarty, and Paula England. 2014. "Queer Women in the Hookup Scene: Beyond the Closet?" *Gender & Society* 28(2):212–235.

Rust, Paula C. 1995. *Bisexuality and the Challenge to Lesbian Politics: Sex, Loyalty, and Revolution*. New York, NY: NYU Press.

Scherrer, Kristin S., Emily Kazyak, and Rachel Schmitz. 2015. "Getting 'Bi' in the Family: Bisexual People's Disclosure Experiences." *Journal of Marriage and Family* 77(3):680–696.

Schilt, Kristen and Laurel Westbrook. 2009. "Doing Gender, Doing Heteronormativity: 'Gender Normals,' Transgender People, and the Social Maintenance of Heterosexuality." *Gender & Society* 23(4):440–464.

Spalding, Leah R. and Letitia Anne Peplau. 1997. "The Unfaithful Lover: Heterosexuals' Perceptions of Bisexuals and Their Relationships." *Psychology of Women Quarterly* 21(4):611–625.

Taub, Jennifer. 1999. "Bisexual Women and Beauty Norms: A Qualitative Examination." *Journal of Lesbian Studies* 3(4): 27–36.

Weiss, Jillian Todd. 2004. "GL vs. BT: The Archaeology of Biphobia and Transphobia within the US Gay and Lesbian Community." *Journal of Bisexuality* 3(3/4):25–55.

Wilson, Bianca D. M., Chiamaka Okwu, and Sandra Mills. 2011. "Brief Report: The Relationship between Multiple Forms of Oppression and Subjective Health among Black Lesbian and Bisexual Women." *Journal of Lesbian Studies* 15(1):15–24.

Worthen, Meredith G. F. 2013. "An Argument for Separate Analyses of Attitudes toward Lesbian, Gay, Bisexual Men, Bisexual Women, MtF and FtM Transgender Individuals." *Sex Roles* 68(11):703–723.

Worthen, Meredith G. F. 2018. "'Gay Equals White'? Racial, Ethnic, and Sexual Identities and Attitudes toward LGBT Individuals among College Students at a Bible Belt University." *The Journal of Sex Research* 55(8):995–1011.

Yon-Leau, Carmen and Muñoz-Laboy. Miguel. 2010. "'I Don't like to Say that I'm Anything': Sexuality Politics and Cultural Critique among Sexual-Minority Latino Youth." *Sexuality Research and Social Policy* 7(2):105–117.

# 11
# BISEXUAL MEN STIGMA

*Males do not represent two discrete populations, heterosexual and homosexual. The world is not to be divided into sheep and goats. Not all things are black nor all things white. It is a fundamental of taxonomy that nature rarely deals with discrete categories. Only the human mind invents categories and tries to force facts into separated pigeon-holes. The living world is a continuum in each and every one of its aspects. The sooner we learn this concerning human sexual behavior the sooner we shall reach a sound understanding of the realities of sex.*

*Alfred Kinsey et al. (1948:639)*

**IMAGE 11.1** Alfred Kinsey (June 23, 1894 – August 25, 1956) was a sexologist who identified as bisexual. He published extensive research about sex and sexuality throughout his career in efforts to normalize sexual behaviors and identities deemed to be socially problematic, including bisexuality.

## The Stigmatization of Bisexual Men

In the survey instrument, the section focusing on attitudes toward bisexual men was preceded by the following statement:

> *Below, please let us know your thoughts, feelings, and predicted behaviors about bisexual men (men who have romantic and sexual attractions to both men and women).*

## The Bisexual Men Stigma Scale

Bisexual men are the fourth least stigmatized among the nine groups examined in this book (recall Figure 7.1). The processes behind the stigmatization of bisexual men are interesting because they overlap somewhat with those associated with both gay men and bisexual women, but negative attitudes toward bisexual men have distinct features as well. These can be better understood by examining the 14 items in the Bisexual Men Stigma Scale as seen in Figure 11.1 and Table 11.1.

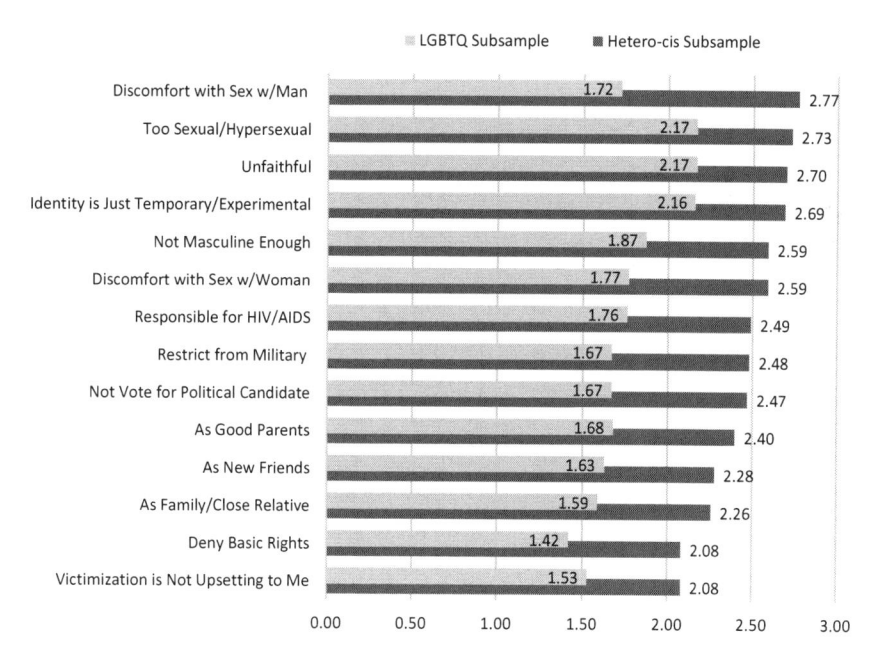

| Item | LGBTQ Subsample | Hetero-cis Subsample |
|---|---|---|
| Discomfort with Sex w/Man | 1.72 | 2.77 |
| Too Sexual/Hypersexual | 2.17 | 2.73 |
| Unfaithful | 2.17 | 2.70 |
| Identity is Just Temporary/Experimental | 2.16 | 2.69 |
| Not Masculine Enough | 1.87 | 2.59 |
| Discomfort with Sex w/Woman | 1.77 | 2.59 |
| Responsible for HIV/AIDS | 1.76 | 2.49 |
| Restrict from Military | 1.67 | 2.48 |
| Not Vote for Political Candidate | 1.67 | 2.47 |
| As Good Parents | 1.68 | 2.40 |
| As New Friends | 1.63 | 2.28 |
| As Family/Close Relative | 1.59 | 2.26 |
| Deny Basic Rights | 1.42 | 2.08 |
| Victimization is Not Upsetting to Me | 1.53 | 2.08 |

**FIGURE 11.1** Bisexual Men Stigma Scale Item Mean Values Rank-Ordered from Most to Least Stigmatizing for the Hetero-cis (n = 1,500) and the LGBTQ (n = 1,604) Subsamples

*Note:* see Table 11.1 for the exact wording for each item. *t*-test results comparing the hetero-cis and LGBTQ subsamples indicate that all means are significantly different from one another at the p < .001 level.

**TABLE 11.1** Bisexual Men Stigma Scale Item Mean Values (Standard Deviations) and *t*-test Results Comparing the Means for the Hetero-cis Subsample and the LGBTQ Subsample

|  | Hetero-cis Subsample | LGBTQ Subsample | *t*-test Results |
|---|---|---|---|
|  | n = 1,500 | n = 1,604 |  |
| *Social and familial relationships* |  |  |  |
| I welcome new friends who are bisexual men.[R] | 2.28 (1.14) | 1.63 (.92) | $t = 17.25^*$ |
| I don't think it would negatively affect our relationship if I learned that one of my close relatives was a bisexual man.[R] | 2.26 (1.15) | 1.59 (.94) | $t = 17.67^*$ |
| Bisexual men are not capable of being good parents. | 2.40 (1.28) | 1.68 (1.11) | $t = 16.59^*$ |
| *Positions of importance and social significance* |  |  |  |
| I would not vote for a political candidate who was an openly bisexual man. | 2.47 (1.32) | 1.67 (1.12) | $t = 18.12^*$ |
| Bisexual men should not be allowed to join the military. | 2.48 (1.36) | 1.67 (1.16) | $t = 17.93^*$ |
| *Basic human rights* |  |  |  |
| I believe bisexual men should have all of the same rights as other people do.[R] | 2.08 (1.13) | 1.42 (.87) | $t = 17.96^*$ |
| It is upsetting to me that bisexual men experience violence, harassment, and discrimination just because they are bisexual men.[R] | 2.08 (1.11) | 1.53 (.97) | $t = 14.57^*$ |
| *Sex act-related stigma* |  |  |  |
| Bisexual men are unfaithful to their romantic partners. | 2.70 (1.16) | 2.17 (1.18) | $t = 12.63^*$ |
| Bisexual men are too sexual (hypersexual). | 2.73 (1.17) | 2.17 (1.16) | $t = 13.48^*$ |
| Bisexual men are mostly responsible for spreading HIV/AIDS. | 2.62 (1.20) | 1.91 (1.12) | $t = 17.17^*$ |
| I am comfortable with the thought of a bisexual man having sex with a man.[R] | 2.77 (1.24) | 1.72 (1.00) | $t = 25.93^*$ |
| I am comfortable with the thought of a bisexual man having sex with a woman.[R] | 2.59 (1.14) | 1.77 (1.00) | $t = 21.22^*$ |
| *Bisexual identity permanency* |  |  |  |
| Most men who call themselves bisexual are just temporarily experimenting with their sexuality. | 2.69 (1.15) | 2.16 (1.17) | $t = 12.77^*$ |

(*Continued*)

**TABLE 11.1** (Cont.)

|  | Hetero-cis Subsample | LGBTQ Subsample | t-test Results |
|---|---|---|---|
| *Achievement of masculinity* | | | |
| Bisexual men are not masculine enough. | 2.59 (1.14) | 1.87 (1.07) | $t = 18.06^*$ |
| α | .90 | .92 | |
| Summed Scale Actual Range | 14-70 | 14-56 | |
| Summed Scale Mean | 34.74 (11.07) | 24.97 (10.17) | $t = 25.55^*$ |

*Notes:* response options were Strongly Disagree–Strongly Agree (range: 1–5). [R] This item is reverse coded. *t-test results allowing for unequal variances indicate that the hetero-cis subsample and LGBTQ subsample means are significantly different from one another at the $p < .001$ level.

## Bisexual Men and Social and Familial Relationships

There are low levels of stigma associated with bisexual men as friends and family members (see Table 11.1). The items in this key area with the lowest mean values for both the hetero-cis subsample and the LGBTQ subsample are: "I welcome new friends who are bisexual men" and "I don't think it would negatively affect our relationship if I learned that one of my close relatives was a bisexual man," both of which were reverse coded. These findings are interesting because as compared to gay men, lesbian women, and bisexual women, bisexual men are least likely to be open about their sexual identities. In particular, only 12% of bisexual men say "most of the important people in their life know they are bisexual" according to U.S. Pew Research Center data (N = 1,197) (Pew Research Center 2013). Qualitative research demonstrates that this lack of disclosure of bisexual identity to friends and family may be especially common among bisexuals who are in long term/married opposite gender relationships (Scherrer, Kazyak, and Schmitz 2015). Despite this, these findings demonstrate low stigma toward bisexual men in social and familial relationships.

The item in this key area with the highest mean values for both subsamples is: "Bisexual men are not capable of being good parents." The bulk of existing media attention and scholarly research has focused on gay and lesbian parents (Brown et al. 2009; Clarke 2001; Crawford et al. 1999; Gander 2018; Joos and Broad 2007; Schacher, Auerbach, and Silverstein 2005) while bisexual parents are often missing from both types of discourse (Carneiro et al. 2017). In fact, nearly all studies to date have clumped gay and bisexual dads together due to small ns (e.g., Power et al. 2012, n = 5 bisexual dads and n = 80 gay dads; Sirota 2009, n = 2 bisexual dads and n = 66 gay dads), thus, we know little about bisexual fathers' experiences. While it is reasonable to expect that a bisexual man who is co-parenting with another man may be thought of negatively in a process similar to the stigmatization of gay dads (e.g., in ways that support the conventional definitions of family (mother + father) as well as norms about masculinity and fatherhood, see Murphy 2013; Schacher, Auerbach, and Silverstein 2005), there are specific negativities toward bisexual dads. These can include stigmatizing attitudes such as "he should just pick a woman to be with if he is going to raise a child" or "he should stop experimenting with men and just settle down with a woman if he's going to bring a baby home." Bisexual dads may also experience particular mental health distresses, anxieties, and discomforts related to feeling their bisexual identities are "invisible," similar to those found in Ross et al.'s (2012) study of bisexual mothers. Though these dynamics are understudied, the stigmatization of bisexual fathers is somewhat evident here.

## Bisexual Men and Positions of Importance and Social Significance

For the two items in this key area: "I would not vote for a political candidate who was an openly bisexual man" and "Bisexual men should not be allowed to join the military," there was relatively low stigmatization with means ranging from 1.67 to 2.48. These perspectives are especially important to examine because bisexual men have only recently become visible political leaders (e.g., Mike Jacobs became the first openly bisexual man state court trial judge in 2018 (in Georgia), Rhode 2018) and there have been no visible bisexual men in high-ranking positions in the U.S. military to date despite the fact that estimates indicate that bisexual men represent a higher percentage of military service membership (2.15% have served) as compared to gay men (.78% have served) (Hoover, Tao, and Peters 2017). Overall, because bisexual men endure stigma in positions of importance and social significance, it is important to continue to examine their experiences.

## Bisexual Men and Sex Act-Related Stigma

Sex act-related stigma directed toward bisexual men is evidenced in Table 11.1. Nearly all items in this area were close to or above 2.0 with some means approaching 3.0 for the hetero-cis subsample. In addition, the top most stigmatizing attitudes toward bisexual men were in this key area for both subsamples (see Figure 11.1). For bisexual men, sex act-related stigma is related to negativities directed toward their presumed sex with men *and* their bisexuality. These intersect to create a particularly stigmatizing experience for bisexual men that is both overlapping and distinct from gay men's and bisexual women's stigma.

While a discussion of many of these dynamics is provided in Chapter 7, an additional review of bisexual men's experiences is notable here because of all nine LGBTQ groups, bisexual men are the most likely to be thought of as unfaithful among both subsamples (recall Figure 7.4 and see Figure 11.1). Thus, across the entire sample, bisexual men were most likely to be stigmatized as "cheaters" in their romantic relationships. Some research supports this sentiment. For example, due to their potential interests in men and women, bisexuals are stereotyped as both anti-monogamous and promiscuous and this may be especially true among bisexual men because they are perceived as more "sexually risky" as compared to bisexual women and heterosexuals (Spalding and Peplau 1997). The actual behaviors of bisexual men also support these scripts. For example, a large-scale U.S. study (N = 63,894) revealed that well over half (63%) of bisexual men reported cheating on their past partner(s) and 15% indicated they were currently cheating—which was nearly double the percentage of current cheating among gay men (8%) and bisexual women (8%), nearly four-times that of heterosexual men (4%), five times that of heterosexual women (3%), and fifteen times that of lesbian women (1%) (Frederick and Fales 2016). Additional research about the clandestine behaviors of men who cheat on their partners by having sex with other men in tearooms, public spaces, and in other "down-low" experiences (Frankis and Flowers 2009; Heath and Goggin 2009; Humphreys 1970) further contributes to the association of unfaithfulness with (perceived as) bisexual men. Thus, the stigmatization of bisexual men is heavily entwined with perceptions about the context of their sexual relationships.

## Bisexual Men Identity Permanency

Similar to perspectives about bisexual women, there is support for stigma associated with bisexual men's identity permanency. As seen in Figure 11.1, across all 14 items in the Bisexual Men Stigma Scale, this item had the second highest mean value for the LGBTQ subsample and the fourth highest for the hetero-cis subsample (2.16 and 2.69 respectively). Thus, there is agreement across the entire sample that "Most men who call themselves bisexual are just temporarily experimenting with their sexuality." Bisexual identity among men can be stereotyped as inauthentic in two interrelated ways. First, there is the belief that bisexuality serves only as a stepping stone to one's "true" gay or lesbian identity (McLean 2008). In other words, people just say they are bisexual because they are not yet ready to admit that they are gay or lesbian. This stereotype has been found to especially associated with bisexual men. For example, in their qualitative study (N = 45) of bisexual identity disclosure, scholars found that bisexual men were most likely to indicate that their families thought that they were "really" gay while bisexual women were more likely to be presumed to be "really" heterosexual (Scherrer, Kazyak, and Schmitz 2015). Both perspectives de-authenticate bisexual identity in general but for men, it is expected that they will "end up" being gay. These processes work together to fully compound the numerous negative stereotypes about the temporary/experimental nature of bisexuality as reviewed in Chapter 10 (e.g., "bisexual people just haven't made up their minds yet," "bisexuals are just confused," "bisexuality is just a phase," and "eventually, he/she/they will just pick one," Hayfield, Clarke, and Halliwell 2014; Weiss 2004).

Second and related, for any man who has sex with another man, there can be a "one-time rule of homosexuality" whereby a single same-sex sexual experience is equated with a gay identity for men (Anderson 2008:105). This stereotype is not uniformly applicable (the same is not true for women) and can also fluctuate based on relationships (Sullivan et al. 2018). However, largely because the masculinities of men who have sexual encounter(s) with men are called into question, their identities can be irreparably effeminized and eternally stigmatized. Together, these stereotypes suggest that there is no truly authentic "bisexuality" among men because a man's single sexual encounter with another man means he is "gay." Thus, the particular set of negativities associated with bisexual men's stigma can be reflected by the stigmatizing sentiment that they are "gay, straight, or lying" (Carey 2005).

### Bisexual Men and the Achievement of Masculinity

There is some support for the statement "Bisexual men are not masculine enough" among the LGBTQ (1.87) and hetero-cis (2.59) subsamples. This item is among the top five most stigmatizing perspectives toward bisexual men for both groups (see Figure 11.1). Similar to the stereotypes associated with gay men's inability to embody masculinity successfully, bisexual men's masculinity is endangered by their involvement in relationships with other men and the types of sex acts they are perceived to be participating in with them (e.g., receptive anal and oral sex, see Chapter 7 for a further discussion). However, because they may participate in relationships with women, bisexual men may be seen as more masculine than gay men (Rosenthal et al. 2012). Masculinities among bisexual men can also be distinct from gay men in ways that inform their experiences with stigma (McCormack, Anderson, and Adams 2014) and with being thought of as "too feminine" (Hart et al. 2019).

### Bisexual Men Stigma Summed Scale

The Bisexual Men Stigma Scale was created by summing together all 14 items. As seen in Table 11.1, Cronbach's alphas were quite high: .90 for the hetero-cis subsample and .92 for the LGBTQ subsample. The actual range in the summed scale values was significantly different between the two subsamples with the highest value for the hetero-cis subsample (70) 14 points higher than the highest value for the LGBTQ subsample (56). As found in the Gay Men Stigma Scale results, a single hetero-cis respondent reported the highest level of stigma on all 14 items in the scale for a value of 70 on the Bisexual Men Stigma Scale. In addition, the summed Bisexual Men Stigma Scale mean values differed quite substantially with the hetero-cis subsample mean (34.74) 9.77 points higher than the LGBTQ subsample mean (24.97). The top most stigmatizing item toward bisexual men also differed between the subsamples. For the hetero-cis subsample, discomfort with bisexual men having sex with men had the highest value. However, the rest of the items in the top were the same for both groups: hypersexuality, unfaithfulness, identity permanency, and masculinity (see Figure 11.1). The overall key area with the highest individual mean values was also the same for both subsamples: sex act-related stigma (though identity permanency was a very close second for both groups). Together, these findings demonstrate that both discomfort with bisexual men's sexual behaviors and the stereotype that their identities are temporary/experimental contribute to the overall stigmatization of bisexual men among both hetero-cis and LGBTQ populations (recall Figure 7.3).

## NCST, Hetero-cis-normativity, Social Power Axes, and the Bisexual Men Stigma Scale

The first set of regression models examine the Bisexual Men Stigma Scale using NCST. The hypotheses are as follows:

- *Hypothesis 1a*: there is a significant positive relationship between the HCN Scale and the Bisexual Men Stigma Scale.
- *Hypothesis 1b*: there are significant relationships between individual social power axes (gender identity, sexual identity, additional gender/sexuality, racial/ethnic identity, basic needs) and the Bisexual Men Stigma Scale.
- *Hypothesis 2a*: the relationship between the HCN Scale and the Bisexual Men Stigma Scale is moderated by interactions between the HCN Scale and axes of social power.
- *Hypothesis 2b*: the relationships between individual social power axes and the Bisexual Men Stigma Scale are moderated by interactions between axes of social power.

Figure 11.2 outlines these relationships and the two models of NCST to be estimated. Specifically, OLS regression is utilized in Table 11.2 to examine NCST and the relationships among hetero-cis-normativity, axes of social power (gender, sexuality, additional gender/sexuality, race/ethnicity, and basic needs), and the Bisexual Men Stigma Scale for the hetero-cis subsample and the LGBTQ subsample. See Chapter 7 for a more complete description of the models. Regarding model fit statistics, the adjusted $R^2$ values ranged from .66 to .68.

## NCST, HCN, Social Power Axes, and the Bisexual Men Stigma Scale: Model 1

In Table 11.2, the relationships between the HCN Scale, axes of social power, and the Bisexual Men Stigma Scale are examined in Model 1. For both groups, the HCN Scale is positively related to the stigmatization of bisexual men, fully

**258** NCST and Understanding LGBTQ Stigma

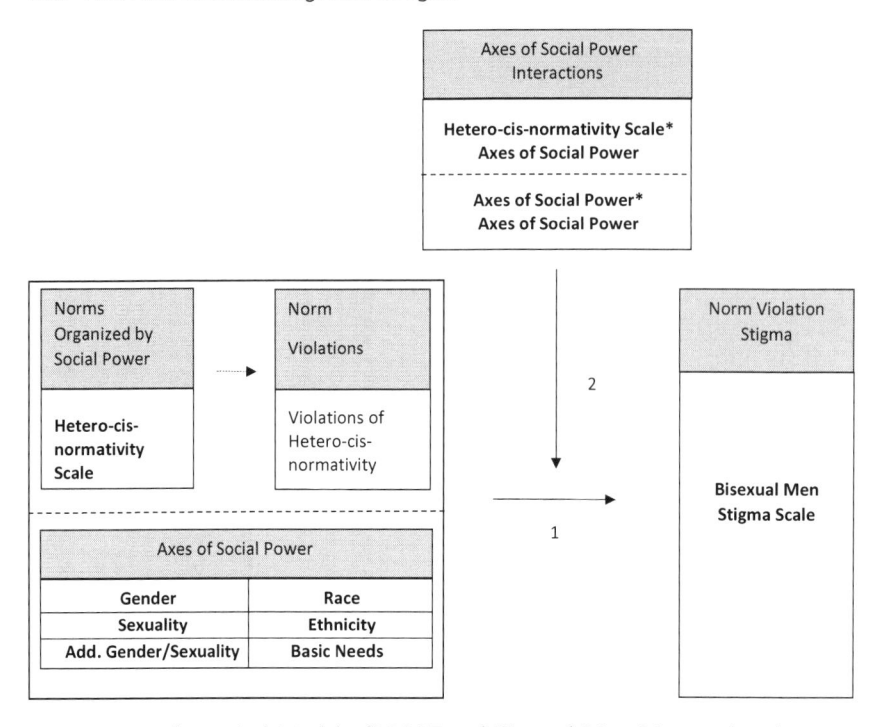

**FIGURE 11.2** Theoretical Model of NCST and Bisexual Men Stigma using the Stigmatizer Lens with Model Numbers to be Examined in Table 11.2

*Notes:* Model 1 estimates the HCN Scale and axes of social power (gender, sexuality, additional gender/sexuality, race, ethnicity, and basic needs) as they relate to the Bisexual Men Stigma Scale. Model 2 estimates interactions among axes of social power and the HCN Scale as they moderate the relationships between the HCN Scale and the Bisexual Men Stigma Scale as well as interactions among axes of social power as they moderate the relationships between the HCN Scale and the Bisexual Men Stigma Scale. The * indicates an interaction.

supporting *Hypothesis 1a*. Individual axes of social power are also significantly related to the Bisexual Men Stigma Scale for the hetero-cis subsample (cis woman, mostly all I need, and often needs not met) and for the LGBTQ subsample (trans woman, bisexual, African American/Black, other race), supporting *Hypothesis 1b*.

## NCST, HCN, Social Power Axes, and the Bisexual Men Stigma Scale: Model 2

Intersections among axes of social power and the HCN Scale as well as interaction effects among axes of social power are examined in Model 2. The HCN Scale remains positively related to the Bisexual Men Stigma Scale for both subsamples. There are also significant HCN Scale and social power interaction effects, though only one is significant for the LGBTQ subsample. Three

**TABLE 11.2** OLS Regression Results Estimating NCST and the Bisexual Men Stigma Scale for the Hetero-cis Subsample (n = 1,500) and the LGBTQ Subsample (n = 1,604)

|  | Hetero-cis Subsample | | LGBTQ Subsample | | Test of Difference |
|---|---|---|---|---|---|
|  | Model 1 | Model 2 | Model 1 | Model 2 |  |
| HCN Scale | .78* | .75* | .74* | .53* | . |
| *Gender identity* | | | | | |
| Cis woman | -1.12* | . | . | . | |
| Trans woman | . | . | 1.94* | . | |
| *Sexual identity* | | | | | |
| Bisexual | . | . | -2.18* | . | |
| *Additional sexual/gender identity* | | | | | |
| SGL | . | . | . | -5.82* | . |
| *Racial/ethnic identity* | | | | | |
| African American/Black | . | . | 1.43* | . | |
| Other race | . | . | 3.07* | 6.49* | . |
| *Basic needs* | | | | | |
| Mostly all I need | -.99* | . | . | . | |
| Often needs not met | -1.53* | . | . | . | |
| *HCN Scale\*social power axes interactions* | | | | | |
| HCN Scale*asexual | — | — | — | .50* | |
| HCN Scale*queer | — | -.38* | — | . | ** |
| HCN Scale*African American/Black | — | -.30* | — | . | ** |
| HCN Scale*mostly all I need | — | .13* | — | . | . |
| HCN Scale*few needs met | — | .34* | — | . | . |
| *Social power axes interactions* | | | | | |
| Bisexual*SGL | — | — | — | 3.66* | |
| Gay/lesbian* Asian American/Pacific Islander | — | — | — | 3.54* | |
| Gay/lesbian*often needs not met | — | — | — | 4.34* | |
| Bisexual*mostly all I need | — | — | — | 4.42* | |
| Bisexual*often needs not met | — | — | — | 4.13* | |
| Queer*few needs met | — | . | — | 4.13* | ** |
| SGL*mostly all I need | — | . | — | -2.02* | . |
| Asian American/Pacific Islander*mostly all I need | — | . | — | 5.63* | . |
| *Controls: common explanations* | | | | | |
| *LGBTQ contact* | | | | | |
| LGBTQ Friends Scale (w/o bisexual men) | . | . | -.22* | -.22* | . |

(*Continued*)

**TABLE 11.2** (Cont.)

|  | Hetero-cis Subsample | | LGBTQ Subsample | | Test of Difference |
| --- | --- | --- | --- | --- | --- |
|  | Model 1 | Model 2 | Model 1 | Model 2 |  |
| *Religiosity* |  |  |  |  |  |
| Church attendance | .39* | .39* | . | . | . |
| *Political perspectives* |  |  |  |  |  |
| Liberal–conservative | .65* | .64* | . | . | ** |
| Openness to new experiences | -1.41* | -1.18* | -1.75* | -1.75* | . |
| *Support laws/policies helping:* |  |  |  |  |  |
| Those in poverty | -1.99* | -1.89* | . | . | ** |
| Women | . | . | 1.18* | 1.12* | ** |
| Non-Christians | -1.18* | -1.07* | -1.42* | -1.47* | . |
| *Beliefs about gender* |  |  |  |  |  |
| Patriarchal Gender Norms Scale | .62* | .59* | .69* | .69* | . |
| *Sociodemographic controls* |  |  |  |  |  |
| Age | .03* | .03* | .04* | .03* | . |
| Adjusted $R^2$ | .68 | .68 | .66 | .66 |  |
| Mean VIF | 1.51 | 1.51 | 1.92 | 1.92 |  |

*Notes:* unstandardized regression coefficients are presented. Only the rows with significant results are displayed here. See Table 11.1 for detailed information about the Bisexual Men Stigma Scale. See Tables 7.1 and 7.2 for details about all other variables and Appendix B Table B.1 for details about the interaction effects.

* $p < .05$; a dot (.) indicates non-statistically significant results. A dash (—) indicates this was not included in the model.

** $p < .05$ for Clogg et al.'s (1995) test of equality of regression coefficients comparing Model 2 for the hetero-cis subsample and Model 2 for the LGBTQ subsample.

are discussed in Chapter 7: the interaction terms between the HCN Scale and queer, the HCN Scale and African American/Black, the HCN Scale and mostly all I need. There is one additional HCN Scale interaction term that is significantly related to the stigmatization of bisexual men for the hetero-cis subsample: the interaction term between the HCN Scale and few needs met is positively related to the Bisexual Men Stigma Scale. As similarly found among the models estimating NCST and the Bisexual Women Stigma Scale (see Table 10.2), hetero-cis-normativity has a greater impact on attitudes toward bisexual men among hetero-cis individuals who are struggling to have their basic needs met in comparison to others with more basic needs stability in the hetero-cis subsample. Such findings mirror previous studies that have found evidence of LGBTQ negativity in working-class settings (Balay 2014; Connell, Davis, and Dowsett 1993; Embrick, Walther, and Wickens 2007).

In addition, among the LGBTQ subsample, the interaction term between the HCN Scale and asexual is positively related to the stigmatization of bisexual men, as similarly found in the models exploring NCST and the stigmatization of lesbian women (Table 8.2) and gay men (Table 9.2). The positive HCN Scale and asexual interaction term indicates that support of hetero-cis-normativity has a more robust effect on asexual individuals' attitudes toward bisexual men as compared to non-asexual individuals' attitudes toward bisexual men. As noted previously, the inclusion of asexual people in the LGBTQ(A) community has caused tension (Colborne 2018; Pinto 2014) and this may impact the relationships between bisexual men negativity, hetero-cis-normativity, and asexuality. Overall, *Hypothesis 2a* is supported: interactions between the HCN Scale and axes of social power moderate the relationship between the HCN Scale and the Bisexual Men Stigma Scale for both subsamples.

Additionally, looking at the findings in rest of the table for Model 2 it is clear that axes of social power shape bisexual men stigmatization in very different ways for the hetero-cis and LGBTQ subsamples. Notably, while there are no significant individual social power axes for the hetero-cis subsample, there are two (SGL and other race) that are significant for the LGBTQ subsample in Model 2. In addition, there are no significant interaction terms among the social power axes for the hetero-cis subsample, but there are eight that are significant for the LGBTQ subsample in Model 2. Including the individual and interaction social power axes terms, there are significant results among sexual identities (SGL, bisexual, gay/lesbian, and queer), racial/ethnic identities (other race and Asian American/Pacific Islander), and basic needs experiences (mostly all I need, often needs not met, and few needs met) for the LGBTQ subsample. Most have positive relationships to the Bisexual Men Stigma Scale. Interestingly, three of these include intersecting experiences of bisexual identity: bisexual and SGL identity, bisexual and mostly all needs met, and bisexual and often needs not met all have positive impacts on the stigmatization of bisexual men. Thus, among bisexuals, intersecting experiences with basic needs and SGL identity shape stigmatizing attitudes toward bisexual men. In contrast, only two social power axes are negative: SGL identity and the interaction term that represents SGL individuals who indicate they have mostly all they need both have negative relationships with the stigmatization of bisexual men. As discussed in Chapter 7, SGL identity has many significant relationships to LGBTQ stigma among the LGBTQ subsample, including bisexual men stigmatization.

It is also interesting that several of these findings overlap with those in other regression models exploring NCST and the LGBTQ Stigma Scales. For example, being other race is positively related to the Bisexual Men Stigma Scale as well as the Lesbian Women Stigma Scale and the Queer Men Stigma Scale (see Tables 11.2, 8.2, and 16.2). Being a gay/lesbian Asian American/Pacific Islander has similar effects on the stigmatization of bisexual men, bisexual women, queer women, and queer men (see Tables 11.2, 10.2, 15.2, and 16.2). Being a bisexual person who indicates that their needs are mostly met is positively related to the stigmatization of bisexual men, gay men, bisexual women, and non-binary/genderqueer individuals (see Tables 11.2, 9.2, 10.2, and 14.2). The interaction term between queer identity and few needs met also has similar effects on the Bisexual Men Stigma Scale, the Trans Women Stigma Scale, and the Trans Men Stigma Scale (see Tables 11.2, 12.2, and 13.2). Such findings suggest that there may be several common and significant underlying factors related to social power axes that contribute to LGBTQ people's stigmatization of other LGBTQ people, as reviewed in Chapter 7.

There are many more significant social power axes among the LGBTQ subsample in comparison to the hetero-cis subsample in Model 2. Additional tests to compare the regression coefficients of the two subsamples reveal some significant differences (Clogg, Petkova, and Haritou 1995). Thus, the specific axes of social power that inform bisexual men stigmatization differ for the hetero-cis and LGBTQ subsamples. These findings continue to parallel other research (e.g., Worthen 2018) that demonstrates different patterns in the stigmatization of bisexual men among heterosexual and LGB subsamples that vary by axes of social power. Overall, *Hypothesis 2b* is only partially supported: interactions between axes of social power moderate the relationship between the individual axes of social power and the Bisexual Men Stigma Scale for the LGBTQ subsample (only).

## Summarizing NCST, HCN, Social Power Axes, and the Bisexual Men Stigma Scale

Overall, Table 11.2 illustrates the importance of examining intersecting experiences of social power to best understand the stigmatization of bisexual men. The differences between the hetero-cis and LGBTQ subsamples are substantial; however, despite these differences, nearly all of the significant findings in Table 11.2 can be seen in other explorations of the LGBTQ stigma scales in this book suggesting that there may also be some commonalities in understanding the relationships between social power axes and the stigmatization of LGBTQ people (as also demonstrated in Chapter 7). By utilizing NCST to explore the Bisexual Men Stigma Scale, we can better understand these patterns.

## Bisexual Men's Experiences

### The Bisexual Men Subsample

The recruitment of bisexual men to participate in this study was successful and the requested quota (n = 330) from Survey Sampling International was nearly met. The study sample included 326 bisexual men (learn more about the data sampling procedures in Chapter 7 and Appendix A). At the beginning of the survey, respondents were asked two questions: (1) "How would you describe yourself?" and (2) "What best describes your gender?" Bisexual men were those who selected "bisexual" for the first question and either "I identify as a man and my assigned sex at birth was male" or "I am transgender: I identify as a man and my assigned sex at birth was female" for the second question. See Table 11.3 for more details about the bisexual men in this study.

**TABLE 11.3** Bisexual Men Characteristics (n = 326)

|  | % | n |
|---|---|---|
| *Gender identity* | | |
| Cis men | 96.3% | 314 |
| Trans men | 3.7% | 12 |
| *Additional gender/sexual identity* | | |
| Queer** | 9.8% | 32 |
| SGL** | 9.2% | 30 |
| Two-Spirit** | 7.5% | 27 |
| Butch | 3.1% | 11 |
| Femme | 3.6% | 13 |
| Leather | 2.5% | 9 |
| Bear** | 9.5% | 34 |
| Twink | 5.0% | 18 |
| Down Low** | 17.6% | 63 |
| *Race/ethnicity* | | |
| Caucasian/White** | 81.9% | 267 |
| African American/Black* | 6.4% | 21 |
| Asian American/Pacific Islander* | 3.6% | 13 |
| Native American/Alaskan Native* | 2.0% | 7 |
| Multi-racial* | 2.8% | 10 |
| Other race* | 2.0% | 7 |
| Latinx race* | 0.3% | 1 |
| Latinx ethnicity** | 10.1% | 36 |
| *Basic needs* | | |
| Everything I need** | 27.0% | 88 |
| Mostly all I need** | 51.8% | 169 |
| Often needs not met* | 15.6% | 56 |
| Few needs met * | 3.6% | 13 |

\* Reference category in analyses in Table 11.5.
\*\* Included in analyses shown in Table 11.5.

## Bisexual Men's Experiences with Gender- and Sexuality-Based DHV

Research indicates that bisexual men report more experiences with childhood trauma, intimate partner violence, sexual assault, and lifetime victimization in comparison to both heterosexual and gay men (Balsam, Rothblum, and Beauchaine 2005; Kalichman et al. 2001; Katz-Wise and Hyde 2012; Meyer 2015; Stephenson and Finneran 2017). Additional studies show that verbal harassment, discrimination, and physical violence are also more common among bisexual men in comparison to gay men (Huebner, Rebchook, and Kegeles 2004) and heterosexual men (Badgett 1994; Mays and Cochran 2001; McCabe et al. 2010).

Figure 11.3 demonstrates that bisexual men are significantly more likely to experience sexuality-based DHV than gender-based DHV with more than one-third (35%) of bisexual men indicating one or more experiences of sexuality-based DHV as compared to half that (18%) indicating one or more experiences of gender-based DHV. Sexuality-based harassment is the most common among these experiences (27%) while gender-based violence is the least common (5%). To better understand bisexual men's gender- and sexuality-based DHV, bisexual men's experiences were compared to the LGBTQ subsample and the men subsample using $t$-tests. Table 11.4 shows that bisexual men are significantly less likely than the overall LGBTQ subsample to experience either form of DHV and do not differ from the all

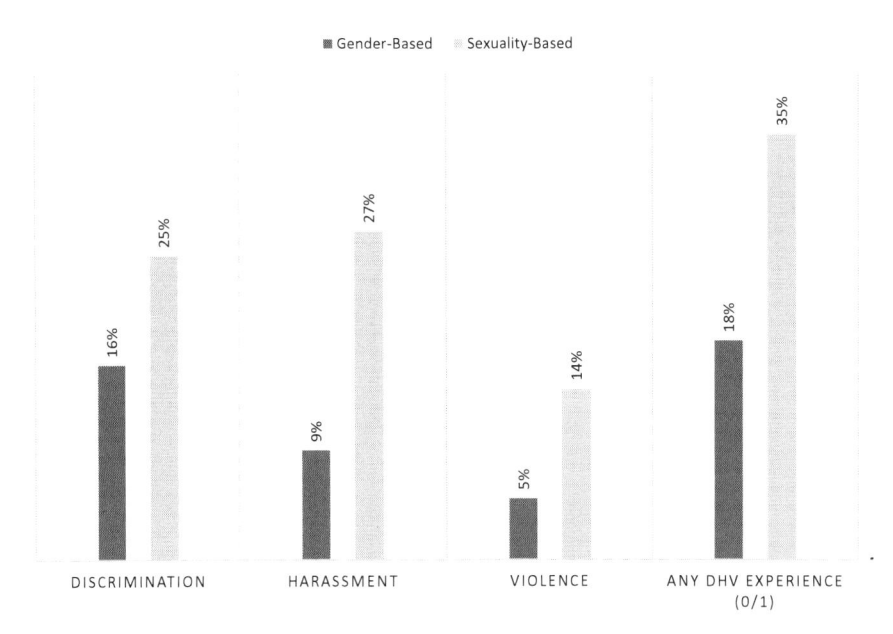

**FIGURE 11.3** Bisexual Men's (n = 326) Experiences with Gender- and Sexuality-Based DHV

*Note*: see Table 11.4 for comparisons of bisexual men's experiences to the LGBTQ subsample and the men subsample.

**TABLE 11.4** Gender- and Sexuality-Based DHV Mean Values (Standard Deviations) among Bisexual Men, the LGBTQ Subsample, and the Men Subsample with *t*-test Results

|  | | Bisexual Men | LGBTQ Subsample | Men Subsample |
|---|---|---|---|---|
| | *n* | 326 | 1604 | 1474 |
| *Gender-based* | | | | |
| Discrimination | | .16 (.36)** | .32 (.47) | .17 (.38) |
| Harassment | | .09 (.29)** | .28 (.45) | .09 (.29) |
| Violence | | .05 (.21)** | .14 (.34) | .07 (.26) |
| Any gender DHV experience (0/1) | | .18 (.39)** | .40 (.49) | .21 (.41) |
| *Sexuality-based* | | | | |
| Discrimination | | .25 (.43)** | .44 (.50) | .23 (.42) |
| Harassment | | .27 (.44)** | .41 (.49) | .24 (.43) |
| Violence | | .14 (.35)** | .20 (.40) | .13 (.34) |
| Any sexuality DHV experience (0/1) | | .35 (.48)** | .53 (.50) | .33 (.47) |

** Bisexual men are significantly different from the LGBTQ subsample (only) at $p < .05$ level.

men subsample in their experiences with gender- or sexuality-based DHV. Thus, compared to all LGBTQ people and all men, bisexual men are not at particular risk for either gender- or sexuality-based DHV.

## NCST and Bisexual Men's Experiences with Gender- and Sexuality-Based DHV

Bisexual men and their experiences with gender- and sexuality-based DHV are examined using NCST with special attention to bisexual men's axes of social power. The hypotheses are as follows:

- *Hypothesis 1*: being a bisexual man (violating hetero-cis-normativity) increases the likelihood of experiencing gender- and sexuality-based DHV (bisexual men stigma).
- *Hypothesis 2*: the relationship between being a bisexual man and gender- and sexuality-based DHV is moderated by interactions among being a bisexual man and axes of social power.

Figure 11.4 outlines these relationships and Table 11.5 displays logistic regression results that examine NCST and the relationships among being a bisexual man, intersections among bisexual men's axes of social power, and any experiences of gender-based DHV (dichotomized as 0/1) or sexuality-based DHV (dichotomized as 0/1) utilizing the LGBTQ subsample (n = 1,604; whereby being a bisexual man is compared to all other LGBTQ people). Because

```
┌─────────────────────────────┐
│   Axes of Social Power      │
│       Interactions          │
├─────────────────────────────┤
│     Bisexual Man*           │
│   Axes of Social Power      │
└─────────────────────────────┘
```

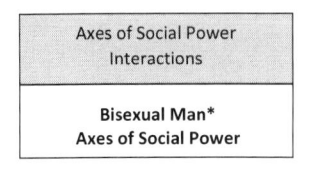

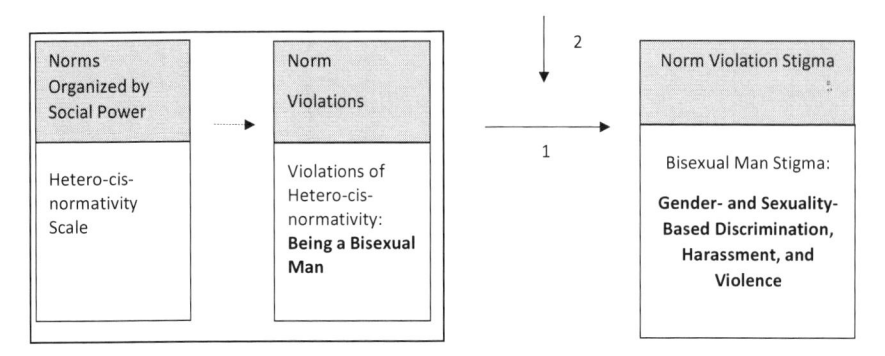

```
┌──────────────┐   ┌──────────────┐        ┌──────────────────┐
│ Norms        │   │ Norm         │   2    │ Norm Violation   │
│ Organized by │   │ Violations   │  ↓     │ Stigma           │
│ Social Power │   │              │        │                  │
├──────────────┤   ├──────────────┤   →    ├──────────────────┤
│ Hetero-cis-  │⤍─▶│ Violations of│   1    │ Bisexual Man     │
│ normativity  │   │ Hetero-cis-  │        │ Stigma:          │
│ Scale        │   │ normativity: │        │ Gender- and      │
│              │   │ Being a      │        │ Sexuality-Based  │
│              │   │ Bisexual Man │        │ Discrimination,  │
│              │   │              │        │ Harassment, and  │
│              │   │              │        │ Violence         │
└──────────────┘   └──────────────┘        └──────────────────┘
```

**FIGURE 11.4** Theoretical Model of NCST and Bisexual Men Stigma using the Stigmatized Lens with Model Numbers to be Examined in Table 11.5

*Notes*: Model 1 estimates being a bisexual man as related to gender- and sexuality-based DHV. Model 2 estimates interactions among bisexual men's axes of social power as they moderate the relationships between being a bisexual man and gender- and sexuality-based DHV. The * indicates an interaction.

bisexual men's experiences are the focus of this exploration (i.e., the stigmatized lens of NCST is being utilized), the bisexual man and social power axes interaction terms are listed at the top of the table and the discussion below only focuses on these variables. However, there are significant corresponding individual effects related to being bisexual and being a man (for example) that are important to recognize. See Chapter 7 for a more complete description of the models and a discussion of overarching trends and patterns. Regarding model fit statistics, the pseudo $R^2$ values ranged from .08 to .16.

## NCST, Bisexual Men, and Gender- and Sexuality-Based DHV: Model 1

In Table 11.5, both Model 1s estimate the relationships between violations of hetero-cis-normativity conceptualized as being a bisexual man and bisexual stigma conceptualized as gender- and sexuality-based DHV. Surprisingly, as compared to other LGBTQ people, being a bisexual man is *not* significantly related to either form of DHV in either Model 1. Such findings do not line up with past research that has found that bisexual men are at a high risk for DHV (Badgett 1994; Balsam, Rothblum, and Beauchaine 2005; Kalichman et al. 2001; Katz-Wise and Hyde 2012; Mays and Cochran 2001). Overall, *Hypothesis 1* is not supported.

**TABLE 11.5** Logistic Regression Results with Odds Ratios and (Standard Errors) Estimating NCST and Gender- and Sexuality-Based DHV as Related to Being a Bisexual Man for the LGBTQ Subsample (n = 1,604)

|  | Gender-Based DHV |  |  |  | Sexuality-Based DHV |  |  |  |
|---|---|---|---|---|---|---|---|---|
|  | Model 1 |  | Model 2 |  | Model 1 |  | Model 2 |  |
|  | OR | SE | OR | SE | OR | SE | OR | SE |
| Bisexual man | . | . | . | . | . | . | 2.55* | (1.15) |
| *Bisexual man social power axes interactions* | | | | | | | | |
|   Bisexual man*queer | — | — | . | . | — | — | .27* | (.13) |
|   Bisexual man*SGL | — | — | . | . | — | — | . | . |
|   Bisexual man*Two-Spirit | — | — | . | . | — | — | . | . |
|   Bisexual man*bear | — | — | . | . | — | — | . | . |
|   Bisexual man*Down Low | — | — | . | . | — | — | . | . |
|   Bisexual man*White | — | — | . | . | — | — | 2.70* | (.96) |
|   Bisexual man*Latinx ethnicity | — | — | . | . | — | — | . | . |
|   Bisexual man*everything I need | — | — | . | . | — | — | . | . |
|   Bisexual man*mostly all I need | — | — | . | . | — | — | . | . |
| *Bisexual man social power axes* | | | | | | | | |
|   Bisexual | . | . | . | . | .36* | (.05) | .37* | (.06) |
|   Man | .19* | (.03) | .19* | (.03) | . | . | . | . |
|   Queer | 2.40* | (.35) | 3.68* | (1.58) | 2.10* | (.30) | 6.77* | (3.07) |
|   SGL | . | . | . | . | . | . | . | . |
|   Two-Spirit | . | . | 2.64* | (1.28) | 1.54* | (.34) | . | . |
|   Bear | . | . | . | . | . | . | . | . |
|   Down Low | . | . | . | . | . | . | . | . |
|   White | . | . | . | . | . | . | . | . |
|   Latinx ethnicity | . | . | . | . | . | . | . | . |
|   Everything I need | .66* | (.12) | . | . | .67* | (.11) | .48* | (.18) |
|   Mostly all I need | .75* | (.11) | . | . | . | . | . | . |
| *Socio-demographic controls* | | | | | | | | |
|   Age | .98* | (.00) | .98* | (.00) | .98* | (.00) | .98* | (.00) |
|   Town type (rural–large city) | . | . | . | . | . | . | . | . |

*(Continued)*

**TABLE 11.5** (Cont.)

|  | Gender-Based DHV | | | | Sexuality-Based DHV | | | |
| --- | --- | --- | --- | --- | --- | --- | --- | --- |
|  | Model 1 | | Model 2 | | Model 1 | | Model 2 | |
|  | OR | SE | OR | SE | OR | SE | OR | SE |
| Education | 1.19* | (.06) | 1.18* | (.05) | 1.10* | (.04) | 1.10* | (.04) |
| Income | . | . | . | . | . | . | . | . |
| Pseudo $R^2$ | .16 | | .16 | | .08 | | .09 | |
| Mean VIF | 1.40 | | 1.40 | | 1.38 | | 1.38 | |

*Notes:* all rows are displayed, including those without significant results. See Table 11.3 for more details about bisexual men.

\* $p < .05$; a dot (.) indicates non-statistically significant results. A dash (—) indicates this was not included in the model.

## NCST, Bisexual Men, and Gender- and Sexuality-Based DHV: Model 2

Intersections among axes of social power and being a bisexual man are included in Model 2 as they relate to gender- and sexuality-based DHV. As seen in Model 1, being a bisexual man remains statistically non-significantly related to gender-based DHV in Model 2. In addition, there are no significant interaction terms for gender-based DHV among bisexual men. In contrast, being a bisexual man emerges as significantly related to sexuality-based DHV in Model 2. Specifically, being a bisexual man increases the likelihood of sexuality-based DHV by 1.55. There are also two significant interaction terms in this Model. First, being a queer bisexual man decreases the likelihood of sexuality-based DHV by .73. While only 10% (n = 32/326) of bisexual men identified as queer, these results suggest that queer identity serves as a protective factor for sexuality-based DHV among bisexual men. Such findings demonstrate that there are likely very real differences between queer bisexual men's and other LGBTQ people's experiences that impact their likelihood of experiencing DHV. As other research has shown (Meyer 2012; Panfil 2017), anti-queer violence differs depending on one's social position. The findings here demonstrate that queer bisexual men may be imbedded in socio-cultural experiences that are less conducive to sexuality-based DHV in comparison to the experiences of non-queer bisexual men.

Second, as compared to other LGBTQ people in all other racial/ethnic groups, being a White bisexual man *in*creases the likelihood of sexuality-based DHV by 1.70. Such findings are surprising because research indicates that LGBTQ people of color endure stigma, harassment, and violence as related to their experiences as both racial/ethnic minorities and gender/sexuality minorities (Battle, Pastrana, and Harris 2017; Han, Proctor, and Choi 2014; Lemelle and Battle 2004; Worthen 2018). There may be something unique about White bisexual men's experiences that puts them at particular risk for sexuality-based DHV. It may be that White bisexual men are more visible in their presentation as bisexual in comparison to bisexual men of color and this may differentially increase their risk of sexuality-based DHV.

Overall, there are significant relationships among being a bisexual man and sexuality-based DHV. Specifically, both the individual effect of being a bisexual man and additional intersecting experiences of social power impact the likelihood of experiencing sexuality-based DHV. However, in stark contrast, there are no statistically significant results related to being a bisexual man among the gender-based DHV models. Thus, *Hypothesis 2* is supported in the sexuality-based DHV models but not in the gender-based DHV models. Interestingly, these results are the exact opposite from those found among bisexual women whereby there were significant findings as related to being a bisexual woman among the gender-based DHV models but not the sexuality-based DHV models. Together, these results demonstrate the importance of exploring bisexual men's and women's DHV experiences separately while centering the importance of intersecting social power axes.

## Summarizing NCST, Bisexual Men, and Gender- and Sexuality-Based DHV

In sum, Table 11.5 indicates that being a bisexual man is not directly related to gender-based DHV but is directly related sexuality-based DHV. In addition, two intersecting measures of social power have opposite effects: queer identity among bisexual men decreases the likelihood of experiencing sexuality-based DHV while White identity among bisexual men increases the likelihood of experiencing sexuality-based DHV. These results largely contrast with previous studies (Badgett 1994; Balsam, Rothblum, and Beauchaine 2005; Battle, Pastrana, and Harris 2017; Han, Proctor, and Choi 2014; Kalichman et al. 2001; Katz-Wise and Hyde 2012; Mays and Cochran 2001; Worthen 2018), and reflect the significance of incorporating multiple layers of intersectionality into continued research that centers bisexual men's experiences with gender- and sexuality-based DHV.

## Summary of Patterns of Bisexual Men Stigma

In line with the three tenets and hypotheses derived from NCST, there are six patterns related to the stigmatization of bisexual men illustrated in this chapter:

1. Bisexual men are largely stigmatized by both hetero-cis and LGBTQ people due to negativities about their sex acts including stereotypes that bisexual men are unfaithful and too sexual/hypersexual in their romantic partnerships.

2. The stigmatization of bisexual men by both hetero-cis and LGBTQ people is also situated within the stereotypes that bisexual men's identities are temporary/experimental and that they are not masculine enough.
3. Hetero-cis-normativity is positively related to bisexual men stigma for both subsamples; however, the interaction effects between the HCN scale and social power axes that moderate these relationships differ for the hetero-cis and LGBTQ subsamples. In addition, there are more significant interaction effects between the HCN Scale and social power axes for the hetero-cis subsample than there are for the LGBTQ subsample.
4. Individual social power axes are significantly related to bisexual men stigma for both subsamples in Model 1 but are only significant for the LGBTQ subsample in Model 2. In addition, the interaction effects between the social power axes only moderate these relationships for the LGBTQ subsample.
5. Bisexual men have nearly twice as many experiences with sexuality-based DHV as compared to gender-based DHV; however, in comparison to the all men and all LGBTQ subsamples, bisexual men experience significantly less DHV.
6. Being a bisexual man is not in and of itself related to the likelihood of gender-based DHV; however, being a bisexual man increases the likelihood of sexuality-based DHV. Also, bisexual men's intersecting experiences with queer identity decrease the likelihood of sexuality-based DHV while White identity among bisexual men increases the likelihood of sexuality-based DHV.

## References

Anderson, Eric. 2008. "'Being Masculine Is Not about Who You Sleep With … ' Heterosexual Athletes Contesting Masculinity and the One-Time Rule of Homosexuality." *Sex Roles* 58(1):104–115.

Badgett, M. V. Lee. 1994. "The Wage Effects of Sexual Orientation Discrimination." *Industrial and Labor Relations Review* 48:726–739.

Balay, Anne. 2014. *Steel Closets: Voices of Gay, Lesbian, and Transgender Steelworkers.* Chapel Hill, NC: University of North Carolina Press.

Balsam, Kimberly F., Esther D. Rothblum, and Theodore P. Beauchaine. 2005. "Victimization over the Life Span: A Comparison of Lesbian, Gay, Bisexual, and Heterosexual Siblings." *Journal of Consulting and Clinical Psychology* 73(3):477–487.

Battle, Juan, Antonio Pastrana and Angelique Harris. 2017. *An Examination of Asian and Pacific Islander LGBT Populations across the United States.* New York, NY: Palgrave Macmillan.

Brown, Suzanne, Susan Smalling, Victor Groza, and Scott Ryan. 2009. "The Experiences of Gay Men and Lesbians in Becoming and Being Adoptive Parents." *Adoption Quarterly* 12(3/4):229–246.

Carey, Benedict. 2005. "Straight, Gay or Lying? Bisexuality Revisited." *The New York Times*, July 5. Retrieved January 30, 2020 (https://www.nytimes.com/2005/07/05/health/straight-gay-or-lying-bisexuality-revisited.html).

Carneiro, Francis A., Fiona Tasker, Fernando Salinas-Quiroz, Isabel Leal, and Pedro A. Costa. 2017. "Are the Fathers Alright? A Systematic and Critical Review of Studies on Gay and Bisexual Fatherhood." *Frontiers in Psychology* 8(1636):1–13.

Clarke, Victoria. 2001. "What about the Children? Arguments against Lesbian and Gay Parenting." *Women's Studies International Forum* 24(5):555–570.
Clogg, Clifford C., Eva Petkova, and Adamantios Haritou. 1995. "Statistical Methods for Comparing Regression Coefficients between Models." *American Journal of Sociology* 100(5):1261–1293.
Colborne, Adrienne. 2018. "Chasing Aces: Asexuality, Misinformation and the Challenges of Identity." *Dalhousie Journal of Interdisciplinary Management* 14:1–13.
Connell, R. W., M. D. Davis and G. W. Dowsett. 1993. "A Bastard of A Life: Homosexual Desire and Practice among Men in Working-Class Milieux." *The Australian and New Zealand Journal of Sociology* 29(1):112–135.
Crawford, Isiaah, Andrew McLeod, Brian D. Zamboni, and Michael B. Jordan. 1999. "Psychologists' Attitudes toward Gay and Lesbian Parenting." *Professional Psychology: Research and Practice* 30(4):394–401.
Embrick, David G., Carol S. Walther, and Corrine M. Wickens. 2007. "Working Class Masculinity: Keeping Gay Men and Lesbians Out of the Workplace." *Sex Roles* 56(11):757–766.
Frankis, Jamie S. and Paul Flowers. 2009. "Public Sexual Cultures: A Systematic Review of Qualitative Research Investigating Men's Sexual Behaviors with Men in Public Spaces." *Journal of Homosexuality* 56(7):861–893.
Frederick, David A. and Melissa R. Fales. 2016. "Upset over Sexual versus Emotional Infidelity among Gay, Lesbian, Bisexual, and Heterosexual Adults." *Archives of Sexual Behavior* 45(1):175–191.
Gander, Kashmira. 2018. "Children Raised by Gay and Lesbian Parents Develop as Well as Kids of Heterosexual Couples, Study Suggests." *Newsweek*. Retrieved January 30, 2020 (https://www.newsweek.com/children-raised-gay-and-lesbian-parents-develop-well-kids-heterosexual-1001515).
Han, Chong-Suk, Kristopher Proctor, and Kyung-Hee Choi. 2014. "We Pretend like Sexuality Doesn't Exist: Managing Homophobia in Gaysian America." *The Journal of Men's Studies* 22(1):53–63.
Hart, Trevor A., Syed W. Noor, Tyler G. Tulloch, Julia R. Buvani Sivagnanasunderam, G. Vernon, David W. Pantalone, Ted Myers, and Liviana Calzavara. 2019. "The Gender Nonconformity Teasing Scale for Gay and Bisexual Men." *Psychology of Men & Masculinities* 20(3):445–457.
Hayfield, Nikki, Victoria Clarke, and Emma Halliwell. 2014. "Bisexual Women's Understandings of Social Marginalisation: 'The Heterosexuals Don't Understand Us but nor Do the Lesbians'." *Feminism & Psychology* 24(3):352–372.
Heath, Jessie and Kathy Goggin. 2009. "Attitudes Towards Male Homosexuality, Bisexuality, and the Down Low Lifestyle: Demographic Differences and HIV Implications." *Journal of Bisexuality* 9(1):17–31.
Hoover, Karen W., Kevin L. Tao, and Philip J. Peters. 2017. "Nationally Representative Prevalence Estimates of Gay, Bisexual, and Other Men Who Have Sex with Men Who Have Served in the U.S. Military." *Plos One* 12(8):e0182222.
Huebner, David M., Gregory M. Rebchook, and Susan M. Kegeles. 2004. "Experiences of Harassment, Discrimination, and Physical Violence among Young Gay and Bisexual Men." *American Journal of Public Health* 94(7):1200–1203.
Humphreys, Laud. 1970. *Tearoom Trade: Impersonal Sex in Public Places*. Piscataway, NJ: Transaction Publishers.

Joos, Kristin E. and K. L. Broad. 2007. "Coming Out of the Family Closet: Stories of Adult Women with LGBTQ Parent(s)." *Qualitative Sociology* 30(3):275–295.

Kalichman, Seth C., Eric Benotsch, David Rompa, Cheryl Gore-Felton, James Austin, Webster Luke, Kari DiFonzo, Jeff Buckles, Florence Kyomugisha, and Dolores Simpson. 2001. "Unwanted Sexual Experiences and Sexual Risks in Gay and Bisexual Men: Associations among Revictimization, Substance Use, and Psychiatric Symptoms." *The Journal of Sex Research* 38(1):1–9.

Katz-Wise, Sabra L. and Janet S. Hyde. 2012. "Victimization Experiences of Lesbian, Gay, and Bisexual Individuals: A Meta-Analysis." *The Journal of Sex Research* 49(2/3):142–167.

Kinsey, Alfred, Wardell Pomeroy, and Clyde Martin. 1948. *Sexual Behavior in the Human Male*. Philadelphia, PA: W. B. Saunders Co.

Lemelle, Anthony and Juan Battle. 2004. "Black Masculinity Matters in Attitudes toward Gay Males." *Journal of Homosexuality* 47(1):39–51.

Mays, Vickie M. and Susan D. Cochran. 2001. "Mental Health Correlates of Perceived Discrimination among Lesbian, Gay, and Bisexual Adults in the United States." *American Journal of Public Health* 91(11):1869–1876.

McCabe, Sean Esteban, Wendy B. Bostwick, Tonda L. Hughes, Brady T. West, and Carol J. Boyd. 2010. "The Relationship between Discrimination and Substance Use Disorders among Lesbian, Gay, and Bisexual Adults in the United States." *American Journal of Public Health* 100(10):1946–1952.

McCormack, Mark, Eric Anderson, and Adrian Adams. 2014. "Cohort Effect on the Coming Out Experiences of Bisexual Men." *Sociology* 48(6):1207–1223.

McLean, Kirsten. 2008. "Inside, Outside, Nowhere: Bisexual Men and Women in the Gay and Lesbian Community." *Journal of Bisexuality* 8(1/2):63–80.

Meyer, Doug. 2012. "An Intersectional Analysis of Lesbian, Gay, Bisexual, and Transgender (LGBT) People's Evaluations of Anti-Queer Violence." *Gender & Society* 26(6):849–873.

Meyer, Doug. 2015. *Violence against Queer People: Race, Class, Gender, and the Persistence of Anti-LGBT Discrimination*. New Brunswick, NJ: Rutgers University Press.

Murphy, Dean A. 2013. "The Desire for Parenthood: Gay Men Choosing to Become Parents through Surrogacy." *Journal of Family Issues* 34(8):1104–1124.

Panfil, Vanessa R. 2017. *The Gang's All Queer: The Lives of Gay Gang Members*. New York, NY: NYU Press.

Pew Research Center. 2013. "Chapter 3: The Coming Out Experience." Retrieved February 6, 2019 (www.pewsocialtrends.org/2013/06/13/chapter-3-the-coming-out-experience/).

Pinto, Stacy Anne. 2014. "ASEXUally: On Being an Ally to the Asexual Community." *Journal of LGBT Issues in Counseling* 8(4):331–343.

Power, Jennifer, Amaryll Perlesz, Ruth McNair, Margot Schofield, Marian Pitts, Rhonda Brown, and Andrew Bickerdike. 2012. "Gay and Bisexual Dads and Diversity: Fathers in the Work, Love, Play Study." *Journal of Family Studies* 18(2/3):143–154.

Rhode, Jason. 2018. "DeKalb Judge Comes Out as Bisexual." *Georgia Voice - Gay & LGBT Atlanta News*, May 1. Retrieved January 20, 2020 (https://thegavoice.com/community/dekalb-judge-comes-out-as-bisexual/).

Rosenthal, A. M., David Sylva, Adam Safron, and J. Michael Bailey. 2012. "The Male Bisexuality Debate Revisited: Some Bisexual Men Have Bisexual Arousal Patterns." *Archives of Sexual Behavior* 41(1):135–147.

Schacher, Stephanie Jill, Carl F. Auerbach, and Louise Bordeaux Silverstein. 2005. "Gay Fathers Expanding the Possibilities for Us All." *Journal of GLBT Family Studies* 1(3):31–52.

Scherrer, Kristin S., Emily Kazyak, and Rachel Schmitz. 2015. "Getting 'Bi' in the Family: Bisexual People's Disclosure Experiences." *Journal of Marriage and Family* 77(3):680–696.

Sirota, Theodora. 2009. "Adult Attachment Style Dimensions in Women Who Have Gay or Bisexual Fathers." *Archives of Psychiatric Nursing* 23(4):289–297.

Spalding, Leah R. and Letitia Anne Peplau. 1997. "The Unfaithful Lover: Heterosexuals' Perceptions of Bisexuals and Their Relationships." *Psychology of Women Quarterly* 21(4):611–625.

Stephenson, Rob and Catherine Finneran. 2017. "Minority Stress and Intimate Partner Violence among Gay and Bisexual Men in Atlanta." *American Journal of Men's Health* 11(4):952–961.

Sullivan, Stephen P., Emily S. Pingel, Rob Stephenson, and José A. Bauermeister. 2018. "'It Was Supposed to Be a Onetime Thing': Experiences of Romantic and Sexual Relationship Typologies among Young Gay, Bisexual, and Other Men Who Have Sex with Men." *Archives of Sexual Behavior* 47(4):1221–1230.

Weiss, Jillian Todd. 2004. "GL vs. BT: The Archaeology of Biphobia and Transphobia within the US Gay and Lesbian Community." *Journal of Bisexuality* 3(3/4):25–55.

Worthen, Meredith G. F. 2018. "'Gay Equals White'? Racial, Ethnic, and Sexual Identities and Attitudes toward LGBT Individuals among College Students at a Bible Belt University." *The Journal of Sex Research* 55(8):995–1011.

# 12
# TRANS WOMEN STIGMA

*No pride for some of us without liberation for all of us.*

Marsha P. Johnson[1]

*We can no longer stay invisible. We should not be ashamed of who we are. We have to show the world that we are numerous. There are many of us out there.*

Sylvia Rivera[2]

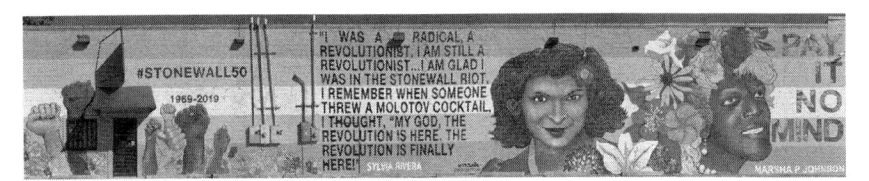

IMAGE 12.1 Mural painted by artist Brian Kenny featuring Sylvia Rivera and Marsha P. Johnson commemorating the 50th anniversary of the Stonewall Uprising. Located in Dallas, TX at 4008 Cedar Springs Road, it is the largest transgender-focused mural in the US. It was commissioned by Arttitude, a not-for-profit organization that serves underrepresented communities by raising visibility through art. Photo credit to Brian Kenny.

## The Stigmatization of Trans Women

In the survey instrument, the section focusing on attitudes toward transgender women was preceded by the following statement:

> Next, we're interested in your thoughts, feelings, and predicted behaviors about transgender women (those who currently identify as women who were assigned 'male' at birth).

### The Trans Women Stigma Scale

Among all nine groups examined in this book, trans women are the fourth most stigmatized. In addition, trans women are the most stigmatized group among all LGBTQ women (recall Figure 7.1). Trans women's marginalized positionality as gender minorities is important to examine as it informs their experiences with stigma. Below, the Trans Women Stigma Scale included in Figure 12.1 and Table 12.1 below is discussed.

### Trans Women and Social and Familial Relationships

In comparison to all other key areas of the scale (with the exception of basic human rights as discussed in Chapter 7), the stigma associated with trans

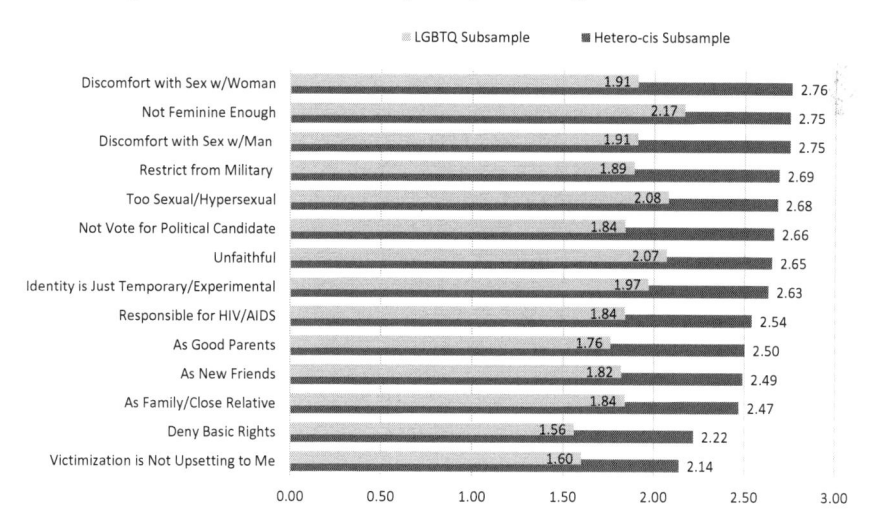

| Item | LGBTQ Subsample | Hetero-cis Subsample |
|---|---|---|
| Discomfort with Sex w/Woman | 1.91 | 2.76 |
| Not Feminine Enough | 2.17 | 2.75 |
| Discomfort with Sex w/Man | 1.91 | 2.75 |
| Restrict from Military | 1.89 | 2.69 |
| Too Sexual/Hypersexual | 2.08 | 2.68 |
| Not Vote for Political Candidate | 1.84 | 2.66 |
| Unfaithful | 2.07 | 2.65 |
| Identity is Just Temporary/Experimental | 1.97 | 2.63 |
| Responsible for HIV/AIDS | 1.84 | 2.54 |
| As Good Parents | 1.76 | 2.50 |
| As New Friends | 1.82 | 2.49 |
| As Family/Close Relative | 1.84 | 2.47 |
| Deny Basic Rights | 1.56 | 2.22 |
| Victimization is Not Upsetting to Me | 1.60 | 2.14 |

FIGURE 12.1 Trans Women Stigma Scale Item Mean Values Rank-Ordered from Most to Least Stigmatizing for the Hetero-cis (n = 1,500) and the LGBTQ (n = 1,604) Subsamples

Note: see Table 12.1 for the exact wording for each item. $t$-test results comparing the hetero-cis and LGBTQ subsamples indicate that all means are significantly different from one another at the $p < .001$ level.

**TABLE 12.1** Trans Women Stigma Scale Item Mean Values (Standard Deviations) and *t*-test Results Comparing the Means for the Hetero-cis Subsample and the LGBTQ Subsample

|  | Hetero-cis Subsample | LGBTQ Subsample | t-test Results |
|---|---|---|---|
|  | n = 1,500 | n = 1,604 |  |
| *Social and familial relationships* |  |  |  |
| I welcome new friends who are trans women.[R] | 2.49 (1.23) | 1.82 (1.08) | t = 16.21* |
| I don't think it would negatively affect our relationship if I learned that one of my close relatives was a trans woman.[R] | 2.47 (1.22) | 1.84 (1.13) | t = 14.90* |
| Trans women are not capable of being good parents. | 2.50 (1.28) | 1.76 (1.13) | t = 17.03* |
| *Positions of importance and social significance* |  |  |  |
| I would not vote for a political candidate who was an openly trans woman. | 2.66 (1.36) | 1.84 (1.23) | t = 17.47* |
| Trans women should not be allowed to join the military. | 2.69 (1.38) | 1.89 (1.27) | t = 16.71* |
| *Basic human rights* |  |  |  |
| I believe trans women should have all of the same rights as other people do.[R] | 2.22 (1.16) | 1.56 (.98) | t = 16.92* |
| It is upsetting to me that trans women experience violence, harassment, and discrimination just because they are trans women.[R] | 2.14 (1.14) | 1.60 (1.03) | t = 13.80* |
| *Sex act-related stigma* |  |  |  |
| Trans women are unfaithful to their romantic partners. | 2.65 (1.11) | 2.07 (1.13) | t = 14.28* |
| Trans women are too sexual (hypersexual). | 2.68 (1.14) | 2.08 (1.12) | t = 14.83* |
| Trans women are mostly responsible for spreading HIV/AIDS. | 2.54 (1.17) | 1.84 (1.12) | t = 17.15* |
| I am comfortable with the thought of a trans woman having sex with a woman.[R] | 2.76 (1.20) | 1.91 (1.06) | t = 20.83* |
| I am comfortable with the thought of a trans woman having sex with a man.[R] | 2.75 (1.18) | 1.91 (1.03) | t = 21.20* |
| *Trans identity permanency* |  |  |  |
| Most women who call themselves transgender are just temporarily experimenting with their gender. | 2.63 (1.17) | 1.97 (1.13) | t = 16.02* |

*(Continued)*

**TABLE 12.1** (Cont.)

|  | Hetero-cis Subsample | LGBTQ Subsample | t-test Results |
|---|---|---|---|
|  | n = 1,500 | n = 1,604 |  |
| *Achievement of femininity* |  |  |  |
| Trans women are not feminine enough. | 2.75 (1.12) | 2.17 (1.16) | t = 14.21* |
| α | .90 | .93 |  |
| Summed scale actual range | 14-68 | 14-67 |  |
| Summed scale mean | 35.91 (11.28) | 26.25 (11.20) | t = 23.95* |

*Note:* response options were Strongly Disagree–Strongly Agree (range: 1–5).[R] This item is reverse coded. *t-test results allowing for unequal variances indicate that the hetero-cis subsample and LGBTQ subsample means are significantly different from one another at the p < .001 level.

women in social and familial relationships is lower, though means are at or above 2.50 for the hetero-cis subsample and are approaching 2.0 for the LGBTQ subsample (see Table 12.1). This demonstrates that there is at least some hostility toward having trans women friends and family members among this sample, but these negativities are not as extreme as those found in most other key areas of the Trans Women Stigma Scale. These findings may be related to the increasing visibility of trans individuals in social and familial networks. For example, an online Harris Poll of U.S. adults (N = 2,024) showed that the number of Americans who indicate that they know or work with a transgender person doubled in less than a decade, from 8% in 2008 to 16% in 2015. This number was nearly three times higher among young people: nearly a quarter (24%) of those aged 18–44 indicate they know/work with a trans person compared to only 9% of those aged 45 and over who indicate as such (Adam and Goodman 2015). In addition, Pew Research Center data (N = 4,573) show that more recent numbers are even higher. Their 2017 poll found that more than one-third (37%) of Americans know/work with a trans person. However, nearly all indicated the trans person they knew was an acquaintance, friend, or co-worker (24%, 9%, and 7%, respectively) and the smallest percentage (6%) indicated they had a trans family member (Brown 2017).

All three items in this key area were very similar for the hetero-cis subsample, ranging by only .03 points; thus, there was not much variation in the stigma associated with friends and family for this group. However, it is interesting that the item with the *lowest* mean value for the LGBTQ subsample (1.76) had the *highest* mean value for the hetero-cis subsample (2.50). This item was: "Trans women are not capable of being good parents." Specific biases toward trans women as capable parents relate to troubling stereotypes about motherhood and family. Some of these can be rooted in overt cis-normative hostilities (e.g., being trans is a sin, being trans is a sickness, being trans is a perversion) and parenting prejudices (e.g., trans parents will disrupt "appropriate" gender identity development in their children) (McGuire et al. 2016; Tornello, Riskind, and Babić 2019; Veldorale-Griffin and Darling 2016). Yet some research suggests that trans mothers endure specific stigma associated with their gender, especially from those that are blatantly unaccepting of their gender identities as women (Haines, Ajayi, and Boyd 2014; Hicks 2013; Hines 2007). In addition, in the U.S. as of 2019, only 5 states and Washington, D.C. have laws that protect transgender people from discrimination by foster care and adoption agencies (Movement Advancement Project 2019). Thus, trans mothers experience both social stigma and legal barriers to becoming mothers which contribute to specific hostilities toward trans women as capable parents.

For the LGBTQ subsample, stigma toward trans women as friends and family members (1.82 and 1.84) was notably higher than feelings about trans women as capable parents (1.76). These patterns may be driven by the historical and sometimes current exclusion of trans people from gay and lesbian spaces. Indeed, both the Gay and Lesbian Movement of the 1970s and onward and more radical separatist feminist movements have outright rejected trans people (Stein 1997; Stryker 2008; Weiss 2004). For example, the "womyn-born womyn" policy at the Michigan Womyn's Music Festival secured the existence of "female-born women's-only" spaces for nearly forty years (1976–2015) and signaled a larger message that trans women did not belong in lesbian spaces (Stone 2009). The 2008-coined term "TERF" (trans exclusionary radical feminist) has further been applied to those who oppose the inclusion of trans women in cis (largely lesbian) women's spaces and who uphold biological/sex-based essentialist beliefs that only those who are assigned "female" at birth are "real women" (Williams 2016). Though many of these anti-trans factions are small, these schisms can shape LGBTQ people's attitudes toward trans people and issues and perhaps especially, attitudes toward trans women as friends and family members (Stone 2009; Worthen 2013).

## Trans Women and Positions of Importance and Social Significance

Among the hetero-cis subsample especially, there was relatively high stigmatization of trans women in positions of importance and social significance. As seen in Figure 12.1, the two items in this key area were amongst the top six most stigmatizing attitudes for the hetero-cis subsample with a mean of 2.66 for "I would not vote for a political candidate who was an openly trans woman" and a mean of 2.69 for "Trans women should not be allowed to join the military."

These perspectives are reflected in the current political landscape in very real ways. For example, though research indicates that 51 trans people ran for office in 2018, there are few currently active trans women politicians in the U.S. (Beachum 2019). A notable stand-out is sitting Virginia General Assembly

Delegate Danica Roem who defeated Republican incumbent Robert Marshall, a vocal supporter of an anti-trans "bathroom bill" designed to exclude trans individuals from using public restrooms that best reflect their gender identities (Beachum 2019). In addition, Amanda Simpson, who was the first ever transgender presidential appointee in 2010, worked in the Pentagon as a civilian employee of the U.S. Army from 2011–2017 as one of the highest ranking transgender people ever in the Department of Defense as well as the federal government (Dawson 2016). Yet trans political and military leaders remain few and far between.

In addition, with President Trump battling to ban their participation in the Armed Forces, U.S. trans military members are at the center of active hostility (Worthen 2019). This is of particular concern because research indicates that trans people serve in the military at up to twice the rates of their cisgender counterparts and some estimates from 2014–2016 showed that there were more than 15,000 trans individuals serving in the U.S. Armed Forces as well as over 100,000 trans veterans (Gates and Herman 2014; James et al. 2016; Elders et al. 2015). Indeed, the Transgender American Veterans Association, founded by two trans women, Army veteran Angela Brightfeather and Navy veteran Monica Helms (who also created the Transgender Pride Flag and served as a delegate in the 2004 Democratic National Convention), currently serves thousands of trans veterans (Allen 2007; TransVeterans.org, n.d.). Overall, hostility toward trans military members remains entrenched in numerous cultural dynamics. As I have discussed elsewhere (Worthen 2019), negativity toward trans military service is cloaked in hetero-cis-normative thinking that is built from pillars of restrictive notions about the exclusivity of cis men in infantry/combat military occupations and combat zones as well as hostility toward women/feminism and LGB people. Together, these perspectives shape opposition and stigmatization toward trans women in positions of importance and social significance.

## Trans Women and Sex Act-Related Stigma

Overall, sex act-related stigma among trans women was relatively high with all means for the five items in this key area above 2.5 among the hetero-cis subsample (ranging from 2.54 to 2.76) and close to 2.0 or higher for the LGBTQ subsample (ranging from 1.84 to 2.08). As seen in Figure 12.1, three of the top six most stigmatizing attitudes toward trans women are found among the sex act-related stigma items for both subsamples (discomfort with sex with men and women and hypersexuality). For trans women, sex act-related stigma is embedded in misinformation and stereotypes about trans women's bodies and their perceived sex acts as well as problematic associations of trans women with sex work.

In Table 12.1, the item with the lowest mean values in the sex act-related stigma key area for both groups is: "Trans women are mostly responsible for spreading HIV/AIDS." This is interesting because although HIV/AIDS-related stigma has been most generally associated with gay, bisexual, and queer men (Dowsett 2009; Herek and Capitanio 1999; McKirnan et al. 1995), trans women are also at risk for both contracting HIV/AIDS and HIV/AIDS-related stigmatization experiences (James et al. 2016; Munro et al. 2017). Yet among this sample, sex act-related stigma directed toward trans women is driven more strongly by other factors.

The two items with the highest mean values in the sex act-related stigma key area for the hetero-cis subsample are: "I am comfortable with the thought of a trans woman having sex with a woman" (2.76) and "I am comfortable with the thought of a trans woman having sex with a man" (2.75) which were both reverse coded because *dis*comfort with trans women engaging in sex acts reflects a stigmatizing attitude toward trans women. The stigmatization of trans women's sexual behaviors is related to stereotypes about trans women's bodies and stereotypes about the types of sex acts they participate in. These can include negative attitudes toward the sexual behaviors of trans women who have undergone gender-affirming/gender-transition surgeries (e.g., "facial feminization, breast augmentation, and surgeries to remove testes (orchiectomy) and create vaginas (vaginoplasty)," Elders et al. 2015:207) but can also include negative attitudes toward trans women who *have not* undergone these procedures. Invasively problematic queries about trans women's body parts, including how they look and how they "work" (or don't), are built into the stigmatization of trans women's sexual behaviors. Harmful beliefs such as trans women "can never be women" and/or "are really men" because they had (or have) penises are also linked to negative perceptions about trans women's sex acts. For example, scholars find that violence toward trans women is strongly related to a process whereby a hetero-cis male claims that a trans woman "deceived" him into thinking she was a "real woman" during a romantic/sexual encounter which caused him to panic and respond with violence (Meyer 2015; Schilt and Westbrook 2009; Wodda and Panfil 2014). Overall, damaging negativities and misinformation work together to shape sex act-related stigma among trans women.

The item with the highest mean value in the sex act-related stigma key area for the LGBTQ subsample (2.08) is: "Trans women are too sexual (hypersexual)" (the mean was also quite high for the hetero-cis subsample at 2.68). The frequent sexual objectification of trans women's bodies along with perceptions that they are involved in sexually "risky" behaviors, including sex work, relate to this stigmatizing attitude (Krüsi et al. 2016; Matsuzaka and Koch 2019; Sausa, Keatley, and Operario 2007; Schilt and Westbrook 2009; Sevelius 2013). For example, qualitative research with trans women of color (N = 22) finds that most (86%) report feeling sexually objectified by men on a regular basis (Sevelius 2013). In addition, a large-scale study conducted by the National Center for Transgender Equality with more than 9,000 trans women respondents found that 1 in

10 trans women (overall) and one-third (33%) of Black trans women indicated that the police officers they interacted with in the past year assumed they were sex workers (James et al. 2016). Together, these intersecting negative stereotypes about trans women's sexualities contribute to their experiences with sex act-related stigma.

## Trans Woman Identity Permanency

The stigmatization of trans women's identity permanency was found among both subsamples. Though the mean for this item was amongst the top four most stigmatizing attitudes for the LGBTQ subsample (1.97), it was mid-range for the hetero-cis subsample (2.63). Thus, attitudes toward the statement "Most women who call themselves transgender are just temporarily experimenting with their gender" drive the stigmatization of trans women among LGBTQ people more than among hetero-cis people. Even so, for both groups, negativity toward trans women's identity as temporary/experimental is relatively strong. This stigma may be associated with a generalized dismissal of trans women's authenticity. For example, research indicates that many trans women encounter skepticism about their gender identity at early ages, especially from family members and even healthcare providers (Alegría 2018; Dowshen et al. 2017; Hill and Menvielle 2009). Experiences with trivializing attitudes such as "it's just a phase" or "she'll (or worse, he'll) grow out of it" may be especially evident among trans girls because negativity toward feminine gender non-conforming behaviors (e.g., "stop acting like a sissy") has been found to be more prominent when compared to negativity toward masculine gender non-conforming behaviors (e.g., "stop acting like a tomboy") (Grossman et al. 2005; see more about trans femininity below). Overall, these perspectives contribute to broader stereotypes about trans women's identity permanency.

## Trans Women and the Achievement of Femininity

Among both subsamples, trans women are stigmatized for the inability to successfully achieve femininity. In fact, across all 14 items in the Trans Women Stigma Scale, this item has the highest mean value for the LGBTQ subsample (2.17) and has the second-highest mean value for the hetero-cis subsample (2.75) (see Figure 12.1). Thus, there is agreement across the entire sample that "Trans women are not feminine enough." Studies indicate that trans women's femininities are often heavily criticized and that their experiences differ from those of trans men in significant ways (McKinnon 2014; Schilt and Westbrook 2009; Serano 2007; Worthen 2016). For example, trans women are ridiculed with horrifically defamatory slurs such as "shemale," "he/she," "shim" or even the dehumanizing "it" (Meyer 2015:35) and offensive public judgements such as "you don't really look like a woman" or "look! a man in a dress!" Trans women are berated because they are perceived as unable to meet the hetero-cis-normative standards of femininity set in place by hetero-cis men for hetero-cis women to attempt to uphold. Trans Studies scholar Julia Serano describes these processes as trans-misogyny: "when a trans person is ridiculed or dismissed not merely for failing to live up to gender norms, but for their expressions of femaleness or femininity" (Serano 2007:14). Indeed, qualitative work (N = 10) reveals that trans women of color are especially likely to experience both transmisogynistic sexual victimization and internalized transmisogyny (Matsuzaka and Koch 2019). Together, the intersectional experiences of being both trans and woman contribute to frequent hostilities associated with the (in)ability to achieve idealized femininity (Arayasirikul and Wilson 2018).

## Trans Women Stigma Summed Scale

In Table 12.1, the Trans Women Stigma Scale was created by summing together all 14 items. Cronbach's alphas were quite high for the hetero-cis subsample (.90) and the LGBTQ subsample (.93). Unlike the stigma scales for lesbian women, gay men, bisexual women, and bisexual men, the actual range in values was nearly identical between the two subsamples for the Trans Women Stigma Scale with the highest value for the hetero-cis subsample (68) only 1 point higher than the highest value for the LGBTQ subsample (67). However, mean values for the summed Trans Women Stigma Scale differed substantially and significantly with the hetero-cis subsample mean (35.91) 9.66 points higher than the LGBTQ subsample mean (26.25). In addition, the key area with the highest individual mean values differed. For the hetero-cis subsample, the highest mean value was among the sex act-related stigma items (discomfort with sex w/woman, 2.76) while for the LGBTQ subsample, the highest mean value was related to trans women's inability to achieve femininity (2.17). However, it is important to note that for the hetero-cis subsample, the top three items were within .01 points of one another and include both sex act-related stigma items and stigma toward trans women's femininity. Similarly, for the LGBTQ subsample, most items in the sex act-related stigma area were also relatively high. Thus, overall, the driving forces behind the stigmatization of trans women are associated with sex act-related stigma and trans women's achievement of femininity (recall Figure 7.3).

## NCST, Hetero-cis-normativity, Social Power Axes, and the Trans Women Stigma Scale

The first set of regression models examine the Trans Women Stigma Scale using NCST. The hypotheses are as follows:

- *Hypothesis 1a*: there is a significant positive relationship between the HCN Scale and the Trans Women Stigma Scale.

- *Hypothesis 1b*: there are significant relationships between individual social power axes (gender identity, sexual identity, additional gender/sexuality, racial/ethnic identity, basic needs) and the Trans Women Stigma Scale.
- *Hypothesis 2a*: the relationship between the HCN Scale and the Trans Women Stigma Scale is moderated by interactions between the HCN Scale and axes of social power.
- *Hypothesis 2b*: the relationships between individual social power axes and the Trans Women Stigma Scale are moderated by interactions between axes of social power.

Figure 12.2 outlines these relationships and the two models of NCST to be estimated. Specifically, OLS regression is utilized in Table 12.2 to examine NCST and the relationships among hetero-cis-normativity, axes of social power (gender, sexuality, additional gender/sexuality, race/ethnicity, and basic needs), and

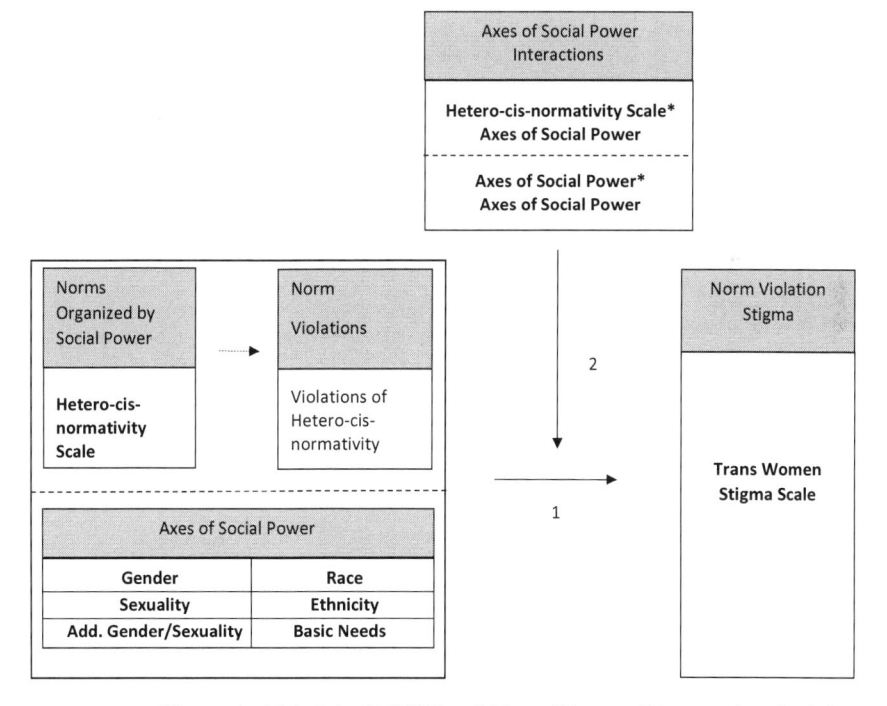

**FIGURE 12.2** Theoretical Model of NCST and Trans Women Stigma using the Stigmatizer Lens with Model Numbers to be Examined in Table 12.2

*Notes:* Model 1 estimates the HCN Scale and axes of social power (gender, sexuality, additional gender/sexuality, race, ethnicity, and basic needs) as they relate to the Trans Women Stigma Scale. Model 2 estimates interactions among axes of social power and the HCN Scale as they moderate the relationships between the HCN Scale and the Trans Women Stigma Scale as well as interactions among axes of social power as they moderate the relationships between the HCN Scale and the Trans Women Stigma Scale. The * indicates an interaction.

the Trans Women Stigma Scale for the hetero-cis subsample and the LGBTQ subsample. See Chapter 7 for a more complete description of the models. Regarding model fit statistics, the adjusted $R^2$ values ranged from .68 to .70.

## NCST, HCN, Social Power Axes, and the Trans Women Stigma Scale: Model 1

In Table 12.2 Model 1, the relationships between the HCN Scale, axes of social power, and the Trans Women Stigma Scale are estimated. For both groups, the HCN Scale is positively related to the Trans Women Stigma Scale in Model 1 alongside the inclusion of established common explanations and sociodemographics as controls. Thus, *Hypothesis 1a* is well supported: hetero-cis-normativity is strongly and positively related to the stigmatization of trans women for both subsamples. Individual axes of social power are also significantly related to the Trans Women Stigma Scale for the hetero-cis subsample (cis woman) and for the LGBTQ subsample (cis woman, queer, few needs met), supporting *Hypothesis 1b*.

**TABLE 12.2** OLS Regression Results Estimating NCST and the Trans Women Stigma Scale for the Hetero-cis Subsample (n = 1,500) and the LGBTQ Subsample (n = 1,604)

|  | Hetero-cis Subsample | | LGBTQ Subsample | | Test of Difference |
|---|---|---|---|---|---|
|  | Model 1 | Model 2 | Model 1 | Model 2 |  |
| HCN Scale | .87* | .84* | .92* | .67* | . |
| *Gender identity* | | | | | |
| Cis woman | -1.36* | . | -1.10* | . | |
| *Additional sexual/gender identity* | | | | | |
| Queer | . | . | -1.25* | . | |
| SGL | . | . | . | -5.20* | ** |
| *Racial/ethnic identity* | | | | | |
| African American/Black | . | . | . | 15.35* | . |
| *Basic needs* | | | | | |
| Few needs met | . | . | 1.57* | . | |
| *HCN Scale\*social power axes interactions* | | | | | |
| HCN Scale\*butch | — | . | — | -.28* | . |
| HCN Scale\*African American/Black | — | -.20* | — | . | . |
| HCN Scale\*Asian American/Pacific Islander | — | -.21* | — | . | . |
| HCN Scale\*mostly all I need | — | .12* | — | .25* | . |
| HCN Scale\*few needs met | — | .31* | — | . | . |

(*Continued*)

**TABLE 12.2** (Cont.)

|  | Hetero-cis Subsample | | LGBTQ Subsample | | Test of Difference |
|---|---|---|---|---|---|
|  | Model 1 | Model 2 | Model 1 | Model 2 |  |
| *Social power axes interactions* | | | | | |
| Gay/lesbian*SGL | — | — | — | 3.50* | |
| Bisexual*SGL | — | — | — | 3.53* | |
| Gay/lesbian*often needs not met | — | — | — | -6.37* | |
| African American/Black*Two-Spirit | — | . | — | -8.19* | ** |
| Queer*often needs not met | — | . | — | 4.30* | . |
| *Controls: common explanations* | | | | | |
| *LGBTQ contact* | | | | | |
| Trans women friends | -1.40* | -1.42* | -1.09* | -1.07* | . |
| LGBTQ Friends Scale (w/o trans women) | -.52* | -.53* | -.17* | . | |
| *Religious identity* | | | | | |
| Protestant—evangelical | 1.49* | . | . | . | |
| *Political perspectives* | | | | | |
| Liberal—conservative | .88* | .82* | . | . | |
| Openness to new experiences | -1.23* | -.95* | -1.57* | -1.56* | . |
| *Support laws/policies helping:* | | | | | |
| Those in poverty | -1.33* | -1.24* | . | . | |
| Racial/ethnic minorities | . | . | -1.49* | -1.29* | . |
| Non-Christians | . | . | . | -1.05* | . |
| *Beliefs about gender* | | | | | |
| Feminist | -.82* | . | -1.20* | -1.11* | . |
| Patriarchal Gender Norms Scale | .50* | .49* | .63* | .65* | . |
| *Sociodemographic controls* | | | | | |
| Outside U.S. | . | . | 2.39* | 2.76* | . |
| Education | . | . | .31* | . | |
| Adjusted $R^2$ | .68 | .68 | .69 | .70 | |
| Mean VIF | 1.51 | 1.51 | 1.93 | 1.93 | |

*Notes:* unstandardized regression coefficients are presented. Only the rows with significant results are displayed here. See Table 12.1 for detailed information about the Trans Women Stigma Scale. See Tables 7.1 and 7.2 for details about all other variables and Appendix B Table B.1 for details about the interaction effects.

* $p < .05$; a dot (.) indicates non-statistically significant results. A dash (—) indicates this was not included in the model.

** $p < .05$ for Clogg et al.'s (1995) test of equality of regression coefficients comparing Model 2 for the hetero-cis subsample and Model 2 for the LGBTQ subsample.

## NCST, HCN, Social Power Axes, and the Trans Women Stigma Scale: Model 2

In Model 2, intersections among axes of social power and the HCN Scale as well as interaction effects among axes of social power are examined. The HCN Scale is positively related to the Trans Women Stigma Scale in Model 2 for both groups. Moving to the HCN Scale interaction terms, there are both positive and negative findings. Two are discussed in Chapter 7: the interaction between the HCN Scale and being African American/Black and the HCN Scale and mostly all I need. Among the hetero-cis subsample, there are two more significant interaction terms. First, there is a negative relationship between the HCN Scale and being Asian American/Pacific Islander such that higher levels of agreement with the HCN Scale have a more robust impact on non-Asian American/Pacific Islander hetero-cis individuals' attitudes toward trans women as compared to Asian American/Pacific Islander hetero-cis individuals' attitudes toward trans women. Second, there is a positive relationship between the HCN Scale and indicating "few needs met" such that higher levels of agreement with the HCN Scale have a more robust impact on attitudes toward trans women among hetero-cis individuals who do not have their basic needs met as compared to hetero-cis individuals who have everything they need and more. Such results contribute to the existing work that highlights how Asian American/Pacific Islander identity and basic needs experiences shape LGBTQ attitudes (Battle, Pastrana, and Harris 2017; Han, Proctor, and Choi 2014) and suggest that opting into hetero-cis-normative thinking relates to attitudes toward trans women in ways that intersect with race/ethnicity and class.

For the LGBTQ subsample, there is also a significant negative relationship between the HCN Scale and being butch whereby higher levels of agreement with the HCN Scale have a more robust impact on non-butch LGBTQ individuals' attitudes toward trans women as compared to butch LGBTQ individuals' attitudes toward trans women. As suggested in some previous work (Bailey et al. 1997; Blair and Hoskin 2015; Johns et al. 2012), being butch can inform perspectives and experiences, especially as related to gender and sexuality. These findings demonstrate the importance of exploring intersectional experiences with butch identity as they impact attitudes toward trans women. Overall, *Hypothesis 2a* is supported: interactions between the HCN Scale and axes of social power moderate the relationship between the HCN Scale and the Trans Women Stigma Scale for both subsamples.

Moving to the rest of the findings, Table 12.2 follows a consistent pattern found in previous chapters: axes of social power shape trans women stigmatization in very different ways for the hetero-cis and LGBTQ subsamples. In fact, no individual social power axes or interactions among the axes of social power are statistically significantly related to the Trans Women Stigma Scale for the hetero-cis subsample. In contrast, there are several significant axes of social power found among the LGBTQ subsample. Specifically, being SGL is negatively related to the stigmatization of trans women for the LGBTQ subsample (though two associated interaction terms are positively related to the Trans Women Stigma Scale: being gay/lesbian and SGL; being bisexual and SGL). In addition, being African American/Black is positively related to the stigmatization of trans women for the LGBTQ subsample (though a corresponding interaction term is negatively related to the Trans Women Stigma Scale: being African American/Black and Two-Spirit). These findings are among the consistent trends discussed in Chapter 7.

There are also two significant interaction terms related to not having one's basic needs met that work in opposite directions: being gay/lesbian and indicating "often needs not met" is negatively related to the stigmatization of trans women while being queer and indicating "often needs not met" is positively related to the stigmatization of trans women. These findings suggest that various intersecting experiences with basic needs, class, and sexual identities contribute to different attitudes toward trans women, as other research has demonstrated (Serano 2007; Worthen 2013, 2016). It may be that gay/lesbian individuals who struggle with their basic needs are well situated to understanding the difficulties that trans women face due to their own experiences with marginalization.

Overall, there are many more significant social power axes among the LGBTQ subsample in comparison to the hetero-cis subsample in Model 2. Additional tests to compare the regression coefficients of the two subsamples reveal some significant differences, though not many (Clogg, Petkova, and Haritou 1995). Even so, these findings suggest that the axes of social power that impact trans women stigmatization may differ for the hetero-cis and LGBTQ subsamples. However, *Hypothesis 2b* is only partially supported: interactions between axes of social power moderate the relationship between the individual axes of social power and the Trans Women Stigma Scale for the LGBTQ subsample (only).

## Summarizing NCST, HCN, Social Power Axes, and the Trans Women Stigma Scale

In sum, the findings in Table 12.2 demonstrate that the stigmatization of trans women works differently for hetero-cis and LGBTQ people. In particular, axes of social power relate to LGBTQ people's attitudes toward trans women in multifaceted, intersecting ways. In contrast, other than interactions with the HCN Scale, social power axes explain less about hetero-cis people's attitudes toward trans women. By centering the importance of hetero-cis-normativity and utilizing NCST to explore the Trans Women Stigma Scale, the mechanisms that shape both negativity and support of trans women are highlighted.

## Trans Women's Experiences

### The Trans Women Subsample

The recruitment of trans women to participate in this study was anticipated to be difficult and the requested quota (n = 100) from Survey Sampling International was not met. The study sample included only 74 trans women (learn more about the data and sampling procedures in Chapter 7 and Appendix A). At the beginning of the survey, respondents were asked "What best describes your gender?" Trans women were those who selected "I am transgender: I identify as a woman and my assigned sex at birth was male." See Table 12.3 for more details about the trans women in this study.

**TABLE 12.3** Trans Women Characteristics (n = 74)

|  | % | n |
|---|---|---|
| *Sexual identity* | | |
| Heterosexual/straight* | 27.0% | 20 |
| Gay/lesbian* | 20.3% | 15 |
| Bisexual** | 37.8% | 28 |
| Pansexual* | 12.2% | 9 |
| Asexual* | 2.7% | 2 |
| *Additional Gender/Sexual Identity* | | |
| Queer | 5.4% | 4 |
| SGL | 18.9% | 14 |
| Two-Spirit | 17.6% | 13 |
| Butch | 18.9% | 14 |
| Femme | 25.7% | 19 |
| Leather | 1.4% | 1 |
| Bear | 2.7% | 2 |
| Twink | 8.1% | 6 |
| Down Low | 4.1% | 3 |
| *Race/ethnicity* | | |
| Caucasian/White** | 56.8% | 42 |
| African American/Black* | 21.6% | 16 |
| Asian American/Pacific Islander* | 16.2% | 12 |
| Native American/Alaskan Native* | 1.4% | 1 |
| Multi-racial* | 1.4% | 1 |
| Other race* | 1.4% | 1 |
| Latinx race* | 1.4% | 1 |
| Latinx ethnicity | 24.7% | 19 |

(*Continued*)

**TABLE 12.3** (Cont.)

|  | % | n |
|---|---|---|
| *Basic needs* | | |
| Everything I need * | 21.6% | 16 |
| Mostly all I need** | 43.2% | 32 |
| Often needs not met* | 28.4% | 21 |
| Few needs met * | 6.8% | 5 |

\* Reference category in analyses in Table 12.5.
\*\* Included in analyses shown in Table 12.5.

## Trans Women's Experiences with Gender- and Sexuality-Based Discrimination, Harassment, and Violence

Studies show that trans women are at high risk for both gender- and sexuality-based stigmatizing experiences in the form of discrimination, harassment, and violence (Greenberg 2012; James et al. 2016; Matsuzaka and Koch 2019; Meyer 2015; Perry and Dyck 2014; Prunas et al. 2018; Schilt and Westbrook 2009; Whitfield et al. 2018). For example, the U.S. Transgender Survey with more than 9,000 trans women respondents found that about 1 in 5 (18%) trans women have lost a job due to their transgender identity, between about 1 in 16 (White) and 1 in 5 (American Indian) trans women were physically attacked in public by a stranger in the past year, many experience intimate partner violence (ranging from 28% among Asian trans women to 57% among American Indian trans women), and more than 1 in 3 (37%) have been sexually assaulted in their lifetimes (James et al. 2016). In addition, the U.S. Human Rights Campaign reports that trans women are at extreme risk for homicide, with nearly 4 out of 5 anti-transgender murder victims being trans women of color (Human Rights Campaign 2018).

As seen in Figure 12.3, about 6 in 10 (61%) trans women have had one or more experiences of sexuality-based DHV and about one-third (32%) have had one or more experiences of gender-based DHV. Sexuality-based discrimination is the most common form (45%) while gender-based violence is the least common (16%). To better understand trans women's gender- and sexuality-based DHV, trans women's experiences were compared to the LGBTQ subsample and the women subsample using *t*-tests. As seen in Table 12.4, as compared to the women subsample, trans women are significantly more likely to experience sexuality-based discrimination and harassment but less likely to experience gender-based harassment. In addition, in comparison to all LGBTQ people and all women, trans women report significantly more experiences with sexuality-based violence. Thus, trans women are at particular risk for sexuality-based DHV but not gender-based DHV and this is especially true for sexuality-based violence.

■ Gender-Based   ▨ Sexuality-Based

```
                                                                61%
        45%
                    39%
32%                                                     32%
            19%              31%
                    16%
```
DISCRIMINATION    HARASSMENT    VIOLENCE    ANY DHV EXPERIENCE
                                                   (0/1)

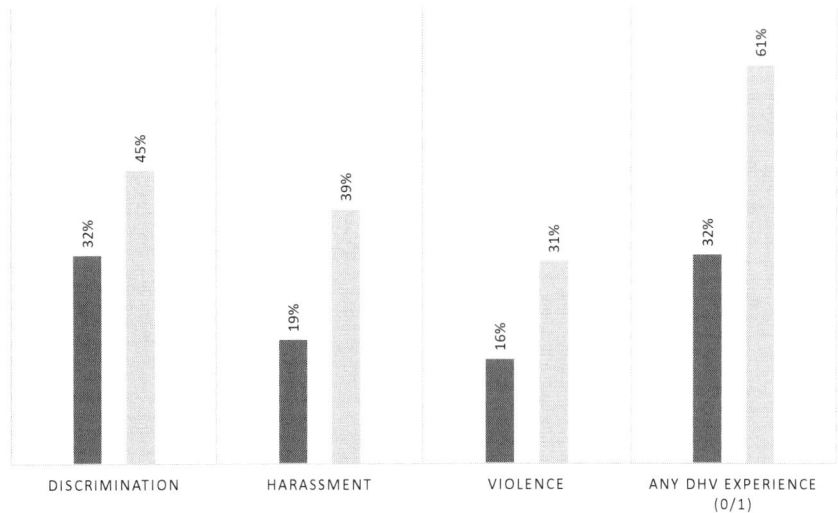

**FIGURE 12.3** Trans Women's (n = 74) Experiences with Gender- and Sexuality-Based DHV

*Note:* see Table 12.4 for comparisons of trans women's experiences to the LGBTQ subsample and the women subsample.

**TABLE 12.4** Gender- and Sexuality-Based DHV Mean Values (Standard Deviations) among Trans Women, the LGBTQ Subsample, and the Women Subsample with *t*-test Results

|  | Trans Women | LGBTQ Subsample | Women Subsample |
|---|---|---|---|
| n | 74 | 1604 | 1535 |
| *Gender-based* | | | |
| Discrimination | .28 (.45) | .32 (.47) | .36 (.48) |
| Harassment | .19 (.39)* | .28 (.45) | .34 (.47) |
| Violence | .16 (.37) | .14 (.34) | .16 (.37) |
| Any gender DHV experience (0/1) | .32 (.47)* | .40 (.49) | .46 (.50) |
| *Sexuality-based* | | | |
| Discrimination | .45 (.50)* | .44 (.50) | .26 (.44) |
| Harassment | .39 (.49)* | .41 (.49) | .23 (.42) |
| Violence | .31 (.47)*** | .20 (.40) | .10 (.31) |
| Any sexuality DHV experience (0/1) | .61 (.49)* | .53 (.50) | .32 (.47) |

* Trans women are significantly different from the women subsample (only) at p < .05 level.

*** Trans women are significantly different from both the LGBTQ and women subsamples at p < .05 level.

## NCST and Trans Women's Experiences with Gender- and Sexuality-Based Discrimination, Harassment, and Violence

The second set of regression models examines trans women and their experiences with gender- and sexuality-based DHV using NCST with special attention to trans women's axes of social power. The hypotheses are as follows:

- *Hypothesis 1*: being a trans woman (violating hetero-cis-normativity) increases the likelihood of experiencing gender- and sexuality-based DHV (trans woman stigma).
- *Hypothesis 2*: the relationship between being a trans woman and gender- and sexuality-based DHV is moderated by interactions among being a trans woman and axes of social power.

Figure 12.4 outlines these relationships and Table 12.5 displays logistic regression results that examine NCST and the relationships among being a trans woman, intersections among trans women's axes of social power, and any experiences of gender-based DHV (dichotomized as 0/1) or sexuality-based DHV (dichotomized as 0/1) utilizing the LGBTQ subsample (n = 1,604; whereby being a trans woman is compared to all other LGBTQ people). Because trans women's

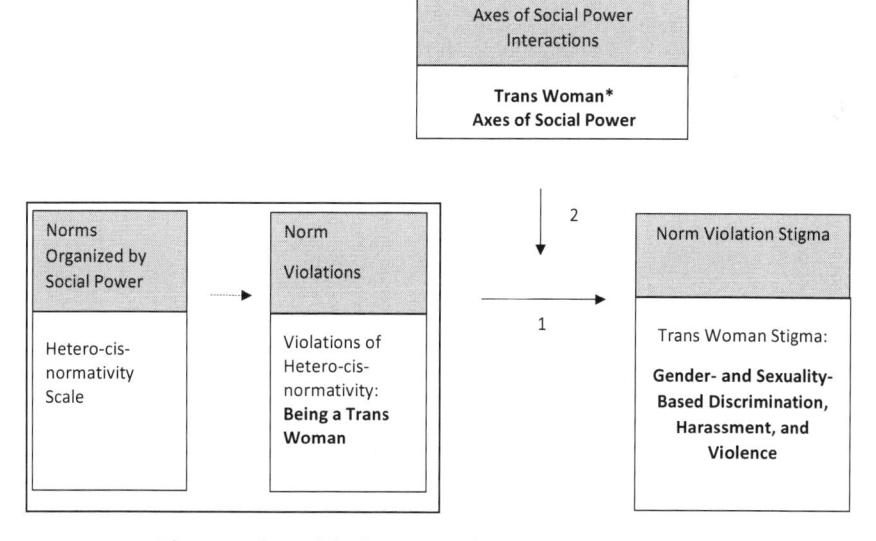

**FIGURE 12.4** Theoretical Model of NCST and Trans Women Stigma using the Stigmatized Lens with Model Numbers to be Examined in Table 12.5

*Notes*: Model 1 estimates being a trans woman as related to gender- and sexuality-based discrimination, harassment, and violence. Model 2 estimates interactions among trans women's axes of social power as they moderate the relationships between being a trans woman and gender- and sexuality-based discrimination, harassment, and violence. The * indicates an interaction.

experiences are the focus of this exploration (i.e., the stigmatized lens of NCST is being utilized), the trans woman and social power axes interaction terms are listed at the top of the table and are the focus of the discussion below. However, there are significant corresponding individual effects related to being White (for example) that are important to recognize. It is also important to note that "woman" was not included in the individual social power axes because the associated gender categories for this study are "trans woman" (which is already included in the interaction effects) or "cis woman" (which does not pertain to this table's focus on trans women). See Chapter 7 for a more complete description of the models and a discussion of overarching trends and patterns. Regarding model fit statistics, the pseudo $R^2$ values were extremely low and ranged from .05 to .06.

## NCST, Trans Women, and Gender- and Sexuality-Based DHV: Model 1

Both Model 1s in Table 12.5 estimate the relationships between violations of hetero-cis-normativity conceptualized as being a trans woman and the stigmatization of trans women conceptualized as gender- and sexuality-based DHV along with sociodemographic controls. Surprisingly, findings show that being a trans woman is not significantly related to gender- or sexuality-based DHV. These results are in direct contrast to past research that demonstrates that trans women are at a high risk for DHV (Human Rights Campaign 2018; James et al. 2016; Schilt and Westbrook 2009). It is important to recall, however, that the comparison group for these models is other

**TABLE 12.5** Logistic Regression Results with Odds Ratios and (Standard Errors) Estimating NCST and Gender- and Sexuality-Based DHV as Related to Being a Trans Woman for the LGBTQ Subsample (n = 1,604)

|  | Gender-Based DHV |  |  |  | Sexuality-Based DHV |  |  |  |
|---|---|---|---|---|---|---|---|---|
|  | Model 1 |  | Model 2 |  | Model 1 |  | Model 2 |  |
|  | OR | SE | OR | SE | OR | SE | OR | SE |
| Trans woman | . | . | . | . | . | . | . | . |
| *Trans woman social power axes interactions* |  |  |  |  |  |  |  |  |
| Trans woman*bisexual | — | — | . | . | — | — | . | . |
| Trans woman*White | — | — | . | . | — | — | .34* | (.18) |
| Trans woman*mostly all I need | — | — | . | . | — | — | . | . |

*(Continued)*

**TABLE 12.5** (Cont.)

|  | Gender-Based DHV || || Sexuality-Based DHV || ||
| | Model 1 || Model 2 || Model 1 || Model 2 ||
| | OR | SE | OR | SE | OR | SE | OR | SE |
|---|---|---|---|---|---|---|---|---|
| *Trans woman social power axes* | | | | | | | | |
|   Trans | . | . | . | . | . | . | . | . |
|   Bisexual | . | . | . | . | .35* | (.04) | . | . |
|   White | . | . | . | . | . | . | 3.41* | (1.76) |
|   Mostly all I need | . | . | . | . | . | . | . | . |
| *Socio-demographic controls* | | | | | | | | |
|   Age | .96* | (.00) | .96* | (.00) | .98* | (.00) | .98* | (.00) |
|   Town type (rural–large city) | . | . | . | . | . | . | . | . |
|   Education | 1.15* | (.05) | 1.15* | (.05) | 1.10* | (.04) | 1.09* | (.04) |
|   Income | . | . | . | . | . | . | . | . |
|     Pseudo $R^2$ | .05 | | .05 | | .06 | | .06 | |
|     Mean VIF | 1.33 | | 1.33 | | 1.34 | | 1.34 | |

*Notes:* all rows are displayed, including those without significant results. See Table 12.3 for more details about trans women.
* $p < .05$; a dot (.) indicates non-statistically significant results. A dash (—) indicates this was not included in the model.

LGBTQ people. Thus, although trans women endure high rates of DHV, being a trans woman (when compared to other LGBTQ people) does not appear to have a direct relationship to the likelihood of experiencing DHV. Overall, *Hypothesis 1* is not supported: being a trans woman is not related to gender- or sexuality-based DHV.

## *NCST, Trans Women, and Gender- and Sexuality-Based DHV: Model 2*

Intersections among axes of social power and being a trans woman are included in Model 2 as they relate to gender- and sexuality-based DHV. Being a trans woman remains statistically non-significantly related to the likelihood of gender- and sexuality-based DHV in Model 2 as seen in Model 1. While there are no significant interaction terms for gender-based DHV among trans women, being a White trans woman decreases the likelihood of sexuality-based DHV by .66. As others have found (Human Rights Campaign 2018; James et al. 2016; Matsuzaka and Koch 2019; Meyer 2015; Schilt and Westbrook 2009), trans women of color endure an especially high risk of DHV. The findings here support this previous work and demonstrate ways racial/ethnic and trans women's indentities intersect to shape their victimization experiences. Overall, *Hypothesis 2* is supported in the sexuality-based DHV models but not in the gender-based DHV models.

## Summarizing NCST, Trans Women, and Gender- and Sexuality-Based DHV

In sum, the findings in Table 12.5 indicate that being a trans woman does not have significant effects on the likelihood of experiencing gender-based DHV. However, the intersecting experiences of being a White trans woman decrease the likelihood of experiencing sexuality-based DHV. Although there are very few significant findings among this small group of trans women (n = 74) and the pseudo $R^2$ values are quite low, by highlighting trans women's identities and social power axes, these results show that there are likely other important factors shaping trans women's DHV experiences (e.g., presentation of femininity). Overall, the use of NCST to explore trans women's gender- and sexuality-based DHV demonstrates that these experiences may not have a direct relationship to being a trans woman, especially in comparison to other LGBTQ people.

## Summary of Patterns of Trans Women Stigma

In line with the three tenets and hypotheses derived from NCST, there are six patterns related to the stigmatization of trans women reviewed in this chapter:

1. Sex-act related stigma is a driving force in the stigmatization of trans women for both hetero-cis and LGBTQ people; however, discomfort with trans women's sex acts with both women and men are most concerning for hetero-cis people while the stigmatizing beliefs that trans women are too hypersexual and unfaithful are most concerning for LGBTQ people.
2. For both hetero-cis and LGBTQ people, there is strong support for the stigmatizing belief that trans women are not feminine enough.
3. Hetero-cis-normativity is positively related to trans women stigma for both subsamples; however, the interaction effects between the HCN Scale and social power axes that moderate these relationships differ for the hetero-cis and LGBTQ subsamples. In addition, there are more significant interaction effects between the HCN Scale and social power axes for the hetero-cis subsample than there are for the LGBTQ subsample.
4. Individual social power axes are significantly related to trans women stigma for both subsamples in Model 1 but are only significant for the LGBTQ subsample in Model 2. In addition, the interaction effects between the social power axes only moderate these relationships for the LGBTQ subsample.

5. Trans women experience high levels of sexuality-based DHV in comparison to the all women subsample and are significantly more likely to experience sexuality-based violence than both the LGBTQ and women subsamples; however, trans women are less likely than both subsamples to experience gender-based DHV.
6. Being a trans woman is not significantly related to the likelihood of gender-based DHV; however, being a White trans woman decreases the likelihood of sexuality-based DHV.

## Notes

1 Born Malcolm Michaels, Jr. on August 24, 1945, in Elizabeth, New Jersey, Marsha P. Johnson moved to New York City in the mid-1960s. She faced many hardships as an African American trans woman and even lived on the streets until she broke into the nightclub scene and became a prominent New York City drag queen. An eccentric woman known for her outlandish hats and glamorous jewelry, she was fearless and bold. Whenever she was asked what the 'P' in her name stood for and when people pried about her gender or sexuality, she quipped back with 'Pay it No Mind.' Her forthright nature and enduring strength led her to speak out against the injustices she saw at Stonewall in 1969. Following the events at Stonewall, Johnson and her friend Sylvia Rivera co-founded the Street Transvestite Action Revolutionaries (STAR) and they became fixtures in the community, especially in their commitment to helping homeless transgender youth in New York City. Sadly, at the age of 46, on July 6, 1992, her body was found floating in the Hudson River off the West Village Piers. The police initially ruled her death a suicide despite claims from her friends and other members of the local community that she was not suicidal. Twenty-five years later, crime victim advocate Victoria Cruz of the New York City Anti-Violence Project (AVP) re-opened this investigation (Worthen 2017). On the 50th anniversary of the Stonewall uprising in June 2019, Johnson was one of fifty inaugural activists inducted into the National LGBTQ Wall of Honor located in the Stonewall Inn (National LGBTQ Task Force 2019).
2 Sylvia Rivera was born on July 2, 1951, in the Bronx, New York. Her Venezuelan grandmother raised her but never fully accepted her for who she was. Experiencing emotional rejection and physical abuse led Rivera to run away from home at the age of 10. She met a group of drag queens while living on the streets of New York City who helped her recognize her identity as Sylvia. In 1969, along with her friend Marsha P. Johnson, Rivera participated in the Stonewall Uprising and co-founded the Street Transvestite Action Revolutionaries (STAR). Rivera left her life of activism for a few decades, feeling her voice was not well represented, but later returned in the mid-1990s to continue to fight for trans rights. On February 19, 2002, Rivera passed away after suffering complications from liver cancer. Like her friend Johnson, Rivera was one of fifty inaugural activists inducted into the National LGBTQ Wall of Honor located in the Stonewall Inn on the 50th anniversary of the Stonewall Uprising in June 2019 (National LGBTQ Task Force 2019).

## References

Adam, Seth and Matt Goodman. 2015. "Number of Americans Who Report Knowing a Transgender Person Doubles in Seven Years, according to New GLAAD Survey." *GLAAD*. Retrieved June 12, 2019 (www.glaad.org/releases/number-americans-who-report-knowing-transgender-person-doubles-seven-years-according-new).

Alegría, Christine. 2018. "Supporting Families of Transgender Children/Youth: Parents Speak on Their Experiences, Identity, and Views." *International Journal of Transgenderism* 19(2):132–143.

Allen, Mariette Pathy. 2007. "Momentum: A Photo Essay of the Transgender Community in the United States over 30 Years, 1978–2007." *Sexuality Research and Social Policy* 4(4):92–105.

Arayasirikul, Sean and Erin C. Wilson. 2019. "Spilling the T on Trans-Misogyny and Microaggressions: An Intersectional Oppression and Social Process among Trans Women." *Journal of Homosexuality* 66(10): 1415-1438.

Bailey, Michael, Peggy Kim, Alex Hills, and Joan Linsenmeier. 1997. "Butch, Femme, or Straight Acting? Partner Preferences of Gay Men and Lesbians." *Journal of Personality & Social Psychology* 73(5):960–973.

Balay, Anne. 2014. *Steel Closets: Voices of Gay, Lesbian, and Transgender Steelworkers*. Chapel Hill, NC: University of North Carolina Press.

Barrett, Donald C. and Lance M. Pollack. 2005. "Whose Gay Community? Social Class, Sexual Self-Expression, and Gay Community Involvement." *The Sociological Quarterly* 46(3):437–456.

Battle, Juan, Antonio Pastrana, and Angelique Harris. 2017. *An Examination of Asian and Pacific Islander LGBT Populations across the United States*. New York, NY: Palgrave Macmillan.

Beachum, Lateshia. 2019. "Transgender Political Candidates Are Increasingly Common. The Money Backing Them Is Not." *Center for Public Integrity*. Retrieved June 19, 2019 (https://publicintegrity.org/federal-politics/elections/transgender-political-candidates-are-increasingly-common-the-money-backing-them-is-not/).

Blair, Karen L. and Rhea Ashley Hoskin. 2015. "Experiences of Femme Identity: Coming Out, Invisibility and Femmephobia." *Psychology & Sexuality* 6(3):229–244.

Brown, Anna. 2017. "Transgender Issues Sharply Divide Republicans, Democrats." *Pew Research Center*. Retrieved June 26, 2019 (www.pewresearch.org/fact-tank/2017/11/08/transgender-issues-divide-republicans-and-democrats/).

Clogg, Clifford C., Eva Petkova and Adamantios Haritou. 1995. "Statistical Methods for Comparing Regression Coefficients between Models." *American Journal of Sociology* 100(5):1261–1293.

Dawson, Fiona. 2016. "In a First, Openly Transgender Service Member Promoted." *NBC News*, September 15. Retrieved January 30, 2020 (https://www.nbcnews.com/feature/nbc-out/first-openly-transgender-service-member-promoted-n648366).

Dowsett, Gilbert. 2009. "The 'Gay Plague' Revisited: AIDS and Its Enduring Moral Panic." Pp. 130–156 in *Moral Panics, Sex Panics: Fear and the Fight over Sexual Rights*, edited by Gilbert Herdt. New York, NY: NYU Press.

Dowshen, Nadia, Susan Lee, Joshua Franklin, Marné Castillo, and Frances Barg. 2017. "Access to Medical and Mental Health Services across the HIV Care Continuum among Young Transgender Women: A Qualitative Study." *Transgender Health* 2(1):81–90.

Elders, M. Joycelyn, George R. Brown, Eli Coleman, Thomas A. Kolditz, and Alan M. Steinman. 2015. "Medical Aspects of Transgender Military Service." *Armed Forces & Society* 41(2):199–220.

Gates, Gary J. and Jody Herman. 2014. *Transgender Military Service in the United States*. Los Angeles, CA: The Williams Institute.

Greenberg, Kae. 2012. "Still Hidden in the Closet: Trans Women and Domestic Violence." *Berkeley Journal of Gender, Law & Justice* 27(2):198–251.

Grossman, Arnold H., Anthony R. D'Augelli, Tamika Jarrett Howell, and Steven Hubbard. 2005. "Parents' Reactions to Transgender Youths' Gender Nonconforming Expression and Identity." *Journal of Gay & Lesbian Social Services* 18(1):3–16.

Haines, Beth A., Alex A. Ajayi and Helen Boyd. 2014. "Making Trans Parents Visible: Intersectionality of Trans and Parenting Identities." *Feminism & Psychology* 24(2):238–247.

Han, Chong-Suk, Kristopher Proctor and Kyung-Hee Choi. 2014. "We Pretend like Sexuality Doesn't Exist: Managing Homophobia in Gaysian America." *The Journal of Men's Studies* 22(1):53–63.

Herek, Gregory M. and John Capitanio. 1999. "AIDS Stigma and Sexual Prejudice." *American Behavioral Scientist* 42(7):1130–1147.

Hicks, Stephen. 2013. "Lesbian, Gay, Bisexual, and Transgender Parents and the Question of Gender." Pp. 149–162 in *LGBT-Parent Families: Innovations in Research and Implications for Practice*, edited by A. E. Goldberg and K. R. Allen. New York: Springer New York.

Hill, Darryl B. and Edgardo Menvielle. 2009. "'You Have to Give Them a Place Where They Feel Protected and Safe and Loved': The Views of Parents Who Have Gender-Variant Children and Adolescents." *Journal of LGBT Youth* 6(2/3):243–271.

Hines, Sally. 2007. *TransForming Gender: Transgender Practices of Identity, Intimacy and Care*. Bristol, England: Bristol University Press.

Human Rights Campaign. 2018. *Dismantling a Culture of Violence: Understanding Anti-Transgender Violence and Ending the Crisis*. Washington, D.C.: Human Rights Campaign Foundation.

James, Sandy, Jody L. Herman, Sue Rankin, Mara Keisling, Lisa Mottet, and Anafi Ma'ayan. 2016. *The Report of the 2015 U.S. Transgender Survey*. Washington, D.C.: National Center for Transgender Equality.

Johns, Michelle Marie, Emily Pingel, Anna Eisenberg, Matthew Leslie Santana, and José Bauermeister. 2012. "Butch Tops and Femme Bottoms? Sexual Positioning, Sexual Decision Making, and Gender Roles among Young Gay Men." *American Journal of Men's Health* 6(6):505–518.

Krüsi, Andrea, Thomas Kerr, Christina Taylor, Tim Rhodes, and Kate Shannon. 2016. "'They Won't Change It Back in Their Heads That We're Trash': The Intersection of Sex Work-Related Stigma and Evolving Policing Strategies." *Sociology of Health & Illness* 38(7):1137–1150.

Matsuzaka, Sara and David E. Koch. 2019. "Trans Feminine Sexual Violence Experiences: The Intersection of Transphobia and Misogyny." *Affilia* 34(1):28–47.

McGuire, Jenifer K., Katherine A. Kuvalanka, Jory M. Catalpa, and Russell B. Toomey. 2016. "Transfamily Theory: How the Presence of Trans* Family Members Informs Gender Development in Families: Transfamily Theory." *Journal of Family Theory & Review* 8(1):60–73.

McKinnon, Rachel. 2014. "Stereotype Threat and Attributional Ambiguity for Trans Women." *Hypatia* 29(4):857–872.

McKirnan, David J., Joseph P. Stokes, Lynda Doll, and Rebecca G. Burzette. 1995. "Bisexually Active Men: Social Characteristics and Sexual Behavior." *Journal of Sex Research* 32(1):65–76.

Meyer, Doug. 2015. *Violence against Queer People: Race, Class, Gender, and the Persistence of Anti-LGBT Discrimination*. New Brunswick, NJ: Rutgers University Press.

Movement Advancement Project. 2019. "Foster and Adoption Laws." Retrieved June 12, 2019 (www.lgbtmap.org//equality-maps/foster_and_adoption_laws).

Munro, Lauren, Zack Marshall, Greta Bauer, Rebecca Hammond, Caleb Nault, and Robb Travers. 2017. "(Dis)integrated Care: Barriers to Health Care Utilization for Trans Women Living with HIV." *Journal of the Association of Nurses in AIDS Care* 28(5):708–722.

National LGBTQ Task Force. 2019. "National LGBTQ Wall of Honor Unveiled at Historic Stonewall Inn." *National LGBTQ Task Force*. Retrieved August 4, 2019 (www.thetaskforce.org/nationallgbtqwallofhonortobeunveiled/).

Perry, Barbara and D. Ryan Dyck. 2014. "'I Don't Know Where It Is Safe': Trans Women's Experiences of Violence." *Critical Criminology* 22(1):49–63.

Prunas, Antonio, Alessandra D. Elisa Bandini, Mario Maggi Fisher, Valeria Pace, Luca Quagliarella, Orlando Todarello, and Maurizio Bini. 2018. "Experiences of Discrimination, Harassment, and Violence in a Sample of Italian Transsexuals Who Have Undergone Sex-Reassignment Surgery." *Journal of Interpersonal Violence* 33(14):2225–2240.

Sausa, Lydia A., JoAnne Keatley and Don Operario. 2007. "Perceived Risks and Benefits of Sex Work among Transgender Women of Color in San Francisco." *Archives of Sexual Behavior* 36(6):768–777.

Schilt, Kristen and Laurel Westbrook. 2009. "Doing Gender, Doing Heteronormativity: 'gender Normals,' Transgender People, and the Social Maintenance of Heterosexuality." *Gender & Society* 23(4):440–464.

Serano, Julia. 2007. *Whipping Girl: A Transsexual Woman on Sexism and the Scapegoating of Femininity*. Berkeley, CA: Seal Press.

Sevelius, Jae M. 2013. "Gender Affirmation: A Framework for Conceptualizing Risk Behavior among Transgender Women of Color." *Sex Roles* 68(11):675–689.

Stein, Arlene. 1997. *Sex and Sensibility: Stories of a Lesbian Generation*. Berkeley, CA: University of California Press.

Stone, Amy L. 2009. "More than Adding a T: American Lesbian and Gay Activists' Attitudes Towards Transgender Inclusion." *Sexualities* 12(3):334–354.

Stryker, Susan. 2008. *Transgender History*. Berkeley, CA: Seal Press.

Tornello, Samantha L., Rachel G. Riskind, and Aleks Babić. 2019. "Transgender and Gender Non-Binary Parents' Pathways to Parenthood." *Psychology of Sexual Orientation and Gender Diversity* 6(2):232–241.

TransVeterans.org. n.d. "Transgender American Veterans Association." *Transgender American Veterans Association*. Retrieved August 21, 2019 (http://transveteran.org/).

Veldorale-Griffin Amanda and Carol Anderson Darling. 2016. "Adaptation to Parental Gender Transition: Stress and Resilience among Transgender Parents." *Archives of Sexual Behavior* 45(3):607–617.

Weiss, Jillian Todd. 2004. "GL vs. BT: The Archaeology of Biphobia and Transphobia within the US Gay and Lesbian Community." *Journal of Bisexuality* 3(3/4):25–55.

Whitfield, Darren L., W. S. Coulter Robert, Lisa Langenderfer-Magruder, and Daniel Jacobson. 2018. "Experiences of Intimate Partner Violence among Lesbian, Gay, Bisexual and Transgender College Students: The Intersection of Gender, Race, and Sexual Orientation." *Journal of Interpersonal Violence* DOI:088626051881207.

Williams, Cristan. 2016. "Radical Inclusion: Recounting the Trans Inclusive History of Radical Feminism." *TSQ: Transgender Studies Quarterly* 3(1/2):254–258.

Wodda, Aimee and Vanessa R. Panfil. 2014. "Don't Talk to Me about Deception: The Necessary Erosion of the Trans Panic Defense." *Albany Law Review*. 78:927–972.

Worthen, Meredith. 2017. "The Stonewall Inn: The People, Place and Lasting Significance of 'Where Pride Began.'" *Biography*. Retrieved August 20, 2019 (www.biography.com/news/stonewall-riots-history-leaders).
Worthen, Meredith G. F. 2013. "An Argument for Separate Analyses of Attitudes toward Lesbian, Gay, Bisexual Men, Bisexual Women, MtF and FtM Transgender Individuals." *Sex Roles* 68(11/12):703–723.
Worthen, Meredith G. F. 2016. "Hetero-cis–normativity and the Gendering of Transphobia." *International Journal of Transgenderism* 17(1):31–57.
Worthen, Meredith G. F. 2019. "Transgender under Fire: Hetero-cis–normativity and Military Students' Attitudes toward Trans Issues and Trans Service Members Post DADT." *Sexuality Research and Social Policy* 16(3):289–308.

# 13
# TRANS MEN STIGMA

*Restrooms have become bio-political battlegrounds attempting to bring order and equilibrium to what is maleness and what is femaleness...[we] must have sound policy...to help protect [transgender people].*

Watkins and Moreno (2017:169–170)

**IMAGE 13.1** Protesters hold signs at a rally against HB2 (otherwise known as the "bathroom bill" designed to exclude trans individuals from using public restrooms that best reflect their gender identities) on April 2, 2016 in Asheville, North Carolina.[1]

## The Stigmatization of Trans Men

In the survey instrument, the section focusing on attitudes toward transgender men was preceded by the following statement:

> *Next, we're interested in your thoughts, feelings, and predicted behaviors about transgender men (those who currently identify as men who were assigned 'female' at birth).*

### The Trans Men Stigma Scale

Trans men are the second most stigmatized among all nine groups examined in this book, just slightly less stigmatized than non-binary/genderqueer people. In addition, trans men are the most stigmatized group among all LGBTQ men (recall Figure 7.1). Though there are some overlaps between trans men's and trans women's experiences, the particular motivations shaping trans men's stigmatization are unique and complex. Figure 13.1 and Table 13.1 provide the mean values for the 14 items in the Trans Men Stigma Scale and are discussed below.

| Item | LGBTQ Subsample | Hetero-cis Subsample |
|---|---|---|
| Discomfort with Sex w/Man | 1.93 | 2.84 |
| Not Masculine Enough | 2.21 | 2.80 |
| Discomfort with Sex w/Woman | 1.95 | 2.79 |
| Restrict from Military | 1.97 | 2.73 |
| Too Sexual/Hypersexual | 2.09 | 2.71 |
| Not Vote for Political Candidate | 1.84 | 2.70 |
| Unfaithful | 2.06 | 2.64 |
| Identity is Just Temporary/Experimental | 1.97 | 2.62 |
| Responsible for HIV/AIDS | 1.88 | 2.61 |
| As Good Parents | 1.83 | 2.54 |
| As Family/Close Relative | 1.88 | 2.53 |
| As New Friends | 1.86 | 2.51 |
| Deny Basic Rights | 1.61 | 2.26 |
| Victimization is Not Upsetting to Me | 1.60 | 2.15 |

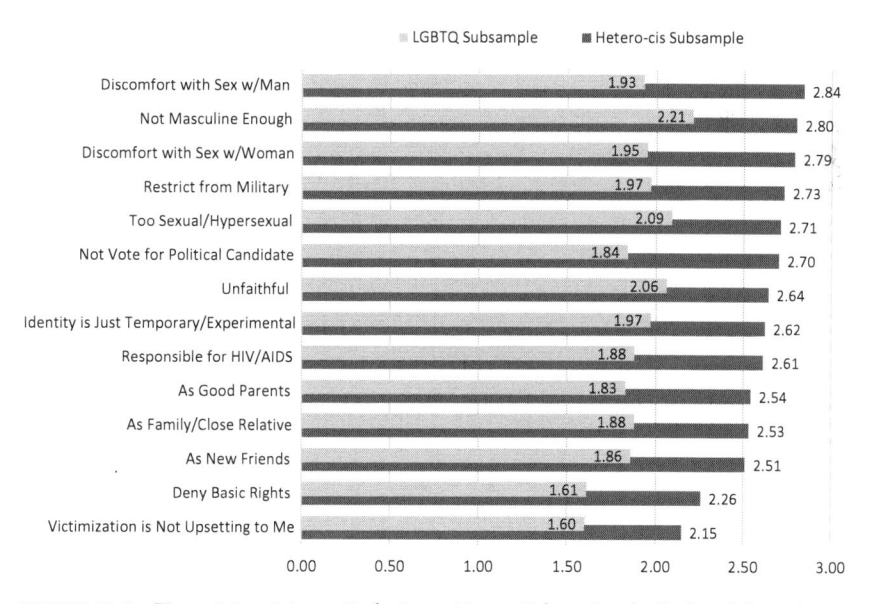

**FIGURE 13.1** Trans Men Stigma Scale Item Mean Values Rank-Ordered from Most to Least Stigmatizing for the Hetero-cis (n = 1,500) and the LGBTQ (n = 1,604) Subsamples

*Notes:* See Table 13.1 for the exact wording for each item. *t*-test results comparing the hetero-cis and LGBTQ subsamples indicate that all means are significantly different from one another at the p < .001 level.

**TABLE 13.1** Trans Men Stigma Scale Item Mean Values (Standard Deviations) and *t*-test Results Comparing the Means for the Hetero-cis Subsample and the LGBTQ Subsample

|  | Hetero-cis Subsample $n = 1,500$ | LGBTQ Subsample $n = 1,604$ | t-test Results |
|---|---|---|---|
| *Social and familial relationships* | | | |
| I welcome new friends who are trans men.[R] | 2.51 (1.25) | 1.86 (1.09) | $t = 15.37^*$ |
| I don't think it would negatively affect our relationship if I learned that one of my close relatives was a trans man.[R] | 2.53 (1.25) | 1.88 (1.14) | $t = 15.17^*$ |
| Trans men are not capable of being good parents. | 2.54 (1.29) | 1.83 (1.14) | $t = 16.08^*$ |
| *Positions of importance and social significance* | | | |
| I would not vote for a political candidate who was an openly trans man. | 2.70 (1.37) | 1.84 (1.22) | $t = 18.41^*$ |
| Trans men should not be allowed to join the military. | 2.73 (1.40) | 1.97 (1.32) | $t = 15.61^*$ |
| *Basic human rights* | | | |
| I believe trans men should have all of the same rights as other people do.[R] | 2.26 (1.19) | 1.61 (1.02) | $t = 16.30^*$ |
| It is upsetting to me that trans men experience violence, harassment, and discrimination just because they are trans men.[R] | 2.15 (1.15) | 1.60 (1.04) | $t = 13.77^*$ |
| *Sex act-related stigma* | | | |
| Trans men are unfaithful to their romantic partners. | 2.65 (1.11) | 2.06 (1.12) | $t = 14.47^*$ |
| Trans men are too sexual (hypersexual). | 2.71 (1.16) | 2.09 (1.13) | $t = 15.06^*$ |
| Trans men are mostly responsible for spreading HIV/AIDS. | 2.61 (1.20) | 1.88 (1.13) | $t = 17.42^*$ |
| I am comfortable with the thought of a trans man having sex with a man.[R] | 2.84 (1.24) | 1.93 (1.07) | $t = 21.67^*$ |
| I am comfortable with the thought of a trans man having sex with a woman.[R] | 2.79 (1.19) | 1.95 (1.07) | $t = 20.51^*$ |

*(Continued)*

**TABLE 13.1** (Cont.)

|  | Hetero-cis Subsample n = 1,500 | LGBTQ Subsample n = 1,604 | t-test Results |
|---|---|---|---|
| *Trans identity permanency* | | | |
| Most men who call themselves transgender are just temporarily experimenting with their gender. | 2.62 (1.17) | 1.97 (1.14) | $t = 15.52$* |
| *Achievement of masculinity* | | | |
| Trans men are not masculine enough. | 2.80 (1.15) | 2.21 (1.22) | $t = 13.92$* |
| α | .90 | .93 | |
| Summed scale actual range | 14-68 | 14-70 | |
| Summed scale mean | 36.42 (11.40) | 26.69 (11.37) | $t = 23.80$* |

* t-test results allowing for unequal variances indicate that the hetero-cis subsample and LGBTQ subsample means are significantly different from one another at the p < .001 level.
Notes: response options were Strongly Disagree–Strongly Agree (range: 1–5). [R] This item is reverse-coded.

## Trans Men and Social and Familial Relationships

Stigma associated with trans men when it comes to social and familial relationships is relatively low, though means are slightly above 2.50 for the hetero-cis subsample and are near 2.0 for the LGBTQ subsample (see Table 13.1). Yet these particular hostilities are not as extreme as those found in most other key areas of the Trans Men Stigma Scale. Indeed, research focusing on transgender friendship patterns finds that trans men are especially likely to have cisgender friends, even more so than trans women (Boyer and Galupo 2018). In addition, as noted in Chapter 12, there has been increasing visibility of trans individuals in social and familial networks according to recent polls with between 16% and 37% of Americans indicating that they know or work with a transgender person (Adam and Goodman 2015; Brown 2017). However, compared to trans acquaintances, friends, and coworkers, a smaller percentage indicate they have a trans family member (Brown 2017). These patterns likely have an impact on stigma directed toward trans men in social and familial relationships.

The three items in this key area ranged by only .03 points for the hetero-cis subsample and .05 points for the LGBTQ subsample indicating that there was not much variation in the stigma associated with friends and family for either group. However, as similarly found among the Trans Women Stigma Scale, the item with the *lowest* mean value for the LGBTQ subsample (1.83) had the *highest* mean value for the hetero-cis subsample (2.54). This item was: "Trans men are not capable of being good parents." Negativity toward trans men as capable parents is certainly linked to cis-normative prejudices (e.g., being trans is a sin, being trans is a sickness, being trans is a perversion) and parenting hostilities (e.g., trans parents will disrupt "appropriate" gender identity development in their children) (McGuire et al. 2016; Tornello, Riskind, and Babić 2019; Veldorale-Griffin and Darling 2016). But these negativities can also be related to more specific stereotypes about trans dads, including the refusal of healthcare personnel and others involved in parenthood practices (e.g., teachers of parenting classes, other parents, school teachers, babysitters) to accept their gender identities as both men and fathers (Downing 2013; Haines, Ajayi, and Boyd 2014; Hicks 2013; Hines 2007). The unique experiences of trans men who become pregnant and give birth while identifying as men are also hampered by palpable stigma and misunderstandings (Hoffkling, Obedin-Maliver, and Sevelius 2017; Karaian 2013; Tornello, Riskind, and Babić 2019). Furthermore, there are very few existing U.S. laws currently in place that protect transgender people from discrimination by foster care and adoption agencies (Movement Advancement Project 2019). As a result, trans dads endure both social and legal obstacles in and to fatherhood.

## Trans Men and Positions of Importance and Social Significance

For both subsamples, stigmatization toward trans men in positions of importance and social significance was relatively high. As seen in Figure 13.1, the item "Trans men should not be allowed to join the military" was the fourth most stigmatizing attitude for the hetero-cis subsample (2.73) and the LGBTQ subsample (1.97) and the item "I would not vote for a political candidate who was an openly trans man" was the sixth most stigmatizing attitude for the hetero-cis subsample (2.70). In addition, among both subsamples, stigma towards trans men in the military is highest in comparison to the other LGBTQ groups (recall Figure 7.4). Trans men (and non-binary/genderqueer individuals) are also the most likely of all groups to be stigmatized as political candidates among the hetero-cis subsample. Overall, the hostility toward trans men in positions of importance and social significance is evidenced across the entire sample.

This negativity can be seen in current issues impacting both trans military membership and trans political candidates. For example, trans men are underrepresented in the U.S. political climate and even among transgender politicians, they comprise only a small percentage (Vikhrov 2018). Minneapolis City Council Member Phillipe Cunningham, the first openly trans man of color in public office in the U.S., joined only two other active trans men politicians in 2017: School Board Members Jay Irwin (Ralston, Nebraska) and Tyler Titus (Erie, Pennsylvania) (Vikhrov 2018). In addition, even though nearly three-fourths (71%) of Americans support openly trans servicemen and women (McCarthy

2019), the vigorous battle to ban trans participation in the U.S. Armed Forces remains of pressing concern because estimates indicate that there may be more than 15,000 trans individuals currently serving in the U.S. military (Elders et al. 2015; Gates and Herman 2014; James et al. 2016; Worthen 2019). Thus, it is clear that there is still very real opposition toward trans men in positions of importance and social significance that deserves further attention.

## Trans Men and Sex Act-Related Stigma

As seen in Table 13.1, sex act-related stigma among trans men was relatively high with all means for the five items in this key area above 2.6 among the hetero-cis subsample (ranging from 2.61 to 2.84) and close to 2.0 or higher for the LGBTQ subsample (ranging from 1.88 to 2.09). Two out of the top three most stigmatizing attitudes toward trans men are found among the sex act-related stigma items for both subsamples (discomfort with sex with men and women for the hetero-cis subsample; hypersexuality and unfaithful for the LGBTQ subsample) (see Figure 13.1).

For both subsamples, the item with the lowest mean values in the sex act-related stigma key area is: "Trans men are mostly responsible for spreading HIV/AIDS." In line with this finding, studies indicate that trans men are significantly less likely to report having HIV/AIDS in comparison to trans women (.3% vs. 3.4% respectively, see James et al. 2016). However, additional research demonstrates that trans men have unique HIV/AIDS risks and those that are living with HIV/AIDS also endure complex stigmatization experiences (Rowniak et al. 2011; Sevelius 2009; Wiewel et al. 2018).

The two items with the highest mean values in the sex act-related stigma key area for the hetero-cis subsample are: "I am comfortable with the thought of a trans man having sex with a man" (2.84) and "I am comfortable with the thought of a trans man having sex with a woman" (2.79) which were both reverse coded because *dis*comfort with trans men engaging in sex acts reflects a stigmatizing attitude toward trans men. This stigmatization process is related to stereotypes about trans men's bodies and misunderstandings about the types of sex acts they take part in. For example, some may be uncomfortable with the sexual behaviors of trans men who have undergone gender-affirming/gender-transition surgeries (e.g., phalloplasty or metoidioplasty) and/or trans men who *have not* undergone these procedures. There continues to be a problematic phallus-focused fascination with trans men's bodies which is a key part of the stigmatization of trans men's sexual behaviors. There are also accompanying damaging beliefs such as trans men "can never be men" and/or "are really women" because they do not have "real" penises that are deeply embedded in trans men's sex act-related stigma (Cromwell 1999; Devor 1997; Rubin 2003; Stein 2018). For example, hypothetical rape-scenario research indicates that trans men are more likely than non-trans victims to be blamed for their sexual assault, in part because they are viewed to be somehow deserving of their attack due to their bodily gender nonconformity (i.e., their lack of a "real" penis) (Davies and Hudson 2011). Additional research indicates that criminal justice system treatment and media representations of trans men further contribute to the stigmatization of trans men's sex acts and their overall negative treatment (Buist and Stone 2014; Stein 2018). These negativities collectively work together to impact trans men's experiences with sex act-related stigma.

The item with the highest mean value in the sex act-related stigma key area for the LGBTQ subsample (2.09) is: "Trans men are too sexual (hypersexual)" (the mean was also quite high for the hetero-cis subsample at 2.71). This finding may be associated with generalized stereotypes about men and hypersexuality (Connell 2005) as well as more specific stereotypes about the effects of testosterone treatment on heightened sexuality that some trans men can experience (Devor 1997; Rubin 2003). For example, studies of Dutch trans men (N = 50) (Wierckx et al. 2011) and Belgian trans men (N = 138) (Wierckx et al. 2014) found that nearly three-fourths (73.9% and 71.0%, respectively) reported an increase in sexual desire after undergoing testosterone treatments and gender-affirming/gender-transition surgeries. A U.S. study also determined that testosterone treatments significantly increased the frequency of sexual fantasies and sexual arousal among trans men (N = 50) (Costantino et al. 2013). In particular, qualitative work (N = 25) reveals that trans men have both an increase in sex drive as well as "a different experience of sex as more urgent and less controllable" after undergoing gender-affirming/gender-transition surgeries (Bockting, Benner, and Coleman 2009:695). Because certainly not all trans men utilize testosterone, beyond these experiences, there may be a larger stigmatizing process associated with these patterns that contributes to the association of trans men with hypersexuality.

## Trans Man Identity Permanency

The stigmatizing attitude that "Most men who call themselves transgender are just temporarily experimenting with their gender" was amongst the top five most stigmatizing attitudes for the LGBTQ subsample (1.97) but was mid-range for the hetero-cis subsample (2.62). However, for both groups, the perspective that trans men's identities are temporary/experimental is evident. Proving one's authenticity as both "self-made men" and "trans enough" are experiences that many trans men endure (Catalano 2015; Rubin 2003; Schilt 2010; Stein 2018). Skepticism about their gender identity from early ages, including trivializing attitudes such as "it's just a phase" or "he'll (or worse, she'll) grow out of it," especially from family members and even healthcare providers, coupled with the dismissive labeling of gender nonconformity as "a tomboy phase" contribute to early stereotypes about trans men's identity permanency (Alegría 2018; Devor 1997; Grossman et al. 2005; Hill and Menvielle 2009; Rubin 2003) that can have long-lasting impacts. Together, these dynamics shape the stigmatizing perspective that trans men's identities are temporary/experimental.

## Trans Men and the Achievement of Masculinity

Among all nine LGBTQ groups, trans men are the most likely to be stigmatized for the inability to achieve masculinity by the LGBTQ subsample and along with queer men, trans men are the most likely to be stigmatized for the inability to achieve masculinity by the hetero-cis subsample (recall Figure 7.4). In addition, across all 14 items in the Trans Men Stigma Scale, the perception that "Trans men are not masculine enough" has the highest mean value for the LGBTQ subsample (2.21) and has the second-highest mean value for the hetero-cis subsample (2.80) (see Figure 13.1). Thus, questions about trans men's masculinities are common amongst this entire sample. Because masculinity is so highly valued, its authenticity is especially regulated. Research demonstrates that both performances and embodiment of masculinity are criticized and that trans men experience such critiques in ways that largely differ from those of both cis men and trans women (Connell 2005; Jauk 2013; Pascoe 2011; Schilt 2010; Schilt and Westbrook 2009; Stein 2018; Worthen 2016). Though the use of testosterone can help trans men to experience less stigma, especially in conjunction with the growth of facial hair (a clear demarcation of masculinity), trans men can be targets of DHV (Dozier 2005; Jauk 2013; Rubin 2003; Schilt 2010). For example, trans men can be publically ridiculed with appallingly offensive slurs often related to their inability to meet the standards of hetero-cis-masculinity (e.g., "pussy" or "fag"). Furthermore, because they can be conceived of as "not real men," the scripts of "you look too feminine" or "you still look like a girl" continue to impact the stigma that trans men endure as related to their inability to achieve masculinity (Cromwell 1999; Devor 1997; Rubin 2003).

## Trans Men Stigma Summed Scale

As seen in Table 13.1, all 14 items were summed together to create the Trans Men Stigma Scale. Cronbach's alphas were quite high for the hetero-cis subsample (.90) and the LGBTQ subsample (.93). Unlike any of the other previously discussed stigma scales (lesbian women, gay men, bisexual women, bisexual men, trans women), the highest value for the Trans Men Stigma Scale was found among the LGBTQ subsample (a single LGBTQ individual indicated the most-stigmatizing response to all 14 items resulting in a score of 70 on the scale). However, the highest value for the hetero-cis subsample was only two points lower (68) and three hetero-cis individuals had this score. The mean values for the summed Trans Men Stigma Scale differed substantially and significantly with the hetero-cis subsample mean (36.42) 9.73 points higher than the LGBTQ subsample mean (26.69). In addition, the key area with the highest individual mean values differed. For the hetero-cis subsample, the highest mean value was among the sex act-related stigma items (discomfort with sex with a man, 2.84) while for the LGBTQ subsample, the highest mean value was related to trans men's inability to achieve masculinity (2.21). However, it is important to note that for the hetero-cis subsample, stigma toward trans men's masculinity was the second most stigmatizing attitude and for the LGBTQ subsample, a sex act-related stigma item (hypersexuality) was second highest. Together, these findings demonstrate that the stigmatization of trans men is largely associated with sex act-related stigma and trans men's achievement of masculinity across the entire sample (recall Figure 7.3).

## NCST, Hetero-cis-normativity, Social Power Axes, and the Trans Men Stigma Scale

The first set of regression models examine the Trans Men Stigma Scale using NCST. The hypotheses are as follows:

- *Hypothesis 1a*: there is a significant positive relationship between the HCN Scale and the Trans Men Stigma Scale.
- *Hypothesis 1b*: there are significant relationships between individual social power axes (gender identity, sexual identity, additional gender/sexuality, racial/ethnic identity, basic needs) and the Trans Men Stigma Scale.
- *Hypothesis 2a*: the relationship between the HCN Scale and the Trans Men Stigma Scale is moderated by interactions between the HCN Scale and axes of social power.
- *Hypothesis 2b*: the relationships between individual social power axes and the Trans Men Stigma Scale are moderated by interactions between axes of social power.

Figure 13.2 outlines these relationships and the two models of NCST to be estimated. Specifically, OLS regression is utilized in Table 13.2 to examine NCST and the relationships among hetero-cis-normativity, axes of social power (gender, sexuality, additional gender/sexuality, race/ethnicity, and basic needs), and the Trans Men Stigma Scale for the hetero-cis subsample and the LGBTQ subsample. See Chapter 7 for a more complete description of the models. Regarding model fit statistics, the adjusted $R^2$ values ranged from .67 to .68.

## NCST, HCN, Social Power Axes, and the Trans Men Stigma Scale: Model 1

In Table 13.2, the relationships between the HCN Scale, axes of social power, and the Trans Men Stigma Scale are estimated in Model 1. Supporting *Hypothesis 1a*, the HCN Scale is positively related to the Trans Men Stigma Scale in Model 1 for both subsamples. Supporting *Hypothesis 1b*, individual axes of

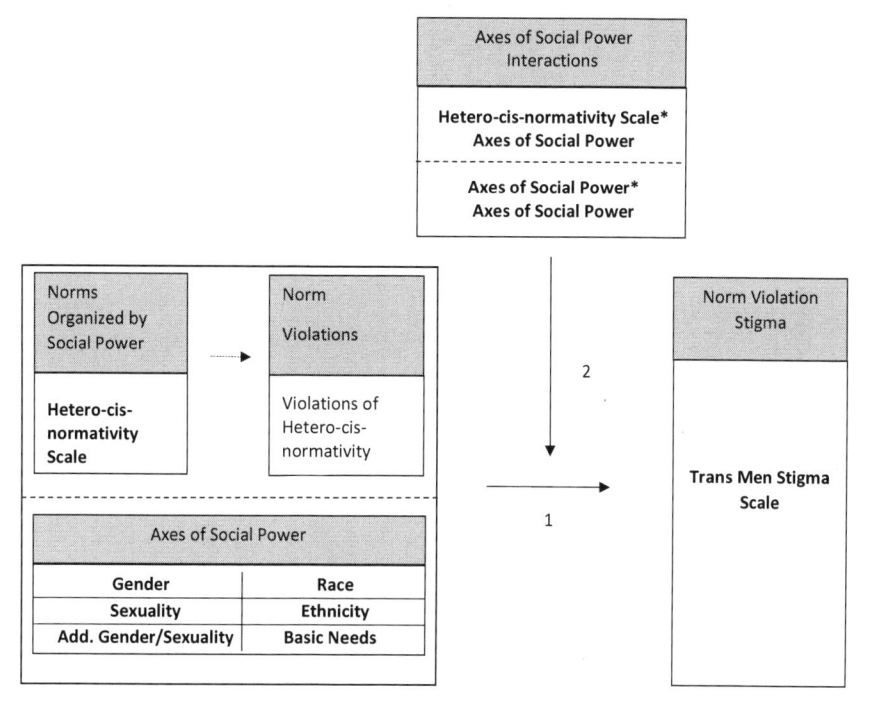

**FIGURE 13.2** Theoretical Model of NCST and Trans Men Stigma using the Stigmatizer Lens with Model Numbers to be Examined in Table 13.2

*Notes:* Model 1 estimates the HCN Scale and axes of social power (gender, sexuality, additional gender/sexuality, race, ethnicity, and basic needs) as they relate to the Trans Men Stigma Scale. Model 2 estimates interactions among axes of social power and the HCN Scale as they moderate the relationships between the HCN Scale and the Trans Men Stigma Scale as well as interactions among axes of social power as they moderate the relationships between the HCN Scale and the Trans Men Stigma Scale. The * indicates an interaction.

social power are also significantly related to the Trans Men Stigma Scale for the hetero-cis subsample (cis woman, bear) and for the LGBTQ subsample (cis woman, queer, butch).

## NCST, HCN, Social Power Axes, and the Trans Men Stigma Scale: Model 2

Intersections among axes of social power and the HCN Scale as well as interaction effects among axes of social power are examined in Model 2. For both subsamples, the HCN Scale is positively related to the Trans Men Stigma Scale in Model 2. Among the significant HCN Scale interaction terms, three are discussed in Chapter 7: the interactions between the HCN Scale and queer, being African American/Black, and mostly all I need. For the hetero-cis subsample, there is one more significant interaction term: there is a positive relationship between the HCN Scale and indicating "few needs met" such that higher levels of agreement with the HCN Scale have a more robust impact on attitudes toward trans men among hetero-cis individuals who do not have their basic needs met as compared hetero-cis individuals who do have everything they need and more. Together, these results show that hetero-cis-normativity, social power axes (gender/sexual, racial, and basic needs experiences), and intersections among them relate to the stigmatization of trans men as suggested in some past research (Balay 2014; Schilt 2010; Worthen 2016). Overall, *Hypothesis 2a* is supported: interactions between the HCN Scale and axes of social power moderate the relationship between the HCN Scale and the Trans Men Stigma Scale for both subsamples.

Looking at the rest of Table 13.2, a familiar set of findings is evident: axes of social power impact attitudes toward trans men in very different ways for the hetero-cis and LGBTQ subsamples. For example, there are no overlapping individual axes of social power that are statistically significantly related to the Trans Men Stigma Scale for both subsamples in Model 2. For the hetero-cis subsample, there is only one significant individual social power axis: being a cis woman is negatively related to the stigmatization of trans men. This is consistent with previous research that finds more supportive attitudes toward trans men among cis women as compared to attitudes among cis men (Carroll et al. 2012; Worthen 2016). However, there are no significant social power axes interaction effects for the hetero-cis subsample.

In contrast, there are both individual and intersecting axes of social power that are significantly related to attitudes toward trans men for the LGBTQ subsample. First, being SGL is negatively related to the Trans Men Stigma Scale. Second, being African American/Black is positively related to the stigmatization of trans men; however, a corresponding interaction term (being African American/Black and Two-Spirit) is negatively related to the Trans Men Stigma Scale. Third, there are two significant interaction terms related to not having one's basic needs met: being queer and indicating "often needs not met" and being Asian American/Pacific Islander and indicating "often needs not met" are both positively related to the stigmatization of trans men. Interestingly, these findings are all among the consistent patterns reviewed in Chapter 7.

Overall, the axes of social power that shape attitudes toward trans men differ for the hetero-cis and LGBTQ subsamples. Additional tests to compare the regression coefficients of the two subsamples reveal several significant differences (Clogg, Petkova, and Haritou 1995). However, *Hypothesis 2b* is only partially supported: interactions between axes of social power moderate the relationship between the individual axes of social power and the Trans Men Stigma Scale for the LGBTQ subsample (only).

**TABLE 13.2** OLS Regression Results Estimating NCST and the Trans Men Stigma Scale for the Hetero-cis Subsample (n = 1,500) and the LGBTQ Subsample (n = 1,604)

|  | Hetero-cis Subsample | | LGBTQ Subsample | | Test of Difference |
|---|---|---|---|---|---|
|  | Model 1 | Model 2 | Model 1 | Model 2 |  |
| HCN Scale | .86* | .79* | 91* | .84* | . |
| *Gender identity* | | | | | |
| Cis woman | -1.62* | -2.62* | -1.53* | . | . |
| *Additional sexual/gender identity* | | | | | |
| Queer | . | . | -.89* | . | |
| SGL | . | . | . | -4.56* | ** |
| Butch | . | . | 1.45* | . | |
| Bear | -2.72* | . | . | . | |
| *Racial/ethnic identity* | | | | | |
| African American/Black | . | . | . | 13.12* | . |
| *HCN Scale\*social power axes interactions* | | | | | |
| HCN Scale*queer | — | -.37* | — | . | ** |
| HCN Scale*African American/Black | — | -.24* | — | . | . |
| HCN Scale*mostly all I need | — | .14* | — | .28* | . |
| HCN Scale*few needs met | — | .33* | — | . | |
| *Social power axes interactions* | | | | | |
| African American/Black*Two-Spirit | — | . | — | -7.67* | ** |
| Queer*often needs not met | — | . | — | 4.29* | ** |
| Asian American/Pacific Islander*often needs not met | — | . | — | 5.51* | ** |
| *Controls: common explanations LGBTQ contact* | | | | | |
| LGBTQ Friends Scale (w/o trans men) | -.78* | -.82* | -.22* | -.23* | ** |
| *Religious identity* | | | | | |
| Protestant—evangelical | 2.22* | 1.97* | . | . | |
| *Political perspectives* | | | | | |
| Liberal—conservative | 1.13* | .1.06* | . | . | ** |
| Openness to new experiences | -1.05* | -.74* | -1.66* | -1.66* | ** |
| *Support laws/policies helping:* | | | | | |
| Immigrants | . | . | -1.10* | -1.37* | . |
| Non-Christians | -1.23* | . | . | . | |

(*Continued*)

**TABLE 13.2** (Cont.)

|  | Hetero-cis Subsample | | LGBTQ Subsample | | Test of Difference |
|---|---|---|---|---|---|
|  | Model 1 | Model 2 | Model 1 | Model 2 |  |
| *Beliefs about gender* |  |  |  |  |  |
| Feminist | -.86* | -.71* | -1.47* | -1.34* | . |
| Patriarchal Gender Norms Scale | .50* | .47* | .65* | .68* | . |
| *Sociodemographic controls* |  |  |  |  |  |
| Age | . | . | .04* | .04* | ** |
| Adjusted $R^2$ | .67 | .67 | .68 | .68 |  |
| Mean VIF | 1.50 | 1.50 | 1.93 | 1.93 |  |

\* $p < .05$; a dot (.) indicates non-statistically significant results. A dash (—) indicates this was not included in the model.

\*\* $p < .05$ for Clogg et al.'s (1995) test of equality of regression coefficients comparing Model 2 for the hetero-cis subsample and Model 2 for the LGBTQ subsample.

*Notes:* unstandardized regression coefficients are presented. Only the rows with significant results are displayed here. See Table 13.1 for detailed information about the Trans Men Stigma Scale. See Tables 7.1 and 7.2 for details about all other variables and Appendix B Table B.1 for details about the interaction effects.

## *Summarizing NCST, HCN, Social Power Axes, and the Trans Men Stigma Scale*

The explorations offered in Table 13.2 show that the processes behind the stigmatization of trans men differ for hetero-cis and LGBTQ people. While axes of social power relate to LGBTQ people's attitudes toward trans men in dynamic, intersectional ways, with the exception of cis woman identity, individual social power axes explain little about hetero-cis people's attitudes toward trans men. Overall, the use of NCST and the HCN Scale to explore the stigmatization of trans men allows us to better understand how social power informs attitudes toward trans men.

## Trans Men's Experiences

### *The Trans Men Subsample*

The recruitment of trans men to participate in this study was anticipated to be difficult and the requested quota (n = 100) from Survey Sampling International was not met. The study sample included only 55 trans men (learn more about the data and sampling procedures in Chapter 7 and Appendix A). At the beginning of the survey, respondents were asked "What best describes your

**TABLE 13.3** Trans Men Characteristics (n = 55)

|  | % | n |
|---|---|---|
| *Sexual identity* | | |
| Heterosexual/straight | 30.9% | 17 |
| Gay/lesbian | 27.3% | 15 |
| Bisexual | 21.8% | 12 |
| Pansexual | 14.5% | 8 |
| Asexual | 5.5% | 3 |
| *Additional gender/sexual identity* | | |
| Queer | 25.5% | 14 |
| SGL | 9.1% | 5 |
| Two-Spirit | 7.3% | 4 |
| Butch | 5.5% | 3 |
| Femme | 16.4% | 9 |
| Leather | 7.3% | 4 |
| Bear | 12.7% | 7 |
| Twink | 12.7% | 7 |
| Down Low | – | 0 |
| *Race/ethnicity* | | |
| Caucasian/White** | 61.8% | 34 |
| African American/Black* | 14.5% | 8 |
| Asian American/Pacific Islander* | 14.5% | 8 |
| Native American/Alaskan Native* | 5.5% | 3 |
| Multi-racial* | 1.8% | 1 |
| Other race* | 1.8% | 1 |
| Latinx race* | – | 0 |
| Latinx ethnicity | 30.9% | 17 |
| *Basic needs* | | |
| Everything I need* | 12.7% | 7 |
| Mostly all I need** | 50.9% | 28 |
| Often needs not met* | 30.9% | 17 |
| Few needs met* | 5.5% | 3 |

\* Reference category in analyses in Table 13.5.
\*\* Included in analyses shown in Table 13.5.

gender?" Trans men were those who selected "I am transgender: I identify as a man and my assigned sex at birth was female." See Table 13.3 for more details about the trans men in this study.

## Trans Men's Experiences with Gender- and Sexuality-Based DHV

Despite evidence that trans men often feel more respected in the workplace, safer in public and in social situations, and less vulnerable to harassment as compared to their

**314** NCST and Understanding LGBTQ Stigma

previous experiences when living as girls/women (Dozier 2005; Jauk 2013; Schilt 2010), research demonstrates that trans men have significant experiences with DHV (Aparicio-García et al. 2018; Buist and Stone 2014; James et al. 2016; Meyer 2015; Schilt 2010; Schilt and Westbrook 2009; Testa et al. 2012). In addition, trans men report very real concerns about potential physical altercations with other men and are especially cognizant of the complexities of sexual violence (Jauk 2013; Moran and Sharpe 2004). For example, the U.S. Transgender Survey with more than 8,500 trans men respondents found that more than one-third (36%) of trans men hid their past gender transition in order to avoid discrimination and about 1 in 7 (14%) lost a job due to their transgender identity (James et al. 2016). In addition, some research indicates that trans men are at extreme risk for violence, with half (51%) indicating experiences with sexual assault in their lifetimes (James et al. 2016) and close to half (45.7%) reporting physical attacks due to their trans identity (Testa et al. 2012).

More than half of trans men in this study have had one or more experiences of gender-based DHV (56%) and 6 in 10 (60%) have had one or more experiences of sexuality-based DHV, as seen in Figure 13.3. Gender-based discrimination is the most common form (53%) while gender-based violence is the least common (22%). To better understand trans men's gender- and sexuality-based DHV, trans men's experiences were compared to the LGBTQ subsample and

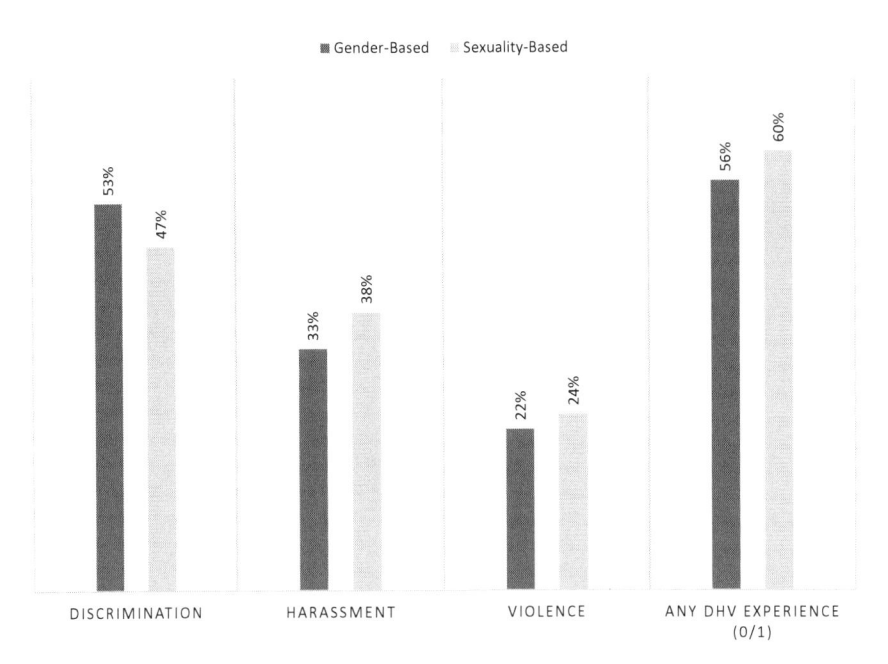

**FIGURE 13.3** Trans Men's (n = 55) Experiences with Gender- and Sexuality-Based DHV

*Note:* see Table 13.4 for comparisons of trans men's experiences to the LGBTQ subsample and the men subsample.

**TABLE 13.4** Gender- and Sexuality-Based DHV Mean Values (Standard Deviations) among Trans Men, the LGBTQ Subsample, and the Men Subsample with $t$-test Results

|  | | Trans Men | LGBTQ Subsample | Men Subsample |
|---|---|---|---|---|
| | $n$ | 55 | 1604 | 1474 |
| *Gender-based* | | | | |
| Discrimination | | .53 (.50)*** | .32 (.47) | .17 (.38) |
| Harassment | | .33 (.47)* | .28 (.45) | .09 (.29) |
| Violence | | .22 (.42)*** | .14 (.34) | .07 (.26) |
| Any gender DHV experience (0/1) | | .56 (.50)* | .40 (.49) | .21 (.41) |
| *Sexuality-Based* | | | | |
| Discrimination | | .47 (.50)* | .44 (.50) | .23 (.42) |
| Harassment | | .38 (.49)* | .41 (.49) | .24 (.43) |
| Violence | | .24 (.43) | .20 (.40) | .13 (.34) |
| Any sexuality DHV experience (0/1) | | .60 (.49)* | .53 (.50) | .33 (.47) |

\* Trans men are significantly different from the men subsample (only) at $p < .05$ level.
\*\*\* Trans men are significantly different from both the LGBTQ and men subsamples at $p < .05$ level.

the men subsample using $t$-tests. Table 13.4 shows that as compared to the men subsample, trans men are significantly more likely to experience gender-based harassment as well as sexuality-based discrimination and harassment. In addition, in comparison to all LGBTQ people and all men, trans men report significantly more experiences with gender-based discrimination and violence. Thus, trans men are at particular risk for both gender- and sexuality-based DHV as compared to all men and this is especially true for gender-based discrimination and violence. These relationships are examined further below.

### NCST and Trans Men's Experiences with Gender- and Sexuality-Based DHV

The second set of regression models examines trans men and their experiences with gender- and sexuality-based DHV using NCST with a focus on trans men's axes of social power. The hypotheses are as follows:

- *Hypothesis 1*: being a trans man (violating hetero-cis-normativity) increases the likelihood of experiencing gender- and sexuality-based DHV (trans man stigma).
- *Hypothesis 2*: the relationship between being a trans man and gender- and sexuality-based DHV is moderated by interactions among being a trans man and axes of social power.

**316** NCST and Understanding LGBTQ Stigma

```
                        ┌─────────────────────────┐
                        │  Axes of Social Power   │
                        │      Interactions       │
                        ├─────────────────────────┤
                        │      Trans Man*         │
                        │  Axes of Social Power   │
                        └─────────────────────────┘
                                    │
                                    │ 2
                                    ▼
┌──────────────┐   ┌──────────────┐     ┌──────────────────────┐
│   Norms      │   │    Norm      │     │ Norm Violation Stigma│
│ Organized by │╌─▶│  Violations  │     ├──────────────────────┤
│ Social Power │   │              │  1  │                      │
├──────────────┤   ├──────────────┤────▶│  Trans Man Stigma:   │
│              │   │              │     │                      │
│ Hetero-cis-  │   │ Violations of│     │ Gender- and Sexuality-│
│ normativity  │   │ Hetero-cis-  │     │ Based Discrimination,│
│ Scale        │   │ normativity: │     │  Harassment, and     │
│              │   │ Being a Trans│     │      Violence        │
│              │   │     Man      │     │                      │
└──────────────┘   └──────────────┘     └──────────────────────┘
```

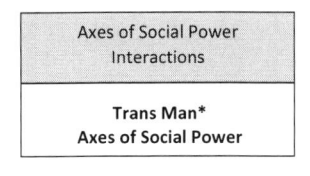

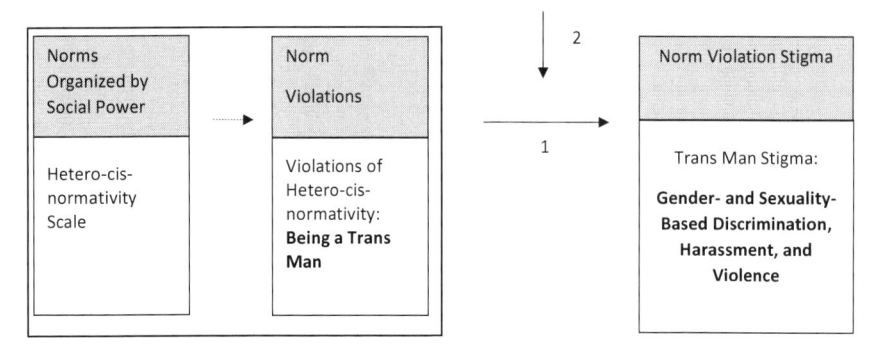

**FIGURE 13.4** Theoretical Model of NCST and Trans Men Stigma using the Stigmatized Lens with Model Numbers to be Examined in Table 13.5

*Notes:* Model 1 estimates being a trans man as related to gender- and sexuality-based DHV. Model 2 estimates interactions among trans men's axes of social power as they moderate the relationships between being a trans man and gender- and sexuality-based DHV. The * indicates an interaction.

Figure 13.4 outlines these relationships and Table 13.5 displays logistic regression results that examine NCST and the relationships among being a trans man, intersections among trans men's axes of social power, and any experiences of gender-based DHV (dichotomized as 0/1) or sexuality-based DHV (dichotomized as 0/1) utilizing the LGBTQ subsample (n = 1,604; whereby being a trans man is compared to all other LGBTQ people). Because trans men's experiences are the focus of this exploration (i.e., the stigmatized lens of NCST is being utilized), the trans man and social power axes interaction terms are listed at the top of the table and are the focus of the discussion below. It is important to note that "man" was not included in the individual social power axes because the associated gender categories for this study are "trans man" (which is already included in the interaction effects) or "cis man" (which does not pertain to this table's focus on trans men). See Chapter 7 for a more complete description of the models and a discussion of overarching trends and patterns. Regarding model fit statistics, the pseudo $R^2$ values were extremely low and ranged from .01 to .05.

## NCST, Trans Men, and Gender- and Sexuality-Based DHV: Model 1

In Table 13.5, Model 1 estimates the relationships between violations of hetero-cis-normativity conceptualized as being a trans man and the stigmatization of trans men

**TABLE 13.5** Logistic Regression Results with Odds Ratios and (Standard Errors) Estimating NCST and Gender- and Sexuality-Based DHV as Related to Being a Trans Man for the LGBTQ Subsample (n = 1,604)

|  | Gender-Based DHV |  |  |  | Sexuality-Based DHV |  |  |  |
|---|---|---|---|---|---|---|---|---|
|  | Model 1 |  | Model 2 |  | Model 1 |  | Model 2 |  |
|  | OR | SE | OR | SE | OR | SE | OR | SE |
| Trans man | 2.07* | (.78) | . | . | . | . | . | . |
| *Trans man social power axes interactions* |  |  |  |  |  |  |  |  |
| Trans man* mostly all I need | — | — | . | . | — | — | . | . |
| Trans man*White | — | — | . | . | — | — | . | . |
| *Trans man social power axes* |  |  |  |  |  |  |  |  |
| Trans | . | . | . | . | . | . | . | . |
| White | . | . | . | . | . | . | . | . |
| Mostly all I need | . | . | . | . | . | . | . | . |
| *Socio-demographic controls* |  |  |  |  |  |  |  |  |
| Age | .96* | (.00) | .96* | (.00) | .98* | (.00) | .98* | (.00) |
| Town type (rural–large city) | . | . | . | . | . | . | . | . |
| Education | 1.15* | (.05) | 1.15* | (.05) | 1.13* | (.04) | 1.13* | (.04) |
| Income | . |  | . |  | . |  | . |  |
| Pseudo R² | .05 |  | .05 |  | .01 |  | .01 |  |
| Mean VIF | 1.23 |  | 1.23 |  | 1.22 |  | 1.22 |  |

\* $p \leq .05$; a dot (.) indicates non-statistically significant results. A dash (—) indicates this was not included in the model.

*Notes:* all rows are displayed, including those without significant results. See Table 13.3 for more details about trans men.

conceptualized as gender- and sexuality-based DHV along with sociodemographic controls. Results show that being a trans man increases the likelihood of gender-based DHV by 1.07 but is not significantly related to sexuality-based DHV. As other research demonstrates (Cromwell 1999; Devor 1997; Rubin 2003; Schilt 2010; Schilt and Westbrook 2009), trans men's gender identity can be challenged and questioned and this can sometimes be directly related to their DHV experiences; however, the sexuality of trans men may be less strongly related to such experiences (James et al. 2016; Testa et al. 2012). This may be especially true for hetero trans men who comprise nearly one-third (31%, n = 17) of the trans men in this sample. Overall, *Hypothesis 1* is partially supported: being a trans man increases the likelihood of gender-based DHV but not sexuality-based DHV.

## NCST, Trans Men, and Gender- and Sexuality-Based DHV: Model 2

In Model 2, intersections among axes of social power and being a trans man are included as they relate to gender- and sexuality-based DHV. There are no significant findings in Model 2 related to being a trans man. Thus, the inclusion of social power axes interaction terms washed out the significance of being a trans man on gender-based DHV. Such findings complement existing research that has highlighted how class experiences shape trans men's stigmatization (Balay 2014; Jauk 2013; Schilt 2010). Furthermore, as found in Model 1, being a trans man remains statistically non-significantly related to the likelihood of sexuality-based DHV in Model 2. Overall, *Hypothesis 2* is not supported.

## Summarizing NCST, Trans Men, and Gender- and Sexuality-Based DHV

In sum, being a trans man increases the likelihood of experiencing gender-based DHV but not sexuality-based DHV. However, overall, there are very few significant findings among this small group of trans men (n = 55) and the pseudo $R^2$ values are extremely low. Even so, by focusing on trans men's experiences, these findings demonstrate that it is important to continue to consider the interactive, intersecting experiences of social power among trans men to best understand their victimization. In particular, it may be that other axes of social power not measured here (e.g., presentation of masculinity) may help to better explain trans men's victimization patterns.

## Summary of Patterns of Trans Men Stigma

In line with the three tenets and hypotheses derived from NCST, there are six patterns related to the stigmatization of trans men reviewed in this chapter:

1. Sex-act related stigma is a driving force in the stigmatization of trans men for both hetero-cis and LGBTQ people; however, discomfort with trans men's sex acts with both men and women are most concerning for hetero-cis people while the stigmatizing beliefs that trans men are too hypersexual and unfaithful are most concerning for LGBTQ people.
2. For both hetero-cis and LGBTQ people, there is strong support for the stigmatizing belief that trans men are not masculine enough.
3. Hetero-cis-normativity is positively related to trans men stigma for both sub-samples; however, the interaction effects between the HCN Scale and social power axes that moderate these relationships differ for the hetero-cis and LGBTQ subsamples. In addition, there are more significant interaction effects

between the HCN Scale and social power axes for the hetero-cis subsample than there are for the LGBTQ subsample.
4. Individual social power axes are significantly related to trans men stigma for both subsamples; however, the interaction effects between the social power axes only moderate these relationships for the LGBTQ subsample.
5. Trans men experience high levels of gender- and sexuality-based DHV in comparison to the all men subsample and are significantly more likely to experience gender-based discrimination and violence than both the LGBTQ and men subsamples.
6. Being a trans man is significantly related to the likelihood of gender-based DHV but being a trans man is not significantly related to the likelihood of sexuality-based DHV.

## Note

1 The Public Facilities Privacy & Security Act, commonly referred to as House Bill 2 or HB2, was a North Carolina statute passed in 2016 and later repealed in 2017. HB2 compelled schools and public facilities to require that public restrooms be used by individuals as related to their sex assigned at birth (not their gender identities) and was strongly opposed by those that support transgender rights.

## References

Adam, Seth and Matt Goodman. 2015. "Number of Americans Who Report Knowing a Transgender Person Doubles in Seven Years, according to New GLAAD Survey." *GLAAD*. Retrieved June 12, 2019 (www.glaad.org/releases/number-americans-who-report-knowing-transgender-person-doubles-seven-years-according-new).

Alegría, Christine. 2018. "Supporting Families of Transgender Children/Youth: Parents Speak on Their Experiences, Identity, and Views." *International Journal of Transgenderism* 19(2):132–143.

Aparicio-García, Marta, Eva Evelia, María Díaz-Ramiro, Susana Rubio-Valdehita, María Inmaculada López-Núñez, and Isidro García-Nieto. 2018. "Health and Well-Being of Cisgender, Transgender and Non-Binary Young People." *International Journal of Environmental Research and Public Health* 15(10):2133.

Balay, Anne. 2014. *Steel Closets: Voices of Gay, Lesbian, and Transgender Steelworkers*. Chapel Hill, NC: University of North Carolina Press.

Bockting, Walter, Autumn Benner, and Eli Coleman. 2009. "Gay and Bisexual Identity Development among Female-to-Male Transsexuals in North America: Emergence of a Transgender Sexuality." *Archives of Sexual Behavior* 38(5):688–701.

Boyer, R. C. and M. Paz Galupo. 2018. "Transgender Friendship Profiles: Patterns across Gender Identity and LGBT Affiliation." *Gender Issues* 35(3):236–253.

Brown, Anna. 2017. "Transgender Issues Sharply Divide Republicans, Democrats." *Pew Research Center*. Retrieved June 26, 2019 (www.pewresearch.org/fact-tank/2017/11/08/transgender-issues-divide-republicans-and-democrats/).

Buist, Carrie L. and Codie Stone. 2014. "Transgender Victims and Offenders: Failures of the United States Criminal Justice System and the Necessity of Queer Criminology." *Critical Criminology* 22(1):35–47.

Carroll, Lynne, Dominik Güss, Kimberly S. Hutchinson, and Andy A. Gauler. 2012. "How Do U.S. Students Perceive Trans Persons?" *Sex Roles: A Journal of Research* 67(9/10):516–527.

Catalano, D. Chase J. 2015. "'Trans Enough?': The Pressures Trans Men Negotiate in Higher Education." *TSQ: Transgender Studies Quarterly* 2(3):411–430.

Clogg, Clifford C., Eva Petkova, and Adamantios Haritou. 1995. "Statistical Methods for Comparing Regression Coefficients between Models." *American Journal of Sociology* 100(5):1261–1293.

Connell, R. W. 2005. *Masculinities*. Oxford, UK: Polity Press.

Costantino, Antonietta, Silvia Cerpolini, Stefania Alvisi, Paolo Giovanni Morselli, Stefano Venturoli, and Maria Cristina Meriggiola. 2013. "A Prospective Study on Sexual Function and Mood in Female-to-Male Transsexuals during Testosterone Administration and after Sex Reassignment Surgery." *Journal of Sex & Marital Therapy* 39(4):321–335.

Cromwell, Jason. 1999. *Transmen and FTMs: Identities, Bodies, Genders, and Sexualities*. Chicago, IL: University of Illinois Press.

Davies, Michelle and Jenefer Hudson. 2011. "Judgments toward Male and Transgendered Victims in a Depicted Stranger Rape." *Journal of Homosexuality* 58(2):237–247.

Devor, Holly. 1997. *FTM: Female-to-Male Transsexuals in Society*. Bloomington, IN: Indiana University Press.

Downing, Jordan B. 2013. "Transgender-Parent Families." Pp. 105–115 in *LGBT-Parent Families: Innovations in Research and Implications for Practice*, edited by A. E. Goldberg and K. R. Allen. New York, NY: Springer New York.

Dozier, Raine. 2005. "Beards, Breasts, and Bodies: Doing Sex in a Gendered World." *Gender & Society* 19(3):297–316.

Elders, M. Joycelyn, George R. Brown, Eli Coleman, Thomas A. Kolditz, and Alan M. Steinman. 2015. "Medical Aspects of Transgender Military Service." *Armed Forces & Society* 41(2):199–220.

Gates, Gary J. and Jody Herman. 2014. *Transgender Military Service in the United States*. Los Angeles, CA: The Williams Institute.

Grossman, Arnold H., Anthony R. D'Augelli, Tamika Jarrett Howell, and Steven Hubbard. 2005. "Parents' Reactions to Transgender Youths' Gender Nonconforming Expression and Identity." *Journal of Gay & Lesbian Social Services* 18(1):3–16.

Haines, Beth A., Alex A. Ajayi and Helen Boyd. 2014. "Making Trans Parents Visible: Intersectionality of Trans and Parenting Identities." *Feminism & Psychology* 24(2):238–247.

Hicks, Stephen. 2013. "Lesbian, Gay, Bisexual, and Transgender Parents and the Question of Gender." Pp. 149–162 in *LGBT-Parent Families: Innovations in Research and Implications for Practice*, edited by A. E. Goldberg and K. R. Allen, New York, NY: Springer.

Hill, Darryl B. and Edgardo Menvielle. 2009. "'You Have to Give Them a Place Where They Feel Protected and Safe and Loved': The Views of Parents Who Have Gender-Variant Children and Adolescents." *Journal of LGBT Youth* 6(2/3):243–271.

Hines, Sally. 2007. *TransForming Gender: Transgender Practices of Identity, Intimacy and Care*. Bristol, England: Bristol University Press.

Hoffkling, Alexis, Juno Obedin-Maliver and Jae Sevelius. 2017. "From Erasure to Opportunity: A Qualitative Study of the Experiences of Transgender Men around Pregnancy and Recommendations for Providers." *BMC Pregnancy and Childbirth* 17(2):332.

James, Sandy, Jody L. Herman, Sue Rankin, Mara Keisling, Lisa Mottet, and Anafi Ma'ayan. 2016. *The Report of the 2015 U.S. Transgender Survey.* Washington, D.C.: National Center for Transgender Equality.

Jauk, Daniela. 2013. "Gender Violence Revisited: Lessons from Violent Victimization of Transgender Identified Individuals." *Sexualities* 16(7):807–825.

Karaian, Lara. 2013. "Pregnant Men: Repronormativity, Critical Trans Theory and the Re(conceive)ing of Sex and Pregnancy in Law." *Social & Legal Studies* 22(2):211–230.

McCarthy, Justin. 2019. "In U.S., 71% Support Transgender People Serving in Military." *Gallup.* Retrieved June 26, 2019 (https://news.gallup.com/poll/258521/support-trans gender-people-serving-military.aspx).

McGuire, Jenifer K., Katherine A. Kuvalanka, Jory M. Catalpa, and Russell B. Toomey. 2016. "Transfamily Theory: How the Presence of Trans* Family Members Informs Gender Development in Families: Transfamily Theory." *Journal of Family Theory & Review* 8(1):60–73.

Meyer, Doug. 2015. *Violence against Queer People: Race, Class, Gender, and the Persistence of Anti-LGBT Discrimination.* New Brunswick, NJ: Rutgers University Press.

Moran, Leslie J. and Andrew N. Sharpe. 2004. "Violence, Identity and Policing: The Case of Violence against Transgender People." *Criminal Justice* 4(4):395–417.

Movement Advancement Project. 2019. "Foster and Adoption Laws." Retrieved June 12, 2019 (www.lgbtmap.org//equality-maps/foster_and_adoption_laws).

Pascoe, C. J. 2011. *Dude, You're a Fag: Masculinity and Sexuality in High School.* (Second Edition). Berkeley, CA: University of California Press.

Rowniak, Stefan, Catherine Chesla, Carol Dawson Rose, and William L. Holzemer. 2011. "Transmen: The HIV Risk of Gay Identity." *AIDS Education and Prevention* 23(6):508–520.

Rubin, Henry. 2003. *Self-Made Men: Identity and Embodiment among Transsexual Men.* Nashville, TN: Vanderbilt University Press.

Schilt, Kristen. 2010. *Just One of the Guys?: Transgender Men and the Persistence of Gender Inequality.* Chicago, IL: University of Chicago Press.

Schilt, Kristen and Laurel Westbrook. 2009. "Doing Gender, Doing Heteronormativity: 'Gender Normals,' Transgender People, and the Social Maintenance of Heterosexuality." *Gender & Society* 23(4):440–464.

Sevelius, Jae. 2009. "'There's No Pamphlet for the Kind of Sex I Have': HIV-Related Risk Factors and Protective Behaviors among Transgender Men Who Have Sex with Nontransgender Men." *Journal of the Association of Nurses in AIDS Care* 20(5):398–410.

Stein, Arlene. 2018. *Unbound: Transgender Men and the Remaking of Identity.* New York, NY: Vintage Books.

Testa, Rylan J., Laura M. Sciacca, Michael L. Florence Wang, Peter Goldblum Hendricks, Judith Bradford, and Bruce Bongar. 2012. "Effects of Violence on Transgender People." *Professional Psychology: Research and Practice* 43(5):452–459.

Tornello, Samantha L., Rachel G. Riskind, and Aleks Babić. 2019. "Transgender and Gender Non-Binary Parents' Pathways to Parenthood." *Psychology of Sexual Orientation and Gender Diversity* 6(2):232–241.

Veldorale-Griffin, Amanda and Carol Anderson Darling. 2016. "Adaptation to Parental Gender Transition: Stress and Resilience among Transgender Parents." *Archives of Sexual Behavior* 45(3):607–617.

Vikhrov, Natalie. 2018. "Where Are The Trans Men In Politics?" *Huff Post.* Retrieved June 26, 2019 (www.huffpost.com/entry/transgender-men-politics_n_5b1172d1e4b 02143b7cc256a).

Watkins, Paul J. and Edward Moreno. 2017. "Bathrooms without Borders: Transgender Students Argue Separate is not Equal." *The Clearing House: A Journal of Educational Strategies, Issues and Ideas* 90(5/6):166–171.

Wierckx, Katrien, Els Elaut, Eva Van Caenegem, Fleur Van De Peer, David Dedecker, Ellen Van Houdenhove, and Guy T'Sjoen. 2011. "Sexual Desire in Female-to-Male Transsexual Persons: Exploration of the Role of Testosterone Administration." *European Journal of Endocrinology* 165(2):331–337.

Wierckx, Katrien, Els Elaut, Birgit Van Hoorde, Gunter Heylens, Griet De Cuypere, Stan Monstrey, Steven Weyers, Piet Hoebeke, and Guy T'Sjoen. 2014. "Sexual Desire in Trans Persons: Associations with Sex Reassignment Treatment." *The Journal of Sexual Medicine* 11(1):107–118.

Wiewel, Ellen W., Alexander B. Harris, Qiang Xia, Demetre Daskalakis, Ansley Lemons, Linda Beer, Teresa Finlayson, Donna Hubbard McCree, Daniel Lentine, and R. Luke Shouse. 2018. "Potential Misclassification of HIV-Positive Persons as Transgender Men/Respond." *American Journal of Public Health* 108(7):E14–15.

Worthen, Meredith G. F. 2016. "Hetero-cis-normativity and the Gendering of Transphobia." *International Journal of Transgenderism* 17(1):31–57.

Worthen, Meredith G. F. 2019. "Transgender under Fire: Hetero-cis-normativity and Military Students' Attitudes toward Trans Issues and Trans Service Members Post DADT." *Sexuality Research and Social Policy* 16(3):289–308.

# 14
# NON-BINARY/GENDERQUEER STIGMA

*It's a difficult place to live, being neither/nor in an either/or world. But the freedom and fun one may derive from navigating that kind of life is well worth any difficulty.*
Kate Bornstein, non-binary activist[1]

IMAGE 14.1 German passport with gender marker "X" issued in 2019. Along with Germany, Australia, Bangladesh, Canada, Iceland, India, Malta, Nepal, the Netherlands, New Zealand, Pakistan and more than twenty states in the U.S. also allow for third gender options on official documents as of 2020.

The explicit use of "non-binary" and "genderqueer" identities is, for the most part, a relatively more recent development than the use of lesbian, gay, bisexual, and transgender identities and perhaps at least partly because of this, non-binary/genderqueer identities may be amongst the most misunderstood. Largely starting in the 1990s, activist/scholars like Kate Bornstein and Riki Wilchins contributed to a growing conversation about gender identities beyond the man/woman dichotomy including both non-binary and genderqueer identities (Bornstein 1994; Wilchins 1997). These identities created a space for individuals who recognize their gender as fluid, androgynous, and/or variant. Alongside this, the self-identification as non-binary and/or genderqueer also grew and continues to be impactful (James et al. 2016; Oakley 2016; Stachowiak 2017). For some, identities such as non-binary and genderqueer are preferential to other self-identity terms, including transgender, because they more accurately capture their experiences as gender diverse. For example, in the U.S. Transgender Survey (N = 27,715), although a majority (65%) identified as transgender, about one-third identified as non-binary (31%) and/or genderqueer (29%) (James et al. 2016). Yet research on non-binary/genderqueer individuals and their experiences is lacking (Marshall et al. 2019).

## The Stigmatization of Non-binary/Genderqueer People

In the survey instrument, the section focusing on attitudes toward non-binary/genderqueer people was preceded by the following statement:

> *We are interested in your thoughts, feelings, and predicted behaviors about people who self-identify as "non-binary" or "genderqueer." Please note that "genderqueer" is often used as an umbrella identity term that encompasses individuals who are gender non-binary or gender fluid and/or those who do not feel they fit within the categories of man or woman.*

### The Non-binary/Genderqueer Stigma Scale

Among all nine groups examined in this book, non-binary/genderqueer individuals are the most stigmatized (recall Figure 7.1). Their experiences beyond the dichotomous gender system of "man" and "woman" inform their stigmatization in dynamic, intersectional ways. To better understand these complexities, the 14 items in the Non-binary/Genderqueer Stigma Scale as seen in Figure 14.1 and Table 14.1 are discussed below.

### Non-binary/Genderqueer Individuals and Social and Familial Relationships

Although the stigmatization of having social and familial relationships with non-binary/genderqueer people is lower in comparison to all other key areas of the

Non-binary/Genderqueer Stigma  325

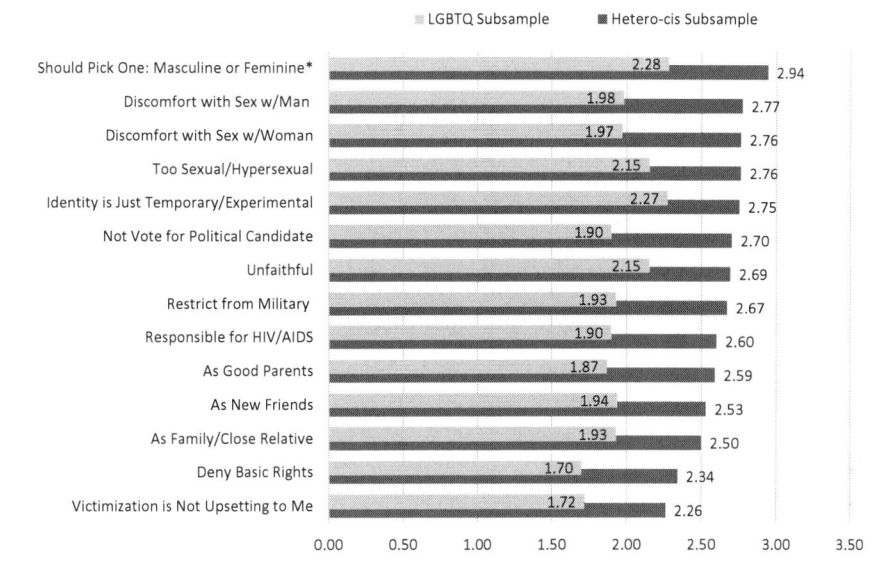

| Item | LGBTQ Subsample | Hetero-cis Subsample |
|---|---|---|
| Should Pick One: Masculine or Feminine* | 2.28 | 2.94 |
| Discomfort with Sex w/Man | 1.98 | 2.77 |
| Discomfort with Sex w/Woman | 1.97 | 2.76 |
| Too Sexual/Hypersexual | 2.15 | 2.76 |
| Identity is Just Temporary/Experimental | 2.27 | 2.75 |
| Not Vote for Political Candidate | 1.90 | 2.70 |
| Unfaithful | 2.15 | 2.69 |
| Restrict from Military | 1.93 | 2.67 |
| Responsible for HIV/AIDS | 1.90 | 2.60 |
| As Good Parents | 1.87 | 2.59 |
| As New Friends | 1.94 | 2.53 |
| As Family/Close Relative | 1.93 | 2.50 |
| Deny Basic Rights | 1.70 | 2.34 |
| Victimization is Not Upsetting to Me | 1.72 | 2.26 |

**FIGURE 14.1** Non-binary/Genderqueer Stigma Scale Item Mean Values Rank-Ordered from Most to Least Stigmatizing for the Hetero-cis (n = 1,500) and the LGBTQ (n = 1,604) Subsamples

*Notes:* see Table 14.1 for the exact wording for each item. *t*-test results comparing the hetero-cis and LGBTQ subsamples indicate that all means are significantly different from one another at the p < .001 level. * This item differs from all other LGBTQ Stigma Scales.

scale (with the exception of basic human rights as discussed in Chapter 7) (see Table 14.1), non-binary/genderqueer people were the most likely of all nine groups to be stigmatized as parents, as friends, and as family members by both the hetero-cis and LGBTQ subsamples (recall Figure 7.4). Thus, there is hostility across the entire sample toward non-binary/genderqueer people in social and familial relationships. Some existing work also highlights the difficulties that non-binary/genderqueer people can experience among friends and family members (Galupo, Henise, and Davis 2014; Stachowiak 2017) and as parents (Tornello, Riskind, and Babić 2019).

Interestingly, the item with the highest mean in this area for the hetero-cis subsample (2.59) had the lowest mean for the LGBTQ subsample (1.87). That item is: "Non-binary/genderqueer people are not capable of being good parents." Hetero-cis individuals in particular may stereotype non-binary/genderqueer people's parenting practices as problematic because they are more inclined to uphold cis-normative and binary gendering parenting ideologies than LGBTQ people are and as a result, they may perceive non-binary/genderqueer parents as unable to appropriately and/or successfully nurture a child's gender identity development (Sutfin et al. 2008). Hetero-cis individuals may also perceive more difficulties with being

**TABLE 14.1** Non-binary/Genderqueer Stigma Scale Item Mean Values (Standard Deviations) and *t*-test Results Comparing the Means for the Hetero-cis Subsample and the LGBTQ Subsample

|  | *Hetero-cis Subsample* | *LGBTQ Subsample* | *t-test Results* |
|---|---|---|---|
|  | n = 1,500 | n = 1,604 |  |
| *Social and familial relationships* |  |  |  |
| I welcome new friends who are non-binary/genderqueer people.[R] | 2.53 (1.18) | 1.94 (1.11) | $t = 14.46^*$ |
| I don't think it would negatively affect our relationship if I learned that one of my close relatives was non-binary or genderqueer.[R] | 2.50 (1.18) | 1.93 (1.15) | $t = 13.63^*$ |
| Non-binary/genderqueer people are not capable of being good parents. | 2.59 (1.27) | 1.87 (1.15) | $t = 16.62^*$ |
| *Positions of importance and social significance* |  |  |  |
| I would not vote for a political candidate who was non-binary or genderqueer. | 2.70 (1.29) | 1.90 (1.21) | $t = 17.84^*$ |
| Non-binary/genderqueer people should not be allowed to join the military. | 2.67 (1.31) | 1.93 (1.23) | $t = 16.25^*$ |
| *Basic human rights* |  |  |  |
| I believe non-binary/genderqueer people should have all of the same rights as other people do.[R] | 2.34 (1.17) | 1.70 (1.07) | $t = 15.99^*$ |
| It is upsetting to me that non-binary/genderqueer people experience violence, harassment, and discrimination just because they are non-binary/genderqueer.[R] | 2.26 (1.15) | 1.72 (1.09) | $t = 13.39^*$ |
| *Sex act-related stigma* |  |  |  |
| Non-binary/genderqueer people are unfaithful to their romantic partners. | 2.69 (1.08) | 2.15 (1.12) | $t = 13.74^*$ |
| Non-binary/genderqueer people are too sexual (hypersexual). | 2.76 (1.11) | 2.15 (1.12) | $t = 15.22^*$ |
| Non-binary/genderqueer people are mostly responsible for spreading HIV/AIDS. | 2.60 (1.15) | 1.90 (1.10) | $t = 17.34^*$ |
| I am comfortable with the thought of a non-binary/genderqueer person having sex with a man.[R] | 2.77 (1.14) | 1.98 (1.07) | $t = 19.73^*$ |

(*Continued*)

**TABLE 14.1** (Cont.)

|  | Hetero-cis Subsample | LGBTQ Subsample | t-test Results |
| --- | --- | --- | --- |
| I am comfortable with the thought of a non-binary/genderqueer person having sex with a woman.[R] | 2.76 (1.13) | 1.97 (1.05) | $t = 20.16$* |
| *Non-binary/genderqueer identity Permanency* | | | |
| Most people who call themselves non-binary/genderqueer are just temporarily experimenting with their gender. | 2.75 (1.09) | 2.27 (1.17) | $t = 11.86$* |
| *Achievement of femininity or masculinity* | | | |
| Non-binary/genderqueer people should just pick one: either be feminine or masculine. | 2.94 (1.12) | 2.28 (1.21) | $t = 15.80$* |
| α | .90 | .94 | |
| Summed scale actual range | 14–70 | 14–70 | |
| Summed scale mean | 36.85 (10.87) | 27.66 (11.79) | $t = 22.58$* |

*Notes:* response options were Strongly Disagree–Strongly Agree (range: 1–5).[R] This item is reverse coded.

* *t*-test results allowing for unequal variances indicate that the hetero-cis subsample and LGBTQ subsample means are significantly different from one another at the p < .001 level.

a non-binary/genderqueer parent than LGBTQ individuals do (Lev 2010; Petit, Julien, and Chamberland 2017; Tornello, Riskind, and Babić 2019). Even so, in this study, both hetero-cis and LGBTQ people indicate the highest stigmatization toward non-binary/genderqueer people in social and familial relationships (recall Figure 7.4).

## Non-binary/Genderqueer Individuals and Positions of Importance and Social Significance

There was moderate stigmatization of non-binary/genderqueer people in this key area. Means for both items ("I would not vote for a political candidate who was non-binary/genderqueer" and "Non-binary/genderqueer people should not be allowed to join the military") were very similar for the hetero-cis subsample (2.70 and 2.67, respectively) and for the LGBTQ subsample (1.90 and 1.93, respectively). Overall, non-binary/genderqueer people were the most likely of all nine groups to be stigmatized as political candidates by both the hetero-cis and LGBTQ subsamples (though the mean was identical for trans men political candidates for the hetero-cis subsample) (recall Figure 7.4). This is not surprising given that though there are celebrities who have self-identified as non-binary and genderqueer (e.g., actors Jonathan Van Ness and Lachlan Watson, musician Sam Smith, see Fuentes 2019), there are no current self-identified non-binary/genderqueer political or military leaders in the U.S. However, there are notable non-binary/genderqueer people working to make changes. For example, in 2020, Bre Kidman became the first openly non-binary person to run for Senate and in doing so, she had the U.S. Senate Select Committee on Ethics add the more gender-neutral "Mx." honorific to the drop-down menu of their e-file system for candidates (Miller 2019) and in 2016, Army veteran Jamie Shupe became the first person in the U.S. to have "non-binary" as the gender marker on their driver's license (Karimi and Stewart 2016). Even so, non-binary/genderqueer people's fights for positions of importance and social significance remain uphill battles.

## Non-binary/Genderqueer Individuals and Sex Act-Related Stigma

Three of the top five most stigmatizing attitudes toward non-binary/genderqueer people were among the sex act-related stigma items for the hetero-cis subsample (hypersexuality and discomfort with sex with both men women) as were two of the top four for the LGBTQ subsample (hypersexuality and unfaithful) (see Figure 14.1). In addition, all means for the five items in this key area were at or above 2.60 among the hetero-cis subsample (ranging from 2.60 to 2.77) and close to 2.0 or higher for the LGBTQ subsample (ranging from 1.90 to 2.15) (see Table 14.1). Sex act-related stigma among non-binary/genderqueer people may be relatively strong because non-binary/genderqueer people's sex acts can be disregarded, and misunderstood (Hammack, Frost, and Hughes 2019; Oakley 2016; Galupo, Lomash, and Mitchell 2017).

For the hetero-cis subsample, the top three highest means in the sex act-related stigma key area were separated by only .01 points. These include: "I am comfortable with the thought of a non-binary/genderqueer person having sex with a man" (reverse coded), "I am comfortable with the thought of a non-binary/genderqueer person having sex with a woman" (reverse coded), and "non-binary/genderqueer people are too sexual (hypersexual)." The stigmatization of non-binary/genderqueer people as hypersexual was also one of the two highest means among the LGBTQ subsample in the sex-act related key area as well as the belief that non-binary/genderqueer people are unfaithful (see Table 14.1).

Non-binary/genderqueer people's sexualities may be stigmatized because they are often missing from both dominant cultural discourse as well as empirical research (Hammack, Frost, and Hughes 2019; Oakley 2016; Galupo et al. 2017; Stachowiak 2017). Yet even amidst this dearth, there is evidence that non-binary/genderqueer people have unique sexual experiences that may relate to their stigmatization. For example, one study (N = 955) found that compared to cisgender men, genderqueer people (n = 57) have significantly higher levels of sexual and relationship anxiety. In addition, these anxieties were found to be related to lower levels of relationship satisfaction, sexual satisfaction, and sexual desire (Mark, Vowels, and Murray 2018). These negative experiences may relate to larger misunderstandings about non-binary/genderqueer people's sexualities. Indeed, research demonstrates that the lack of cultural recognition of their romantic and relationship experiences impacts the ways that non-binary/genderqueer people feel about their sexual selves (Oakley 2016; Galupo, Lomash, and Mitchell 2017). Overall, because non-binary/genderqueer people's sexualities continue to be disregarded and misunderstood, non-binary/genderqueer sex act-related stigma remains apparent.

## *Non-binary/Genderqueer Individuals Identity Permanency*

The stigmatizing perspective that "Most people who call themselves non-binary/genderqueer are just temporarily experimenting with their gender" was evident in both subsamples. Specifically, this was the second most stigmatizing attitude among the LGBTQ subsample and the fifth most stigmatizing attitude among the hetero-cis subsample (however, the mean was only .01–.02 points lower than the items three items ranked above this item for the hetero-cis-subsample). There are two related stereotypes that contribute to the questioning of non-binary/genderqueer people's identity permanency. First, because non-binary/genderqueer identities are often defined as fluid (Davidson 2007; Oakley 2016; Stachowiak 2017) some may wrongly perceive non-binary/genderqueer identity as inauthentic. This perspective may also be related the "temporary" quality that can be assigned to non-binary/genderqueer people's identities and associated dismissive attitudes (Clarke 2018; Vanderburgh 2009). For example, in the U.S. Transgender Discrimination Survey (n = 9,769 non-binary/genderqueer respondents), when asked why they do not correct those who wrongly assume they are cis men or cis women, 63% of non-binary/genderqueer respondents indicated that "most people dismiss [their non-binary identity] as not being a real identity or a 'phase'" (James et al. 2016:49).

Second, because non-binary/genderqueer is a relatively new self-proclaimed identity (Davidson 2007; Kuper, Nussbaum, and Mustanski 2012; Oakley 2016; Stachowiak 2017), some may see non-binary/genderqueer identity as a short-lived youthful trend among those who are already regularly dismissed and disregarded as going through "phases" related to their gender identities (James et al. 2016; Vanderburgh 2009). Consistent with one online convenience sample of transgender spectrum/gender variant adults across the globe (N = 292, n = 161 genderqueer individuals) (Kuper, Nussbaum, and Mustanski 2012) and another online study conducted in Australia (N= 7,479, n = 579 non-binary individuals) (Whyte, Brooks, and Torgler 2018) that both found that younger individuals are more likely to identify as non-binary or genderqueer, in this sample, the mean age of non-binary/genderqueer individuals (33.42 years) was close to seven years younger than the mean age of those that did not identify as non-binary/genderqueer (40.40 years). In addition, half (50.5%, n = 48/95) of non-binary/genderqueer individuals were aged 35 years or younger in this sample. Overall, these perspectives and patterns contribute to stereotypes about non-binary/genderqueer people's identity permanency.

## Non-binary/Genderqueer Individuals and the Achievement of Femininity or Masculinity

The item in this key area differed from all other LGBTQ stigma scales. For the Non-binary/Genderqueer Stigma Scale, this item was: "Non-binary/genderqueer people should just pick one: either be feminine or masculine." Non-binary/genderqueer people were strongly stigmatized for their lack of adherence to either femininity or masculinity. In fact, this item had the highest mean value as compared to all other items in all of the LGBTQ stigma scales (126 items in total) for the hetero-cis subsample (2.94) and had the second-highest mean for the LGBTQ subsample (2.28). In addition, across all 14 items in the Non-binary/Genderqueer Stigma Scale, this item has the highest mean value for both subsamples (see Figure 14.1). Thus, there is agreement across the entire sample that non-binary/genderqueer people should make a decision about being either feminine or masculine and this perspective is particularly strong compared to other stigmatizing attitudes toward other LGBTQ people.

Because non-binary/genderqueer identity is often fluid, those who identify as non-binary/genderqueer may express gender and sexuality in diverse ways which can contrast strongly with hetero-cis-normative expectations (Davidson 2007; Richards, Bouman, and Barker 2017; Stachowiak 2017). For example, one qualitative study (N = 10) found that genderqueer individuals felt that their gender expression was regularly policed by others, especially parents, in ways that attempted to reinforce hetero-cis-normativity (Stachowiak 2017). Yet genderqueer individuals also described their genderqueer identities as creating freedom to (re)grow gender in a way that is authentic to their selves which often involved the embodiment of both femininity and masculinity (Stachowiak 2017).

In addition, non-binary/genderqueer individuals may opt out of hormonal and surgical gender affirming treatments/surgeries (that can sometimes reinforce cisnormative expectations) in favor of developing their gender expressions in more variant and fluid ways (Kuper, Nussbaum, and Mustanski 2012). Specifically, in comparison to trans individuals, non-binary/genderqueer individuals may feel that more permanent transitions may be less in line with their desires to express their fluid gender identities. For example, in one study of trans and genderqueer U.S. adults (N = 166; about one third of whom identified as genderqueer, 31.3%, n = 52), genderqueer people were more likely to indicate they had no interest in hormone treatment as compared to trans men and trans women (21.9% vs. 0% and 0% respectively) and no interest in genital surgery (64.1% vs. 31.4% and 14.0% respectively) (Factor and Rothblum 2008). In the U.S. Transgender Discrimination Survey (n = 9,769 non-binary/genderqueer respondents), compared to trans men, non-binary/genderqueer respondents with female on their original birth certificate were significantly more likely to indicate that do not ever want top surgeries (chest reduction/reconstruction, 3% vs. 21%) or bottom surgeries (metoidioplasty, 24% vs. 72%; phalloplasty, 35% vs. 79%). In addition, compared to trans women, non-binary/genderqueer respondents with male on their original birth certificate were significantly more likely to indicate that do not ever want top surgeries (augmentation mammoplasty, 19% vs. 47%) or bottom surgeries (vaginoplasty or labiaplasty, 12% vs. 59%; orchiectomy, 20% vs. 53%) (James et al. 2016).

Overall, because Western cultures actively uphold and maintain hetero-cis-normativity and non-binary/genderqueer individuals challenge this through their gender expressions and gender identities, they experience stigma. In particular, the need for non-binary/genderqueer people to squarely and consistently fit into the categories of either "feminine" or "masculine" is a strongly stigmatizing attitude among both subsamples in this study. As noted above, across all 126 items in the 9 LGBTQ stigma scales, this perspective is the most stigmatizing attitude toward *all* LGBTQ people held among hetero-cis people and the second-most stigmatizing attitude held among LGBTQ people.

### Non-binary/Genderqueer Stigma Summed Scale

In Table 14.1, the Non-binary/Genderqueer Stigma Scale was created by summing all 14 items together. Cronbach's alphas were quite high for the hetero-cis subsample (.90) and the LGBTQ subsample (.94). Similar to the Trans Women Stigma Scale (but unlike the stigma scales for lesbian women, gay men, bisexual women, and bisexual men), the actual range in values for the Non-binary/Genderqueer Stigma Scale was identical for the two subsamples (14–70) with one hetero-cis person and two LGBTQ people indicating the most stigmatizing attitudes on all 14 items in the scale. However, mean values for the summed Non-binary/Genderqueer Stigma Scale differed substantially and significantly with the hetero-cis subsample mean (36.85) 9.25 points higher than the LGBTQ subsample mean (27.66). In addition, the key area with the highest individual mean value was the same for both subsamples: achievement of femininity or masculinity. In addition, stigma toward non-binary/genderqueer identity permanency and hypersexuality were high for both subsamples. For the hetero-cis subsample, non-binary/genderqueer people's sex acts were also highly stigmatized. However, it is important to note that for the hetero-cis subsample, the mean scores ranked second through fifth were very close to one another (ranging by only .02 points). Thus, overall, the stigmatization of non-binary/genderqueer people is largely associated with the belief that non-binary/genderqueer people should just be either masculine or feminine, identity permanency, and sex act-related stigma (recall Figure 7.3).

## NCST, Hetero-cis-normativity, Social Power Axes, and the Non-binary/Genderqueer Stigma Scale

The first set of regression models examine the Non-binary/Genderqueer Stigma Scale using NCST. The hypotheses are as follows:

- *Hypothesis 1a*: there is a significant positive relationship between the HCN Scale and the Non-binary/Genderqueer Stigma Scale.
- *Hypothesis 1b*: there are significant relationships between individual social power axes (gender identity, sexual identity, additional gender/sexuality, racial/ethnic identity, basic needs) and the Non-binary/Genderqueer Stigma Scale.
- *Hypothesis 2a*: the relationship between the HCN Scale and the Non-binary/Genderqueer Stigma Scale is moderated by interactions between the HCN Scale and axes of social power.
- *Hypothesis 2b*: the relationships between individual social power axes and the Non-binary/Genderqueer Stigma Scale are moderated by interactions between axes of social power.

Figure 14.2 outlines these relationships and the two models of NCST to be estimated. Specifically, OLS regression is utilized in Table 14.2 to examine

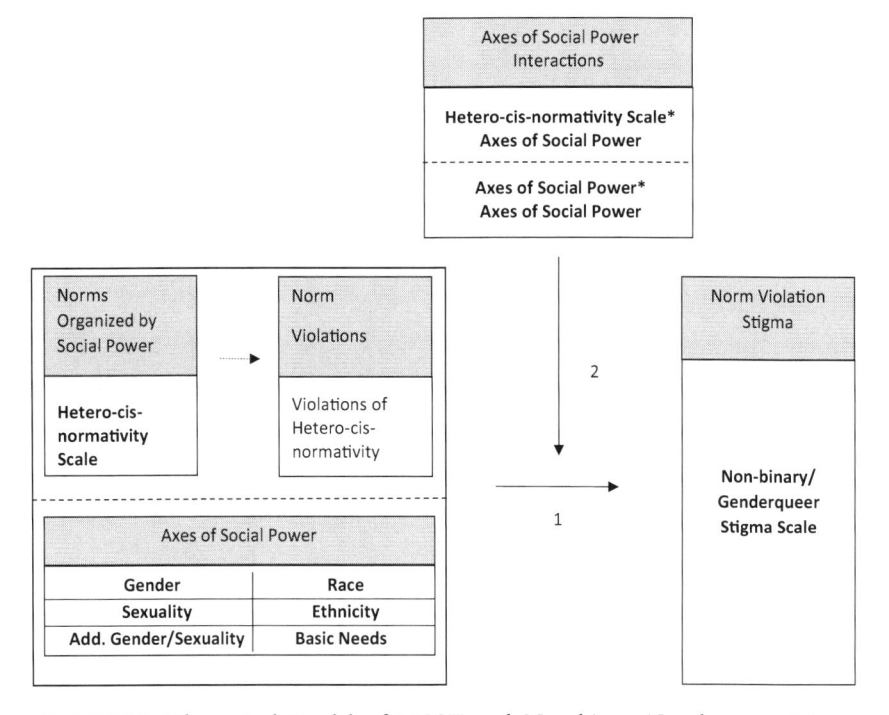

**FIGURE 14.2** Theoretical Model of NCST and Non-binary/Genderqueer Stigma using the Stigmatizer Lens with Model Numbers to be Examined in Table 14.2

*Notes*: Model 1 estimates the HCN Scale and axes of social power (gender, sexuality, additional gender/sexuality, race, ethnicity, and basic needs) as they relate to the Non-binary/Genderqueer Stigma Scale. Model 2 estimates interactions among axes of social power and the HCN Scale as they moderate the relationships between the HCN Scale and the Non-binary/Genderqueer Stigma Scale as well as interactions among axes of social power as they moderate the relationships between the HCN Scale and the Non-binary/Genderqueer Stigma Scale. The * indicates an interaction.

NCST and the relationships among hetero-cis-normativity, axes of social power (gender, sexuality, additional gender/sexuality, race/ethnicity, and basic needs), and the Non-binary/Genderqueer Stigma Scale for the hetero-cis subsample and the LGBTQ subsample. See Chapter 7 for a more complete description of the models. Regarding model fit statistics, the adjusted $R^2$ values ranged from .64 to .65.

## NCST, HCN, Social Power Axes, and the Non-binary/Genderqueer Stigma Scale: Model 1

In Table 14.2 Model 1, the relationships between the HCN Scale, social power axes, and the Non-binary/Genderqueer Stigma Scale are estimated. For both groups, the HCN Scale is positively related to the Non-binary/Genderqueer Stigma Scale in Model 1. Thus, *Hypothesis 1a* is well supported: hetero-cis-normativity is strongly and positively related to the stigmatization of non-binary/genderqueer people for both subsamples. Supporting *Hypothesis 1b*, individual axes of social power are also significantly related to the Non-binary/Genderqueer Stigma Scale for the hetero-cis subsample (cis woman) and for the LGBTQ subsample (cis woman, queer, Two-Spirit, and African American/Black).

**TABLE 14.2** OLS Regression Results Estimating NCST and the Non-binary/Genderqueer Stigma Scale for the Hetero-cis Subsample (n = 1,500) and the LGBTQ Subsample (n = 1,604)

|  | Hetero-cis Subsample | | LGBTQ Subsample | | Test of Difference |
|---|---|---|---|---|---|
|  | Model 1 | Model 2 | Model 1 | Model 2 |  |
| HCN Scale | .83* | .81* | 87* | .71* | . |
| *Gender identity* | | | | | |
| Cis woman | -1.32* | -3.77* | -1.14* | . | |
| *Additional gender/sexual identity* | | | | | |
| Queer | . | . | -1.25* | . | |
| Two-Spirit | . | . | -1.63* | -4.81* | . |
| *Race/ethnicity* | | | | | |
| African American/Black | . | . | 1.42* | 11.08* | . |
| *HCN Scale*social power axes interactions* | | | | | |
| HCN Scale*cis woman | — | .16* | — | . | . |
| HCN Scale*queer | — | -.34* | — | . | ** |
| HCN Scale*femme | — | -.33* | — | . | . |
| HCN Scale*African American/Black | — | -.26* | — | . | ** |

(*Continued*)

**TABLE 14.2** (Cont.)

|  | Hetero-cis Subsample | | LGBTQ Subsample | | Test of Difference |
|---|---|---|---|---|---|
|  | Model 1 | Model 2 | Model 1 | Model 2 | |
| HCN Scale*Multi-racial | — | .60* | — | . | ** |
| HCN Scale*mostly all I need | — | . | — | .26* | ** |
| *Social power axes interactions* | | | | | |
| Cis woman*few needs met | — | -4.01* | — | . | ** |
| Bisexual*mostly all I need | — | — | — | 5.93* | |
| African American/Black*femme | — | . | — | -3.59* | . |
| SGL*few needs met | — | . | — | -5.45* | . |
| *Controls: common explanations* | | | | | |
| *LGBTQ contact* | | | | | |
| Genderqueer friends | -1.14* | -1.16* | -1.44* | -1.61* | . |
| LGBTQ Friends Scale (w/o non-binary and genderqueer) | -.47* | -.51* | -.26* | -.28* | . |
| *Religious identity* | | | | | |
| Catholic | 1.22* | . | . | . | |
| Protestant—mainline | 1.74* | . | . | . | |
| Protestant—evangelical | 2.55* | . | . | . | |
| *Political perspectives* | | | | | |
| Liberal—conservative | .95* | .89* | .48* | .46* | . |
| Openness to new experiences | -1.23* | -.96* | -1.38* | -1.47* | . |
| *Support laws/policies helping:* | | | | | |
| Immigrants | . | . | . | -1.29* | . |
| Non-Christians | . | . | -1.13* | -1.20* | . |
| *Beliefs about gender* | | | | | |
| Feminist | -.91* | . | -2.14* | -1.97* | ** |
| Patriarchal Gender Norms Scale | .45* | .41* | .60* | .60* | . |
| *Sociodemographic controls* | | | | | |
| Education | . | . | .29* | . | |
| Adjusted $R^2$ | .64 | .65 | .64 | .64 | |
| Mean VIF | 1.50 | 1.50 | 1.93 | 1.93 | |

*Notes:* unstandardized regression coefficients are presented. Only the rows with significant results are displayed here. See Table 14.1 for detailed information about the Non-binary/Genderqueer Stigma Scale. See Tables 7.1. and 7.2 for details about all other variables and Appendix B Table B.1 for details about the interaction effects.

\* $p < .05$; a dot (.) indicates non-statistically significant results. A dash (—) indicates this was not included in the model.

\*\* $p < .05$ for Clogg et al.'s (1995) test of equality of regression coefficients comparing Model 2 for the hetero-cis subsample and Model 2 for the LGBTQ subsample.

## NCST, HCN, Social Power Axes, and the Non-binary/Genderqueer Stigma Scale: Model 2

In Model 2, axes of social power and intersections among axes of social power and the HCN Scale are examined as they moderate the relationship between the HCN Scale and the Non-binary/Genderqueer Stigma Scale. The HCN Scale is positively related to the Non-binary/Genderqueer Stigma Scale in Model 2 for both groups. Among the HCN Scale interaction terms, four are discussed in Chapter 7: the interactions between the HCN Scale and queer identity, African American/Black identity, Multi-racial identity, and indicating "mostly all I need." In the hetero-cis subsample, there are two additional significant interaction terms: the interactions between the HCN Scale and cis woman and femme identities are both related to the Non-binary/Genderqueer Stigma Scale but in opposite directions. Higher levels of agreement with the HCN Scale have a more robust impact on attitudes toward non-binary/genderqueer people among hetero-cis women as compared hetero-cis men. Although hetero-cis women are more overall supportive of non-binary/genderqueer people than hetero-cis men are (means on the Non-binary/Genderqueer Stigma Scale of 34.72 vs. 38.98, respectively, are significantly different from one another at the $p < .001$ level), for hetero-cis women who opt into hetero-cis-normative ways of thinking, this strongly impacts their perspectives about non-binary/genderqueer people. This finding extends previous research that has underscored the significance of gender in shaping LGBT attitudes (Herek 1988, 2000, 2002; Worthen 2012, 2016).

In addition, higher levels of agreement with the HCN Scale have a more robust impact on attitudes toward non-binary/genderqueer people among hetero-cis individuals who do *not* identify as "femme" as compared hetero-cis individuals who do identify as "femme." Because non-femme-identified hetero-cis individuals are less stigmatizing toward non-binary/genderqueer individuals than femme-identified hetero-cis individuals are (means on the Non-binary/Genderqueer Stigma Scale of 36.57 vs. 42.14, respectively, are significantly different from one another at the $p < .001$ level), hetero-cis-normative ways of thinking among non-femme-identified hetero-cis individuals strongly inform their attitudes toward non-binary/genderqueer people. Such findings complement existing work on femme- and non-femme identified individuals and their experiences (Blair and Hoskin 2015; Hoskin 2017; Levitt and Horne 2002). Overall, *Hypothesis 2a* is supported: interactions between the HCN Scale and axes of social power moderate the relationship between the HCN Scale and the Non-binary/Genderqueer Stigma Scale for both subsamples.

As seen in all previous chapters, there are no overlapping individual axes of social power that are statistically significantly related to the Non-binary/Genderqueer Stigma Scale for both subsamples in Model 2. Thus, axes of social power shape perspectives about non-binary/genderqueer people for the hetero-cis and LGBTQ subsamples in very different ways. For example, among the individual social power axes, only one is significantly related to the Non-binary/Genderqueer Stigma Scale for the hetero-cis subsample: being a cis woman is negatively related to the stigmatization of non-binary/genderqueer people. The corresponding interaction effect between being a cis woman and having few basic needs met is also negative. These findings are among the consistent trends related to being a cis woman and LGBTQ attitudes as discussed in Chapter 7.

In contrast, there are many more significant results among the individual social power axes and the interaction effects among the social power axes for the LGBTQ subsample. Among the individual effects, being Two-Spirit is negatively related to the Non-binary/Genderqueer Stigma Scale. Because Two-Spirit is an identity that can sometimes overlap with gender fluid identities (Walters et al. 2006), Two-Spirit individuals may be less likely to stigmatize non-binary/genderqueer people. For example, in this study, about 1 in 7 (13.7%, n = 13/95) non-binary/genderqueer individuals identified as Two-Spirit. This overlap in gender fluid identities likely contributes to these findings.

In addition, being African American/Black is positively and robustly related to the stigmatization of non-binary/genderqueer people among the LGBTQ subsample. However, there is one corresponding interaction term that is negatively related to the stigmatization of non-binary/genderqueer people: being African American/Black and femme. Those who identify as LGBTQ, African American/Black, and femme may be less stigmatizing toward non-binary/genderqueer people because they may be more open to diverse, non-hetero-cis-normative gender expressions. Indeed, research indicates that African American lesbian sexual cultural dynamics actively resist dominant hegemonic gender and sexual scripts in numerous ways that intersect with the femme/butch-stud dynamic (Wilson 2009). Thus, although the individual effect of being African American/Black is positively related to the Non-binary/Genderqueer Stigma Scale, the intersection of being LGBTQ, African American/Black, and femme has the opposite effect on the stigmatization of non-binary/genderqueer people.

There are two significant interaction terms among the LGBTQ subsample related to basic needs that do not have corresponding individual effects. Being bisexual and having most needs met is positively related to the Non-binary/Genderqueer Stigma Scale. Such findings indicate that there may be some tension between bisexual and non-binary/genderqueer people. For example, one study found that bisexuality can be described as discriminatory toward non-binary/genderqueer people because bisexuality enforces a binary and in doing so, ignores and/or rejects non-binary/genderqueer people (Flanders et al. 2016). Coupled with class privilege among those who have mostly all they need, these findings indicate some evidence of strains between bisexual and non-binary/genderqueer people.

In contrast, being SGL and having few needs met is negatively related to the Non-binary/Genderqueer Stigma Scale. Because SGL identity can be encompassing of diverse gender expression, SGL individuals may be more supportive of non-binary/genderqueer people. This finding aligns with some past work that found evidence of fluidity of sexual and gender practices among SGL men (Truong et al. 2016). Together, the experiences of struggling to meet one's basic needs and navigating an SGL identity interact to shape supportive perspectives toward non-binary/genderqueer people.

Overall, the findings indicate that the axes of social power that shape perspectives about non-binary/genderqueer people are largely different for the hetero-cis and LGBTQ subsamples. Additional tests to compare the regression coefficients of the two subsamples also reveal several significant differences (Clogg, Petkova, and Haritou 1995). These results provide support for *Hypothesis 2b*: interactions between axes of social power moderate the relationship between the individual axes of social power and the Non-binary/Genderqueer Stigma Scale for both subsamples.

## Summarizing NCST, HCN, Social Power Axes and the Non-binary/Genderqueer Stigma Scale

Table 14.2 shows that hetero-cis and LGBTQ people's attitudes toward non-binary/genderqueer people differ. In particular, different intersecting experiences with hetero-cis-normativity and social power impact the stigmatization of non-binary/genderqueer people for hetero-cis and LGBTQ people. Though some previous research has examined some of these mechanisms (Davidson 2007; Galupo, Lomash, and Mitchell 2017; Stachowiak 2017), overall, NCST's intersectional focus on hetero-cis-normativity and axes of social power help us to better understand the stigmatization of non-binary/genderqueer people.

## Non-binary/Genderqueer People's Experiences

### The Non-binary/Genderqueer Subsample

In this study, there was no requested quota from Survey Sampling International for non-binary/genderqueer individuals yet the sample included 95 non-binary/genderqueer individuals (learn more about the data and sampling procedures in Chapter 7 and Appendix A). At the beginning of the survey, respondents were asked "What best describes your gender?" Non-binary/genderqueer people were those who selected either "I am gender non-binary, gender fluid, or genderqueer and my assigned sex at birth was male" (n = 32) or "I am gender non-binary, gender fluid, or genderqueer and my assigned sex at birth was female" (n = 63). These groups were combined to create the non-binary/genderqueer subsample (n = 95). See Table 14.3 for more details about the non-binary/genderqueer people in this study.

**TABLE 14.3** Non-binary/Genderqueer Subsample Characteristics (n = 95)

|  | % | n |
|---|---|---|
| *Sexual identity* | | |
| Heterosexual/straight* | 12.6% | 12 |
| Gay/lesbian* | 24.2% | 23 |
| Bisexual** | 34.7% | 33 |
| Pansexual* | 15.8% | 15 |
| Asexual* | 12.6% | 12 |
| *Additional gender/sexual identity* | | |
| Queer** | 42.2% | 40 |
| SGL | 15.8% | 15 |
| Two-Spirit | 13.7% | 13 |
| Butch | 8.4% | 8 |
| Femme | 20.0% | 19 |
| Leather | 10.9% | 6 |
| Bear | 10.9% | 6 |
| Twink | 5.5% | 3 |
| Down Low | 9.1% | 5 |
| *Race/ethnicity* | | |
| Caucasian/White** | 67.4% | 64 |
| African American/Black* | 15.8% | 15 |
| Asian American/Pacific Islander* | 2.1% | 2 |
| Native American/Alaskan Native* | 6.3% | 6 |
| Multi-racial* | 6.3% | 6 |
| Other race* | – | 0 |
| Latinx race* | 1.8% | 1 |
| Latinx ethnicity | 23.6% | 13 |
| *Basic needs* | | |
| Everything I need* | 14.7% | 14 |
| Mostly all I need** | 43.2% | 41 |
| Often needs not met** | 26.3% | 25 |
| Few needs met* | 15.8% | 15 |

\* Reference category in analyses in Table 14.5.
\*\* Included in analyses shown in Table 14.5.

## Non-binary/Genderqueer People's Experiences with Gender- and Sexuality-Based DHV

Some research indicates that non-binary/genderqueer people are at risk for DHV (Davidson and Halsall 2016; James et al. 2016; Lubitow et al. 2017; Nadal et al. 2016; Reineck 2017; Sterzing et al. 2017; Tabaac, Perrin, and Benotsch

2018; Walker et al. 2018; Wyss 2004). For example, in the U.S. Transgender Discrimination Survey (n = 9,769 non-binary/genderqueer respondents), more than one-third (39%) were treated negatively on public transportation in the past year, more than half (53%) avoided public restrooms in the past year in fear of DHV, and more than half (55%) experienced sexual assault in their lifetimes (James et al. 2016). In addition, about 1 in 5 non-binary individuals reported losing a job (19%) and being denied a job promotion (21%) (Davidson and Halsall 2016). Another smaller scale study of non-binary youth (n = 68) found that over half experienced discrimination when looking for a job (55.1%) and verbal attacks (56%) (Aparicio-García et al. 2018).

Figure 14.3 shows that over half of non-binary/genderqueer people have had one or more experiences of gender-based DHV (55%) and one or more experiences of sexuality-based DHV (51%). Sexuality-based discrimination is the most common form (47%) while sexuality-based violence is the least common (20%). To better understand non-binary/genderqueer people's gender- and sexuality-based DHV, non-binary/genderqueer people's experiences were compared to the LGBTQ subsample, the women subsample, and the men subsample using *t*-tests. Table 14.4 demonstrates that in comparison to all LGBTQ people, all women, and all men, non-binary/genderqueer people are significantly more likely to experience gender-based violence. In

**FIGURE 14.3** Non-binary/Genderqueer People's (n = 95) Experiences with Gender- and Sexuality-Based DHV

*Notes:* see Table 14.4 for comparisons of being a non-binary/genderqueer people's experiences to the LGBTQ subsample, the men subsample, and the women subsample.

**TABLE 14.4** Gender- and Sexuality-Based DHV Mean Values (Standard Deviations) among Non-binary/Genderqueer People, the LGBTQ Subsample, the Women Subsample, and the Men Subsample with *t*-test Results

|  | | Non-binary /Genderqueer | LGBTQ Subsample | Women Subsample | Men Subsample |
|---|---|---|---|---|---|
| | *n* | 95 | 1604 | 1535 | 1474 |
| *Gender-based* | | | | | |
| Discrimination | | .45 (.50) *** | .32 (.47) | .36 (.48) | .17 (.38) |
| Harassment | | .41 (.49) *** | .28 (.45) | .34 (.47) | .09 (.29) |
| Violence | | .25 (.43)**** | .14 (.34) | .16 (.37) | .07 (.26) |
| Any gender DHV experience (0/1) | | .55 (.50) *** | .40 (.49) | .46 (.50) | .21 (.41) |
| *Sexuality-based* | | | | | |
| Discrimination | | .47 (.50) ** | .44 (.50) | .26 (.44) | .23 (.42) |
| Harassment | | .41 (.49) ** | .41 (.49) | .23 (.42) | .24 (.43) |
| Violence | | .20 (.40) * | .20 (.40) | .10 (.31) | .13 (.34) |
| Any sexuality DHV experience (0/1) | | .51 (.50) ** | .53 (.50) | .32 (.47) | .33 (.47) |

\* Non-binary/genderqueer people are significantly different from the women subsample (only) at p < .05 level.

\*\* Non-binary/genderqueer people are significantly different from both the women and men subsamples at p < .05 level.

\*\*\* Non-binary/genderqueer people are significantly different from both the LGBTQ and men subsamples at p < .05 level.

\*\*\*\* Non-binary/genderqueer people are significantly different from the LGBTQ subsample, the women subsample, and men subsample at p < .05 level.

addition, non-binary/genderqueer people report significantly more experiences with gender-based discrimination and harassment as well as any gender-based DHV in comparison to both the LGBTQ and men subsamples. Non-binary/genderqueer people are also significantly more likely than both the women and men subsamples to experience sexuality-based discrimination and harassment as well as any sexuality-based DHV. Non-binary/genderqueer people also report significantly more sexuality-based violence comparison to the women subsample. Overall, compared to the other LGBTQ groups, non-binary/genderqueer individuals (and bisexual women) experience the highest percentage of gender-based violence (recall Figure 7.7). Thus, non-binary/genderqueer people are at particular risk for both gender- and sexuality-based DHV. Non-binary/genderqueer people's DHV experiences are examined further below.

## NCST and Non-binary/Genderqueer People's Experiences with Gender- and Sexuality-Based DHV

The second set of regression models examines non-binary/genderqueer people and their experiences with gender- and sexuality-based DHV using NCST with a focus on non-binary/genderqueer people's axes of social power. The hypotheses are as follows:

- *Hypothesis 1*: being a non-binary/genderqueer person (violating hetero-cis-normativity) increases the likelihood of experiencing gender- and sexuality-based DHV (non-binary/genderqueer stigma).
- *Hypothesis 2*: the relationship between being a non-binary/genderqueer person and gender- and sexuality-based DHV is moderated by interactions between being a non-binary/genderqueer person and axes of social power.

Figure 14.4 outlines these relationships and Table 14.5 displays logistic regression results that examine NCST and the relationships among being a non-binary/genderqueer person, non-binary/genderqueer people's axes of social power and intersections among non-binary/genderqueer people's axes of social power, and any experiences of gender-based DHV (dichotomized as 0/1) or sexuality-based DHV

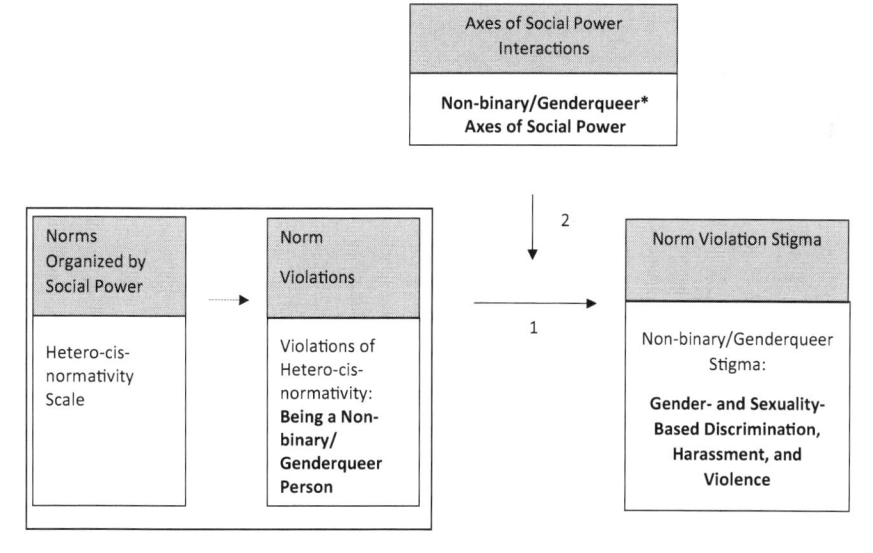

**FIGURE 14.4** Theoretical Model of NCST and Non-binary/Genderqueer Stigma using the Stigmatized Lens with Model Numbers to be Examined in Table 14.5

*Notes:* Model 1 estimates being a non-binary/genderqueer person as related to gender- and sexuality-based DHV. Model 2 estimates interactions among non-binary/genderqueer people's axes of social power as they moderate the relationships between being a non-binary/genderqueer person and gender- and sexuality-based DHV. The * indicates an interaction.

(dichotomized as 0/1) utilizing the LGBTQ subsample (n = 1,604; whereby being a non-binary/genderqueer person is compared to all other LGBTQ people). Because non-binary/genderqueer people's experiences are the focus of this exploration (i.e., the stigmatized lens of NCST is being utilized), the non-binary/genderqueer and social power axes interaction terms are listed at the top of the table and are the focus of the discussion below. However, there are significant corresponding individual effects related to being bisexual and being queer (for example) that are important to recognize. See Chapter 7 for a more complete description of the models and a discussion of overarching trends and patterns. Regarding model fit statistics, the pseudo $R^2$ values were low and ranged from .07 to .08.

## NCST, Non-binary/Genderqueer People, and Gender- and Sexuality-Based DHV: Model 1

In Table 14.5, both Model 1s estimate the relationships between violations of hetero-cis-normativity conceptualized as being a non-binary/genderqueer person and the stigmatization of non-binary/genderqueer people conceptualized as gender- and sexuality-based DHV along with sociodemographic controls. Being a non-binary/genderqueer person is not significantly related to gender-based DHV but is significantly related to sexuality-based DHV in Model 1. However, results are in the opposite direction from predicted. Specifically, being a non-binary/genderqueer person *decreases* the likelihood of sexuality-based DHV by .41. This is in direct contrast with past research that has identified relationships between non-binary/genderqueer identity and DHV (Aparicio-García et al. 2018; James et al. 2016; Lubitow et al. 2017; Nadal et al. 2016; Reineck 2017; Sterzing et al. 2017; Tabaac, Perrin, and Benotsch 2018; Walker et al. 2018; Wyss 2004). Thus, *Hypothesis 1* is not supported.

TABLE 14.5 Logistic Regression Results with Odds Ratios and (Standard Errors) Estimating NCST and Gender- and Sexuality-Based DHV as Related to Being a Non-binary/Genderqueer Person for the LGBTQ Subsample (n = 1,604)

|  | Gender-Based DHV |  |  |  | Sexuality-Based DHV |  |  |  |
|---|---|---|---|---|---|---|---|---|
|  | Model 1 |  | Model 2 |  | Model 1 |  | Model 2 |  |
|  | OR | SE | OR | SE | OR | SE | OR | SE |
| Non-binary/ genderqueer | . | . | . | . | .59* | (.14) | .27* | (.16) |
| *Non-binary/genderqueer social power axes interactions* |  |  |  |  |  |  |  |  |
| Non-binary/ genderqueer*bisexual | — | — | . | . | — | — | .26* | (.13) |

(*Continued*)

**TABLE 14.5** (Cont.)

|  | Gender-Based DHV | | | | Sexuality-Based DHV | | | |
| --- | --- | --- | --- | --- | --- | --- | --- | --- |
|  | Model 1 | | Model 2 | | Model 1 | | Model 2 | |
|  | OR | SE | OR | SE | OR | SE | OR | SE |
| Non-binary/genderqueer*queer | — | — | . | . | — | — | . | . |
| Non-binary/genderqueer*White | — | — | . | . | — | — | . | . |
| Non-binary/genderqueer*mostly all I need | — | — | . | . | — | — | . | . |
| Non-binary/genderqueer*often needs not met | — | — | . | . | — | — | . | . |
| *Non-binary/genderqueer social power axes* | | | | | | | | |
| Bisexual | . | . | . | . | .35* | (.04) | . | . |
| Queer | 1.98* | (.27) | 3.14* | (1.52) | 2.20* | (.32) | . | . |
| White | . | . | . | . | . | . | . | . |
| Mostly all I need | . | . | . | . | . | . | . | . |
| Often needs not met | . | . | . | . | 1.46* | (.24) | 4.19* | (2.62) |
| *Socio-demographic controls* | | | | | | | | |
| Age | .96* | (.00) | .96* | (.00) | .98* | (.00) | .98* | (.00) |
| Town type (rural–large city) | . | . | . | . | . | . | . | . |
| Education | 1.14* | (.05) | 1.14* | (.05) | . | . | . | . |
| Income | . | . | . | . | . | . | . | . |
| Pseudo $R^2$ | .07 | | .07 | | .08 | | .08 | |
| Mean VIF | 1.15 | | 1.15 | | 1.15 | | 1.15 | |

*Notes:* all rows are displayed, including those without significant results. See Table 14.3 for more details about non-binary/genderqueer people.
* $p < .05$; A dot (.) indicates non-statistically significant results. A dash (—) indicates this was not included in the model.

## NCST, Non-binary/Genderqueer People, and Gender- and Sexuality-Based DHV: Model 2

Intersections among axes of social power and being a non-binary/genderqueer person are included as they relate to gender- and sexuality-based DHV in Model 2. Among the gender-based DHV models, being a non-binary/genderqueer person remains non-statistically significant and there are no significant non-binary/genderqueer social power interaction terms in this Model 2. In contrast, being non-binary/genderqueer remains significantly related sexuality-based DHV in Model 2. Specifically, being non-binary/genderqueer person *decreases* the likelihood of experiencing sexuality-based DHV by .73. In addition, among the interaction effects, being a non-binary/genderqueer bisexual person *decreases* the likelihood of experiencing sexuality-based DHV by .74. These results are surprising and contrary to previous studies (James et al. 2016; Nadal et al. 2016; Sterzing et al. 2017; Walker et al. 2018; Wyss 2004). The findings here suggest that in comparison to other LGBTQ identities, non-binary/genderqueer identity and bisexuality among those who identify as non-binary/genderqueer may be protective factors for sexuality-based DHV experiences. Because they may be more likely to express gender in more non-conforming and/or fluid ways as compared to others in the LGBTQ community, this may make non-binary/genderqueer people less vulnerable to sexuality-based DHV. Overall, *Hypothesis 2* is supported in the sexuality-based DHV models but not in the gender-based DHV models.

## *Summarizing NCST, Non-binary/Genderqueer People, and Gender- and Sexuality-Based DHV*

In sum, being a non-binary/genderqueer person has significant effects on the likelihood of experiencing sexuality-based DHV but not gender-based DHV; however, contrary to expectations, being a non-binary/genderqueer person *decreases* the likelihood of sexuality-based DHV. Specifically, compared to other LGBTQ people, being a non-binary/genderqueer person may serve as a protective factor to sexuality-based DHV. However overall, there are very few significant findings in this table and the pseudo $R^2$ values are quite low. Even so, focusing on non-binary/genderqueer identities and social power axes allows us to better understand non-binary/genderqueer people's experiences with both gender- and sexuality-based DHV.

## Summary of Patterns of Non-binary/Genderqueer Stigma

In line with the three tenets and hypotheses derived from NCST, there are six patterns related to the stigmatization of non-binary/genderqueer people reviewed in this chapter:

1. Sex-act related stigma is a driving force in the stigmatization of non-binary/genderqueer people for both hetero-cis and LGBTQ people, especially the damaging perspectives that non-binary/genderqueer people are too sexual; however, discomfort with non-binary/genderqueer people's sex acts are also quite concerning for hetero-cis people and the perspective that non-binary/genderqueer people are unfaithful is evident among the LGBTQ subsample.

2. For both hetero-cis and LGBTQ people, there is strong support for the stigmatizing beliefs that non-binary/genderqueer people's identities are temporary and that they should be either masculine or feminine.
3. Hetero-cis-normativity is positively related to non-binary/genderqueer stigma for both subsamples; however, the interaction effects between the HCN Scale and social power axes that moderate these relationships differ for the hetero-cis and LGBTQ subsamples. In addition, there are more significant interaction effects between the HCN Scale and social power axes for the hetero-cis subsample than there are for the LGBTQ subsample.
4. Individual social power axes are significantly related to non-binary/genderqueer stigma for both subsamples; however, the interaction effects between the social power axes that moderate these relationships differ for the hetero-cis and LGBTQ subsamples. In addition, there are more significant interaction effects between the social power axes for the LGBTQ subsample than there are for the hetero-cis subsample.
5. Non-binary/genderqueer people experience extremely high levels of gender-based DHV in comparison nearly all other groups and higher levels of sexuality-based discrimination in comparison to both the women and men subsamples (but not the LGBTQ subsample).
6. Being a non-binary/genderqueer person is not significantly related to gender-based DHV; however, being a non-binary/genderqueer person and bisexual identities among non-binary/genderqueer people *decrease* the likelihood of sexuality-based DHV.

## Note

1 Katherine Vandam "Kate" Bornstein (born in 1948) is an activist, performer, and educator who identifies as non-binary. They has written several books including *Gender Outlaw: On Men, Women, and the Rest of Us* (Bornstein 1994). According to their website, "Kate's work is taught in five languages, in over 300 high schools, colleges, and universities around the world" (Bornstein n.d.).

## References

Aparicio-García, Marta, Eva Evelia, María Díaz-Ramiro, Susana Rubio-Valdehita, María Inmaculada López-Núñez, and Isidro García-Nieto. 2018. "Health and Well-Being of Cisgender, Transgender and Non-binary Young People." *International Journal of Environmental Research and Public Health* 15(10):2133.
Blair, Karen L. and Rhea Ashley Hoskin. 2015. "Experiences of Femme Identity: Coming Out, Invisibility and Femmephobia." *Psychology & Sexuality* 6(3):229–244.
Bornstein, Kate. 1994. *Gender Outlaw: On Men, Women and the Rest of Us* (First Edition). New York, NY: Routledge.
Bornstein, Kate. n.d. "Kate Bornstein." *Kate Bornstein*. Retrieved August 21, 2019 (http://katebornstein.com/).
Clarke, Jessica A. 2018. "They, Them, and Theirs." *Harvard Law Review* 132:894–991.

Clogg, Clifford C., Eva Petkova, and Adamantios Haritou. 1995. "Statistical Methods for Comparing Regression Coefficients between Models." *American Journal of Sociology* 100(5):1261–1293.

Davidson, Megan. 2007. "Seeking Refuge under the Umbrella: Inclusion, Exclusion, and Organizing within the Category Transgender." *Sexuality Research and Social Policy* 4(4):60–80.

Davidson, Skylar and Jamie Halsall. 2016. "Gender Inequality: Nonbinary Transgender People in the Workplace." *Cogent Social Sciences* 2(1):1–12.

Factor, Rhonda and Esther Rothblum. 2008. "Exploring Gender Identity and Community among Three Groups of Transgender Individuals in the United States: MTFs, FTMs, and Genderqueers." *Health Sociology Review* 17(3):235–253.

Flanders, Corey E., Margaret Robinson, Melissa Marie Legge, and Lesley A. Tarasoff. 2016. "Negative Identity Experiences of Bisexual and Other Non-Monosexual People: A Qualitative Report." *Journal of Gay & Lesbian Mental Health* 20(2):152–172.

Fuentes, Tamara. 2019. "'Queer Eye' Star Jonathan Van Ness Reveals that He is Nonbinary." *Seventeen*. Retrieved July 10, 2019 (www.seventeen.com/celebrity/g27702340/Non-binary-celebrities/).

Galupo, M. Paz, Shane B. Henise, and Kyle S. Davis. 2014. "Transgender Microaggressions in the Context of Friendship: Patterns of Experience across Friends' Sexual Orientation and Gender Identity." *Psychology of Sexual Orientation and Gender Diversity* 1(4):461–740.

Galupo, M. Paz, Edward Lomash, and Renae C. Mitchell. 2017. "'All of My Lovers Fit into This Scale': Sexual Minority Individuals' Responses to Two Novel Measures of Sexual Orientation." *Journal of Homosexuality* 64(2):145–165.

Hammack, Phillip L., David M. Frost, and Sam D. Hughes. 2019. "Queer Intimacies: A New Paradigm for the Study of Relationship Diversity." *Journal of Sex Research* 56(4/5):556–592.

Herek, Gregory M. 1988. "Heterosexuals' Attitudes toward Lesbians and Gay Men: Correlates and Gender Differences." *Journal of Sex Research* 25(4):451–477.

Herek, Gregory M. 2000. "Sexual Prejudice and Gender: Do Heterosexuals' Attitudes toward Lesbians and Gay Men Differ?" *Journal of Social Issues* 56(2):251–266.

Herek, Gregory M. 2002. "Gender Gaps in Public Opinion about Lesbians and Gay Men." *Public Opinion Quarterly* 66(1):40–66.

Hoskin, Rhea Ashley. 2017. "Femme Theory: Refocusing the Intersectional Lens." *Atlantis: Critical Studies in Gender, Culture & Social Justice* 38(1):95–109.

James, Sandy, Jody L. Herman, Sue Rankin, Mara Keisling, Lisa Mottet, and Ma'ayan Anafi. 2016. *The Report of the 2015 U.S. Transgender Survey*. Washington, D.C.: National Center for Transgender Equality.

Karimi, Faith and Dani Stewart. 2016. "Nonbinary: Army Veteran Legally Not Male or Female, Judge Rules." *CNN*, June 12. Retrieved January 31, 2020 (https://www.cnn.com/2016/06/11/us/jamie-shupe-non-binary/index.html).

Kuper, Laura, Robin Nussbaum, and Brian Mustanski. 2012. "Exploring the Diversity of Gender and Sexual Orientation Identities in an Online Sample of Transgender Individuals." *The Journal of Sex Research* 49(2/3):244–254.

Lev, Arlene Istar. 2010. "How Queer! The Development of Gender Identity and Sexual Orientation in LGBTQ-Headed Families." *Family Process* 49(3):268–290.

Levitt, Heidi M. and Sharon G. Horne. 2002. "Explorations of Lesbian-Queer Genders: Butch, Femme, Androgynous or 'Other.'." *Journal of Lesbian Studies* 6(2):25–39.

Lubitow, Amy, JaDee Carathers, Maura Kelly, and Miriam Abelson. 2017. "Transmobilities: Mobility, Harassment, and Violence Experienced by Transgender and Gender Nonconforming Public Transit Riders in Portland, Oregon." *Gender, Place & Culture* 24(10):1398–1418.

Mark, Kristen P., Laura M. Vowels and Sarah H. Murray. 2018. "The Impact of Attachment Style on Sexual Satisfaction and Sexual Desire in a Sexually Diverse Sample." *Journal of Sex & Marital Therapy* 44(5):450–458.

Marshall, Zack, Vivian Welch, Alexa Minichiello, Michelle Swab, Fern Brunger, and Chris Kaposy. 2019. "Documenting Research with Transgender, Nonbinary, and Other Gender Diverse (Trans) Individuals and Communities: Introducing the Global Trans Research Evidence Map." *Transgender Health* 4(1):68–80.

Miller, Hayley. 2019. "First Openly Non-binary Senate Candidate Seeks To Make Politics More Inclusive." *Huff Post*. Retrieved July 10, 2019 (www.huffpost.com/entry/bre-kidman-Non-binary-maine-senate_n_5d13c36fe4b09ad014f9f470).

Nadal, Kevin L., Chassitty N. Whitman, Lindsey S. Davis, Tanya Erazo, and Kristin C. Davidoff. 2016. "Microaggressions toward Lesbian, Gay, Bisexual, Transgender, Queer, and Genderqueer People: A Review of the Literature." *The Journal of Sex Research* 53(4/5):488–508.

Oakley, Abigail. 2016. "Disturbing Hegemonic Discourse: Nonbinary Gender and Sexual Orientation Labeling on Tumblr." *Social Media + Society* 2(3):1–12.

Petit, Marie-Pier, Danielle Julien, and Line Chamberland. 2017. "Negotiating Parental Designations among Trans Parents' Families: An Ecological Model of Parental Identity." *Psychology of Sexual Orientation and Gender Diversity* 4(3):282–295–322.

Reineck, Katie. 2017. "Running from the Gender Police: Reconceptualizing Gender to Ensure Protection for Non-binary People." *Michigan Journal of Gender & Law* 24:265–322.

Richards, Christina, Walter Pierre Bouman, and Meg-John Barker (eds). 2017. *Genderqueer and Non-binary Genders*. London, UK: Palgrave Macmillan.

Stachowiak, Dana M. 2017. "Queering It Up, Strutting Our Threads, and Baring Our Souls: Genderqueer Individuals Negotiating Social and Felt Sense of Gender." *Journal of Gender Studies* 26(5):532–543.

Sterzing, Paul R., G. Allen Ratliff, Rachel E. Gartner, Briana L. McGeough, and Kelly C. Johnson. 2017. "Social Ecological Correlates of Polyvictimization among a National Sample of Transgender, Genderqueer, and Cisgender Sexual Minority Adolescents." *Child Abuse & Neglect* 67:1–12.

Sutfin, Erin L., Megan Fulcher, Ryan P. Bowles, and Charlotte J. Patterson. 2008. "How Lesbian and Heterosexual Parents Convey Attitudes about Gender to Their Children: The Role of Gendered Environments." *Sex Roles* 58(7):501–513.

Tabaac, Ariella, Paul B. Perrin and Eric G. Benotsch. 2018. "Discrimination, Mental Health, and Body Image among Transgender and Gender-Non-binary Individuals: Constructing a Multiple Mediational Path Model." *Journal of Gay & Lesbian Social Services* 30(1):1–16.

Tornello, Samantha L., Rachel G. Riskind, and Aleks Babić. 2019. "Transgender and Gender Non-binary Parents' Pathways to Parenthood." *Psychology of Sexual Orientation and Gender Diversity* 6(2):232–241.

Truong, Nhan, Amaya Perez-Brumer, Melissa Burton, June Gipson, and DeMarc Hickson. 2016. "What's in a Label?: Multiple Meanings of 'MSM' among Same-Gender-Loving Black Men in Mississippi." *Global Public Health* 11(7/8):937–952.

Vanderburgh, Reid. 2009. "Appropriate Therapeutic Care for Families with Pre-Pubescent Transgender/Gender-Dissonant Children." *Child and Adolescent Social Work Journal* 26(2):135–154.

Walker, Allyson, Lori Sexton, Jace Valcore, Jennifer Sumner, and Aimee Wodda. 2018. "Transitioning to Social Justice." Pp. 220–233 in *Routledge Handbook of Social, Economic, and Criminal Justice*, edited by C. Roberson. New York, NY: Routledge.

Walters, Karina L., Jane M. Teresa Evans-Campbell, Theresa Ronquillo Simoni, and Rupaleem Bhuyan. 2006. "'My Spirit in My Heart': Identity Experiences and Challenges among American Indian Two-Spirit Women." *Journal of Lesbian Studies* 10(1/2):125–149.

Whyte, Stephen, Robert C. Brooks, and Benno Torgler. 2018. "Man, Woman, 'Other': Factors Associated with Nonbinary Gender Identification." *Archives of Sexual Behavior* 47(8):2397–2406.

Wilchins, Riki Anne. 1997. *Read My Lips: Sexual Subversion and the End of Gender*. Ithaca, NY: Firebrand Books.

Wilson, Bianca D. M. 2009. "Black Lesbian Gender and Sexual Culture: Celebration and Resistance." *Culture, Health & Sexuality* 11(3):297–313.

Worthen, Meredith G. F. 2012. "Understanding College Student Attitudes toward LGBT Individuals." *Sociological Focus* 45(4):285–305.

Worthen, Meredith G. F. 2016. "Hetero-cis-normativity and the Gendering of Transphobia." *International Journal of Transgenderism* 17(1):31–57.

Wyss, Shannon E. 2004. "'This Was My Hell': The Violence Experienced by Gender Non-conforming Youth in US High Schools." *International Journal of Qualitative Studies in Education* 17(5):709–730.

# 15
# QUEER WOMEN STIGMA

*It was a rebellion, it was an uprising, it was a civil rights disobedience—it wasn't no damn riot.*

(Stonewall Veterans' Association 2019)
Stormé DeLarverie, activist and Stonewall Uprising participant[1]

IMAGE 15.1 The Stonewall Inn pictured in 1969 just days after the Stonewall Uprising in New York City. A message from the Mattachine Society on the window reads: "WE HOMOSEXUALS PLEAD WITH OUR PEOPLE TO PLEASE HELP MAINTAIN PEACEFUL AND QUIET CONDUCT ON THE STREETS OF THE VILLAGE—MATTACHINE."

The modern "queer" identity largely gained popularity alongside the emergence of queer theorizing and "queer" reclamation (Brontsema 2004; Butler 1993; Gamson 1995). Thus, compared to lesbian, gay, trans, and bisexual identities, modern queer identities are relatively new. In addition, queer identities can be more inclusive but also, more ambiguous. Queer identity creates a space for those who do not think that LGBT identities adequately or fully capture their experiences, for those who want to break through the status quo and challenge existing hierarchies, and/or for those who feel "queer" (Brontsema 2004; Butler 1993; Gamson 1995). In this study, about 1 in 8 overall (12.7%, n = 393/3,104) and nearly 1 in 5 LGBTQ people (19.5%, n = 313/1,604) identified as "queer." Because this study utilized a U.S. nationally representative sampling frame, it is especially noteworthy that queer identity was so pronounced. Yet the particulars of attitudes toward queer people and queer people's experiences remain in surprisingly uncharted territory for the most part.

## The Stigmatization of Queer Women

In the survey instrument, the section focusing on attitudes toward queer women was preceded by the following statement:

> *Next we'd like to ask you for your thoughts, feelings, and predicted behaviors about women who self-identify as "queer." Please note that "queer" is often used as an umbrella identity term that encompasses individuals who do not feel they fit within the categories of heterosexual, lesbian, gay, or bisexual, and/or those who are attracted to people of many genders, and/or those who feel their sexual identity is fluid.*

## The Queer Women Stigma Scale

Queer women occupy a midpoint among all nine groups examined in this book as the fifth most and fifth least stigmatized. In addition, following the same patterns as the other LGBTQ groups, queer women are less stigmatized than queer men (recall Figure 7.1). However, the stigmatization of queer women has both similar and different motivations when compared to the other LGBTQ groups. As seen in Figure 15.1 and Table 15.1, the Queer Women Stigma Scale can help us to better understand these complexities.

### *Queer Women and Social and Familial Relationships*

The stigma associated with queer women's social and familial relationships is lower in comparison to all other key areas of the scale (with the exception of basic human rights as discussed in Chapter 7), though means are above 2.4 for the

## Queer Women Stigma 351

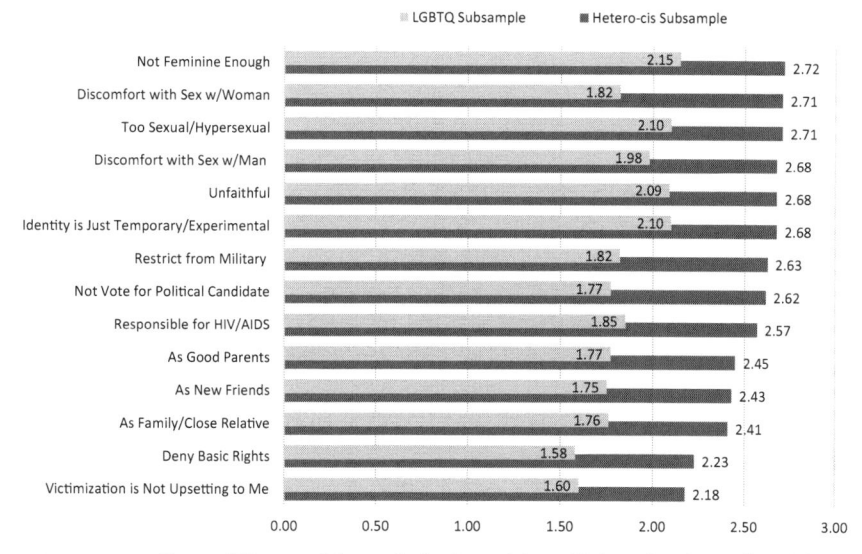

|   | LGBTQ Subsample | Hetero-cis Subsample |
|---|---|---|
| Not Feminine Enough | 2.15 | 2.72 |
| Discomfort with Sex w/Woman | 1.82 | 2.71 |
| Too Sexual/Hypersexual | 2.10 | 2.71 |
| Discomfort with Sex w/Man | 1.98 | 2.68 |
| Unfaithful | 2.09 | 2.68 |
| Identity is Just Temporary/Experimental | 2.10 | 2.68 |
| Restrict from Military | 1.82 | 2.63 |
| Not Vote for Political Candidate | 1.77 | 2.62 |
| Responsible for HIV/AIDS | 1.85 | 2.57 |
| As Good Parents | 1.77 | 2.45 |
| As New Friends | 1.75 | 2.43 |
| As Family/Close Relative | 1.76 | 2.41 |
| Deny Basic Rights | 1.58 | 2.23 |
| Victimization is Not Upsetting to Me | 1.60 | 2.18 |

**FIGURE 15.1** Queer Women Stigma Scale Item Mean Values Rank-Ordered from Most to Least Stigmatizing for the Hetero-cis (n = 1,500) and the LGBTQ (n = 1,604) Subsamples.

*Note:* see Table 15.1 for the exact wording for each item. *t*-test results comparing the hetero-cis and LGBTQ subsamples indicate that all means are significantly different from one another at the $p < .001$ level.

hetero-cis subsample and are approaching 2.0 for the LGBTQ subsample (see Table 15.1). Few researchers have specifically examined these relationships, however, one Canadian study (N = 466) found that compared to LGB women, queer women (n = 206) experienced the highest levels of stigma associated with their identity (Logie and Earnshaw 2015). Specifically, queer women's experiences with stigma included losing straight friends because of their identity (58.4% of all LGBQ women indicated as such, no estimates were provided for queer women specifically) and feeling their family was hurt and embarrassed because of their identity (75.5% of all LGBQ women indicated as such). In particular, queer women's familial relationships were especially strained (Logie and Earnshaw 2015). Another small scale project (N = 60, n = 3 queer women) also found that queer women experienced more difficulties than lesbian, bisexual, and heterosexual women connecting to social communities (Rothblum 2010). Yet in this study (as demonstrated in Table 15.1), there was not much variation in the stigma associated with friends and family for either group with all three items in this key area ranging by only .02–.04 points. Overall, although there is evidence of some negativity toward having queer women friends and family members among this sample and others (Logie and Earnshaw 2015), these hostilities are not as severe as those found in most other key areas of the Queer Women Stigma Scale.

**TABLE 15.1** Queer Women Stigma Scale Item Mean Values (Standard Deviations) and *t*-test Results Comparing the Means for the Hetero-cis Subsample and the LGBTQ Subsample

|  | Hetero-cis Subsample $n = 1{,}500$ | LGBTQ Subsample $n = 1{,}604$ | *t*-test Results |
|---|---|---|---|
| *Social and familial relationships* | | | |
| I welcome new friends who are queer women.[R] | 2.43 (1.18) | 1.75 (1.00) | $t = 17.22^*$ |
| I don't think it would negatively affect our relationship if I learned that one of my close relatives was a queer woman.[R] | 2.41 (1.20) | 1.76 (1.05) | $t = 16.06^*$ |
| Queer women are not capable of being good parents. | 2.45 (1.24) | 1.77 (1.15) | $t = 15.87^*$ |
| *Positions of importance and social significance* | | | |
| I would not vote for a political candidate who was an openly queer woman. | 2.62 (1.32) | 1.77 (1.15) | $t = 19.09^*$ |
| Queer women should not be allowed to join the military. | 2.63 (1.34) | 1.82 (1.20) | $t = 17.86^*$ |
| *Basic human rights* | | | |
| I believe queer women should have all of the same rights as other people do.[R] | 2.23 (1.14) | 1.58 (.98) | $t = 16.96^*$ |
| It is upsetting to me that queer women experience violence, harassment, and discrimination just because they are queer women.[R] | 2.18 (1.15) | 1.60 (1.00) | $t = 14.82^*$ |
| *Sex act-related stigma* | | | |
| Queer women are unfaithful to their romantic partners. | 2.68 (1.12) | 2.09 (1.12) | $t = 14.78^*$ |
| Queer women are too sexual (hypersexual). | 2.71 (1.13) | 2.10 (1.12) | $t = 15.17^*$ |
| Queer women are mostly responsible for spreading HIV/AIDS. | 2.57 (1.16) | 1.85 (1.12) | $t = 17.66^*$ |
| I am comfortable with the thought of a queer woman having sex with a woman.[R] | 2.71 (1.18) | 1.82 (1.00) | $t = 22.71^*$ |
| I am comfortable with the thought of a queer woman having sex with a man.[R] | 2.68 (1.14) | 1.98 (1.09) | $t = 17.54^*$ |
| *Queer identity permanency* | | | |
| Most women who call themselves queer are just temporarily experimenting with their sexuality. | 2.68 (1.13) | 2.10 (1.15) | $t = 14.03^*$ |

(*Continued*)

**TABLE 15.1** (Cont.)

|  | Hetero-cis Subsample | LGBTQ Subsample | |
| --- | --- | --- | --- |
|  | n = 1,500 | n = 1,604 | t-test Results |
| *Achievement of femininity* | | | |
| Queer women are not feminine enough. | 2.72 (1.12) | 2.15 (1.16) | t = 13.94* |
| α | .91 | .93 | |
| Summed scale actual range | 14-70 | 14-70 | |
| Summed scale mean | 35.70 (11.19) | 26.13 (11.13) | t = 23.88* |

*Notes:* response options were Strongly Disagree–Strongly Agree (range: 1–5).[R] This item is reverse coded.

* t-test results allowing for unequal variances indicate that the hetero-cis subsample and LGBTQ subsample means are significantly different from one another at the p < .001 level.

## Queer Women and Positions of Importance and Social Significance

There was moderate stigmatization of queer women in positions of importance and social significance. Means were similar for both items in this key area ("I would not vote for a political candidate who was an openly queer woman" and "Queer women should not be allowed to join the military") for the hetero-cis subsample (2.62 and 2.63 respectively) and the LGBTQ subsample (1.77 and 1.82 respectively). In comparison to the other 14 items in the scale, stigma toward queer women in positions of importance and social significance was midrange for both subsamples (see Figure 15.1). This is somewhat surprising because though there are women celebrities who have openly discussed their queer identities (e.g., actress Evan Rachel Wood, actress Sara Ramirez, journalist Natalie Morales, and singer/actress Janelle Monáe; see Juhasz 2018; Renfro 2019), there are no clearly recognizable openly self-identified queer U.S. political or military women leaders. Media discussions about "queerness" do include leaders such as U.S. Senator Tammy Baldwin who did not refute the claim that she was "the first openly queer person ever to be elected to Congress and the Senate" in an interview with Refinery29, a website focused on young women's empowerment (González-Ramírez 2019). Yet Baldwin has not publically self-identified as "queer" nor have any other current American women politicians or high-ranking military officials. Even so, it appears that there is some openness to the idea of queer women in positions of importance and social significance in this sample.

## Queer Women and Sex Act-Related Stigma

As seen in Figure 15.1, three of the top five most stigmatizing attitudes toward queer women were among the sex act-related stigma items for both subsamples (hypersexuality, discomfort with sex with men, and unfaithfulness). In addition, all means for the five items in this key area were above 2.5 among the hetero-cis subsample (ranging from 2.57 to 2.71) and close to 2.0 or higher for the LGBTQ subsample (ranging from 1.82 to 2.10). Overall, because queer women have been found to be more sexually fluid than others, including bisexual women (Mereish, Katz-Wise, and Woulfe 2017), they can also be at higher risk for sexual stigma.

Interestingly, in the the sex act-related stigma key area, the item with the *lowest* mean for the LGBTQ subsample (1.82) is one of the two with the *highest* means for the hetero-cis subsample (2.71). That item is: "I am comfortable with the thought of a queer woman having sex with a woman" which was reverse coded because *dis*comfort with queer women engaging in sex acts reflects a stigmatizing attitude toward queer women. Because sex acts between women violate heteronormativity, it makes sense that hetero-cis people feel more hostility toward queer women having sex with other women than LGBTQ people feel. In addition, LGBTQ people were more stigmatizing in their feelings about the contrasting survey item, "I am comfortable with the thought of a queer woman having sex with a man." Somewhat similar to the ideas discussed in Chapter 10 as related to bisexual women stigmatization, among attitudes toward queer-identified women, woman + man duos are least stigmatized by the hetero-cis subsample, but for the LGBTQ subsample, woman + woman duos are viewed as most acceptable.

The item with the highest mean value in the sex act-related stigma key area for the LGBTQ subsample (2.10) and the item that is one of the two with the highest means for the hetero-cis subsample (2.71) is: "Queer women are too sexual (hypersexual)." The stereotyping of sexual- and gender-diverse women as "hypersexual" spans many identities (as discussed in this book, lesbian, bisexual, and trans women to name a few). Women interacting sexually with other women garners public attention, especially from heterosexual men, which can contribute strongly to this stereotype (Hamilton 2007; Rupp and Taylor 2010; Rupp et al. 2014). However, beyond this, there is additional research that demonstrates differences in queer women's sexualities as compared to others. For example, one study (N = 489) found that queer women (n = 86) were significantly more likely than bisexual women (n = 403) to have active sex lives (both in the past year and in their lifetimes) (Mereish, Katz-Wise, and Woulfe 2017). In addition, queer women indicated more gender diversity in their sex partners (men, women, transgender, and/or genderqueer individuals) than bisexual women did (Mereish, Katz-Wise, and Woulfe 2017). Overall, because queer women's identities can reflect an openness to diverse sexualities and sexual experiences (Mereish, Katz-Wise, and Woulfe 2017; Rupp et al. 2014), they can be over-sexualized as "up for anything" sexually and this can translate into a very palpable hypersexual stigma among queer women.

## *Queer Woman Identity Permanency*

Stigma directed toward queer women's identity permanency was evident among both subsamples. Specifically, "Most women who call themselves queer are just temporarily experimenting with their sexuality" was the second most stigmatizing attitude among the LGBTQ subsample (the mean was identical for the item about queer women's hypersexuality, 2.10), and the third most stigmatizing attitude among the hetero-cis subsample (the mean was identical for the item about discomfort with sex with a man and the item about queer women being unfaithful, 2.68). Two overlapping stereotypes contribute to the questioning of queer women's authenticity. First, because queer identity often signifies some form of flexibility and fluidity for most women (Mereish, Katz-Wise, and Woulfe 2017; Rupp et al. 2014), some may erroneously believe that queer identity is inauthentic. This can be entwined with similar damaging perspectives about bisexual women and the "temporary" quality stereotypically assigned to their identities (see Chapter 10). Second, because queer as a modern self-proclaimed identity is relatively new (Brontsema 2004; Gamson 1995), some may see queer identity as a fleeting trend among "young" people whose non-hetero-cis-normative genders and sexualities are already regularly dismissed and disregarded as "phases" (Alegría 2018; Dowshen et al. 2017; Hayfield, Clarke, and Halliwell 2014; Hill and Menvielle 2009; Weiss 2004). This perspective is enhanced by particular hostilities among older generations of gay men and lesbian women who actively oppose the reclamation of "queer" (Brontsema 2004). Consistent with Australian research (N = 2,220) that found that queer identity is most common among younger people (Morandini, Blaszczynski, and Dar-Nimrod 2017), in this sample, the mean age of queer-identified individuals (35.84 years) was close to five years younger than the mean age of non-queer-identified individuals (40.19 years) and well over half (61.8%, n = 243/393) of queer-identified individuals were aged 35 years or younger. Together, these patterns shape broader stereotypes about queer women's identity permanency.

## *Queer Women and the Achievement of Femininity*

Queer women are stigmatized for the inability to successfully achieve femininity. In fact, across all 14 items in the Queer Women Stigma Scale, this item has the highest mean value for the hetero-cis subsample (2.72) and the LGBTQ subsample (2.15) (see Figure 15.1). Thus, there is agreement across the entire sample that "Queer women are not feminine enough." The often fluid and flexible quality of queer identity can contribute to diverse expressions of femininity and gender among queer women which may not align with hetero-cis-normative expectations (Dahl and Volcano 2009; Reddy-Best and Pedersen 2015). For example, one study of lesbian and queer women in the UK (N = 31) found that queer femininity can be femme, butch, or both, depending on context (Eves 2004). Because some queer-identified women are stereotyped as being butch or masculine (Eves 2004; Levitt and Horne 2002; Mishali 2014), this contributes to a larger set of stigmatizing beliefs that queer women cannot ever be and/or "are not feminine enough."

## Queer Women Stigma Summed Scale

In Table 15.1, all 14 items were summed together to create the Queer Women Stigma Scale. Cronbach's alphas were quite high for the hetero-cis subsample (.91) and the LGBTQ subsample (.93). Similar to the Trans Women Stigma Scale and the Non-binary/Genderqueer Stigma Scale (but unlike the stigma scales for lesbian women, gay men, bisexual women, and bisexual men), the actual range in values for the Queer Women Stigma Scale was identical for the two subsamples (14–70). However, mean values for the summed Queer Women Stigma Scale differed substantially and significantly with the hetero-cis subsample mean (35.70) 9.57 points higher than the LGBTQ subsample mean (26.13). Even so, the key area with the highest individual mean values was the same for both subsamples: queer women's inability to achieve femininity. However, it is important to note that for the hetero-cis and LGBTQ subsamples, the top three mean scores were very close to one another (ranging by only .04 points and .06 points respectively) and include both sex act-related stigma items and stigma toward queer women's identity permanency. Thus, overall, queer women's stigmatization is associated with the achievement of femininity, identity permanency, and sex act-related stigma (recall Figure 7.3).

## NCST, Hetero-cis-normativity, Social Power Axes, and the Queer Women Stigma Scale

The first set of regression models examine the Queer Women Stigma Scale using NCST. The hypotheses are as follows:

- *Hypothesis 1a*: there is a significant positive relationship between the HCN Scale and the Queer Women Stigma Scale.
- *Hypothesis 1b*: there are significant relationships between individual social power axes (gender identity, sexual identity, additional gender/sexuality, racial/ethnic identity, basic needs) and the Queer Women Stigma Scale.
- *Hypothesis 2a*: the relationship between the HCN Scale and the Queer Women Stigma Scale is moderated by interactions between the HCN Scale and axes of social power.
- *Hypothesis 2b*: the relationships between individual social power axes and the Queer Women Stigma Scale are moderated by interactions between axes of social power.

Figure 15.2 outlines these relationships and the two models of NCST to be estimated. Specifically, OLS regression is utilized in Table 15.2 to examine NCST and the relationships among hetero-cis-normativity, axes of social power (gender, sexuality, additional gender/sexuality, race/ethnicity, and basic needs), and the Queer Women Stigma Scale for the hetero-cis subsample and the LGBTQ subsample. See Chapter 7 for a more complete description of the models. Regarding model fit statistics, the adjusted $R^2$ values ranged from .67 to .69.

## NCST, HCN, Social Power Axes, and the Queer Women Stigma Scale: Model 1

In Table 15.2 Model 1, the relationships between the HCN Scale, social power axes, and the Queer Women Stigma Scale are estimated. Supporting *Hypothesis 1a*, the HCN Scale is positively related to the Queer Women Stigma Scale in Model 1 for both subsamples. Supporting *Hypothesis 1b*, individual axes of social power are also significantly related to the Queer Women Stigma Scale for the hetero-cis subsample (cis woman and femme) and for the LGBTQ subsample (queer and African American/Black).

## NCST, HCN, Social Power Axes, and the Queer Women Stigma Scale: Model 2

Axes of social power and intersections among axes of social power and the HCN Scale are examined in Model 2. The HCN Scale is positively related to the Queer Women Stigma Scale for both groups. Moving to the HCN Scale interaction terms, all three are discussed in Chapter 7: the interaction between the HCN Scale and queer identity, Multi-racial identity, and indicating "mostly all I need." Together, these results show how the intersections between hetero-cis-normativity, gender/sexual identities, racial identities, and basic needs experiences relate to the stigmatization of queer women. In particular, opting into hetero-cis-

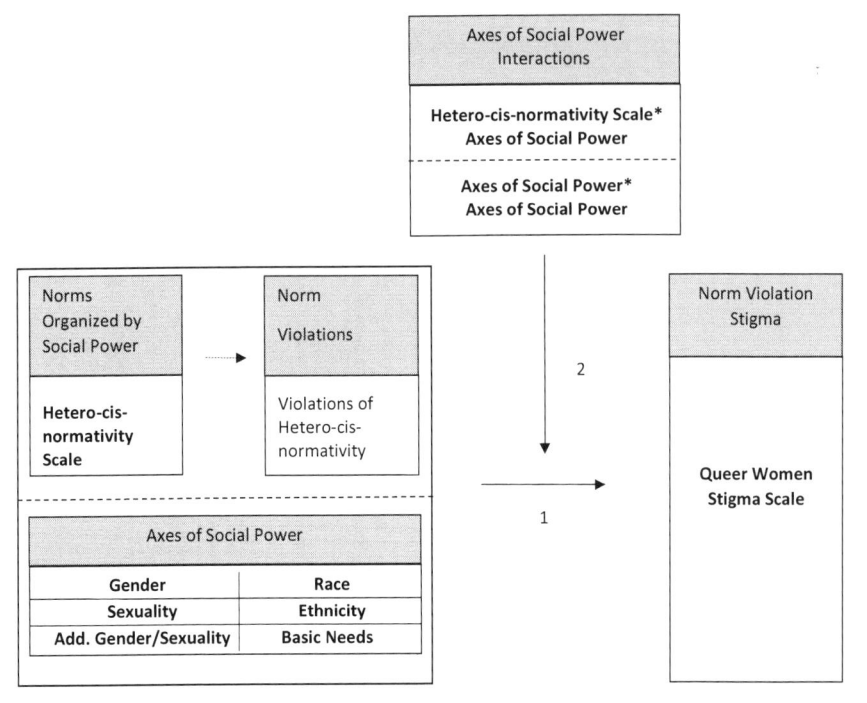

**FIGURE 15.2** Theoretical Model of NCST and Queer Women Stigma using the Stigmatizer Lens with Model Numbers to be Examined in Table 15.2

*Notes:* Model 1 estimates the HCN Scale and axes of social power (gender, sexuality, additional gender/sexuality, race, ethnicity, and basic needs) as they relate to the Queer Women Stigma Scale. Model 2 estimates interactions among axes of social power and the HCN Scale as they moderate the relationships between the HCN Scale and the Queer Women Stigma Scale as well as interactions among axes of social power as they moderate the relationships between the HCN Scale and the Queer Women Stigma Scale. The * indicates an interaction.

normative thinking has differential impacts on attitudes toward queer women that are shaped by intersecting experiences with social power. Overall, *Hypothesis 2a* is supported: interactions between the HCN Scale and axes of social power moderate the relationship between the HCN Scale and the Queer Women Stigma Scale for both subsamples.

As similarly seen in previous chapters, different axes of social power shape perspectives about queer women for the hetero-cis and LGBTQ subsamples. For example, as discussed in Chapter 7, being a cis woman is negatively related to the stigmatization of queer women for the hetero-cis subsample. There are also two significant interaction terms related to having "mostly all" your basic needs met that work in opposite directions: being Two-Spirit and indicating that you have mostly all your basic needs met is negatively related to the Queer Women Stigma Scale while identifying as a bear and indicating "mostly

**TABLE 15.2** OLS Regression Results Estimating NCST and the Queer Women Stigma Scale for the Hetero-cis Subsample (n = 1,500) and the LGBTQ Subsample (n = 1,604)

|  | Hetero-cis Subsample | | LGBTQ Subsample | | Test of Difference |
|---|---|---|---|---|---|
|  | Model 1 | Model 2 | Model 1 | Model 2 |  |
| HCN Scale | .84* | .79* | 93* | .63* | . |
| *Gender identity* | | | | | |
| Cis woman | -.95* | -2.20* | . | . | . |
| *Additional gender/sexual identity* | | | | | |
| Queer | . | . | -1.36* | . | . |
| Femme | 2.20* | . | . | . | . |
| *Racial identity* | | | | | |
| African American/Black | . | . | 1.66* | . | . |
| *Basic needs* | | | | | |
| Few needs met | . | . | . | 10.84* | . |
| *HCN Scale\*social power axes interactions* | | | | | |
| HCN Scale*queer | — | -.35* | — | . | ** |
| HCN Scale*Multi-racial | — | .59* | — | . | . |
| HCN Scale*mostly all I need | — | . | — | .22* | . |
| *Social power axes interactions* | | | | | |
| Gay/lesbian*Asian American/Pacific Islander | — | — | — | 3.41* | . |
| Two-Spirit*mostly all I need | — | -4.89* | — | . | . |
| Bear*mostly all I need | — | 4.95* | — | . | ** |
| African American/Black*few needs met | — | . | — | -6.42* | . |
| *Controls: common explanations* | | | | | |
| *LGBTQ contact* | | | | | |
| Queer women friends | . | . | -1.26* | -1.38* | . |
| LGBTQ Friends Scale (w/o queer women) | -.52* | -.51* | . | . | ** |
| *Religious identity* | | | | | |
| Protestant—evangelical | 2.10* | 2.02* | . | . | ** |
| *Political perspectives* | | | | | |
| Liberal—conservative | .66* | .62* | . | . | ** |
| Openness to new experiences | -1.50* | -1.24* | -1.33* | -1.32* | . |
| *Support laws/policies helping:* | | | | | |
| Those in poverty | -1.13* | -1.13* | . | . | . |
| *Beliefs about gender* | | | | | |
| Feminist | -.88* | . | -1.07* | -.94* | . |
| Patriarchal Gender Norms Scale | .58* | .55* | .62* | .61* | . |

(*Continued*)

**TABLE 15.2** (Cont.)

|  | Hetero-cis Subsample | | LGBTQ Subsample | | Test of Difference |
|---|---|---|---|---|---|
|  | Model 1 | Model 2 | Model 1 | Model 2 |  |
| *Sociodemographic controls* |  |  |  |  |  |
| Age | . | . | .03* | . |  |
| Outside U.S. | . | . | 2.99* | 4.00* | ** |
| Education | . | . | .25* | . |  |
| Adjusted $R^2$ | .67 | .68 | .69 | .69 |  |
| Mean VIF | 1.51 | 1.51 | 1.94 | 1.94 |  |

*Notes:* unstandardized regression coefficients are presented. See Table 15.1 for detailed information about the Queer Women Stigma Scale. See Tables 7.1 and 7.2 for details about all other variables and Appendix B Table B.1 for details about the interaction effects. Only the rows with significant results are displayed here.

\* $p < .05$; a dot (.) indicates non-statistically significant results. A dash (—) indicates this was not included in the model.

\*\* $p < .05$ for Clogg et al.'s (1995) test of equality of regression coefficients comparing Model 2 for the hetero-cis subsample and Model 2 for the LGBTQ subsample.

all I need" is positively related to the stigmatization of queer women. Past research has found that Two-Spirit identities can be inclusive of queer women (Walters et al. 2006) while bear culture has been found to be exclusionary to women in some regards (Hennen 2005). Together, these findings suggest that there are important dynamics in some Two-Spirit communities that may work to cultivate the support of queer women while some aspects of bear culture may contribute to hostilities toward queer women.

For the LGBTQ subsample, indicating that few of your basic needs are met is positively related to the Queer Women Stigma Scale. This type of relationship has been associated with other experiences with class identity as well. For example some class experiences, including higher levels of education, have been found to be related to an increased likelihood of identifying as queer as compared to identifying as bisexual among women (Mereish, Katz-Wise, and Woulfe 2017). Indeed, some scholars suggest that identifying as "queer" within the LGBTQ community can be associated with privilege in and of itself (Alimahomed 2010; Brontsema 2004; Logie and Rwigema 2014). Because queer identity among women is linked to experiences with class privilege, negativity toward queer women may be more pervasive among those who struggle to meet their basic needs.

However, a related interaction term between being African American/Black and having few needs met is actually negatively related to the stigmatization of queer women among the LGBTQ subsample. The intersecting marginalized experiences of being African American/Black, struggling to meet one's needs, and being LGBTQ may allow for a particular way of thinking about these issues. For example, scholars find that both being African American/Black and being LGBTQ can result in feeling and thinking like an "outsider within" (Alimahomed 2010; Collins 1986). This vantage point can help shape empathy and sympathy with marginalized others, including queer women.

In contrast, being gay/lesbian and Asian American/Pacific Islander is positively related to the Queer Women Stigma Scale among the LGBTQ subsample. Negativity toward queer women among Asian communities may be especially palpable due to intersecting cultural and sexual scripts (Alimahomed 2010; Battle, Pastrana, and Harris 2017). For example, one study in Canada (N = 466) found that South Asian LGBQ women (n = 18) experienced significantly higher levels of stigma associated with their LGBQ identities as compared to White/Caucasian LGBQ women (Logie and Earnshaw 2015). Indeed, being a queer Asian American/Pacific Islander woman has been found to have profound impacts on experiences with stigma (Alimahomed 2010). Overall, these results continue to demonstrate how the interlocking experiences of gay/lesbian and Asian American/Pacific Islander identities shape queer women stigmatization in important ways.

In sum, in Table 15.2, findings indicate that the axes of social power that relate to attitudes toward queer women are largely different for the hetero-cis and LGBTQ subsamples. Additional tests to compare the regression coefficients of the two subsamples also reveal significant differences (Clogg, Petkova, and Haritou 1995). Thus, interactions between axes of social power moderate the relationship between the individual axes of social power and the Queer Women Stigma Scale for both subsamples, supporting *Hypothesis 2b*.

## Summarizing NCST, HCN, Social Power Axes, and the Queer Women Stigma Scale

Overall, hetero-cis and LGBTQ people's attitudes toward queer women are influenced by hetero-cis-normativity and social power experiences in dynamic and intersectional ways. By utilizing NCST to explore the Queer Women Stigma Scale and centering the importance of hetero-cis-normativity and social power, the mechanisms that shape both negativity and support of queer women are better contextualized.

## Queer Women's Experiences

### The Queer Women Subsample

Though a definition of "queer" was provided during the attitudes/perspectives section as described at the beginning of this chapter, survey respondents self-identified as queer (or not) at the start of the survey (prior to the attitudes/perspectives questions) and there was no definition of queer provided in the self-identity question which followed two separate questions about sexual identity (heterosexual, gay/lesbian, bisexual, pansexual, or asexual) and gender identity (cis man, cis woman, trans man, trans woman, or non-binary/genderqueer). Specifically, the survey item was "I identify as (select all that apply):" and "queer" was the first of these options that respondents could select. Thus, all people in this study had a sexual, gender, and queer (or not queer) identity. This allows for the examination of those that identify as both "queer" and "bisexual" (for example) as seen in some other research (Galupo, Mitchell, and Davis 2015; Rupp et al. 2014) but goes against some scholarly work that suggests that "queer" pushes back against more restrictive LGBT identity terms (Brontsema 2004; Gamson 1995; Jones 2015). For some, queer identity can be political, confrontational, and activist-oriented, for others, queer identity can be used more as a "shorthand" or "catchall" term for all LGBTQ people, or sometimes, any non-hetero-cis-normative or deviantized gender/sexual identity or experience which may or not be connected to queer politics (Brontsema 2004; Gray and Desmarais 2014). Because "queer" can have multiple and evolving meanings, people who self-identify as queer may have different reasons for doing so.

In this study, there was no requested quota from Survey Sampling International for queer women yet the sample included 144 queer women (learn more about the data and sampling procedures in Chapter 7 and Appendix A). Nearly all (94%) of queer women were lesbian/gay (n = 61), bisexual (n = 55), pansexual (n = 16), or asexual (n = 3); however, there were a small number of heterosexual queer women (n = 9). To keep the DHV investigations consistently focused on LGBTQ people's DHV experiences as seen in all other chapters, queer heterosexual women were removed from this investigation. The final sample size of queer LGBTQ women was 135. See Table 15.3 for more details about the queer women in this study.

## Queer Women's Experiences with Gender- and Sexuality-Based DHV

Because queer women have intersecting marginalized identities as both women and queer people, it is imperative to examine queer women's experiences with stigma (i.e., the stigmatized lens). More specifically, queer women can endure both gender- and sexuality-based stigmatizing experiences in the form of DHV. Some small-scale research indicates that queer-identified women may be at high risk for stigma and discrimination (Alimahomed 2010; Friedman and Leaper 2010; Logie and Earnshaw 2015; Reddy-Best and Pedersen 2015). For example, compared to LGB women, queer women were found to experience the highest levels of stigma associated with their identity in one online Canadian study (N = 466, n = 206

**TABLE 15.3** Queer LGBTQ Women Characteristics (n = 135)

|  | % | n |
|---|---|---|
| *Sexual identity* | | |
| Gay/lesbian** | 45.2% | 61 |
| Bisexual* | 40.7% | 55 |
| Pansexual* | 11.9% | 16 |
| Asexual* | 2.2% | 3 |
| *Gender identity* | | |
| Cis women | 97.0% | 131 |
| Trans women | 3.0% | 4 |
| *Additional gender/sexual identity* | | |
| SGL** | 18.5% | 25 |
| Two-Spirit | 1.5% | 2 |
| Butch | 9.6% | 13 |
| Femme** | 23.0% | 31 |
| Leather | – | 0 |
| Bear | – | 0 |
| Twink | 3.6% | 2 |
| Down Low | 3.6% | 2 |
| *Race/ethnicity* | | |
| Caucasian/White** | 83.7% | 113 |
| African American/Black* | 5.2% | 7 |
| Asian American/Pacific Islander* | 4.4% | 6 |
| Native American/Alaskan Native* | 1.5% | 2 |
| Multi-racial* | 7.3% | 4 |
| Other race* | 3.6% | 2 |
| Latinx race* | 1.8% | 1 |
| Latinx ethnicity | 32.7% | 18 |
| *Basic needs* | | |
| Everything I need** | 18.5% | 25 |
| Mostly all I need** | 54.8% | 74 |
| Often needs not met* | 32.2% | 30 |
| Few needs met * | 4.4% | 6 |

\* Reference category in analyses in Table 15.5.
\*\* Included in analyses shown in Table 15.5.

queer women) (Logie and Earnshaw 2015). Another study with U.S. college students (N = 83, n = 21 queer women) found that "lesbian/queer" women were more likely to endure experiences with discrimination as related to their sexual identity when compared to bisexual women (Friedman and Leaper 2010). However, no large-scale U.S. research has explored DHV experiences specifically among queer-identified women.

As seen in Figure 15.3, more than three-quarters (78%) of queer women have had one or more experiences of gender-based DHV and close to three-fourths (72%) have had one or more experiences of sexuality-based DHV. Sexuality-based discrimination is the most common form (64%) while sexuality-based violence is the least common (23%). To better understand queer women's gender- and sexuality-based DHV, queer women's experiences were compared to the LGBTQ subsample and the women subsample using $t$-tests. As seen in Table 15.4, in comparison to all LGBTQ people and all women, queer women are significantly more likely to experience all types of gender-based DHV as well as sexuality-based discrimination and harassment. In addition, queer women report significantly more experiences with sexuality-based violence in comparison to the all women subsample. Overall, compared to the other LGBTQ groups, queer women experience the highest percentage of three types of DHV (gender-based discrimination, sexuality-based discrimination, and gender-based harassment) and they report the highest percentage of any gender- or sexuality-based DHV experience (recall Figure 7.7) (though it is important to note that queer men report the same percentage of any sexuality-based DHV as queer women do). Thus, queer women are at particular risk for both gender- and sexuality-based DHV.

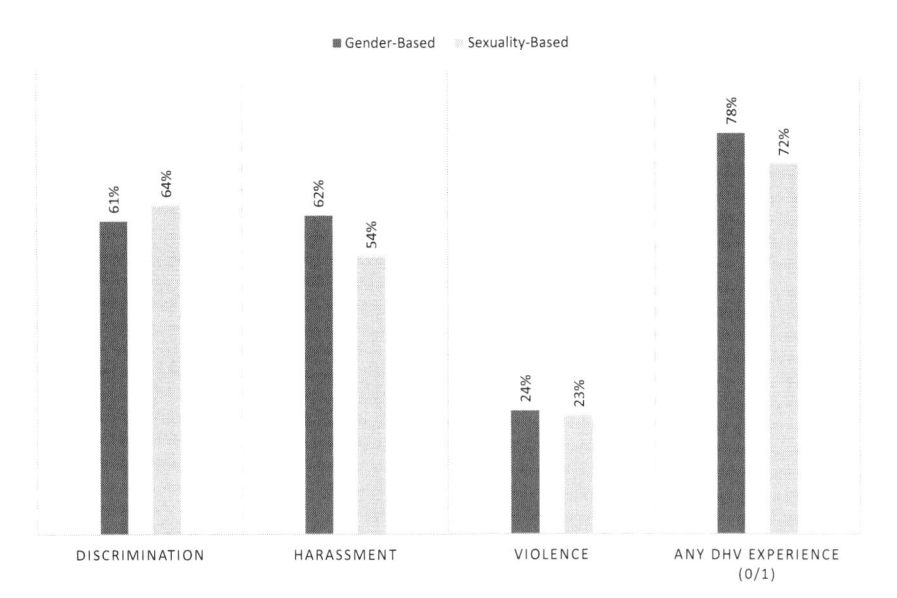

**FIGURE 15.3** Queer LGBTQ Women's (n = 135) Experiences with Gender- and Sexuality-Based DHV

*Notes:* see Table 15.4 for comparisons of queer LGBTQ women's experiences to the LGBTQ subsample and the women subsample.

**TABLE 15.4** Gender- and Sexuality-Based DHV Mean Values (Standard Deviations) among Queer LGBTQ Women, the LGBTQ Subsample, and the Women Subsample with *t*-test Results

|  | | Queer LGBTQ Women | LGBTQ Subsample | Women Subsample |
|---|---|---|---|---|
| | *n* | 135 | 1604 | 1535 |
| *Gender-based* | | | | |
| Discrimination | | .61 (.49) *** | .32 (.47) | .36 (.48) |
| Harassment | | .62 (.49) *** | .28 (.45) | .34 (.47) |
| Violence | | .24 (.43) *** | .14 (.34) | .16 (.37) |
| Any gender DHV Experience (0/1) | | .78 (.42) *** | .40 (.49) | .46 (.50) |
| *Sexuality-based* | | | | |
| Discrimination | | .64 (.48) *** | .44 (.50) | .26 (.44) |
| Harassment | | .54 (.50) *** | .41 (.49) | .23 (.42) |
| Violence | | .23 (.42)* | .20 (.40) | .10 (.31) |
| Any sexuality DHV experience (0/1) | | .72 (.45)*** | .53 (.50) | .32 (.47) |

* Queer women are significantly different from the women subsample (only) at $p < .05$ level.
*** Queer women are significantly different from both the LGBTQ and women subsamples at $p < .05$ level.

## NCST and Queer Women's Experiences with Gender- and Sexuality-Based DHV

The second set of regression models examines queer women and their experiences with gender- and sexuality-based DHV using NCST with a focus on queer women's axes of social power. The hypotheses are as follows:

- *Hypothesis 1*: being a queer woman (violating hetero-cis-normativity) increases the likelihood of experiencing gender- and sexuality-based DHV (queer women stigma).
- *Hypothesis 2*: the relationship between being a queer woman and gender- and sexuality-based DHV is moderated by interactions among being a queer woman and axes of social power.

Figure 15.4 outlines these relationships and Table 15.5 displays logistic regression results that examine NCST and the relationships among being a queer woman, intersections among queer women's axes of social power, and any experiences of gender-based DHV (dichotomized as 0/1) or sexuality-based DHV (dichotomized as 0/1) utilizing the LGBTQ subsample (n = 1,604; whereby being a queer woman is compared to all other LGBTQ people). Because queer women's experiences are the focus of this exploration (i.e., the stigmatized lens of NCST is being utilized), the queer woman and social power axes interaction terms are listed at the top of the table and are the focus of the discussion below. However, there are significant corresponding individual effects related to being queer and being a woman (for example) that are important to recognize. See Chapter 7 for a more complete description of the models and a discussion of overarching trends and patterns. Regarding model fit statistics, the pseudo $R^2$ values were low and ranged from .09 to .15.

## NCST, Queer Women, and Gender- and Sexuality-Based DHV: Model 1

In Table 15.5, both Model 1s estimate the relationships between violations of hetero-cis-normativity conceptualized as being a queer woman and the stigmatization of queer women conceptualized as gender- and sexuality-based DHV along with sociodemographic controls. Surprisingly, being a queer woman is not significantly related to gender- or sexuality-based DHV. These findings contrast with past research that has found that queer identity is a risk factor for DHV among women (Logie and Earnshaw 2015). Recall, however, that LGBTQ people are the comparison group for these models. Thus, although queer women have very high rates of DHV, being a queer woman (when compared to other LGBTQ people) does not appear to have a direct relationship to the likelihood of experiencing DHV. Thus, *Hypothesis 1* is not supported.

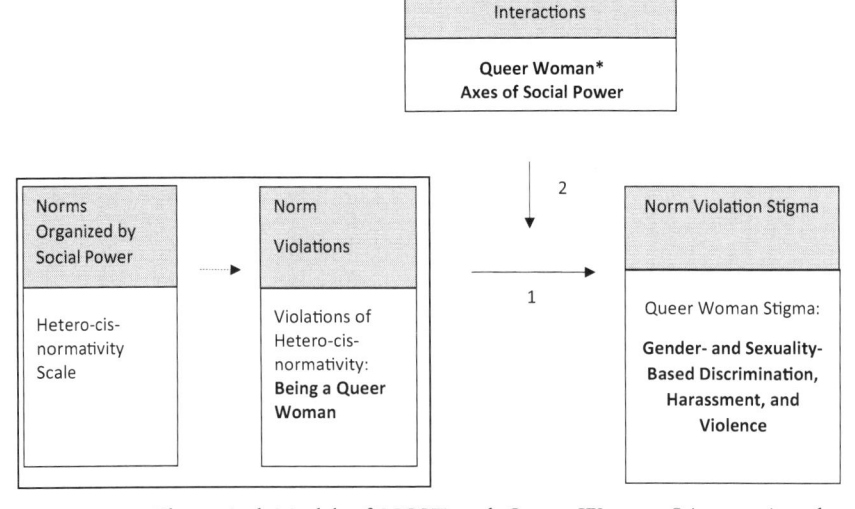

**FIGURE 15.4** Theoretical Model of NCST and Queer Women Stigma using the Stigmatized Lens with Model Numbers to be Examined in Table 15.5

*Notes:* Model 1 estimates being a queer woman as related to gender- and sexuality-based DHV. Model 2 estimates interactions among queer women's axes of social power as they moderate the relationships between being a queer woman and gender- and sexuality-based DHV. The * indicates an interaction.

**TABLE 15.5** Logistic Regression Results with Odds Ratios and (Standard Errors) Estimating NCST and Gender- and Sexuality-Based DHV as Related to Being a Queer Woman for the LGBTQ Subsample (n = 1,604)

|  | Gender-Based DHV ||||  Sexuality-Based DHV  ||||
|  | Model 1 || Model 2 || Model 1 || Model 2 ||
|  | OR | SE | OR | SE | OR | SE | OR | SE |
|---|---|---|---|---|---|---|---|---|
| Queer woman | . | . | . | . | . | . | . | . |
| *Queer woman social power axes interactions* | | | | | | | | |
| Queer woman*gay/lesbian | — | — | . | . | — | — | . | . |
| Queer woman*SGL | — | — | . | . | — | — | . | . |
| Queer woman*femme | — | — | . | . | — | — | . | . |
| Queer woman*White | — | — | .34* | (.18) | — | — | . | . |
| Queer woman*everything I need | — | — | . | . | — | — | . | . |
| Queer woman*mostly all I need | — | — | . | . | — | — | . | . |
| *Queer woman social power axes* | | | | | | | | |
| Queer | 2.73* | (.52) | 2.74* | (.52) | 2.26* | (.43) | 2.25* | (.43) |
| Woman | 4.11* | (.56) | 4.13* | (.57) | . | . | . | . |
| Gay/lesbian | . | . | . | . | 3.41* | (.41) | 2.41* | (1.03) |
| SGL | . | . | . | . | . | . | . | . |
| Femme | . | . | . | . | . | . | . | . |
| White | . | . | . | . | . | . | . | . |
| Everything I need | .63* | (.11) | . | . | .64* | (.10) | . | . |
| Mostly all I need | .71* | (.10) | . | . | . | . | . | . |
| *Socio-demographic controls* | | | | | | | | |
| Age | .98* | (.00) | .97* | (.00) | .98* | (.00) | .98* | (.00) |
| Town type (rural–large city) | . | . | . | . | . | . | . | . |
| Education | 1.17* | (.05) | 1.16* | (.05) | 1.41* | (.21) | . | . |
| Income | . | . | . | . | . | . | . | . |
| Pseudo $R^2$ | .14 || .15 || .09 || .09 ||
| Mean VIF | 1.37 || 1.37 || 1.37 || 1.37 ||

*Notes:* all rows are displayed, including those without significant results. See Table 15.3 for more details about queer LGBTQ women.

* $p < .05$; a dot (.) indicates non-statistically significant results. A dash (—) indicates this was not included in the model.

## NCST, Queer Women, and Gender- and Sexuality-Based DHV: Model 2

Model 2 includes intersections among axes of social power and being a queer woman as they relate to gender- and sexuality-based DHV. As seen in the results for both Model 1s, being a queer woman remains non-statistically significant. However, there is one significant social power interaction term for the gender-based DHV models: being a White queer woman decreases the likelihood of experiencing gender-based DHV by .66. These results overlap with previous research that finds that as compared to White LGBTQ women, LGBTQ women of color endure more stigma and violence (Alimahomed 2010; Battle, Pastrana, and Harris 2017; Logie and Earnshaw 2015; Worthen 2018). However, there are no significant results related to being a queer woman for the sexuality-based DHV models. Overall, *Hypothesis 2* is supported in the gender-based DHV models but not in the sexuality-based DHV models.

## Summarizing NCST, Queer Women, and Gender- and Sexuality-Based DHV

Despite the fact that queer women are at the highest risk for three types of DHV (gender-based discrimination, sexuality-based discrimination, and gender-based harassment) and they report the highest percentage of any gender- or sexuality-based DHV as compared to other LGBTQ groups (recall Figure 7.7), surprisingly, Table 15.5 shows that being a queer woman does not have significant effects on the likelihood of experiencing gender- or sexuality-based DHV in Model 1. In addition, only one intersecting social power experience (being a White queer woman) impacts gender-based DHV among queer women in Model 2. In fact, there are very few significant findings in this table and the pseudo $R^2$ values are quite low. However, by focusing on queer women's identities and social power axes, it becomes clear that there are likely other important factors that contribute to queer women's DHV experiences that deserve further investigation. In particular, other axes of social power not measured here (e.g., presentation of femininity) may help to better explain the DHV experiences of queer women.

## Summary of Patterns of Queer Women Stigma

In line with the three tenets and hypotheses derived from NCST, there are six patterns related to the stigmatization of queer women reviewed in this chapter:

1. Sex-act related stigma is a driving force in the stigmatization of queer women for both hetero-cis and LGBTQ people, especially the damaging

perspectives that queer women are too sexual and unfaithful; however, discomfort with queer women's sex acts with both women and men are also quite concerning for hetero-cis people.
2. For both hetero-cis and LGBTQ people, there is strong support for the stigmatizing belief that queer women are not feminine enough and that their identities as queer women are just temporary or experimental.
3. Hetero-cis-normativity is positively related to queer women stigma for both subsamples; however, the interaction effects between the HCN Scale and social power axes that moderate these relationships differ for the hetero-cis and LGBTQ subsamples.
4. Individual social power axes are significantly related to queer women stigma for both subsamples; however, the interaction effects between the social power axes that moderate these relationships differ for the hetero-cis and LGBTQ subsamples.
5. Queer women experience extremely high levels of gender- and sexuality-based DHV in comparison nearly all other groups.
6. Surprisingly, the individual effect of being a queer woman is not significantly related to the likelihood of gender- or sexuality-based DHV; however, being a White queer woman decreases the likelihood of gender-based DHV.

## Note

1 Stormé DeLarverie (December 24, 1920–May 24, 2014) was a life-long LGBTQ rights activist. From 1955 to 1969, DeLarverie served as the emcee (and only drag king) of the Jewel Box Revue, the first racially integrated drag show in the U.S. On June 28, 1969, she was one of several (some say *the first*) who fought back against the police during their raid at the Stonewall Inn in New York City, an event which many believe was a catalyst to the Gay and Lesbian Rights Movement (Stonewall Veterans' Association 2019). DeLarverie went on to become an active participant in the Stonewall Veterans' Association and served as the "self-appointed guardian of lesbians in the Village … patrolling the sidewalks and checking in at lesbian bars" until she was nearly 90 years old (Yardley 2014). As life-long friend Lisa Cannistraci puts it, "She literally walked the streets of downtown Manhattan like a gay superhero. She was not to be messed with by any stretch of the imagination" (Yardley 2014). On the 50th anniversary of the Stonewall Uprising in June 2019, DeLarvarie was one of fifty inaugural activists inducted into the National LGBTQ Wall of Honor located in the Stonewall Inn (National LGBTQ Task Force 2019).

## References

Alegría, Christine. 2018. "Supporting Families of Transgender Children/Youth: Parents Speak on Their Experiences, Identity, and Views." *International Journal of Transgenderism* 19(2):132–143.

Alimahomed, Sabrina. 2010. "Thinking Outside the Rainbow: Women of Color Redefining Queer Politics and Identity." *Social Identities* 16(2):151–168.

Battle, Juan, Antonio Pastrana, and Angelique Harris. 2017. *An Examination of Asian and Pacific Islander LGBT Populations across the United States*. New York, NY: Palgrave Macmillan.

Brontsema, Robin. 2004. "A Queer Revolution: Reconceptualizing the Debate over Linguistic Reclamation." *Colorado Research in Linguistics* 17(1):1–17.

Butler, Judith. 1993. "Critically Queer." *GLQ: A Journal of Lesbian and Gay Studies* 1(1):17–32.

Clogg, Clifford C., Eva Petkova, and Adamantios Haritou. 1995. "Statistical Methods for Comparing Regression Coefficients between Models." *American Journal of Sociology* 100(5):1261–1293.

Collins, Patricia Hill. 1986. "Learning from the Outsider Within: The Sociological Significance of Black Feminist Thought." *Social Problems* 33(6):S14–32.

Dahl, Ulrika and Del LaGrace Volcano. 2009. *Femmes of Power: Exploding Queer Femininities*. London, UK: Serpent's Tail.

Dowshen, Nadia, Susan Lee, Joshua Franklin, Marné Castillo, and Frances Barg. 2017. "Access to Medical and Mental Health Services across the HIV Care Continuum among Young Transgender Women: A Qualitative Study." *Transgender Health* 2(1):81–90.

Edmonds, Shaun E. and Susan G. Zieff. 2015. "Bearing Bodies: Physical Activity, Obesity Stigma, and Sexuality in the Bear Community." *Sociology of Sport Journal* 32(4):415–435.

Eves, Alison. 2004. "Queer Theory, Butch/Femme Identities and Lesbian Space." *Sexualities* 7(4):480–496.

Friedman, Carly and Campbell Leaper. 2010. "Sexual-Minority College Women's Experiences with Discrimination: Relations with Identity and Collective Action." *Psychology of Women Quarterly* 34(2):152–164.

Galupo, M. Paz, Renae C. Mitchell, and Kyle S. Davis. 2015. "Sexual Minority Self-Identification: Multiple Identities and Complexity." *Psychology of Sexual Orientation and Gender Diversity* 2(4):355–364.

Gamson, Joshua. 1995. "Must Identity Movements Self-Destruct? A Queer Dilemma." *Social Problems* 42(3):390–407.

Gilley, Brian Joseph. 2006. *Becoming Two-Spirit: Gay Identity and Social Acceptance in Indian Country*. Lincoln, NE: University of Nebraska Press.

González-Ramírez, Andrea. 2019. "Tammy Baldwin On The Next Battle For LGBTQ+ Rights." *Refinery29*. Retrieved July 2, 2019 (www.refinery29.com/en-us/2019/03/226505/tammy-baldwin-equality-act-lgbtq-anti-discrimination-federal-law).

Gray, Amy and Serge Desmarais. 2014. "Not All One and the Same: Sexual Identity, Activism, and Collective Self-Esteem." *Canadian Journal of Human Sexuality* 23(2):116–122.

Hamilton, Laura. 2007. "Trading on Heterosexuality: College Women's Gender Strategies and Homophobia." *Gender & Society* 21(2):145–172.

Hayfield, Nikki, Victoria Clarke, and Emma Halliwell. 2014. "Bisexual Women's Understandings of Social Marginalisation: 'The Heterosexuals Don't Understand Us but nor Do the Lesbians.'" *Feminism & Psychology* 24(3):352–372.

Hennen, Peter. 2005. "Bear Bodies, Bear Masculinity: Recuperation, Resistance, or Retreat?" *Gender & Society* 19(1):25–43.

Hill, Darryl B. and Edgardo Menvielle. 2009. "'You Have to Give Them a Place Where They Feel Protected and Safe and Loved': The Views of Parents Who Have Gender-Variant Children and Adolescents." *Journal of LGBT Youth* 6 (2/3):243–271.

Jones, Richard G. 2015. "Queering the Body Politic: Intersectional Reflexivity in the Body Narratives of Queer Men." *Qualitative Inquiry* 21(9):766–775.

Juhasz, Aubri. 2018. "25 Famous Women on Coming Out." *The Cut*. Retrieved July 1, 2019 (www.thecut.com/article/coming-out-stories-famous-queer-women.html).

Levitt, Heidi M. and Sharon G. Horne. 2002. "Explorations of Lesbian-Queer Genders: Butch, Femme, Androgynous or 'Other'." *Journal of Lesbian Studies* 6 (2):25–39.

Logie, Carmen H. and Valerie Earnshaw. 2015. "Adapting and Validating a Scale to Measure Sexual Stigma among Lesbian, Bisexual and Queer Women." *Plos One* 10(2): e0116198.

Logie, Carmen H. and Marie-Jolie Rwigema. 2014. "'The Normative Idea of Queer Is a White Person': Understanding Perceptions of White Privilege among Lesbian, Bisexual, and Queer Women of Color in Toronto, Canada." *Journal of Lesbian Studies* 18 (2):174–191.

Mereish, Ethan H., Sabra L. Katz-Wise, and Julie Woulfe. 2017. "We're Here and We're Queer: Sexual Orientation and Sexual Fluidity Differences between Bisexual and Queer Women." *Journal of Bisexuality* 17(1):125–139.

Mishali, Yael. 2014. "Feminine Trouble: The Removal of Femininity from Feminist/Lesbian/Queer Esthetics, Imagery, and Conceptualization." *Women's Studies International Forum* 44:55–68.

Morandini, James S., Alexander Blaszczynski, and Ilan Dar-Nimrod. 2017. "Who Adopts Queer and Pansexual Sexual Identities?" *The Journal of Sex Research* 54 (7):911–922.

National LGBTQ Task Force. 2019. "National LGBTQ Wall of Honor Unveiled at Historic Stonewall Inn." *National LGBTQ Task Force*. Retrieved August 4, 2019 (www.thetaskforce.org/nationallgbtqwallofhonortobeunveiled/).

Reddy-Best, Kelly L. and Elaine L. Pedersen. 2015. "Queer Women's Experiences Purchasing Clothing and Looking for Clothing Styles." *Clothing and Textiles Research Journal* 33(4):265–279.

Renfro, Kim. 2019. "33 Celebrities Who Don't Identify as either Straight or Gay." *INSIDER*. Retrieved July 1, 2019 (www.thisisinsider.com/celebrities-who-are-bisexual–2017-9).

Rothblum, Esther. 2010. "Where Is the 'Women's Community?' Voices of Lesbian, Bisexual, and Queer Women and Heterosexual Sisters." *Feminism & Psychology* 20(4):454–472.

Rupp, Leila J. and Verta Taylor. 2010. "Straight Girls Kissing." *Contexts* 9(3):28–32.

Rupp, Leila J. Verta Taylor, Alison C. Shiri Regev-Messalem, K. Fogarty, and Paula England. 2014. "Queer Women in the Hookup Scene: Beyond the Closet?" *Gender & Society* 28(2):212–235.

Stonewall Veterans' Association. 2019. "Stormé DeLarverie, S.V.A. Stonewall Ambassador." *Stonewall Veterans' Association*. Retrieved August 4, 2019 (www.stonewallvets.org/StormeDeLarverie.htm).

Walters, Karina L., Jane M. Teresa Evans-Campbell, Theresa Ronquillo Simoni, and Rupaleem Bhuyan. 2006. "'My Spirit in My Heart': Identity Experiences and Challenges among American Indian Two-Spirit Women." *Journal of Lesbian Studies* 10 (1/2):125–149.

Weiss, Jillian Todd. 2004. "GL vs. BT: The Archaeology of Biphobia and Transphobia within the US Gay and Lesbian Community." *Journal of Bisexuality* 3(3/4): 25–55.

Worthen, Meredith G. F. 2018. "'Gay Equals White'? Racial, Ethnic, and Sexual Identities and Attitudes toward LGBT Individuals among College Students at a Bible Belt University." *The Journal of Sex Research* 55(8):995–1011.

Yardley, William. 2014. "Storme DeLarverie, Early Leader in the Gay Rights Movement, Dies at 93." *The New York Times*, May 29. Retrieved February 21, 2020 (https://www.nytimes.com/2014/05/30/nyregion/storme-delarverie-early-leader-in-the-gay-rights-movement-dies-at-93.html).

# 16
# QUEER MEN STIGMA

*A Pride month night of celebration and fun—the weekly Latin Night at the popular Orlando club, Pulse, focused on Latin music, performances and dancing—turned into a morning of mass death and devastation. But the brutal reality that jarred Orlando's LGBT community, and the entire nation, is something that LGBT people have always experienced, as gay and lesbian bars and clubs have been targeted consistently by those who harbor hate toward LGBT people. And it's a reminder of the animus against LGBT people that still exists, and the ever present danger with which we still live.*

Michelangelo Signorile (2016), HuffPost editor-at-large[1]

**IMAGE 16.1** Flowers and photos memorializing the 49 dead and 53 wounded in the attacks on June 12, 2016 are displayed in front of Pulse nightclub in Orlando, Florida as Secretary of Homeland Security Jeh Johnson shakes hands with a chaplain who helped those impacted by the shooting. Official DHS photo by Jetta Disco.

## The Stigmatization of Queer Men

In the survey instrument, the section focusing on attitudes toward queer men was preceded by the following statement:

> *Next we'd like to ask you for your thoughts, feelings, and predicted behaviors about men who self-identify as "queer." Please note that "queer" is often used as an umbrella identity term that encompasses individuals who do not feel they fit within the categories of heterosexual, lesbian, gay, or bisexual, and/or those who are attracted to people of many genders, and/or those who feel their sexual identity is fluid.*

## The Queer Men Stigma Scale

Queer men are the third most stigmatized among all nine groups examined in this book, just slightly less stigmatized than trans men and non-binary/genderqueer people (recall Figure 7.1). Queer men have unique experiences with stigma that both overlap and differ from queer women and other LGBT men. To better understand these patterns, the mean values for the 14 items in the Queer Men Stigma Scale provided in Figure 16.1 and Table 16.1 are discussed below.

| Item | LGBTQ Subsample | Hetero-cis Subsample |
|---|---|---|
| Discomfort with Sex w/Man | 1.84 | 2.81 |
| Not Masculine Enough | 2.20 | 2.80 |
| Too Sexual/Hypersexual | 2.20 | 2.78 |
| Discomfort with Sex w/Woman | 1.84 | 2.76 |
| Responsible for HIV/AIDS | 1.98 | 2.71 |
| Unfaithful | 2.15 | 2.68 |
| Identity is Just Temporary/Experimental | 2.04 | 2.68 |
| Restrict from Military | 1.85 | 2.63 |
| Not Vote for Political Candidate | 1.80 | 2.63 |
| As Good Parents | 1.77 | 2.50 |
| As New Friends | 1.76 | 2.46 |
| As Family/Close Relative | 1.75 | 2.44 |
| Deny Basic Rights | 1.56 | 2.23 |
| Victimization is Not Upsetting to Me | 1.62 | 2.17 |

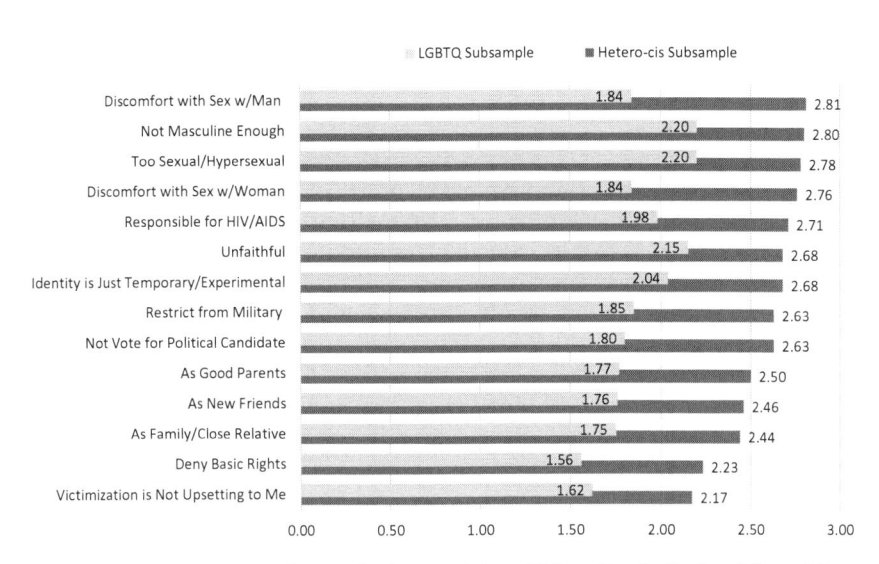

**FIGURE 16.1** Queer Men Stigma Scale Item Mean Values Rank-Ordered from Most to Least Stigmatizing for the Hetero-cis (n = 1,500) and the LGBTQ (n = 1,604) Subsamples

*Notes:* see Table 16.1 for the exact wording for each item. *t*-test results comparing the hetero-cis and LGBTQ subsamples indicate that all means are significantly different from one another at the $p < .001$ level.

**TABLE 16.1** Queer Men Stigma Scale Item Mean Values (Standard Deviations) and *t*-test Results Comparing the Means for the Hetero-cis Subsample and the LGBTQ Subsample

|  | Hetero-cis Subsample | LGBTQ Subsample | t-test Results |
|---|---|---|---|
|  | n = 1,500 | n = 1,604 |  |
| *Social and familial relationships* |  |  |  |
| I welcome new friends who are queer men.[R] | 2.46 (1.21) | 1.76 (1.02) | *t* = 17.29* |
| I don't think it would negatively affect our relationship if I learned that one of my close relatives was a queer man.[R] | 2.44 (1.19) | 1.75 (1.03) | *t* = 17.08* |
| Queer men are not capable of being good parents. | 2.50 (1.27) | 1.77 (1.12) | *t* = 17.01* |
| *Positions of importance and social significance* |  |  |  |
| I would not vote for a political candidate who was an openly queer man. | 2.63 (1.33) | 1.80 (1.17) | *t* = 18.37* |
| Queer men should not be allowed to join the military. | 2.63 (1.34) | 1.85 (1.24) | *t* = 16.81* |
| *Basic human rights* |  |  |  |
| I believe queer men should have all of the same rights as other people do.[R] | 2.23 (1.17) | 1.56 (.97) | *t* = 17.22* |
| It is upsetting to me that queer men experience violence, harassment, and discrimination just because they are queer men.[R] | 2.17 (1.14) | 1.62 (1.02) | *t* = 14.23* |
| *Sex act-related stigma* |  |  |  |
| Queer men are unfaithful to their romantic partners. | 2.68 (1.12) | 2.15 (1.17) | *t* = 13.06* |
| Queer men are too sexual (hypersexual). | 2.78 (1.17) | 2.20 (1.18) | *t* = 14.02* |
| Queer men are mostly responsible for spreading HIV/AIDS. | 2.71 (1.20) | 1.98 (1.16) | *t* = 17.17* |
| I am comfortable with the thought of a queer man having sex with a man.[R] | 2.81 (1.21) | 1.84 (1.01) | *t* = 24.15* |
| I am comfortable with the thought of a queer man having sex with a woman.[R] | 2.76 (1.17) | 2.06 (1.13) | *t* = 16.83* |
| *Queer identity permanency* |  |  |  |
| Most men who call themselves queer are just temporarily experimenting with their sexuality. | 2.68 (1.13) | 2.04 (1.11) | *t* = 15.96* |
| *Achievement of masculinity* |  |  |  |
| Queer men are not masculine enough. | 2.80 (1.14) | 2.20 (1.19) | *t* = 14.53* |
| α | .91 | .93 |  |
| Summed scale actual range | 14–70 | 14–70 |  |
| Summed scale mean | 36.28 (11.24) | 26.57 (11.17) | *t* = 24.12* |

*Notes*: response options were Strongly Disagree–Strongly Agree (range: 1–5). [R] This item is reverse coded.
* *t*-test results allowing for unequal variances indicate that the hetero-cis subsample and LGBTQ subsample means are significantly different from one another at the $p < .001$ level.

## Queer Men and Social and Familial Relationships

In comparison to all other key areas of the scale, the stigmatization of having queer men as friends and family members is lower (with the exception of basic human rights as discussed in Chapter 7) (see Table 16.1). All three items in this key area ranged by only .06 points for the hetero-cis subsample and .02 points for the LGBTQ subsample. Thus, there was little variation in the stigma associated with queer men's social and familial relationships for either subsample. One small qualitative study (N = 5) found that queer-identified men navigate complex and sometimes hostile relationships with family members and peer groups (Jones 2015). Another project examining queer Latino men (N = 15, n = 5 queer men) also revealed difficulties in familial relationships, including regular experiences with anti-queer microaggressions from family members (Duran and Pérez 2017). Overall, however, in this study, negativity toward queer men as friends and family members is not as extreme as seen in most other key areas of the Queer Men Stigma Scale.

## Queer Men and Positions of Importance and Social Significance

For the items in this key area ("I would not vote for a political candidate who was an openly queer man" and "Queer men should not be allowed to join the military"), there was moderate stigmatization. Means were identical for the hetero-cis subsample (2.63 and 2.63 respectively) and were similar for the LGBTQ subsample (1.80 and 1.85 respectively). Stigma toward queer men in positions of importance and social significance was midrange in comparison to the other 14 items in the scale for both groups (see Figure 16.1). This is somewhat unexpected because as similarly noted in Chapter 15, though there are men celebrities who have unmistakably self-identified as "queer" (e.g., actor Ezra Miller; see Renfro 2019), self-identified queer political or military men leaders in the U.S. are not as clearly noticeable. Openly gay U.S. politician and Navy veteran Pete Buttigieg referred to himself in passing as "the first out queer person to get this far" and as "a good candidate who happens to be queer" in an interview with *The Advocate* about his campaign for the 2020 presidency (Masters 2019). Openly gay Massachusetts Senator Julian Cyr also referred to himself in passing as "a young, queer member of the senate" in an interview with LGBT news site NewNowNext (Braithwaite 2018). Yet in both cases, it is unclear if these remarks indicate that these men actually self-identify as "queer" or if they are using this term as a collective, catchall phrase in response to the interviewers' use of "queer." Whatever the case may be and despite this lack of recognizable self-identified queer political or military men leaders in the U.S., in this sample, there is some support for queer men in positions of importance and social significance.

## *Queer Men and Sex Act-Related Stigma*

Four of the top five most stigmatizing attitudes toward queer men were among the sex act-related stigma items for the hetero-cis subsample (hypersexuality, discomfort with sex with both men women, and HIV/AIDS) as were three of the top five for the LGBTQ subsample (hypersexuality, unfaithful, and HIV/AIDS) (see Figure 16.1). Furthermore, all means for the five items in this key area were above 2.7 among the hetero-cis subsample (ranging from 2.71 to 2.81) and close to 2.0 or higher for the LGBTQ subsample (ranging from 1.84 to 2.20). Because queer men's sex acts can be both misunderstood and deviantized (Iasenza 2010; Jones 2015; Galupo, Lomash, and Mitchell 2017; Scheim, Adam, and Marshall 2019), sex act-related stigma among queer men may be especially strong.

As seen in Table 16.1, the item with the *lowest* mean value in the sex act-related stigma key area for the hetero-cis subsample (2.68), "Queer men are unfaithful to their romantic sexual partners," actually had the second-*highest* mean for the LGBTQ subsample (2.15). In fact, for the LGBTQ subsample, the mean for the item "Queer men are too sexual (hypersexual)" was only .05 points higher and this item had the second highest mean for the hetero-cis subsample (2.78) and the highest mean among the LGBTQ subsample in the sex-act related key area (2.20) (see Table 16.1). This is especially significant because queer men were the most likely among all nine LGBTQ groups to be stigmatized for being too hypersexual by the hetero-cis subsample (recall Figure 7.4).

These findings may be associated with generalized stereotypes about men's hypersexuality (Connell 2005) as well as their clandestine sexual behaviors (Heath and Goggin 2009; Humphreys 1970). However, because queer-identified men have described their own experiences with sex-related negativity and misunderstandings in small scale studies (Jones 2015; Galupo et al. 2017; Scheim, Adam, and Marshall 2019), it is likely that queer men endure more specific sexual stigmatization related to their queer selves. As reviewed in Chapter 7, like gay and bisexual men, queer men are perceived as participating in penile-anal sex with other men and this can be especially stigmatizing (Heflick 2010). However, because queer men's sexualities are particularly under-examined and culturally misunderstood (Hammack, Frost, and Hughes 2019; Jones 2015; Galupo, Lomash, and Mitchell 2017; Scheim, Adam, and Marshall 2019), they may be especially likely to be perceived of as involved in other stigmatized and hypersexualized behaviors such as kink, leather, and BDSM (Dominguez 1994; Iasenza 2010; Sprott and Hadcock 2018) as well as fetishized bear and twink subcultures/communities (for example) (Hennen 2005, 2008). Indeed, one study found that "kink" identity was more common among "queer" individuals as compared to gay, lesbian, bisexual, pansexual, and asexual individuals (Galupo, Mitchell, and Davis 2015). In this study's sample, queer men were the most likely to identify as "leather," "bear," and "twink" among all nine LGBTQ groups. Overall, queer men's hypersexuality was a common stigmatizing perspective among both subsamples and in comparison to all others, queer men are especially likely to be stigmatized in this way by the hetero-cis subsample.

Among all nine LGBTQ groups, queer men were most likely to be stigmatized by both subsamples as being "mostly responsible for spreading HIV/AIDS" (recall Figure 7.4). Though the dominant discourse about HIV/AIDS in the 1980s was focused on "gay" and "bisexual" men (Dowsett 2009; Herek and Capitanio 1999), largely starting with the founding of Queer Nation in 1990, HIV/AIDS activism became entwined with "queer" identity/politics (Brontsema 2004; Gamson 1995). In particular, as an offshoot of the HIV/AIDS activist group AIDS Coalition to Unleash Power (ACT-UP), Queer Nation spearheaded a force of HIV/AIDS activism that was decidedly "queer" (Brontsema 2004). Because of this as well as the associated largely stigmatized sex acts of queer men as discussed above and in Chapter 7, both LGBTQ and hetero-cis people may be especially likely to link queer men with HIV/AIDS-related stigma.

The findings related to comfort/discomfort with queer men's sex acts followed similar patterns as found in previous chapters. In the sex act-related stigma key area, the item with the *lowest* mean for the LGBTQ subsample (1.84) has the *highest* mean for the hetero-cis subsample (2.81). That item is: "I am comfortable with the thought of a queer man having sex with a man" which was reverse coded because *dis*comfort with queer men engaging in sex acts reflects a stigmatizing attitude toward queer men. Hetero-cis people may feel more hostility toward queer men having sex with other men than LGBTQ people feel because sex acts between men violate heteronormativity. However, LGBTQ people indicated more stigma toward the contrasting survey item, "I am comfortable with the thought of a queer man having sex with a woman." Somewhat similar the ideas discussed in Chapter 15 as related to queer women stigmatization, among attitudes toward queer-identified men, man + man duos are viewed as most acceptable by the LGBTQ subsample but woman + man duos are least stigmatized by the hetero-cis subsample.

## *Queer Man Identity Permanency*

The stigmatizing perspective that "Most men who call themselves queer are just temporarily experimenting with their sexuality" was evident in both subsamples. Specifically, this was the fourth most stigmatizing attitude among the LGBTQ subsample and the sixth most stigmatizing attitude among the hetero-cis subsample (the mean was identical for the item about queer men being unfaithful in the hetero-cis subsample, 2.68). As similarly described in Chapter 15, there are two overlapping stereotypes that contribute to this finding: (1) the flexible and fluid qualities associated with queer identity for men (Jones 2015; Morandini, Blaszczynski, and Dar-Nimrod 2017) (and in some related ways, for bisexual men, see Chapter 11), and (2) the youthful and (perceived to be) fleeting "trend" of adopting a queer identity (Brontsema 2004; Gamson 1995). Because queer identity is seen as both malleable and "trendy" by both hetero-cis and LGBTQ people, this contributes to broader questions about the permanency of queer men's identities.

### Queer Men and the Achievement of Masculinity

Queer men's masculinity is strongly criticized. In fact, queer men (and trans men) are most likely among all LGBTQ groups to be stigmatized for not being "masculine enough" by the hetero-cis subsample (recall Figure 7.4). In addition, across all 14 items in the Queer Men Stigma Scale, this item has the second-highest mean value for the hetero-cis subsample (2.80) and has one of the two highest mean values for the LGBTQ subsample (2.20) (see Figure 16.1). Thus, there is agreement across the entire sample that queer men do not meet the dominant cultural criteria of masculinity. Because queer identity is often fluid, queer men can have diverse expressions of masculinity, gender, and sexuality which can contrast with hetero-cis-normative standards (Jones 2015; Galupo, Lomash, and Mitchell 2017). For example, one small qualitative study (N = 5) found that queer men actively rejected hegemonic masculinity and "played" with creating their own "queer masculinities" in ways that were authentic to their queer identities (Jones 2015). Even so, there is a strong stigmatizing perspective that queer men "are not masculine enough" among both subsamples in this study.

### Queer Men Stigma Summed Scale

In Table 16.1, the Queer Men Stigma Scale was created by summing all 14 items together. Cronbach's alphas were quite high for the hetero-cis subsample (.91) and the LGBTQ subsample (.93). Similar to the Trans Women Stigma Scale, the Non-binary/Genderqueer Stigma Scale, and the Queer Women Stigma Scale (but unlike the stigma scales for lesbian women, gay men, bisexual women, and bisexual men), the actual range in values for the Queer Men Stigma Scale was identical for the two subsamples (14–70). However, mean values for the summed Queer Men Stigma Scale differed substantially and significantly with the hetero-cis subsample mean (36.28) 9.71 points higher than the LGBTQ subsample mean (26.57). In addition, the key area with the highest individual mean value differed for the subsamples. For the hetero-cis subsample, discomfort with queer men's sex acts was most stigmatized while queer men's inability to achieve masculinity and hypersexuality had the highest means for the LGBTQ subsample. However, it is important to note that for the hetero-cis subsample, the top three mean scores were very close to one another (ranging by only .03 points) and include stigma toward queer men's inability to achieve masculinity and hypersexuality. Thus, overall, queer men's stigmatization is associated with the achievement of masculinity and sex act-related stigma (recall Figure 7.3).

## NCST, Hetero-cis-normativity, Social Power Axes, and the Queer Men Stigma Scale

The first set of regression models examine the Queer Men Stigma Scale using NCST. The hypotheses are as follows:

- *Hypothesis 1a*: there is a significant positive relationship between the HCN Scale and the Queer Men Stigma Scale.
- *Hypothesis 1b*: there are significant relationships between individual social power axes (gender identity, sexual identity, additional gender/sexuality, racial/ethnic identity, basic needs) and the Queer Men Stigma Scale.
- *Hypothesis 2a*: the relationship between the HCN Scale and the Queer Men Stigma Scale is moderated by interactions between the HCN Scale and axes of social power.
- *Hypothesis 2b*: the relationships between individual social power axes and the Queer Men Stigma Scale are moderated by interactions between axes of social power.

Figure 16.2 outlines these relationships and the two models of NCST to be estimated. Specifically, OLS regression is utilized in Table 16.2 to examine NCST and the relationships among hetero-cis-normativity, axes of social power (gender, sexuality, additional gender/sexuality, race/ethnicity, and basic needs), and the Queer Men Stigma Scale for the hetero-cis subsample and the LGBTQ subsample. See Chapter 7 for a more complete description of the models. Regarding model fit statistics, the adjusted $R^2$ values ranged from .67 to .68.

### NCST, HCN, Social Power Axes, and the Queer Men Stigma Scale: Model 1

The relationships between the HCN Scale, social power axes, and the Queer Men Stigma Scale are estimated in Table 16.1, Model 1. For both groups, *Hypothesis 1a* is well supported: the HCN Scale is positively related to the Queer Men Stigma Scale. Supporting *Hypothesis 1b*, individual axes of social power are also significantly related to the Queer Men Stigma Scale for the hetero-cis subsample (cis woman) and for the LGBTQ subsample (queer, African American/Black, other race, and Multi-racial).

### NCST, HCN, Social Power Axes, and the Queer Men Stigma Scale: Model 2

In Model 2, axes of social power and intersections among axes of social power and the HCN Scale are examined. The HCN Scale continues to be positively related to the Queer Men Stigma Scale in Model 2 for both subsamples. Among the HCN

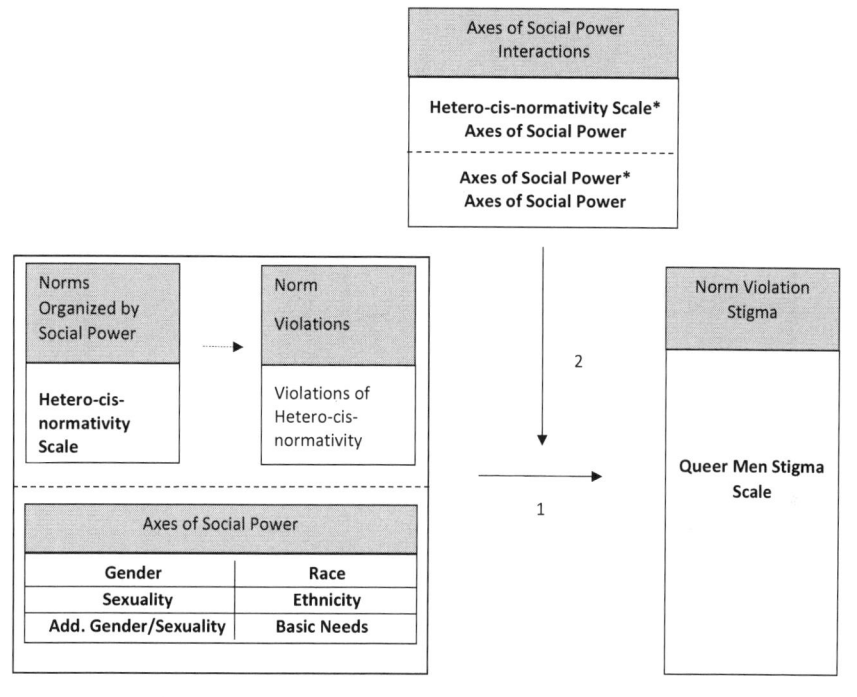

**FIGURE 16.2** Theoretical Model of NCST and Queer Men Stigma using the Stigmatizer Lens with Model Numbers to be Examined in Table 16.2

Notes: Model 1 estimates the HCN Scale and axes of social power (gender, sexuality, additional gender/sexuality, race, ethnicity, and basic needs) as they relate to the Queer Men Stigma Scale. Model 2 estimates interactions among axes of social power and the HCN Scale as they moderate the relationships between the HCN Scale and the Queer Men Stigma Scale as well as interactions among axes of social power as they moderate the relationships between the HCN Scale and the Queer Men Stigma Scale. The * indicates an interaction.

Scale interaction terms, two are discussed in Chapter 7: the interactions between the HCN Scale, Multi-racial identity, and indicating "mostly all I need." In the hetero-cis subsample, there are two additional significant interaction terms: the interactions between the HCN Scale and femme and bear identities are both negatively related to the Queer Men Stigma Scale. Higher levels of agreement with the HCN Scale have a more robust impact on attitudes toward queer men among hetero-cis individuals who do *not* identify as "femme" or "bear" as compared hetero-cis individuals who do identify as femme or bear. Though most research focuses on femme and bear identities in the LGBTQ community (Hennen 2005; Levitt and Horne 2002), about one fourth (24%, 74/303) of femmes were hetero-cis and more than one-third (39%, 59/153) of bears were hetero-cis in this study. The findings here demonstrate that hetero-cis-normative thinking impacts attitudes toward queer men among

**TABLE 16.2** OLS Regression Results Estimating NCST and the Queer Men Stigma Scale for the Hetero-cis Subsample (n = 1,500) and the LGBTQ Subsample (n = 1,604)

|  | Hetero-cis Subsample |  | LGBTQ Subsample |  | Test of Difference |
|---|---|---|---|---|---|
|  | Model 1 | Model 2 | Model 1 | Model 2 |  |
| HCN Scale | .85* | .80* | 88* | .76* | . |
| *Gender identity* |  |  |  |  |  |
| Cis woman | -1.24* | -2.46* | . | . | . |
| *Additional gender/sexual identity* |  |  |  |  |  |
| Queer |  |  | -1.16* | . | . |
| *Race/ethnicity* |  |  |  |  |  |
| African American/Black | . | . | 1.62* | 12.69* | . |
| Other race | . | . | 3.84* | 7.48* | . |
| Multi-racial | . | . | -2.14* | . | . |
| *Basic needs* |  |  |  |  |  |
| Few needs met | . | . | . | 9.55* | . |
| *HCN Scale\*social power axes interactions* |  |  |  |  |  |
| HCN Scale*femme | — | -.33* | — | . | . |
| HCN Scale*bear | — | -.29* | — | . | ** |
| HCN Scale*Multi-racial | — | .61* | — | . | . |
| HCN Scale*butch | — | . | — | -.30* | . |
| HCN Scale*Asian American/Pacific Islander | — | . | — | -.37* | . |
| HCN Scale*mostly all I need | — | . | — | .17* | . |
| *Social power axes interactions* |  |  |  |  |  |
| Cis woman*Two-Spirit | — | . | — | 3.26* | . |
| Gay/lesbian*Asian American/Pacific Islander | — | — | — | 3.51* | . |
| African American/Black*Two-Spirit | — | . | — | -6.54* | ** |
| African American/Black*often needs not met | — | . | — | -4.66* | . |
| African American/Black*few needs met | — | . | — | -6.13* | . |
| *Controls: common explanations* |  |  |  |  |  |
| *LGBTQ contact* |  |  |  |  |  |
| Queer men friends | -1.68* | -1.85* | -1.52* | -1.50* | . |
| LGBTQ Friends Scale (w/o queer men) | -.45* | -.46* | . | . | ** |

(Continued)

**TABLE 16.2** (Cont.)

|  | Hetero-cis Subsample | | LGBTQ Subsample | | Test of Difference |
| --- | --- | --- | --- | --- | --- |
|  | Model 1 | Model 2 | Model 1 | Model 2 |  |
| *Religious identity* |  |  |  |  |  |
| Protestant—evangelical | 2.17* | 2.02* | . | . | . |
| Atheist | 1.96* | 2.35* | . | . | ** |
| *Political perspectives* |  |  |  |  |  |
| Liberal—conservative | .90* | .83* | . | . | ** |
| Openness to new experiences | -1.37* | -1.09* | -1.50* | -1.52* | . |
| *Support laws/policies helping:* |  |  |  |  |  |
| Those in poverty | -1.16* | -1.12* | -1.15* | . | . |
| Racial/ethnic minorities | . | . | -1.31* | -1.15* | ** |
| Immigrants | . | . | . | -1.02* | . |
| Women | -1.07* | -1.01* | . | . | ** |
| *Beliefs about gender* |  |  |  |  |  |
| Feminist | . | . | -1.17* | -1.09* | . |
| Patriarchal Gender Norms Scale | .52* | .49* | .61* | .63* | . |
| *Sociodemographic Controls* |  |  |  |  |  |
| Age | . | . | .04* | . | . |
| Outside U.S. | . | . | . | 2.62* | . |
| Education | . | . | .32* | . | . |
| Adjusted $R^2$ | .67 | .67 | .68 | .68 |  |
| Mean VIF | 1.51 | 1.51 | 1.94 | 1.94 |  |

*Notes:* Unstandardized regression coefficients are presented. See Table 16.1 for detailed information about the Queer Men Stigma Scale. See Tables 7.1 and 7.2 for details about all other variables and Appendix B Table B.1 for details about the interaction effects. Only the rows with significant results are displayed here.

* $p < .05$; a dot (.) indicates non-statistically significant results. A dash (—) indicates this was not included in the model.
** $p < .05$ for Clogg et al.'s (1995) test of equality of regression coefficients comparing Model 2 for the hetero-cis subsample and Model 2 for the LGBTQ subsample.

femmes and bears in intersecting ways. It may be that these groups are less open to "queer" expressions. For example, scholars find hetero-cis femmes are more inclined toward essentialist definitons of femininity (Blair and Hoskin 2005) and similarly, hetero-cis bears may rely on essentialist constructions of masculinity (Hennen 2005). Together these findings suggest that there may be something unique about the cultural experiences of hetero-cis femmes and bears that contributes to their stigmatization of queer men.

For the LGBTQ subsample, interactions between the HCN Scale and butch and Asian American/Pacific Islander identities are both negatively related to the Queer Men Stigma Scale. Higher levels of agreement with the HCN Scale have a more robust impact on attitudes toward queer men among LGBTQ individuals who do *not* identify as "butch" or "Asian American/Pacific Islander" as compared LGBTQ individuals who do identify as "butch" or "Asian American/Pacific Islander." The intersections of butch identity and Asian identity have been found to impact LGBTQ experiences (Bailey et al. 1997; Battle, Pastrana, and Harris 2017; Han, Proctor, and Choi 2014; Johns et al. 2012). The results in Table 16.2 further suggest that hetero-cis-normativity effects hostilities toward queer men in ways that vary by the sexual identity (butch) and race (Asian American/Pacific Islander) of the stigmatizer. Indeed, "butch" can be a contested identity in some queer spaces (Halberstam 1998) and queer identity among Asian American/Pacific Islander individuals exists in a nexus of complexities (Eng and Hom 1998; Kumashiro 1999). Thus, these findings underscore how stigmatizing attitudes toward queer men are shaped by butch and Asian American/Pacific Islander identities. Overall, *Hypothesis 2a* is supported: interactions between the HCN Scale and axes of social power moderate the relationship between the HCN Scale and the Queer Men Stigma Scale for both subsamples.

As noted in prior chapters, axes of social power shape perspectives about queer men in different ways for the hetero-cis and LGBTQ subsamples. For example, among the individual social power axes, only one is significantly related to the Queer Men Stigma Scale for the hetero-cis subsample: being a cis woman is negatively related to the stigmatization of queer men. This finding is among the consistent trends discussed in Chapter 7. However, there are no significant interaction terms among the social power axes for the hetero-cis subsample. In contrast, there are numerous significant results for the LGBTQ subsample. Among the individual social power axes, being African American/Black, being other race, and indicating that few of your basic needs are met are all positively related to the Queer Men Stigma Scale. However, there are three corresponding interaction terms that are negatively related to the stigmatization of queer men: being African American/Black and Two-Spirit, being African American/Black and often not having one's needs met, and being African American/Black and having few needs met. As noted in Chapter 15, the intersecting marginalized experiences of being African American/Black, LGBTQ, and experiencing basic needs strains can work together to shape unique and empathic perspectives about marginalized others, including queer men (Alimahomed 2010; Collins 1986; Rosenberg 2018). Thus, although the individual effects of being African American/Black and struggling to meet one's basic needs are positively related to the Queer Men Stigma

Scale, the intersections of these experiences have the opposite effect on the stigmatization of queer men.

There are two significant interaction terms among the LGBTQ subsample that do not have corresponding individual social power axes effects: (1) being a cis woman and Two-Spirit and (2) being gay/lesbian and Asian American/Pacific Islander are both positively related to the Queer Men Stigma Scale. Some research indicates that there is some tension among Two-Spirit and other LGBTQ groups and communities (Gilley 2006, 2010; Walters et al. 2006) as well as Asian American/Pacific Islander LGBTQ negativity within LGBTQ groups and communities (Battle, Pastrana, and Harris 2017; Han, Proctor, and Choi 2014). Part of this can relate to the privileges associated with some LGBTQ identities commonly associated with Whiteness (e.g., gay, and queer) and the marginalization that some LGBTQ people of color experience (Choi et al. 2011; Han, Proctor, and Choi 2014; Walters et al. 2006; Worthen 2018). Some cis Two-Spirit women and gay/lesbian Asian American/Pacific Islander individuals may stigmatize queer men because they may see identifying as "queer" and "man" as intersecting and problematic privileges within the LGBTQ community (Alimahomed 2010; Brontsema 2004; Heasley 2005; Logie and Rwigema 2014). Together, these interlocking identities impact the stigmatization of queer men.

Findings in Table 16.2 demonstrate differences in the axes of social power that relate to attitudes toward queer men for the hetero-cis and LGBTQ subsamples. Additional tests to compare the regression coefficients of the two subsamples also some reveal significant differences, but not many (Clogg, Petkova, and Haritou 1995). Overall, interactions between axes of social power moderate the relationship between the individual axes of social power and the Queer Men Stigma Scale for the LGBTQ subsample (only), partially supporting *Hypothesis 2b*.

## Summarizing NCST, HCN, Social Power Axes, and the Queer Men Stigma Scale

In sum, Table 16.2 shows that axes of social power relate to hetero-cis and LGBTQ people's attitudes toward queer men in different ways. In particular, while both hetero-cis-normativity and the HCN Scale interaction terms are significant for the hetero-cis and LGBTQ subsamples, individual and intersecting social power experiences work together to shape the stigmatization of queer men among the LGBTQ subsample much more so than among the hetero-cis subsample. Thus, as suggested in some past studies (Duran and David 2017; Jones 2015; Morandini, Blaszczynski, and Dar-Nimrod 2017; Galupo, Lomash, and Mitchell 2017), hetero-cis and LGBTQ people's attitudes toward queer men are differentially impacted by intersecting experiences with social power. Overall, NCST's intersectional focus on hetero-cis-normativity and axes of social power contributes to a deeper understanding of the stigmatization of queer men.

## Queer Men's Experiences

### The Queer Men Subsample

In this study, there was no requested quota from Survey Sampling International for queer men yet the sample included 209 queer men (learn more about the "queer" survey item and survey response options in Chapter 15 and the data and sampling procedures in Chapter 7 and Appendix A). The majority (65%) of queer men were gay (n = 95), bisexual (n = 32), pansexual (n = 5), or asexual (n = 4); however, over one-third (35%, n = 71) were hetero-cis queer men (n = 2 were hetero trans queer men). Although there is fascinating existing research focusing on queer heterosexual men (Heasley 2005), to parallel the previous DHV investigations in this book, only queer LGBTQ men's DHV experiences were explored. The final sample size of queer LGBTQ men was 138. See Table 16.3 for more details about the queer men in this study.

**TABLE 16.3** Queer LGBTQ Men Characteristics (n = 138)

|  | % | n |
|---|---|---|
| *Sexual identity* | | |
| Heterosexual* | 1.4% | 2 |
| Gay** | 68.8% | 95 |
| Bisexual* | 23.2% | 32 |
| Pansexual* | 3.6% | 5 |
| Asexual* | 2.9% | 4 |
| *Gender identity* | | |
| Cis men | 89.9% | 124 |
| Trans men | 10.1% | 14 |
| *Additional gender/sexual identity* | | |
| SGL** | 18.1% | 25 |
| Two-Spirit | 7.2% | 10 |
| Butch | 9.4% | 13 |
| Femme | 8.7% | 12 |
| Leather | 8.0% | 11 |
| Bear | 12.3% | 17 |
| Twink | 8.7% | 12 |

(*Continued*)

**TABLE 16.3** (Cont.)

|  | % | n |
|---|---|---|
| Down Low | 7.2% | 10 |
| *Race/ethnicity* | | |
| Caucasian/White** | 76.8% | 106 |
| African American/Black* | 10.9% | 15 |
| Asian American/Pacific Islander* | 5.8% | 8 |
| Native American/Alaskan Native* | 2.2% | 3 |
| Multi-racial* | 2.9% | 4 |
| Other race* | 0.7% | 1 |
| Latinx race* | 0.7% | 1 |
| Latinx ethnicity | 15.9% | 22 |
| *Basic needs* | | |
| Everything I need** | 28.3% | 39 |
| Mostly all I need** | 50.0% | 69 |
| Often needs not met* | 14.5% | 20 |
| Few needs met* | 7.2% | 10 |

\* reference category in analyses in Table 16.5.
\*\* included in analyses shown in Table 16.5.

## Queer Men's Experiences with Gender- and Sexuality-Based DHV

Some research indicates that queer-identified men experience stigma in various forms (Duran and David 2017; Jones 2015; Meyer 2015; Morandini, Blaszczynski, and Dar-Nimrod 2017; Galupo, Lomash, and Mitchell 2017). Yet queer men's DHV experiences have not been previously explored in any large-scale studies. Figure 16.3 shows that close to three-fourths (72%) of queer men have had one or more experiences of sexuality-based DHV and close to one-third (32%) have had one or more experiences of gender-based DHV. Sexuality-based discrimination is the most common form (60%) while gender-based violence is the least common (14%). To better understand queer men's gender- and sexuality-based DHV, queer men's experiences were compared to the LGBTQ subsample and the men subsample using *t*-tests. Table 16.4 demonstrates that in comparison to all LGBTQ people and all men, queer men are significantly more likely to experience all types of sexuality-based DHV as well as gender-based harassment. In addition, queer men report significantly more experiences with gender-based discrimination and violence in comparison to the all men subsample. Overall, compared to the other LGBTQ groups, queer men experience the highest percentage of two types of DHV (sexuality-based harassment and sexuality-based violence) and they report the highest

■ Gender-Based    Sexuality-Based

DISCRIMINATION: 28%, 60%
HARASSMENT: 19%, 59%
VIOLENCE: 14%, 37%
ANY DHV EXPERIENCE (0/1): 32%, 72%

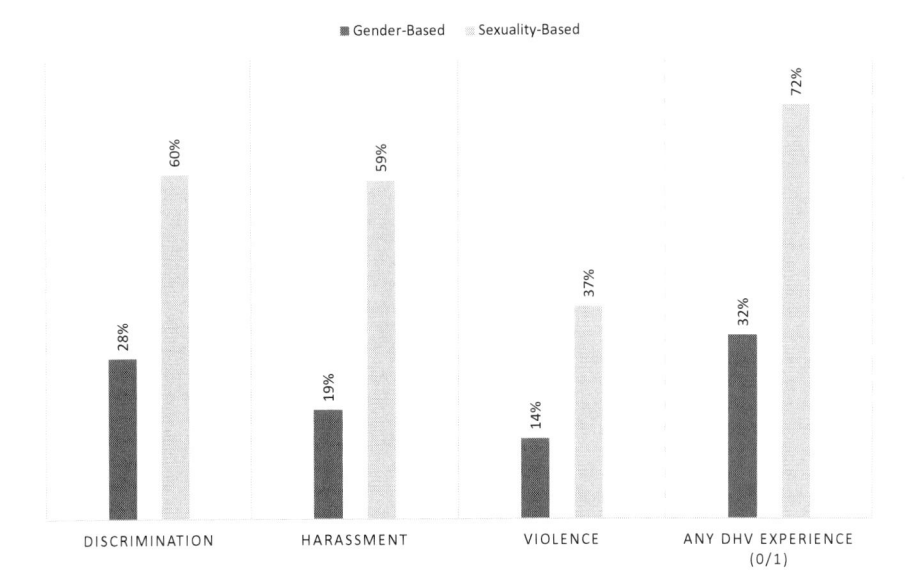

**FIGURE 16.3** Queer LGBTQ Men's (n = 138) Experiences with Gender- and Sexuality-Based DHV

*Note:* see Table 16.4 for comparisons of queer LGBTQ men's experiences to the LGBTQ subsample and the men subsample.

**TABLE 16.4** Gender- and Sexuality-Based DHV Mean Values (Standard Deviations) among Queer LGBTQ Men, the LGBTQ Subsample, and the Men Subsample with *t*-test Results

|  | Queer LGBTQ Men | LGBTQ Subsample | Men Subsample |
|---|---|---|---|
| n | 138 | 1604 | 1474 |
| *Gender-based* | | | |
| Discrimination | .28 (.45) * | .32 (.47) | .17 (.38) |
| Harassment | .19 (.39) *** | .28 (.45) | .09 (.29) |
| Violence | .14 (.35) * | .14 (.34) | .07 (.26) |
| Any gender DHV experience (0/1) | .32 (.47) * | .40 (.49) | .21 (.41) |
| *Sexuality-based* | | | |
| Discrimination | .60 (.49) *** | .44 (.50) | .23 (.42) |
| Harassment | .59 (.49) *** | .41 (.49) | .24 (.43) |
| Violence | .37 (.48) *** | .20 (.40) | .13 (.34) |
| Any sexuality DHV experience (0/1) | .72 (.45) *** | .53 (.50) | .33 (.47) |

\* Queer men are significantly different from the men subsample (only) at p < .05 level.

\*\*\* Queer men are significantly different from both the LGBTQ and men subsamples at p < .05 level.

percentage of any sexuality-based DHV experience (recall Figure 7.7) (though it is important to note that queer women report the same percentage of any sexuality-based DHV as queer men do). Thus, queer men are at particular risk for both gender- and sexuality-based DHV.

## NCST and Queer Men's Experiences with Gender- and Sexuality-Based DHV

The second set of regression models examines queer men and their experiences with gender- and sexuality-based DHV using NCST with a focus on queer men's axes of social power. The hypotheses are as follows:

- *Hypothesis 1*: being a queer man (violating hetero-cis-normativity) increases the likelihood of experiencing gender- and sexuality-based DHV (queer men stigma).
- *Hypothesis 2*: the relationship between being a queer man and gender- and sexuality-based DHV is moderated by interactions among being a queer man and axes of social power.

Figure 16.4 outlines these relationships and Table 16.5 displays logistic regression results that examine NCST and the relationships among being a queer man, intersections among queer men's axes of social power, and any experiences of gender-based DHV (dichotomized as 0/1) or sexuality-based DHV (dichotomized as 0/1) utilizing the LGBTQ subsample (n = 1,604; whereby being a queer man is compared to all other LGBTQ people). Because queer men's experiences are the focus of this exploration (i.e., the stigmatized lens of NCST is being utilized), the queer man and social power axes interaction terms are listed at the top of the table and are the focus of the discussion below. However, there are significant corresponding individual effects related to being queer and being a man (for example) that are important to recognize. See Chapter 7 for a more complete description of the models and a discussion of overarching trends and patterns. Regarding model fit statistics, the pseudo $R^2$ values were low and ranged from .09 to .16

## NCST, Queer Men, and Gender- and Sexuality-Based DHV: Model 1

Both Model 1s estimate the relationships between violations of hetero-cis-normativity conceptualized as being a queer man and the stigmatization of queer men conceptualized as gender- and sexuality-based DHV along with sociodemographic controls in Table 16.5. Contrasting strongly with past research that has identified relationships between queer identity among men and DHV (Jones 2015;

```
                    ┌─────────────────────┐
                    │ Axes of Social Power│
                    │    Interactions     │
                    ├─────────────────────┤
                    │     Queer Man*      │
                    │ Axes of Social Power│
                    └─────────────────────┘
                              │
                              │ 2
                              ▼
┌──────────────┐   ┌──────────────┐        ┌──────────────────┐
│    Norms     │   │     Norm     │        │ Norm Violation   │
│ Organized by │   │  Violations  │        │     Stigma       │
│ Social Power │   │              │        │                  │
├──────────────┤──▶├──────────────┤───1───▶├──────────────────┤
│ Hetero-cis-  │   │ Violations of│        │Queer Man Stigma: │
│ normativity  │   │ Hetero-cis-  │        │Gender- and Sexu- │
│ Scale        │   │ normativity: │        │ality-Based Dis-  │
│              │   │ Being a Queer│        │crimination, Har- │
│              │   │ Man          │        │assment, and      │
│              │   │              │        │Violence          │
└──────────────┘   └──────────────┘        └──────────────────┘
```

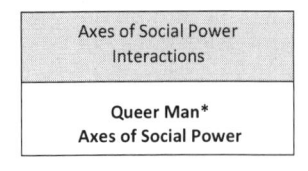

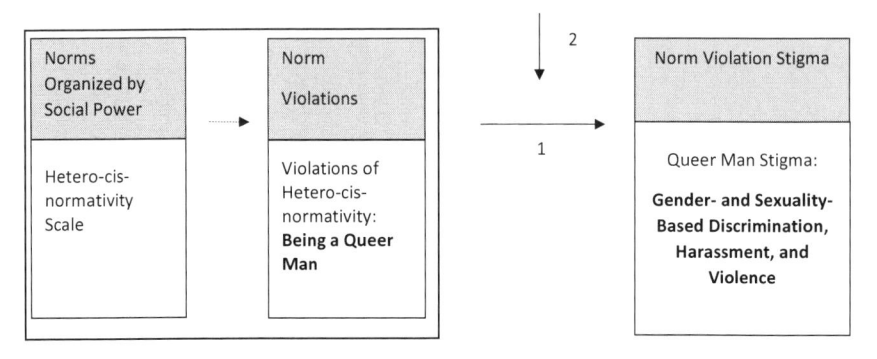

**FIGURE 16.4** Theoretical Model of NCST and Queer Men Stigma using the Stigmatized Lens with Model Numbers to be Examined in Table 16.5

*Notes:* Model 1 estimates being a queer man as related to gender- and sexuality-based DHV. Model 2 estimates interactions among queer men's axes of social power as they moderate the relationships between being a queer man and gender- and sexuality-based DHV. The * indicates an interaction.

Meyer 2015), being a queer man is not significantly related to gender- or sexuality-based DHV. Thus, *Hypothesis 1* is not supported.

## NCST, Queer Men, and Gender- and Sexuality-Based DHV: Model 2

In both Model 2s, intersections among axes of social power and being a queer man are included as they relate to gender- and sexuality-based DHV. As seen in Model 1, being a queer man remains non-statistically significantly related to gender- and sexuality-based DHV in Model 2. However, in the gender-based DHV models, there are three significant queer man social power interaction terms. First, being a gay queer man increases the likelihood of experiencing gender-based DHV by 3.27. Queer men who identify as gay may be at higher risk for gender-based DHV experiences because they may be more likely to express gender in nonconforming and/or fluid ways as compared to other queer men in the LGBTQ community who do not identify as gay (Jones 2015). Because "queer" identity can represent diverse gender expression which can encompass effeminacy among queer gay men (Brontsema 2004), this may relate to

**TABLE 16.5** Logistic Regression Results with Odds Ratios and (Standard Errors) Estimating NCST and Gender- and Sexuality-Based DHV as Related to Being a Queer Man for the LGBTQ Subsample (n = 1,604)

|  | Gender-Based DHV |  |  |  | Sexuality-Based DHV |  |  |  |
|---|---|---|---|---|---|---|---|---|
|  | Model 1 |  | Model 2 |  | Model 1 |  | Model 2 |  |
|  | OR | SE | OR | SE | OR | SE | OR | SE |
| Queer man | . | . | . | . | . | . | . | . |
| *Queer man social power axes interactions* |  |  |  |  |  |  |  |  |
| Queer man*gay | — | — | 4.27* | (2.09) | — | — | . | . |
| Queer man*SGL | — | — | .20* | (.12) | — | — | . | . |
| Queer man*White | — | — | 3.17* | (1.53) | — | — | . | . |
| Queer man* everything I need | — | — | . | . | — | — | . | . |
| Queer man* mostly all I need | — | — | . | . | — | — | . | . |
| *Queer man social power axes* |  |  |  |  |  |  |  |  |
| Queer | 2.55* | (.51) | 2.54* | (.50) | 1.88* | (.36) | 1.87* | (.36) |
| Man | .21* | (.03) | .21* | (.03) | . | . | . | . |
| Gay | . | . | .23* | (.11) | 3.42* | (.41) | . | . |
| SGL | . | . | 5.51* | (3.04) | . | . | . | . |
| White | . | . | .35* | (.16) | . | . | 2.49* | (1.10) |
| Everything I need | .67* | (.12) | . | . | .64* | (.10) | . | . |
| Mostly all I need | .75* | (.11) | . | . | . | . | . | . |
| *Socio-demographic Controls* |  |  |  |  |  |  |  |  |
| Age | .98* | (.00) | .98* | (.00) | .98* | (.00) | .98* | (.00) |
| Town type (rural–large city) | . | . | . | . | . | . | . | . |
| Education | 1.18* | (.05) | 1.18* | (.05) | . | . | . | . |
| Income | . | . | . | . | . | . | . | . |
| Pseudo R² | .15 |  | .16 |  | .09 |  | .09 |  |
| Mean VIF | 1.40 |  | 1.40 |  | 1.38 |  | 1.38 |  |

*Notes:* all rows are displayed, including those without significant results. See Table 16.3 for more details about queer LGBTQ men.

* $p < .05$; a dot (.) indicates non-statistically significant results. A dash (—) indicates this was not included in the model.

their higher likelihood of experiencing gender-based DHV. Second, and in contrast, being a SGL queer man decreases the likelihood of experiencing gender-based DHV by .80. Perhaps because SGL identity can be distinct from "gay" or other marginalized identities (Truong et al. 2016), SGL identity can have a protective effect on queer men's experiences of gender-based DHV.

Third, compared to queer men of all other racial identities, being a White queer man actually *increases* the likelihood of experiencing gender-based DHV by 2.17. This is surprising because existing research indicates that LGBTQ people of color are at higher risk for stigma and violence as compared to White LGBTQ people (Battle, Pastrana, and Harris 2017; Han, Proctor, and Choi 2014; Lemelle and Battle 2004; Ramirez, Gonzalez, and Galupo 2018). There may be something unique about White queer men's experiences that differentially impacts their gender-based DHV. White queer men may be more open and visible in their expressions of gender in ways that differ from queer men of color and this may contribute to their gender-based victimization experiences.

In contrast to the gender-based DHV models, there are no significant results related to being a queer man for the sexuality-based DHV models. Thus, social power experiences have different impacts on queer men's gender- and sexuality-based DHV. Overall, *Hypothesis 2* is supported in the gender-based DHV models but not in the sexuality-based DHV models.

## *Summarizing NCST, Queer Men, and Gender- and Sexuality-Based DHV*

In sum, while queer men's intersecting experiences with other axes of social power (gay, SGL, and White identities) relate to gender-based DHV among queer men, being a queer man does not directly relate to the likelihood of sexuality-based DHV as compared to other LGBTQ people. This is surprising because 72% of queer men report having an experience of sexuality-based DHV (see Figure 16.3). It may be that other axes of social power not measured here (e.g., presentation of masculinity) would help us to better understand queer men's DHV experiences. Overall, there are very few significant findings in this table and the pseudo $R^2$ values are quite low. Even so, by focusing on queer men's identities and social power axes, it is clear that queer identity among men has differential effects on men's experiences with both gender- and sexuality-based DHV.

## Summary of Patterns of Queer Men Stigma

In line with the three tenets and hypotheses derived from NCST, there are six patterns related to the stigmatization of queer men reviewed in this chapter:

1. Sex-act related stigma is a driving force in the stigmatization of queer men for both hetero-cis and LGBTQ people, especially the damaging perspectives that queer men are too sexual; however, discomfort with queer men's sex acts with men are also quite concerning for hetero-cis people.
2. For both hetero-cis and LGBTQ people, there is strong support for the stigmatizing belief that queer men are not masculine enough.
3. Hetero-cis-normativity is positively related to queer men stigma for both subsamples; however, the interaction effects between the HCN Scale and social power axes that moderate these relationships differ for the hetero-cis and LGBTQ subsamples.
4. Individual social power axes are significantly related to queer men stigma for both subsamples; however, the interaction effects between the social power axes that moderate these relationships differ for the hetero-cis and LGBTQ subsamples. In addition, there are more significant interaction effects between the social power axes for the LGBTQ subsample than there are for the hetero-cis subsample.
5. Queer men experience extremely high levels of gender- and sexuality-based DHV in comparison nearly all other groups.
6. Queer men's intersecting experiences with social power (gay, SGL, and White identities) are significantly related to the likelihood of gender-based DHV; however, being a queer man is not significantly related to the likelihood of sexuality-based DHV.

## Note

1 On June 12, 2016, Omar Mateen entered Pulse, an LGBTQ nightclub in Orlando, Florida at 2 a.m. and opened fire with a semi-automatic Sig Sauer MCX rifle and handgun in a rage-filled rampage, holding 15 to 20 people hostage in an attack that lasted nearly three hours and left 49 people dead and 53 injured. At the time, the massacre was described as the "Deadliest Mass Shooting In U.S. History" (Murdock, Campbell, and Frej 2016). (In 2017, Stephen Paddock killed 59 people and injured more than 500 others when he opened fire into a crowd of more than 20,000 people attending a country music festival in Las Vegas, Nevada (Blankstein et al. 2017)).

## References

Alimahomed, Sabrina. 2010. "Thinking Outside the Rainbow: Women of Color Redefining Queer Politics and Identity." *Social Identities* 16(2):151–168.

Bailey, Michael, Peggy Kim, Alex Hills, and Joan Linsenmeier. 1997. "Butch, Femme, or Straight Acting? Partner Preferences of Gay Men and Lesbians." *Journal of Personality & Social Psychology* 73(5):960–973.

Battle, Juan, Antonio Pastrana, and Angelique Harris. 2017. *An Examination of Asian and Pacific Islander LGBT Populations across the United States*. New York, NY: Palgrave Macmillan.

Blankstein, Andrew, Pete Williams, Rachel Elbaum, and Elizabeth Chuck. 2017. "59 People Killed, More than 500 Hurt in Las Vegas Strip Shooting." *NBC News*. Retrieved August 4, 2019 (www.nbcnews.com/storyline/las-vegas-shooting/las-vegas-police-investigating-shooting-mandalay-bay-n806461).

Blair, Karen L. and Rhea Ashley Hoskin. 2015. "Experiences of Femme Identity: Coming Out, Invisibility and Femmephobia." *Psychology & Sexuality* 6(3):229–244.

Braithwaite, Lester. 2018. "Queer and Roving on the Campaign Trail: The Only Openly Gay Member of the Massachusetts Senate." *NewNowNext*. Retrieved July 3, 2019 (www.newnownext.com/queer-and-roving-on-the-campaign-trail-part-1/10/2018/?fbclid=IwAR32eUVeMpvoI-zg3IYdnCcRSrWgXrFsyc_wLQ3V6R8pGzVzWWy4qGkVIg).

Brontsema, Robin. 2004. "A Queer Revolution: Reconceptualizing the Debate over Linguistic Reclamation." *Colorado Research in Linguistics* 17(1):1–17.

Choi, Kyung-Hee, Chong-suk Han, Jay Paul, and George Ayala. 2011. "Strategies for Managing Racism and Homophobia among U.S. Ethnic and Racial Minority Men Who Have Sex with Men." *AIDS Education and Prevention* 23(2):145–158.

Clogg, Clifford C., Eva Petkova, and Adamantios Haritou. 1995. "Statistical Methods for Comparing Regression Coefficients between Models." *American Journal of Sociology* 100(5):1261–1293.

Collins, Patricia Hill. 1986. "Learning from the Outsider Within: The Sociological Significance of Black Feminist Thought." *Social Problems* 33(6):S14–32.

Connell, R. W. 2005. *Masculinities*. Oxford, UK: Polity Press.

Dominguez, Ivo. 1994. *Beneath the Skins: The New Spirit and Politics of the Kink Community* (Second Edition). Los Angeles, CA: Daedalus Publishing.

Dowsett, Gilbert. 2009. "The 'Gay Plague' Revisited: AIDS and Its Enduring Moral Panic." Pp. 130–156 in *Moral Panics, Sex Panics: Fear and the Fight over Sexual Rights*, edited by Gilbert Herdt. New York, NY: NYU Press.

Duran, Antonio and Pérez. David. 2017. "Queering La Familia: A Phenomenological Study Reconceptualizing Familial Capital for Queer Latino Men." *Journal of College Student Development* 58(8):1149–1165.

Eng, David and Alice Hom. 1998. *Q & A Queer and Asian: Queer & Asian in America*. Philadelphia, PA: Temple University Press.

Galupo, M. Paz, Edward Lomash, and Renae C. Mitchell. 2017. "'All of My Lovers Fit into This Scale': Sexual Minority Individuals' Responses to Two Novel Measures of Sexual Orientation." *Journal of Homosexuality* 64(2):145–165.

Galupo, M. Paz, Renae C. Mitchell and Kyle S. Davis. 2015. "Sexual Minority Self-Identification: Multiple Identities and Complexity." *Psychology of Sexual Orientation and Gender Diversity* 2(4):355–364.

Gamson, Joshua. 1995. "Must Identity Movements Self-Destruct? A Queer Dilemma." *Social Problems* 42(3):390–407.

Gilley, Brian Joseph. 2006. *Becoming Two-Spirit: Gay Identity and Social Acceptance in Indian Country*. Lincoln, NE: University of Nebraska Press.

Gilley, Brian Joseph. 2010. "Native Sexual Inequalities: American Indian Cultural Conservative Homophobia and the Problem of Tradition." *Sexualities* 13(1):47–68.

Halberstam, Judith 1998. "Transgender Butch: Butch/FTM Border Wars and the Masculine Continuum." *GLQ: A Journal of Lesbian and Gay Studies* 4(2):287–310.

Hammack, Phillip L., David M. Frost, and Sam D. Hughes. 2019. "Queer Intimacies: A New Paradigm for the Study of Relationship Diversity." *Journal of Sex Research* 56(4/5):556–592.

Han, Chong-Suk, Kristopher Proctor, and Kyung-Hee Choi. 2014. "We Pretend like Sexuality Doesn't Exist: Managing Homophobia in Gaysian America." *The Journal of Men's Studies* 22(1):53–63.

Heasley, Robert. 2005. "Queer Masculinities of Straight Men: A Typology." *Men and Masculinities* 7(3):310–320.

Heath, Jessie and Kathy Goggin. 2009. "Attitudes Towards Male Homosexuality, Bisexuality, and the Down Low Lifestyle: Demographic Differences and HIV Implications." *Journal of Bisexuality* 9(1):17–31.

Heflick, Nathan. 2010. "EWWW....Anal Sex Is Icky!" *Psychology Today*. Retrieved April 1, 2019 (www.psychologytoday.com/us/blog/the-big-questions/201002/ewwwanal-sex-is-icky).

Hennen, Peter. 2005. "Bear Bodies, Bear Masculinity: Recuperation, Resistance, or Retreat?" *Gender & Society* 19(1):25–43.

Hennen, Peter. 2008. *Faeries, Bears, and Leathermen: Men in Community Queering the Masculine*. Chicago, IL: University of Chicago Press.

Herek, Gregory M. and John Capitanio. 1999. "AIDS Stigma and Sexual Prejudice." *American Behavioral Scientist* 42(7):1130–1147.

Humphreys, Laud. 1970. *Tearoom Trade: Impersonal Sex in Public Places*. Piscataway, NJ: Transaction Publishers.

Iasenza, Suzanne. 2010. "What Is Queer about Sex?: Expanding Sexual Frames in Theory and Practice." *Family Process* 49(3):291–308.

Johns, Michelle Marie, Emily Pingel, Anna Eisenberg, Matthew Leslie Santana, and José Bauermeister. 2012. "Butch Tops and Femme Bottoms? Sexual Positioning, Sexual Decision Making, and Gender Roles among Young Gay Men." *American Journal of Men's Health* 6(6):505–518.

Jones, Richard G. 2015. "Queering the Body Politic: Intersectional Reflexivity in the Body Narratives of Queer Men." *Qualitative Inquiry* 21(9):766–775.

Kumashiro, Kevin K. 1999. "Supplementing Normalcy and Otherness: Queer Asian American Men Reflect on Stereotypes, Identity, and Oppression." *International Journal of Qualitative Studies in Education* 12(5):491–508.

Lemelle, Anthony and Juan Battle. 2004. "Black Masculinity Matters in Attitudes toward Gay Males." *Journal of Homosexuality* 47(1):39–51.

Levitt, Heidi M. and Sharon G. Horne. 2002. "Explorations of Lesbian-Queer Genders: Butch, Femme, Androgynous or 'Other'." *Journal of Lesbian Studies* 6(2):25–39.

Logie, Carmen H. and Marie-Jolie Rwigema. 2014. "'The Normative Idea of Queer Is a White Person': Understanding Perceptions of White Privilege among Lesbian, Bisexual, and Queer Women of Color in Toronto, Canada." *Journal of Lesbian Studies* 18(2):174–191.

Masters, Jeffrey. 2019. "We Sat Down With Pete Buttigieg To Talk About Gay Stuff." *The Advocate*. Retrieved July 3, 2019 (www.advocate.com/politics/2019/4/22/we-sat-down-pete-buttigieg-talk-about-gay-stuff).

Meyer, Doug. 2015. *Violence against Queer People: Race, Class, Gender, and the Persistence of Anti-LGBT Discrimination*. New Brunswick, NJ: Rutgers University Press.

Morandini, James S., Alexander Blaszczynski, and Ilan Dar-Nimrod. 2017. "Who Adopts Queer and Pansexual Sexual Identities?" *The Journal of Sex Research* 54(7):911–922.

Murdock, Sebastian, Roque Planas Campbell, and Willa Frej. 2016. "New Details Emerge about Deadliest Mass Shooting in U.S. History." *HuffPost*. Retrieved August 4, 2019 (www.huffpost.com/entry/terror-shooting-at-gay-club_n_575d5938e4b0e39a28add1b4).

Ramirez, Johanna L., Kirsten A. Gonzalez, and M. Paz Galupo. 2018. "'Invisible during My Own Crisis': Responses of LGBT People of Color to the Orlando Shooting." *Journal of Homosexuality* 65(5):579–599.

Renfro, Kim. 2019. "33 Celebrities Who Don't Identify as either Straight or Gay." *INSIDER*. Retrieved July 1, 2019 (www.thisisinsider.com/celebrities-who-are-bisexual-2017-9).

Rosenberg, Shoshana. 2018. "Coming In: Queer Narratives of Sexual Self-Discovery." *Journal of Homosexuality* 65(13):1788–1816.

Scheim, Ayden I., Barry D. Adam, and Zack Marshall. 2019. "Gay, Bisexual, and Queer Trans Men Navigating Sexual Fields." *Sexualities* 22(4):566–586.

Signorile, Michelangelo. 2016. "The Orlando Massacre: A Reminder of the Dangers LGBT People Live with Every Day." *HuffPost*. Retrieved August 4, 2019 (www.huffpost.com/entry/orlando-pulse-shooting-lgbt-dangers_n_575d6615e4b0e39a28add385).

Sprott, Richard A. and Bren Benoit Hadcock. 2018. "Bisexuality, Pansexuality, Queer Identity, and Kink Identity." *Sexual and Relationship Therapy* 33(1/2):214–232.

Truong, Nhan, Amaya Perez-Brumer, Melissa Burton, June Gipson, and DeMarc Hickson. 2016. "What's in a Label?: Multiple Meanings of 'MSM' among Same-Gender-Loving Black Men in Mississippi." *Global Public Health* 11(7/8):937–952.

Walters, Karina L., Jane M. Teresa Evans-Campbell, Theresa Ronquillo Simoni, and Rupaleem Bhuyan. 2006. "'My Spirit in My Heart': Identity Experiences and Challenges among American Indian Two-Spirit Women." *Journal of Lesbian Studies* 10(1/2):125–149.

Worthen, Meredith G. F. 2018. "'Gay Equals White'? Racial, Ethnic, and Sexual Identities and Attitudes toward LGBT Individuals among College Students at a Bible Belt University." *The Journal of Sex Research* 55(8):995–1011.

# 17
# LGBTQ STIGMA, NCST, AND FUTURE RESEARCH

In this book, I argued for separate but interconnected discussions about the experiences of lesbian women, gay men, bisexual women, bisexual men, trans women, trans men, non-binary/genderqueer people, queer women, and queer men (Worthen 2013). In addition, I demonstrated that a norm-centered intersectional and social-power-focused examination of hetero-cis-normativity is integral to best understand the spectrum of stigmatizing attitudes toward LGBTQ people and LGBTQ people's experiences with stigma (discrimination, harassment, and violence (DHV)). Specifically, NCST's three tenets were upheld throughout this investigation:

- *Tenet #1*: There is a culturally dependent and reciprocal relationship between hetero-cis-normativity and LGBTQ stigma.
- *Tenet #2*: The relationship between hetero-cis-normativity and LGBTQ stigma is organized by social power dynamics between LGBTQ people and those that stigmatize LGBTQ people.
- *Tenet #3*: LGBTQ stigma is inclusive of negativity and social sanctions directed toward violations and violators of hetero-cis-normativity justified through social power dynamics and situated on a spectrum.

Together, these findings demonstrate both the utility of NCST in understanding stigma more generally as well as the centrality of hetero-cis-normativity in explaining LGBTQ negativity and stigmatizing experiences more specifically. In addition, the importance of axes of social power in these relationships was clearly demonstrated across the spectrum of LGBTQ stigma that was developed throughout this text. In particular, as seen in Figure 17.1, when considering both gender and sexual identity, we can see that non-binary/genderqueer people are the most stigmatized group and

## 398 NCST and Understanding LGBTQ Stigma

| Non-binary/ Genderqueer People | Trans Men | Queer Men | Trans Women | Queer Women | Bisexual Men | Gay Men | Bisexual Women | Lesbian Women |

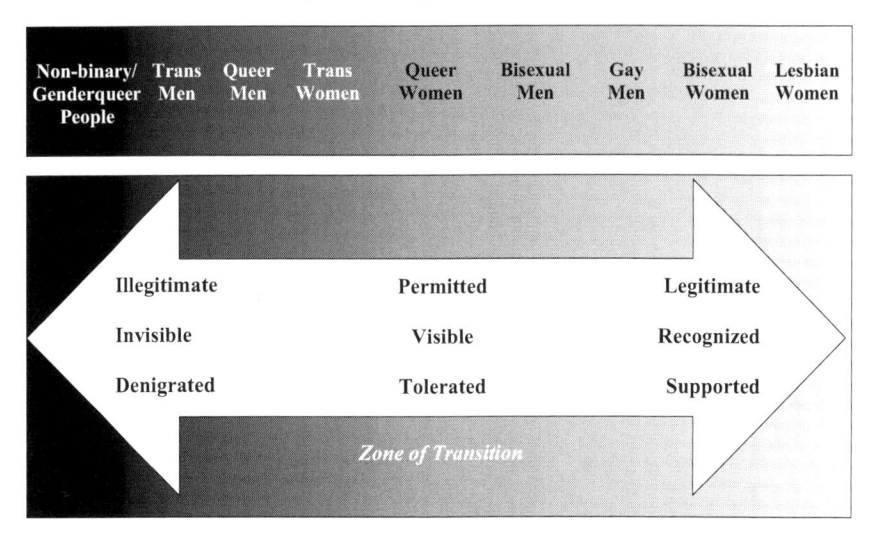

Illegitimate — Permitted — Legitimate

Invisible — Visible — Recognized

Denigrated — Tolerated — Supported

*Zone of Transition*

**FIGURE 17.1** Spectrum of Stigma with LGBTQ Stigma Scales Findings

lesbian women are the least stigmatized group according to the LGBTQ stigma scales. These dynamics also inform LGBTQ people's experiences with discrimination, harassment, and violence in complex ways that support the intersectional framework of NCST.

## Policy Implications

The results presented throughout this text demonstrate variation in the stigmatizing experiences of LGBTQ people but also provide evidence of parallels across the LGBTQ groups. Thus, these findings suggest that policy makers should be careful to consider both similarities and differences in the experiences LGBTQ people's lives as they pertain to equal access and protections from discrimination. In addition, by illuminating the experiences of groups that are often swept into the "monolithic" "LGBTQ community" such as bisexual individuals, non-binary/genderqueer individuals, and queer men and women, it is clear that policies should be more inclusive. Indeed, while advancements such as marriage equality indicate positive shifts toward inclusivity of same-gender couples, numerous obstacles remain including but not limited to adoption and state family leave protections as well as employment and housing non-discrimination laws for all LGBTQ people based on *both* sexual and gender identity (Becker 2014; Goldberg et al. 2014; Movement Advancement Project 2019). Furthermore, trans and non-binary people face unique challenges related to their identity documents and bathroom usage as well as banishment from U.S. military service (to name a few) (James et al. 2016; Liptack 2019; Movement Advancement Project 2019). Together, the findings in this book lead to many possible policy implications including the following:

- Because being a lesbian woman was found to be related to an increased likelihood of experiencing gender-based DHV, gender non-discrimination and victim protection policies should be explicitly inclusive of lesbian women. In addition, workplace and law enforcement personnel should be made aware of the ways lesbian women can be targeted for gender-based DHV.
- With negativity toward gay men highly centered around sex act-related stigma and queer men experiencing the highest levels of HIV/AIDS stigma, policies focusing on HIV/AIDS intervention and education should be encompassing of ways to address the stigmatizing experiences that gay and queer men endure as related to their sexualities and their sexual behaviors. In addition, healthcare workers should be particularly cognizant of how these dynamics impact gay and queer men's lives.
- Because bisexual women are especially likely to be navigating the false belief that their "identity is just experimental," efforts should be made to unambiguously include and validate bisexual women's experiences when it comes to policies focusing on equal access and protections from discrimination.
- With bisexual men enduring an increased likelihood of sexuality-based DHV, policies focusing on sexuality non-discrimination and victim protections should be designed to be clearly inclusive of bisexual men. In addition, workplace and law enforcement personnel should be made aware of the ways bisexual men can be targeted for sexuality-based DHV.
- Because trans women are highly stigmatized, especially in comparison to other LGBQ women, their marginalized intersecting experiences as both trans and as women should be considered when designing policies for protections from discrimination and equal access. Efforts should also be made to educate law enforcement and workplace personnel about their unique experiences with DHV.
- With trans men being highly stigmatized as political candidates and military members, more support for trans men currently in or running for these positions is needed. In addition, efforts to design policy to be more supportive and inclusive of trans men in these positions and to educate about the barriers that trans men face in these positions are essential.
- Because non-binary/genderqueer people experience high levels of stigma (including the denial of basic human rights) and 1 in 4 report at least one experience with gender-based violence, human rights, victim protections, and non-discrimination policies should clearly identify non-binary/genderqueer people and identities in their verbiage. In addition, efforts should be made to be more inclusive of non-binary/genderqueer people and educate others about their experiences across all social institutions.

- With three out of four queer women and queer men reporting at least one experience with gender- and/or sexuality-based DHV, policy makers should explicitly include queer people in all equal access and protections language. In addition, ways queer men and women can be targeted for sexuality-based DHV should be made clear to all workplace and law enforcement personnel.

## Additional Considerations and Future Research

There are numerous additional avenues of research that would both complement and extend the findings in this book. These include (1) more diversity, identities, and groups, (2) more norms, and (3) more types of research. These are discussed below.

### *More Diversity, Identities, and Groups*

Beyond the nine LGBTQ groups examined in this study, there are many additional identities that deserve attention. For example, it is important to examine the stigmatization of pansexual, asexual, and intersex people. Investigations of other identities including agender, androgynous, bigender, pangender, and/or genderfluid are also essential. Queer as singular identity (as opposed to queer *and* bisexual, for example) as well as trans and non-binary as a dual identity would also be especially helpful to explore. Additional intersectional experiences, such as those among queer-identified heterosexual men (Heasley 2005) as well as intersecting experiences with age (both the young and the elderly especially), ability, cultural origin, and religious identity are integral to the conversation about LGBTQ stigma (D'Augelli and Hershberger 1993; Worthen 2018; Worthen, Lingiardi, and Caristo 2017). There are also many subcultures and groups within and connected to the LGBTQ community such as diesel dykes, lipstick lesbians, ball/ballroom culture, drag kings and queens, cross dressing/cross dressers, kink, polyamory, the deaf queer community, and the sisters of perpetual indulgence, to name a few. Investigations of the experiences of these groups are essential to better recognize the interconnectedness of identity and stigma.

### *More Norms*

Norms (specifically hetero-cis-normativity) are integral to understanding LGBTQ stigma. However, in addition to hetero-cis normativity, further exploration of other norms and normative perspectives would be ideal. For example, norms associated with marriage and family and political perspectives could help elucidate why LGBTQ people are stigmatized. In addition, norms related to community and culture, urbanicity, age, race, and ethnicity could help further expand our knowledge about LGBTQ people's experiences. Overall, by centering the importance of norms, we can work toward a better awareness of the experiences of those who violate norms and who experience enduring negativity associated with their "deviant," non-normative socio-cultural status.

## More Research

More research focusing on the experiences of LGBTQ people is needed. In particular, qualitative research can help bring LGBTQ voices to the forefront of the conversation. For example, while many have concentrated on the negative life experiences of LGBTQ people, the resilience and natural strengths of LGBTQ people to move beyond their oppression and marginalization are an ideal area of continued research. Qualitative work that highlights lived experiences can work toward a deeper understanding of the ways LGBTQ people navigate stigma alongside their ability to flourish (Higgins, Sharek, and Glacken 2016; Meyer 2010). In addition, more quantitative research utilizing NCST to understand LGBTQ stigma would also be beneficial. Together, both qualitative and quantitative studies that focus on LGBTQ people's intersectional lives can help us build an incredible wealth of knowledge about the experiences of LGBTQ people and work toward ameliorating LGBTQ negativity.

## Revisiting Goals and Concluding Remarks

Overall, the goals of this text (as outlined in Chapter 1) were as follows:

1. To introduce a theory about stigma that is testable and grounded in previous research (NCST).
2. To highlight the significance of hetero-cis-normativity and intersectionality in understanding LGBTQ stigmatization (stigmatizer lens) and the stigmatizing experiences of LGBTQ people (stigmatized lens).
3. To continue to stress the importance of separate but interconnected discussions about lesbian women, gay men, bisexual women, bisexual men, trans women, trans men, non-binary/genderqueer people, queer women, and queer men to uncover both similarities and differences across their experiences.

Throughout this text, I have offered a novel approach to understanding LGBTQ stigma. I have broken LGBTQ stigma down into separate but related experiences and I have woven these pieces back together. I have demonstrated overlap while still pointing to the importance of separate considerations. In all, hetero-cis-normativity remains at the core of LGBTQ stigma and NCST helps us to empirically examine these relationships with a critical focus on intersectionality. With these tools, as both scholars and as people, we can focus on "queers and bis" and begin to dismantle "straight lies."

## References

Becker, Amy. 2014. "Employment Discrimination, Local School Boards, and LGBT Civil Rights: Reviewing 25 Years of Public Opinion Data." *International Journal of Public Opinion Research* 26(3):342–354.

D'Augelli, Anthony R. and Scott L. Hershberger. 1993. "Lesbian, Gay, and Bisexual Youth in Community Settings: Personal Challenges and Mental Health Problems." *American Journal of Community Psychology* 21(4):421–448.

Goldberg, Abbie E., Lori A. Kinkler, April M. Moyer, and Elizabeth Weber. 2014. "Intimate Relationship Challenges in Early Parenthood among Lesbian, Gay, and Heterosexual Couples Adopting via the Child Welfare System." *Professional Psychology: Research and Practice* 45(4):221–230.

Heasley, Robert. 2005. "Queer Masculinities of Straight Men: A Typology." *Men and Masculinities* 7(3):310–320.

Higgins, Agnes, Danika Sharek, and Michele Glacken. 2016. "Building Resilience in the Face of Adversity: Navigation Processes Used by Older Lesbian, Gay, Bisexual and Transgender Adults Living in Ireland." *Journal of Clinical Nursing* 25:3652–3664.

James, Sandy, Jody L. Herman, Sue Rankin, Mara Keisling, Lisa Mottet, and Anafi Ma'ayan. 2016. *The Report of the 2015 U.S. Transgender Survey*. Washington, DC: National Center for Transgender Equality.

Liptack, Adam. 2019. "Supreme Court Revives Transgender Ban for Military Service." *New York Times*. January 22. Retrieved January 31, 2020 (https://www.nytimes.com/2019/01/22/us/politics/transgender-ban-military-supreme-court.html).

Meyer, Ilan H. 2010. "Identity, Stress, and Resilience in Lesbians, Gay Men, and Bisexuals of Color." *The Counseling Psychologist* 38(3):442–454.

Movement Advancement Project. 2019. "Equality Maps." Retrieved August 29, 2019 (www.lgbtmap.org/home).

Worthen, Meredith G. F. 2013. "An Argument for Separate Analyses of Attitudes toward Lesbian, Gay, Bisexual Men, Bisexual Women, MtF and FtM Transgender Individuals." *Sex Roles* 68(11/12):703–723.

Worthen, Meredith G. F. 2018. "'Gay Equals White'? Racial, Ethnic, and Sexual Identities and Attitudes toward LGBT Individuals among College Students at a Bible Belt University." *The Journal of Sex Research* 55(8):995–1011.

Worthen, Meredith G. F., Vittorio Lingiardi, and Chiara Caristo. 2017. "The Roles of Politics, Feminism, and Religion in Attitudes toward LGBT Individuals: A Cross-Cultural Study of College Students in the USA, Italy, and Spain." *Sexuality Research and Social Policy* 14(3):241–258.

# APPENDIX A
Data and Methods

**Survey Sample Data and Comparisons to the U.S. Census**

A nationally representative sample of U.S. adults aged 18–64 stratified by U.S. census categories of age, gender, race, ethnicity, and census region was obtained for this study in November 2018. As seen in Appendix A Table 1, characteristics for the total sample as well as the hetero-cis and LGBTQ subsamples are similar to 2017 U.S. population census characteristics (U.S. Census Bureau 2017; see also Flores et al. 2016). However, there are some differences. For example, the study population has more Caucasian/White respondents but fewer African American/Black respondents as compared to the U.S. Census data. For age, the study population includes more of those aged 25–34 years but fewer of those aged 45–54 years. For education, the study population includes fewer of those with less than high school or high school/GED education levels but more of those with Bachelor's degrees and higher. For income, the study population includes more of those with incomes ranging from $25,000 to $99,999 but fewer of those with $100,000 and greater incomes. Among the subsample comparisons (final column of Table A.1), the hetero-cis subsample is largely similar to the LGBTQ subsample with most differences at 2 percentage points or less. However, the LGBTQ subsample includes fewer Asian American/Pacific Islander individuals and fewer of those aged 25–34 but more of those aged 45–54. In addition, the LGBTQ subsample includes fewer of those indicating only a high school/GED education level but more of those indicating a college degree greater than a Bachelor's.

TABLE A.1 U.S. Census Population Characteristics in Comparison to Total Sample (N = 3104), the Hetero-cis Subsample (n = 1500), and the LGBTQ Subsample (n = 1604) in Percentages

| | All U.S. Adults (Census) | Total Sample | ± vs. Census | Hetero-cis Subsample | ± vs. Census | LGBTQ Subsample | ± vs. Census | ± Hetero-cis vs. LGBTQ |
|---|---|---|---|---|---|---|---|---|
| **Gender** | | | | | | | | |
| Men | 49.2 (male) | 45.7 (cis man) | -3.5 | 50.0 (cis man) | +0.8 | 41.7 (cis man) | -7.5 | -8.3 |
| Women | 50.8 (female) | 47.1 (cis woman) | -3.7 | 50.0 (cis woman) | -0.8 | 44.3 (cis woman) | -6.5 | -5.7 |
| Transgender women | No data available* | 2.4 | — | — | — | 4.6 | — | — |
| Transgender men | No data available* | 1.8 | — | — | — | 3.4 | — | — |
| Non-binary/genderqueer | No data available | 3.0 | — | — | — | 5.9 | — | — |
| **Race/ethnicity** | | | | | | | | |
| Caucasian/White | 72.3 | 78.1 | +5.8 | 77.2 | +4.9 | 79.0 | +6.7 | +1.8 |
| African American/Black | 12.7 | 9.6 | -3.1 | 10.2 | -2.5 | 9.1 | -3.6 | -1.1 |
| Asian American/Pacific Islander | 5.8 | 6.2 | +0.4 | 7.7 | +1.9 | 4.7 | -1.1 | -3.0 |
| Native American/Alaskan Native | 0.8 | 1.7 | +0.9 | 2.0 | +1.2 | 1.5 | +0.7 | -0.5 |
| Multi-racial | 3.3 | 2.6 | -0.7 | 1.9 | -1.4 | 3.3 | 0 | +1.4 |

| | | | | | | | | |
|---|---|---|---|---|---|---|---|---|
| Other race** | 5.1 | 0.8 | -4.3 | 0.5 | -4.6 | 1.0 | -4.1 | +0.5 |
| Latinx race** | — | 0.8 | — | 0.9 | — | 0.7 | — | -0.2 |
| Latinx ethnicity | 18.1 (Hispanic) | 13.4 | -4.7 | 13.9 | -4.2 | 13.0 | -5.1 | -0.9 |
| *Age* | | | | | | | | |
| 18-24 | 15.3 | 14.3 | -1.0 | 13.9 | -1.4 | 14.7 | -0.6 | +.08 |
| 25-34 | 22.3 | 27.5 | +4.2 | 29.5 | +7.2 | 25.6 | +3.3 | -3.9 |
| 35-44 | 20.4 | 19.7 | -0.7 | 20.5 | -.01 | 18.9 | -1.5 | -1.6 |
| 45-54 | 21.0 | 15.2 | -5.8 | 13.4 | -7.6 | 16.8 | -4.2 | +3.4 |
| 55-64 | 20.9 | 23.4 | +2.5 | 22.6 | +1.7 | 24.1 | +3.2 | +1.5 |
| *Education* | | | | | | | | |
| < High school | 12.1 | 3.2 | -8.9 | 3.1 | -9.0 | 3.2 | -8.9 | +0.1 |
| High school or GED | 27.7 | 21.6 | -6.1 | 23.7 | -4.0 | 19.7 | -8.0 | -4.0 |
| Some college*** | — | 25.4 | — | 24.3 | — | 26.3 | — | +2.0 |
| College degree (Associate's)*** | — | 12.1 | — | 11.9 | — | 12.3 | — | +0.4 |
| Combined*** | 30.8 | 36.2 | +5.7 | 36.5 | +5.4 | 38.6 | +7.8 | +2.0 |
| College degree (Bachelor's) | 18.6 | 24.0 | +5.4 | 25.1 | +6.5 | 22.9 | +4.3 | -2.2 |
| College degree > than Bachelor's | 10.8 | 13.7 | +2.9 | 11.7 | +.09 | 15.6 | +4.8 | +3.9 |
| *Income* | | | | | | | | |
| Less than $5,000 | — | 6.1 | — | 5.9 | — | 6.3 | — | +0.4 |
| Less than $10,000 | 6.5 | — | — | — | — | — | — | — |
| $5,000-$24,999 | — | 18.5 | — | 18.5 | — | 18.5 | — | 0 |

(*Continued*)

TABLE A.1 (Cont.)

| | All U.S. Adults (Census) | Total Sample | ± vs. Census | Hetero-cis Subsample | ± vs. Census | LGBTQ Subsample | ± vs. Census | ± Hetero-cis vs. LGBTQ |
|---|---|---|---|---|---|---|---|---|
| $10,000–$24,999 | 13.8 | — | — | — | — | — | — | — |
| $25,000–$49,999 | 21.8 | 26.3 | +4.5 | 26.6 | +4.8 | 26.0 | -4.2 | -0.6 |
| $50,000–$99,999 | 30.1 | 31.6 | +1.5 | 32.2 | +2.1 | 31.1 | +1.0 | -1.1 |
| $100,000 and greater | 27.8 | 17.4 | -10.4 | 16.7 | -11.1 | 18.1 | -9.7 | +1.4 |

\* Utilizing the CDC Behavioral Risk Factor Surveillance System, Flores et al. (2016) determined that 0.6% of U.S. adults identify as transgender. Their report does not specify the gender breakdown of the transgender U.S. population (i.e., transgender men or transgender women).

\*\* To keep in line with the study's coding strategy, "other race" does not include those coded as Latinx Race (n = 25).

\*\*\* For those aged 18–24, the 2017 American Community Survey (ACS) includes a combined category of "Some college or Associate's." For those aged 25 and over, these categories are separate ("Some college" and "Associate's"). In order to understand the educational attainment of all those aged 18+ in the ACS, these categories were collapsed for the census column and combined for comparison purposes for the survey data columns. The ± column compares the combined groups to one another.

*Notes:* the characteristics for all U.S. adults come from the U.S. Census Bureau's 2017 American Community Survey (ACS) and include all those in the ACS aged 18+. For the age breakdown only, percentages were calculated for those aged 18–64. The characteristics for the total sample are limited to those aged 18–64 due to IRB restrictions on those aged 65+ who are identified as a vulnerable population.

## OLS Method of Analysis for the NCST, Social Power Axes, and LGBTQ Stigma Scales

OLS regression was chosen as the method of analysis for the models exploring NCST, social power axes, and the LGBTQ Stigma Scales. A three-step process was utilized to determine if OLS was the appropriate modeling technique. First, histograms of all the dependent variables (the LGBTQ Stigma Scales) were visually examined for skewness. Upon inspection, there was not strong evidence of skewness for any of the LGBTQ Stigma Scales. Second, the kurtosis values for the LGBTQ Stigma Scales were examined. All kurtosis values were less than 2.5 (see Table A.2). Thus, the kurtosis values met the established criteria of less than 7 for determining substantial non-normality (Kim 2013). Third, the skewness values for the LGBTQ Stigma Scales were examined. All skewness values were less than .50 (see Table A.2). Thus, the skewness values met the established criteria of less than 2 for determining substantial non-normality (Kim 2013).

TABLE A.2 Kurtosis and Skewness Values of the LGBTQ Stigma Scales

|  | Kurtosis | Skewness |
|---|---|---|
| Lesbian Woman Stigma Scale | 2.06 | .46 |
| Gay Man Stigma Scale | 2.22 | .44 |
| Bisexual Woman Stigma Scale | 1.90 | .30 |
| Bisexual Man Stigma Scale | 1.97 | .27 |
| Trans Woman Stigma Scale | 1.88 | .13 |
| Trans Man Stigma Scale | 1.98 | .13 |
| Non-binary/Genderqueer Scale | 1.93 | -.03 |
| Queer Woman Stigma Scale | 1.84 | .10 |
| Queer Man Stigma Scale | 2.00 | .14 |

## References

Flores, Andrew R., Jody L. Herman, Gary J. Gates, and Taylor N. Brown. 2016. "How Many Adults Identify as Transgender in the United States?" *The Williams Institute.*

Kim, Hae-Young. 2013. "Statistical Notes for Clinical Researchers: Assessing Normal Distribution (2) Using Skewness and Kurtosis." *Restorative Dentistry & Endodontics* 38 (1):52–54.

U.S. Census Bureau. 2017. American Community Survey 2017 Year Estimates. Retrieved June 1, 2019 (https://factfinder.census.gov/faces/tableservices/jsf/pages/productview.xhtml?src=bkmk#).

# APPENDIX B
## Supplemental Tables

**TABLE B.1** N values of Interaction Terms

|  | n |  | n |  | n |
|---|---|---|---|---|---|
| *Gender\*sexuality (25 interaction terms total, 9 interaction terms n > 25)* | | | | | |
| Cis man*heterosexual | 750 | Cis woman*heterosexual | 750 | Trans woman*heterosexual | 20[x] |
| Cis man*gay/lesbian | 330 | Cis woman*gay/lesbian | 331 | Trans woman*gay/lesbian | 15[x] |
| Cis man*bisexual | 314 | Cis woman*bisexual | 330 | Trans woman*bisexual | 28 |
| Cis man*pansexual | 11[x] | Cis woman*pansexual | 36 | Trans woman*pansexual | 9[x] |
| Cis man*asexual | 14[x] | Cis woman*asexual | 14[x] | Trans woman*asexual | 2[x] |
| Trans man*heterosexual | 17[x] | Non-binary*heterosexual | 12[x] | | |
| Trans man*gay/lesbian | 15[x] | Non-binary*gay/lesbian | 23[x] | | |
| Trans man*bisexual | 12[x] | Non-binary*bisexual | 33 | | |
| Trans man*pansexual | 8[x] | Non-binary*pansexual | 15[x] | | |
| Trans man*asexual | 3[x] | Non-binary*asexual | 12[x] | | |
| *Gender\*additional sexuality/gender (45 interaction terms total, 15 interaction terms n > 25)* | | | | | |
| Cis man*queer | 195 | Cis woman*queer | 140 | Trans woman*queer | 4[x] |
| Cis man*SGL | 148 | Cis woman*SGL | 160 | Trans woman*SGL | 14[x] |
| Cis man*Two-Spirit | 97 | Cis woman*Two-Spirit | 50 | Trans woman*Two-Spirit | 13[x] |

(*Continued*)

## TABLE B.1 (Cont.)

| | n | | n | | n |
|---|---|---|---|---|---|
| Cis man*butch | 64 | Cis woman*butch | 65 | Trans woman*butch | 14[x] |
| Cis man*femme | 54 | Cis woman*femme | 202 | Trans woman*femme | 19[x] |
| Cis man*leather | 61 | Cis woman*leather | 2[x] | Trans woman*leather | 1[x] |
| Cis man*bear | 129 | Cis woman*bear | 9[x] | Trans woman*bear | 2[x] |
| Cis man*twink | 74 | Cis woman*twink | 8[x] | Trans woman*twink | 6[x] |
| Cis man*Down Low | 103 | Cis woman*Down Low | 18[x] | Trans woman*Down Low | 3[x] |

| | | | | | |
|---|---|---|---|---|---|
| Trans man*queer | 14[x] | Non-binary*queer | 40 | | |
| Trans man*SGL | 5[x] | Non-binary*SGL | 15[x] | | |
| Trans man*Two-Spirit | 4[x] | Non-binary*Two-Spirit | 13[x] | | |
| Trans man*butch | 3[x] | Non-binary*butch | 8[x] | | |
| Trans man*femme | 9[x] | Non-binary*femme | 19[x] | | |
| Trans man*leather | 4[x] | Non-binary*leather | 6[x] | | |
| Trans man*bear | 7[x] | Non-binary*bear | 6[x] | | |
| Trans man*twink | 7[x] | Non-binary*twink | 3[x] | | |
| Trans Man*Down Low | 0[x] | Non-binary*Down Low | 5[x] | | |

*Gender\*race/ethnicity (40 interaction terms total, 13 interaction terms n > 25)*

| | n | | n | | n |
|---|---|---|---|---|---|
| Cis man*White | 1125 | Cis woman*White | 1160 | Trans woman*White | 42 |
| Cis man*Black | 125 | Cis woman*Black | 135 | Trans woman*Black | 16[x] |
| Cis man*Asian | 99 | Cis woman*Asian | 70 | Trans woman*Asian | 12[x] |
| Cis man*Native | 20[x] | Cis woman*Native | 24[x] | Trans woman*Native | 1[x] |
| Cis man*Multi-racial | 25 | Cis woman*Multi-racial | 49 | Trans woman*Multi-racial | 1[x] |
| Cis man*other race | 14[x] | Cis woman*other race | 8[x] | Trans woman*other race | 1[x] |
| Cis man*Latinx race | 10[x] | Cis woman*Latinx race | 13[x] | Trans woman*Latinx race | 1[x] |
| Cis Man*Latinx ethnicity | 188 | Cis woman*Latinx ethnicity | 180 | Trans woman*Latinx ethnicity | 19[x] |

| | | | | | |
|---|---|---|---|---|---|
| Trans man*White | 34 | Non-binary*White | 64 | | |
| Trans man*Black | 8[x] | Non-binary*Black | 15[x] | | |
| Trans man*Asian | 8[x] | Non-binary*Asian | 2[x] | | |
| Trans man*Native | 3[x] | Non-binary*Native | 6[x] | | |

*(Continued)*

**TABLE B.1** (Cont.)

| | n | | n | | n |
|---|---|---|---|---|---|
| Trans man*Multi-racial | 1[x] | Non-binary*Multi-racial | 6[x] | | |
| Trans man*other race | 1[x] | Non-binary*other race | 0[x] | | |
| Trans man*Latinx race | 0[x] | Non-binary*Latinx race | 1[x] | | |
| Trans man*Latinx ethnicity | 17[x] | Non-binary*Latinx ethnicity | 13[x] | | |
| *Gender\*basic needs (20 interaction terms total, 12 interaction terms n > 25)* ||||||
| Cis man*everything I need | 492 | Cis woman*everything I need | 364 | Trans woman*everything I need | 16[x] |
| Cis man*mostly all I need | 685 | Cis woman*mostly all I need | 778 | Trans woman*mostly all I need | 32 |
| Cis man*often needs not met | 180 | Cis woman*often needs not met | 259 | Trans woman*often needs not met | 12[x] |
| Cis man*few needs met | 62 | Cis woman*few needs met | 60 | Trans woman*few needs met | 8[x] |
| Trans man*everything I need | 7[x] | Non-binary*everything I need | 14[x] | | |
| Trans man*mostly all I need | 28 | Non-binary*mostly all I need | 41 | | |
| Trans man*often needs not met | 17[x] | Non-binary*often needs not met | 25 | | |
| Trans man*few needs met | 3[x] | Non-binary*few needs met | 15[x] | | |
| *Sexuality\*additional sexuality/gender (45 interaction terms total, 23 interaction terms n > 25)* ||||||
| Heterosexual*queer | 84 | Gay/lesbian*queer | 168 | Bisexual*queer | 103 |
| Heterosexual*SGL | 69 | Gay/lesbian*SGL | 178 | Bisexual*SGL | 82 |
| Heterosexual*Two-Spirit | 85 | Gay/lesbian*Two-Spirit | 20[x] | Bisexual*Two-Spirit | 65 |
| Heterosexual*butch | 38 | Gay/lesbian*butch | 82 | Bisexual*butch | 25 |
| Heterosexual*femme | 85 | Gay/lesbian*femme | 94 | Bisexual*femme | 101 |
| Heterosexual*leather | 43 | Gay/lesbian*leather | 17[x] | Bisexual*leather | 11[x] |
| Heterosexual*bear | 65 | Gay/lesbian*bear | 47 | Bisexual*bear | 36 |
| Heterosexual*twink | 47 | Gay/lesbian*twink | 25 | Bisexual*twink | 22[x] |
| Heterosexual*Down Low | 31 | Gay/Lesbian*Down Low | 22[x] | Bisexual*Down Low | 73 |
| Pansexual*queer | 28 | Asexual*queer | 10[x] | | |
| Pansexual*SGL | 9[x] | Asexual*SGL | 4[x] | | |
| Pansexual*Two-Spirit | 3[x] | Asexual*Two-Spirit | 4[x] | | |
| Pansexual*butch | 6[x] | Asexual*butch | 3[x] | | |
| Pansexual*femme | 20[x] | Asexual*femme | 3[x] | | |

(*Continued*)

## TABLE B.1 (Cont.)

| | $n$ | | $n$ | | $n$ |
|---|---|---|---|---|---|
| Pansexual*leather | $1^x$ | Asexual*leather | $2^x$ | | |
| Pansexual*bear | $3^x$ | Asexual*bear | $2^x$ | | |
| Pansexual*twink | $4^x$ | Asexual*twink | $0^x$ | | |
| Pansexual*Down Low | $2^x$ | Asexual*Down Low | $1^x$ | | |
| *Sexuality\*race/ethnicity (40 interaction terms total, 15 interaction terms n > 25)* | | | | | |
| Heterosexual*White | 1179 | Gay/lesbian*White | 576 | Bisexual*White | 580 |
| Heterosexual*Black | 170 | Gay/lesbian*Black | 67 | Bisexual*Black | 53 |
| Heterosexual*Asian | 125 | Gay/lesbian*Asian | 35 | Bisexual*Asian | $23^x$ |
| Heterosexual*Native | $22^x$ | Gay/lesbian*Native | $8^x$ | Bisexual*Native | $1^x$ |
| Heterosexual*Multi-racial | 30 | Gay/lesbian*Multi-racial | $14^x$ | Bisexual*Multi-racial | 30 |
| Heterosexual*other race | $9^x$ | Gay/lesbian*other race | $5^x$ | Bisexual*other race | $10^x$ |
| Heterosexual*Latinx race | $13^x$ | Gay/lesbian*Latinx race | $8^x$ | Bisexual*Latinx race | $4^x$ |
| Heterosexual*Latinx ethnicity | 219 | Gay/lesbian*Latinx ethnicity | 88 | Bisexual*Latinx ethnicity | 90 |

| | | | | | |
|---|---|---|---|---|---|
| Pansexual*White | 60 | Asexual*White | 30 | | |
| Pansexual*Black | $2^x$ | Asexual*Black | $7^x$ | | |
| Pansexual*Asian | $4^x$ | Asexual*Asian | $4^x$ | | |
| Pansexual*Native | $5^x$ | Asexual*Native | $3^x$ | | |
| Pansexual*Multi-racial | $7^x$ | Asexual*Multi-racial | $1^x$ | | |
| Pansexual*Other race | $0^x$ | Asexual*Other race | $0^x$ | | |
| Pansexual*Latinx race | $0^x$ | Asexual*Latinx race | $0^x$ | | |
| Pansexual*Latinx ethnicity | $14^x$ | Asexual*Latinx ethnicity | $6^x$ | | |
| *Sexuality\*basic needs (20 interaction terms; 13 interaction terms n > 25)* | | | | | |
| Heterosexual*everything I need | 508 | Gay/lesbian*everything I need | 210 | Bisexual*everything I need | 153 |
| Heterosexual*mostly all I need | 734 | Gay/lesbian*mostly all I need | 391 | Bisexual*mostly all I need | 373 |
| Heterosexual*often needs not met | 240 | Gay/lesbian*often needs not met | 82 | Bisexual*often needs not met | 151 |
| Heterosexual*few needs met | 67 | Gay/lesbian*few needs met | 31 | Bisexual*few needs met | 40 |

*(Continued)*

**TABLE B.1** (Cont.)

|  | n |  | n |  | n |
|---|---|---|---|---|---|
| Pansexual*everything I need | 12$^x$ | Asexual*everything I need | 10$^x$ | | |
| Pansexual*mostly all I need | 44 | Asexual*mostly all I need | 22$^x$ | | |
| Pansexual*often needs not met | 19$^x$ | Asexual*often needs not met | 10$^x$ | | |
| Pansexual*few needs met | 4$^x$ | Asexual*few needs met | 3$^x$ | | |
| *Additional sexuality/gender\*race/ethnicity (72 interaction terms total, 20 interaction terms > 25)* | | | | | |
| Queer*White | 302 | SGL*White | 254 | Two-Spirit*White | 117 |
| Queer*Black | 41 | SGL*Black | 54 | Two-Spirit*Black | 35 |
| Queer*Asian | 23$^x$ | SGL*Asian | 18$^x$ | Two-Spirit*Asian | 16$^x$ |
| Queer*Native | 11$^x$ | SGL*Native | 3$^x$ | Two-Spirit*Native | 4$^x$ |
| Queer*Multi-racial | 10$^x$ | SGL*Multi-racial | 7$^x$ | Two-Spirit*Multi-Racial | 3$^x$ |
| Queer*other race | 3$^x$ | SGL*other race | 1$^x$ | Two-Spirit*other race | 1$^x$ |
| Queer*Latinx race | 3$^x$ | SGL*Latinx race | 4$^x$ | Two-Spirit*Latinx race | 0$^x$ |
| Queer*Latinx ethnicity | 64 | SGL*Latinx ethnicity | 54 | Two-Spirit*Latinx ethnicity | 37 |

| Butch*White | 95 | Femme*White | 214 | Leather*White | 44 |
|---|---|---|---|---|---|
| Butch*Black | 33 | Femme*Black | 55 | Leather*Black | 21$^x$ |
| Butch*Asian | 11$^x$ | Femme*Asian | 15$^x$ | Leather*Asian | 6$^x$ |
| Butch*Native | 7$^x$ | Femme*Native | 3$^x$ | Leather*Native | 1$^x$ |
| Butch*Multi-racial | 5$^x$ | Femme*Multi-racial | 14$^x$ | Leather*Multi-racial | 1$^x$ |
| Butch*other race | 1$^x$ | Femme*other race | 2$^x$ | Leather*other race | 1$^x$ |
| Butch*Latinx race | 1$^x$ | Femme*Latinx race | 0$^x$ | Leather*Latinx race | 0$^x$ |
| Butch*Latinx ethnicity | 32 | Femme*Latinx ethnicity | 50 | Leather*Latinx ethnicity | 13$^x$ |

| Bear*White | 110 | Twink*White | 60 | Down Low*White | 92 |
|---|---|---|---|---|---|
| Bear*Black | 22$^x$ | Twink*Black | 22$^x$ | Down Low*Black | 18$^x$ |
| Bear*Asian | 12$^x$ | Twink*Asian | 9$^x$ | Down Low*Asian | 9$^x$ |
| Bear*Native | 3$^x$ | Twink*Native | 1$^x$ | Down Low*Native | 0$^x$ |
| Bear*Multi-racial | 3$^x$ | Twink*multi-racial | 4$^x$ | Down Low*Multi-racial | 8$^x$ |

(*Continued*)

**TABLE B.1** (Cont.)

|  | n |  | n |  | n |
|---|---|---|---|---|---|
| Bear*other race | 3[x] | Twink*other race | 1[x] | Down Low*Other race | 2[x] |
| Bear*Latinx race | 0[x] | Twink*Latinx race | 0[x] | Down Low*Latinx race | 0[x] |
| Bear*Latinx ethnicity | 23[x] | Twink*Latinx ethnicity | 31 | Down Low*Latinx ethnicity | 24[x] |
| *Additional Sexuality/Gender\*Basic Needs (36 interaction terms total, 24 interaction terms n > 25)* ||||||
| Queer*everything I need | 123 | SGL*everything I need | 121 | Two-Spirit*everything I need | 75 |
| Queer*mostly all I need | 172 | SGL*mostly all I need | 155 | Two-Spirit* mostly all I need | 64 |
| Queer*often needs not met | 68 | SGL*often needs not met | 41 | Two-Spirit*often needs not met | 20[x] |
| Queer*few needs met | 30 | SGL*few needs met | 25 | Two-Spirit*few needs met | 1[x] |
| Butch*everything I need | 44 | Femme*everything I need | 88 | Leather*everything I need | 28 |
| Butch*mostly all I need | 75 | Femme*mostly all I need | 134 | Leather*mostly all I need | 27 |
| Butch*often needs not met | 20[x] | Femme*often needs not met | 56 | Leather*often needs not met | 8[x] |
| Butch*few needs met | 15[x] | Femme*few needs met | 25 | Leather*few needs met | 11[x] |
| Bear*everything I need | 61 | Twink*everything I need | 44 | Down Low*everything I need | 34 |
| Bear*mostly all I need | 59 | Twink*mostly all I need | 38 | Down Low*mostly all I need | 74 |
| Bear*often needs not met | 19[x] | Twink*often needs not met | 9[x] | Down Low*often needs not met | 11[x] |
| Bear*few needs met | 14[x] | Twink*few needs met | 7[x] | Down Low*few needs met | 10[x] |
| *Race/ethnicity\*basic needs (32 interaction terms total, 16 interaction terms n > 25)* ||||||
| White*everything I need | 707 | Black*everything I need | 96 | Asian*everything I need | 56 |
| White*mostly all I need | 1231 | Black*mostly all I need | 128 | Asian*mostly all I need | 101 |
| White*often needs not met | 387 | Black*often needs not met | 47 | Asian*often needs not met | 31 |
| White*few needs met | 100 | Black*few needs met | 28 | Asian*few needs met | 3[x] |
| Native*everything I need | 11[x] | Multi-racial*everything I need | 12[x] | Other race*everything I need | 6[x] |
| Native*mostly all I need | 25 | Multi-racial*mostly all I need | 45 | Other race*mostly all I need | 13[x] |

(*Continued*)

**TABLE B.1** (Cont.)

|  | n |  | n |  | n |
|---|---|---|---|---|---|
| Native*often needs not met | 16[x] | Multi-racial*often needs not met | 15[x] | Other race*often needs not met | 4[x] |
| Native*few needs met | 2[x] | Multi-racial*few needs met | 10[x] | Other race*few needs met | 1[x] |
| Latinx race*everything I need | 5[x] | Latinx ethnicity*everything I need | 116 |  |  |
| Latinx race*mostly all I need | 17[x] | Latinx ethnicity*mostly all I need | 226 |  |  |
| Latinx race*often needs not met | 2[x] | Latinx ethnicity*often needs not met | 53 |  |  |
| Latinx race*few needs met | 1[x] | Latinx ethnicity*few needs met | 22[x] |  |  |

[x] Items were excluded from regression models due to low n values (n < 25)

**TABLE B.2** Final "Other Race" Variable Responses (n = 24)

| Response | Response Option in Survey | n |
|---|---|---|
| Middle Eastern | Middle Eastern | 11 |
| Human | Other (please specify) | 3 |
| American | Other (please specify) | 2 |
| A little Spanish | Other (please specify) | 1 |
| Brown | Other (please specify) | 1 |
| Caribbean | Other (please specify) | 1 |
| Indian | Other (please specify) | 1 |
| Irish | Other (please specify) | 1 |
| Italian | Other (please specify) | 1 |
| Mediterranean | Other (please specify) | 1 |
| Spanish | Other (please specify) | 1 |

*Notes:* the final "other race" variable includes those who responded to "*Please select the racial category with which you most closely identify*" with "other race" and wrote in responses that did not fit into any of the existing racial categories. In addition, those who responded with "Middle Eastern" were collapsed into the "other race" category due to the small number of respondents.

Table B.3 "Other Race" Write-In Responses Collapsed into Existing Racial Categories (n = 8)

| Write-In Response | Collapsed into Existing Racial Category | n |
|---|---|---|
| Asian | Asian American/Pacific Islander | 2 |
| Chinese | Asian American/Pacific Islander | 1 |
| ColoRed Dark Brown A.I. | Native American/Alaskan Native | 1 |
| Biracial | Multi-racial | 1 |
| Mixed | Multi-racial | 1 |
| Nordic, Irish, Cherokee | Multi-racial | 1 |
| Puerto Rican, African American, Finnish | Multi-racial | 1 |

*Notes:* those who responded to "*Please select the racial category with which you most closely identify*" with "other race" who wrote in responses that fit into the existing racial categories were collapsed into them.

**TABLE B.4** Latinx Race Variable Responses (n = 25)

| Response | Response Option in Survey | n |
| --- | --- | --- |
| Hispanic | Other (please specify) | 12 |
| Honduran | Other (please specify) | 1 |
| Latin | Other (please specify) | 1 |
| Latino | Other (please specify) | 2 |
| Latino/Hispanic | Other (please specify) | 1 |
| Mexican | Other (please specify) | 4 |
| Mexican American | Other (please specify) | 2 |
| Puerto Rican | Other (please specify) | 2 |

*Notes:* the "Latinx race" variable includes those who responded to "*Please select the racial category with which you most closely identify*" with "other race" and wrote in responses that were Latinx-oriented.

**TABLE B.5** Protestant—Evangelical Religion Variable Responses (n = 282)

| Response | Response Option in Survey | n |
| --- | --- | --- |
| Protestant—evangelical | Protestant—evangelical | 242 |
| Christian/non-denominational | Other (please specify) | 23 |
| Pentecostal | Other (please specify) | 9 |
| Born again Christian | Other (please specify) | 2 |
| Christian reform/reformed | Other (please specify) | 2 |
| A follower of Christ | Other (please specify) | 1 |
| Christian who follows the King James Bible | Other (please specify) | 1 |
| Red Letter Christian | Other (please specify) | 1 |
| Southern Baptist | Other (please specify) | 1 |

*Notes:* the "Protestant—Evangelical" variable includes those who responded to "*Which religion do you identify with most?*" with response categories of "Protestant—Evangelical" or with "Other (please specify)" and wrote in some other Evangelical-related term.

**TABLE B.6** Christian/Other Christian Religion Variable Responses (n = 143)

| Response | Response Option in Survey | n |
| --- | --- | --- |
| Christian/Christianity/Christ | Other (please specify) | 122 |
| Orthodox/Eastern/Greek Orthodox | Other (please specify) | 5 |
| Jehovah's Witness | Other (please specify) | 4 |
| Quaker | Other (please specify) | 4 |
| First Century Christian | Other (please specify) | 1 |
| Apostolic | Other (please specify) | 1 |
| Backslidden Christian | Other (please specify) | 1 |
| Brethren | Other (please specify) | 1 |
| Church of God | Other (please specify) | 1 |
| More into the book of Enoch the man behind the dead sea scrolls | Other (please specify) | 1 |
| Progressive Christianity | Other (please specify) | 1 |
| Yahvist | Other (please specify) | 1 |

*Notes:* the "Christian/other Christian religion" variable includes those who responded to "*Which religion do you identify with most?*" with "other (please specify)" and wrote in responses of "Christian" or some other Christian-related term or religion that resulted in total n values < 25.


**TABLE B.7** Pagan/Wiccan Responses (n = 46)

| Response | Response Option in Survey | n |
| --- | --- | --- |
| Pagan/Paganism | Other (please specify) | 22 |
| Wiccan | Other (please specify) | 18 |
| Witch/I practice witchcraft | Other (please specify) | 3 |
| Norse Pagan | Other (please specify) | 1 |
| Odinism | Other (please specify) | 1 |
| Pagan/Celtic Irish Pantheon | Other (please specify) | 1 |

*Notes:* The "Pagan/Wiccan" variable includes those who responded to "*Which religion do you identify with most?*" with "Other (please specify)" and wrote in a response that included the words "pagan" or "wiccan" or some other pagan/wiccan-related term.

**TABLE B.8** Other Non-Christian Religion Variable Responses (n = 71)

| Response | Response Option in Survey | n |
|---|---|---|
| Muslim | Other (please specify) | 11 |
| Hindu | Other (please specify) | 7 |
| Unitarian Universalist | Other (please specify) | 7 |
| Taoist | Other (please specify) | 3 |
| My own | Other (please specify) | 2 |
| Pantheist | Other (please specify) | 2 |
| American Indian Religion/Native American | Other (please specify) | 2 |
| Satanism/Satanist | Other (please specify) | 2 |
| Islam | Other (please specify) | 2 |
| Agnostic Christian | Other (please specify) | 1 |
| Antitheist | Other (please specify) | 1 |
| Black | Other (please specify) | 1 |
| Christian/Wiccan | Other (please specify) | 1 |
| Combination of Buddhist, Hindu, and Wiccan beliefs | Other (please specify) | 1 |
| Discordian | Other (please specify) | 1 |
| Don't really subscribe to just one form | Other (please specify) | 1 |
| Esoteric Christianity | Other (please specify) | 1 |
| Ex-Catholic | Other (please specify) | 1 |
| Former Lutheran | Other (please specify) | 1 |
| Freemasonry | Other (please specify) | 1 |
| God | Other (please specify) | 1 |
| Holy Roller | Other (please specify) | 1 |
| Honestly I've been leaning more and more towards Aztec. I find myself really liking Tezcatlipoca. | Other (please specify) | 1 |
| Ifa | Other (please specify) | 1 |
| J | Other (please specify) | 1 |
| Jewatholic | Other (please specify) | 1 |
| Just me | Other (please specify) | 1 |
| Love | Other (please specify) | 1 |
| Mix of everything sorta | Other (please specify) | 1 |

(*Continued*)

**TABLE B.8** (Cont.)

| Response | Response Option in Survey | n |
|---|---|---|
| New Thought | Other (please specify) | 1 |
| Omnistic | Other (please specify) | 1 |
| Religious | Other (please specify) | 1 |
| Santeria | Other (please specify) | 1 |
| Secular Humanist | Other (please specify) | 1 |
| Self-healing and universal peace | Other (please specify) | 1 |
| Shamanism | Other (please specify) | 1 |
| Shinto | Other (please specify) | 1 |
| Sidha Yoga | Other (please specify) | 1 |
| Sinner that is HOPEFULLY saved by Grace in the end. | Other (please specify) | 1 |
| Taoist or Pagan | Other (please specify) | 1 |
| Toltec | Other (please specify) | 1 |
| All religions | Other (please specify) | 1 |

*Notes:* the "other non-Christian religion" variable includes those who responded to "*Which religion do you identify with most?*" with "other (please specify)" and wrote in a non-Christian or mixed-non-Christian/Christian response that resulted in total n values < 25.

# INDEX

achievement of: femininity or masculinity (key area of LGBTQ Stigma Scales) 3, 101, **102**, 114, 116, *131*, *133*, *325*, **327**, 330–331; femininity (key area of LGBTQ Stigma Scales) *131*, *133*, *167*, **168**, 173–174, *223*, **225**, 229, *275*, **277**, 281–282, *351*, **353**, 355–356; masculinity (key area of LGBTQ Stigma Scales) *131*, *133*, *197*, **198**, 202, *251*, **253**, 256, *301*, **303**, 307–308, *374*, **375**, 379
activo/pasivo 31, 48
Adams, John 116
Adams, John Q. 116
adoption, same-sex couples 1, 169, 199, 278, 304, 398
African American/Black LGBTQ experiences *see* Chapter 3
AIDS Coalition to Unleash Power (ACT-UP) 378
Allport, Gordon 61–62, 64, 76n1
anal sex 46–48, 51, 111, 117n7, 132, 202, 256, 377
Anderson, Elijah 45
anti-LGBTQ language/slurs 91, 106, 174, 228, 281, 307
Armed Forces *see* United States Military
asexual/asexuality 179, 377, 400
Asian American/South Asian, Southeast Asian, Pacific Islander LGBTQ experiences *see* Chapter 3

Attitudes Regarding Bisexuality Scale (ABRS), Mohr and Rochlen's (1999) 92

Balay, Anne 41, 44
Baldwin, Tammy 353
basic human rights (key area of LGBTQ Stigma Scales) 3, 101, **102**, 105–108, 129, *130*, *133*, *167*, **168**, *197*, **198**, *223*, **224**, *251*, **252**, *275*, **276**, *301*, **302**, *325*, **326**, 350, *351*, **352**, *374*, **375**, 376, 399
bathroom bill/law 1, 279, 300, 319n1
bear/bear community 46, 49, 93, 111, **135**, *147*, **184**, *210*, **214**, **215**, *232*, 234, **237**, *263*, **267**, **288**, 309, **311**, **313**, **338**, 358, **359**, 360, *363*, 377, 381, **382**, 383, **386**
beliefs about gender 2, 60, 66, 70–73, 75, **142**; *see also* feminist/feminism and patriarchal gender norms
Bérubé, Allan 40
biblical/scriptural literalism/literalists **63**, 64–66, 73, **139**, 169, **206**
bi-invisibility/bi-erasure 87
bisexual men: *see* Chapter 11; achievement of masculinity *251*, **252–253**, 256–257, 270; basic human rights *130*; DHV experiences 264–265; effeminacy 256; findings (DHV models) *155*, *157*, *158*, 265–269, 270; findings (stigma scale models) *147*, *150*, *151*, 257–262, **259–260**; findings (summary of patterns)

269–270; HIV/AIDS 112, 132, *251*, **252–253**, 378; hypersexuality 47–48, *251*, **252–253**, 254–255, 269; identity permanency *131*, *251*, **252–253**, 255–256, 257, 270; military/armed forces *251*, **252–253**, 254; monogamy 254–255; out 253; parents *251*, **252–253**, 253–254; political candidates *251*, **252–253**, 254; positions of importance and social significance *251*, **252–253**, 254; sex act-related stigma 47–48, *131*, *147*, *150*, *151*, *251*, **252–253**, 254–255; sexuality 47–48, 254–255, 257; social and familial relationships *251*, **252–253**, 253–254; stigma scale *128*, *251*, **252–253**, 256–257; subsample details 262–263, **263**; theoretical model (DHV models) *266*; theoretical model (stigma scale models) *258*; unfaithful *133*
Bisexual Rights Movement 86, 245n1
bisexual women: *see* Chapter 10; achievement of femininity *223*, **224–225**, 229; basic human rights *130*; DHV experiences *156*, *238*, **239**; experimental identity *223*, **224–225**; findings (DHV models) *155*, *157*, *158*, 239–244; findings (stigma scale models) *147*, *150*, *151*, 230–236; findings (summary of patterns) 244–245; friendships 225; hetero-femininity 48, 227, 229; HIV/AIDS *223*, **224–225**; hypersexuality 48, *223*, **224–225**, 227; identity permanency *131*, *133*, *223*, **224–225**, 228–229; lesbian hostility 228; men's eroticization of 48, 227; military/armed forces *223*, **224–225**, 226; monogamous 227; out 225; parents *223*, **224–225**, 225–226; political candidates *223*, **224–225**, 226; positions of importance and social significance *223*, **224–225**, 226; sex act-related stigma *131*, *223*, **224–225**, 226–228; social and familial relationships *223*, **224–225**, 225–226; stigma scale *128*, *147*, *150*, *151*, *223*, **224–225**, 229–230; subsample details 236, **237**; theoretical model (DHV models) ; theoretical model (stigma scale models) *231*
bisexuality, general stereotypes about 48, 86–87, 228, 255
Black church 66, 76n2

blameworthy, LGBTQ people for their assaults 50–51, 107–108, 280, 305–306
Blokker, Scott 200
Bogardus' Social Distance Scale 101–102
Bornstein, Kate 89, 323–324, 345n1
*Bowers v. Hardwick* 111, 116–117n7
boy scouts 1
Brightfeather, Angela 279
Brown, Kate 226
Buchanan, James 116
butch 31, 46, 91, 132, **135**, **150**, **155**, 174, **178**, 182, **184**, **188**, 189–190, **210**, **214–215**, 216–218, **237**, 234, **263**, **284**, **286**, **288**, 309, **311**, **313**, 336, **338**, 356, **363**, **382**, 384, **386**
Butler, Judith 2, 19, 24, 350
Buttigieg, Pete 376

Carroll, Aengus 107
Catholic/Catholicism 65, 67, 140, 334
cheating/cheaters *see* unfaithful/ unfaithfulness
Chechnya, concentration camps 107, 116n5
childhood, anti-LGBTQ experiences 71, 104, 264, 281, 306
Christianity 30, 116, **140**, **416–417**
closet/closeted/closeting 32, 41, 45, 52, 66–67, 110, 114, 116, 166
Collins, Patricia Hill 2, 19–20, 24, 361, 384
coming out 113, 199
Compton's Cafeteria Riot 34, 54n2
Compton's Transgender Cultural District 54n2
compulsive heterosexuality 44
Confucianism 66
Connell, Raewyn 72
conservative politics/political perspectives 68–70, 73–74, 76n2, **141**, **178**, 182, **206**, **233**, **260**, **285**, **311**, **334**, **359**, **383**
Contact hypothesis 61
conversion therapy/therapies 113, 115, 202
Cox, Laverne 35, 88
Crenshaw, Kimberlé 2, 19, 24
criminalization of LGBTQ people *see* homosexuality, criminalization of and homosexuality, punishable by death
Cunningham, Phillipe 304
Cyr, Julian 376

D'Emilio, John 67
DADT *see* United States Military, Don't Ask, Don't Tell, Don't Pursue (DADT)
data, description of 125–126, 403, **404–406**
Daughters of Bilitis 40, 54n4, 166, 190n1
Davis, Kathy 2, 19, 24
deception/deceit 50–51, 107, 280
dees 31
dehumanization 107, 281
DeLarverie, Stormé 34, 349, 369n1
democrat 68–69
Diagnostic and Statistical Manual of Mental Disorders (DSM): and homosexuality as mental illness 85, 108–109, 112, 130–131; DSM-I 108, 130–131; DSM-II 108–109, 130–131; DSM-II-Revised 109; DSM-III 109; DSM-IV 109; DSM-V 88, 109–110
dissident femininity *see* hegemonic femininity
double-stigmatization 87
Down Low 41, 52, 110, **135**, **184**, **210**, **237**, 255, **263**, **267**, **288**, **313**, **338**, **363**, **387**
DSM *see* Diagnostic and Statistical Manual of Mental Disorders (DSM)

effeminate/effeminacy 31, 41, 48, 202, 390
Eliason, Michele 86
eroticization 46, 48–50, 93, 171–173, 189, 227
etymology of gay and lesbian 84
Evangelical Protestants 65, **140**, **178**, **206**, **233**, **285**, **311**, **334**, **359**, **383**, **416**
ex-gay movement 113

Falk, Gerhard 9
familismo 32, 67
family support 30
Fanning, Eric 201
FBI 107–108, 116n6, 187, 215
femininity *see* achievement of femininity
feminist/feminism 70, 72–75, **142**, *151*, 152–153, 278–279, **285**, **312**, **334**, **359**, **383**
femme 31, 46, 48, 91, 132, **135**, *155*, 172, **184**, **188**, **189**, **205**, **207**, **210**, 216, 227, 229, **237**, **241**, 243, 245, *263*, **288**, **313**,

**333–334**, 335–336, **338**, 356–357, **359**, **363**, **367**, 381, **382**, 383, **386**
fetish/fetishizing 45, 48–50, 110, 216, 377
Fillmore, Millard 116
findings patterns among: both subsamples (stigma scales models) 145–146; common explanations and sociodemographic controls (stigma scales models) 151–153; hetero-cis subsample (stigma scales models) 147–149; key independent variables (DHV models) **155**, 155–156; LGBTQ subsample (stigma scales models) 149–151; social power axes and controls 156–160

Gallup poll 169, 199–200
gay, as improper placeholder for all LGBTQ 88
Gay Activists Alliance 34
Gay and Lesbian Rights Movements 19, 34, 84, 369n1
gay equals rich norm 2, 24
gay equals White norm 2, 24, 28–32
Gay Liberation Front 84
gay men: *see* Chapter 9; achievement of masculinity *197*, **198**, 202, 217; basic human rights *130*; DHV experiences *211*, **212**, 218; effeminacy 202; findings (DHV models) *155*, *157*, *158*, 212–217; findings (stigma scale models) *147*, *150*, *151*, 203–209; findings (summary of patterns) 217–218; friendships 199–200; HIV/AIDS *197*, **198**, 217; hypersexuality 47–50, *133*, *197*, **198**, 217; identity permanency *197*, **198**, 202; military/armed forces *197*, **198**, 200–201; out 199; parents *197*, **198**, 199–200; political candidates *197*, **198**, 200–201; positions of importance and social significance *197*, **198**, 199–201; radical separatism 200; sex act-related stigma 47–50, *131*, *133*, *197*, **198**, 201, 203, 217; social and familial relationships *197*, **198**; stigma scale *128*, *147*, *150*, *151*, *197*, **198**, 202–203; subsample details 209, **210**; theoretical model (DHV models) *213*; theoretical model (stigma scale models) *204*
gay panic defense 107
gay plague 112, 201
gay-related immune deficiency (GRID) 112

gender deceivers (stereotype about trans women) 50–51, 107, 280
Gender Dysphoria 88, 109
Gender Identity Disorder 88, 109
gender inequality, *see* patriarchy
gender norm violations/gender nonconformity prejudice 26, 88, 106–107, 109, 112–113, 306
gender performance 26, *26*, 114–115
gender-Bashing (Hill's 2002 concept) 89
genderism (Hill's 2002 concept) 89
Genderism and Transphobia Scale (GTS) 89
genderqueer *see* non-binary/genderqueer
genderqueer spectrum 90
genital label/labeling *see* sex assigned at birth
goals, of the text 4, 401
god 62–63, 65, 139, **417–418**
Goffman, Erving 2, 9–14, 16–17, 20

h word (problematic use of "homosexual") 85
Harding, Warren 116
hate crimes, LGBTQ 42, 68, 107, 116n6, 130
Hay, Harry 54n3, 196, 218n1
HB2 *see* bathroom bill/law
heaven 63, 65
hegemonic femininity 44–45
hegemonic masculinity 44–45, 379
hell 65
Helms, Monica 279
Herek, Gregory 16–17
hetero-cis-normative sex 45, 47, 51, 227
hetero-cis-normativity *see* Chapter 3
hetero-cis-normativity scale *see* measurement, hetero-cis-normativity
heteronormativity 16–17, 19, 24, 105, 182, 354, 318
heterosexual assumption (Herek) 16
heterosexual prowess 44
hijra 39, 52
HIV/AIDS 9, 14–15, 93, **102**, 109, 112, 132, *133*, *167*, **168**, 171–172, *197*, **198**, 201, 203, 217, *223*, **224**, *251*, **252**, *275*, **276**, 279–280, *301*, **302**, 305, *325*, **326**, *351*, **352**, *374*, **375**, 377–378, 399
homophobia 29–33, 41–42, 71, 83–85, 102
Homophobia Scale (Kenneth Smith, 1971) 83

homophobic discourse, *see* anti-LGBTQ language/slurs
homosexual: identity, origins of 113–114; as associated with men only 29, 47, 85–86, 170; changing use of term 84–86
homosexuality: as mental illness 9, 85–86, 88, 108–109, 112, 130–131; criminalization of 42, 46, 84–86, 109, 111; punishable by death 46, 181
human Rights, worthiness of LGBTQ people 106
Humphreys, Laud 110
hypersexuality, as a diagnosis 110
hypersexuality/hypersexualization 93–94, *102*, 109–112, 132, *133*, *167*, **168**, 171–172, 174, 190, *197*, **198**, 201, 203, 217, *223*, **224**, 227, 230, 244, *251*, **252**, 257, 269, *275*, **276**, 279–280, 294, *301*, **302**, 305–306, 308, 318, *325*, **326**, 328, 331, *351*, **352**, 354–355, *374*, **375**, 377, 379

ideal type (Goffman) 13–14
identity documents **36–38**, 52, 323, 398
insertive sex 31, 47–48, 132, 202
International Lesbian, Gay, Bisexual, Trans and Intersex Association (ILGA) 107
intersectionality 2, 4, 19, 21, 24–53, 160, 181, 269, 401
invisible/invisibility 17, *18*, 27–30, 32–33, 45, 52, 87, 93, 113–114, 226, 254, 274, *398*
Irwin, Jay 304

Jackson, Andrew 116
Jacobs, Mike 254
Jefferson, Thomas 116
Jehovah's Witness 65, 417
Jenner, Caitlyn 33–35, 88
John and Mary Doe, original plaintiffs in *Bowers v. Hardwick* 116–117n7
Johnson, Andrew 116
Johnson, Marsha P. 34, 274, 295n1
Jorgensen, Christine 33–34, 53–54n1, 88

kathoey 39, 52
Kenny, Brian 274
Khayatt, Didi 91
kidman, Bre 328
Kink 46, 377, 400
Kinsey, Alfred 250

Laaksonen, Touko 49; *see also* Tom of Finland
labeling/labeling theory 9, 12, 14–16
lady boys *see* kathoey
Latinx/o/a LGBTQ experiences *see* Chapter 3
Lavender Scare 108–109, 112, 115
*Lawrence v. Texas* 111
leather 93, 111, 135, 175, **177**, **184**, **210**, 231, **232**, **237**, **263**, **288**, **313**, **338**, **363**, **377**, **386**
Leatherman/leathermen 46, 49, 135, 216
left wing 68
Leitenberg, Harold 87
lesbian women: *see* Chapter 8; achievement of femininity *131*, *167*, **168**, 173–174; androgyny 174; basic human rights *130*; DHV experiences 183–185, 190; experimental sexuality 173; findings (DHV models) *155*, *157*, *158*, 186–189; findings (stigma scale models) *147*, *150*, *151*, 175–183; findings (summary of patterns) 189–190; friendships *167*, **168**, 169–170; HIV/AIDS *167*, **168**, 171–172; hypersexuality *167*, **168**, 171–172, 190; identity permanency *131*, *167*, **168**, 173; masculinity 174; men's eroticization of 172–173; military/armed forces *167*, **168**, 170–171; out 169; parents *167*, **168**, 169; political candidates *167*, **168**, 170–171; positions of importance and social significance *167*, **168**, 170–171; radical separatism 170, 181, 200, 278; sex act-related stigma *131*, *133*, *167*, **168**, 171–173, 189; social and familial relationships *167*, **168**, 169; stigma scale *128*, *147*, *150*, *151*, *167*, **168**, 174; subsample details 183, **184**; theoretical model (DHV models) *186*; theoretical model (stigma scale models) *176*
LGBTQ bodies 45–51
LGBTQ Groups: Rank Ordered *128*; with the Highest Gender- and Sexuality-Based DHV Experiences *156*; with the Highest Means for the Individual LGBTQ Stigma Scale Items *133*
LGBTQ identity permanency (key area of LGBTQ Stigma Scales) 3, *131*, **168**, 173–174, 190, **198**, 202, **224**, 228, 230, **252**, 255, 257, **276**, 281, **303**, 306, **327**, 329, 331, 352, 355–356, **375**, 378
LGBTQ rights/protections 1, 105–108, 130, 398–400
LGBTQ Stigma Scale Items by Key Area of Stigma **102**
LGBTQ Stigma Scales **102**, *167*, **168**, *197*, **198**, *223*, **224**, *251*, **252**, *275*, **276**, *301*, **302**, *325*, **326**, *351*, **352**, *374*, **375**; *see also* Chapter 6
LGBTQ Stigma Scales, Key Areas with the Highest Mean Values *131*
LGBTQ stigma: and correlates *see* Chapters 3 and 4; and intersectionality (race/ethnicity, class, basic needs) *see* Chapter 3
LGBTQ umbrella 180
liberal politics/political perspectives 68–70, 73–74, 76n2, **141**, *178*, 182, **206**, **233**, **260**, **285**, **311**, **334**, **359**, **383**
liberal vs. conservative, foundations of 69–70
Lincoln, Abraham 116
Link, Bruce 9
lipstick (femme presentation) 172, 174, 189, 227, 400
lumberjack 49, 216
Lyon, Phyllis 166, 190n1

MacDonald, A. P. 86
machismo 32, 67, 71
male gaze 45, 48, 51, 173
marionismo 32, 71
Martin, Del 166, 190n1
masculinity *see* achievement of masculinity
Mattachine Society 40, 54n3, 54n4, 196, 218n1, 349
Mattachine steps 196
Measurement Principles: #1, LGBTQ (defined) 86; #2, LGBTQ (defined) 87; #3, LGBTQ (defined) 89; #4, LGBTQ (defined) 90; #5, LGBTQ (defined) 92; #6, LGBTQ (defined) 94; #7, LGBTQ (defined) 95
measurement, attitudes toward: bisexuals 86–87; homosexuals 83–86; non-binary and genderqueer individuals 90; queer individuals 90–92; trans individuals 87–89
measurement of: hetero-cis-normativity 94–95; intersections of gender and sexual identity (overview) 92–94; LGBTQ stigma *see* Chapter 5

media, LGBTQ representations in 21, 31, 33–35, 40, 54n1, 67–68, 85, 88, 103, 169, 172–173, 199, 225, 227, 253, 306, 353
Miller, Ezra 376
modeling strategy of: DHV models 132, 134; stigma scales models 154
Modern Homophobia Scale (MHS) (Raja and Stokes 1998) 92
Monáe, Janelle 353
Morales, Natalie 353
Mormon 65, **140**, **233**
MSM (men who have sex with men) 32, 40–41
Museum of Contemporary Art (MOCA), Los Angeles, CA 49
Museum of Modern Art (MOMA), New York, NY 49
Museum of Modern Art, San Francisco, CA 49
Mx. (honorific) 328

National Center for Transgender Equality U.S. Transgender Survey *see* National Transgender Discrimination Survey
National LGBTQ Wall of Honor 53–54n1, 190n1, 218n1, 295n1, 295n2, 369n1
National Transgender Discrimination Survey 35, *36–38*, **43**, 50, 90, 72, 280–281, 289, 314, 324
Native American LGBTQ experiences *see* Chapter 3
NCST: hypotheses 20, 53, 175, 186, 203, 212–213, 230, 239, 257, 265, 282–283, 291, 308, 315, 332, 341, 357, 365, 380, 389; zone of transition 17–19, 27–28, 33, *398*
NCST tenets: #1 10–12, 53, 397; #2 12–14, 53, 397; #3 15–17, 53, 397
NCST theoretical models: 20, *21;* of hetero-cis-normativity and LGBTQ stigma **25, 176, 186, 204, 213, 231, 240, 258, 266, 283, 291, 309, 316, 332, 341, 358, 366, 381, 390**
NCST/Norm-Centered Stigma Theory *see* Chapter 2
*New York Times* 1, 85
non-binary, employment 339
non-binary/genderqueer identity, and age 39, 329; as new 114, 324, 329
non-binary/genderqueer people *see* Chapter 14; achievement of femininity or masculinity *131, 325*, **326**, 330, 345; basic human rights *130, 133*; bodies 330–331; DHV experiences *156,* 338–340, 345; findings (DHV models) *155, 157, 158,* 341–344; findings (stigma scale models) *147, 150, 151,* 331–337; findings (summary of patterns) 344–345; gender affirming treatments/ surgeries 330–331; hypersexuality *325,* **326**, 344; identity permanency *131, 325,* **326**, 329; military/armed forces *325,* **326**, 327; parents *133, 325,* **326**; political candidates *133, 325,* **326**, 327; positions of importance and social significance *325,* **326**; sex act-related stigma *131, 325,* **326**, 327–329, 344; sexual and relationship anxiety 328; social and familial relationships 324, *325,* **326**, 327; stigma scale *128, 147, 150, 151,* 324, *325,* **326**, 331; subsample details 337, **338**; theoretical model (DHV models) *341;* theoretical model (stigma scale models) *332*
non-binary/genderqueer vs. binary people's experiences 39, 41, 90, 328–331
norm centrality 10, 12, 14, 16–17, 21, 27, 75, 95, 116, 160
norms, defined 10; followers/following 11, 13, 15, 20, 24, 26, 33, 61, 63, 94; violators/violations 3, 10–17, 19–20, **21, 24, 25, 176, 186, 204, 213, 231, 240, 258, 266, 283, 291, 309, 316, 332, 341, 358, 366, 381, 390**, 401

Obama, Barak 116
objectification 2, 16, 25, 43, 45–46, 48, 50–52, 93, 100, 171, 189, 227, 243, 280
Obscene File (FBI) 108
Ochs, Robyn 222, 245n1
one-time rule of homosexuality 256
openness to new experiences 69, 137, **141**, *151,* 152–153, **178, 206, 233, 260, 285, 311, 334, 359, 383**
oral sex 47–48, 111, 117n7, 202, 256
*Orange is the New Black* 35

pansexual/pansexuality 126, **134, 177**, 180–182, **232**, 235–236, **288**, 313, **338**, 362, **363, 377, 386**, 400
paraphilia 88, 109

*Parents* (magazine) 200
pariah femininity *see* hegemonic femininity
Pascoe, C. J. 44
passport *see* identity documents
patriarchal gender norms 16, 67, 70–72, 137, *142*, *151*, 152–153, **178**, **206**, **233**, **260**, **285**, **312**, **334**, **359**, **383**
patriarchy 16, 44–45, 67, 70–73
pedophiles (stereotype about LGBTQ people) 108, 171, 199
penile-anal intercourse 47, 132, 377
penile-vaginal intercourse 47, 111
People's Liberation Army (of China) 105
Pew Research Center data/study 60, 62, **63**, 64, 66–67, 69, 106, 129, 169–171, 199, 225, 253, 277
phase, LGBTQ identities are 113, 173, 228, 255, 281, 306, 329, 355
Phelan, Jo 9
policy implications 398–400
Polis, Jared 201
political perspectives *see* conservative politics/political perspectives and Liberal politics/political perspectives
Polk, James 116
positions of importance and social significance (key area of LGBTQ Stigma Scales) 3, 101, **102**, 104, **168**, 170, **198**, 200–201, **224**, 226, **252**, 254, **276**, 278–279, **302**, 304–305, **326**, 327, **352**, 353, **375**, 376
poverty, LGBTQ 35, 42, **43**, 50–51
predators (stereotype about LGBTQ people) 84, 108
Pulse (nightclub) shootings 243, 373, 393n1

queer identity, age and 355; as "catchall" 362, 376; as new 114, 350, 355; multiple meanings 362
queer men *see* Chapter 16; achievement of masculinity *131*, *133*, *374*, **375**, 379, 393; basic human rights *130*; bear and 376; DHV experiences *156*, 387–389, 393; findings (DHV models) *155*, *157*, *158*, 389–392; findings (stigma scale models) *147*, *150*, *151*, 380–386; findings (summary of patterns) 392–393; HIV/AIDS 112, 132, *133*, *374*, **375**, 376; hypersexuality *133*, *374*, **375**, 376; identity permanency *374*, **375**, 378–379; kink and 376; leather and 376; military/armed forces *374*, **375**, 376; political candidates *374*, **375**, 376; positions of importance and social significance *374*, **375**, 376; sex act-related stigma *131*, *374*, **375**, 377–378, 393; social and familial relationships *374*, **375**, 376; stigma scale *128*, *147*, *150*, *151*, *374*, **375**, 379; subsample details **386–387**; theoretical model (DHV models) *390*; theoretical model (stigma scale models) *381*; twink and 376
Queer Nation (HIV/AIDS activism group) 378
queer theory/theorists 19, 24, 91–92, 350
queer women *see* Chapter 15; achievement of femininity *131*, *351*, **352**, 355–356, 368; basic human rights *130*; DHV experiences *156*, 362–365, 368; experimental sexuality 355, 368; findings (DHV models) *155*, *157*, *158*, 365–368; findings (stigma scale models) *147*, *150*, *151*, 356–361; findings (summary of patterns) 368–369; hypersexuality *351*, **352**, 354, 368; identity permanency *131*, *351*, **352**, 355, 368; masculinity 356; military/armed forces *351*, **352**, 353; political candidates *351*, **352**, 353; positions of importance and social significance *351*, **352**; sex act-related stigma *131*, *351*, **352**, 354–357, 368; social and familial relationships 350–353, *351*, **352**; stigma scale *128*, *147*, *150*, *151*, *351*, **352**, 356; subsample details 361–362, **363**; theoretical model (DHV models) *366*; theoretical model (stigma scale models) *358*
queer, as derogatory 91; as reclaimed 91, 350, 355

radical separatism 170, 181, 200, 278
Ramirez, Sara 353
receptive sex 31, 47–48, 132, 202, 256
religiosity: attendance **63**, 64–67, 76, 137, 139, **178**, **206**, **233**, **260**; generalized religiousness 62, **63**, 63–66, 137, 139; U.S. views about "homosexuality" 62, **63**, 64–66
religious/holy scripture *see* biblical/scriptural literalism/literalists
republican 68, 73–74, 279

restrooms, public *36–37*, 279, 300, 339, 319n1; *see also* bathroom bill/law
right wing 68
Rivera, Sylvia 34, 274, 295n1, 295n2
Roem, Danica 279

same-gender-loving (SGL) 29–30, 52, 93, 132, **135**, 137, 149, *150*, *155*, **177–178**, 180–182, **184**, **188**, **205**, 207–209, **210**, **214–215**, 216–218, **232**, **236**, **237**, **241**, 243, 245, **259**, 261, **263**, **267**, **284–285**, 286–287, **288**, 310, **311**, **313**, **334**, 336–337, **338**, **363**, **367**, **386**, **391**, 392–393
same-sex/gender marriage 1, 64, 68, 106, 398
sample characteristics/sampling frames, description of 125–126
Schur, Edwin 16
Second World War-era Perverts in Government Service File (FBI) 108
Sedgwick, Eve Kosofsky 2, 19, 24
sex act-related stigma (key area of LGBTQ Stigma Scales) 3, **102**, 108–109, 112, 129, 130, *131*, 132, **168**, 171–172, 174, **198**, 201, 203, 217, **224**, 226–227, 230, 244, **252**, 254, 257, **276**, 279–282, **302**, 305–308, **326**, 328–329, 331, **352**, 354, 356, **375**, 377–379, 399
sex assigned at birth 25, **26**, 27, 50, 88–89, 114, 328, 391n1
Sex Deviates File/Program (FBI) 108
sex objects *see* objectification
sex work/sex workers 42, 46, 50–51, 279–281
sex, criminalization of LGBTQ *see* homosexuality, criminalization of homosexuality, punishable by death
sex/gender marker *see* sex assigned at birth
sex/sexualization, LGBTQ 45–51, 93, 227–228
sexual behaviors 45–51, 109–113, 130, 132, 171–172, 250, 257, 280, 305, 377, 399; *see also* anal sex, oral sex, penile-vaginal sex, and penile-anal sex
sexual deviants 108–109, 171, 199
sexual dysfunctions 88
sexual stigma (Herek) 16–17
Shaun T 200
Shupe, Jamie 328
Simpson, Amanda 279

Sinema, Kyrsten 226
Slavin, Lesley 87
Smith, Sam 327
social and familial relationships (key area of LGBTQ Stigma Scales) 3, 101, **102**, 103–104, *167*, **168**, 169, 197, *197*, **198**, 199, **224**, 225, **252**, 253, *275*, **276**, 277, **302**, 303–304, 324, *325*, **326–327**, 350, *351*, **352–353**, 353, **375**, 376
social distancing 65, 73, 101–103
social justice/injustice 65, 69, 129, 153, 180
social power: defined 10; and foundations in norms/stigma *see* Chapter 2; as justification 15–17, 95, 116, 160; as organizational 12–15, 95,116, 160
sociopathic personality disturbances (DSM) 85, 108
sodomy laws 84, 111–112, 116–117n7
spectrum of stigma 11, 17–20, 24, 26–27, 33, 35, 52, 89, 95, 116, 160, 397, *398*
Stafford, Mark 11–12, 21n1
status quo 69–70, 104, 350
*Steel Closet* (Balay)/steel mill sex/ steelworkers 41, 44
Stein, Arlene 84, 170, 200, 278
stereotypes 2, 10–12, 14–15, 19, 25, 28, 31, 33, 35, 43, 46–48, 50–52, 70, 86–87, 89, 109–111, 113–115, 125, 129, 132, 169, 171–174, 189, 199, 201–202, 227–228, 244, 255–257, 269–270, 277, 279–281, 304–306, 325, 329, 354–356, 377–378
stigma, defined 10
stigma, foundational work *see* Chapter 2
*Stigma: Notes on the Management of Spoiled Identity* (by Goffman) 9
stigmatized lens 3, 4, 14–15, 20, 53, 76, 93, 116, 125, 153–154, 160, *186*, *213*, *240*, *266*, *291*, *316*, *341*, *366*, *390*, 401
stigmatizer lens 3, 4, 14–15, 20, 53, 60–61, 75, 125, 132, 153, 160, *176*, *204*, *231*, *258*, *283*, *309*, *332*, *358*, *381*, 401
Stonewall Inn 54n1, 190n1, 218n1, 349, 369n1
Stonewall Uprising 28, 34, 54n1, 54n2, 84, 190n1, 218n1, 274, 295n1, 295n2, 349, 369n1
Stonewall Veterans' Association 349, 369n1
straight girls kissing 48, 51, 173, 228

Street Transvestite Revolutionaries (STAR) 34, 295n1, 295n2
Stryker, Susan 1, 32–33, 54n2, 89, 278
survey: design and implementation of 126–127; identity quotas 126–127; sampling frame and characteristics 126–127

Taft, William Howard 116
Taoism 66
tearooms 41, 110, 255
Teena, Brandon 88
TERF (trans exclusionary radical feminist) 278
*The Ladder* 166
third gender 39, 323
*Time* magazine 35
Titus, Tyler 304
Tom of Finland 49
toms/tom boys 31
traditional: gender roles 27, 66, 70–71, 117n7, 153, 182, 199, 229; values/expectations 30, 69, 104–105, 180
trans equals White norm 2, 24, 28
trans men *see* Chapter 13; achievement of masculinity 113, 133, 301, **302–303**, 306, 318; basic human rights 130; blameworthy for own assault 305–306; bodies 305–306; DHV experiences 313–315, 318; findings (DHV models) *155*, *157*, *158*, 315–318; findings (stigma scale models) *147*, *150*, *151*, 308–312; findings (summary of patterns) 318–319; gender affirming treatments/surgeries 305–306; HIV/AIDS 301, **302–303**, 305; hypersexuality 301, **302–303**, 305–306; identity permanency 301, **302–303**, 306; military/armed forces 133, 301, **302–303**, 304–305; parents 301, **302–303**, 303–304; political candidates 133, 301, **302–303**, 304–305; positions of importance and social significance 301, **302–303**, 304–305; pregnant 304; sex act-related stigma 113, 301, **302–303**, 305–310, 318; social and familial relationships 301, **302–303**, 303–304; stigma scale *128*, *147*, *150*, *151*, 301, **302–303**, 307–308; subsample details 312, **313**; testosterone 306–307; theoretical model (DHV models) *316*; theoretical model (stigma scale models) *309*

trans panic defense 107
trans women *see* Chapter 12; achievement of femininity *131*, 275, **276–277**, 281–282; basic human rights *130*; bodies 279–280; deception/deceit 50–51, 107, 280; DHV experiences 289–290, 295; findings (DHV models) *155*, *157*, *158*, 291–294; findings (stigma scale models) *147*, *150*, *151*, 282–287; findings (summary of patterns) 294–295; gender affirming treatments/surgeries 54n1, 280; HIV/AIDS 275, **276–277**, 279–280; hypersexuality 50–51, 275, **276–277**, 280, 294; identity permanency 275, **276–277**, 281; military/armed forces 275, **276–277**, 278–279; parents 275, **276–277**, 278; police interactions with 54n2, 281, 295n1; political candidates 275, **276–277**, 278–279; positions of importance and social significance 275, **276–277**, 278–279; radical separatism 170, 278; sex act-related stigma 50–51, *131*, 275, **276–277**, 279–281, 294; sex work, *see* sex work/sex workers; social and familial relationships 275, **276–277**, 278; stigma scale *128*, *147*, *150*, *151*, 275, **276–277**, 282; subsample details **288–289**; theoretical model (DHV models) *291*; theoretical model (stigma scale models) *283*
Transgender American Veterans Association 279
transgender pride flag 279
transgender, employment/workplace **36–38**, 42, *43*; family rejection **36–38**; health care 35, **36–38**, *43*, 281, 304, 306; homelessness 34, **36–38**, 295n1, 295n2; identity documents *see* identity documents; intimate partner violence (IPV) 35, **36–38**, 50, 289; mental health **36–38**; physical attacks **36–38**, 289, 314; police interactions **36–38**, 54n2, 281, 295; poverty 35, 42, *43*, 50–51; public restrooms *see* restrooms, public and bathroom bill/law; school harassment **36–38**; sexual assault 35, **36–38**, 50, 289, 305, 314, 339; suicide 35, **36–38**; verbal harassment **36–38**
trans-misogyny 282
transphobia 89, 92
transsexualism/transexuality 87, 88, 91

transvestism 108, 131
*triple jeopardy* 29
twink 46, 93, 111, 132, **135**, *147*, **184**, **205**, 208, **210**, **233**, 235, **237**, **263**, **288**, **313**, **338**, **363**, **377**, **386**
Two-Spirit 30–31, 39, 52, 93, 132, **135**, *147*, **150**, **178**, 180, 182, **184**, **205**, 208, **210**, **237**, **241**, **263**, **267**, **285**, 287, **288**, 310, **311**, **313**, **333**, 336, **338**, 358, **359**, 360, **363**, **382**, 384–385, **386**

unblushing female (Goffman's ideal type); *see also* ideal type 16
unblushing male (Goffman's ideal type); *see also* ideal type 13, 16
unfaithful/unfaithfulness **102**, 109–112, 132, *133*, *167*, **168**, *351*, 171, 190, *197*, **198**, *223*, **224**, 227, 230, 244, *251*, **252**, 254–255, 257, 269, *275*, **276**, 294, *301*, 302, 305, 318, *325*, **326**, 328, 344, 351, 352, 354–355, 369, *374*, **375**, 377–378
Unitarian Universalist/Unitarian Universalist Association (UUA) 65, 116n4, **418**
United Nations' Universal Declaration of Human Rights 105–108
United States Census, comparison to study sample 403, **404–406**
United States Department of Defense (DoD) 105, 279
United States Federal Protections, LGBTQ 1, 106, 111, 130, 279, 398–400
United States Military: Don't Ask, Don't Tell, Don't Pursue (DADT) 105, 115, 171, 191n2; LGBTQ members 105, 115, 171, 191n2, 279, 305; transgender ban 105, 279, 305
United States Presidents, hetero-cis-normativity of 104
United States Supreme Court rulings *see Bowers v Hardwick* and *Lawrence v Texas*

Van Ness, Jonathan 327
variables: controls list of **138–144**; dependent (DHV models) 154; independent variables key patterns (stigma scales models) *147*, *150*, *151*; independent variables list of (stigma scales models) **134–136**
veteran/Veterans (military) 1, 34, 279, 328, 376
victim-blaming 107
von Schrenck-Notzing, Albert 113

Washington, George 116
Watson, Lachlan 327
Weinberg, George 83
Weiss, Jillian Todd 86–88, 228, 255
Whiteness 28–29, 32–34, 67, 150, 385
Wilchins, Riki 324
Wilde, Oscar 113
womyn-born womyn policy (trans women exclusion) 278
Wood, Evan Rachel 353
working-class closet 41, 45, 52
World Professional Association for Transgender Health 88

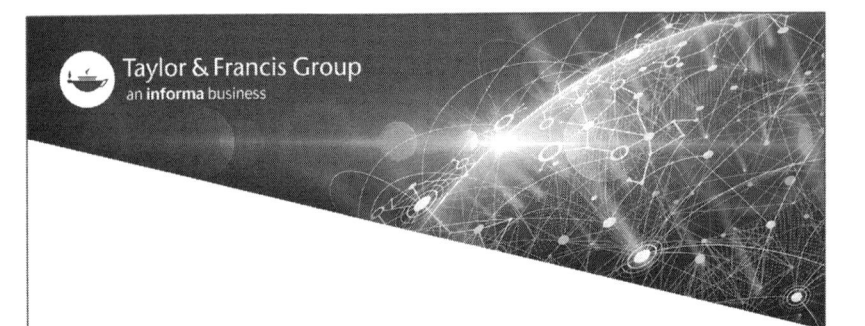

Printed in Great Britain
by Amazon